DIGITAL SOCIOLOGY

We now live in a digital society. New digital technologies have had a profound influence on everyday life, social relations, government, commerce, the economy and the production and dissemination of knowledge. People's movements in space, their purchasing habits and their online communication with others are now monitored in detail by digital technologies. We are increasingly becoming digital data subjects, whether we like it or not, and whether we choose this or not.

The sub-discipline of digital sociology provides a means by which the impact, development and use of these technologies and their incorporation into social worlds, social institutions and concepts of selfhood and embodiment may be investigated, analysed and understood. This book introduces a range of interesting social, cultural and political dimensions of digital society and discusses some of the important debates occurring in research and scholarship on these aspects. It covers the new knowledge economy and big data, reconceptualising research in the digital era, the digitisation of higher education, the diversity of digital use, digital politics and citizen digital engagement, the politics of surveillance, privacy issues, the contribution of digital devices to embodiment and concepts of selfhood, and many other topics.

Digital Sociology is essential reading not only for students and academics in sociology, anthropology, media and communication, digital cultures, digital humanities, internet studies, science and technology studies, cultural geography and social computing, but for other readers interested in the social impact of digital technologies.

Deborah Lupton is Centenary Research Professor in the News and Media Research Centre, Faculty of Arts & Design, University of Canberra.

DIGITAL SOCIOLOGY

Deborah Lupton

Routledge
Taylor & Francis Group

LONDON AND NEW YORK

First published 2015
by Routledge
2 Park Square, Milton Park, Abingdon, Oxon OX14 4RN

and by Routledge
711 Third Avenue, New York, NY 10017

Routledge is an imprint of the Taylor & Francis Group, an informa business

British Library Cataloguing-in-Publication Data
A catalogue record for this book is available from the British Library

Library of Congress Cataloging-in-Publication Data
Lupton, Deborah.
Digital sociology / Deborah Lupton.
  pages cm
ISBN 978-1-138-02276-8 (hardback)—ISBN 978-1-138-02277-5 (paperback)—ISBN 978-1-315-77688-0 (ebook)   1. Digital media—Social aspects.   2. Sociology.   3. Technology—Sociological aspects.
I. Title.
HM851.L864 2014
302.23'1—dc23

2014014299

ISBN: 978-1-138-02276-8 (hbk)
ISBN: 978-1-138-02277-5 (pbk)
ISBN: 978-1-315-77688-0 (ebk)

Typeset in Bembo
by RefineCatch Limited, Bungay, Suffolk

Printed and bound in the United States of America by
Edwards Brothers Malloy on sustainably sourced paper

CONTENTS

CHAPTER 1

Introduction

Life is digital

Life is Digital: Back It Up
> (Headline of an online advertisement used by a
> company selling digital data-protection products)

Let me begin with a reflection upon the many and diverse ways in which digital technologies have permeated everyday life in developed countries over the past thirty years. Many of us have come to rely upon being connected to the internet throughout our waking hours. Digital devices that can go online from almost any location have become ubiquitous. Smartphones and tablet computers are small enough to carry with us at all times. Some devices – known as wearable computers ('wearables' for short) – can even be worn upon our bodies, day and night, and monitor our bodily functions and activities. We can access our news, music, television and films via digital platforms and devices. Our intimate and work-related relationships and our membership of communities may be at least partly developed and maintained using social media such as LinkedIn, Facebook and Twitter. Our photographs and home videos are digitised and now may be displayed to the world if we so desire, using platforms such as Instagram, Flickr and YouTube. Information can easily be sought on the internet using search engines like Google, Yahoo! and Bing. The open-access online collaborative platform Wikipedia has become the most highly-used reference source in the world. Nearly all employment involves some form of digital technology use (even if it is as simple as a website to promote a business or a mobile phone to communicate with work-mates or clients). School curricula and theories of learning have increasingly been linked to digital technologies and focused on the training of students in using these technologies. Digital global positioning systems give us directions and help us locate ourselves in space.

In short, we now live in a digital society. While this has occurred progressively, major changes have been wrought by the introduction of devices and platforms over the past decade in particular. Personal computers were introduced to the public in the mid-1980s. The World Wide Web was invented in 1989 but became readily accessible to the public only in 1994. From 2001, many significant platforms and devices have been released that have had a major impact on social life. Wikipedia and iTunes began operation in 2001. LinkedIn was established in 2003, Facebook in 2004, Reddit, Flickr and YouTube a year later, and Twitter in 2006. Smartphones came on the market in 2007, the same year that Tumblr was introduced, while Spotify began in 2008. Instagram and tablet computers followed in 2010, Pinterest and Google+ in 2011.

For some theorists, the very idea of 'culture' or 'society' cannot now be fully understood without the recognition that computer software and hardware devices not only underpin but actively constitute selfhood, embodiment, social life, social relations and social institutions. Anthropologists Daniel Miller and Heather Horst (2012: 4) assert that digital technologies, like other material cultural artefacts, are 'becoming a constitutive part of what makes us human'. They claim against contentions that engaging with the digital somehow makes us less human and authentic that, 'not only are we just as human in the digital world, the digital also provides many new opportunities for anthropology to help us understand what makes us human'. As a sociologist, I would add to this observation that just as investigating our interactions with digital technologies contributes to research into the nature of human experience, it also tells us much about the social world.

We have reached a point where digital technologies' ubiquity and pervasiveness are such that they have become invisible. Some people may claim that their lives have not become digitised to any significant extent: that their ways of working, socialising, moving around in space, engaging in family life or intimate relationships have changed little because they refuse to use computerised devices. However, these individuals are speaking from a position which only serves to highlight the now unobtrusive, taken-for-granted elements of digitisation. Even when people themselves eschew the use of a smartphone, digital camera or social media platform, they invariably will find themselves interacting with those who do. They may even find that digital images or audio files of themselves will be uploaded and circulated using these technologies by others without their knowledge or consent.

Our movements in public space and our routine interactions with government and commercial institutions and organisations are now mediated via digital technologies in ways of which we are not always fully aware. The way in which urban space is generated, configured, monitored and managed, for example, is a product of digital technologies. CCTV (closed-circuit television) cameras that monitor people's movements in public space, traffic light and public transport systems, planning and development programmes for new buildings and the ordering, production and payment systems for most goods, services and public utilities are all digitised. In an era in which mobile and wearable digital devices are becoming increasingly common, the digital recording of images and audio by people interacting in private and public spaces, in conjunction with security and commercial surveillance technologies that are now part of public spaces and everyday transactions, means that we are increasingly becoming digital data subjects, whether we like it or not, and whether we choose this or not.

Digitised data related to our routine interactions with networked technologies, including search engine enquiries, phone calls, shopping, government agency and banking interactions, are collected automatically and archived, producing massive data sets that are now often referred to as 'big data'. Big data also include 'user-generated content', or information that has been intentionally uploaded to social media platforms by users as part of their participation in these sites: their tweets, status updates, blog posts and comments, photographs and videos and so on. Social media platforms record and monitor an increasing number of features about these communicative acts: not only what is said, but the profiles of the speaker and the audience, how others reacted to the content: how many 'likes', comments, views, time spent on a page or 'retweets' were generated, the time of day interaction occurred, the geographical location of users, the search terms used to find the content, how content is shared across platforms and so on. There has been increasing attention paid to the value of the big data for both commercial and non-commercial enterprises. The existence of these data raises many questions about how they are being used and the implications for privacy, security and policing, surveillance, global development and the economy.

How we learn about the world is also digitally mediated. Consider the ways in which news about local and world events is now gathered and presented. Many people rely on journalists' accounts of events for their knowledge about what is going on in the world. They are now able to access news reports in a multitude of ways, from the traditional (print newspapers, television and radio news programmes) to the new digital media forms: Twitter feeds, Storify accounts, online versions of newspapers, live news blogs that are constantly updated. Twitter is now often the most up-to-date in terms of reporting breaking news, and many journalists use tweets as a source of information when they are constructing their stories. Journalists are now also drawing on the expertise of computer scientists as part of using open-source digital data as a source of news and to present data visualisations (sometimes referred to as 'data journalism'). Further, the ability of people other than trained journalists to report on or record news events has expanded significantly with the advent of digital technologies. 'Citizen journalists' can video or photograph images and tweet, blog or write on Facebook about news happenings, all of which are available for others to read and comment on, including professional journalists. Traditional news outlets, particularly those publishing paper versions of newspapers, have had to meet the challenges of new digital media and construct new ways of earning income from journalism.

Digital technologies have also been used increasingly for mass citizen surveillance purposes, often in ways about which citizens are unaware. This element of the digital world became highlighted in mid-2013, when an American contractor working for the US National Security Agency (NSA), Edward Snowden, leaked thousands of classified documents he had secretly obtained as part of his work to the *Guardian* and *Washington Post* newspapers. These documents revealed the extent of the American and other anglophone (British, Australian, Canadian and New Zealand) governments' digital surveillance activities of their own citizens and those in other countries. The documents showed that these activities included accessing telephone records, text messages, emails and tracking mobile phone locations in the US, UK and Europe, as well as surveillance of citizens' internet interactions and the phone call data of many political and business leaders. It was revealed that the NSA and its British counterpart, the Government Communications Headquarters (GCHQ), were able to access users' personal metadata from major American internet companies, including Google, Apple, Microsoft and Facebook as well as intercepting data from fibre-optic telephone and internet networks.

This book on digital sociology examines many aspects of digital society. Given the spread of digital technologies into most nooks and crannies of everyday life for people in developed countries (and increasingly in developing countries), it is impossible for one book to cover all the issues and topics that could be incorporated under a sociology of digital technologies. My more modest aim in this book is to introduce a range of interesting social, cultural and political dimensions of digital society and to discuss some of the important debates occurring in research and scholarship on these aspects. I contend that sociologists should not only be thinking about and studying how (other) people use digital technologies but also how they themselves are increasingly becoming 'digitised academics' and the implications for the practice and definition of the discipline of sociology.

Some sociologists have speculated that in a context in which many diverse actors and organisations can collect and analyse social data from digital sources, the claim of sociologists that they have superior knowledge of researching social life and access to social data is challenged. The internet empires of Google, Facebook and Amazon as well as many other companies and agencies have become expert at managing data collection, archiving and interpretation in ways about which sociologists and other social scientists working in higher education can only dream. Is there a 'coming crisis' of empirical sociology (Savage and Burrows 2007, 2009), and indeed has it now arrived? Must sociologists suffer from 'data envy' (Back 2012: 19) or what otherwise has been termed 'Google envy' (Rogers 2013: 206) in this age of the corporatisation of big data? How can they manage the vastness of the digital data that are now produced and the complexities of the technologies that generate them? Is there still a role for sociologists as social researchers in this era in which other research professionals can easily access and analyse large data sets? As I will demonstrate in this book, rather than constituting a crisis, the analysis of digital society offers new opportunities for sociologists to demonstrate their expertise in social analysis and take the discipline in new and exciting directions.

If it is accepted that 'life is digital' (as the advertisement quoted at the beginning of this chapter put it so succinctly), I would argue that sociology needs to make the study of digital technologies central to its very remit. All of the topics that sociologists now research and teach about are inevitably connected to digital technologies, whether they focus on the sociology of the family, science, health and medicine, knowledge, culture, the economy, employment, education, work, gender, risk, ageing or race and ethnicity. To study digital society is to focus on many aspects that have long been central preoccupations of sociologists: selfhood, identity, embodiment, power relations and social inequalities, social networks, social structures, social institutions and social theory.

This book develops ideas and discusses ideas in which I have been interested for about two decades now. In the mid-1990s I began thinking and writing about how people conceptualised and used the types of computers that were available in those days: personal computers, the large, heavy objects that sat on people's desks, or the bulky laptops that they lugged around in the early version of 'mobile' computers. I first became intrigued by the sociocultural dimensions of computer technologies when I began to notice the ways in which computer viruses were discussed in popular culture in the early 1990s. Personal computers had been in use for some time by then, and people were beginning to recognise how much they had begun to depend on computer technologies and also what could go wrong when hackers developed 'malware' (or malicious software) in attempts to disrupt computer systems. My research interests at that time were in health, medicine, risk and embodiment (including writing about the metaphors of and social responses to HIV/AIDS). I was fascinated by what the metaphor of the computer virus revealed about our understandings of both computer technologies and human bodies (which have increasingly come to be portrayed as computerised systems in relation to the immune system and brain function) and the relationships between the two.

These interests first culminated in an article on what I described as 'panic computing' where I examined the viral metaphor in relation to computers and what this revealed about our feelings towards computers, including the common conceptualisations of computers as being like humans (Lupton 1994). I followed up with another piece reflecting on what I described as 'the embodied computer/user' (Lupton 1995). As this term suggests, the article centred on such features as the ways we thought of our personal computers as extensions of or prosthetics of our bodies/selves, blurring the conceptual boundaries between human body and self and the computers people use. An empirical project with Greg Noble then built on this initial work to investigate how personal computers were conceptualised and used in the academic workplace, including identifying the ways in which people anthropomorphised them, gave them personalities and invested them with emotions (Lupton and Noble 1997, 2002; Noble and Lupton 1998). Two other interview-based projects with Wendy Seymour addressed the topic of how people with disabilities used computer technologies, again focusing on such features as people's emotional and embodied relationships with these technologies (Lupton and Seymour 2000, 2003; Seymour and Lupton 2004).

Some of these earlier interests are taken up and re-examined in this book in a context in which computers have moved off the desktop, significantly shrunk in size and connect to the internet in almost any location. Now, more than ever, we are intimately interembodied with our computing technologies. We are not only embodied computer/ users; we are digitised humans. In the wake of the different ways in which people are now using digital technologies, I have become interested in investigating what the implications are for contemporary concepts of self, embodiment and social relations.

My more recent research has also involved the active use of many forms of digital tools as part of academic professional practice. Since 2012 I have been engaging in what might be called a participant observation study of the use of digital media in academia, trying various tools and platforms to see which are the most useful. I established my own blog, 'This Sociological Life', and began blogging not only about my research but also my observations about using social and other digital media for academic purposes. I joined Twitter and used platforms such as Facebook, Pinterest, Slideshare, Storify, Prismatic, Delicious, Scoop.it and Bundlr for professional academic purposes. The contacts and interactions I have made on Twitter and in following other academics' blogs, in particular, have been vital in keeping up to date with others' research and exchanging ideas about digital society. All of this research and the practical use of social and other digital media, from my earlier forays to my contemporary work, inform the content of this book.

KEY TERMS

When referring to digital technologies I mean both the software (the computer coding programs that provide instructions for how computers should operate) and the hardware (physical computer devices) that work together using digital coding (otherwise known as binary coding), as well as the infrastructures that support them. Contemporary digital technologies use computing platforms, the underlying environment in which software operates, including operating systems, browsers, applications (or apps) and the processing hardware that supports the software and manages data movement in the computer.

The digital is contrasted with analogue forms of recording and transmitting information that involve continuous streams of information, or with non-electronic formats of conveying information such as printed paper or artworks on canvas. Non-digital media technologies include landline telephones, radio, older forms of television, vinyl records, audio and visual tape cassettes, print newspapers, books and magazines, paintings, cameras using film and so on. While all of these 'old' or 'traditional' media and devices still exist, and some of them are still used regularly by large numbers of people, they can also be rendered into digital formats. Artefacts and artworks in museums and art galleries, for example, are now often photographed using digital cameras and these images are uploaded to the museum's or gallery's website for viewing by those who cannot view them in person.

This leads to the concept of digital data. When referring to digital data I mean the encoded objects that are recorded and transmitted using digital media technologies. Digital information is conveyed by non-continuous sequences of symbols (often 0s and 1s). Digital data include not only numerical material (how many likes a Facebook page receives, how many followers one has on Twitter) but also audio and visual data such as films and photos and detailed text such as blog posts, status updates on social media, online news articles and comments on websites. As I emphasise in this book, digital data are not just automatically created objects of digital technologies. They are the products of human action. Human judgement steps in at each stage of the production of data: in deciding what constitutes data; what data are important to collect and aggregate; how they should be classified and organised into hierarchies; whether they are 'clean' or 'dirty' (needing additional work to use for analysis); and so on.

The transferability of digital formats to different technologies capable of interpreting and displaying them is pivotal for the convergence of the new digital technologies: the fact that they can share information with each other easily and quickly. These technologies can also perform a multitude of functions. Smartphones not only make telephone calls but connect to the web, take digital photographs and videos, run apps, record voice data and play music, television programmes and films. Games consoles such as Nintendo's Wii can now browse the internet and connect to social media platforms. Various devices used each day – smartphones, cameras, MP3 players, desktops, laptops, tablets, wearable computers – can share information between themselves, facilitated by common interfaces and cloud computing (which involves the use of a network of a large number of computers connected to remote servers hosted on the internet to store, manage and process digital data).

It has been argued that to speak of 'the internet' these days is to inaccurately represent it as a singular phenomenon, when it is in fact comprised of a multitude of different digital platforms that are interconnected (Hands 2013). The internet has not always been this complex, however. In its early days it was a technology designed to establish data communication networks for the sharing of resources between separate computers (hence the term 'internet') that previously had been used mainly by the military, universities and information technology experts and enthusiasts. The World Wide Web (often referred to as 'the web' for short), invented by Sir Tim Berners-Lee in 1989, provided the infrastructure to use hyperlinks to access the internet. However the web was only readily available to the general public via the first commercial provider in 1994. The web, therefore, is not synonymous with the internet, but rather is a convenient way of accessing the internet. Web browsers such as Google Chrome and Internet Explorer provide the means by which the web can be searched and interacted with. Browsers are able to access Uniform Resource Locators (URLs) or hyperlinks that are used to identify and locate web resources such as web pages, images or videos.

The digital technologies of the last century (now often retrospectively referred to as 'Web 1.0') were based on websites and devices such as desktop or laptop computers. People could view information online and use facilities such as emails, online banking and shopping, but for the most part had little role to play in creating online content (although some users did interact with others in internet chat rooms, listservs, discussion groups and multi-player online games). Computers at first connected to the internet via telephone lines, and thus their users were physically limited in the extent to which they could be online. Software applications were loaded on to individual desktops or laptops.

Since the early years of the twenty-first century, the emergence of platforms and websites that were accessible online rather than loaded individually on to one's desktop computer, the development of technologies such as wireless ('wi-fi') and broadband internet access and related devices have resulted in a proliferation of technologies. Ubiquitous wireless computing technologies allow for users to be connected to the internet in almost any location at any time of the day using their mobile devices that can easily be carried around with them. Some digital devices can be worn on the body, such as self-tracking wristbands or headbands used to collect biometric data, smartwatches and Google Glass, a device that is worn on the face like spectacles. Social media sites such as Facebook, Twitter, Google+, Instagram and YouTube that facilitate the online sharing of personal information and images with potentially many others have become extremely popular among internet users. These developments have been characterised as 'Web 2.0' (or 'the social web') by many commentators. An 'Internet of Things' is now beginning to develop (also often referred to as 'Web 3.0'), in which digitised everyday objects (or 'smart things') are able to connect to the internet and with each other and exchange information without human intervention, allowing for joined-up networks across a wide range of objects, databases and digital platforms.

There is some contention about when exactly the features of Web 2.0 emerged in terms of a history of the internet, given that some of the aspects described above, such as Wikipedia and some early versions of social media sites, had already been around for some years by the time the term Web 2.0 had entered common use. It is difficult, therefore, to designate a specific and precise timeframe in which the apparent Web 2.0 began. The names given to the different manifestations of internet technologies ('1.0', '2.0', '3.0' and so on) mimic the terminology developed by software developers, but do not do justice to the complexity and messiness of how the internet has developed over the years (Allen 2013).

Whatever terminology is chosen, there is little doubt that the ways in which we communicate with other people, access news, music and other media, play computer games and conduct our working lives have changed dramatically in many aspects over the past decade. While websites designed mainly to communicate information in a one-way format are still available and used for some purposes, they have been complemented by a multitude of online platforms that allow, and indeed encourage, users to contribute content and share it with other users in real time. These activities have been dubbed 'prosumption' (a combination of production and consumption) by some internet researchers to convey the dual nature of such interaction with digital technologies (Beer and Burrows 2010; Ritzer 2014; Ritzer *et al.* 2012). Prosumption using digital media includes such activities as writing blog posts, contributing information to support or fan forums, uploading images, status updates and tweets, and commenting on, liking, retweeting, curating or sharing other users' content. These activities represent a significant shift in how users interact with and make use of digital technologies compared to the very early days of the internet. The ethos of prosumption conforms to the democratic ideals of citizen participation and sharing that are central features of discourses on contemporary digital media use, particularly social media platforms (Beer and Burrows 2010; John 2013). Prosumption had been a feature of some activities before the advent of digital technologies or the internet (among fan cultures or as part of craftwork, for example). However, digital media have afforded the rapid expansion as well as new forms of prosumption (Ritzer 2014).

The classification practices, or tagging (also sometimes called 'folksonomy'), in which users engage comprise another form of prosumption. Users choose whatever words or terms they wish to tag digital content. These can sometimes be sarcastic or critical as part of efforts to entertain others or denote one's emotional responses to content. One common example is the use of the hashtag symbol (#) on Twitter, which not only serves to classify content (for example, I often use #digitalsociology when posting on Twitter about topics related to this subject) but is also often used as a way of expressing opinion or evaluation (#excited, #disgusted). These tagging practices produce 'metadata', or information that indicates the categories into which content may fall, and are therefore vital to allowing others to find content. This is a form of classification, a practice that is vitally important to the way in which the content of Web 2.0 platforms and devices is organised, accessed and circulated (Beer and Burrows 2013).

When I write a blog post or journal article, for example, I engage in the production of metadata by deciding what tags (or 'key words', the term used by academic journals) best describe the content of that particular piece of writing. Once I have tagged the piece, the metadata produced by the tags I have selected helps others to find it when they engage in online searches. If I have not used the most relevant or obvious terms, this may mean that my content may not be found as easily, so tagging practices can be very important in making content 'discoverable'. Metadata also include such features of mobile phone calls as the numbers called, the length of the calls and the geographical location from which they were made, as well as the terms people enter into search engines, what websites they visit, how long they spend browsing websites, to whom they send emails and so on. While the detailed content of these communications is not revealed by metadata, such information can reveal much about people's use of digital technologies, particularly if aggregated from various sources.

I use the term 'algorithm' often throughout the book. An algorithm is a sequence of computer code commands that tells a computer how to proceed through a series of instructions to arrive at a specified endpoint. In short, algorithms are used to solve problems in software. Computer algorithms are becoming increasingly important in facilitating the ways in which digital technologies collect data about users, sort and make sense of these data and generate predictions about the user's future behaviour or make suggestions about how the user should behave. Thus, for example, when Amazon sends users an email making suggestions about books they might be interested in, it has used algorithms to determine each individual's possible interests (and purchasing choices) based on their previous searches or purchases on its platform. The Google Go app (once authorised by the user) can draw on the user's Gmail content and Google searches, using algorithms, to calculate what information the user might require next. The study of algorithms in recent social scholarship has focused attention not only on the increasingly important role played by these types of computer codes in digital society, but also on their cultural and political dimensions.

SCOPING DIGITAL SOCIOLOGY

Sociological research into computer technologies has attracted many different names, dispersed across multiple interests, including 'cyber sociology', 'the sociology of the internet', 'e-sociology', 'the sociology of online communities', 'the sociology of social media' and 'the sociology of cyberculture'. When computer technologies first began to be used widely, researchers often used the terms 'information and communication technologies' (ICTs) or 'cyber technologies' to describe them. The terms 'digital', 'Web 2.0' and 'the internet' have superseded that of the 'cyber' to a large extent in both the academic literature and popular culture. The term 'digital' is now frequently employed in both the popular media and the academic literature to describe the expanding array of material that has been rendered into digital formats and the technologies, devices and media that use these formats. As part of this general discursive move, 'digital sociology' is beginning to replace older terms. This change in terminology is consonant with other sub-disciplines that focus on digital technologies, including digital humanities, digital cultures, digital anthropology and digital geography.

While there certainly have been a number of sociologists who have been interested in researching computer technologies since they attracted popular use, in general sociologists have devoted less significant and sustained attention to this topic compared to their colleagues in communication and media and cultural studies. In the context of the US, Farrell and Petersen (2010), in remarking upon what they term 'the reluctant sociologist' in relation to internet-based research, express their surprise at this lack of interest, particularly given that sociologists have traditionally been in the forefront of adopting and testing new research methods and sources of data for social research studies. While the occasional argument has appeared in journals that US sociologists should be researching online media technologies (DiMaggio *et al.* 2001), it would appear that sociologists in that country tended to abandon communication and media research in general when it moved to journalism schools and an accompanying focus on the social psychology of persuasion in the middle of the last century. As a consequence, although the sociology of culture has flourished in the US, for quite some time American sociologists tended to eschew research into the mass media (Farrell and Petersen 2010; Nichols 2009; Pooley and Katz 2008).

In the UK, the interdisciplinary field of cultural studies (often conjoined with media studies) that emerged in the 1970s dominated research and theorising relating to the mass media and, subsequently, computer technologies. Cultural studies scholars were particularly interested in 'cyberculture', rather than the rather more banal terms 'information society' and 'sociology of information technologies' that tended to be employed in sociology (Webster 2005). Indeed, the choice of terms is telling. The 'cyber' focus of cultural studies emphasises the futuristic, science-fiction dimensions of computerised technologies, while terms referring to 'information technologies' direct attention at the grounded, factual and utilitarian use of such devices for accessing information (Webster 2005).

For a long time, when cultural studies scholars were writing about cyberculture and other aspects of media and popular culture, British sociologists remained focused on such topics as work, crime and social class. Researchers in cultural studies were more interested in the uses people made of popular culture, while sociologists of culture tended towards examining the constraints to their freedoms posed by social structures such as social class, gender and ethnicity (Webster 2005). Few connections were made between these bodies of literature. Thus, for example, the influential and wide-ranging volume *The Cybercultures Reader* (Bell and Kennedy 2000) was edited by Britons David Bell, a critical geographer, and Barbara Kennedy, an academic in film, media and cultural studies. While the work of a few sociologists (including myself) was included in this reader, most other contributions were from academics affiliated with communication, media and cultural studies, literary studies, critical theory or technoscience.

My own country, Australia, like the US, has experienced the introduction of schools of journalism and mass media studies and a resultant withdrawal – to some extent – of sociologists from mass and digital media research. The British cultural studies tradition is also strong in Australia. Cultural studies in Australia as an academic discipline tends to be very separate from both media and communication studies and sociology. Each one – media and communication, sociology and cultural studies – has its own individual association and annual conferences, and there tends to be little communication between researchers associated with each discipline. Media studies and communication studies in Australia have oriented themselves towards the US tradition, while sociology and cultural studies are more influenced by British scholarship. Here again the bulk of Australian research on digital technologies has been published by researchers located within media and communication or cultural studies departments and in journals devoted to these disciplines, rather than by sociologists.

The situation is quickly changing, however. In recent years interest in digital society finally appears to be growing in sociology, and 'digital sociology' has recently become used more frequently. The first journal article published to use the term 'digital sociology' of which I am aware was by an American sociologist in an American journal (Wynn 2009). In this piece Wynn outlined various ways in which digital technologies can be used both for research purposes (using digital devices to conduct ethnographic research, for example) and in teaching. Digital sociology as a term and an endeavour is most commonly found in the British context. At the end of 2012 the British Sociological Association approved a new study group in digital sociology which held its first event in July 2013. Goldsmiths, University of London, offers the first masters degree in digital sociology. The first book with this title was published in 2013 (Orton-Johnson and Prior 2013), a collection edited by two British sociologists featuring contributions predominantly from other sociologists located in the UK and continental Europe. While digital sociology is still not a term that is used to any obvious extent by American sociologists, the American Sociological Association now has a thriving section entitled 'Communication and Information Technologies' that incorporates research on all things digital. In Australia as well digital sociology has not been used very commonly until very recently. A breakthrough was achieved when two sessions under the title digital sociology were held for the first time at the Australian Sociological Association's annual conference in November 2013.

A particular feature of sociological enquiry and theorising is the tendency to be reflexive, including in relation to one's own practices as a sociologist. Sociologists view the world with a particular sensibility (Gane and Back 2012; Holmwood 2010) that is part of the sociological imagination, a term drawn from one of the most influential writers in the discipline, the American C. Wright Mills, that is frequently employed to gloss an approach to studying the world that is distinctively sociological. The sociological sensibility adopts critique not only of other disciplines but of sociology itself. Drawing on the work of another classic sociologist, Pierre Bourdieu, Holmwood (2010: 650) uses the term 'sociological habitus' to suggest that sociology is a habituated set of practices and dispositions that often leads to self-subversion and a tendency to internal interdisciplinarity in its stance. According to Savage (2010), such intensely introspective and reflexive critiques of sociology and agonising over its future may itself be considered a sociological peculiarity, rarely found in other academic disciplines.

What is notable about digital sociology as it has recently emerged as a sub-discipline, particularly in the UK, is not only the focus on the new technologies that have developed since the turn of the twenty-first century, but also the development of a distinctive theoretical and methodological approach that incorporates this reflexive critique. Digital sociology is not only about sociologists researching and theorising about how other people use digital technologies or focusing on the digital data produced via this use. Digital sociology has much broader implications than simply studying digital technologies, raising questions about the practice of sociology and social research itself. It also includes research on how sociologists themselves are using social and other digital media as part of their work. The same types of concerns and theoretical approaches tend to be shared by sociologists writing on digital media and others commenting on related issues such as the future of sociology as a discipline, which types of research methods should be employed and how they should be conceptualised, the ways in which issues of measure and value have become prominent in contemporary societies, the emergence of a knowledge economy and the new political formations and relations of power that are evident. While not all of these scholars may categorise themselves as specifically digital sociologists, their work has contributed significantly to the distinctive direction of the sub-discipline as it has recently emerged.

It should be emphasised here that digital scholarship is necessarily a multidisciplinary area. Sociology itself, like any other discipline, is a permeable and dynamic entity. Accordingly I certainly do not limit my discussion in this book to publications by those writers who would identify themselves as sociologists. Scholars in several other disciplines have had interesting things to say about the social and cultural dimensions of digital media technologies that are directly relevant to the concerns of this book. The fields of mass communication, media studies, cultural geography and digital anthropology in particular, and even some aspects of computer science research, such as that focusing on human–computer relations, have much to offer, as do interdisciplinary areas, such as science and technology studies, internet studies and digital cultures. Discrete areas of research have begun to develop as well that examine the social, cultural and political dimensions of specific features of the digital world, including software studies, game studies, mobile media studies and platform studies. Ideally, these fields should be engaging with and benefiting from each other's work.

While others may have their own views on what digital sociology encompasses, I have developed a four-fold typology that summarises my definition of the sub-discipline. This is as follows:

- *professional digital practice*: using digital tools as part of sociological practice – to build networks, construct an online profile, publicise and share research and instruct students;

- *analyses of digital technology use*: researching the ways in which people's use of digital technologies configures their sense of self, their embodiment and their social relations, and the role of digital media in the creation or reproduction of social institutions and social structures;
- *digital data analysis*: using naturally occurring digital data for social research, either quantitative or qualitative; and
- *critical digital sociology*: undertaking reflexive analysis of digital technologies informed by social and cultural theory.

Professional digital practice

As I observed above, the working lives and identities of sociologists have already been profoundly affected by digitisation. Many aspects of academic research and teaching have been transformed by new digital technologies. Professional digital practice relates to how sociologists (and other academics) are using these tools. In general sociologists have been slow to personally engage in using social media and other digital technologies for professional practice (Daniels and Feagin 2011; Farrell and Petersen 2010; Mitchell 2000). This is slowly beginning to change, however, as more and more sociologists and other academics realise the potential of such tools in generating networks with people both inside and outside the academic world, disseminating research widely, increasing the impact of their research and learning about others' research. Some sociologists have contended that using social media and open-access platforms for publishing has become a vital aspect of engaging as a public sociologist, by facilitating public engagement and interest in and access to research findings. Professional digital use, however, carries with it potential risks as well as possibilities. Sociologists have begun to recognise and write about these various dimensions from a sociologically informed perspective.

Analyses of digital technology use

While, as I observed above, sociologists in general have devoted comparatively little attention to computer technologies in favour of other research topics, since the introduction of personal computers and then the internet a body of sociological literature has developed addressing how people use these technologies. More recently the widespread use of digital technologies, their entry into all realms of everyday life and their use in establishing and maintaining social networks have generated sociological interest in how the self is presented via digital technologies, their incorporation into everyday routines and activities, how people learn about the world using them, the differences in access to and use of these technologies, their uses for surveillance and the implications for concepts of privacy. The big data phenomenon has also sparked a growing scholarly interest in the ethical and political aspects of large digital data sets. The popularity of social media sites has incited sociological enquiries into how best to access and analyse people's engagement with these media. To investigate these topics, sociologists have applied both qualitative methodologies (such as interviews, focus groups and ethnographic research) and quantitative approaches such as surveys. This kind of digital sociological research has clear overlaps with research in digital anthropology, digital cultures, internet studies and digital geography. Central to most sociological analyses of the digital world, however, are questions of power relations and how they operate to affect and produce social relations, self or group identities and social and economic disadvantage and privilege.

Digital data analysis

Another dimension of digital sociology is the use of large digital data sets to conduct social research. Titles such as 'digital social research', 'webometrics', 'web social science' and 'computational social science' tend to be used to refer to conducting this type of 'e-research'. The focus of this strand of research is on the collection and use of data and the tools to analyse these data. Followers adopt an approach that is drawn largely from computer science, and are interested in the most efficient use of tools to store and analyse digital data. Their methods use 'naturally' or incidentally generated data that are already collected by various web platforms (for example, Facebook and Twitter posts, Instagram images, search engines, text messages and GPS data). Some researchers who adopt this approach to digital data analysis are also interested in ways of recording and analysing data for qualitative analysis, including images, videos and audio data. While these approaches seem quite widely used in such fields as information science and technology and communication studies, thus far they seem little used by sociologists, perhaps because few sociologists have training in how to access and analyse these big data sets.

Critical digital sociology

A number of major themes have emerged in recent years in the sociological literature cohering around how the new digital media, the data they produce and the actors involved in the collection, interpretation and analysis of these data confront sociology as a discipline. These issues and questions go to the heart of debates and discussion about how sociology as a discipline should be conceptualised and carried out. Some sociologists have begun to interrogate the ways in which the use of new digital technologies may affect their employment conditions and their presentation of their professional selves. They have offered critiques not only of digital society as a whole but of their own position as increasingly digitised subjects, and of how sociology should deal with the challenges of the new forms of knowledge that are produced by digital technologies. A perspective on digital social research that acknowledges that the methods and devices used to conduct this research are themselves constitutive of social life and society has developed. Other sociologists have begun to investigate ways of using digital technologies and digital data as part of creative, inventive and innovative ways of conducting sociology in research and teaching.

THIS BOOK

The chapters in this book address all of these dimensions of digital sociology. Chapter 2 provides a foundation for the ensuing chapters by reviewing the major theoretical perspectives that are developed in the book. These include analyses of the global information economy and new forms of power, the sociomaterial perspective on the relationship between humans and digital technologies, prosumption, neoliberalism and the sharing subject, the importance of the archive, theories of veillance (watching) that are relevant to digital society and theories concerning digitised embodiment. In Chapter 3 I move on to new ways of conceptualising research in the digital era. This chapter summarises many of the methods that are currently employed by digital social researchers, providing numerous examples of innovative and creative projects that have contributed to innovative ways of rethinking sociology. The discussion also raises the issue of theorising methods, drawing on a body of literature that has developed on positioning the methodological device as itself a sociocultural artefact and agent in the conduct of research.

Chapter 4 addresses the topic of the digitised academic by outlining the ways in which sociologists and other academics use digital technologies as part of their professional practice. The discussion in the chapter adopts a sociological perspective on this topic by examining not only the possibilities and limitations of using social media as an academic, but the deeper implications for professional identity and the politics of digital public engagement. Chapter 5 develops a critical sociology of big data. After reviewing the emergence of the big data and its rapid diffusion into commercial, government and personal enterprises, I identify the social, cultural, ethical and political aspects of this phenomenon, again adopting the perspective that positions digital data as sociomaterial objects.

The final three substantive chapters address the ways in which people interact with digital technologies. Chapter 6 examines the diversity of digital technology use across social groups and geographical locations. I begin with 'the big picture', drawing on several large-scale reports that have identified trends in use both within certain countries and cross-nationally. The chapter then moves on to discuss the more contextually based qualitative investigations that provide insights into the complexities of digital social inequalities and the culturally situated expectations and norms that structure digital engagement practices. The gendered nature of digital technology use is discussed in detail, and the potential for digital technology use to exacerbate social marginalisation and discrimination against minority groups is also canvassed.

Chapter 7 follows on from some of these issues. I examine the politics of digital veillance, activism, privacy debates, calls for openness of digital data and citizen digital public engagement. It is argued that while digital activism and moves to render digital data more open to citizens can be successful to some extent in achieving their aims, claims that they engender a major new form of political resistance or challenge to institutionalised power are inflated. Indeed, digital technologies can provide a means by which activists can come under surveillance and be discredited by governments. Other negative aspects of citizen digital engagement are outlined, including the ways in which the internet can incite discrimination and vigilantism and promote the dissemination of false information.

In Chapter 8 I address embodiment and selfhood as they are enacted via the use of digital technologies. I argue that digital software and hardware now have far more of a capacity to be intimately involved in our lives. More than ever, they are becoming part of our identities as they store more data about our experiences, our social relationships and encounters and our bodily functioning. Their material design and use are also experienced at an embodied and affective level – elements of digital society that are often neglected in sociological analyses.

The brief conclusion in Chapter 9 summarises the main themes and arguments of the book and makes a case for an optimistic and forward-thinking view of what digital sociology can offer.

CHAPTER 2

Theorising digital society

In this chapter I introduce the dominant theoretical perspectives that will be drawn upon and developed further in the other chapters. These perspectives are by no means exhaustive of all the interesting work that has been published relating to digital society, but they represent some of the approaches that I have found some of the most intriguing for developing digital sociology.

THE GLOBAL INFORMATION ECONOMY AND NEW FORMS OF POWER

Contemporary social theory has increasingly represented societies in the developed world as characterised by networks, across which information circulates and spreads. The emergence of new ways of developing social networks via online technologies such as social media platforms has inspired many sociologists and other social theorists to devote their attention to how these technologies are shaping and reshaping social lives.

Manuel Castells is one influential writer on the sociology of digital networks. His concept of 'network society', as expressed in several books and articles (e.g. Castells 2000a, 2000b, 2012), positions networks as the basis for contemporary societies' structure and power relations. In what Castells characterises as 'the information age', industrial processes have been superseded by electronic communications facilitated by the new information technologies. Power is now multidimensional, residing in networks such as the global financial, political, military–security, information production, criminal and multimedia networks. All these networks are involved in defining the rules and norms of societies. Castells asserts that digitally mediated information has become key to economic productivity. Knowledge-based information technologies produce even more knowledge and information, contributing to a new information-based economy that is dispersed globally and is highly interconnected, using digital and other networking technologies and practices. According to Castells, digital technologies such as social media have played a major role in creating a new social structure, global economy and a new virtual culture. His work has led the way in acknowledging the importance of these technologies in contemporary social formations.

The features of new ways of knowing about the world, new forms of information and novel commercial uses for digital data have received attention from several other sociologists. They have argued that digital technologies have changed the ways in which economic value is produced and distributed and commodities conceptualised (Beer 2013a; Featherstone 2009; Lash 2007; Mackenzie 2005; Savage and Burrows 2007). According to these writers, knowledge itself has become transformed via these processes. Many cite Nigel Thrift's (2005, 2006) writings on the information economy and what he entitles 'knowing capitalism' to support their position. Thrift argues that the capitalist economic system is increasingly turning to information as a source of profit, underpinned by increasing the rate of innovation and invention through refigurings of space and time. The affordances of the internet have contributed to this move. Digitisation has the effect of rendering knowledge into information that can easily be accessed via digital technologies. The internet is configuring a new scholarly apparatus that engenders different modes of research, scholarship and communication (Featherstone 2009).

The internet empires (or 'megaplatforms') of the Google, Facebook, Apple and Amazon companies have dominated the digital world and changed the ways in which knowledge is produced and reproduced. The term 'Googilization' (Vaidhyanathan 2011) has been used to describe the ways in which the Google company has expanded its influence into many domains of social, economic and political life. Google is viewed as exerting a powerful effect not only on the ways in which search engines operate and the aesthetics of platforms and apps, but also education, academia, information services, social research, advertising, geographic services, email, publishing and web commerce.

On a broader level, each act of communication via digital media has become a valuable entity by being transformed into digital data that can be aggregated into massive data sets. Whether it is a like on Facebook, a comment on Twitter or a search engine enquiry, these acts of communication have become commoditised. Many commercial and government agencies and organisations now collect and use digital data as part of their operation. A digital data economy has developed, built on techniques of accessing digital data from the various archives in which they are stored for commercial purposes. Where once it was the physical labour of workers that produced surplus value, now the intellectual labour of the masses has monetary value, constituting a new information economy in which thought has become reified, public and commodified (Smith 2013; Thrift 2005, 2006).

It has been contended that power relations are shifting now that the digitised coding of people, things and places has become ubiquitous. Power now operates principally through modes of communication (Lash 2007; Mackenzie 2005; Mackenzie and Vurdubakis 2011; Smith 2013). Instead of the structural model of power that tended to represent societies as systems of largely fixed hierarchies, this approach views power as horizontal, rhizomatic, fluid and dynamic. The mass media are no longer viewed and theorised as 'top-down' mass persuaders, able to manipulate the masses to which they are disseminated and representative of the monopolistic concentration of power over public representations. Rather, it is acknowledged that the new mobile and interactive media embodied in Web 2.0 platforms and devices are dispersed, multimodal, a web of nodes that incorporate prosumption but also constant surveillance and information-gathering on users (Beer 2013a; Beer and Burrows 2010; Lash 2007; Smith 2013). The old media exerted power over the content of the messages they disseminated but had little knowledge of their audiences. In contrast, the new media not only incorporate content from their audiences but know their audiences in ever finer-grained detail (Beer 2013a; Best 2010; Featherstone 2009).

This is a perspective that adopts a Foucauldian approach to power in its emphasis not on the merely repressive dimensions of power relations (the traditional sovereign model of power in which an authoritative individual or group exerts power coercively over subjugated citizens), but on its everyday, dispersed and often voluntary nature. Power produces capabilities and choices at the same time as it delimits them (Foucault 1995). Lash (2007: 70) argues that via the newly digitised information economy and its 'neo-commodities' of data, a type of 'post-hegemonic power' operates in increasingly subtle ways. This 'leaking out' of power from the traditional hegemonic institutions to everyday, taken-for-granted practices means that the age of ubiquitous computing and ubiquitous media is also that of ubiquitous politics. Power becomes immanent to forms of life, and thus is not recognised as such because of its invisible and taken-for-granted nature (Lash 2007: 75).

For Lash (2005, 2006), the global information society is character-ised by openness of systems, non-linear movement and flux as well as flows of information. Lash (2006) notes that flux is characterised by tensions, struggles for power, whereas pure flow presupposes unrestricted movement. He argues for the importance of 'putting flux back into the flows': to problematise the smoothness of flows of information, 'to develop a global politics of flux versus flow' (Lash 2005: 17). This distinction between flux and flow of digital networks and data is an important one. It contravenes a dominant representation of digital data as circulating freely (as in the more utopian visions of writers such as Castells), and emphasises that there are difficulties and blockages in the flows inherent to the global information society.

DIGITAL TECHNOLOGIES AND DATA AS SOCIOMATERIAL OBJECTS

The focus on the ceaseless movement of digital data, while accurately articulating the networked nature of contemporary societies and the speed and ease with which information travels across the networks, also tends to obscure certain dimensions of digitisation. As sociologists and other social theorists have begun to argue, digital data are neither imma-terial nor only minuscule components of a larger material entity. This perspective adopts a sociomaterial approach drawn from science and technology studies, an interdisciplinary field which has provided a critical stance on media technologies in general, and computerised technologies more specifically. In recent years, actor network theory, drawing on the work of sociologist of science Bruno Latour (e.g. Latour 1987, 2005), has achieved a dominant position in science and technology studies. In emphasising the role and agency of non-human actors in shaping human actors, actor network theory directs attention at the materiality and heterogeneous nature of human experience and subjectivity. Exponents contend that humans are always imbricated within networks comprised of human and non-human actors and cannot be isolated from these networks. This perspective has proven to be an insightful approach in scholarship on digital society, particularly in relation to understanding such digital phenomena as networks, social media platforms and data.

The concept of the assemblage is a useful way of understanding the hybrid phenomena that form when human and non-human actors interact. Drawing on actor network theory as well as Deleuzian philosophy, the assemblage concept denotes an intermingling of the human and non-human in various dynamic ways (Haggerty and Ericson 2000; Latour 2005; Latour *et al.* 2012; Marcus 2006; Palmås 2011). The assemblage provides an approach to understanding the individual's relationship to and use of digital technologies that emphasises that each actor, whether human or non-human, shapes the other in a mutually constitutive relationship. It also provides a theoretical basis for understanding how nonhuman actors interact with each other, as takes place in the Internet of Things.

Assemblages are viewed as 'messy objects' in their complexity and mutability (Fenwick and Edwards 2011). Thus, for example, Fenwick and Edwards (2011) discuss the ways in which data and the devices used to create them have become a driving force in contemporary education, shaping decisions about what to teach students and how to use resources. By this process, the education system is rendered accountable to the data that are collected, used to monitor and calculate student learning outcomes. This massive and complex data-gathering assemblage used for governance purposes, however, is precarious, open to contingencies and messiness by virtue of its sheer size and complexity, its enrolment of many diverse agents and the possibility for gaming the system or engaging in resistant acts: cheating on test scores, for instance, or when teachers refuse to administer standardised tests, or when the data are subjected to contestations and challenges about what they really demonstrate. Counter-networks emerge to challenge existing networks, so that the power of a network of actors is never assured.

In this literature, the digital data objects that are brought together through digital technologies – including 'like' or 'share' buttons, individuals' browser histories, personalised recommendations and comments on social media posts as well as the hardware and software that structure the choices available to users – are assemblages of complex interactions of economic, technological, social and cultural logics (Caplan 2013; Langois and Elmer 2013; Mackenzie 2005; Mackenzie and Vurdubakis 2011). Representing digital phenomena as objects serves the purpose of acknowledging their existence, effects and power (Caplan 2013; Hands 2013; Langois and Elmer 2013; Marres 2012).

The cultural and political analysis of computer software is sometimes referred to as software studies. Writers in software studies place an emphasis not on the transmission or reception of messages, as in the old model of communication, but rather have developed a socio-material interest in the ways in which acts of computation produce and shape knowledges. Computer codes are positioned as agents in configurations and assemblages (Fuller 2008), producing what Kitchin and Dodge (2011) refer to as 'coded assemblages'. Indeed, the pervasive nature of software in everyday life is such that Manovich (2013b) argues that it has become 'a universal language, the interface to our imagination and the world'. He contends, therefore, that social researchers should be conceptualising people's interactions with digital technologies as 'software performances' which are constructed and reconstructed in real time, with the software constantly reacting to the user's actions.

Software is no longer static: it is constantly responding to inputs from its users and from other networked systems: updating data, recognising location as the user moves around in space, noticing what activities the user is engaging in on her or his device (Helmond 2013; Manovich 2013a; Rogers 2013). Manovich (2013a: 36) gives the example of a user engaging with the Google Earth platform. Due to the constantly updated nature of Google Earth, each time the user accesses the platform she or he is viewing a 'new Earth', with new data available. Similarly, many Wikipedia entries are dynamic, being updated or edited regularly. Users can also create 'mashups' by bringing information from a range of digital platforms together in completely new and individually customised ways. Because these technologies are interactive platforms, they are subject to constant renewal and change, including changes contributed by users themselves. This is a completely new way of understanding and experiencing the nature of 'information' itself. As Manovich (2013b) comments, humans and software interact in ways that can be difficult to disentangle from each other:

> What are interactive-media 'data'? Software code as it executes, the records of user interactions (for example, clicks and cursor movements), the video recording of a user's screen, a user's brain activity as captured by an EEG or fMRI? All of the above, or something else?

Digital data are also positioned as sociomaterial objects in this literature. Whereas many commentators in the popular media, government and business world view digital data as the ultimate forms of truth and accurate knowledge, sociologists and other social theorists have emphasised that these forms of information, like any other type, are socially created and have a social life, a vitality, of their own. Digital data objects structure our concepts of identity, embodiment, relationships, our choices and preferences and even our access to services or spaces. There are many material aspects to digital data. They are the product of complex decisions, creative ideas, the solving and management of technical problems and marketing efforts on the part of those workers who are involved in producing the materials that create, manage and store these data. They are also the product of the labour of the prosumers who create the data. These are the 'invisible' material aspects of digital data (Aslinger and Huntemann 2013).

Algorithms play an important role in configuring digital data objects. Without the knowledge of digital technology users, algorithms measure and sort them, deciding what choices they may be offered. Digital data objects aggregated together, often from a variety of sources, configure 'metric assemblages' (Burrows 2012) or 'surveillant assemblages' (Haggerty and Ericson 2000) that produce a virtual *doppelgänger* of the user. Algorithms and other elements of software, therefore, are generative, a productive form of power (Beer 2009; 2013a; boyd and Crawford 2012; Cheney-Lippold 2011; Mackenzie 2005; Mackenzie and Vurdubakis 2011; Ruppert *et al.* 2013).

Scholars who have adopted a sociomaterial perspective have also highlighted the tangible physicality of aspects of digital technology manufacture and use. Despite the rhetoric of seamless, proficient operation that so commonly is employed to discuss the internet and ubiquitous computing, the maintenance that supports this operation is messy and contingent, often involving pragmatic compromises, negotiations and just-in-time interventions to keep the system working. Geographical, economic, social, political and cultural factors – including such basic requirements as a stable electricity supply and access to a computer network – combine to promote or undermine the workings of digital technologies (Bell 2006a; Bell and Dourish 2007, 2011; Dourish and Bell 2007). The materiality of digital hardware becomes very apparent when devices that are no longer required must be disposed of, creating the problem of digital waste (or 'e-waste') that often contains toxic materials (Gabrys 2011; Miller and Horst 2012).

Given the high turnover of digital devices, their tendency towards fast obsolescence and the fact that they are often replaced every few years in wealthy countries by people seeking the newest technologies and upgrades, vast quantities of digital waste are constantly generated. The vast majority of discarded digital devices end up in landfill. Only a small minority are recycled or reused, and those that are tend to be sent from wealthy to poor countries for scrap and salvaging of components. When they are outmoded and discarded, the once highly desirable, shiny digital devices that were so full of promise when they were purchased simply become another form of rubbish – dirty, unsightly and potentially contaminating pollutants (Gabrys 2011). The electricity supplies that power digital technologies and digital data storage units themselves have environmental effects on humans and other living things, such as the release of smoke and particles from coal-fired electricity generating plants. 'The digital is a regime of energies: human energy and the energy needed for technological machines' (Parikka 2013).

The materiality of digital objects is also apparent in debates over how and where digital data should be stored, as they require ever-larger physical structures (servers) for archiving purposes. Despite the metaphor of the computing 'cloud', digital data do not hover in the ether but must be contained within hardware. Furthermore, digital data are very difficult to erase or remove, and thus can be very stubbornly material. At the same time, however, if stored too long and not used, they may quickly become obsolete and therefore useless, if contemporary technologies can no longer access and make use of them. Digital data, therefore, may be said to 'decay' if left too long, and may be lost and forgotten if they are not migrated to new technological formats. Digital memory is volatile because the technologies used to store and access data change so quickly. Analogue materials that are rendered into digital form for archival purposes and then destroyed may therefore be lost if their digital forms can no longer be used (Gabrys 2011).

PROSUMPTION, NEOLIBERALISM AND THE SHARING SUBJECT

As noted above, in the global information economy a kind of digital vitality has been generated, in which information and data have taken on value in themselves. The practices of prosumption are major contributors to this economy, providing constant streams of information about the preferences, habits and opinions of digital technology users that can then be used for targeted marketing, advertising and other commercial promotional purposes (Beer 2009; Beer and Burrows 2013; Ritzer *et al.* 2012). Many users of social media enjoy creating content such as writing comments or blogs, producing fan sites or making mashups or digital graphic visualisations. Such activities can be a form of creative work. The opportunity for others to acknowledge or demonstrate their appreciation of the content can be a powerful motivating force for prosumption (Beer and Burrows 2013).

Some writers on digital society have discussed the broader political implications of the use and impact of digital technologies. Several have remarked upon the ways in which these technologies serve a neoliberal political mode of governance. Neoliberalism is a political orientation that has taken hold across the developed world. Its main tenets are the notion of the atomised human actor who is responsible for her or his life chances and outcomes, the power of the market economy and competition in achieving the best outcomes for all and the withdrawal of the state from providing support services to the socioeconomically disadvantaged. The ideal subject, according to neoliberal principles, is self-regulated and takes responsibility for her or his own destiny. Individuals are expected and encouraged to be self-reflexive, or to view their lives as projects that require entrepreneurial investment of time and energy (Ventura 2012). Neoliberalism underpins many dimensions of sociological theorising in response to digital technologies, including sociologists' identification of the ways in which the surveillance and monitoring functions afforded by these technologies may be used in the interests of promoting self-management and competitive behaviours over state regulation and intervention.

Prosumption may also be theorised taking up Foucault's work on the practices of selfhood that make up human actors: those activities that are directed at self-care or self-improvement (Foucault 1988). Through these technologies, people learn about their environment and the other people with whom they share their lives. Indeed, it has been argued that social media platforms such as Instagram and Facebook encourage the production and circulation of greater intimate knowledge about and between participants than ever before. These technologies, via status updates and visual imagery, allow friends and family members who may not live in the same geographical area and who rarely meet face-to-face to engage regularly with each other across space and time. They construct a chronological account of various aspects of a person's life that they wish to share with friends or followers: in the terminology of Facebook, indeed, a 'timeline' combining words with photos or videos to present the user's persona. However, the regular and continued use of these technologies also demands a type of work – social labour – to conform to the demands of these media and those with whom users interact (Fuchs 2012; Lambert 2013; Marwick 2012; M. Sauter 2013).

Foucault's writings on the confession in his *History of Sexuality* (1979) have also been taken up to theorise the ways in which people configure and represent themselves on social media sites as part of ethical self-formation. It is argued that as part of the moral economy of many forms of social media, users of these media are incited to confess or reveal aspects of their private lives to other observers, who may choose to comment on or otherwise demonstrate approval or disapproval through such functions as 'liking' or sharing the content.

By both revealing the intimate details of their lives and responding to others' reactions, users may engage in self-reflection and self-improvement as well as participating in the evaluation of others' actions and practices. Such social media use may therefore be thought as an ethical and social practice that contributes not only to self-formation but the reproduction of social norms and expectations to which people are expected to adhere (Boellstorff 2013; Marwick 2012; T. Sauter 2013).

Theorists who have sought to position social media participation in the context of the global knowledge economy have contended that digital entrepreneurs and companies are able to sell more to consumers through the harnessing of the enthusiasms of consumer communities, the automating and mass dissemination of 'word of mouth' and the use of algorithms to make suggestions about future purchases based on past choices. The commodity is not only the item that is sold but information about the item and its consumers as well as the communities that form around consumption that themselves generate value by producing information and innovative ideas as well as generate experiences for the consumers involved that have value for them (Beer 2013a; Beer and Burrows 2013; Thrift 2005, 2006).

Cultural studies scholars such as Henry Jenkins and his collaborators (Ford *et al.* 2013) are interested in what they term 'spreadable media' or media produced digitally that circulate or 'spread' across multiple sites, platforms and cultures in messy and difficult to govern ways. They contend that users' choices about sharing digital content with others are reshaping the media landscape, representing a shift from distribution to circulation. Producers of content attempt to make their content in ways that will inspire users to share it with their friends or followers via social media. To achieve this, the content has to be meaningful in some way to the person who redistributes it, thus involving active participation and decision-making on their part (Ford *et al.* 2013). The term 'spreadable' is used to denote the properties of media content that render it more or less easy to share and distribute. It includes technical resources, economic structures, attributes of the content itself and the social networking devices and software that facilitate circulation. It differs from, although is related to, 'sticky' content or 'destination viewing' – content that is located in a specific media site to which the content producers attempt to attract audiences. 'Sticky' content becomes 'spreadable' when it moves from a static position on a media site to other destinations across the cultural landscape (Ford *et al.* 2013).

The concept of the sharing subject is central to spreadable media. The sharing subject seeks to recirculate content as part of their identity and participation in social networks and communities, harbouring the belief that such sharing will have an impact on their networks and contribute to conversations (John 2013; Payne 2012). In 'communicative capitalism' (Payne 2012), media companies and corporations actively seek to monetise content sharing and circulation – to achieve 'virality' – and to direct this in ways that contribute financially to themselves but not to the creators of the content. The media industry quickly learned to co-opt the creative efforts of fans engaging in prosumption, for example, as part of their attempts to sell ever more products to these fans. Fans were manipulated into becoming the marketers for media products, helping to publicise them by their prosumption practices and their generation of metadata (Bird 2011).

Thus simultaneous discourses of participatory democracy (Beer 2009, 2013a) and (far less overt) that of capitalising upon and delimiting this freedom operate in many social media platforms. Critics contend that these technologies are one dimension of a vast network of systems of monitoring, measuring and regulating the population and subgroups within the population that direct attention at individual behaviours rather than social processes. Social media, for example, are often represented as promoting individual creativity and freedom via the opportunities they offer for prosumption. But there remain well-defined limits to how this creativity and freedom of expression are allowed to operate. Some writers draw on political economy perspectives to highlight the lack of access many people still face and the discrimination and exploitation that are inherent in many digital relationships and in the manufacture of the technologies themselves. Marxist thought lives on in several critiques of digital technologies, as particularly exemplified by the work of Fuchs and collaborators, who have written about the exploitation of prosumers on sites such as Facebook and also the poor working conditions faced by paid workers engaged by the computer hardware and internet empires (Fuchs 2011, 2012, 2014b; Fuchs and Dyer-Witheford 2013).

These commentators emphasise that many platforms that encourage prosumption practices are also attempting to monetise these activities in classical capitalist endeavours. Counter to the idealised notion of the sharing subject that can be creative and resistant to dominant discourses, industry has begun to use this ideal for its own ends. Differential power relations and exploitation, therefore, are reproduced on the internet just as they are in other social sites, challenging taken-for-granted assumptions about the 'democratic' nature of the internet. The interests of the corporate entities that established the Web 2.0 tools and platforms that encourage content creation and sharing often differ from those who are creating the content, who are seeking democratic participation and support the ethos of sharing as a gift (John 2013). The 'moral economy' of content creation and sharing conflicts with the capitalist economy of those who seek to gain financially. Content producers and sharers are engaging in unpaid labour which, to them, has affective and moral value, the surplus value of which financially benefits others (Bird 2011; Ford *et al.* 2013; Fuchs 2012; Fuchs and Dyer-Witheford 2013; Lupton 2014a; Payne 2012). The terms of service of the platforms that prosumers use are more frequently making clear that the content they contribute to these platforms does not belong to them, but rather to the developers of the platforms (Lupton 2014a). People's creative efforts, therefore, have become harnessed to the media and data industries, but many of them may not be fully aware of this, particularly if they do not closely read the terms and conditions of the platforms they use or if the platforms are vague about how they use the data that are uploaded by users.

THE IMPORTANCE OF THE ARCHIVE

The specific features of how digital data are produced and the ways in which these data are now archived are vital to how they are understood as new forms of social data. The internet is a living archive: it generates, stores, distributes and transmits data (Smith 2013). Online archives have become complex and self-referential, such that 'There are archives on the Internet. There are archives of archives on the Internet. There are archives of the Internet. And then there is the Internet itself as an archive and as archival' (Smith 2013: 383). Digital archives render digital data searchable and distributable, both essential features that contribute to their apparent value. Given that the current global information economy depends on these processes, questions arise concerning the politics of the knowledge kept in these archives, the politics of ownership and control of these data and the politics of the human, or the privacy rights and identities that may be challenged by the existence of these archives (Smith 2013).

Beer and Burrows (2013) identify four components of popular cultural digital data archives. These components include profiles, or the information that users enter about themselves to take part in online activities and linkages and data intersectionality, or the connections that are made between digital devices, sites or platforms, each containing data derived from different methods. Another component feature of digital data is metadata or tagging practices. The final component feature is that of play: the ludic dimensions of using digital media as part of popular culture that generates data. Beer and Burrows then go on to outline a framework of four interrelated and overlapping types of digital archives related to popular culture in which these data are stored, based on the content. The first is that of transactional data, or data produced via the vast range of routine activities in which computer users engage online, whether using their own device or as part of a broader organisation's digital system. These data are produced via such activities taking place online as banking and purchasing, searches, customer loyalty programmes, ticket booking, interactions with government agencies and the like. Examples of these types of archives include Amazon, Spotify and iTunes. These archives contain both the cultural forms that are consumed and the data that users generate as part of their consumption (on their preferences, for example). Next, Beer and Burrows suggest the archive of the everyday, in which digital data about people's everyday activities, social relationships, likes, friends and followers are stored via such platforms as Twitter, Facebook, Tumblr, YouTube, Flickr and Instagram. The third type of digital archive they identify is that comprised of viewpoint or opinion commentaries, typically expressed on digital forums such as online news sites, blogs/micro-blogs and websites that specifically elicit users' opinions or ratings on goods, products, services or celebrities, such as Patient Opinion, Amazon and Trip Advisor and various websites that have been established for the fans of celebrities or sports teams. Finally, there is the crowdsourcing archive, created by users contributing data specifically to create new forms of knowledge via aggregates of data or to raise money for enterprises. Examples of this archive are Wikipedia, Kickstarter, Quora and PatientsLikeMe.

Many other digital data archives that are not directly related to popular culture exist, such as those generated by government agencies, educational institutions, healthcare services, security organisations and corporations. Many organisations are realising the value of digitising and archiving data. Census data, for example, is archived by the government agency that collects it. Increasing numbers of digital data sets are collected by educational institutions to monitor and track their students' progress by creating 'learning profiles'. Various healthcare agencies and services are attempting to bring together medically related digital data on the patients they treat, including electronic medical records. Museums and libraries are increasingly using digital methods to preserve material in their archives. Organisations such as the New York Philharmonic have created digital repositories for such material as programmes, scores, images, business documents and audio material. Universities use e-repositories to collect their researchers' output, and academic journals now publish their material online in searchable archives.

Much of this material remains accessible on the web, perhaps permanently, meaning that retrospective surveillance over a historical time period can easily be performed. What has been described as 'the right to be forgotten' has subsequently received much attention by media and legal researchers as part of the new legal specialisation of digital privacy rights (Rosen 2012). It has been argued, indeed, that we are now living in an era characterised by 'the end of forgetting', in which digital data linger indefinitely as forms of recording and archiving information (Bossewitch and Sinnreich 2013). Because they are machines, and not the fleshly brain-matter upon which traditional memory relies, digital technologies are viewed as providing more accurate records of events. Digital technologies act as 'cognitive prostheses', their records extending, enhancing and even replacing memories (Bossewitch and Sinnreich 2013: 226).

DIGITAL VEILLANCE

Another important theoretical perspective that is relevant to digital sociology is that offered by scholars contributing to the literature on veillance (watching) in contemporary societies. Due to digital and other surveillance technologies, the social sphere has become heavily mediated, with new technologies extending the field of vision in public space and opportunities for monitoring and recording the actions of individuals (Biressi and Nunn 2003; Bossewitch and Sinnreich 2013). Watching in everyday life, frequently undertaken using digital technologies, has become normalised as a life-practice, part of the constellation of the configuration of identity and embodiment (Ball 2014; Rosenzweig 2012).

It has been observed by many commentators that the vast masses of digital data that are generated by security technologies, devices and apps and stored on platform archives may be used for various forms of watching. The data that are collected when people use the internet, as well as the content that they upload and share with others as part of their prosumption practices, are subject to monitoring and oversight by various other actors, including digital developers and companies and one's friends and followers on social media. Indeed, this type of monitoring and collection of data on the users of online technologies has become a central dimension of the digital information economy. Digital veillance is not only an apparatus of government security agencies, but is integral to the commercial economy and such institutions as healthcare, policing and the education system. Facilitated by the internet, a global surveillance economy and multifaceted surveillant assemblage has developed, in which nations both collaborate in providing digital surveillance systems and advice and monitor each other using these systems (Ball and Murakami Wood 2013). The full extent of espionage activity that is undertaken using access to digital data has only recently been revealed by the Snowden files, which demonstrated that many nations are engaging in major, detailed digital surveillance of their own citizens.

Writers on the social, cultural and political dimensions of veillance have identified a number of different modes. In simple terms, surveillance denotes 'watching over', or 'watching from above', usually in relation to those in power watching over others (Mann and Ferenbok 2013). Digital surveillance is undertaken using technologies such as CCTV cameras, radio frequency identification chips (RFIDs) and the biometric monitoring that is undertaken by various agencies as part of security arrangements, as well as the surveillance practices carried out by commercial enterprises seeking to extract monetary value from digital data created by users. Sometimes people are aware that they are being watched using these technologies; sometimes such surveillance is covert. Digital surveillance may be coercive, used to punish or overtly discipline individuals or social groups, or it may be benign, a form of security or governance designed for efficiency and promoting economic growth or physical wellbeing.

Digital surveillance technologies differ from previous forms of watching in their pervasiveness, the scope of data they are able to collect and store, their potential longevity and the implications for privacy they evoke. These types of surveillance operate via digital recording of people's activities, the storage of these data in archives and the use of algorithms to generate and manipulate the data and to make predictions about people's behaviour. These surveillance data have a much longer life and capacity to be disseminated across time and space than previous forms of surveillance (Bossewitch and Sinnreich 2013; Mann and Ferenbok 2013; Werbin 2011).

Lyon and Bauman's (2013) book on 'liquid surveillance' makes extensive reference to the ways in which digital data circulate as part of systems of veillance. Building on Bauman's extensive writings on 'liquid modernity' and Lyon's body of work on surveillance societies, this book emphasises that due to the new practices and technologies emerging in late modernity, surveillance has become uncontained and pervasive. Liquid surveillance is the apotheosis of the move towards monitoring and measuring humans and non-humans. The mobility and ubiquitous nature of new surveillance technologies (many of which are digital) mean that it has become increasingly difficult for people to know when they are being monitored. Surveillance, thus, is 'seeping and spreading into many life areas where once it had only marginal sway' (Lyon and Bauman 2013: 3).

Digital technologies have intensified or generated new forms of veillance. I referred earlier in this chapter to the term 'surveillant assemblage', which has been employed to describe the ways in which digital data are used to create 'data doubles' (Haggerty and Ericson 2000). The surveillant assemblage is configured via the production and aggregating of various forms of digital data, producing a new kind of assemblage that is constantly changing as more data are produced. Bodies and identities are fragmented into a series of discrete components as digital data and reassembled via this process of reconfiguration. This assemblage then becomes the target of various forms of intervention: greater security measures, increases or reductions in social security payments, medical therapies, educational interventions and so on. Groups that once were not subject to routine surveillance are now targeted by the dispersed liquid technologies of digital surveillance (Haggerty and Ericson 2000).

Foucault's writings have been very influential in writings on veillance, including those referring to digital devices. His work on biopolitics and biopower in particular has delineated the forms of watching and exclusion that involve the detailed monitoring of both individuals and populations. Foucault's writings on governmentality, or the managing of populations by specific political rationalities, have also been taken up by scholars writing about forms of veillance that are used for such management. The influential concept of panoptic surveillance (Brignall 2002; Elmer 2003) draws on Foucault's use of the metaphor of the panopticon in his *Discipline and Punish* (1995), itself derived from the writings of the English philosopher Jeremy Bentham. Panoptic surveillance is a feature of non-coercive disciplinary power involving the few watching the many. The panopticon is an exemplary prison in which a small number of prison guards watch a large number of prisoners from a central hidden position. The idea of this concept of watching is that because the prisoners are never able to tell when they are being watched, they learn to engage in self-discipline, internalising the guards' regulatory gaze. The concept of CCTV cameras as a security measure relies to some extent upon this assumption: we are never quite sure if an operator is monitoring the images produced by the cameras, or even if they are actually turned on, so we may modify our behaviour accordingly.

Panoptic surveillance contributes to a politics of exclusion and inclusion that continues to operate in relation to the field of public visibility configured through and with digital surveillance technologies. People from specific social groups that are categorised as the undesirable Other by virtue of their race, ethnicity or nationality, age or social class are subjected to far more intensive monitoring, identification as 'dangerous' or 'risky', and exclusion on the basis of these factors than are those from privileged social groups (Biressi and Nunn 2003; Werbin 2011). The term ban-optic surveillance (a variation of panoptic surveillance) has been employed to more specifically describe the use of data to ban or exclude certain individuals and social groups from particular regions, countries or public spaces, or from access to employment, social services, insurance and so on (Ajana 2013; Pavone and Esposti 2012; Sutrop and Laas–Mikko 2012).

Panspectric veillance (also sometimes referred to as dataveillance) refers to a broader range of digital technologies and uses of data. The panspectron is a concept developed by DeLanda (1991), again in response to the concept of the panopticon. DeLanda contrasted the panspectron with the panopticon, noting that the latter relies on human senses (mainly vision), while the former uses mostly digital sensors and signals to create large data sets for veillance purposes. DeLanda was writing almost twenty-five years ago, when the use of personal computer technologies was in its infancy, the internet was not available for widespread access and social media had yet to be invented. A more recent application of his concept of panspectric veillance notes its relevance to contemporary business practices involving the generation and use of large digital data sets about consumer behaviour. This generation of data also often involves the use of RFID chips embedded in consumer products to trace their distribution and consumers' buying patterns (Palmås 2011).

It is here that big data, algorithms and predictive analytics are playing important roles. Given these developments in the use of digital data, I would argue that yet another form of veillance using digital technologies has developed that is used increasingly more often as part of dataveillance and ban-optic surveillance: that of algorithmic veillance. The algorithms used to make decisions and predictions about the value of some consumers compared with others, based on their digital consumption activities, or even in some cases about the threat they may pose to others (as in identifying potential terrorists, criminals or illegal immigrants), act to exclude some individuals at the same time as they privilege and work to include others (Crawford and Schultz 2014; Lyon and Bauman 2013).

The practices of sousveillance (literally meaning 'watching from below') have also been promoted by the emergence of digital technologies that provide ordinary people with the means to watch others. Sousveillance involves citizens not only watching each other but also conducting surveillance of those in authority. Many people now have access to devices such as smartphones, wearable computing (like Google Glass) and sensor-embedded technologies to capture images or information for their own use. It is often used in relation to citizen participation, citizen journalism and political transparency, as it is argued that the democratisation of surveillance has the effect of empowering citizens to watch and report on abuses of power on the part of the powerful (Ganascia 2010; Kingsley 2008; Mann and Ferenbok 2013).

Some writers have used the term synoptic veillance (Doyle 2011), the inverse of panoptic veillance, to describe social and other forms of watching which involve the many watching the few. This takes place in relation to fandom cultures, for example, in which celebrities post content on social media that is viewed and followed by many others. It also occurs when material that individuals who are non-celebrities have uploaded to social media sites such as YouTube 'goes viral', or attracts many viewers or followers. More specifically, a further new concept of veillance, social surveillance (Marwick 2012), has been employed to describe the interactive watching of each other that takes place on social media sites. Social surveillance may be viewed as one form of participatory veillance, which involves the voluntary engage-ment in watching or being watched by others. Participatory veillance is a feature of signing up to use social media platforms, when people consent to their data being collected as part of the conditions of their use of these sites, or other technologies, such as customer loyalty schemes (enshrined in such features as 'terms and conditions' and 'privacy policy' that are included on digital sites or agreement to the acceptance of 'cookies') (Best 2010; Lupton 2014a). It also takes place when people engage in self-monitoring practices of their bodies or everyday habits (Lupton 2012) or share their geo-location details with others (Hjorth and Pink 2014).

Another form of veillance, dubbed uberveillance, is also often participatory, but can be used for imposed, covert or coercive surveil-lance measures that may challenge people's rights to privacy. This term has been invented to denote, in particular, the use of tracking tech-nologies that can be inserted within or worn upon the body. These include wearable computing used for monitoring biometric data and identifying spatial location, as well as RFID chips. RFID chips are being used increasingly in such technologies as electronic passports, credit and debit cards, motor vehicle driving monitoring systems and medical technologies such as heart pace-makers and prosthetic knees to assist with post-operation analytics and for monitoring patients with dementia. These devices can be used to track individuals' movements and activities in real time. Many users of such technologies are unaware of the capacity of the digital signals they emit to identify their geo-location and the ways in which these data may be used for surveillance purposes (Michael and Clarke 2013; Michael and Michael 2013).

THEORISING DIGITISED EMBODIMENT

From the perspective of the sociomaterial approach, the ways in which nonhuman actors interact with humans are a central topic of understanding social life, subjectivity and embodiment. This approach moves away from a focus on the discursive that had dominated social and cultural theory for some time, to addressing the material dimensions of social relations and human experience. So, too, the sociology of the body that was a dominant interest of scholars at the end of the last century has engendered a greater awareness of human embodiment and interembodiment: the fleshly dimensions of human subjects and their interactions with others' bodies and with objects.

Theories of material cultures and consumption in anthropology and cultural studies are also enlightening to understand the ways in which the new digital media are 'appropriated' or 'domesticated' into everyday practices and routines (Hartmann 2013). Scholars who are interested in material culture focus their attention on the ways in which material artefacts are invested with social, cultural and personal meaning when they are manufactured and used as part of everyday life. They contend that study of such things is vital to understanding both the ways in which cultures are enacted and reproduced and the significance that objects have in specific cultural contexts. Many digital anthropologists are associated with this approach (Miller and Horst 2012). Writers in cultural and media studies have focused attention for some decades now on the ways in which people engage with and use media as part of their everyday routines in the home and at work, including digital devices (Lupton and Noble 2002; Richardson 2009; Salovaara *et al.* 2011). The concept of appropriation refers to the incorporation of objects into habitual practices, while that of domestication relates to the ways in which objects are altered in some way via these routine practices.

Importantly, this research emphasises the active participation of individuals in taking up media. It goes beyond the prosumption perspective by contending that *all* consumption involves some kind of work on the part of the user when they are incorporating an object into their everyday routines. It focuses on the enabling and constraining dimensions of the use of objects and how objects shape or discipline users just as users reconfigure objects. From this perspective, consumption is viewed broadly as the interaction of human bodies with objects in specific contexts and spaces. People consume objects by incorporating and domesticating them, bringing them into their everyday worlds, melding them to their bodies/selves and bestowing these objects with their own biographically specific meanings. They become 'territories of the self', marked by individual use, and therefore redolent of personal histories (Nippert-Eng 1996). This concept of territories of the self acknowledges that bodies and selves are not contained within the fleshly envelope of the individual body, but extend beyond this into space and connect and interconnect with other bodies and objects. These processes are inevitably relational because they involve embodied interactions and affective responses at both the conscious and unconscious levels.

The period spanning the two decades from the early 1980s to the first few years of the twenty-first century was the era of 'the cyber' in social, cultural and political theory and research. During this cyber era, frequent references were made not only to the cyborg but also to cyberspace, cyberfeminism, cybercultures, cybercrime, cyber-racism, postcolonial cyborgs, cyberpunk, cyber-queer, cyber-bullying and so on. Cyberspace was portrayed as a virtual, non-physical network in which users interacted with each other by employing computer technologies. The term at first tended to suggest an experience that was disembodied, comprised of one's digital avatar moving through another world that was entirely separate and different from that of the material world. The term 'virtual reality' also signified an experience that was different from material reality, not quite real.

Despite the cultural currency of all things cyber late last century, it is clear that these terms and their accompanying theoretical insights have lost momentum, and now have 'almost an antique feel' (Bell 2007: 2). These days, referring to cyberspace seems inappropriate, old-fashioned and clunky, too closely tied to the imaginaries of science fiction and failing to recognise the ordinary and taken-for-granted nature of computer technologies. The terms 'posthuman' and 'transhuman' also circulated in earlier writing on technocultures, and continue to be frequently used in the literature on the human–technology encounters. Yet these terms too fail to recognise the routine incorporation of new digital technologies into everyday lives. To be human, as I argued in Chapter 1, means for many the use of digital technologies on a regular basis. More contemporary terms focus on the technical features or capabilities of the technologies rather than attempting to position these technologies as somehow offering an alternative world separate from a more 'real' experience (Paasonen 2009). There is no need to jettison cyber theory altogether, however. Indeed, I would assert that there is significant value and scope in revisiting cyborg theory in the light of new technologies that have become so seamlessly incorporated and domesticated into everyday life.

The technoscience feminist scholar Donna Haraway's seminal writings on the cyborg remain important in conceptualising the ontology and politics of human–digital encounters. Her essay 'Manifesto for cyborgs' (Haraway 1985) is one of the most influential pieces of writing in cyberculture studies. In this work, Haraway argues that there are two types of cyborg that operate at different ontological levels. One type is the material cyborg that is configured via the military–industrial–entertainment complex. In the 1980s, when Haraway was writing, this was the cyborg of science-fiction films, the warrior macho human–machine or the medicalised body that is normalised by technologies and earns profits for pharmaceutical and medical device companies. This literal cyborg continues to exist and has become increasingly digitised in the context of mobile and wearable digital devices.

The second type of cyborg identified by Haraway, and the one that represents her substantial contribution to the theoretical literature on technocultures, is that of the metaphorical or ontological cyborg. The cyborg is a figure that challenges assumptions and binaries, that is politically disruptive, progressive and oppositional in its hybridity and liminality. It is this cyborg as metaphor that Haraway seeks to take up and use to support her theorising of the interrelationship of humans and nonhumans. Haraway adopts a strongly relative sociomaterial perspective on human actors as they interact with other actors, both living (such as animals) and non-living. In her concept of the cyborg she is trying to express the broader idea that no human bodies/selves are stable or natural. Rather, we are multiple bodies and multiple selves, depending on the context in which we find ourselves and the other bodies and nonhuman entities with which we interact.

The material cyborg is only one such assemblage that may be configured. For Haraway, therefore, the cyborg represents the actor-network assemblage both literally and metaphorically (and, indeed, she acknowledges the influence of Latour in developing her ideas; see Penley et al. 1991). In an article published in 2012, Haraway notes that she no longer views cyborgs as machine–organism hybrids 'or indeed hybrids at all', but rather as 'imploded entities, dense material semiotic "things" – articulated string figures of ontologically heterogeneous, historically situated, materially rich, virally proliferating relatings of particular sorts' (Haraway 2012: 301). Haraway's reference to 'string figures' relates to the cat's cradle game, played using string manipulated on the hands to produce complicated patterns, and which can be swapped from one pair of hands to another as part of sharing the creation. She employs this metaphor in her later work as a means of emphasising the intertwinings, complicated patternings, knottings, webbings and collaborations of technoscience and the bodily assemblages it configures.

The metaphor of entanglement is now frequently adopted in sociomaterial writings. Like Haraway's cat's cradle metaphor, the entanglement metaphor emphasises the inextricably intertwined relationship of human subjects with material objects. However, the entanglement metaphor, more than that of the cat's cradle, bespeaks messiness, occasional chaos, disorder. Unlike the cat's cradle, which is highly ordered and patterned, entanglements may be completely spontaneous and unanticipated and therefore unpredictable in their forms and consequences. Unlike metaphors such as 'cloud computing', which tend to represent digital technologies as seamless, stable and pure, the entanglement metaphor acknowledges the heterogeneity and instability of technological agents' interactions with human actors (Shepard 2013).

This chapter has covered an extensive theoretical ground. All of the approaches and perspectives I have discussed have much to offer a sociocultural analysis of the politics of digital technologies; new forms of knowledge formation and power relations in digital society; the various ways in which digital veillance operates; and how computer software and hardware act to configure subjectivity, embodiment and social relations. In the next chapter I discuss research methods, but do so in a way that also incorporates social theory. A body of literature in sociology has developed that has begun to theorise methods of research, thus breaking down the traditional distinctions between theory and method. As this chapter shows, the scholars who have contributed to this literature offer a way forward for both conceptualising and undertaking digital sociology research.

CHAPTER 3

Reconceptualising research in the digital era

This chapter focuses on sociological and other social research in the digital era. The aim of the discussion is not to outline how to do digital research in detail (there are several fine introductory handbooks available for these purposes). Rather I present an overview not only of some of the approaches that are available and their possibilities and limitations, but also of the more theoretical and critical stances that sociologists are taking to digital social research. I also devote attention to innovative ways of performing digital social research that are part of attempts to invigorate sociological research practice as a way of demonstrating the new and exciting directions in which sociology can extend in response to digital society.

DIGITAL SOCIAL RESEARCH METHODS

Before detailing the ways in which digital social research may be undertaken, it is important to provide the context for debates about how research practices relate to the future direction of sociology. One of the main contentions of several sociologists writing on digital sociology is that sociologists in general should develop new ways of 'doing sociology' in response to the digital age, particularly if practitioners of the discipline are to retain their pre-eminent position as experts in social research. This is not to contend that older-style social research methods should necessarily be discarded in favour of those using new digitised approaches. Sociologists should both investigate the various approaches that can be adopted to undertake digital social research and continue to interrogate these approaches themselves for how they shape and interpret the data they produce. These debates confront broader questions about the nature of the discipline itself, including the future of sociological research and theorising in the digital era.

As I briefly outlined in Chapter 1, there are various ways of approaching researching digital society. In the past sociologists and other researchers have employed both qualitative and quantitative methods to investigate how people are using digital technologies. Quantitative methods have included surveys asking people what technologies they use and why, and discerning differences between social groups. Qualitative approaches have employed one-to-one interviews or focus groups to promote more detailed discussion, while ethnographic techniques involve the researcher making observations of how people interact with digital technologies, often in specific sites that are defined by geographical locations.

These time-honoured approaches to social research are still valuable ways of enquiring into the nature of digital society and its implications for self-identity, embodiment, everyday life, group membership, social institutions and social inequality, all traditional questions of interest for sociologists and other social researchers. There are many different ways in which digital devices and platforms can be used for social research, both to generate and record data. Even the older-style methods of research have themselves become digitised. Social surveys are now often completed on computers and the data automatically entered into a database, and paper surveys are digitised when the data are eventually entered into a computerised system for analysis. Online surveys are now used increasingly by both academic and commercial social researchers. They are attractive options as they are able to attract very large numbers of respondents at little expense, and can reach respondents who might otherwise be difficult to access.

Qualitative research methods can also be conducted using online tools and digital devices. One-to-one interviews are now usually conducted using digital sound recorders and the resultant data analysed using computerised methods. Specialised software is now available not only for analysing and coding verbal transcripts but also images-based material, such as videos. Such techniques as video-conferencing, Skype, chat rooms, internet discussion groups and social media platforms can be employed as ways of conducting interviews or group discussions. Field notes may be recorded using mobile digital devices such as tablet computers, note-taking software or voice-recording functions on smartphones. Digital tools such as cameras, video recorders and geo-location devices can be employed as part of ethnographic fieldwork and research participants' own collection of data.

Unlike forms of social research that require the intervention of researchers to collect the data they want to analyse from their respondents, the vast bulk of digital data is generated unobtrusively, as part of other routine activities. These include moving around in public space, making telephone calls, sending emails, browsing the web, using search engines, engaging with government services, purchasing goods online or using customer loyalty schemes, all of which produce digital data on users' activities, as well as more deliberate content-generation practices, such as blogging and uploading status updates, images, likes, tweets and retweets or comments to social media platforms and so on. These masses of aggregated, quantifiable digital data that are generated as an outcome of internet use are variously referred to as transactional, trace, by-product or big data.

As outlined in Chapter 2, another more analytical term that has begun to be employed by digital social researchers is that of 'digital data objects'. Rogers (2013) makes the case for drawing a distinction between 'digitised data objects' and 'natively digital data objects'. The former relates to material that was in a pre-existing analogue form and then has become digitised ('migrated to the web', as Rogers puts it). This includes images, films, audio recordings, documents, books or artefacts that have been scanned, re-recorded or photographed to make new digital versions that can be uploaded to websites such as online museum displays or historical archives. People working in the digital humanities have devoted a great deal of time to digitising such materials. Natively digital data objects are produced from properties of the web formulated for specific purposes as part of its operation ('born in the web'). They are attractive to digital social researchers because they appear to offer a truthfulness and validity that researcher-generated data do not. They provide a window into social practices and identities that take place when people are not consciously aware that they are being surveyed, interviewed or otherwise canvassed for their opinion.

Ways of accessing data archives and the skills to analyse the data stored therein are key methodological issues for researchers who wish to use them. For sociologists, these digital data objects pose a number of questions and challenges. The quantity of such digital data that are available and their continual, unrelenting production are unique features that hitherto have not been encountered by sociologists and other social researchers. The scale of these data offers great opportunities but it can also be daunting, raising questions about how to delimit the field of research.

I referred in Chapter 1 to the argument put forward by some that empirical sociology is facing a crisis of legitimacy and claims to exclusiveness in the face of widespread access to massive digital data sets and tools to analyse these data on the part of a range of actors, from government organisations and security agencies such as the NSA, to commercial enterprises, to digital technology users themselves. It has been contended by a number of sociologists that, as a consequence, the position of sociologists as pre-eminent empirical researchers – skilled collectors, analysers and interpreters of social data – has been subjected to major challenges (Savage 2013; Savage and Burrows 2007, 2009). Social research in any context is a 'shared accomplishment' rather than the sole endeavour of the researcher, including not only human actors but the technologies involved (Marres 2012: 140). This has become even more the case in relation to digitally enacted social research. Other researchers and organisations outside the university have always been involved in social research. With the advent of big data, however, social research has been redistributed across a wider range of entities capable of conducting such research, as well as across a diverse array of methods and devices (Marres 2012; Marres and Weltevrede 2013; Ruppert 2013; Ruppert *et al.* 2013).

Not only are sociologists faced by the fact that other actors or agencies can make use of digital data objects and thus jostle for position with sociologists as social research experts; they may also experience difficulties in grappling with the computing skills required by large digital data sets. A small group of social scientists are highly skilled at quantitative digital data analysis and are able to engage in the types of computer coding and software use required to better access and analyse digital data. Computational social scientists have for some years engaged in various forms of computer-based research using quantifiable data. Their approaches are influenced by network science techniques drawn from computing science, social network researchers, webometrics (the use of statistical techniques to identify characteristics of websites and platforms) and quantitative methods in media and communication studies (for an overview of the methods they adopt, see Ackland 2013).

Despite its title, computational social science is not an approach that is common in the academic social sciences but is instead employed in corporate environments and government agencies. Some sociologists are proficient in these approaches, but they are few. Indeed several commentators have contended that sociologists and other social researchers may experience a digital analysis divide, in which only a small number may have the tools and experience to easily engage in digital media analysis while the vast majority will not (Mahrt and Scharkow 2013; Manovich 2012; Savage and Burrows 2007). The more sophisticated uses of digital data for which there are not ready-made and accessible tools may require sociologists to acquire expertise in computing or to collaborate with computer scientists or digital tool developers in research (Aslinger and Huntemann 2013; Bruns 2013; Halford *et al.* 2013; Marres 2012; Marres and Weltevrede 2013).

TOWARDS A LIVE SOCIOLOGY

This emphasis on the need for computing skills, however, is only one small dimension of rethinking how sociology should move forward in the context of digital society. A new way of conceptualising how the discipline should be defined and what its practitioners should attempt to achieve has been called for by some sociologists. These arguments often refer to the need to incorporate digital technologies into socio-logical practice in innovative and inventive ways, both as the objects and conduits of enquiry. Several sociologists have contended that if social, economic and political lives have become increasingly experi-enced in and through digital technologies, if we are to 'know these lives' we must rethink sociological practice (Ruppert *et al.* 2013: 24).

These new ways of doing sociology may not necessarily involve highly technical data science or coding literacy, but they do incorpo-rate various types of digital technologies to generate, analyse and visu-alise social data. Older social research methods require reassessment in the context of the opportunities offered by natively digital data objects and the devices that can be used to configure, analyse and visualise them. For Latour and colleagues (2012), the data generated by users' interactions with digital technologies provide the opportunity for nothing less than the opportunity to rethink social theory. They assert that in the age of the digital, where information about people can be found on search engines, actors have become defined by their digital networks: 'the more you wish to pinpoint an *actor*, the more you have to deploy its *actor-network*' (Latour *et al.* 2012: 592; emphasis in the original).

This reconsideration of what social researchers should attempt to achieve and the methods and objects that they employ is an element of a trend in sociological writing that is beginning to critically examine the status of contemporary sociology. Back and Puwar (Back 2012; Back and Puwar 2012) call for a 'live sociology' to deal with 'lively

data' – creative, imaginative, playful and new ways of performing sociology that are also public and critical. Rather than being inhibited by
the alternative forms of social research now available to many actors
other than sociologists, Back and Puwar argue for the challenge of
inventing new methods of research, new sociological devices. Back
defines 'dead sociology' as that which tends to render the data it
analyses (quantitative or qualitative) as lifeless, not recognising the
vitality inherent within them. It also tends to employ 'zombie concepts'
drawn from 'old sociology' that do not fit well the current state of the
dynamic, fluid social world. Importantly for the topic of this book,
Back argues that dead sociology fails to come to terms with the digitised nature of social life, expressed in a kind of technophobia expressed
by sociologists for learning about or using new digital media as well as
a failure to conduct research into digital technologies. A final aspect of
dead sociology he identifies is its parochial nature, its failure to recognise the globalised, dispersed nature of social relations and institutions
(a phenomenon that again is implicated in the emergence of digital
society).

Here, then, is a vision of a different kind of sociological sensibility,
one that retains the sociological imagination and reflexivity of previous
approaches but which incorporates new modes of practice, or what
Back and Puwar (2012) refer to as 'sociological craft'. They define live
methods for sociology as incorporating a number of dimensions or
approaches, including new tools for 'real-time' and 'live' investigation
as parts of social research (particularly those that can harvest and
analyse digital transactional data), but also retaining a longer view of
the historical context of these data and their futures. This is where
digital technologies can be employed as part of the practice or craft of
live sociology.

Dave Beer (2014), for his part, has invented the term 'punk sociology' to similarly encapsulate his contentions that sociology needs to
avoid becoming moribund and that sociologists should actively take
up the challenge to consider new approaches. In Beer's formulation,
punk sociology looks outward, is subversive and willing to try new
approaches, and also is ready to engage with alternative forms of
knowledge outside sociology. It means investigating forms of research
and representations of social life that are beyond the textual, such
as audio-visual material, and, as Beer (2014: 38) puts it, coaching
'ourselves to see sociology in sources where we may not be expecting
to see it'. It also includes working with, rather than on, participants in
sociological research, and experimenting with different approaches to
writing about one's work: blogging, podcasts, YouTube videos and
tweets, for example. Beer asserts that sociology needs to be reactive,

energetic and nimble and even confronting like the original punk musicians were, in response to the social changes that are continually occurring and new forms of social research that are emerging (particularly those related to digital media and digital data). He encourages sociologists to take courage in conveying ideas that may still be raw and engaging with others' responses to them, a practice that social media avenues encourage.

THEORISING METHODS

Another important move in sociology and other social theory is the developing literature that examines the ways in which social research methods are themselves socially configured objects. This approach to research methods moves away from the traditional division between 'theory' and 'methods' by, in effect, theorising methods. It includes not only interrogating the research practices or methods that are employed but also seeing the objects that are used as part of sociological craft as actors, shaping how sociologists conduct their research. From this perspective, social research methods both produce and are configured by the social world: they are both material and social (Law and Ruppert 2013; Lury and Wakeford 2012b).

The term 'methodological devices' is frequently used in this literature to denote the material objects and immaterial ideas that come together to configure ways of conducting social research. This discursive use of 'devices' is not to be confused with my more general use of the term in relation to digital devices: that is, computer hardware such as desktop computers, tablets, smartphones, MP3 players, wearable computers and so on. The term 'device' in this literature rather acknowledges the relationship between method and object: that they are linked together and constitute each other (Law and Ruppert 2013; Lury and Wakeford 2012a; Ruppert *et al.* 2013). Methodological devices, like other devices, 'do things' (Law and Ruppert 2013: 229). It is emphasised by these sociologists that social research methods are not only themselves sociocultural artefacts but also work to 'make up' and may profoundly influence the phenomena they set out to study: 'Possessed of a double social life, they are shaped *by* the social, and in turn they act as social operators to *do* the social' (Law and Ruppert 2013: 233; emphasis in the original).

From this perspective, a methodological device can be viewed as an assemblage of material artefacts, human users, practices, ideas and spaces that is constantly subject to change. Such devices are not only methods for research, but also themselves may be viewed as objects of analysis. It is therefore difficult to disentangle the distinctions between object, subject and technique of research. The focus of enquiry into methodological devices is not simply how appropriate, accurate or ethical they are for various purposes, but rather their potentialities, capacities and limitations, how they configure the objects they are attempting to study and measure and how they serve political purposes. Social research methods are themselves assemblages even as they work to configure other types of assemblages: it is in this sense that they may be said to possess a 'social life' (Savage 2013), and even histories and biographies, of their own.

So, too, when sociologists and other social researchers enact research, they are entering into assemblages of human, methodological research devices and data that shift and move as the conditions under which research takes place change. These research assemblages in turn produce research object assemblages. These different assemblages are configured and interrelate with each other: social research assemblages, social researcher assemblages and research object assemblages.

In relation to research using digital technologies and digital data, how digital data objects are identified, formatted and analysed using the various techniques that are available to social (and other) researchers becomes an interesting research question in itself. When applied to digital sociology, this debate centres not simply on 'how to do research' but on the very nature of the generation of knowledge and information as this is performed on the web (Rogers 2013). When analytic formats and categories are already formed by the available digital data analysis tools, these formats and categories may themselves become a subject for research (Marres and Weltevrede 2013; Postill and Pink 2012; Rogers 2013). As scholars writing in software studies have contended, the software that structures the working of digital objects has its own politics (Fuller 2008; Kitchin and Dodge 2011; Manovich 2013a). These objects (including digital hardware and software) are not always predictable, manageable or orderly. They have a structuring and shaping effect on what data are able to be collected, what data are considered important and what data can be stored for analysis.

Thus, for example, search engines possess what Rogers (2013: 19) refers to as 'algorithmic authority' and act as 'socio-epistemological machines': they exert power over what sources are considered important and relevant. From this perspective, the results that come from search engine queries are viewed not solely as 'information', but also as social data that are indicative of power relations. These investigations can reveal how topics, events, organisations and individuals achieve prominence in public debates and framings of some issues over others and how social relationships and power relationships are constituted and maintained.

The digital data object as a research object assemblage can also become the focus of social analysis. Langois and Elmer (2013) argue that the digital data object is comprised of three distinct characteristics. As a media object it is comprised of a semantic layer (drawn from content such as images or texts posted on platforms). As a network object, it connects to other media objects and their networks. Finally, as a phatic object, it establishes specific types of presence and relation between users, by demonstrating users' preferences, tastes and opinions (for example, through their use of the Facebook 'like' button, the content of Pinterest boards that they construct or their choice of links that they share on Twitter). All three of these elements of the digital object work together to configure its meaning and all three can be analysed by researchers interested in their social effects.

CREATIVE WAYS OF DOING DIGITAL SOCIAL RESEARCH

Digital methods of research may bring together multiple forms of data derived from different sources, overlaying them or juxtaposing them in efforts to create knowledges and understandings (Mackenzie and McNally 2013). Sensor-based devices and visualisation tools, for example, can be combined with other forms of qualitative data elicitation, such as interviews and ethnographic observations, to produce rich portraits of social lives.

Ethnographic research, particularly as undertaken by anthropologists, has contributed major insights into how people in various cultural and geographical locations use digital technologies. However, the very ubiquity and dispersal of new digital devices have challenged traditional notions of ethnographic research. Given the dispersal of the internet across many different types of device, platform and tool, and the complex relationship between 'the online' and 'the offline' worlds, the notion of undertaking fieldwork as a participant observer in a specific and well-defined 'field site' has become problematised. The ethnographic field of the digital is a messy and constantly changing site of research, involving intersections and collaborations between the different technologies and human actors involved. The internet is not just one thing; it is many, used in different combinations by different people for different purposes in specific cultural and geographical contexts (Miller 2011; Miller and Horst 2012; Postill and Pink 2012).

Digital anthropologists have begun to grapple with these complexities and are able to offer insights that are useful for other social researchers. For example, Sarah Pink (2009) has developed the concept of the 'ethnographic place' which need not necessarily be only or solely a material space, a bounded locality, but rather a collection of interrelated objects, people and places that are drawn together for the purposes of the researcher. Adopting this approach, the digital technology use of a group, including their activities both online and offline (where distinctions between the two can easily become blurred) and the interactions between these worlds, can be conceptualised as the (digital) ethnographic place of investigation. It incorporates the understanding that the site of research is not static but rather dynamic, constantly changing. There is also the recognition that ethnographers themselves are participating in the configuration of this ethnographic place by following the social media posts and updates of participants, sometimes by contributing to them and by recording or archiving them (Postill and Pink 2012).

Developing techniques for the analysis of digital visual images and the use of digital visualising tools for sociological research is also important. The sub-discipline of visual sociology includes elements of the creative representation and documenting of social issues and problems as well as the interpretation of these images as parts of sociological analysis. Traditionally using images drawn from photography and videos, as well as artwork, visual sociology lends itself to digitised imaging technologies (Graham *et al.* 2011; Lapenta 2011). Visual sociology seeks to identify the implications of these technologies and to use them productively to analyse the contemporary social world.

New digital visual technologies act in various ways that are integral to and have profound effects on social life, social institutions and social relations. They participate in the management and creation of personal social space and in achieving and comprising connections between people, spaces and objects (Graham *et al.* 2011). Digital media technologies constitute new kinds of visual production and audiences for these productions online, ranging from the highly intimate to the highly public. Mobile and wearable devices, such as smartphones and tablets, and platforms, such as Flickr, YouTube, Facebook and Twitter, facilitate constant visual documentation of one's own life and the sharing of this material to a worldwide audience. Location-based and spatial mapping technologies ('geomedia'), such as Google Earth, and digital games rely on sophisticated imaging, while digital editing software affords the creation and manipulation of a wide variety of images (Lapenta 2011). These devices, which 'constitute new epistemologies of space, place and information' (Lapenta 2011: 2), provide fertile opportunities for sociologists to engage in ethnographic and participant observation research using a wealth of visual images. As Les Back puts it, their use involves not so much a sociology 'of' but a sociology 'with' (Back 2012: 33).

Tracking and mapping devices have been used as part of artistic works to create new visualisations of cities. In the Amsterdam Real-Time project, conducted in 2002, 60 volunteers moving around the city carried a GPS-enabled device for a week. Their data were used to plot their individual movements together with those of the other volunteers to produce a visual map of how they encountered space in the city of Amsterdam. These people's movements produced a new map of the city, one that displayed the everyday use of space. The GPS devices thus enable artistic and imaginative expression, serving to visually display everyday practices and use of space as part of quotidian routines and relationships, producing 'personal portraits' of spaces such as cities (Pinder 2013).

The practice of ethno-mining combines quantitative digital data with situated and rich ethnographic research that is able to provide a sociocultural context for the data (Aipperspach *et al.* 2006; Anderson *et al.* 2009; Boase 2013). It is an approach that developed from the use of sensor-based technologies that could automatically track people's movements as part of projects by researchers in the field of human–computer interaction. Anthropologists have since taken up the approach to conduct ethnographic research informed by digital data derived from sensors and other technologies. In a series of projects by anthropologists working for Intel addressing computer use and temporality, the participants' time spent on their digital devices and their geo-locative data derived from their mobile phones were tracked and visualised using digital graphic tools. The visualisations were shown to the study participants, who collaborated with the researchers to produce interpretations of what the data were demonstrating about their habits of use of digital devices (Anderson *et al.* 2009).

In another ethno-mining study, participants in four households and their laptop computers were outfitted with a location-tracking tag and software was installed on each computer to log keyboard and mouse activity, application use and power status. Qualitative data were collected via interviews and observations of the participants' behaviour in their homes, both focusing on where people spent time in this space in relation to the use of their laptops. The quantitative data that were collected were processed using an algorithm that was developed from the researchers' ethnographic observations of and interviews with the participants, while the data generated by the sensor-based and automatic logging technologies contributed insights to the ethnographic data. The researchers developed graphic maps showing the participants' customary movements around their homes in relation to their laptop use, and again used these visualisations to prompt further discussions with the participants (Aipperspach *et al.* 2006).

In Back's writing on live sociology he highlights the importance of moving in space as a researcher, documenting not only what people say about their experiences and thoughts but also the material dimensions of their lived environments: the sensations and emotions that are produced through these environments and experiences (Back 2012; Back and Puwar 2012). His Live Sociology project trained researchers in the use of digital technologies, including using these technologies for collecting, analysing, archiving and curating ethnographic social research. Research participants were involved as co-collaborators in these processes to promote a diversity of socio-logical vantage points. The research trainees were asked to walk around with digital cameras and audio recorders to conduct listening experi-ments of local phenomena (Back 2012). One of Back's current projects is Every Minute of Every Day (2013), an experiment in real-time ethnography which uses digital technologies to record sound and images as well as written texts to document the relationship of local communities with hospices located in their areas. The local residents as research co-collaborators used these technologies to create their own data as contributions to the project.

Artists, designers and sociologists can work together to engage in creative forms of social research, addressing digital technology use or using digital devices to research other aspects of social life. In an example of playful and provocative social research, a research team comprised of designers used objects they entitled 'Domestic Probes' to explore the possible new roles of technology in the home (Boehner *et al.* 2012). Participants in the research were given packets containing the following probes:

- a 'dream recorder' (a repackaged digital memo-taker that allowed participants to record details of a vivid dream for ten seconds);
- a 'listening glass' (a drinking glass packaged with instructions for participants to use it to amplify interesting sounds they noticed in their homes and then to write on it what they had heard);
- a 'bathroom pad' (a paper notepad with about 20 pages, each one featuring a short news item to which participants were invited to respond in writing on the page);
- a disposable camera with a list of instructions for participants to take images around their homes;
- a piece of paper with a grid pattern, intended for participants to draw floor plans of their homes;

- a 'friends and family map' (a piece of paper upon which participants were requested to draw a map of their closest social ties);
- pieces of paper upon which participants were asked to write down their household rules;
- a large sheet of photographic paper with instructions asking participants to place household objects on it and make a collage of their shapes;
- a pinhole camera to take an image of 'an interesting view' from the home;
- a telephone jotter pad with various questions printed on it for participants to respond to in words or drawings; and
- a visitor pad with space for visitors to the home to record comments about their visits.

The participants were asked to keep these items for a while in their homes and to respond to them as and when they felt like it. After about a month, the researchers returned to their homes and collected the probes. They used the participants' responses in developing prototypes for new household objects and to think about the use of technology in the home in different ways. The point of such activities, argue the designers, was not to undertake standard social research that led to findings or results about existing practices, but rather to stimulate both participants and designers to think in unexpected and inventive ways.

While this project was about technology (in terms of designing new technologies) and used various forms of devices and technologies, it was not specifically directed at *digital* technologies. Nonetheless, such innovative approaches could be taken up by sociologists to engage in live sociology related to researching digital media technologies. The researchers on this project suggest using probes to start a conversation and to enliven traditional social research methods such as questionnaires or interviews.

Another example of the potential of this approach is a study in which one of the designers on the above project, William Gaver, collaborated with sociologist Mike Michael (Michael 2012; Michael and Gaver 2009). This project involved using digital technologies as 'threshold devices', again in the context of the home, that are designed to 'look out' of the domestic setting as part of exploring concepts of home and the boundaries between the home and outside. One device that was employed was a 'video window', which displayed views from the outside of the home that could not usually be seen via windows using a digital video camera and a wall-mounted display of the images it portrayed. These technologies were used as part of a broader investigation into the complexities of the relationship of the home with its natural–cultural environment, and, more specifically, how technologies mediate the world outside the home and act to configure the home.

USING NATIVE DIGITAL DATA OBJECTS

The approaches outlined above are essentially variations on generating social research data using new digital technologies. As I observed above, however, digital technologies themselves generate and archive data as part of their operation. As devices 'that observe and follow activities and "doings"' and thereby 'track the doing subject' (Ruppert *et al.* 2013: 34, 35), they configure native digital data objects. Native digital data objects are often already cleaned, ordered and formulated ready for research because the companies or government agencies that collect them use them for their own purposes. However, to some extent, they can be repurposed in various ways by academic researchers, market researchers, policy think-tanks and other commercial enterprises. Such researchers now often refer to 'harvesting', 'mining' or 'scraping' the web to gain access to these data.

Using digital data analysis tools, free or otherwise, individuals from various kinds of occupations or with diverse political motivations can access big data and employ these data for their own ends. Commercial companies also frequently use 'text mining' or 'sentiment analysis', particularly in relation to social media content, or the analysis of fragments of statements used when users are commenting on issues, using such methods as natural language-processing software. These analyse the structure and content of the words used in social media texts in relation to each other, or more simplistically, software that simply counts the number of times words are used (Andrejevic 2013; Breur 2011).

There are various open-source tools that are freely available to any internet user to engage in forms of social research using digital data. These all involve some form of web scraping. Once the data are scraped, the tools provide the opportunity to analyse or visualise the data collected. Many of these digital research tools, as well as some that have been developed by members of the Digital Initiatives group led by Richard Rogers, are listed on its website (Digital Methods Initiative). This website is an invaluable resource which provides details and hyperlinks to digital scraping tools in five categories: media analysis, data treatment, natively digital, device centric and spherical. These tools are able to perform a multitude of analyses, including monitoring online media outputs, capturing and analysing social media content, such as tweets, identifying the time-stamps of websites (or when they were last modified), checking whether a URL has been censored and harvesting metadata and content from iTunes, Wikipedia, Twitter, Facebook and Amazon.

Many tools are available to represent digital data visually, including graphs, social network and word cloud visualisations. Tools such as Topsy provide the opportunity for anyone to search the web for words or terms across social media platforms. Topsy generates a list of mentions of these words or terms and links to each of them, and also provides numbers and graphs of these mentions and a sentiment score. It can compare words and terms as well and graphically represent how often each one is mentioned compared to the others.

Google offers several free web scraping tools. These include Google Trends (which analyses the popularity of search terms entered into Google) and Google Books Ngram Viewer (which draws on a corpus of millions of books published between the 1500s and 2008 that have been digitised by Google). Thus, for example, I can very easily produce a graph using Google Trends that can show how often the term 'digital sociology' has been entered into Google as a search term compared with 'digital anthropology' and 'digital cultures', to provide an indication of interest in these terms relative to each other. As an exponent of digital sociology, the resultant graph gives me some indication of when people using the Google search engine began to use the term 'digital sociology' (for the record, it was May 2009), and how much interest there is in the term in comparison to the others that I have put in the tool. Using the Topsy social media analysis tool, I can see how often these terms have been tweeted about in a defined time period comparative to each other, as well as trace mentions of each one across the internet, thus allowing more detailed analysis of social media discussions of these topics.

Google Ngram Viewer has been used to engage in linguistic research tracing changes in the use and meaning of words or terms over centuries. A group of computational linguistics researchers, including several who were involved in developing the Ngram Viewer project (Michel *et al.* 2011), for example, conducted an analysis of the evolution of grammar, and compared how the use of English irregular verbs (such as burned/burnt, strived/strove, dwell/dwelt) changed over the centuries between 1800 and 2000 and also how these words were used in the UK compared with the USA. It has been argued that this approach to online news items can identify changes in tone in the material that may predict political unrest and economic events. One study used a digitised global news archive over a period of 30 years to examine 'global news tone'. The researcher went beyond the standard analysis by seeking to identify the geographical location and latent tone of the words employed and quantifying these dimensions of the news texts. Using this analysis, he was able to forecast such events as the revolutions in Egypt, Tunisia and Libya (Leetaru 2011).

To try Ngram Viewer for myself, I searched for the terms 'cyberspace' and 'cyborg' to test my argument that these terms have lost some of their currency since the early 2000s. When I searched for these terms between 1980 and 2008, I found that this was indeed the case, at least as demonstrated by the number of mentions of these words during this period in the corpus digitised by Google. Both words hardly appeared in the Google Books database until 1988, when they began a gradual rise in number of mentions, reaching a peak in 2000 for cyberspace and in 2002 for cyborg, after which the frequency of their use declined. Cyberspace was far more commonly used than cyborg, although both terms had similar trajectories of use. Unfortunately, as Google Ngram Viewer currently only includes books published before 2009, I was unable to trace the frequency of further mentions over the past few years, a period in which I would predict these words would have been used less often in books.

Several digital social researchers have been interested in tracing the history of internet sites, including cultural change as it occurs over time on these sites. Identifying the history of searches on engines provides 'stories' relating to the politics of knowledge: of how content is manipulated, how some views are prioritised and others excluded on search engines. Here the search engine is understood as 'an authoring device' in constructing a particular story or viewpoint (Rogers 2013). Thus, for example, Rogers (2013) and colleagues made a collection of Iraqi websites stretching back some years to determine the types of information that had been available on Iraqi society that differed from official government accounts. They also compared Wikipedia articles on the fall of Srebrenica, the Srebrenica massacre and genocide written in Dutch, Serbian and Bosnian, examining the edit history over six years and the sources used as a means of tracing the political nature of knowledge generation and manipulation on that site. Such genealogies of websites are important ways of tracking and identifying how issues come to the fore, whose voices are given prominence and whose are ignored or censored. This type of research is able to provide insights into how knowledge is generated and negotiated online, and also the gaps and inconsistences involved in this process.

The quantities of data that big digital data sets provide lend themselves to graphic visualisation as a means of most easily identifying patterns in the data (Bruns 2012). Graphic visualisation tools can be employed to analyse social networks and investigate how social media use is socially and culturally contextual. Several free tools are available to perform social media network analysis. One such tool is Gephi, a free and open-source interactive visualisation and exploration platform for networks and complex systems. Bruns (2012) used Gephi to graphically visualise Twitter activity data cohering around specific hashtags and replies to individual users to examine the networks established between users. This analysis allowed him to identify shifts in the hashtag network, including changing participation by contributors and the response of the overall hashtag community to new stimuli, such as the entry of new participants or the availability of new information. The study focused on how Twitter operates as a space for conversation in relation to specific topics (as designated by hashtags used in front of key terms).

For people who are interested in exploring the types of metadata that are generated by their own use of social media, various tools are available that allow them to scrape their own data from their email, Facebook or LinkedIn account and produce statistics, graphs and other data visualisations that show data on who they are linked to, how these people may be linked with each other in various networks and the frequency of interactions one has with them. I used the LinkedIn Maps tool for this purpose to see what data it produced. Drawing on my LinkedIn connections, the tool produced a multi-coloured image of network clusters that showed how my contacts were linked with each other. This was an interesting exercise in demonstrating who knew who among my contacts and how the clusters identified were distinct as well as overlapping. Not surprisingly, the clusters were structured around predominantly the features of geography and field of research, so that the British sociologists, for example, were closely clustered, as were my Australian academic contacts and colleagues from my university. There were also several connections identified in the cluster map of people that I had no idea were linked in any way.

In a far more complex project involving the use of visual images, Hochman and Manovich (2013) analysed images that were uploaded to the photo-sharing social media platform Instagram. In their 'big visual data' research they identified what they call 'the visual signatures' of 13 global cities, drawing on 2.3 million Instagram images from these cities. Their research was directed at identifying patterns of Instagram use that reveal local social and cultural events by using techniques that draw on metadata but also the visual content of the actual images. They describe their approach as 'data ethnography', as they are able to move between large-scale analyses of tens of thousands of images and more detailed analysis that can reveal patterns of individual users. For example, they examined the photos shared on Instagram by people located in the Brooklyn area of New York City when Hurricane Sandy hit that city and those taken by users in Tel Aviv on national memorial days. They argue that this new paradigm is able to analyse individual users of digital media not through hierarchies and categories but rather through relations, transitions and sequences. Their website – Phototrails – provides many examples of the data visualisations produced as part of this research project.

Very few sociologists have yet made use of web harvesting techniques in their research practices. One exception is Dave Beer (2012c), who has experimented with using the social media data aggregator Insightlytics to compare the ways in which the terms 'sociology' and 'celebrity' were employed on Twitter. He looked at how often these appeared over a defined time period, the geographical origins of the tweets, the other terms combined with each word, the influential commentators who made reference to the terms, the sentiment accompanying the mention of the terms and aspects of individual tweets employing the terms. As Beer notes, there are significant limitations to this kind of broad-brush analysis. While it can be useful in identifying basic patterns in a vast number of data, this technique should only be viewed as a starting point for social analysis. Digital transactional data and the algorithms used to sort them were not created with the purposes of social researchers in mind. They therefore can often be unwieldy and inconvenient for researchers to use, and do not fit their specific research questions. This may result in the data that are available for use shaping the generation of research questions, rather than the opposite occurring (Beer and Taylor 2013).

Two other sociologists, Noortje Marres and Esther Weltevrede, have also experimented with web scraping devices and reflected on the ways in which such devices, as sociomaterial objects, shape social research practices and how 'the social' is defined. They contend that 'scraping disturbs the distinction between the "inside" and the "outside" of social research' (Marres and Weltevrede 2013: 315). Web scraping tools and practices operate under different conditions and assumptions from those that are usually employed in academic social research. The data these strategies access, as native digital data objects, come already formatted. Scrapers act as 'analytical machines' because they define and order, and thus pre-format, the data they scrape according to certain conventions embedded within the software (Marres and Weltevrede 2013: 326). Like Beer, Marres and Weltevrede remark that there are limitations to what academic researchers can do with web scraping tools as they must accept the conventions and structures of the platforms in which these data are generated. However, they extend this observation by contending that addressing the ways in which this formatting takes place can become a focus of sociological enquiry. Web scraping is both an automatic process generated by the software being employed and a social process, subject to the decisions of those who code the software, to the sharing of the data thus generated and to discussion among those employing different tools as to which work the best. Social researchers can both use the tool and analyse how the tool operates as a form of web epistemology (Rogers 2013) that shapes the content, forms and categories of knowledge that can become available.

THE LIMITATIONS OF DIGITAL DATA ANALYSES

Digital social research offers many possibilities. However, there are also significant limitations for social researchers who are interested in employing big digital data sets, online data collection and analytic tools, some of which have already been touched upon in this chapter. Not everyone has equal access to big digital data sets. I remarked earlier in this chapter about the lack of computing skills most sociologists possess, and how this may limit their opportunities to go beyond the simple analyses offered by open-source analytic tools. There is a growing divergence in the ways in which big data can be accessed and used. The move towards open-source data initiatives and the provision of tools to access and analyse these data have led to some forms of digital data becoming more widely available for analysis. These types of tools enable any interested person to engage in social research, without requiring any training in research methods. Yet, while some digital data are open to the use of all, as the massive data sets collected by commercial internet corporations have become increasingly valuable entities access to them has been progressively closed off.

Social media platforms such as Facebook, YouTube, Flickr and Twitter began purely as means of online communication, the sharing of images and networking, but as their popularity and influence have grown, they have become commercialised, forums for advertising and tools for the provision of data that can be mined and sold on. While the content that is prosumed on these platforms appears to be a transparent and rich source of data for social researchers, this increasing move towards ownership of the data limits the extent to which researchers may access them by scraping. The number of times a user can visit a website to scrape data is now often limited by 'terms and conditions'. Platforms such as Twitter and Facebook have instituted rules around data mining which limit it to use of their own application program interfaces (APIs). A two-tier system now may operate, in which some access to data is freely available to all but access to more detailed data is limited to those willing to pay for these data (Bruns 2012, 2013; Burgess and Bruns 2012; Langois and Elmer 2013). Manovich (2012: 470) subsequently argues that three categories of actors (or, to use his term, 'data classes') may now be identified in the context of digital data. The first category is comprised of those who create the data, either inadvertently or deliberately (anyone who uses or is monitored by digital technologies). The second category includes the people or organisations that have the means to archive these data (a far smaller group). The third and even smaller category is made up of those individuals or organisations that are able to access and analyse the data from these archives.

The data that are freely available using the platform's APIs represent only a tiny fraction of all the data collected and stored by the platform, which raises questions about the representativeness of the data that may be analysed (boyd and Crawford 2012; Bruns 2012; Burgess and Bruns 2012; Edwards *et al.* 2013; Vis 2013). The issue of representativeness has been raised by other critics, who have pointed out that researchers often simply choose to use the data that are conveniently available rather than engage with issues of representative sampling. Twitter or Facebook users, for example, are from certain defined social groups, and are by no means representative of the general public. This lack of representativeness can also be a problem with other forms of eliciting data using online tools. For example, online surveys may attract respondents who are not representative of the general population. This occurred in the Great British Class Survey (Savage *et al.* 2013), which was conducted by sociologists in conjunction with the BBC. Although a large number of respondents completed the online survey, they were skewed towards the typical BBC viewer class profile: the well educated and economically privileged in professional occupations. The researchers were then forced to conduct a second survey using standard quota sampling procedures and face-to-face questioning conducted by a social research company that were able to attract responses from a more socially-diverse group.

In addition to these difficulties faced by academic researchers who are interested in social media analysis, Bruns (2013) raises a number of others. He observes that the sheer quantities of digital data that researchers are faced with mean that they must constantly make choices about how to select certain data to analyse. They simply cannot analyse all the data on a particular topic or from a particular social media platform, for example. Technical matters such as data storage capacity are also integral to the decisions that researchers interested in online material must make. Bruns also cautions that academic researchers invest blind trust in the open sources or commercial social media analysis tools that are available to them uncritically, without raising questions about their validity and reliability. It is also very difficult to replicate the findings of other researchers, given that the tools and data sets used are often unstable, and social media platforms often do not allow researchers to publicly share their data sets.

Many broader concerns have been articulated in relation to social research practices using native digital data. As I explain in more detail in Chapter 5, digital data are as subject as any other forms of data (quantitative or qualitative) to inaccuracy, bias, distortions and errors at any stage of their production and analysis. Despite the aura of objectivity and scientific neutrality that surrounds digital data (because they are generated by computer technologies, often in vast quantities), like any other form of data, digital data are the product of human decision-making. The content of online material may change over time as it is revised or even removed altogether from the internet. Much of the big data analysed can only provide very partial information, often devoid of contextual features such as the gender, age, ethnicity, geographical location, social class and education level of the contributors of the data (boyd and Crawford 2012; Edwards *et al.* 2013; Mahrt and Scharkow 2013).

A further difficulty in terms of judging the validity of the data is that some contributors attempt to game the system, or conduct hoaxes, posting incorrect information or doctored images represented as factual (Procter *et al.* 2013). The people who are the sources of these data manipulate them in certain ways for their own ends, choosing to upload certain images over others, for example, or sharing or retweeting carefully selected items to present a certain persona to friends and followers on social networks. Search engine results or Twitter trending topics can be manipulated by those seeking commercial or political advantage (Lazer *et al.* 2014). So, too, digital data such as 'likes', 'shares' and 'followers' can easily be gamed (by being bought or by using bots, for example; see Baym 2013).

Regardless of the validity of big data, several critics have pointed out that while they include many digital data objects, massive data sets are limited in terms of their explanatory power. They are able in the main to provide counts and evidence of correlations and connections between different variables, but beyond this they are not particularly insightful. Big data provide little explanation of the context in which they are produced (Andrejevic 2013; Uprichard 2012, 2013). The meaning of the data may be lost or misunderstood because other indicators of meaning may not be included in the digitised materials: the social and cultural context in which the original texts were produced, or the relevance of words or texts to each other. For example, the interpretation of 'sentiment' in social media data is undertaken by natural language-processing algorithms. But because these are generated by computer codes, rather than interpretations by humans, such analysis easily misses nuances and ambiguities of meaning. Words and other elements of cultural texts become reduced to computer data alone (Beer and Taylor 2013; Gooding 2013). Without detailed knowledge of the context, it is often difficult to judge the tenor of content when users are commenting on social media, such as whether they are being serious or sarcastic.

Notes of caution have also been articulated in relation to the increasing digitisation of materials. Gooding (2013: 1), for example, has referred to archives of digitised material as potentially constituting 'a virtual rubbish dump of our cultural heritage'. He writes that several major concerns have been expressed within the humanities about digitisation of materials. One is that quantification and information will come to be privileged over the traditional, more in-depth and interpretative analyses of cultural material that involve close reading or examination of the texts. Another concern is that little has been published about the use of large-scale digital archives of cultural material for purposes other than quantification. Furthermore, the mass digitisation of materials may be of poor quality compared to small digitised collections that have been developed with a high degree of human intervention to ensure standards are high. Large-scale digitisation, which often relies on automated mass scanning techniques, can often result in poor metadata and mistakes in the digitisation process so that important information is lost. The value of these data, therefore, may be compromised for researchers.

Some critics have addressed the ethical issues of using data from online communities and forums for research. These issues incite consideration of such questions as whether or not such communities constitute public or private space or whether researchers should make themselves known to communities when studying their interactions. Some researchers have contended that if information that users post about themselves is posted on public websites and platforms, then such data should not be considered private or confidential, and should be open to researchers to use regardless of whether or not the individuals know their content is being used for research. Others argue that researchers should take care to let people know that they are using their data, particularly if they are posting about personal matters (Boase 2013; Mahrt and Scharkow 2013; Moreno *et al.* 2013). As I discuss in greater detail in Chapters 5 and 7, the use and commercialisation of big data by digital companies and government agencies has raised many issues concerning the extent to which people understand how their data are being used and whether they should be able to gain access to their own data.

By virtue of the long tradition of social research in sociology, sociologists have been sensitised to the ethical and political dimensions of the processes of sorting and classification that are intrinsic to the production and use of data (Uprichard 2013). Sociologists and other critical analysts, therefore, play a vital role in continuing to challenge the accepted truths of big data or digital social data. It is in the emphasis of the contextual and constructed nature of digital data, including their political purposes and effects, that sociologists and other social and cultural scholars are able to develop insights. Data mean nothing without interpretation and contextualisation, and these scholars are trained to achieve precisely this. Due to these caveats, big data analyses should be considered as only a small part of an analysis of social behaviour. It is here that the types of innovative approaches outlined earlier in this chapter offer ways of incorporating digital technologies into creative and insightful sociological enquiry.

THE CRITICAL REFLEXIVE POSITION

Digital sociology can contribute to the revitalising of 'dead sociology' in many important ways. Digital technologies as methodological devices and as subjects for research provide exciting, creative and innovative new ways of conducting sociological research. They offer an opportunity to enliven sociology and other social research by contributing new forms of data and ways of including research participants as co-collaborators in research projects. Sociologists offer many important perspectives on digital social research. Not only are they able to investigate people's digital technology use from both broad and in-depth perspectives, they are able to position this use within the social, cultural and political context in which it takes place. They are able to interrogate their own position as researchers and to query the nature of research methods from a critical perspective. All of these perspectives contribute to a potentially rich and vital sociology in which practitioners reflect upon their own positioning as researchers and site their approaches within a theoretical perspective that acknowledges the ways in which social research practices both document and create social lives.

Adopting a critical reflexive sociological perspective on sociologists as digital media researchers, one could ask the following questions.

What are sociologists doing when they seek to analyse digital media? To what extent are they simply taking up digital media analysis tools to harvest data and to what extent are they challenging these tools' usefulness or even focusing attention on the tools (and digital platforms and digital data) themselves as objects of research? There are different layers of analysis that can be engaged in by sociologists, each of which adopts a somewhat different perspective on the epistemologies and ontologies of digital devices, software and data. We can use computer functions and tools such as Google Ngram, Google Trends, Google Search and autocomplete simply as *search* tools, as any digital users do, but we can also position them as *research* tools, ways of exploring and revealing social and cultural conventions, norms and discourses. At the same time, as reflexive digital sociologists, we need to view these tools as very blunt instruments, and acknowledge that in using them we are required to invest our faith in the validity and reliability of the data they produce. And further, as critical analysts of the digital, we can reflect on how these tools position ourselves as researchers and their implications for social research in general.

Thus, for example, when I use a tool such as Google Trends, as a sociologist I may do so in various ways. I may use the tool and accept the results it produces unproblematically. Here the data it produces is my main interest. I may be interested in investigating how the tool produces and structures the data, challenging the 'black box' of its inner workings and logic. The tool itself is here becoming the object of my analysis. I may want to explore the social and political implications of how Trends is part of the Google apparatus of shaping and structuring knowledge, or the 'Googilization' of the world (Vaidhyanathan 2011). I may want to do all of these things simultaneously. All of these are intriguing ways of investigating the digital world sociologically.

This chapter has examined the issue of how digital sociology may be practised in terms of research methods. In the next chapter, I go on to outline more specifically the use of digital technologies for professional practice as a sociologist. As in the present chapter, the discussion takes a reflexive position by not only outlining what kinds of strategies may be adopted by sociologists (and other academics) to 'digitise' themselves, and the possible benefits and drawbacks of adopting these strategies, but also examining the deeper implications for concepts of academic identities and work.

CHAPTER 4

The digitised academic

In this chapter I look at how academics are becoming digitised knowledge workers, with a particular focus on sociologists. The higher education workplace has become increasingly digitised, with many teaching and learning resources and academic publications moving online and the performance of academics and universities monitored and measured using digital technologies. Some sociologists and other academics are also beginning to use social media as part of their academic work. Digital technologies are therefore becoming an important element of constructing and performing the professional self for many workers in higher education. I examine the benefits and possibilities offered by digital technologies but also identify the limitations, drawbacks and risks that may be associated with becoming a digitised academic and the politics of digital public engagement. Throughout the chapter I will make reference to findings from my own online survey of academics who use social media for professional purposes (see the Appendix for further details).

DIGITAL PUBLIC SOCIOLOGY

As part of the continuing reflexive critique in which sociologists like to participate as part of their sociological sensibility, periodically there are examinations by sociologists about the future of their discipline.

Many of these enquiries contend that public sociology is a vital aspect of what contemporary sociology should be attempting to achieve. What the term 'public sociology' involves has itself been subjected to lengthy analysis and debate (Burawoy 2005; Holmwood 2007). For some, public sociology involves engaging in political activism, agitating for social justice and human rights and challenging inequalities, while for others, it is more broadly related to engaging in public discourse to audiences outside the academy as expert commentators on contemporary social issues: that is, to be public intellectuals.

One of the most well-known pieces on public sociology is 'For public sociology', an article by American sociologist Michael Burawoy (2005), derived from his presidential address to the American Sociology Association's annual conference in 2004. In the article Burawoy (2005: 4) defines the challenge of public sociology as 'engaging multiple publics in multiple ways'. He discusses the importance of making sociology visible to those outside the profession as part of legitimising and bolstering support for it, showing people how important and relevant it is. Such arguments suggest that sociologists have retreated into their ivory towers and become focused on internal debates and professional advancement instead of engaging directly with the social groups that are the topics of their research (Holmwood 2007). It is clear, however, that many sociologists view public engagement as integral to their professional work for a number of reasons, including a personal belief that such engagement should be fundamental to the praxis of sociologists.

Burawoy (2005: 7) comments on the potential of public sociology to bring sociology into 'a conversation with publics, understood as people who are themselves involved in a conversation'. The recursive nature of public engagement by academics who conduct social research is evident in this statement. Sociology itself is about the examination of social processes and institutions, of which the discipline and its practitioners are parts. Sociologists study the social world and their research findings may in turn have an influence on social relations and social structures. Furthermore, sociologists themselves are part of society and thus contribute to the understanding and construction of the entity of which they are members. As I go on to contend below, this has implications for the ways in which sociologists use social and other digital media as part of their presentation of their professional selves or in their research.

When Burawoy was writing about public sociology, social media had not begun to enter private and professional worlds. A decade after his talk, the concept of digital public sociology may now be introduced, relating to the practice of using social and other digital tools to perform public sociology. The higher education sphere has become profoundly transformed by digital technologies in the past ten years. As participants in the digitised knowledge economy, the work and output of academics has become increasingly presented online. In many cases scholars' 'academic personae' may have been constructed for academics using defined formats by their universities (the information webpage about their research, teaching and qualifications that is part of the university website, for example), the academic journals and books that publish their work, sites such as Amazon and Google Books which publicise their books and invite reviews of them, the libraries that purchase their books, the other academics who publish course readings, articles or blog posts referring to their work, or readers who review their work on review websites. As a result of all this internet-based activity, many academics have a far greater online presence than many other professionals. However, much of this kind of representation of academics is beyond their control, as it is produced, or at least shaped, by others.

Institutional imperatives are also beginning to encourage sociologists and other academics to render their research findings more accessible. The increasing move towards open-access publishing – including mandates from public research funding bodies in several countries for academics to make their research readily available to the public – also supports the concept of public sociology. While the traditional mass media, particularly the news media, provided a major forum for such public commentary, the new digital media offer far more ways to do this. They allow sociologists to have more control over the tenor of the messages they wish to disseminate in public forums, as scholars are able to publish material themselves, without a mediator. Blogging, tweeting, curating Facebook pages, editing Wikipedia entries, engaging in professional networking websites such as Academia.edu, ResearchGate and LinkedIn, making podcasts and YouTube videos and so on are all ways of employing digital media for professional academic purposes.

So, too, in recent years there has been increasing interest in offering higher education in online formats, including not only the relatively small-scale offerings from universities as part of their accredited courses that have been available for many years now, but 'massive open online courses' (MOOCs). MOOCs have been offered by prestigious universities such as Princeton, California Berkeley, MIT, Harvard and Stanford since 2012. They provide access to higher education to people from around the globe who may previously have been prevented from undertaking university-level study because of their geographical location or lack of money. MOOCs have been viewed by some commentators on higher education as potentially trans-forming the ways in which university education is delivered and funded. Many questions have been raised about how MOOCs will affect the higher education sector, including their quality, their success in terms of retaining a high proportion of the large numbers of students who enrol, whether they offer a viable business model (how will universities be able to continue to fund them?) and the extent to which they may offer a viable alternative to the traditional model of learning and degree accreditation. Most providers of MOOCs have not charged fees, but there is evidence that at least some of the univer-sities offering them will begin to charge students and offer accredita-tion towards diplomas and degrees. Such forms of teaching also require universities to examine how their teaching staff are trained to offer them effectively. Both smaller-scale courses and MOOCs require those academics who are involved in them to acquire digital tech-nology skills and understand the complexities of teaching effectively in online formats.

Only a small proportion of academics currently actively and regu-larly use social and other digital media as part of their professional work. This number appears to be slowly growing, however, as moves towards making research data and publications and teaching materials available outside the academy become more dominant in higher education. Perhaps unsurprisingly, given the focus of their work, academics in media and communication studies have been at the fore-front of employing digital media to present their professional selves (Barbour and Marshall 2012). Martin Weller (2011), an academic specialising in educational technology, has discussed the concept of 'the digital scholar' in detail in his book bearing this title, with the subtitle 'How technology is transforming scholarly practice'. At least one handbook has been published on the subject, entitled *Social Media for Academics: A Practical Guide* (Neal 2012). As these signs suggest, a momentum appears to be developing in which academics are begin-ning to realise the benefits of using digital media for scholarly practice and learning how to do so.

Sociologists are only beginning to recognise the value of digital media, although websites such as the LSE's Impact of the Social Sciences are providing many useful accounts of and guides to how to use these tools. It has been argued by some commentators that engaging in professional digital use as part of sociological practice will do much to raise the profile of sociology and demonstrate its rele-vance and importance in an era in which a shrinking academic employment market, suspicion among conservative governments of social scientists and general economic austerity are threatening funding for sociological research and teaching and subsequent employment opportunities for sociologists. It can also serve to encourage students to take up sociology, if they are exposed to greater public engagement on the part of the academics teaching them and to methods of using digital tools themselves. Engaging in digital sociology, therefore, may be viewed as a 'social impact investment' for future research and teaching (Casilli 2012).

Using social media platforms can be a highly efficient way of connecting with other academics working in a similar area as well as interested people from outside academia. These tools allow participants to join networks arranged around topic or discipline areas and to contribute in discussions and sharing information within these networks. Blogging sites such as WordPress and micro-blogging platforms such as Twitter can be used as easily accessible forums in which academics can communicate their ideas in short form. Unlike traditional journal articles that are locked behind paywalls, these platforms are free to access and material can be instantly published, allowing academics to share some of their research findings quickly. They therefore allow scholars to promote their research and share it with a far greater audience than they would usually find in the traditional forums for publication. Links can be provided to journal articles so that longer academic pieces can be followed up by readers.

Blogs and micro-blogging platforms also allow interested readers to comment and engage with authors, thus facilitating public engagement. Individuals can ask a question in a blog or Twitter post and receive responses, or readers may simply choose to use the comments box to make remarks on a piece that has been published. Sites such as Academia.edu, ResearchGate and LinkedIn, as well as academics' university profile webpages, are ways of providing information about themselves. In Academia.edu and ResearchGate, both of which were designed specifically for academics, users can list and upload their articles, conference papers and books, follow other individuals and topic areas and be followed in turn, and engage in discussions with colleagues. LinkedIn provides opportunities to link not only to academic colleagues but also those outside, and to join special interest groups.

Curation and sharing platforms such as Delicious, Google+, SlideShare, Pinterest, Scoop.it, Pearltrees, Bundlr, Paper.li and Storify, as well as referencing tools such as Mendeley, CiteuLike and Zotero, allow academics to easily gather and present information and, importantly, to then make the information public and share it with others online. On SlideShare, PowerPoint or Prezi presentations may be uploaded to the internet and the referencing tools allow you to gather lists of references on specific topics and then share these with others. Several of these tools, including Pinterest, Bundlr and Storify, allow users to insert their own comments or analysis on the material that they have gathered. These media can also be used as teaching tools, providing new ways of engaging with students both through classroom teaching and in student assignments, where students can use the tools themselves to collect, curate and present information.

Social media are also being increasingly used as part of academic conferences. For example, academics often 'live tweet' about the content of the presentations they attend, providing a 'back-channel' of communication that can be shared with both those participating and those who cannot attend. These tweets can then be presented and preserved in platforms such as Storify as a record of the conference to which anyone can have access, and conference attendees also sometimes blog about the proceedings.

As noted above, the judicious use of social media allows academics to exercise better control and manage the content of their online professional persona (sometimes referred to as 'e-profile') in a context in which search engines are constantly collating information about them. Even apparently trivial practices such as bestowing titles and key words on one's articles, books or chapters and the words chosen for abstracts can be very important in how a scholar's work is accessible to others, now that most academic outputs are digitised. It has been argued that, given that the words used in a title are assigned particular importance by search engine algorithms, a strategy for maximising visibility should be adopted. If the title contains key words that are likely to be entered into search engines by those looking for research on those topics, it is far more likely to rank highly on the search engines' returns (Dunleavy 2014). Many journals now advise their authors on how to maximise visibility of their articles by ensuring that they choose their titles, abstracts and key words judiciously for search engine optimisation.

It has become evident that using social and other digital media can have positive effects on academics' impact, both in the higher education domain and outside it. Academic blog posts are now commonly cited as academic publications in other scholarly writing (I do this frequently myself, including throughout this book). Some sociology blogs, such as Sociological Images, have become very successful, with a readership of millions, thus successfully achieving a high level of public awareness of sociological research (Wade and Sharp 2013). While the vast majority of sociological blogs do not enjoy anywhere near this level of reach, they are still able to have an impact as accessible public discussions of sociological research and analysis. It has been demonstrated that using tools such as blogs and Twitter to discuss and publicise research outcomes has a measurable positive effect on resultant academic citations (Eysenbach 2011). One academic traced the effects of tweeting and blogging about papers she had placed on an institutional repository. She noted a clear and major increase in the number of times papers were viewed and downloaded, even for papers that were not recent (Terras 2012).

Using social media can also be viewed as part of facilitating access to academic research as part of open-access initiatives. Over the past few years a high level of attention has been devoted to open-education and open-access issues. Discussion has focused on how university-based researchers, who are often funded by the public to undertake research, can release their findings to members of the general public, the vast majority of whom do not have free access to scholarly journals and books (Kitchin *et al.* 2013; Weller 2013). Using social media outlets can also provide a way of facilitating the communication of research findings to the public as well as to other researchers. Researchers are therefore beginning to include these as part of research funding applications as a means of demonstrating public engagement and impact (Kitchin *et al.* 2013).

RESEARCH ON THE DIGITISED ACADEMIC

As all of this suggests, academic practices and identities are increasingly becoming shaped by the affordances and demands of digitisation. As noted in Chapter 2, the use of social media may be viewed as part of the heterogeneous practices that individuals may adopt in their project of configuring and presenting their identities. This is the case for academics as much as for any other individuals. Academic blogging and other social media use may be viewed as techniques of the professional self, allowing users to actively construct and maintain a public identity for themselves (Kirkup 2010).

While becoming a digitised academic offers many possibilities and benefits, the possible negative dimensions also need acknowledgement. In adopting a critical reflexive approach to all this additional production of content via social media and other digital outlets, we need to ask questions:

- What happens when academic research goes open and is presented in less formal formats?
- What are the implications and effects of new ways of measuring academic output and impact via digital technologies?

- Will academics, many of whom already report feeling overworked, underappreciated and stressed, find themselves under further pressure to engage as digital academics?
- How will MOOCs and other attempts to render education more accessible via online technologies affect pedagogies, funding, workloads and employment levels in the higher education sector?
- How will the conventions of academic publishing respond to open-access initiatives?

Sociologists need to stand back and take a reflexive perspective on these developments in academic life: not necessarily solely to condemn them, but also to acknowledge their contribution to the making up of contemporary academic selves and to the pleasures as well as the privations of academic work. Here the implications of digital public sociology for the private lives and subjectivities of academics require attention.

My own more recent survey of academics who use social media as part of their work found that not surprisingly, given the publicising of the survey using social media networks and especially Twitter, 90 per cent of my respondents said that they used Twitter for professional purposes, with 60 per cent using LinkedIn, 49 per cent Academia.edu, 42 per cent Facebook, 33 per cent ResearchGate, 32 per cent a personal blog, 25 per cent YouTube, 21 per cent Google+ and 20 per cent online referencing tools, such as Mendeley or Zotero. Other social media tools, such as multi-authored blogs (16 per cent), Wikipedia as an author/editor (7 per cent), Pinterest (9 per cent), SlideShare (13 per cent), Instagram (3 per cent), Tumblr (5 per cent), Flickr (5 per cent), Storify (9 per cent), curation tools (7 per cent), Google Scholar (1 per cent) and Quora (1 per cent), attracted fewer responses. When asked which of these social media they found 'most useful' for their academic work, Twitter again featured very strongly (83 per cent), followed by a very long margin by Academia.edu (23 per cent), a personal blog (16 per cent), Facebook (14 per cent), LinkedIn (14 per cent), online referencing tools (11 per cent), YouTube (10 per cent), a multi-authored blog (7 per cent), Google+ (5 per cent), SlideShare (5 per cent) and curation tools (4 per cent). Other tools listed – Wikipedia (as author/editor), Pinterest, Instagram, Tumblr, Flickr and Quora – attracted fewer than 2 per cent of responses.

While the many academics who responded to my survey use only a small number of digital media tools for a limited number of purposes, several reported employing a wider range. One example is a female academic from the UK who is an early career researcher. This is what she had to say about her use of social media:

[I use] Twitter – useful to follow people doing similar work, connect at conferences, enables me to discover articles, resources, organisations, ongoing projects. I use Twitter to tell others about ongoing work or resources and to have conversations, throw ideas around etc. I find interesting presentations on SlideShare, gives me ideas about content and is a way to follow work of people in a variety of fields. I blog as part of my work on a WordPress platform – it is an official department blog where multiple team members contribute. I find blogging great for slightly longer pieces about projects or activities (which I can then tweet links to) and I also follow quite a few blogs to keep up to date with work in other institutions or work of individuals. I use a Facebook group with students to keep in touch, they respond quicker to questions posted there rather than direct email.

As this account suggests, at least some academics are engaging in social media tools in sophisticated and complex ways and perceive many advantages of this use. In my survey, when asked what they saw as the benefits of using social media as an academic, many people mentioned the connections or networks they had established with other academics and also those outside academia. Several made reference to the wide scope of these connections, which allowed them to interact with people across the globe and from diverse communities. It was common for the respondents to also note that their social media use enabled them to make connections with people or groups that they otherwise may never have come across. Their professional networks, therefore, were expanded via social media in sometimes unpredictable and serendipitous ways. Some respondents observed that not only were their social media networks broad, they were also horizontal and democratic, enabling more junior academics and postgraduate students to more easily interact with senior academics. As a female early career academic from the UK wrote:

I like Twitter especially because it allows me to follow a lot of people doing similar (or even better: not so similar) research as I do and keep track of what they're working on/publication/struggles they're having. What's particularly great is that these people come from all levels of research (other students to senior academics) and all over the world.

The respondents said that they also valued the speed and immediacy of social media, enabling them to keep up to date with recent publications and event announcements and to chat with others in their networks in real time about issues of mutual interest. Several mentioned using social media in their teaching, as they engage their students and offer a way in which online students in particular can easily connect with academic staff and each other. Many respondents mentioned the opportunities for promoting their own research and discussing their ideas in early form with colleagues. Some identified being able to access research participants using social media. As noted by an American female early career academic:

> I am actually tracking an international movement and so following key players on Twitter has been useful in terms of getting leads, reaching new informants, etc. I also have a network of colleagues on Facebook who suggest citations, theoretical frameworks, etc.

Surprisingly little research has focused on how academic practices become habituated and routine, part of tacit knowledges, using any kind of technology, digital or otherwise. One recent study sought to explore this aspect of academic work, drawing on interviews with and observations of scholars using a range of technologies as part of their work (Löfgren 2014). This research found that writing practices have changed with the advent of computerised word processing that enables edits to be easily and quickly made to an academic piece of writing, and accessing journal articles no longer requires hunting down hard copies of journals and then photocopying them, with journals now online. Note-taking has become digitised for many scholars, as have searching for information and systems of filing. Scholars develop customised routines of using search engines, making decisions about what information is important and following hyperlinks that are often difficult to articulate because they have become so habituated and unconscious, involving 'gut feelings' (Löfgren 2014).

As has been found in other research addressing the negotiation of work/home boundaries for knowledge workers in digital society (Gregg 2011; Humphry 2011), traditional models of space and time and work and leisure are challenged by the use of digital technologies. For academics and other knowledge workers, mobile devices such as smartphones, laptops and tablet computers allow the constant switching between work and personal activities, even in bed at night or upon first waking (Löfgren 2014). For researchers who focus on social practices, such as anthropologists, sociologists and those in media, communication and cultural studies, it is difficult not to continually observe social life. Digital media facilitate and intensify such observations. Digital devices are used for both personal and work-related purposes and their mobility and continuous connection to the internet result in work being potentially present at any time of the day.

Most available scholarship on the use of social media for academic purposes focuses on blogging. It has been observed by several writers that in the early years of academic blogging, there was often suspicion of the practice on the part of other academics. People who maintained blogs were in some cases discriminated against when seeking tenure or promotion or otherwise viewed with disdain for being self-aggrandising or wasting time (Gregg 2006; Kirkup 2010; Maitzen 2012). Although negative views of academic blogging have certainly not disappeared, they appear to be slowly changing as universities seek to demonstrate that they are engaging with the public and conforming to open-access mandates and policies.

Academic blogging has been described as 'conversational scholar-ship', a means by which academics can attempt to loosen their formal style of writing as part of communicating to a wider audience (Gregg 2006). It has been argued that the practice forces academics to think about their research and writing in new ways, bearing in mind the multiplicity of potential audiences and the ways readers can respond to the material presented (Kitchin 2014; Kitchin *et al.* 2013). Some bloggers use their writing as a way of developing ideas and seeking engagement with others before they formalise their ideas into a more traditional academic piece (Adema 2013; Carrigan 2013; Daniels 2013a; Estes 2012; Gregg 2006; Maitzen 2012). Daniels (2013a) has described a trajectory by which she has tweeted about an issue during a sociology conference, followed this up with a series of longer blog posts and then collected these posts together, expanded upon her argument and produced an academic journal article. I have also often experienced this process of beginning with a tweet or a blog post and then producing a much more detailed piece of academic writing from these initial thoughts; indeed, parts of this book began in exactly this fashion. Those who use social media in this way have been described as 'open-source academics' (Carrigan 2013).

Public digital scholarship practices such as blogging are also some-times represented as overtly political and resistant acts. It is argued that these types of practices allow for scholars to experiment with digital publishing and engagement at the same time as resisting the dictates of the scholarly publishing industry and producing new forms of knowl-edge dissemination (Adema 2013; Gregg 2006, 2009). The content itself of blog posts, Twitter comments and other social media commu-nications may be directly political, with these tools providing a forum for academics to challenge government policies and programmes (Kitchin 2014; Kitchin *et al.* 2013; Wade and Sharp 2013). They can also provide an opportunity for academics to share their frustrations about higher education procedures and policies and their own experiences as academic workers (Adema 2013; Gregg 2006, 2009; Mewburn and Thomson 2013). In my survey, several postgraduate students and early career researchers wrote that social media connections often gave them emotional as well as academic support, which they found particularly important at their stage of academic career.

THE ACADEMIC GIFT ECONOMY AND NEW FORMS OF PUBLISHING

Several scholars discussing academic blogging have asserted that using this medium often serves the purpose of sharing information and providing advice as part of a gift economy of producing material to share freely with others. From this perspective, scholarship and knowledge are not viewed as a marketable commodity but rather as a social good (Adema 2013; Gregg 2006; Hall 2013a, 2013c; Mewburn and Thomson 2013). Here, the general sharing ethos and participatory democracy that are viewed as characteristic of social media engagement more generally are interpreted in a more specialist academic context.

Academic blogs and other forms of writing on digital platforms are also beginning to reinvent scholarly publishing modes. Blog posts are now often cited in more traditional academic forums, some scholarly journals are incorporating blogs, multimedia or open-access repositories as part of their online presence, and academic presses are experimenting with new digital modes of publication, including shorter online book formats with shorter-than-usual turnaround times between acceptance of the manuscript and publication. Scholarly publishing is developing as hybrid and multiple, drawing both on legacy forms of publishing and on novel modes introduced by digital formats and platforms.

Some academics have taken the concept of 'open scholarship' even further, bringing the concept of the academic gift economy together with the ideals of new approaches to academic publishing. Cultural and media theorist Gary Hall, for example, has developed the concept of the 'open book' on his website (Hall 2013b) and in other writings (Hall 2013c). Hall is part of a movement in 'new cultural studies' that is interested in the performative aspects of scholarship in cultural studies (Hall and Birchall 2006) and in challenging concepts of academic publishing (Hall 2013c). Hall has published material from his book *Media Gifts* on his website of the same title. He describes it as 'the working title of an open, distributed, multi-medium, multi-platform, multi-location, multiple identity book' (Hall 2013b). Here, Hall is pushing the concept of academic writing as part of a gift economy as far as he can. He has experimented with the concept of 'pirated' academic texts by inviting readers to 'steal' or 'pirate' versions of his work as a deliberate attempt to call into question concepts of intellectual property, content creation, authorship and copyright in scholarly writing and publishing.

Hall is also the co-editor of a series of scholarly open publications on Open Humanities Press, including an open-access journal, *Culture Machine*, and two experimental edited book series, Living Books about Life (to which I have contributed a volume – Lupton 2013b) and Liquid Books. These book series, constructed using a wiki platform, are attempts to produce open-access digital books that are 'living' or 'liquid' in the sense that they may be added to at any time after their original publication date, not only by the original volume editors but by any other contributor in a model similar to the Wikipedia format. As these books are digital, it is also possible to include audio-visual material, links to websites and so on as part of the books' contents. These books' 'free-content' approach means that the material contained within can be altered, added to, remixed, reformatted and edited by others as part of a challenge to the concept of the traditional authored or edited scholarly book.

These projects are part of Hall's and his collaborators' experiments with the concept of what Hall calls 'media gifts', or 'using digital media to actualise or creatively perform critical and cultural theory' (Hall 2013a). He views these activities as gifts because they are freely available rather than protected as intellectual property, and as performative because they are directed not at representing or documenting the world but at interacting or acting with it, adopting creative and inventive forms of analysis and critique. Another example of Hall's media gifts project is 'Liquid Theory TV', a collaborative project with Clare Birchall and Pete Woodbridge aimed at developing a series of internet-hosted television programmes for the discussion of intellectual ideas (Hall 2013a).

Hall (2013c) envisages a future scholarly publishing environment in which academics publish their work across a range of formats and platforms, from the more traditional journal, book chapter or monograph published by traditional scholarly presses to the diverse array of forms made available by self-publishing and open-access platforms now available on the internet, including multi-media formats, animation, graphics, photography, film, music and so on. From this perspective, he argues, the concept of 'publication' is challenged and extended. There is no longer an end-point to a publication, as its online form can be continually reworked, revised, mashed up and otherwise transformed continually. This brings us to the idea of the circulation of digital material on the internet and how such material may be constantly reinvented in ways in which the original author may never have intended or expected.

ACADEMIC METRIC ASSEMBLAGES AND AUDIT CULTURE

One important dimension of the increasing digitisation of academic work is the way in which higher education has become subject to quantified monitoring and measuring. Academics are now, whether voluntarily or unwillingly, engaging in presentations of professional selves that incorporate these kinds of measurements and ranking. They possess constantly changing academic data doubles that incorporate digital quantitative data that may be gathered on their professional activities without their specific knowledge or consent (Burrows 2012; Kelly and Burrows 2011; Smith and Jeffery 2013).

Measurement and quantification are not novel practices in the higher education workplace. Even before the advent of digital technologies academics had been counting elements of their work for a long time as part of their professional practice and presentation of the self. The 'publish or perish' maxim refers to the imperative for a successful academic to constantly produce materials such as books, book chapters and peer-reviewed journal articles in order to maintain their reputation and place in the academic hierarchy. Academic curricula vitae invariably involve lists of these outputs under the appropriate headings, as do university webpages for academics. They are required for applications for promotions, new positions and research funding.

Nonetheless, the detail involved and the use of continuous digitised measurements for monitoring and quality assessment purposes is a new phenomenon, as is the opportunity to track some academic metrics in real time. There is now a multitude of ways in which academic performance is monitored, measured and assessed. The performance of sociologists and other academics and the departments and universities which they inhabit are now constantly compared against norms and standards: teaching assessments are carried out; graduate destinations and satisfaction ratings are recorded; research assessment exercises are undertaken; university, department and discipline league tables are published; quality of journals is ranked; academics' citation numbers are counted; and so on. Many of these quantification and quality assessments take place using digital technologies.

Members of such academic open-access digital platforms as Academia.edu and ResearchGate are informed of metrics such as how many people are following them, how often their profile has been viewed, how often their papers have been viewed or downloaded, and, in the case of Academia.edu, who has used search engines to search for them, what key words were used and in what country the searcher is located. LinkedIn tells academic members what new jobs the people they follow have moved to, and makes suggestions for members about which of the jobs advertised on the site they might be suitable for. Academics who blog, use Facebook or Twitter can easily see how many people visit their site or follow them.

Many academic journals now publish figures showing their lists of the most highly cited and highly read articles in their journals, as well as viewing and download statistics for each article individually. Some journals now run their own blogs or tweet links to their newly published articles and monitor and display metrics such as how often articles are shared via social media. The *Journal of Medical Internet Research*, for example, shows 'tweetations', or number of tweets an article published in the journal has attracted, while the PLoS suite of journals lists the number of Facebook or Twitter shares an article has attracted next to its title. Individual journals publish their impact factors and their ranking in relation to other journals in their field. The citation to academics' publication metrics can now be easily viewed by anyone on Google Scholar.

In response to these new ways of measuring and assessing the impact of scholarly publications, an innovative approach to impact entitled 'altmetrics' (short for 'alternative metrics') has been developed. Altmetrics tools can be used to aggregate various uses of academics' work, including monitoring not only traditional forms of citation (in other academic journals, books or chapters) but also the extent to which the work is viewed or referred to in online media texts, such as blogs, tweets and online reference managers such as Mendeley, CiteuLike or Zotero (Galligan and Dyas-Correia 2013; Liu and Adie 2013). Altmetrics views and citations are much more quickly gathered and computed than traditional academic citations (in academic journals and books). If universities begin to accept altmetrics as a valid way of measuring academic impact and influence, then these data will also contribute to assessments of academics' work.

An increasingly managerial approach in higher education has contributed to and encouraged the proliferation of practices of monitoring, measuring and ranking of the performance of individuals, departments, faculties and universities, in what Holmwood (2010) refers to as 'governance by audit'. Some sociologists and other critical commentators view this growth of the audit culture in academia as a significant problem, viewing it as a repressive form of micromanagement and encouraging the inappropriate fostering of a competitive ethos among academics and between universities. It has been contended that the digitisation of academic output as part of the audit culture has had the effect of producing academics as 'metric assemblages' (Burrows 2012) who are encouraged to demonstrate certain kinds of attributes to achieve recognition and status (Barbour and Marshall 2012; Holmwood 2011; Kelly and Burrows 2011).

Some critics propose that these processes have resulted in academic work being given a new kind of value – one that can be quantified – to the exclusion of other ways of assessing the impact and quality of this work. Burrows (2012: 359), for example, has written on the ways in which metrics such as the 'h-index' and 'impact factor', constructed via digital citation indices, contribute to 'a complex data assemblage that confronts the individual academic'. While the results of some of this auditing of academic performance take place at an internal level that is not accessible to the public, many others are publicly available via online sites in ways outlined above. These metrics have become integral to the ways in which academics, academic units and universities receive funding and are ranked against others, and, in the case of individual academics, to their prospects for employment and promotion. They are thus a part of the ways in which other academics judge colleagues' worth and increasingly the judgement of their value – their 'quality' – by their institutions or departments or funding bodies. As such, these metrics can play an enormously important role in the career trajectory and prospects of the contemporary academic. Academics may find it well-nigh impossible to 'opt out' of such measurement and assessment of their value.

The academic metric assemblage may even be viewed as part of a growing trend towards the 'gamification' of the self, including in the workplace setting. Gamification is a term derived from computer science and behavioural economics, denoting the use of gaming strategies and an appeal to fun and the competitive urge in areas that traditionally have been considered non-game environments. In the workplace, gamification is viewed as a tool for increasing employee productivity and efficiency. The concept has become popular in corporate and business contexts, especially advertising and marketing, and is moving into other domains as a strategy for using measuring and monitoring to motivate people and encourage behavioural change (Jagoda 2013). More than 50 American government organisations, as well as the US army, navy and air force, use online games to crowd-source ideas from the general population, as do many corporations (McCormick 2013). The provision of such statistics in ways that provide the opportunity to easily measure oneself or one's department or university against others promotes a gamification mentality, in which there are winners and losers. Comparing one's Google Scholar citation or Twitter follower metrics against others, and the process of using altmetrics itself, may be considered a form of gamification of academic performance, as may the lists of top universities that appear regularly (in which the 'winners' are those universities that achieve the highest rankings, while the 'losers' are those languishing at the bottom).

Some academics are now concerned that in the quest to achieve community engagement and impact, universities will begin to pressure academics to use social media tools, albeit under restrictive guidelines developed by the university and in the interests of anodyne public relations rather than to challenge ideas or engage in political activism (Mewburn and Thomson 2013). In a workplace in which many academics are already feeling overworked and under continuing stress to produce research publications as well as attract students, such demands may be viewed as unreasonable. It has been contended by some observers that the constant measuring and quantifying of academic work has led to significant changes in the ways in which academics view their activities, resulting, in many cases, in feelings of despair, anxiety, depression, stress and exhaustion, a sense that they are never quite 'good enough' (Burrows 2012; Gill 2010). This suggestion has been supported by a 2013 survey of British workers in higher education, which found that they reported higher levels of stress than members of the general population. Almost three-quarters of the respondents agreed that they found their job stressful and the majority noted that they often neglected their personal needs because of the demands of their work. Academics in teaching and research positions reported the highest levels of stress (Kinman and Wray 2013).

My survey of academics' use of social media found that while many respondents reported that using these tools had many benefits (including, for some, higher efficiency and better organisation of their work), use also contributed to time pressures. Several remarked about their concern that universities may be adding digital public engagement to the already long list of obligations demanded of their academic staff. As a male early career academic from Canada wrote: 'My concern is that it is time consuming and it is yet another PR job downloaded into faculty already stretched beyond reason'. A European male early career researcher commented that social media 'shouldn't be considered an obligation. It may contribute to the "the publish or perish" tyranny'. Several others talked about the 'time-drain' of using social media or of the importance of not becoming 'addicted' to using them to the detriment of other work.

However, it is important to emphasise here that although the sociological response to the audit culture and the metricised academic has largely been negative, there are alternative ways of viewing these new technologies of professional practice and identities. As I outlined above, there are undeniable positive dimensions and benefits for academics of participating in digital public engagement. Becoming a metricised assemblage is not necessarily a negative transformation. For many academics, collecting data on their professional selves can engender feelings of achievement, satisfaction and pride in their accomplishments. One might also consider metric assemblages as ways for some academics to resist marginalisation. Citation counts, for example, that offer a quantitative way to support academics' claims of their research impact thus provide a 'bargaining chip' for those who may be traditionally discriminated against in what is still very much an 'old boys' network' in the higher ranks of academia. Traditional academic networks of power still rest on notions of patronage and discriminate against women, those from minority racial or ethnic groups, those who might be considered 'too old' or 'too young' for a position or for a promotion and those who have had a career break for reasons such as caring for others. For such groups, indices such as citation counts and h-indexes may prove vital to supporting their claims to academic achievement and influence as a form of resistance to covert systems of patronage. As this suggests, these digitised metric devices should not simply be considered repressive of academics' autonomy or freedom: quite the opposite, they may offer a means to counter discrimination by virtue of their very power as apparently neutral 'numbers'.

OPENNESS AND THE CIRCULATION OF KNOWLEDGES

Many universities worldwide have begun to privilege the concepts of openness and engagement as parts of their operations. Open learning strategies such as MOOCs and initiatives promoting open access to research publications and data have become key to discussions of the future of higher education and research. As outlined above, academics are now frequently encouraged to deposit their publications in open-access forums, consider developing online courses and take steps to promote engagement of their ideas with other members of the community.

Academics who use digital media tools as part of their professional identities need to think carefully about how best to manage their private and public personae when doing so: how formal their self-presentation is, to what extent they make personal comments about themselves or others, the nature of images of themselves that they upload, to what extent they allow – or respond to – comments from others (Barbour and Marshall 2012). Many academics who responded to my online survey on social media use raised this issue about the blurring of boundaries between professional and private lives on social media. Respondents observed that it can be difficult to maintain these boundaries. This concerned some people because they thought that their academic persona may be undermined by personal content on social media: 'Some caution is required – I feel as there is the potential for some academics to disclose too much of their professional and personal lives' (female early career academic, UK). In negotiating this issue, many people mentioned using some platforms for professional purposes only and maintaining others for private or personal use. As one female early career academic from Australia/New Zealand put it: 'I use Facebook, Flickr, Pinterest and a personal blog for personal rather than academic purposes. [I] don't want to let my professional identity enter those spaces because I like having work/life separation to at least some extent'.

Another issue identified by respondents in my online survey was the lack of credibility that using social media for academic purposes was given by other academics, who viewed such practices as frivolous or time-wasting: 'Some senior scientists at my university still consider social media as useless or a waste of time. It's not always easy to justify a social media presence and activity' (European female postgraduate student). A further potential pitfall of using social media is the extent to which academics become part of their students' social networks and vice versa. Academics need to consider carefully the politics of following or 'friending' students and allowing them to reciprocate in the context of a relationship that is essentially an unequal one, particularly if the academics depart from strictly professional interactions in online forums (American Association of University Professors 2013). This issue again relates to the presentation of the professional academic self on social media, and the extent to which the content academics create and share and the people with whom they interact are related to their academic work and networks or are about their private lives and opinions.

The freedom of expression that forums such as blogs and social media sites offer academics can also be the cause of their downfall. It has been alleged, for example, that an American political scientist, Juan

Cole, was found unacceptable for a job position in 2006 at a prestigious American university because of anti-war sentiments he had expressed on his personal blog (Barbour and Marshall 2012). Several other cases exist involving the censure or disciplining of academics for statements that they made on social media sites of which their university disapproved (American Association of University Professors 2013). More recently, the Twitter comment expressed in 2013 by another American academic, evolutionary psychologist Geoffrey Miller, received a high level of social media attention and opprobrium when he asserted that he would not accept 'obese PhD applicants' as postgraduate students because their body size was evidence of their lack of 'willpower to stop eating carbs'. Although he later claimed that the tweet was part of a research project, Miller was denounced as a 'fat-shaming professor' and the case came under the examination of his university's Institutional Review Board (Ingeno 2013). Academics have also been the targets of libel actions instigated by people offended by comments they have made on social media (American Association of University Professors 2013). In response to these issues, some universities are beginning to institute restrictive guidelines that limit the freedom of academics to engage in social media as part of their professional practice.

The phenomenon of what is often termed 'trolling' or 'cyber bullying' – or the use of online media to engage in harassment and verbal abuse of other users – has received a high level of attention both in academic research and the popular media. The vast proportion of this discussion, however, has focused on children or adolescents. There is much less research about or wider discussion of the use of digital media to engage in the harassment of or malicious commentary about adults in the context of the workplace, including in higher education. I have observed that female academics who engage in fat activism using online forums or traditional media outlets are frequently targeted by vituperative comments about their appearance, lack of self-discipline and the like. (Ironically, these comments often serve only to demonstrate further the contentions of these academics concerning fat stigma and discrimination.) Sexual harassment has also been experienced by some female academics who have engaged in debates in public forums or who have used social media to communicate their research findings. Some female academics have described their experiences of their appearance and their sexual attractiveness being remarked upon following their participation in social media outlets or in the traditional mass media. In some cases, contributions from anonymous commentators have detailed sexual fantasies about the women, while in others the women's appearance has been aggressively criticised (Beard 2013; Mitchell 2013). Non-white academics have also been subjected to racist comments, and female black academics have experienced both sexism and racism (Cottom McMillan 2012).

Those academics who express their opinions on controversial issues, who identify as gay or who challenge powerful institutions or commercial interests are also often the targets of comments questioning their professional integrity, as well as hate messages and even death threats (American Association of University Professors 2013; Chapman 2012; Cottom McMillan 2012; Kitchin 2014; Kitchin *et al.* 2013; Wade and Sharp 2013). Such abusive and overly racist, misogynistic or homophobic comments, which are often on public display and can be accessed via search engines, may be very confronting and disturbing for their targets, particularly if sexual violence or other violent acts against the targets are suggested. This is a wider problem of the affordances of online technologies: anyone who engages online is open to abusive comments that cannot easily be removed from internet archives (see further discussion of these issues in Chapters 6 and 7).

This was a concern that was expressed by several respondents in my survey, who identified their worry about being open to attack by using social media. Such attacks may descend into outright aggression, hate speech or harassment. Thus, for example, an Asian female mid-career academic noted: 'It can be a nasty unmediated space. If something goes wrong, unlikely upper management of Uni will support you. Trolling. Ick place if your work is non-normative: e.g. feminist, queer'. For a male early career academic from Australia/New Zealand, 'Visibility is an issue; there is always a concern about trolling and/or tweets posted appearing out of context in mainstream media'. A British female mid-career academic commented: 'I've had problems with trolls that have been quite disturbing'.

Early career researchers may be more vulnerable to trenchant criticism of their views at a time when they are still establishing their careers and seeking employment. More than established academics, who have less to lose, such junior academics are caught in a double-bind. Using social media such as blogs can be an important way for junior academics to establish a foothold in their field, get their name and research known, establish valuable networks with colleagues, and demonstrate to potential employers that they are engaging with the public in approved ways. On the other hand, however, some early career academics, particularly if they also come from marginalised social groups or are working in less prestigious universities, may find their opinions open to attack to a greater extent compared with more senior and socially privileged academics (Gregg 2009).

Significant concern about jeopardising their academic career or future job prospects was evident in the comments written by respondents who were early career researchers or postgraduate students, and, to a lesser extent, some more senior academics in my online survey. Several mentioned this concern as one of the issues they worried or were cautious about when using social media. For example, a British male mid-career academic wrote that he was worried that 'sometimes forthright expression of views could cause issues for employers and affect my reputation. Use has to carefully balance professionalism and discretion with academic freedom and freedom of speech'. A British female postgraduate student noted that being too open in the content she shares on social media may make her vulnerable: 'My Twitter mixes personal with academic online activity. I worry that my (left) politics and my openness about being queer may disadvantage me in getting jobs'. For others, the possibility that they may lose their jobs because of remarks they made on social media influenced their engagement on these sites. As an American female postgraduate student put it:

> [I worry] that my university will fire me due to some public post, even though on 'public' social media I am very careful/self-censored (like Twitter) and on my more 'private' channels I use a pseudonym (like Tumblr). But I'm still nervous. All universities seem to be making some very questionable decisions and actions against their faculty.

Some writers have commented on the vulnerability that social media engagement such as blogging may engender in scholars who are used to formal academic writing styles and traditional procedures of publishing, in which one's writing is vetted by one's peers before it reaches an audience, and people outside academia do not have the opportunity to comment on one's research (Estes 2012; Gregg 2006; Kirkup 2010; Kitchin *et al.* 2013; Maitzen 2012). As Gregg (2006: 154) points out,

> Blogs reveal the mind of the critic as impressionable and open to persuasion, for the writer is rarely able to sustain the confidence and assurance of a fixed position. Such a function contrasts with conventional modes of academic performance premised on expertise and mastery.

This concern was evident in the responses written by some respondents in my survey. One European female postgraduate student wrote that she was concerned about 'coming across as dumb!', while a female mid-career academic from Australia/New Zealand mentioned the risk of 'putting a half-baked idea on the public record'. A male post-graduate student from the UK wrote: 'I occasionally worry that having many "works in progress" sitting around on the internet may provoke a negative reaction if people judge them by the same standards as, say, journal articles'.

Posting one's work on online media may also be considered a risky practice because of the loss of control that eventuates. New digital technologies offer great potential for sharing and disseminating these knowledges far more widely and rapidly than ever before, at the same time as allowing scope for greater transformation of these knowledges in ways which the original authors may not anticipate or approve. Academics need to be aware of the multitude of ways in which the content created by one author or group of authors may be reused and transmitted via different modes of publishing (reblogged or excerpted on other people's blogs; tweeted in tiny 'grabs'; commented upon; and so on). Using new media technologies, the product of sociologists' and other academics' labour may be reappropriated and transformed in ways that are unprecedented and may pose a challenge to traditional concepts of academic research and publication (Beer 2013b). Their comments can be deliberately misquoted, placed out of context and otherwise used in ways that would not be approved of by the original authors (Kitchin *et al.* 2013).

These processes of reuse and transformation have always been the subject of sociological research published in more traditional academic forums. Journal articles, books or reports are taken up and reappropriated by those who cite them in their own work, or by journalists reporting on their findings, in ways that may be unpredictable and which are completely out of the control of the original author. Sociologists have often been unhappy about the way their research has been reported in the traditional news media, for example, by being overly simplified and reduced to sound bites and controversial headlines. The difference in the new digital media era is the scale of such circulations and potential transformations of sociological knowledges that have escaped the academy.

As part of the digital knowledge economy of circulation and recursion, once digital data are generated they regenerate other data and are linked to each other. Prosumers continually create new or modified versions of data in a never-ending cycle, including creating new metadata through classification practices such as tagging related to the data (Beer and Burrows 2013). Algorithms and practices of classification play important roles in structuring and shaping the ways in which online academic content is used and discovered. They serve to identify some research as relevant and ignore others, while users' practices in tagging of others' contents serve as another way of making research more or less visible to others and making some connections between topics and writers while excluding others that are equally valid. The use of predictive algorithms of the types that are employed by Amazon and Google Go may begin to benefit academics by making recommendations of their work to others who are interested in the topics about which they write (Beer 2012a).

To some extent, some journal websites themselves have begun to operate in this way – by providing lists of related articles available in the journal when one is reading an article on a particular topic, or by displaying the articles that have cited the article one is perusing and providing hyperlinks that give ready access to these articles. Google Scholar now also provides a useful automatic customised alert service to users of articles that have been identified as related to topics on which the users have published. The growing scholarly community on Twitter can also play a role in sharing or retweeting links to articles and blog posts by other researchers working in common areas of interest and by using hashtags to organise content. The practice of tagging to produce metadata, therefore, plays a role in the ordering, organising and classification of academic knowledge in online forums. The value of the ideas and the quality of the writing are not necessarily the most important (or the only) features of whether or not a particular piece of work is widely circulated and read.

An example of this process from my own experience of social media use is when I publish blog posts. I tweet the link to the blog post when it is published, which is then retweeted by some of my followers (and perhaps by their followers to their own followers, and so on). I may receive some comments in my blog's comments section, and sometimes people re-blog the post on their own blogs, add it to a curated digital collection on a platform like Scoop.it or Bundlr, or write about it on their own blogs, providing a hyperlink back to the original post. They may give the material tags that may be different from those that I used for my original post. Sometimes I come across references to my blog posts in unexpected places. I have found my posts referenced in academic journal articles and, as I remarked earlier in this chapter, I sometimes draw on them myself to write traditional academic material. I may also link to my own previously published blog posts in new blog posts. Some of this use is under my control (when I use my own material for my purposes); most of it is not.

The possibilities of plagiarism have also been raised by some academics as a risk of engaging in digital public scholarship. Some academics who blog have noticed that their content has been used by others, sometimes verbatim, without any form of attribution to its original source. This experience has led them to reconsider the benefits of blogging (see, for example, an account by Williams 2013). This issue was also brought up by some of the academics who responded to my survey. As a British female early career academic mused: 'how much can/should you share of your research via social media before it's published, and who, if anyone, cites pre-article material (and how)?'

It is not known, however, whether blogs are more open to plagiarism than are other forms of academic publication. Given that blog posts carry the name of the author as well as the date of publication, both of which can be easily verified and cited by anyone wanting to refer to this material, there is no justification for such material to be plagiarised, apart from the fact that it is more accessible to the public than is academic writing that is published in journals that require a subscription or payment of an article fee to access. Indeed, many major style guides now provide guidelines for how to cite blog posts and tweets in academic writing. More difficult to control is the sharing of one's scholarly content via other forms of social media. Some academics are concerned that if their conference papers are live-tweeted at conferences, audio- or videotaped, blogged about, or otherwise shared on social media by others their new and original ideas may be misrepresented or stolen before they have a chance to fully develop them. The same argument has been made about teaching resources in terms of preserving intellectual property rights and the right of academics to privacy in relation to comments they may make in classes or emails to students (American Association of University Professors 2013).

Beer (2012a, 2013b) argues that this increasing potential of publishing in a variety of forums beyond the traditional academic journal and book may also lead to a proliferation of sociological material being available, much of which may struggle to find an audience. While high-profile academics may receive even more attention by using new digital platforms of expression, maintaining a digital presence to bolster their credentials, others may be ignored and fail to receive adequate acknowledgement of their work. Beer observes that this has happened to the music industry in the wake of digitisation. Large numbers of musicians are publishing their work online and making it freely available, but are failing to achieve a desired level of impact or to receive adequate remuneration for their work. According to Beer, if digital outlets for publication and dissemination of sociological research become valued in the university, it will be those academics who are skilled at marketing themselves and using digital tools who will benefit, while those who are unwilling or unable to employ these technologies will be disadvantaged.

A debate has also developed in response to the proliferation of online courses, which has caused many commentators to question the pedagogical value of these courses and their implications for employment levels and academic workloads. Some critics view online courses as yet another opportunity for governments to withdraw funding for face-to-face teaching in favour of what are viewed as less expensive forms of instruction via online technologies (Smith and Jeffery 2013). From this critical perspective, if there is a push to encourage academics to learn about and use social media, open-education technologies and open-access publication forums solely as parts of their universities' imperatives for public engagement and impact, the digitised academic may be positioned as yet another facet of the neoliberal ethos of the contemporary university (Burrows 2012; Gill 2010; Holmwood 2010).

Open-access initiatives have also been subjected to critique. The basic tenet of open access is clearly a sensible one: it is difficult to argue against the idea that researchers' insights should be rendered accessible outside the walls of the academy. However, it has been noted by some that these initiatives, while clearly providing opportunities for researchers to publish their work in ways to which members of the public can gain access, have begun to be monetised by some publishers to the detriment of some academics. There are now three methods of open access:

- 'green' – publishing without charge in such places as university e-repositories or sites such as one's personal website, Academia.edu and ResearchGate;
- 'gold' – paying academic journals an article-processing fee upon acceptance of the article for it to be rendered open access by the journal; and
- 'platinum' – in which open-access journals publish an article free of charge.

Critics have questioned how researchers from traditionally underfunded disciplines such as the humanities and social sciences will find the money to pay article-processing fees if they wish to publish in a journal that has adopted the 'gold' open-access approach.

The apparent co-option of traditional academic publishers of open-access initiatives for commercial gain has attracted much critique and disquiet. Many academics in science, medicine and technology have embraced open-access publishing and there are several well-established open-access journals in their fields. However, some academics in the humanities and social sciences have felt pushed into rendering their material open access by funding bodies or their own institutions, and they are now concerned that this will affect their chances of publishing in the more established publication forums that have higher reputations (LSE Public Policy Group 2013; Weller 2013).

So too, the notion that publishing in digital formats is somehow easier, less expensive, more permanent and less a product of human labour than traditional forms of scholarly publication has been challenged (Drucker 2014). As I contended in Chapter 1, digital data are material artefacts and their production and storage consume material resources. Digitised publications are subject to deterioration and loss of access if they are not carefully maintained and the platforms on which they reside constantly upgraded. Costs are associated with preserving digital archives and providing the energy resources to support servers. If a publication exists only in a digital format and the platform upon which it is archived is removed, then it simply disappears. Digital academic texts still need careful reviewing, editing and proofing, their format needs to be attractive and readable, and they need to be distributed and publicised, all of which requires the labour of the author or others in the production process (Drucker 2014).

In this chapter, I have adopted a reflexive sociological stance on the use of social and other digital media as parts of digital sociology, outlining a number of considerations and complexities related to 'digitising' oneself as an academic. As I have shown, using social media is a very effective way of facilitating openness and engagement. However, there are some pitfalls and risks associated with rendering one's ideas 'open' to the public. Academics who engage in digital public engagement may be subjected to public criticism of their ideas, unfounded or legitimate, as part of receiving wider attention. This criticism disproportionately affects specific social groups within higher education. Further, while using these media for academic work is always a performance of professional selfhood, it matters whether this performance is mandated by employers or springs from a genuine desire or interest on the part of the academic in engaging as a digital public scholar. As such, there may said to be a politics of digital engagement, in which some academics, particularly those who are members of marginalised social groups or who are junior academics seeking tenure or those in short-term employment contracts, may need to be very cautious about the types of opinions they express in open digital forums. Quite simply, engaging as a digitised public scholar may be too confronting for some academics.

CHAPTER 5

A critical sociology of big data

In recent years, there has been extensive discussion of and publicity about the possibilities for social research, commercial enterprise and efficient government offered by the massive digital data sets – big data – that are now collected via individuals' online activities. In the popular media and in data science, business, global development, policing and security, politics, healthcare, education and agriculture, much is made of the potential offered by these ever-expanding data sets. Big data are viewed as offering greater precision and predictive powers to improve efficiency, safety, wealth generation or resource management. The capacity of digital technologies to harvest, mine, store and analyse data is represented as superior to other forms of knowledge, offering greater opportunities than ever before to delve into human behaviours. From a critical sociological perspective, however, there is much more to say about big data as sociocultural artefacts.

Following an overview of the ways in which big data discourses and practices have achieved dominance in many social spheres, I discuss how digital data assemblages and algorithms possess power and authority, the metaphors used to describe big data and what these reveal about our anxieties and concerns about this phenomenon, big data hubris and rotted data, and the ethical issues relating to big data.

THE BIG DATA PHENOMENON

Data that are digitally generated or stored via digital means have been in existence since the early years of computing. What the 'big data' term refers to is the major expansion in the contemporary era of the quantities of digital data that are generated as the products of users' transactions with and content generation via digital media technologies, as well as digital surveillance technologies such as CCTV cameras, RFID chips, traffic monitors and sensors monitoring the natural environment. Digital data objects are not only constantly generated but they are also highly detailed, able to pinpoint many users' activities with great precision. Mobile devices such as smartphones collect data on who the user calls, what websites and platforms they browse and search terms they use and also details on the location and body movements of their users through their embedded GPS receivers, compasses, gyroscopes and accelerometers. These data are considered 'bigger' than other forms of data because of their ever-increasing volume, constant state of generation, the variety of sites from which they are produced, the capacity to search within and compare the data sets, and their potential to link to each other to create new and more detailed data sets. These features of digital data, it is argued, require new ways of storing, processing and analysing the data (boyd and Crawford 2012; Dumbill 2013).

The term 'big data' is appearing with ever-greater frequency in the popular media, government reports and business-related blogs. I conducted a Google Trends graph of the frequency of searches for the term 'big data' from January 2004 to March 2014 (appropriately enough using a big data tool to research big data). This showed that the frequency of searches remained low until the end of 2010. From 2011, however, the term was searched for increasingly frequently, and has risen steadily, reaching its peak (at the time of writing) in March 2014. The Google Trends analysis also demonstrated that the regional interest in big data, as indicated by Google searches, was by far the greatest in Asia, with India demonstrating the most relative interest, followed by Singapore, South Korea, Taiwan and Hong Kong.

As individuals, corporations and government agencies gather more data and become aware of its apparent value, a breathless rhetoric has emerged around the concept of big data. It is assumed that the more data are gathered and analysed, the better. Such an approach is evident in the first book to be published about the potential of big data for a popular readership, entitled *Big Data: A Revolution That Will Transform How We Live, Work and Think* (Mayer-Schonberger and Cukier 2013). The book's dramatic title is indicative of the authors' view that big data represents a revolutionary phenomenon. *Big Data for Dummies*

(Hurwitz *et al.* 2013) is also now available to instruct lay readers in the uses and potential of big data. A report with somewhat more gravitas by the British House of Commons Public Administration Select Committee (2014) represents digital data sets as containing 'unused knowledge that otherwise goes to waste, which can be used to empower citizens, to improve public services, and to benefit the economy and society as a whole'. The US federal government has also supported open digital data initiatives. The Data.gov website has been established as a platform for centralising government data and providing access to these data, with over 85,000 searchable data sets made available.

Online users' activities and choices become converted into precious data commodities that can be sold on to third parties or used by the corporations that collect the data for their own purposes. A growing industry has developed that is directed at harvesting – or scraping – the web for data, and the profession of 'data brokering' has emerged, which involves the accessing and selling on of data for profit. A kind of digital vitality has been generated, in which information and data have taken on value in themselves, contributing to the digital knowledge economy discussed in Chapter 2. As one marketer was quoted as remarking: 'From a marketer's perspective, this new class of data is a goldmine. Just think what we can do with minute-by-minute tracking of body movements, physical reaction to external stimulus (like ads!), weight and body changes and geolocation' (Anonymous 2013).

According to the editor of the new data science journal *Big Data*, a shared assumption in public discourse on big data is 'the notion that we might compute our way to better decisions' (Dumbill 2013: 1). The authors of a report by the McKinsey Global Institute, the research arm of a large global management company, put it in these terms: big data 'will become a key basis of competition, underpinning new waves of productivity growth, innovation and consumer surplus ... Leaders in every sector will have to grapple with the implications of big data, not just a few data-oriented managers' (Manyika *et al.* 2011: n.p.). The authors go on to contend that big data can make information 'transparent and usable at much higher frequency', can provide 'more accurate and detailed performance information' for organisations who collect and analyse these data, to 'help make better management decisions', to allow 'ever-narrower segmentation of customers' for more targeted marketing efforts, to 'substantially improve decision-making' and to 'improve the next generation of products and services' (Manyika *et al.* 2011: n.p.). Practitioners of data science are now frequently portrayed in news reports and blogs as the newest hot profession, and their scarcity is bemoaned. Indeed, according to the *Harvard Business Review*, data science is 'the sexiest job of the 21st century' (Davenport and Patil 2013).

While prosumption has been a feature of capitalist economies for some time, the new digital media technologies have provided the conditions for an expansion of these activities and the surveillance of consumption habits in real time (Ritzer 2014). The data they prosume are used to construct profiles of consumer habits and to market to consumers in ever more detailed and personalised ways. As data can now be merged from multiple databases, their precision and predictive power have become enhanced. Marketing companies now seek to combine various approaches to eliciting and analysing consumer sentiment with statistics about their purchasing habits, and large digital data sets are viewed as contributing major insights to the understanding of consumer behaviour and direct marketing efforts in what is sometimes referred to as 'data fusion'. They view 'clickstream analysis' data (recordings of web users' activities) as providing more accurate and less expensive information about consumer habits and preferences (Breur 2011).

Social media and digital information companies such as Facebook, Microsoft and Google, as well as major retailing companies like Amazon, Target and Walmart, have led the way in realising the ways in which the data that users voluntarily contribute about themselves may be used to in turn target the users for product development and advertising that is tailored and customised. These companies are currently building huge digital data storage centres (Lesk 2013). One of the largest companies engaged in database marketing, Axiom, claims to have digital data records on hundreds of millions of Americans taken from a wide array of data sets. It is able to compile digital profiles based on these data sets that can identify such features as a person's age, gender, ethnicity or race, number of children, education level, place of residence, type of car they drive and so on. Axiom sells these data profiles to its customers, which include large banks, credit card issuers, telecom/media companies and insurance companies (Marwick 2014).

Many retailers now have customer loyalty schemes, in which customers are issued with cards that are swiped at the checkout when they are paying for their purchases. Data about the purchases are then archived by the supermarket and used for marketing purposes or sold on to their own clients. Customers are enticed to join up by winning discounts or products once they have accumulated enough points. If retailers are able to connect enough databases, they are able to market their products in ever more detailed and customised ways to consumers. It has been estimated that the American retailing giant Walmart has gathered online consumer data on more than 60 per cent of American adults and it shares its digital database with over 50 third-party partners. Walmart not only collects data on what its customers purchase but also tracks their movements around its stores using in-store wi-fi technology (Center for Media Justice, ColorOfChange, Sum of Us 2013). Target, another major American retailer, uses combined customer purchases to estimate not only if a female customer is pregnant, but even what her due date may be, by analysing patterns of purchasing. If a woman begins purchasing unscented lotion or lotion advertised to help alleviate stretch marks, cotton balls, hand sanitiser and pregnancy vitamins, she is deemed to be pregnant and accordingly sent baby-related vouchers by the company. Once Target realised that customers may become 'creeped out' by how much it knew about them, it began to send pregnant women baby vouchers combined with other non-pregnancy-related products to allay their suspicions (Duhigg 2012).

In Australia, the Woolworths supermarket chain also owns an insurance company and petrol stations and has a 50 per cent share in a data analytics company. Using the combined databases drawn from their customer loyalty programme and insurance company and employing the skills provided by their data analytics company, Woolworths were able to demonstrate that they could target consumers for insurance packages based on their supermarket purchasing habits. They found that customers of their supermarkets who purchased higher quantities of milk and red meat were better car insurance risks than those who purchased high quantities of pasta and rice, filled their cars with petrol at night and drank spirits. Based on the information in these datasets the two groups of customers were then targeted for offering different insurance packages involving different premium costs (Wallace and Whyte 2013).

The other major Australian supermarket chain, Coles, released a detailed description of its privacy policy for its customer loyalty and online shopping schemes in March 2014. The updated policy revealed how many other companies with which it shared customers' personal data (30 companies owned by the corporation that also owns Coles) and that these data were sold to third parties in at least 23 other countries. The new privacy policy also revealed that personal information Coles collected on customers, including name, contact and household details, transaction history and buying habits, can be used for conducting risk assessments for credit and insurance, products also sold by the corporation (Thomson 2014).

As more objects become digitised and 'smart', attached to sensors and connected to the internet, some devices have been developed that are able to closely monitor and measure human behaviour, either for commercial or administrative purposes. As mentioned above, retailers such as Walmart monitor the movements of shoppers in their stories using wi-fi. A growing number of developers of health self-tracking apps and platforms are selling the data they produce to third parties.

Users download the apps for free, but the data they generate are the products that are sold by the app developers (Dredge 2013; McCowen 2013). Another example is the black box recorder that can be attached to a car engine and transmit regular reports on driver behaviour, including driving times, locations, speed, braking and cornering forces. As part of the 'telematic insurance' phenomenon, these data are sent wirelessly to insurance companies for their use in determining how risky drivers are considered to be and therefore whether they should be offered insurance and at what level of premium (McCowen 2013). Through the use of these types of technologies, assessments of risk become ever more personalised and fine-grained.

Sensor-based technologies have also been used to generate digital data on phenomena in the organic world, such as animals, soil, waterways and plants. Workers in the agricultural sector have identified the potential of big data derived from databases of climate, crop yields, soil analyses and livestock behaviours to develop 'precision agriculture' or 'smart farming'. Farmers are increasingly using sensor-based devices, RFID tagging of livestock and big data to improve their productivity. Many tractors and combine harvesters are equipped with digital technologies that collect data on geo-location, crops and soil. The developers of 'prescription planting' technologies use aggregated data from farmers and meteorological data to create algorithms that direct users how to most efficiently use their resources to improve their yields. The giant seed company Monsanto had led the way in developing technologies using big data, including its acquisition of Climate Corp, a weather data–mining company. Its FieldScripts application suite uses agricultural and climate data in conjunction with its own data on the genetic properties of its seeds to make recommendations to farmers about how they should best plant their seeds (Bunge 2014).

Australia's peak scientific research body, the Commonwealth Scientific and Industrial Research Organisation (CSIRO), recently published a report on 'smart farming'. This report referred to the potential of objects equipped with sensor-based technologies to contribute data to maximise the productivity of Australian agriculture by creating an Internet of Things, sharing data with each other, such as pasture vegetation, soil moisture, livestock movements and farm equipment. A key feature of 'smart farming', the report's authors contend, is the ability to use cloud computing to aggregate these data from numerous farms to provide big data analytics. These analytics can predict such features as pasture growth and the early detection of subclinical diseases in livestock and enhance monitoring of crop yield, pasture quality, feed allocation systems and animal reproductive performance, weight, growth rates and health (Griffith *et al.* 2013).

The potential for humanitarian uses of big data has also been identified. The World Economic Forum (2011) has represented digital data as creating new opportunities for wealth creation and alleviating social disadvantage and ill-health. Personal data are described as 'the new oil' and 'a valuable resource of the 21st century' in its report on 'personal data as the new asset class' (World Economic Forum 2011: 5). According to a United Nations report (Letouze 2012), open access to 'real-time' digital data offers major opportunities for global development. The United Nations has launched its Global Pulse initiative, which is directed at using big data to track and monitor the impacts of global and local socioeconomic crises and to mitigate the risks of these. Google now offers several tools that draw on data from Google searches to provide indications of outbreaks of diseases such as influenza and dengue fever (Google Flu Trends and Google Dengue Trends), locations of crises and natural disasters such as floods and bushfires (Google Public Alerts and Google Crisis Map) and assistance in locating people who may have been dislocated in times of crisis or natural disasters (Google Person Finder).

The lure of big data has had a major impact upon healthcare policy. Many public health units, hospitals and other healthcare facilities are putting into place data management systems in an attempt to better deal with and plan for demands on their services. There is now much focus on and discussion concerning the power of the vast data archives gathered by digital technologies both to inform patients about their own bodies and to provide information to healthcare providers about the health states of populations and the use of healthcare. Numerous reports and journal articles have been published on the predicted benefits that generating and using big data sets will bring for medicine and public health, including improving healthcare delivery as well as disease monitoring and prevention (e.g. Barrett *et al.* 2013; Hay *et al.* 2013; Murdoch and Detsky 2013; Swan 2013). Several countries are attempting to transfer patient records into electronic form and are investigating the ways in which these data may be mined for insights into patterns of health, illness and medical treatment to improve the quality of healthcare (Garrety *et al.* 2014). The English National Health Service (NHS), for example, launched the care.data initiative in 2014, directed at digitising medical records of patients in its system, both from general practitioners and hospitals, and combining them into a massive database, with the motto 'Better information means better care'. The data from the care.data database was planned not only for research into healthcare services but also to serve a commercial function, with the NHS selling the data to private enterprises such as health insurance companies.

In the domain of school education there is increasing interest in using digitised data drawn from many data sets and combining them to provide increasingly detailed data profiles of students. 'Learning analytics' are used to create 'learning profiles' for individual students that diagnose their strengths and weaknesses and ways of learning. Across groups of students (segmented by gender, age, socioeconomic status and ethnicity/race), predictive analytics are employed in the attempt to identify features of performance that can then be used to improve learning (Grant 2013). This is also taking place at the level of higher education in some countries. Some American colleges, for example, are using predictive analytics combining data from students' grades, number of hours they are enrolled during each semester, number of hours they are working outside university and the level of financial assistance from their families as well as other factors to determine which new students are most likely to encounter problems once enrolled (Ungerleider 2013).

Policing and security agencies are also tapping into big data to identify security threats and behaviour patterns, patterns in crime and potential suspects or terrorists and as part of 'predictive policing' make predictions about who might commit criminal or terrorist acts and where. The American Federal Bureau of Investigation enters details of date, time, type and location of recent crimes into databases and combines this information with historical crime data to produce algorithmically generated 'crime hotspots' at which greater surveillance and other policing resources are directed. Law enforcement and security agencies also attempt to identify suspicious groups or individuals who are targeted for surveillance, further investigation, search or detention (Crawford and Schultz 2014). As was evident from the documents released by Edward Snowden, the American and other anglophone governments have been engaging in extensive surveillance activities of their own citizens by accessing digital data collected by commercial enterprises. Given the extent of these surveillance data-gathering activities, it is not surprising that the NSA is building a massive data centre for its own storage purposes (Lesk 2013).

DIGITAL DATA ASSEMBLAGES AND ALGORITHMIC AUTHORITY

In information or data science, data are generally represented as if they are the raw materials for information and algorithms as the neutral agents for processing these pieces of information. They are represented as the scientifically produced, *a priori* basis for developing 'information' when structured or arranged in a particular context (moving from 'raw data' to analysed data), which in turn is used to construct 'knowledge', which may involve meaning, cultural beliefs and value judgements (Räsänen and Nyce 2013). As I contended in Chapter 2, sociologists and other scholars interested in media and communication have developed a different perspective on the big data phenomenon and on the algorithms that are used to collect, classify and process big data. They emphasise that big data are not as objective, complete and neutral as they are portrayed in mainstream representations. The production and use of big data are political, social and cultural processes.

From this perspective, numbers are sociotechnical devices that are inseparable from the practices that seek to enumerate the materials they measure (Uprichard 2013; Verran 2012). They are 'semiotically agential', used for particular rhetorical and discursive purposes: 'the workings of numbers are deeply embedded in and constitutive of the real – they lubricate its happening' (Verran 2012: 112). In other words, numbers can play a part in constituting phenomena, bringing them into being, making them as well as making sense of them. Numbers are not neutral and objective, although they are widely believed to be so, particularly in relation to qualitative sources of knowledge. They have an inextricable relationship to what is considered to be valuable, used both to produce value and to measure value, and also standing for what is considered valuable to quantify in the first place (West 2014).

The digital data objects that are rendered into numbers by digital technologies are both the products of sociotechnical devices and such devices themselves, possessing their own agency and power. There is no such thing as 'raw' data – indeed, according to the memorable title of one book on this subject, 'raw data' is an oxymoron (Gitelman 2013). There are conventions and practices of seeking out, recording, archiving and categorising data that are themselves configured via specific beliefs, judgements, values and cultural assumptions that 'cook' the data from the very beginning so that they are never in a 'raw' state (Baym 2013; boyd and Crawford 2012; Gitelman and Jackson 2013; Räsänen and Nyce 2013). Rather than pre-existing items of information, digital data are co-produced or co-authored by those who make the software and devices that elicit and archive them, the coders who generate the algorithms in the software and those who use these technologies. Those individuals or institutions who archive data have an important role to play in how the data are ordered and classified, and, therefore, in the ways in which they are accessed and retrieved by potential users (Beer 2013a).

At each step in the process of generating digital data, human decision-making, judgement, interpretation and action are involved. Some phenomena are selected to be collected as 'data' while others are not; some of these data are considered important to analyse while others are not; some are rendered visible while others remain invisible (Andrejevic 2013; boyd and Crawford 2012; Vis 2013). Problems and practices are produced via algorithms, as are solutions to problems (Beer 2009, 2013a; Cheney-Lippold 2011; Lash 2007; Rogers 2013). Once the data are produced, interpretations are made about how they should be classified, what they mean and how they should best be represented. These interpretations again rely on subjective decision-making: 'we tell stories about the data and essentially these are the stories we wish to tell' (Vis 2013).

The algorithms that shape the ways in which digital data are collected and classified are the result of human action and decision-making, but they possess their own agential power. Algorithms do not simply describe data; they also make predictions and play a part in the configuring of new data. For example, search engines possess what Rogers (2013: 97) refers to as 'algorithmic authority' and act as 'socio-epistemological machines': they influence what sources are considered important and relevant. Algorithms play an influential role in ranking search terms in search engines, ensuring that some voices are given precedence over others. From this perspective, the results that come from search engine queries are viewed not solely as 'information' but as social data that are indicative of power relations. Google's Page Rank system has enormous influence in determining which webpages appear when a search term is used, and therefore which tend to be viewed more often, which in turn affects the algorithms dictating page ranking.

It has been asserted by some scholars that traditional concepts of knowledge have become challenged by big data. In the global digital knowledge economy, knowledge that is quantifiable, distributable and searchable via online technologies is represented as superior (Andrejevic 2013; Smith 2013). At the same time, information has become limitless and more difficult to define. The logic of the predictive and analytic power of big data is that all information about everyone is important, because it cannot be known in advance what data may become vital to use. Hence the incessant need to generate and store data. Data mining is therefore speculative as well as comprehensive (Andrejevic 2013).

So, too, new ways of conceptualising people and their behaviours have been generated by big data discourses and practices. Indeed, it has been contended that our 'data selves' as they are configured by the data we and others collect on ourselves represent human subjects as archives of data: 'digitised humans' or 'data-generating machines' (McFedries 2013). For some commentators, this is having the effect not only of turning people into data but also encouraging them to view themselves as data assemblages above other ways of defining identity and selfhood: 'We are becoming data ... So we need to be able to understand ourselves as data too' (Watson 2013). Not only are people represented as data-generating objects in these discourses, by virtue of the commercially valuable data that consumers generate they are portrayed simultaneously as commodities. It has now become a common saying in relation to the digital data economy that 'you are the product'.

Algorithms are constitutive of new types of selfhood: they create 'algorithmic identities' (Cheney-Lippold 2011). The digital data that are collected on populations are a specific means of constructing certain types of assemblages of individuals or populations from a variety of sources. Algorithms join together various data fragments. Digital data are both drawn from the actions and interactions of individuals and also shape them, either by external agencies using the numbers to influence or act upon individuals or by individuals themselves who use the data to change their behaviour in response. A continual interactive loop is therefore established between data and behaviour (Ruppert 2011; Smith 2013). Using digital databases, individuals and social groups or populations are rendered into multiple aggregations that can be manipulated and changed in various ways depending on what aspects are focused on or searched for. Behaviours and dispositions are interpreted and evaluated with the use of the measuring devices, complex algorithms and opportunities for display afforded by these technologies, allowing for finer detail to be produced on individuals, groups and populations. The metrics derived from digital databases make visible aspects of individuals and groups that are not otherwise perceptible, because they are able to join up a vast range of details derived from diverse sources. Organisations use algorithms to confer types of identities upon users (employing categories such as gender, race, location, income status and so on) and in doing so redefine what these categories come to mean (Cheney-Lippold 2011; Ruppert 2012).

Furthermore, as outlined earlier in this chapter, the analysis of big data is playing an increasingly integral role in identifying certain behaviours, activities or outcomes as appropriate or 'normal' and others as deviating from the norm. The rhetorical power that is bestowed upon big data has meant that they are viewed as arbiters of drawing distinctions between acceptable and unacceptable practices and behaviours: in effect, shaping definitions of 'normality'. Here again, algorithmic authority has political and economic consequences. Big digital data have begun to shape and define concepts of 'dangerous', 'safe', 'unhealthy', 'risky', 'under-achieving', 'productive' and so on, thus producing and reproducing new forms of value. Via such data assemblages, norms are constructed using vast aggregated masses of data against which individuals are compared. Individuals or social groups are identified as 'problems' as part of this process of normalisation, and the solutions for ameliorating these problems are often themselves digital devices or technologies. Thus, for example, the solution for patients who lack healthcare facilities is often touted as providing them with digital self-monitoring and self-care devices; students who are diagnosed as under-achievers are prescribed digital learning packages; individuals who are deemed a risk to society are required to wear RFID devices so that their movements may be digitally tracked.

Algorithms have become increasingly important in both generating and accessing knowledge. As discussed in Chapter 2, one important element introduced by Google is its customisation of the experience of internet use. It is different for each user now that searches and hyperlinks are customised for each individual based on the archiving and algorithmic manipulation of their previous searches. As a result, Google search engine results are 'co-authored by the engine and the user'; or, in other words, 'the results you receive are partly of your own making' (Rogers 2013: 9). This means that the returns from the same search term may be different for every user, as the search engine uses its algorithms to determine the most appropriate results for each individual based on previous search histories. The authority of the algorithm that operates via such technologies means that users' capacity to search the web and the types of information they find are delimited by their previous interactions with Google.

It has also been contended that as a consequence of predictive analytics, digital technology users may end up living in a 'filter bubble' or an 'echo chamber' (Lesk 2013). If Amazon is continually recommending books to people based on past search or purchasing habits, if Google Search customises search terms for each individual enquirer, if Facebook and Twitter target direct marketing to users or suggest friends or followers based on their previous searches, likes, comments and follower/friendship groups, then they are simply reinforcing established opinions, preferences and viewpoints, with little to challenge them. The Google autocomplete function, which suggests the format of search terms before they are completely typed in by the user, depends on predictive algorithms that are based on not only your own but other users' previous searches. Thus, users and the software comprise a digital assemblage of content creation and recreation, of co-authorship and mutual decision-making about what content is relevant (Rogers 2013).

Cheney-Lippold (2011) adopts a Foucauldian perspective to characterise algorithmic authority as a kind of 'soft power' operating in the domain of biopolitics and biopower – the politics and power relations concerned with the regulation, monitoring and management of human populations. This theoretical position, as expressed in the participatory surveillance perspective (Chapter 2), emphasises the indirect and voluntary nature of accepting the disciplinary directives offered by algorithmic authority. Various possibilities are offered, from among which users are invited to select as part of 'tailoring [life's] conditions of possibility' (Cheney-Lippold 2011: 169). The digital subject is made intelligible via the various forms of digital data produced about it using algorithms, as are the conditions of possibility that are made available. This is a form of power but one that configures and invites choice (albeit by also structuring what choices are generated) based on the user's previous and predicted actions, beliefs and preferences. It should be emphasised, however, that algorithmic identities are not always linked only to soft biopower but also to coercive and exclusionary modes of power ('hard biopower'), as when predictive analytics are used to identify and target potential criminals or terrorists or certain categories of individuals are denied access to social services or insurance. Such strategies participate in a ban-optic approach to surveillance by identifying groups or individuals who are considered risky or threatening in some way and attempting to control, contain them or exclude them from specific spaces or social support.

When concepts of identity are structured via the impregnable logic and soft power of the algorithm, traditional forms of resistance to biopower are difficult to sustain (Cheney-Lippold 2011). The 'black boxes' that are the software and coding protocols that organise and order these technologies are invisible to the user. We do not know how algorithms are working as part of the surveillance of our internet activities or movements in space. All we are aware of are the results of algorithmic calculation: when we are excluded from certain choices and offered others. As a result, this form of power is difficult to identify or resist. We may disagree with how the algorithm defines it, but opportunities to challenge or change this definition are few, particularly in a context in which computer coding and data manipulation are considered politically neutral, authoritative and always accurate.

BIG DATA ANXIETIES

While big data have been lauded in many forums, there is also evidence of disquiet in some popular representations. The ways in which big digital data are described rhetorically reveal much about their contemporary social and cultural meanings. As Thomas (2013) writes in her book *Technobiophilia: Nature and Cyberspace*, organic metaphors drawn from the natural world have been continually used to describe computer technologies since their emergence. Such natural terms as the web, the cloud, bug, virus, root, mouse and spider have all been employed in attempting to conceptualise and describe these technologies. These have sometimes resulted in rather mixed metaphors, such as 'surfing the web'. Thomas argues that because of the ambivalence we hold towards these technologies, we attempt to render them more 'natural', and therefore less threatening and alienating. This approach to naturalising computer technologies may adopt the view of nature that sees it as nurturing and good. However, nature is not always benign: it may sometimes be wild, chaotic and threatening, and these meanings of nature may also be bestowed upon digital technologies.

This ambivalence is clearly evident in the metaphorical ways in which big data are described, both in popular culture and in the academic literature. By far the most commonly employed metaphors to discuss big data are those related to water: streams, flows, leaks, rivers, oceans, seas, waves, fire hoses and even floods, deluges and tsunamis of data are commonly described. Thus, for example, in an academic article, Adkins and Lury (2011: 6) represent digital data in the following terms: 'Neither inert in character nor contained or containable in any straightforward sense, data increasingly feeds back on itself in informational systems with unexpected results: it moves, flows, leaks, overflows and circulates beyond the systems and events in which it originates'. In a blog post about how data philanthropy can operate, again the notion of the excess and fluidity of data is evident: 'We are now swimming in an ocean of digital data, most of which didn't exist even a few years ago' (Kirkpatrick 2011).

These rather vivid descriptions of big data as a large, fluid, uncontrollable entity possessing great physical power emphasise the fast nature of digital data object movements, as well as their unpredictability and the difficulty of control and containment. It draws upon a current move in social theory towards conceptualising social phenomena in general as liquidities, fluxes and flows, circulating within and between social entities (Sutherland 2013). The metaphor is evident, for example, in the title of Lyon and Bauman's book *Liquid Surveillance* (2013). Writers on digital technologies also commonly employ these concepts when discussing the circulation and flow of digital data. These metaphors build on older metaphors that represented the internet as a 'super highway', or information as passing along the internet via a series of conduits, tunnels and passageways. Information here is viewed as substances that can pass easily and quickly along defined channels (Markham 2013). Some commentators have suggested, indeed, that 'cybercultures are cultures of flow', given the circulation of meaning, data, communities and identities around and through the conduits of the internet. This suggests that cybercultures, communities and digital information have no limitations or boundaries and cannot easily be controlled (Breslow and Mousoutzanis 2012: xii).

Digital data objects, thus, are frequently described and conceptualised not as static pieces of information, but as participating in a dynamic economy in which they move and circulate. This discourse is an attempt to convey the idea that many types of digital data, particularly those generated and collected by social media platforms and online news outlets, constantly move around various forums rather than sit in archives. In the process they may mutate as they are reused in a multitude of ways, configuring new social meanings and practices. Digital data objects are described as recursive, doubling back on each other or spreading out and moving back again. Indeed, it has been contended that a performativity of circulation has been generated, as well as an economy of likes/clicks/retweets, in which the value of data is generated by how often they have been reused, approved of and circulated (Beer 2013a; Beer and Burrows 2013). The liquidity, permeability and mobility of digital data, therefore, are often presented as central to their ontology and as contributing to their novelty and potential as valuable phenomena.

I would argue, however, that this liquidity metaphor is underpinned by an anxiety about the ubiquity and apparent uncontained nature of digital technologies and the data they produce. It suggests an economy of digital data and surveillance in which data are collected constantly and move from site to site in ways that cannot easily themselves be monitored, measured or regulated. Both academic and popular cultural descriptions of big data have frequently referred to the 'fire hose' of data issuing from a social media site such as Twitter and the 'data deluge' or 'tsunami' that as internet users we both contribute to and which threatens to 'swamp' or 'drown us'. Such phraseology evokes the notion of an overwhelming volume of data that must somehow be dealt with, managed and turned to good use. We are told that 'the amount of data in our world is exploding', as researchers at the McKinsey Global Institute put it in a report on the potential of big data (Manyika *et al.* 2011). Instead of 'surfing the net' – a term that was once frequently used to denote moving from website to website easily and playfully, riding over the top of digital information and stopping when we feel like it – we now must cope with huge waves of information or data that threaten to engulf us. The apparent liquidity of data, its tendency to flow freely, can also constitute its threatening aspect, its potential to create chaos and loss of control.

Other metaphors that are sometimes employed to describe the by-product data that are generated include data 'trails', 'breadcrumbs', 'exhausts', 'smoke signals' and 'shadows'. All these tend to suggest the notion of data as objects that are left behind as tiny elements of another activity or entity ('trails', 'breadcrumbs', 'exhausts'), or as the ethereal derivatives of the phenomena from which they are viewed to originate ('smoke signals', 'shadows'). Digital data are also often referred to as living things, as having a kind of organic vitality in their ability to move from site to site, morph into different forms and possess a 'social life' (Beer and Burrows 2013). The 'rhizome' metaphor is sometimes employed to describe how digital data flow from place to place or from node to node, again employing a concept that suggests that they are part of a living organism such as a plant (Breslow and Mousoutzanis 2012). The rhizomatic metaphor also suggests a high level of complexity and a network of interconnected tubes and nodes. Another metaphor that represents the digital data system as a living entity, even a human body, is that which refers to a change from the 'digital exoskeleton' that supported businesses and government agencies by providing information to a 'digital nervous system' that is an inherent part of any organisation. The 'digital nervous system' metaphor is used by Dumbill (2013: 2) to denote both the importance of digital systems to organisations and their reactivity and even unpredictability: 'in a very real sense, algorithms can respond to and affect their environments'.

Such a metaphorical linking of digital technologies with living creatures, including human bodies, has long been evident. I have previously written about the ways in which popular cultural representations of the threats of computer viruses in the 1990s depicted personal computers as human entities becoming ill from viral infection. This metaphor suggested the presence of a malevolent alien invader within the computer causing malfunction (Lupton 1994). While the term 'virus' has become taken-for-granted in its use in relation to digital technologies, its use underpins our tendency to want to conceptualise computers as living entities like ourselves. I suggested in this earlier analysis that discourses of computer viruses suggest our ambivalence about computer technologies: our desire to incorporate them into everyday life unproblematically and to strip them of their alienating meanings as complex machines, but also our very awareness of our dependence on them and their technological complexity that many of us do not understand.

Viruses as organic entities do not possess nervous systems, intelligence or the capacity for independent life, but are parasitic, living in the body of the organic creature they inhabit. Digital systems and the data they produce, when referred to as part of a 'digital nervous system', are endowed with far more capacity for independence and authority. There is the suggestion in this metaphor that somehow digital data-generating technologies are beginning to know more about us in their capacity to gather and aggregate information about us than we might like. While the computer virus afflicts and infects our machines, the digital nervous system quietly gathers information about us. This information, when it contributes to vast, ever-moving streams or floods of digital data, then potentially moves beyond our control.

The blockages and resistances, the solidities that may impede the fluid circulation of digital data objects, tend to be left out of such discussions (Fuchs and Dyer-Witheford 2013; Lash 2007; Sutherland 2013). One of the most highly valued attributes of digital technologies is their seamlessness, their lack of 'friction' when used. Yet many technologies fail to achieve this ideal. The ideology of free streams of flowing communication tends to obscure the politics and power relations behind digital and other information technologies, the ways in which a discourse of liberation due to free-flowing data hides the neoliberal principles underpinning it. As I will discuss in further detail in Chapter 6, the continuing social disadvantage and lack of access to economic resources (including the latest digital devices and data download facilities) that many people experience belie the discourse of digital data and universal, globalised access to and sharing of these data (Fuchs and Dyer-Witheford 2013; Sutherland 2013).

The Snowden files alerted many people to the reality that much of their personal digital data is easily accessible to government and other security agencies. The documents he made public have revealed that apps are one among many types of digital technologies that government security organisations have targeted as part of their data collection (Ball 2014). People have only just begun to realise how personal digital data can be harvested and employed by such security agencies and by commercial enterprises or even other citizens themselves using open-source tools to access data such as Facebook Graph Search.

The predictive analytics that some platforms offer which recommend products or websites based on users' previous internet use provide an online experience that some people find disturbing in terms of what digital technologies 'know' about oneself. New predictive apps, such as Google Now, billed as 'intelligent personal assistants', are able to make predictions based on past actions, search habits, location data and data archived in the Gmail account of the user. Before a user even thinks to make a query, Google Now attempts to predict what the user needs to know and informs users accordingly. Thus, for example, the app is able to use the information that the user may be about to catch a plane and will automatically send a message to tell the user that the flight is delayed, what the weather will be like at the destination and recommendations for the best hotels to stay in. The app can also tell friends and family about the user's location (if authorised by the user). For several commentators in popular media, these predictive functions of Google Now are viewed as 'creepy' because Google seems to know too much about the user due to monitoring and recording data about users' interactions and diary entries. For example, in one hyperbolic headline in a blog post for the *Forbes* magazine website, it was claimed that Google Now's 'insights into its users' were 'terrifying, spine-tingling, bone chilling' (Hill 2012).

BIG DATA HUBRIS AND ROTTED DATA

The term 'big data hubris' has been employed to describe 'the implicit assumption that big data are a substitute for, rather than a supplement to, traditional data collection and analysis' (Lazer *et al.* 2014: 1203). I would extend this definition to include the grandiose claims that are often made that big data offer nothing less than a new and better form of knowledge. More critical commentators have begun to draw attention to the limitations and ethical dimensions of big data. It has been argued that while big data do offer large quantities of data in unprecedented volume, questions need to be posed about their usefulness. Some of the shortcomings of using big data as research objects were outlined in Chapter 3, including their validity and their claims to representativeness. As I noted in that chapter, sociologists and other social scientists have expressed concern that they do not have the skills or resources to deal with huge digital data sets. But even expert data analysts have commented on the difficulty and complexity of using available data analysis tools that were not designed to deal with such large and constantly growing data sets (Madden 2012).

The neatness and orderliness of big data sets are compelling, and part of their cultural power and resonance, but are mirages. Big data sets, while large in size, are not necessarily 'clean', valid or reliable (Lazer *et al.* 2014). The problem of 'dirty data', or data that are incomplete or incorrect, becomes even greater when the data sets are enormous. Such data are useless until they are 'cleaned', or rendered into usable forms for analysis (boyd and Crawford 2012; Waterman and Hendler 2013). Ensuring that data are 'clean' and usable, and employing experts who are able to manipulate the data, can be very expensive.

In addition to discussing the metaphors of data as 'raw' and 'cooked' (referred to earlier in this chapter), Boellstorff (2013) draws further on the work of the anthropologist Claude Lévi-Strauss to introduce the concept of 'rotted' data. This metaphor highlights the ways in which digital data are transformed in ways in which their original creators may not have intended or imagined. It also acknowledges the materiality of data and the ways in which data storage, for example, may result in the deterioration or loss of data. The concept of 'rotted' data draws attention to the impurity of data, thereby contravening dominant concepts of digital data as clean, objective and pure. The ways in which digital data are produced, transferred and stored are not failsafe. The relationships between hyperlinks on the web are not always seamless and fluid. If the metaphor of the 'web' or the 'internet' tends to suggest an interlinking of threads or ropes, then the language of the 'broken web' or 'blocked sites' demonstrates that these interlinks can fail to connect with each other, become tangled and therefore useless. The web may be 'broken' at various points due to websites going down or not being updated, links not working and sites being censored by governments (Rogers 2013: 127).

The underlying assumptions that configure the collection and interpretation of big data also require emphasis in critical analyses of the phenomenon. As Baym (2013) notes, 'In a time when data appear to be so self-evident and big data seem to hold such promise of truth, it has never been more essential to remind ourselves what data are not seen, and what cannot be measured.' The decisions that are made relating to big data, such as which are important, how phenomena should best be categorised to render them into data, serve to obscure ambiguities, contradictions and conflicts (Baym 2013; boyd and Crawford 2012; Gitelman and Jackson 2013; Uprichard 2013; Verran 2012; Vis 2013).

One example of how digital data can be corrupted is that of the Google Flu Trends and Google Dengue Trends websites. Google created Flu Trends in 2008 to demonstrate the value of using its search terms to monitor outbreaks of infectious diseases such as influenza. The Dengue Trends website was created in 2011 with a similar objective. Both use daily tallies of search terms related to these illnesses to estimate how many people are infected over a particular time period, thus – in theory – providing information that may demonstrate influenza or dengue fever outbreaks before public health surveillance systems are able to identify them, and particularly season start and peak data. When comparing their data against official public health surveillance figures from the US Centers for Disease Control and Prevention, Google analysts found that in the United States' 2012/13 influenza season their predictions significantly overestimated the incidence of that disease. The reason they suggested for this lack of accuracy was that there was heightened media coverage of the influenza epidemic during this time which in turn generated a high rate of Google searches for the disease by people who may have been worried about the epidemic and wanted to find out more about it, but did not themselves have the illness. Their algorithms had to be adjusted to allow for such spikes (Copeland *et al.* 2013). Nevertheless, it has been contended that Google Flu Trends remains highly imprecise in its estimates of influenza, and not more useful than traditional projection models in identifying current prevalence of the disease (Lazer *et al.* 2014).

In addition to these difficulties, it has been pointed out that Google's search algorithm model itself influences – and indeed works to configure – the data that it produces on influenza in Google Flu Trends. Google's algorithms have been established to provide users with information quickly. Search returns are based on other users' searches as well as the individual's previous searches. If many people are using a specific search term at the time at which a user decides to search for the same term, then the relative magnitude of certain searches will be increased. Thus users' searches for 'influenza'/'flu' (and indeed for any search term) are influenced by all these factors and are not valid indicators of the disease's prevalence (Lazer *et al.* 2014). Phrased differently, 'search behavior is not just exogenously determined, but is also endogenously cultivated by the service provider' (Lazer *et al.* 2014: 1204). This is a clear example of the algorithmic authority of software such as search engines and the role they play in the production of knowledge.

The superficiality of big data has also attracted criticism from some social researchers, who have contended that the growing use of big data to attempt to make sense of social behaviours and identities serves to leave out the multitude of complexities, contradictions, interconnections and therefore the meaning of these phenomena. Despite their status as constituting superior knowledges, big data do not offer many insights into why people act the way they do (boyd and Crawford 2012; Uprichard 2013). Big data are sometimes compared with 'small', 'deep', 'thick' or 'wide' data. These latter terms are a response to the 'bigness' of digital data in emphasising that massive quantities of data are not always better. 'Small data' is a term that is often used to refer to personalised information that individuals collect about themselves or their environment for their own purposes. 'Deep data' refers to information that is detailed, in-depth and often drawn from qualitative rather than quantitative sources. The term 'wide data' has been used to describe various forms of gathering information and then using them together to provide greater insights. The term 'thick data' highlights the contextuality of data, or that data can only ever be understood in the specific contexts in which they are generated and employed (Boellstorff 2013).

BIG DATA ETHICS

There are also many significant ethical and political implications of big data. The terms 'good data' and 'bad data' are now sometimes used to describe the implications of big data use by corporations and government agencies (Lesk 2013). 'Good data' provide benefits for commercial enterprises and government agencies, contribute to important research (such as that on medical topics) and assist security and safety measures without disadvantaging consumers and citizens or infringing on their privacy or civil liberties (when they become viewed as 'bad data'). Discussions of data 'deluges' and 'tsunamis' – or, less dramatically, the dynamic, multiplying and interrelated nature of digital data – underpin concerns about privacy and data security issues. It has been estimated that data about a typical American are collected in more than 20 different ways, and that this is twice as many compared with 15 years ago due to the introduction of digital surveillance methods (Angwin and Valentino-Devries 2012). Private details, such as police officers' home addresses, whether someone has been a victim of a rape or has a genetic disease, cancer or HIV/AIDS, have been sold on from databases by third-party data brokers. Although many digital data sets remove personal details – such as names and addresses – the joining-up of a number of data sets that include the details of the same people can work to de-anonymise data (Crawford 2014).

Many app developers store their data on the computing cloud, and not all name identifiers are removed from the data uploaded by individuals. Several companies that have developed self-tracking technologies are now selling their devices and data to employers as part of workplace 'wellness programmes' and also to health insurance companies seeking to identify patterns in health-related behaviours in their clients (McCarthy 2013). Some health insurance companies offer users the technology to upload their health and medical data to platforms that have been established by these companies. The data that are collected on their own biometrics by people who self-track are viewed as opportunities to monitor individuals as part of reducing healthcare costs both by private enterprises and government agencies. Health insurance companies and employers in the US have already begun to use self-tracking devices and online websites involving the disclosure of health information and even such topics as whether or not clients are separated or divorced, their financial status, whether they feel under stress at work and the nature of their relationships with co-workers as a means of 'incentivising' people to engage in behaviours deemed to be healthy. Those people who refuse to participate may be required to pay a hefty surcharge to their health insurance company (Dredge 2013; Shahani 2012; Singer 2013). Questions remain about the future linking of users' health-related data to their health insurance policies in such platforms, and what might happen in the future if these companies purchase control over health app data by buying the apps and their data (Dredge 2013).

Until very recently, many mobile app users viewed the information stored on their apps to be private, not realising the extent to which the apps' developers used these data for their own purposes, including selling the data on to third parties (Urban *et al.* 2012). App and platform developers have not always taken appropriate steps to safeguard the often very personal data that are collected, including data on sexual practices and partners and reproductive functions that are collected by some apps (Lupton 2014b). For example, a recent study of privacy policies on mobile health and fitness-related apps found that many lacked any kind of privacy policy, few took steps to encrypt the data they collect and many sent the data collected to a third party not disclosed by the developer on its website (Ackerman 2013).

The secret information exposed in Edward Snowden's leaked documents has made it ever more apparent that the security of private information in both commercial and government databases is much less than many people have realised. Government databases have been subject to several other privacy breaches and concerns about who is allowed access to these data. National initiatives to combine patient medical records into giant databases, for example, have been subject to controversy. Garrety *et al.* (2014) argue that such initiatives are inevitably controversial because they challenge the social, moral and medico-legal orders governing the production, ownership, use of and responsibility for medical records. When policy-makers seek to push them through without acknowledging these assumptions and this meaning, key stakeholders are alienated and resistant. The different groups involved often have contrasting interests and agendas which contribute to resistances to the introduction of the digitisation of medical records.

The NHS care.data initiative described earlier in this chapter attracted a high level of negative publicity when it was revealed that the data would be sold to commercial companies. Critics questioned whether this use of the data was the major purpose for constructing the database and wondered how well the security and anonymity of the data would be protected. They also identified the lack of information given to patients concerning their right to opt out of the system and the difficulty in doing so (Anonymous 2014). Research undertaken by the Wellcome Trust involving interviews with Britons about the use of their personal data found that many interviewees expressed the idea that while sharing data about individuals within the NHS could benefit the individual (so that different healthcare providers could access the same set of medical records), the sensitive and often intensely personal nature of such data required a high level of data security. Most interviewees contended that these data should not be shared with entities outside the NHS, and especially not private health insurers, employers and pharmaceutical companies (Wellcome Trust 2013).

The notion that users have lost control of their data is becoming evident in popular forums and news coverage of these issues. For example, some people engaging in voluntary self-tracking using digital devices are beginning to question how their data are being used and to call for better access so that they can use and manipulate these data for their own purposes (Lupton 2013c; Watson 2013). The open data movement also focuses on promoting open access to large databases held by government agencies (see more on this in Chapter 7). Yet, as contended in Chapter 3, many big data sets, and especially those archived by commercial internet companies, are becoming increasingly shut off from free access due to recognition by these companies of their economic value. Governments are also beginning to consider the economic benefits of privatising the data they collect on their citizens, thus moving these data from open-access to pay-for-use status. The British government, for example, has sold its postcode and address data sets as part of the privatisation of the Royal Mail service. This sale was subject to trenchant critique by the House of Commons' Public Administration Committee (2014). In their report advising on the use of big data collected by the government, the members of this committee revealed that they were strong supporters of open public data. They contended that the Royal Mail data set should have been maintained as a national public asset, as should all public sector data.

More seriously, big data can have direct effects on people's freedoms and citizen rights. Crawford and Schultz (2014) have identified what they call the 'predictive privacy harms' that may be the result of predictive analytics. Because big data analytics often draw on metadata rather than the content of data, they are able to operate outside current legal privacy protections (Polonetsky and Tene 2013). Predictive privacy harm may involve bias or discrimination against individuals or groups who are identified by big data predictive analytics and the cross-referencing of data sets. People are rarely aware of how their metadata may be interpreted through the use of disparate and previously discrete data sets to reveal their identity, habits and preferences and even their health status and produce information about them that may have an impact on their employment and/or access to state benefits or insurance (Crawford and Schultz 2014). Concerns have been raised about the use of digital data to engage in racial and other profiling that may lead to discrimination and to over-criminalisation and other restrictions. It has been argued that the big data era has resulted in a major policy challenge in determining the right way to use big data to improve health, wellbeing, security and law enforcement while also ensuring that these uses of data do not infringe on people's rights to privacy, fairness, equality and freedom of speech (Crawford and Schultz 2014; Laplante 2013; Polonetsky and Tene 2013).

Journalist Julia Angwin (2014) wrote in *Time* magazine's online site about her discoveries when she reviewed her Google searches over the past few years and realised how much they revealed about her current and future interests and habits. She described these details as 'more intimate than a diary. It was a window into my thoughts each day – in their messiest, rawest form – as I jumped from serious work topics to shopping for my kids'. Angwin wrote of her concerns that such personal details might be sold on to third parties, perhaps denying her access to credit in the future by aggregating all the data Google had gathered on her. She was aware that Google has been subjected to legal action for abusing users' data privacy and also that their data archives have been accessed by US security agents. Angwin subsequently decided to migrate from Google and use other platforms that did not retain users' data.

This chapter has detailed the many and diverse uses to which big data have been applied in recent times and the multitude of claims that have been made about the use of big data across a range of commercial, government, humanitarian and personal endeavours. As I have demonstrated, like other digital data objects, big data sets are systems of knowledge that are implicated in power relations. Big data are both the product of social and cultural processes and themselves act to configure elements of society and culture. They have their own politics, vitality and social life.

CHAPTER 6

The diversity of digital technology use

There has been much discussion of the so-called 'digital divide', or the lack of access to digital technologies that some social groups experience. While this term is subject to some contention, it is clear that some social groups and those living in certain geographical regions use digital technologies less frequently than others. It is important to acknowledge that the utopian discourses of democratic participation, community-building, sharing and prosumption that often circulate in mainstream accounts of the possibilities offered by digital technologies often fail to recognise the political aspects of these technologies. This chapter addresses these issues, examining the use of digital technologies in different areas of the globe and how socioeconomic, cultural and political factors shape, promote or delimit the use of these technologies. It moves from reviewing the findings of large-scale surveys involving large numbers of respondents from specific countries or cross-nationally to in-depth qualitative investigations that are able to provide the detailed context for differences in internet use.

THE BIG PICTURE

A number of large-scale research reports have been published recently by both academic and corporate researchers on the attitudes to and use of digital technologies in various geographical locations. In this section I discuss some of the findings from these reports, some of which draw on vast collections of data globally, which provide some important quantitative information about the 'big picture'. Their findings reveal continuing differences between countries in access to the internet and attitudes to digital technologies in various social groups within nations.

According to an estimate presented in a report published by the International Telecommunication Union (2013), by the end of 2013 there would be almost as many mobile phone subscriptions as people on the planet. It was also estimated that almost 100 per cent of people globally can now access a mobile phone signal. However, not everyone owns a mobile phone or has access to the internet, and clear disparities are evident when comparing wealthy with middle-income and developing countries. As the report notes, by the end of 2013 although an estimated 2.7 billion people were using the internet, this left even more (4.4 billion) who were not online. Across the globe there had been a strong growth in household internet access over the previous three years, particularly in developing countries, to the point that it has been estimated that over 40 per cent of households had access (International Telecommunication Union 2013: 1). However, when this figure is compared for developed versus developing countries, while almost 80 per cent of people living in developed countries had household internet access at the end of 2013, this compared with only 28 per cent in the developing regions. Those living in Africa have the least access (6.7 per cent), followed by Asia (32.7 per cent). The main reasons for this disparity are the cost of obtaining internet access and the availability of internet infrastructure, particularly in rural areas (International Telecommunication Union 2013: 7–9).

Our Mobile Planet is a report commissioned by Google about the ownership and use of smartphones in 47 countries globally (although no findings are provided on any African countries). On the Our Mobile Planet website, extensive details are provided about the results of the global survey that was undertaken by research firms for Google using an online questionnaire in three waves: in 2011, 2012 and 2013. The focus of the survey is commercial: Google was interested in the penetration of smartphone use in the countries surveyed and how users employed their phones, particularly in relation to commercial information seeking and purchasing decisions.

The findings of Our Mobile Planet, as shown on the website, indicate that smartphone ownership has risen significantly in every country included in the study in the past two years. However, there is a clear difference when regional areas are compared. Wealthy Middle Eastern countries have the highest rate of smartphone ownership: 74 per cent of residents of the United Arab Emirates and 73 per cent in Saudi Arabia own them. These countries are closely followed by middle-income Asian countries such as South Korea (73 per cent), Singapore (72 per cent) and Hong Kong (63 per cent) and the anglophone countries (65 per cent in Australia, 62 per cent in the UK, 56 per cent in both the US and Canada and 54 per cent in New Zealand). In China 47 per cent of the population own smartphones. Interestingly, the Google data show that the Japanese are not yet high adopters of the smartphone, with only 25 per cent of people in that country owning this device. However, this statistic is somewhat misleading, as it does not reflect the fact that the Japanese were leaders in mobile phone technology and a high number have been using the Japanese version of internet-enabled mobile phones (called 'feature phones') for many years.

The Google data demonstrate that Eastern European, Southern European and Central and South American countries do not have high rates of smartphone ownership (in Argentina, 31 per cent own smartphones, while in Brazil it is 26 per cent and in Mexico 37 per cent). Poor South and South-East Asian countries have very low smartphone ownership (20 per cent in Vietnam and 13 per cent in India, for example). While it is not surprising that less wealthy countries do not have a high rate of smartphone ownership, the interesting difference is between wealthy countries. According to Google's data, the residents of European countries (52 per cent in the Netherlands, 45 per cent in Finland, 42 per cent in France and 40 per cent in Germany, for example) are somewhat less enthusiastic about smartphone ownership than are those living in some anglophone nations. Central European nations also do not have high smartphone ownership (Greece 33 per cent, Poland 35 per cent, Hungary 34 per cent).

Other data have been retrieved from the Alexa company, which aggregates data from millions of internet users, and rendered into visual form on a global map by the Information Geographies team (Mark Graham and Stefano De Sabbata) at the Oxford Internet Institute. Their map (Oxford Internet Institute 2013) shows the reach and spread of Google and Facebook. The map shows that Google is the most visited website in most of Europe, North America and Oceania (including Australia and New Zealand). Facebook is the most visited site in the Middle East, North Africa and most of the countries in the Spanish-speaking Americas, but Google/YouTube (Youtube is owned by Google) are the second-most visited sites in these countries. The countries where Google is the most visited website account for half of the entire population with access to the internet. In Asia, however, local competitors dominate. Baidu is the most used search engine in China and South Korea, while the Japanese version of

Yahoo! and Yahoo! Taiwan dominate in those countries respectively and the search engine Yandex is the most visited site in Russia.

Another survey-based study covering several countries was commissioned by Intel. It identified attitudes to and use of digital technologies in Brazil, China, France, India, Indonesia, Italy, Japan and the USA (IntelPR 2013). The Intel Innovation Barometer found that most of the respondents said that digital technologies made their lives easier and enhanced their relationships with family and friends. More than one-third of the respondents agreed with the idea that the technologies they use should learn about their behaviours and preferences as they use them, as this makes technology use more efficient.

The Intel report also identified some interesting differences between social groups. According to Intel, the group they describe as 'millennials' (young people aged 18 to 24) were somewhat ambivalent about digital technologies. They recognised the value of technologies in their lives and were willing to allow their devices to track their preferences and to share their data with others, advocating for a more 'personal experience' in using them. But members of this group were also concerned about users becoming over-reliant on their technologies and that using technologies made people 'less human'. In comparison, women aged 45 or older, as well as those living in the developing countries included in the survey, were the most positive about digital technologies. These respondents viewed digital technologies as contributing to a country's wellbeing in such areas as employment, transport, education and healthcare. They tended to agree, therefore, that people should use technology more often. Higher-income respondents were more likely to own and regularly use digital devices, be willing to share their personal data anonymously to support important research such as that related to health, and to allow monitoring of their work habits in the interests of greater personal efficiency.

Two other recent reports focused more specifically on internet use in the US and the UK. The US-based Pew Research Center, which describes itself as a nonpartisan fact tank, conducts regular surveys of Americans' use of the internet as part of its Internet & American Life Project. It recently undertook a major survey to mark the twenty-fifth anniversary of the invention of the World Wide Web by Sir Tim Berners-Lee (Pew Research Center 2014). The findings detailed in this report underline the major changes that have taken place over this quarter of a century in the US in relation to digital devices and online access. Pew's research in 1995 found that more than half of Americans had never heard of the internet while a further 20 per cent only vaguely understood the concept and only 14 per cent said that they could access it. Its latest research found that 87 per cent of Americans reported that they use the internet, with almost all of those living in a high-income household, in the 18 to 29 years age group and with a university degree doing so. Sixty-eight per cent of Americans connect to the internet using mobile devices, and 58 per cent own smart-phones. This Pew report also noted that education levels, household income and age continue to be major factors in influencing computer use: far more university-educated, wealthier and younger people use computer technologies compared to other groups. These differentials have remained stable since Pew's 1990 research.

This survey also asked respondents about their overall judgement of the internet. The researchers found that 90 per cent of the respondents who used the internet said that it was a positive experience for them and 76 per cent thought it was a good thing for society, while 53 per cent of users said that they would find it very difficult to give up using the internet, both for work-related purposes and as part of personal relationships with family and friends. Indeed 67 per cent of internet users reported that the technology had strengthened their personal ties. Only 25 per cent reported negative experiences with other users, such as being treated unkindly or being attacked verbally online.

In a previous report (Zickuhr 2013), Pew focused on the 15 per cent of Americans who do not use the internet (this had reduced to 13 per cent by the time of the 2014 survey). When asked why, these respondents gave the following answers: 35 per cent said that the internet was not relevant to them, 32 per cent said that they thought it was not easy to use or that they were worried about privacy issues, 19 per cent referred to the expense of connecting to the internet and 7 per cent said that they lacked access. The survey found that non-use of the internet was strongly correlated with age, income, ethnicity and educational attainment: 44 per cent of Americans aged 65 and older did not use the internet, and nor did 41 per cent of those respondents with a lower educational attainment, 24 per cent of Hispanics and 24 per cent of those with low income levels. These responses suggest that lack of access is not the main reason why Americans choose not to use the internet, but rather that they do not see what internet access can offer them.

Other Pew Research Center findings have demonstrated that in the US people's health status and whether or not they have a disability are also highly influential factors in their online use. Americans with chronic health conditions use the internet less often than those who do not have these conditions, even when other variables such as age, ethnicity, income and education levels are controlled for (Fox and Duggan 2013). Americans with disabilities are far less likely to go online compared with others (54 per cent compared with 81 per cent) and less likely to own a smartphone, desktop or laptop computer (Fox and Boyles 2012).

Yet another report by Pew (Duggan and Smith 2013) found that 73 per cent of the American adults they surveyed who use the internet are on social network sites. Nearly all of these (71 per cent) used Facebook. Those aged 18 to 29 were the most likely to use Facebook: 84 per cent compared to 45 per cent of internet users aged 65 and above. Over all age groups, women (76 per cent) were more likely to use Facebook than men (66 per cent). Of adults online, 18 per cent were Twitter users, split equally between men and women, although African Americans (29 per cent) and younger Americans (31 per cent of those aged 18 to 29 compared to only 5 per cent of those aged 65 and over) were far more likely to be on Twitter than other ethnic and age groups. The survey found that 17 per cent of online adults used Instagram and 21 per cent used Pinterest, with far more women (33 per cent) than men (9 per cent) using the latter platform. Not surprisingly the professional networking site LinkedIn, with 22 per cent of online adults using it, attracted far more users with university degrees, who were employed, with a higher income and older.

The Oxford Internet Institute, based at the University of Oxford, undertakes an extensive survey of internet use in the UK every two years. Its latest report (Dutton and Blank 2013) demonstrated that the use of the internet had risen to 78 per cent of the population aged 14 years and over. The researchers identified five broad 'cultures' of internet use. These included the following:

- 'e-mersives' (12 per cent of internet users), or those who feel comfortable being online, use it as an escape and for feeling part of a community, and have a high rate of use;
- 'techno-pragmatists' (17 per cent of users), who use the internet to save time and make their lives easier;
- 'cyber-savvies' (19 per cent of users), who demonstrated ambivalent feelings about the internet, both enjoying and finding enjoyable aspects of their use but also expressing concern about privacy and time-use issues;
- 'cyber-moderates' (37 per cent of users), who express mixed attitudes but are more moderate in their views than the 'cyber-savvy' group; and
- 'adigitals' (14 per cent of users), who find the internet difficult or frustrating to use.

The report identifies 18 per cent of respondents who said that they had no interest in using the internet. As in the Pew Research Center survey, these uninterested people were more likely to belong to the older age group and include people with disabilities and those holding lower educational qualifications.

DIGITAL SOCIAL INEQUALITIES

The kinds of broad-scale research described above are necessary in developing an understanding of how digital technologies are used in different social and cultural contexts. While these data can identify differences, they cannot explain them: for this we need to turn to more detailed research based on ethnographic and other forms of qualitative methods.

The term 'digital divide' has become commonly used in discussions of the diversity of digital technology use among different social, cultural and geographical groups. However, some researchers have identified what they view as a simplistic perspective in the use of this term. For example, Halford and Savage (2010) have critiqued the concept of the digital divide for the tendency of those who use it to separate 'the social' from 'the technological'. They contend that understandings of both social inequity and access to digital media technologies need to acknowledge their interlinking and their dynamic nature. Each acts to constitute the other, but this is a fluid, unstable process. Halford and Savage propose instead the concept of 'digital social inequality' to denote the interconnectedness of social disadvantage and lack of access to digital technologies. They argue further that rather than understanding access to and use of digital technologies as a unidirectional process (social disadvantage leading to lack of access), it may be more productive to understand the relationship in terms of mutual configuration (or what they term 'co-constitution') between social structural factors and digital technology use.

To refer to a single 'digital divide' also fails to acknowledge the complexities of access to and use of digital technologies. Having access to a high enough income to pay for devices and internet access, and living in a region in which internet access is readily available, are clear factors influencing people's use of digital technologies. A somewhat less obvious factor is the specific practices in which they engage when access is available (Hargittai and Hinnant 2008; Robinson 2009). Four dimensions of access barriers to digital technologies have been identified. These include the following:

• lack of elementary digital experience caused by low interest, anxiety about using the technologies or design elements of the technologies that discourage use;

- lack of access to the technologies, such as not owning a digital device or not having a connection to the internet;
- lack of digital skills due to low levels of use or unfamiliarity with new versions of technologies; and
- lack of significant usage opportunities due to time constraints and competition over access in the domestic or workplace setting.

(van Dijk and Hacker 2003)

Even when people have a similar level of access to and interest in using digital technologies, differential skills and practices are evident. People with lower levels of income and education use digital technologies differently from those with higher levels. The latter group are able to use digital technologies to reinforce their cultural and economic capital and social status, thus maintaining their advantages (Halford and Savage 2010). Research has shown that people of lower education level may spend more time online in their free time than those of higher education levels, but do so in different ways. They engage in social interaction and gaming more often, for example, rather than using digital technologies for education, seeking information or work-related reasons (van Deursen and van Dijk 2014), or what has been referred to as 'capital enhancing activities' (Hargittai and Hinnant 2008: 602).

Digital technologies are not neutral objects: they are invested with meanings relating to such aspects as gender, social class, race/ethnicity and age. It can be difficult to resist or overcome these meanings even when people have an overt political agenda in attempting to do so. This was evident from Dunbar-Hester's (2010) study of media activists based in Philadelphia who were attempting to broaden access to communication technologies and the skills related to using technologies. Their project was to 'demystify' media technologies by engaging in pedagogical activities with traditionally excluded groups in relation to community radio and community wi-fi technologies. As Dunbar-Hester observes, social identities may be open to change but are not endlessly fluid. They are structured by and through encounters with technologies, including their discursive and material dimensions. The media activists in her study found that despite their best efforts to encourage people who traditionally were excluded from access to or engagement with digital and other communication technologies (individuals who did not conform to the white male social identity), they were confronted by the continuing persistence of gendered and racial stereotypes in relation to communication technologies.

Some people, as the Oxford Internet Institute report referred to above observed, simply do not see the relevance of digital technologies to their lives. This is particularly the case for the elderly, who often report lacking interest in using these technologies (Hakkarainen 2012; Olphert and Damodaran 2013). Few in–depth studies have sought to investigate the issues related to this lack of interest. However, one Finnish project (Hakkarainen 2012) investigated written accounts by people aged 60 years and over explaining why they refuse to use the internet. The researchers found that for these older people, the computer was understood as a tool or sophisticated gadget, but they viewed it as one that they did not perceive as useful to their everyday lives. They compared the computer with other tools that they were accustomed to using (such as their hands, pens, pencils or their own brains) and said that it was unable to offer more than these tools could. The notion of the computer as offering access to a virtual world where one could interact socially with others or access information was absent from these Finns' notions. They also represented computers and the internet negatively as promoting addictive behaviours that caused users to deprive themselves of other life experiences. These people also often represented computers and the internet as dangerous, posing a threat to such valued aspects of their lives as time reserves, security, simple living, traditional skills and face-to-face human contact.

Popular portrayals of internet users in developed countries tend to represent young people as 'digital natives', who use digital technologies, particularly mobile phones and social media, avidly, often and with expertise. This stereotype fails to recognise the substantial proportion of young people who do not engage actively with these technologies. A nationwide study of young adult Americans aged 18 to 23 found that those who did not use social media tended to have caregiving responsibilities (for their own children or other family members), experienced economic and employment instability and fractured educational histories, relied upon their families for economic assistance and focused on finding and keeping jobs rather than developing a career. Few of these non–adopters lacked access to a computer. However, they were in shared living conditions with other family members, which may have limited their opportunities to use social media. Several of the study participants lacked confidence about using computers and were socially isolated with few friends, or in difficult family relationship circumstances. The researchers concluded that lack of social media use for these young adults was both an outcome and a contributor to their disadvantaged positions and lack of close social ties (Bobkowski and Smith 2013).

The affordances of specific platforms and the nature of other users also have a significant impact on how and why people use them.

As older people migrate to social media sites such as Facebook, younger people (especially their children or grandchildren) tend to leave. Facebook announced in November 2013 that the site was seeing a decrease in the number of teenagers using it daily. Young people are beginning to use mobile phone messaging apps such as WhatsApp, Pinger and WeChat as alternatives to more mainstream social media sites. WhatsApp in November 2013 had more active users than Twitter worldwide. These new apps afford greater privacy, as they allow users to engage with each other and share images in a forum that is not public, only including others that they specifically wish to communicate with. Young people also appreciate that these messages and images are not archived permanently on the web, as they are when other social media sites are used (Olson 2013).

The materiality of the design of both software and hardware are features that are frequently neglected in accounts of digital social inequalities. These aspects are particularly relevant to people with disabilities. As noted above, surveys in the UK and US have revealed that fewer people with disabilities use digital technologies compared with those without disabilities. To what extent this difference is influenced by disabilities themselves or by people with disabilities' greater likelihood to experience economic disadvantage is not clear, however.

On the positive side, people with disabilities who do use digital technologies often report finding these technologies offer a way of communicating and expressing themselves, of achieving greater participation in social relationships (Ellis and Goggin 2014; Ginsburg 2012; Lupton and Seymour 2003; Newell and Goggin 2003; Seymour and Lupton 2004). As commented by one of the participants in the study Wendy Seymour and I conducted (Lupton and Seymour 2003), she felt 'comforted', 'safe', 'more relaxed' and 'at peace with myself' and 'normal' when communicating with others online. The people with whom she interacted could not see the facial and body tics that were part of her Tourette's syndrome. This interviewee therefore could feel free to participate without feeling self-conscious about these involuntary movements. Another interviewee with mobility difficulties found communicating on the internet an opportunity to escape social isolation as well as retreat from social interactions when she felt tired, in pain or unwell.

Ginsburg (2012) gives the example of an American woman with autism who does not communicate verbally but uses YouTube very effectively to demonstrate how she sees the world and express her experiences. Ginsburg also found that people with disabilities often enjoy using the virtual world of Second Life to interact with others and therefore alleviate the social isolation that they previously experienced. She further remarks on the expansion of online support and activist networks, blogs related to the experiences of having a disability and social media groups for people with disabilities. Similarly, as Ellis and Goggin (2014) point out, Twitter is popular with people with visual impairments because sound-based technologies can be used to turn tweets into audible messages. Some smartphones and tablet computers include these technologies in ways that are easy for people with visual and mobility impairments to use. Ellis and Goggin (2014) also single out support groups (now often mediated via Facebook), Second Life, YouTube and personal blogs (including audio and video blogs) as having an important role to play as providing platforms by which people with disabilities can present themselves in ways that counter stigmatising and limiting representations in other popular culture portrayals.

More negatively, however, the design of digital devices can result in people with disabilities experiencing difficulties using them (Ellis and Goggin 2014; Lupton and Seymour 2003; Newell and Goggin 2003; Seymour and Lupton 2004). Many social media platforms are difficult for people with disabilities to use and they are thus excluded from yet another arena of social life. Just as with the other physical environments with which people with disabilities interact, the design of digital technologies may serve to configure disability in their neglect of accessibility for a wide range of users and bodily capacities. For example, my interview study with Seymour found that some people with mental impairments commented that they found it difficult to keep up with a high pace of interaction in real-time online discussions, as did those with physical disabilities who found it difficult or painful to type on computer keyboards (Lupton and Seymour 2003; Seymour and Lupton 2004).

GENDERED TECHNOLOGIES

An extensive literature exists on the gendered aspects of digital technologies and their use. In the 1980s and 1990s, scholars adopting a 'cyberfeminist' perspective on digital technologies sought to construct a critique of the gendered aspects of their design and use. I referred in Chapter 2 to the important work of Donna Haraway in theorising digital technologies. One of Haraway's major contributions was to articulate a feminist approach to computer technologies that recognised difference and diversity and included the role of material agents in understanding the human–computer relationship. Haraway's concept of the cyborg brought the body and its permutations, differences and ambiguities – its performative configurations – into focus as an object for political critique and action. She argued for a view of the subject/ body that is inevitably split and contradictory, providing for ambivalence and ambiguity. Haraway (1985) saw this approach as important both for feminist and technoscientific critique. What Haraway was trying to argue in her metaphor of the cyborg is that human bodies are not essentialised, they cannot easily be categorised as one thing or another in a binary definition. She brought together Marxist with technoscience and feminist theory in what she viewed as a socialist feminist politics.

Cyberfeminists building on Haraway's work foresaw a technologically mediated world in which gender (and other bodily related attributes) would no longer constrain choice and action. Like many other writers on cyborgs and cyberculture, some cyberfeminists saw cyberspace as a virtual space of freedom and transcendence from the body, including gendered identities (Brophy 2010; Daniels 2009b; Luckman 1999; Wajcman 2004). Given the apparent anonymity of the internet, where other users could not detect one's gender, age, race and other bodily features of identity, some cyberfeminists were positive about the opportunity to freely engage in the use of computer technologies without dealing with assumptions about their capabilities based on their gender. Using computer technologies was positioned as a way of taking back technology from men. There was much discussion in the 1990s of a utopian future in which the 'wetware' of the fleshly body could be left behind in cyberspace as part of entering virtual reality and online gaming communities. Some women chose to use male names when engaging in these activities as part of their attempts to experiment with different gender identities (Luckman 1999).

One way to understand the interplay of gender and technology use is to highlight the performative and constraining nature of both as well as their inextricable meanings. Gender and digital technologies 'are both discourses and apparatuses that enable/limit what we can do online. Each apparatus is an articulation of body-medium' (Brophy 2010: 942). As such, a digital technology user's agency is shaped both by the design and meaning of the device she is using and the agencies of other users and the meanings they give to the technologies. These technologies reproduce pre-existing gender norms (and norms and stereotypes concerning age, race and ethnicity) and also reinforce them. Thus, as some cyberfeminists contended, such practices as women using male names when engaging online simply reinforced the notion that cyberspace was a place of masculine privilege and entitlement, and thus failed to challenge existing power relations and inequalities. These scholars focused on directing attention at the masculinised nature of discourses on cyberspace and attempted new ways of thinking about computer technologies that resisted these discourses (Luckman 1999). These included creative artworks that re-imagined cybercultures in blatantly feminised and sexualised ways to highlight the fleshly nature of these technologies (Paasonen 2011). As a result, the cyborg as reimagined by some cyberfeminists was a highly sexually charged figure, filled with erotic pleasure in its transgression of body boundaries, its fluidity and what was viewed as the emotional and sensual fusion of human organism and technology (Luckman 1999).

As many feminist scholars have contended, gender norms tend to influence the ways in which women and men use digital technologies and which technologies they prefer to use. Technological design, in turn, supports assumptions and norms about gender (Paasonen 2011; Wajcman 2004). The connection of the internet with the military and the discourses of cyberpunks, cyberspace and hackers that dominated discussion of computer technologies in the 1980s and 1990s invariably represented the cyber-world as a masculine environment (Lupton 1995; Wajcman 2004). Early computer technologies were represented as requiring arcane technical and mathematical skills for coding, programming and setting up the technologies for use, which in turn were portrayed as male rather than female practices. Men tend to be taught technical skills related to electronics while women are still often excluded from this type of education and hence a gendered difference in skills and confidence in using such technologies begins early (Dunbar-Hester 2010).

Many studies undertaken since personal computers became available for purchase have demonstrated that women tend to be less inclined to learn computer science and demonstrate greater levels of technophobia and lower levels of computer proficiency and self-assessed confidence in using computers than men. The archetypal computer user/expert has traditionally been an anglophone, white (or occasionally Asian), middle-class young man. The figure of the 'hacker' tends to be represented as a white male who is very clever and technologically skilled but often has malicious or criminal intent. The archetypal computer 'nerd' or 'geek' is another type of white male: again highly intelligent and accomplished in matters of computer science, but physically unattractive, socially awkward and friendless (Kendall 2011; Lupton 1995). These archetypes may act to exclude others from positioning themselves as expert at computer technologies or even wanting to demonstrate interest in acquiring skills, given that they are persistently negative in their representation of 'nerds' and 'geeks' (Dunbar-Hester 2010; Kendall 2011). They position not only women as antithetical to the image of the accomplished computer user but also racial groups other than white, and men who prefer to view themselves as socially accomplished and popular rather than nerds (Kendall 2011).

With the advent of social media and mobile devices, to a large extent computer technologies have lost their mystique of the arcane and technical. As part of their widespread use and entry into most locations of everyday life, and particularly with smartphones and tablets, digital technologies have become domesticated and taken-for-granted. The everyday computer user, therefore, may now be viewed as crossing gender and racial or ethnic boundaries (and, as I noted above, even grandparents use Facebook). Using readily available and easy-to-use devices and software, however, is different from possessing knowledge about the technical aspects of digital technologies. Men still dominate over women in having this kind of expertise. Women studying computer science and working in the field remain in the minority (Cozza 2011).

In terms of domestic use, research suggests that at least in the developed countries of the cultural North, women and men, regardless of their race or ethnicity, now access the internet in equal numbers. The latest Pew findings demonstrate that there is now very little difference in computer use by women compared to men, rural compared to city residents or between the major racial groups in the US (Pew Research Center 2014). The International Telecommunication Union's (2013: 12) report found that globally women tend to use the internet more for educational use than do men, that men access the internet more than women in commercial internet facilities, and that men tend to be online more frequently than women. The report noted that there remains a gender disparity, with 11 per cent more men than women using the internet worldwide. This difference is particularly striking in developing countries, where 16 per cent more men are online, while there is only a 2 per cent gap between men and women in developed countries. The authors relate this difference to gender disparities in education level and income. This finding is supported by a study of data sets of computer use in 12 Latin American and 13 African countries, which found that once the variables of employment, education and income levels were controlled for, women were more active users of digital technologies than men in those countries (Martin 2011). This research demonstrates that in some cultural contexts, education and income levels may be more influential in structuring access to digital technologies than are gender and race/ethnicity.

Nonetheless, gender differences in internet use persist in developed countries, where education levels tend to be equal for women and men. A team of researchers who looked at British female and male students' internet use first in 2002 and then again ten years later found that at both time periods a significant gender difference was evident, which was even more marked in the 2012 research. In the 2012 study, male students demonstrated a greater breadth of internet use. They used it more for games and entertainment purposes, such as downloading and playing music and videos and accessing adult content sites, than did the women who were surveyed. The female students used the internet more for communication, including email, internet phone calls and social media sites, compared to the male students surveyed (Joiner *et al.* 2012). Gender differences are evident from childhood, as demonstrated by research on Portuguese children's uses of digital technologies. The boys in the study were more likely to play online games or game apps involving cars, football and fighting, while the girls enjoyed games related to dressing up, dolls, make-up and hairstyles and were more likely than the boys to use social media networking sites (de Almeida *et al.* 2014).

A study on home internet use that drew on interview data with men and women who were part of couples living together in both Australia and Germany similarly found that men tended to be online more often, and to use the internet for recreational purposes, such as playing online games, and to seek time on their own away from domestic or childcare duties. In contrast the women who were interviewed, particularly those with children, viewed going online as part of their domestic duties. They used the internet to engage in online shopping for groceries or clothing or paying bills, for example, or to keep in touch with family members. They therefore tended to view the internet as another household appliance with practical value in managing family-related responsibilities (Ahrens 2013).

Some women may find themselves forced to use digital technologies as part of workplace demands or to maintain family ties or both. Research on the use of various types of digital media by Filipino women working in foreign countries as domestic workers showed that, despite their initial reluctance to use these technologies, they were forced to do so to keep in touch with the children they had left behind in the Philippines. The internet allowed these women to conform to their own and others' expectations about the importance of mothers keeping in touch with their children, particularly when they lived in a different country. Their use of digital media and devices thus drew upon traditional concepts of femininity related to 'the good mother' (Madianou and Miller 2012). Like the Australian and German women in the research discussed above, digital technologies for these women were modes of performing the relational, care-giving and domestic tasks required of them by norms of motherhood and domestic duties. Such use may be conceptualised as affective labour, a specific form of the broader unpaid labour of prosumption upon which the internet empires and data brokers rely for their profits (Jarrett 2014). For the Filipino workers, their use of digital media serves to allow them to engage in paid labour and in the affective unpaid work of motherhood simultaneously.

There is very little specific research comparing gender difference in the use of social media platforms. As noted earlier, statistics are available from the US and the UK that demonstrate that women and men in those countries use some social media sites differently. Gender performances also structure the types of content that women and men upload to social media. A study of young Canadian women's use of Facebook (Bailey *et al.* 2013) found that the images they tend to upload of themselves conformed to normative expectations about the desirable (sexually attractive, fun-loving, heterosexual, popular) young woman. Young women have to deal and negotiate with gender stereotypes constraining their use of this social media site. When interviewed about the material about themselves they uploaded to Facebook, the study participants were aware of the importance of treading a fine line between representing themselves as popular and attractive without appearing to be superficial or 'slutty'. They noted that young women, compared with young men, were much more likely to be harshly judged or ridiculed by others if they misjudged the ways they represented themselves on Facebook. The researchers suggest, therefore, that rather than challenging gender norms and allowing users greater freedom of self-expression, social media sites such as Facebook work to limit the ways in which young women can represent themselves in a context of intense surveillance and judgement from others. Another Facebook research study focused on how gender norms and expectations were performed on that platform by identifying stereotypes in the profile images uploaded by a selection of male and female users. It was found that the men tended to present themselves – through their images – as active, dominant and independent. Women, in contrast, uploaded photos that portrayed them as attractive and dependent (Rose *et al.* 2012).

There is often a lack of acknowledgement in cyberfeminist writings of the diversity of women's use of digital technologies, including the intersections of gender with race, ethnicity, social class and geographical location. Just as discourses on computer technologies have often assumed a white, middle-class, male user, some cyberfeminist writings position the female technology user as almost exclusively white and middle class and located in wealthy countries. The lived, embodied relationship to and use of digital technologies for disadvantaged women, those who live in rural or remote regions, or those who experience discrimination based on their race, ethnicity or sexual preference, often differ significantly from those of privileged women living in urban regions in the cultural North (Daniels 2009b). These assumptions fail to recognise the role that women in developing countries play in working in digital industries such as microchip factories and call centres (Philip *et al.* 2012). They also do not acknowledge the lack of access that many women in these contexts have to computers and internet connections (Daniels 2009b; Gajjala 2003), and that more men than women have access to education that teaches them the English they require to use many internet sites (Bell 2006a).

Despite these constraints, women in developing countries or living under repressive political regimes have employed digital technologies as part of their efforts to improve their social and economic conditions and to engage in political activism, including on a global level (Daniels 2009b; Newsom and Lengel 2012). Social media outlets may allow for women living in cultures where their political participation and ability to demonstrate in public spaces may be limited to express their views and opinions. During the Arab Spring citizen uprisings, for example, feminist activists and activist organisations in Tunisia and Egypt used online networking technologies extensively in their attempts to incite political change (Newsom and Lengel 2012).

ETHNOGRAPHIES OF DIGITAL TECHNOLOGY USE

As noted above, many discussions of digital technology use tend to assume a certain social group and cultural context: that inhabited by the privileged citizens of the global North. Philip *et al.* (2012) use the term 'postcolonial computing' to outline a critical perspective that seeks to draw attention to the lack of acknowledgement of the extensive diversity of cultural, social and geographical contexts in which digital technologies are used. They argue for a focus on the productive possibilities for researchers of emphasising difference and how it operates and expresses itself across cultural boundaries. Difference here is not conceptualised as inherent, but rather as a product of specific contexts. Designers, manufacturers, planners, the digital objects that they shape and the diverse users of these objects are part of an assemblage that is subject to transformation and reconfiguration as different actors enter and leave. Categories such as female, Asian, European and human are not fixed and do not exist independently of technology, but rather are the products of complex entanglements of power, politics, institutions and technologies. This is a similar argument to that made by some of the cyberfeminists discussed above, who have emphasised the mutual constitution of the categories of gender and technology.

Digital anthropologists have led the way in highlighting the multitudes of different ways in which the internet is used in specific geographical and cultural contexts. By engaging in ethnographic fieldwork, digital anthropologists are able to generate rich, highly contextualised data (the 'thick data' referred to in the previous chapter) about the incorporation of digital technologies into everyday life and the meanings that are assigned to these devices. Bell (2006a, 2006b), for example, conducted fieldwork in more than 50 households in four South Asian countries (India, Malaysia, Singapore and Indonesia). She spent time with the families in their houses, observing how they engaged with digital technologies and participating in these activities, as well as using interviews, taking photographs and making technology inventories. She undertook observations in key public spaces, such as shopping areas, and noted key artefacts and icons relevant to the research. Finally Bell sought the help of key area specialists to help her contextualise her data and provide alternative perspectives.

This fieldwork was undertaken before the advent of Web 2.0 technologies. As noted in Chapter 3, the emergence of ubiquitous digital media and social media networks has stimulated media researchers to '"rethink" ethnography and ethnographic practice' and to recognise their diversity (Horst *et al.* 2012: 87). Digital anthropologists have developed new ways of engaging in ethnographic research in their attempt to study in detail the cultural and social dimensions of the ways in which people engage with online technologies. For example, Postill and Pink (2012) spent time in Barcelona observing the use of social media by activist groups there. They investigated the content of the social media texts produced by the groups on Facebook, Twitter, blogs and YouTube and also participated on these sites, as well as interviewing members of the groups, attending events and researching online news sites related to the groups' activities and interests. As these researchers observe, the social media field site or research site is dispersed among a number of online platforms as well as offline sites. Their knowledge of these groups' activities was generated not only from what they did or produced online, but also from face-to-face interactions with the group members.

Outside the anglophone countries, there are major differences between the cultural contexts in which people are able (or not) to access digital technologies and the protocols of use. Such features as infrastructure and education levels, as well as cultural notions of which people should be given access to digital technologies, are influential in structuring digital use among and between social groups. In illustrating this point, Goggin and McLelland (2009: 3) compare examples of the experiences of two adolescent girls in very different cultural contexts: a Japanese girl in Tokyo and a Palestinian girl in the Occupied Territories. The former young woman is highly digitally literate and part of a culture which has embraced digital technologies for decades. She has access to all the latest technologies and years of experience using them. The latter is illiterate even in her own language, and is attempting to access the internet for the first time. Even if this young Palestinian girl is provided with the technologies, she lacks the required literacy to be able to make use of them.

The 'internet', therefore, is not a universal phenomenon across regions and cultures: it has different histories and configurations in different countries. Not only are assumptions and beliefs concerning digital use shifting between cultural contexts, so are the material infrastructures that support access to the internet: download speeds; the type of access (broadband or otherwise) that is available; the presence and reliability of electricity supplies; the cost of software packages and devices; government regulations concerning internet access of citizens; and so on. In several Asian countries, for example, personal computers first began to be used in the (middle-class) home rather than in the workplace. As a result computers were initially given meaning as domestic devices that were part of home life rather than work life, particularly with the purpose of assisting children with their education. Furthermore, their early use was inextricably interbound with accessing the internet, and this was their primary function (Bell 2006a).

Goggin and McLelland (2009) provide further examples to underline the cultural and historical diversity of the use of digital technologies across geographical regions. They note that while personal computers were not as commonly used in Japan as in anglophone countries, locally made phones that could connect to the internet were taken up years earlier in that country. South Koreans also used mobile internet-enabled phones earlier and had access to broadband well before countries such as the US because of the high population density and topography of their country that allowed for wide coverage to be provided (see also Bell and Dourish 2007, 2011; Dourish and Bell 2007). Similarly, as Bell and Dourish (2007) note, the geographical features of the small, highly urban island nation of Singapore, in conjunction with a relatively well-off and highly technologically literate population and government with a tradition of a high level of regulation of its citizens' everyday life, have allowed it to lead the way in adopting ubiquitous computing technologies. As

Google's *Our Mobile Planet* survey of global smartphone use showed, Singaporeans and South Koreans, together with residents of the United Arab Emirates and Saudi Arabia, lead the world in smartphone ownership. In Singapore and South Korea, however, with this development of a technologically connected 'intelligent island' has come a high level of government control, regulation and surveillance of citizens' internet use and access, including regulation and censorship of websites (see more on this issue in Chapter 7).

Digital anthropologists have also demonstrated the ways in which digital devices and platforms may be invested with meanings that resist or change those intended by their developers. Bell (2006b, 2011) gives the example of the use of paper replicas of digital technologies such as iPhones and iPads used in Chinese communities as offerings of love, piety and respect to dead ancestors. These replicas stand as symbols of wealth and Western culture, but are also viewed more spiritually as devices for the dead to communicate with each other as they were used to in the world of the living. Here these technologies have taken on a symbolic form wholly unimagined and unintended by their developers. With Dourish, Bell (Dourish and Bell 2007) also comments on the specific design of a mobile phone aimed at Muslims, which enables them to locate Mecca, read the Koran or hear it read to them, hear the call to prayer from Mecca live and be notified of prayer times. This device has taken on an overtly spiritual meaning as a supportive means for users to practise their faith.

Christie and Verran (2013) use the term 'postcolonial digital lives' to describe the ways in which members of the Yolngu Aboriginal communities with which they worked use digital technologies as part of their cultural archiving practices. The digital lives enacted via these practices are resistant to colonialising impulses that attempt to separate people and place. Their Yolngu co-researchers did not view constructing digital databases as appropriate for their purposes. Such databases represented the reproduction of Western ordering and taxonomic practices that did not fit with Yolngu concepts of preserving cultural artefacts, stories and traditions and interacting with them in dynamic ways. The method that was culturally appropriate required a fluid data structure in which the only *a priori* distinctions were those between file types (texts, audio files, movies and images).

Such anthropological research and the insights it provides go well beyond concepts of the digital divide or digital social inequalities to acknowledge that digital technologies are themselves invested with cultural assumptions drawn from the Western tradition. However, they may also be reinvested with alternative or resistant meanings that are culturally appropriate and meaningful to the people using them.

DISCRIMINATION ON DIGITAL SITES

It is important to acknowledge that despite the opportunities that social media and other websites afford for the promotion of forms of participatory democracy and freedom of expression, they may also reproduce and exacerbate discrimination and attempts to silence the members of social minority groups. The 'openness' of the internet and the growth of social media platforms that allow individuals and organisations to broadcast their opinions have resulted in greater opportunities to attack, discriminate against and marginalise already disadvantaged social groups. It has been argued that increasing use of online platforms by marginalised groups may in turn lead to more visibility and greater opportunity for others to attack them in these open forums (Ellis and Goggin 2014; Soriano 2014), a point I made about academic online engagement (Chapter 4).

It is all too evident that continuing sexism, racism, homophobia and other forms of discrimination and hate speech exist on the web. Online sites provide forums for the expression, reproduction and support of stigmatising and discriminatory statements that are aimed at social divisiveness rather than cohesiveness. Members of social minority groups tend to be subjected to far more hate speech, trolling, flaming, threats of violence and other forms of online harassment than are those who are part of the hegemonic social group – white, able-bodied, middle-class men living in the cultural North (Daniels 2013b; Humphreys and Vered 2014).

Racist and misogynist abuse and threats of violence are common on online sites. Social media platforms provide an opportunity for racist, homophobic and misogynist groups to attract members and engage in hate speech. Online forums such as news sites frequently attract racist hate speech, to the point that some news organisations no longer allow anonymous comments because of the vitriol that was expressed in them by people using pseudonyms. They also commonly use bots to search for racial epithets and profanity before approving comments to appear on their sites. Some online news sites have simply closed their comments sections because of the time and expense involved in moderating comments for racist and other offensive language and opinions (Hughey and Daniels 2013). Some websites established by white supremacist and other overtly racist organisations feature racist jokes as part of their rhetoric (Weaver 2011). Facebook groups such as 'Kill a Jew Day' and 'I Hate Homosexuals' and neo-Nazi websites have allowed people a forum for their opinions and to foment violence against their targets (Citron and Norton 2011).

Several of these types of racist propaganda websites are 'cloaked', meaning that they are published by individuals or groups who conceal or obfuscate authorship or pretend to have another agenda to attract views and achieve legitimacy. Such websites at first glance appear legitimate, but further examination reveals their racist propaganda agendas (Daniels 2009a; Hughey and Daniels 2013). One such website is entitled 'Martin Luther King: A True Historical Examination'. The website appears to be a tribute to King, but the website includes material and links to other websites that demonstrate its true agenda: to discredit him. Partly because they are cloaked, these websites often appear towards the top of search engine results for individuals such as King, bolstering their claims to veracity and credibility (Daniels 2009a).

Racist behaviour often takes place on what is referred to as the 'deep web', 'invisible web' or 'dark web'. The 'surface web' is that which any user can access using the usual search engines and browsers. In contrast, the 'deep web' is structured so that it uses encrypted and private networks and therefore is hidden and difficult to access. It is many times larger than the surface web and requires special browsers for access. The deep web is used for criminal or malicious purposes, such as drug and arms dealing, the hiring of assassins, disseminating child pornography or 'snuff' films (real footage of people being killed) as well as inciting racism or terrorism.

Some types of digital shaming and vigilantism (discussed further in Chapter 7) are also overtly racist, as in the website 419eater.com, which encourages participants to engage in 'scam baiting' of people who often originate from non-Western countries (frequently blacks from African countries such as Nigeria). This involves answering scam emails and attempting to engage the scammer in time-wasting or humiliating activities, such as posing for photographs holding signs in English that they do not understand but which humiliate them or otherwise position them in abject ways or even getting tattooed as directed by the scam baiter who promises them money if they do so.

Mobile apps also perpetuate racism, sexism and other forms of social discrimination and stigmatisation. There are several apps available that list racist jokes or use racist stereotypes as part of games, for example. A list of 'the 10 most racist smartphone apps ever created' refers to Mariachi Hero Grande, a game developed by Norwegians that featured a Mexican wearing a dirty poncho whose goal is to squash cockroaches while shooting tequila bottles; Jew or Not Jew, a French app aimed at providing details of Jewish celebrities; and Illegal Immigration: A Game, an alleged game that uses prejudiced subtext in discussing true or false 'facts' about immigrants to the US (Bracetti

2012). Other apps that were at first included by Google on its app store but then banned following complaints invited users to convert a photo of themselves into a different ethnic or racial group by adding such features as slanted eyes, a Fu Manchu moustache and yellow skin to 'make me Asian'. This game also used racial stereotypes to supposedly transform white faces into blacks, Native Americans and a victim of the Auschwitz concentration camp.

Overt discrimination and hate speech against women is also common on the internet. It is not only female academics who have been subjected to sexual harassment and threats of violence and rape (Chapter 4). Many other women who engage in digital public engagement, such as feminist activists, bloggers or journalists, have experienced highly misogynist comments, stalking and threats of violence, often couched in extremely explicit and aggressive terms. Women are disproportionately targeted by hate speech and abuse online when compared to male users of digital media (Citron 2009). One well-known case is that of English student Caroline Criado-Perez, who led a campaign to petition the British government to put more women on that country's banknotes. In mid-2013 she was subjected to many rape, violence and death threats on Twitter. In response to several online petitions, Twitter eventually developed a button allowing people to report abusive or violent messages on that platform.

The Google autocomplete function has been identified as having significant political and ethical implications. For example, an advertising campaign developed for the UN Women organisation identified the digitised discrimination against women evidenced in autocomplete Google searches (UN Women 2013). When the campaign's developers performed a search using the terms 'Women should', 'Women shouldn't' and 'Women need', Google autocompleted them with such phrases as 'Women need to be disciplined' and 'Women shouldn't have rights'. When I performed my own Google search in November 2013 using 'Women should ...', the autocomplete on my computer came up with 'not play sports', 'be silent', 'stay at home' and 'not be educated'. As another experiment I did a search using the words 'Muslims should ...'. The autocomplete came up with 'leave Australia', 'go home', 'be banned', 'be killed' and 'leave the UK'. When I entered the words 'Gay people should ...' the top suggestions provided by autocomplete included 'die', 'not be allowed to adopt' and 'be shot'. These autocomplete suggestions reveal the most often searched-for terms by other users, and hence the entrenched discrimination against women, some religious and ethnic or racial groups and gay people among many anglophone digital users. It could also be argued that by continuing to allow autocomplete to display these terms, this discrimination is perpetuated whenever the words are entered by reinforcing the views that are displayed. The autocomplete algorithms, therefore, are not simply acting to draw on search data; they are also actors in the construction and reproduction of social attitudes.

Racist, misogynistic, homophobic and other forms of threats and harassment are often trivialised and are not adequately dealt with by the law. However, they can have significant emotional effects on their victims and restrict opportunities for marginalised groups to participate freely in digital public engagement, including earning an income from such participation (Citron 2009; Citron and Norton 2011).

This chapter has addressed the multiple ways in which people engage with digital technologies across a range of socioeconomic and cultural contexts. The examples provided demonstrate that even when digital technologies have global reach, local 'technoscapes' or 'cultures of use' shape the ways in which they are used (Goggin and McLelland 2009: 4). Geographical location is important in determining physical access to technologies, but so too are the norms, practices and expectations that characterise societies within those locations. As I have argued, digital social inequalities are expressed and reproduced in a range of ways, including cultures of use as well as lack of access. Social inequalities and marginalisation may also be perpetuated and exacerbated online. Some of these topics are discussed further in the next chapter, in which I turn my attention to aspects of digital politics as they are expressed in relation to digital data veillance, digital activism, the open data movement and citizen participation.

CHAPTER 7

Digital politics and citizen digital public engagement

There is a growing literature on the use of digital media, particularly social media platforms, as means of facilitating and inciting social activism and political protest and on the open data movement and sousveillance strategies as examples of the production and use of digital data for political purposes on the part of citizens. This chapter begins with an overview of the politics of digital veillance, an issue that has become increasingly important in the age of big data and revelations about how governments are conducting covert dataveillance of their citizens. The chapter goes on to address the politics of privacy and to review the uses of digital media technologies for citizen political initiatives. A critical perspective is adopted on the claims that are often made about the unique power of social media to influence social change and achieve greater openness and access to digital data. The discussion will also draw attention to the ways in which the apparent 'truths' produced via such activities as citizen journalism may be falsified for political purposes or sheer perverseness, how misinformation may be disseminated, and how activism via social media may sometimes descend into vigilantism and forms of social marginalisation and discrimination.

▉ THE POLITICS OF DIGITAL WATCHING

In Chapter 2 I outlined the various forms of watching (veillance) that are applicable to digital technologies. I pointed out that surveillance may be voluntary and involuntary, overt and hidden, benign or coercive, restrictive of personal freedoms or productive of liberty. As outlined in Chapter 2, it has been recognised that we are now living in a post-panoptic world, where the panoptic model of surveillance has been complemented or superseded by new forms of power relations cohering around observation and monitoring. Panoptic surveillance was a feature of 'solid modernity', confined as it was to specific locations and times. Traditional panoptic data were static, recorded in one place and gathering dust in that location. They moved in one direction only: from the surveilled to the surveillants. The information that is gathered via contemporary digital veillance techniques is different. In liquid modernity (Lyon and Bauman 2013) surveillance is everywhere and is agile and fast-moving.

There is no denying that coercive and social exclusionary modes of surveillance may be facilitated by digital technologies, particularly in institutions such as prisons, in the screening of immigrants and asylum-seekers using digital profiling and as part of security measures, such as the identification of potential criminals or terrorist suspects and the use of CCTV in public spaces (Bossewitch and Sinnreich 2013; Hintjens 2013; Mann and Ferenbok 2013). This is surveillance as a mode of authoritarian power to which those who are monitored do not always give their explicit agreement (or, indeed, are asked to do so), and those who monitor others do not acquiesce to a similar level of transparency of their own actions.

Many activities of everyday life involve digital surveillance to which one has not directly agreed and which may be covert. The data that are collected via some technologies are not generally made available to those who are monitored, even though the data are about them. These surveillance strategies are proliferating, often without the knowledge or consent of those who are being watched. For example, in the US the licence plates and location of cars in some areas are routinely photographed by police officers, private companies and CCTV cameras at intersections. The resultant data are used for identifying criminals but also in routine surveillance by police, even of citizens about whom they have no suspicions, and for commercial purposes (such as for use by car repossession companies) (Angwin and Valentino-Devries 2012). Some companies have begun to gather data from people moving in public spaces using the wireless signals that automatically issue from smartphones searching for wi-fi networks. The smartphone owners do not have to be using their phones for these data to be accessed and are unaware that their movements are being tracked (Crawford 2014).

It is known that intelligence and law enforcement agencies have been monitoring the content and metadata of content on social media platforms for several years, as well as using customised social media platforms to share data among themselves (Werbin 2011). However, it was not until Snowden's revelations concerning the extent of government agencies' surveillance of digital users that many citizens became aware of how their personal data may have come under the scrutiny of such agencies. The popular media have warned for some time that commercial entities such as Google and Facebook as well as government agencies are spying on citizens through their accumulation of data about them, and may end up knowing too much about individuals through the increasingly detailed information produced from aggregating various data sets (Wallace and Whyte 2013). The Snowden documents demonstrated the extent to which even democratic Western governments have secretly accessed digital media sites in their attempts to monitor the activities of individuals engaged in political activism.

Not only have the NSA and other Western intelligence agencies used digital media data for surveillance, they have also sought to employ social media platforms to discredit political activists and movements such as WikiLeaks and Anonymous. 'The Five Eyes Alliance' is a security cooperative comprised of intelligence agencies in the USA, the UK, Australia, Canada and New Zealand. Its activities go well beyond engaging in surveillance of internet material to actively intervening in digital content to create false information. Snowden's documents have shown that the British spy agency GCHQ's Joint Threat Intelligence Group engages in such practices as contributing false material to internet platforms about its targets to discredit them and destroy their reputations and manipulating online discussions to generate outcomes that fit its agenda. This includes falsely attributing online material to someone else, changing the target's online photos, writing blogs pretending to be a victim of the individual or group it is attempting to discredit and posting negative information on online forums. One GCHQ document that outlines these tactics refers to the 'four Ds' that are part of its 'online covert operation': deny, disrupt, degrade, deceive (Greenwald 2014). The GCHQ also secretly monitored visitors to a WikiLeaks site and by tapping into fibre-optic cables was able to collect the IP addresses of visitors in real time, as well as identifying the search terms that they used to find the website (Greenwald and Gallagher 2014).

Ban-optic surveillance is a major feature of contemporary digital surveillance. Several writers have noted how this mode of surveillance is central to the establishment and maintenance of borders: between 'normal' and 'deviant', 'pure' and 'contaminated', 'healthy' and 'sick', 'legal' and 'illegal' and so on. It involves a kind of social sorting, in which certain social groups are identified as posing various levels of danger-ousness or threat and their movements or actions allowed or limited as a result (Ajana 2013; Muller 2008). Ban-optic surveillance therefore conforms to a political rationality that deems border and boundary control as vitally important to the governance of populations. The tech-nologies used to produce data for the purposes of exclusion often employ biometric data such as fingerprints and facial images to check against online databases as part of measures designed to control risk as part of 'risk profiling'. These have been described as 'first-generation biometrics'. 'Second-generation biometrics' involve the monitoring of people's behaviours with the aims of identifying and measuring suspi-cious or hostile intentions (Sutrop and Laas-Mikko 2012). As this social sorting becomes increasingly mobilised via second-generation biomet-rics, the individuals who are subject to this monitoring are less aware that they are being monitored, due to the invisible nature of many of these technologies (Sutrop and Laas-Mikko 2012).

As the latest form of surveillance in a long history of the close monitoring of such groups, digital surveillance technologies offer even more detail of such practices as individuals' expenditure of social security payments. As another example, immigrant groups in coun-tries such as the US are subjected to forms of biometric surveillance (such as fingerprint scanning) to prove their identity and residence status to which other groups do not have to submit. When people lack social power as well as digital literacy or access, they are less able to resist governmental digital surveillance. They have fewer options to withdraw from digital surveillance than do more privileged social groups because their income, access to social services or right to work may depend on submitting to these demands. Concerns about such monitoring and regulation have led to a focus on what has been termed 'digital human rights' (Eubanks 2014).

It is very difficult to anticipate how the digital data that are gener-ated now may be used in the future with new developments in data mining and algorithmic processing (Andrejevic 2013). As discussed in Chapter 5, there is growing evidence that previously anonymised data from various sources can be used together to trace the originator of the data, hence destroying anonymity. 'Digital fingerprinting' tech-niques allow for the linking of diverse data sets gathered from different digital devices about an individual to identify them, if not necessarily by name then by their habits, preferences and practices (Andrejevic 2013). Even if data remain anonymous, they can have significant implications for individuals' rights and freedoms. Whether or not an individual's data are included in big data sets, other people's data are used to make decisions for them, often limiting their choices (Andrejevic 2013). Once it has been demonstrated, for example, that people of a certain body weight or alcohol intake, or those who drive their cars in certain ways, are more likely to be at risk of disease or a car accident, then they become liable to pay higher insurance premiums. If individuals from a particular gender, age and ethnicity are identified as security risks, then all people who fit this specific profile become targeted as potential criminals or terrorists.

Practices of tagging and other forms of content categorisation of such material in producing data subjects are open to errors and misinterpretations that can have severe repercussions for the individuals that they target. As Werbin (2011: 1260) points out, 'social media does not forget. Not only is its memory persistent and difficult to correct, but it is also parsed and distributed and thus open to recombinant logics and endless accumulations and endless forms across indefinite platforms'. Inaccuracies and errors can therefore persist indefinitely, not only masking the ways in which these errors are produced, but multiplying their effects. This has led to individuals being identified on 'no fly' and other security watch lists and prevented from entering other countries, for example, even if these categorisations were made in error (Bossewitch and Sinnreich 2013; Werbin 2011).

THE POLITICS OF PRIVACY

The distinction between public and private has become challenged and transformed via digital media practices. Indeed it has been contended that via the use of online confessional practices, as well as the accumulation of masses of data that are generated about digital technology users' everyday habits, activities and preferences, the concept of privacy has changed. Increasingly, as data from many other users are aggregated and interpreted using algorithms, one's own data has an impact on others by predicting their tastes and preferences (boyd 2012). The concept of 'networked privacy' developed by danah boyd (2012) acknowledges this complexity. As she points out, it is difficult to make a case for privacy as an individual issue in the age of social media networks and sousveillance. Many people who upload images or comments to social media sites include other people in the material, either deliberately or inadvertently. As boyd (2012: 348) observes, 'I can't even count the number of photos that were taken by strangers with me in the background at the Taj Mahal'.

Many users have come to realise that the information about themselves and their friends and family members that they choose to share on social media platforms may be accessible to others, depending on the privacy policy of the platform and the ways in which users have operated privacy settings. Information that is shared on Facebook, for example, is far easier to limit to Facebook friends if privacy settings restrict access than are data that users upload to platforms such as Twitter, YouTube or Instagram, which have few, if any, settings that can be used to limit access to personal content. Even within Facebook, however, users must accept that their data may be accessed by those that they have chosen as friends. They may be included in photos that are uploaded by their friends even if they do not wish others to view the photo, for example.

Open-source data harvesting tools are now available that allow people to search for their friends' data. Using a tool such as Facebook Graph Search, people who have joined that social media platform can mine the data uploaded by their friends and search for patterns. Such elements as 'photos of my friends in New York' or 'restaurants my friends like' can be identified using this tool. In certain professions, such as academia, others can use search engines to find out many details about one's employment history and accomplishments (just one example is Google Scholar, which lists academics' publications as well as how often and where they have been cited by others). Such personal data as online photographs or videos of people, their social media profiles and online comments can easily be accessed by others by using search engines.

Furthermore, not only are individuals' personal data shared in social networks, they may now be used to make predictions about others' actions, interests, preferences or even health states (Andrejevic 2013; boyd 2012). When people's small data are aggregated with others to produce big data, the resultant data sets are used for predictive analytics (Chapter 5). As part of algorithmic veillance and the production of algorithmic identities, people become represented as configurations of others in the social media networks with which they engage and the websites people characterised as 'like them' visit. There is little, if any, opportunity to opt out of participation in these data assemblages that are configured about oneself.

A significant tension exists in discourses about online privacy. Research suggests that people hold ambivalent and sometimes paradoxical ideas about privacy in digital society. Many people value the use of dataveillance for security purposes and for improving economic and social wellbeing. It is common for digital media users to state that they are not concerned about being monitored by others online because they have nothing to hide (Best 2010). On the other hand, however, there is evidence of unease about the continuous, ubiquitous and pervasive nature of digital surveillance. It has become recognised that there are limits to the extent to which privacy can be protected, at least in terms of individuals being able to exert control over access to digital data about themselves or enjoy the 'right to be forgotten' (Rosen 2012; Rosenzweig 2012). Some commentators have contended that notions of privacy, indeed, need to be rethought in the digital era. Rosenzweig (2012) has described previous concepts as 'antique privacy' and asserts that these need challenging and reassessment in the contemporary world of ubiquitous dataveillance. He argues that in weighing up rights and freedoms, the means, ends and consequences of any dataveillance program should be individually assessed.

Recent surveys of Americans by the Pew Research Center (Rainie and Madden 2013) have found that the majority still value the notion of personal privacy but also value the protection against criminals or terrorists that breaches of their own privacy may offer. Digital technology users for the most part are aware of the trade-off between protecting their personal data from others' scrutiny or commercial use, and gaining benefits from using digital media platforms that collect these data as a condition of use. This research demonstrates that the context in which personal data are collected is important to people's assessments of whether their privacy should be intruded upon. The Americans surveyed by Rainie and Madden were more concerned about others knowing the content of their emails than their internet searches, and were more likely to experience or witness breaches of privacy in their own social media networks than to be aware of government surveillance of their personal data.

Another study using qualitative interviews with Britons (Wellcome Trust 2013) investigated public attitudes to personal data and the linking of these data. The research found that many interviewees demonstrated a positive perspective on the use of big data for national security and the prevention and detection of crime, improving government services, the allocation of resources and planning, identifying social and population trends, convenience and time-saving when doing shopping and other online transactions, identifying dishonest practices and making vital medical information available in an emergency. However, the interviewees also expressed a number of concerns about the use of their data, including the potential for the data to be lost, stolen, hacked or leaked and shared without consent, the invasion of privacy when used for surveillance, unsolicited marketing and advertising, the difficulty of correcting inaccurate data on oneself and the use of the data to discriminate against people. Those interviewees of low socioeconomic status were more likely to feel powerless about dealing with potential personal data breaches, identity theft or the use of their data to discriminate against them.

DIGITAL ACTIVISM

The use of social media and other digital technologies for social activist purposes has been investigated by researchers from a variety of disciplines within the social sciences, including not only sociology but also anthropology, media and communication studies and cultural studies. Manuel Castells is one of the most well-known writers on the use of social media for activism. In one of his most recent accounts of networked societies, Castells (2012) turns his attention to the ways in which contemporary social movements and activism are facilitated using digital social networks. He views these newer forms of networks as operating to pose a significant challenge to the operation of established power by forming new public spaces, or the networked space that is configured between the digital and the urban space.

Several cultural studies and media and communication academics have written about such aspects as the use of digital media for political activism, the creation of political media content by users on online forums and other forms of public participation. Researchers of online activism have focused in particular on the use of social media such as Twitter, YouTube, Facebook and blogs in the Arab Spring protests and the activities of the Occupy Wall Street movement, both occurring in 2011 (Bruns *et al.* 2013; Gleason 2013; Howard and Hussain 2011; Murthy 2013). Indeed, Tufekci and Freelon (2013: 843) contend that digital media technologies are now so influential in political activism that 'it no longer makes sense to ask if digital technologies will exercise influence; rather, we can and should be looking at how and, also crucially, through which mechanisms'.

The WikiLeaks movement and the activities of the Anonymous activist hacker alliance have also gained some attention for their interventions into making previously secret government documents available on the internet, in the case of the former, and in engaging in hacking activities seeking to challenge government power, as Anonymous seeks to do (Cammaerts 2013; Curran and Gibson 2013; Postill 2013; M. Sauter 2013). Several digital anthropologists have explored the ways in which subjugated groups have used social and other digital media as part of their efforts to achieve justice and recognition. John Postill, for example, has written a number of accounts of the use of internet activism and social protest in countries such as Malaysia (Postill 2008) and Spain (Postill and Pink 2012).

Some research has also been conducted on the use of online platforms for feminist activism and consciousness-raising. This research suggests that digital media can be important in mobilising support for protests and allowing previously silenced women, including those from racial or ethnic or sexual identity minorities or located in the global South, to be given a voice (Friedman 2007; Merithew 2004; Rapp *et al.* 2010). A recent example of digital feminist activism from Australia is the 'Destroy the Joint' campaign. Twitter and Facebook were used by Australian feminists to protest against the comments in 2013 of a well-known conservative radio commentator, Alan Jones, on his radio programme that women leaders and politicians such as the then-Prime Minister Julia Gillard were 'destroying the joint' – that is, that they were allegedly having a detrimental effect on Australia. After adopting the hashtag '#destroythejoint', feminist activists quickly used Twitter to draw attention to Jones's sexist comments, often by using ironic comments about how they planned to 'destroy the joint', and gathered many supporters and retweeters of their comments. Jones's further negative comments in a speech at a political function about Gillard, labelling her a liar, also drew these social media activists' attention and criticism. Commercial advertisers responded to the negative publicity engendered by the 'Destroy the Joint' campaign by withdrawing their funding from Jones's radio programme. He was forced to make a public apology for the comments he made in his speech about Gillard.

I noted in the previous chapter that many people with disabilities have found support from online communities. Members of other socially marginalised groups have also found the internet to be a source of support and political mobilisation. People who identify as queer or transgender have used online technologies for these purposes, sometimes finding the internet the only safe space for expressing their sexual identity. Lesbian, gay, bisexual and transsexual activists have frequently employed digital media outlets to muster support and engage in political activism, attempting to challenge heteronormative stereotypes and challenge discrimination (Fraser 2010; Soriano 2014). Via such activities, an online 'queer community' has developed as well as many political groups and support networks (Soriano 2014). There are numerous Tumblr sites, for example, devoted to celebrating and expressing queer identities and inviting participation from other queer-identified users, with titles such as 'Radically Queer', 'I Knew I Was Queer When …', 'Queer Resistance' and 'What I Love about Being Queer', as well as a number of others devoted to gay, lesbian, transsexual or transgender identities.

People who self-identify as fat have also taken up online activism in their efforts to challenge and resist fat stigma. They blog about fat pride, engage in information-sharing and activism using Facebook pages, Tumblr and Twitter feeds and post images that represent fat bodies as normal, healthy and attractive. The image curation site Pinterest, for example, features many pages established by fat acceptance supporters and fat activists that display images of fat bodies that have been selected for their positive representations of this body type. They include images of fat celebrities looking glamorous, vintage images of attractive fat bodies, erotic portrayals of curvy bodies, artistic representations, fat acceptance posters and products such as badges and t-shirts and photographs of ordinary people wishing to express their confidence in their bodies. The term 'fatosphere' has been used to denote these efforts (Meleo-Erwin 2011).

There is a multitude of health-related digital media sites directed at information provision and sharing and patient support for specific diseases and conditions. Some of the members of these online groups and organisations also attempt to engage in political activism to achieve more positive representations of people with specific illnesses or conditions, agitate for greater access to medical care or healthcare policy changes, or challenge medical orthodoxies (Meleo-Erwin 2011). Disability activists have begun to use social media to draw attention to such issues as government cuts to services. One example is the 2012 British 'We Are Spartacus' campaign. Organised around a Twitter hashtag, this campaign began with a small number of activists tweeting about a report that outlined the British government's disability living allowance reform. The report itself was written with the help of social media contributions from people with illnesses and disabilities describing their experiences and the effects the proposed cuts to their disability living allowance would have on their lives. The campaign was vastly helped by the participation of the celebrity Stephen Fry, who has millions of Twitter followers, as well as influential politicians who also tweeted about the report and other well-known British public figures. The British mainstream news media picked up on the story once it became clear that the topic was trending on Twitter, and the resulting publicity exerted pressure on the politicians involved (Butler 2012).

OPEN DATA AND DATA PROTECTION INITIATIVES

As discussed in Chapter 5, it has been contended that individuals' and organisations' digital data may come to be viewed as marketable commodities to the extent that they may be viewed as a form of valuable property and therefore should be protected and stored in ways that secure it from outside use unless permission is given. There is, therefore, a debate between those who argue that individuals and organisations should protect their rights to their own data, and those who claim that these data should be viewed as a public asset and shared as such (Kirkpatrick 2011). Indeed, a new form of philanthropy has been identified – 'data philanthropy' – in which individuals and corporations are encouraged to 'donate' their data for the benefit of all (Kirkpatrick 2011). This has been championed, for example, by the humanitarian organisation Global Pulse.

So valuable are digital data objects now considered that reference is frequently made to individuals' 'data assets' and consideration given to what should happen to these following a person's death. It has been argued by some commentators that digital users should establish a personal computing cloud repository in which all their data interactions may be stored that they can then use, trade or sell as they wish and that 'do not track' browser settings may become common ways of preventing corporate platforms from mining users' personal data. Some commentators have contended that people need to be more conscious of their metadata, or what others can discover about them online, and become more aware of what data are collected about them and how they can be used (Horning 2013; Watson 2013).

There is a move towards liberating data from the archives used by platform and website developers so that they can be accessed by individuals for purposes other than commercial ones. The data assemblage here becomes a commodity that users may use themselves rather than allowing it to be monetised by platform developers (Vaughn 2013). If it is accepted that 'you are your data', the argument continues that one's own data should be owned and available for use by oneself (Watson 2013). This valorisation of digital data does not centre solely on economic imperatives, but incorporates others related to how data may be used to improve individuals' lives. This perspective is articulated in a multitude of forums in relation to many other aspects of individuals' lives, including healthcare, employment and education. When people are able to collect 'small data', as in the case of people using digital self-tracking devices or engaging in citizen science or citizen journalism practices, they are contributing to 'home-made big data' that may be used for broader research or political as well as personal purposes. Indeed, this is one of the stated aims of the Quantified Self movement, as expressed on its website: to produce data on oneself to meet one's own objectives that can also be aggregated with others' data to create broader insights into human behaviours. Providing open data sources to the public is also represented as a way for citizens to engage in their own research using big data (Halavais 2013).

Digital strategies of attempting to take control of dataveillance have begun to emerge. These include using programs that can reveal how people's online activities are being monitored and who is gaining access to personal data. Browsers and search engines can also be used as alternatives to those offered by the internet empires that do not track users' queries, as are online services that encrypt messages and phones that do not identify users' geo-locations. Ad-blocking tools that both prevent ads from appearing on devices' screens and stop advertisers collecting data about users are becoming popular browser extensions. Programs are available that can provide users with a snapshot of what information they are sharing in social media sites and online services such as Google. They inform users when their privacy settings are weak and send alerts when sites make changes to their privacy policies. Other tools can show users which companies have access to information such as their credit-card details, phone number and email addresses or remove an individual's public profile and personal information from sites that gather data about people from the internet. Some people clear the cookies that companies use to track users' browsing behaviours or set their devices to disable, block or turn off cookies (Dwoskin 2014).

On a more politically activist level, some critics and activists have begun to call for people to engage in resistant acts to counter others collecting data on their activities for commercial or surveillance purposes. They assert that digital data should be made available to citizens to use for the benefit of themselves or their communities. Several social media scholars view it as important to personally participate in public debates about digital media as part of their own political activism (see, for example, Ford *et al.* 2013; Fuchs 2014b; Jenkins 2014). In April 2014, a group of internet scholars, media practitioners, librarians, activists and media policy-makers, including the prominent Marxist media theorist Christian Fuchs, released *The 2014 Vienna Declaration on Freedom of Information and Expression*, which they circulated on various scholarly forums calling for other academics to sign. The declaration called for 'public vigilance to defend freedom of information and expression as key democratic rights', particularly in relation to internet dataveillance and corporate and state control of the media (Avaaz.org 2014).

'Open' has become a buzzword in relation to digital technologies, with many advocating for open-source software, open data, open online education and, as discussed in Chapter 4 in relation to academic research, open access to scholarly publications. The term 'open data movement' has been employed to describe a political perspective that valorises access to the data archives of government bodies. The open-data movement assumes that government bodies tend at best to be inefficient, wasteful in their spending and lack attention to issues that citizens consider important, and at worst corrupt, and that opening their data archives will reveal this. There is much focus on key words such as 'transparency', 'accountability', 'citizen empowerment' and 'participation' in open-data initiatives. It is contended that such practices not only involve greater democratic participation, but also may lead to the generation of new industries and innovations. There is talk of producing a global ecosystem of data to which communities from all over the world may have access for their own purposes (Davies and Bawa 2012).

'Community informatics' is a term that is also often used in relation to community members engaging in their own data collection and analysis, while 'citizen sensing' or 'participatory sensing' is employed more specifically to denote the activities that involve citizens gathering data, particularly environmentally related, using sensor-enabled technologies. These include sensors that may be worn by individuals as wearable computing, mounted on vehicles (including bicycles), attached to balloons and installed in people's houses or on street furniture (Kamel Boulos *et al.* 2011). An increasing number of calls have been made for children to learn computer coding from an early age as part of the school curriculum, supported by the argument that digital and coding literacies are as important in the contemporary digital society as are the more traditional forms of literacies. Coding literacy is represented in such arguments as helping children and young people to become equipped for a future workplace that may require such skills and also to protect themselves against incursions against the privacy of their personal digital data (Williamson 2013a, 2013b).

Various organisations and groups have developed for the purposes of helping people learn about creating and using digital data. The School of Data and Open Data Institute in the UK, for example, offers courses and activities for non-commercial organisations, social activists, journalists and citizens to instruct them in creating, accessing and using digital data. Many initiatives are now in operation to support digitally enabled citizen science activities, assisting people to use digital technologies to gather data about environmental conditions in their locality, for example, so that they can use these data to agitate for change. The Mapping for Change initiative is one such example. This organisation provides mapping, geographical analysis and community engagement services, including helping communities create online interactive maps demonstrating geographical information about such features as community services or environmental pollution. Some of these mapping activities involve the use of digital sensors and other digital technologies, such as social media for generating data, so that participants are able to collect their own data and then represent these data visually on an online map. We the Data's website (which, interestingly, is a joint partnership between what the website describes as 'friends', 'TED Fellows' and 'some visionaries' from the computer giant Intel) outlines a number of activities it promotes in the interests of enhancing citizens' access to their digital data: platform openness, data literacy, digital access and digital trust (defined as 'the ability to control our personal data "exhaust" and build systems of reputation and accountability').

It is evident that increasing numbers of people are learning about gathering and interpreting data using digital tools. When Typhoon Haiyan hit the Philippines in late 2013, for instance, volunteers were called into action to use social media data to inform aid efforts. Faced with a lack of information about how citizens were faring in the more far-flung regions, particularly given the lack of landline telephone access due to damage from the typhoon, social media messages – supported by emergency digital technology infrastructure, such as inflatable broadband antennae – were able to provide details. Workers using the MicroMappers platform were able to pinpoint where people were asking for help by using volunteers to sift through tweets and other digital media updates, noting descriptions of the situation and the content of any images uploaded. The online mapping tool OpenStreetMap was used by other volunteers to create new versions of digital maps that showed changes to the topography of affected regions to promote better access for relief workers (MacKenzie 2013). In other developing countries, citizens have used open government data to monitor politicians' actions (Ghana), demonstrate waste in government spending (Nigeria) and engage in political action designed to improve public sanitation and access to clean water (India) (Firth 2013).

CRITICAL PERSPECTIVES

Despite the many examples of successful uses of social and other digital media for political activism and citizen participation, some critics have challenged what they identify as an overly utopian and simplistic perspective on what these practices can achieve. They suggest that the apparent power of the new digital media in facilitating protest and social change, championing their liberating potential, tends to present an overly simplistic view of digital media's role. A more complex approach acknowledges the interaction of digital media with traditional media and other forms of disseminating information and inciting action is complex and multifaceted, involving a heterogeneous collection of actors, both human and nonhuman, and both old and new media. Community and social network concepts tend to be employed in internet research as if they are bounded and unidimensional, rather than heterogeneous and dynamic. Postill (2008) proposes instead the concept of the 'social field', a space in which social agents compete or collaborate, including both local residents who may be agitating for change and the authorities resisting change. A diverse range of different human actors are contributing to the current convergence of digital freedom activism and popular protest, including computer geeks and hackers, journalists and lawyers specialising in copyright and internet issues, other knowledge producers such as academics as well as social activists and citizens. An equally diverse range of actors may seek to limit, contain or repress such activities (Fuchs 2011, 2014b; Postill 2013; Tufekci and Freelon 2013).

The human and nonhuman actors that work together to produce digital data – the developers, coders, web hyperlinks, algorithms, search engines and engineering of the infrastructure of the internet itself – structure and delimit the ways in which people are able to search for and find relevant information or indeed upload and manipulate their own data (Ruppert and Savage 2011). Castells has been criticised for neglecting discussion of surveillance and privacy issues and for his assumptions that all citizens have equal access to the internet (Fuchs 2014a; van Dijk 2010). As shown in Chapter 6, many people continue to lack expertise in using digital technologies or even the kind of access to them that utopian visions of community mobilisation via the internet tend to assume. A significant disparity exists online in terms of skills and expertise to use digital media for political purposes. A high-profile digital presence is often a result of access to funds to pay for it. Those groups and organisations that have access to greater resources are able to pay for technical expertise and for their websites to achieve greater visibility (Adams 2011; Halford et al. 2013; Mager 2009).

Regardless of citizen data initiatives, as described in Chapter 5, the internet empires retain a firm hold of the data they collect and archive. While the ideals of sharing and participatory democracy that are promoted in Web 2.0 cultures suggest that average citizens can both contribute to and benefit from the affordances of digital media technologies, the people who create the data rarely benefit financially from them. It is Google, Amazon, Facebook, Twitter and the like and the corporations to which they sell their data who are able to make money from these data. While 'transparency' is a major discourse in the big data rhetoric, many collectors of big data sets do not reveal how they are collected or to what purposes they are put. While big data analytics are used to generate decisions and predictions about individuals, those individuals often have no idea how these were made, and thus how they can be challenged (Richards and King 2013). Big digital companies still exert power over the content that they allow on the social media sites they have developed. Continuing battles over Facebook's refusal to allow women to upload photos of themselves breastfeeding as this is considered to be publishing inappropriate images of female nudity is one example.

While social media allow social activists and political protesters to organise their movements, they are also a source of data for intelligence and policing agencies to mobilise against them and for use in legal charges (Werbin 2011). Governments can move to shut down, prohibit or censor digital media sites. In countries like Singapore (Bell and Dourish 2007), Syria (Richards and King 2013) and China (Tang and Sampson 2012), for example, the government exerts tight censorship over both the traditional media and internet sites. While there is some opportunity for the citizens of these countries to use the internet as part of social protest and activism, there is much less freedom to do so compared to countries with less government intervention. Indeed, Singapore was targeted by Anonymous in November 2013 for its censorship activities. An example of such repression of free speech on social media occurred in March 2014, when the Prime Minister of Turkey, Recep Erdoğan, restricted access to Twitter in his country as part of his attempts to silence political dissent and challenges to his political power. Twitter and other social media platforms had been used by dissidents to leak documents and wire-tapped recordings that allegedly provided evidence of corruption among Erdoğan's inner circle.

In addition to censoring social media political activism or dissent, some government regimes have themselves employed the internet to conduct surveillance on political activists and organisers. They have used social media data to identify and arrest them, thus turning the communicative and networking functions of online technologies against attempts at free speech and political change (Fuchs 2014a). Thus, for example, the Syrian government used the social media output of pro-democracy activists working as part of the Arab Spring to secretly profile and identify them (Richards and King 2013).

A further critique of the assumptions and ideologies underpinning advocacy of digital activism argues that advocates represent digital activism as unfailingly productive and positive. There is little questioning of the rhetoric of openness and participation that suffuses these assumptions. The privileging of leaderless and horizontal organising and an aversion to hierarchies tend to be part of the rhetoric of digital activism, as is the representation of social media as vibrant and progressive compared to previous forms of political organising (Kavada 2014). Here the discourses of digital utopianism and technological determinism are as evident as they are in other spheres of human endeavour. Advocates of digital activism tend to represent traditional media as obsolete and inefficient in organising political activism, even as 'dead' and corrupt, while positioning new digital media as progressive and revolutionary (Natale and Ballatore 2014). Indeed, it has been asserted that both the popular media and certain academic portrayals of digital activism have tended to romanticise such activism (Markham 2014; Natale and Ballatore 2014). Fuchs (2014a) speculates whether events such as the Arab Spring and Occupy Wall Street protests would have taken place without the use of digital technologies. He concludes that these protests would still have occurred, albeit using different forms of media and organisation of activists.

Critics have also pointed out that prosumption has various levels of political and economic participation, some of which are minor and some of which have more major implications. Uploading detailed content agitating for political change on social media platforms and actively using digital media networks to collaborate on political activities and encourage membership of dissident groups, for example, are very different practices from simply sharing or liking others' social media content. In the increasingly commercialised environment of prosumption, some forms of digital participation are revolutionary and resistant to current modes of power. Other forms are part of dominant, powerful institutions and support their power: for example, economically powerful corporations such as Google, Apple and Amazon (Fuchs 2011, 2014b; Jenkins 2014). As Jenkins (2014: 10) contends, the Web 2.0 business model seeks 'to capture, commodify and control the public's desire for meaningful participation'. Some of the sites that have been established for the communication of resistant political ideas or to enhance support among marginalised groups have become commercialised (Lupton 2014a; Soriano 2014).

Some commentators have challenged the ideals of citizens learning to gather and manipulate digital data or to learn computer coding. It has been asserted that these ideals may be interpreted as yet further examples of citizens encouraged to act as responsible in the context of neoliberal politics, enjoined to participate in coding, data gathering and data analysis for political purposes (Bates 2012) or in the interests of commercial enterprises (Williamson 2013a). It may be argued that such utopian ideals tend to discount the realities of the messiness, inaccuracies, partial nature and incompleteness of the data with which citizens may be encouraged to grapple (Davies and Bawa 2012), as well as the fact that collecting data, coding and data analysis practices are themselves often complex to teach and learn. Even professional coders struggle to keep up with changes in programming languages, coding packages and operating systems, and are largely unaware of the social and economic consequences of their coding work (Williamson 2013a).

Furthermore, releasing data sets to render them 'open' in itself is not an emancipatory or politically progressive act: the conditions in which this occurs, the quality of the data and the uses to which they are put all structure how this process operates and is interpreted. Bates's (2012) analysis of the Open Government Data initiative in the UK found that powerful political interests attempted to shape the release of data and represent this process as serving commercial interests rather than progressive social policy. Open data initiatives, therefore, are the sites of significant social and political struggle, with community groups attempting to access data sometimes subject to continuing efforts to co-opt and exploit them in the interests of elite groups. The project of 'releasing data' is far more complex and politically contested than some of its advocates are willing to acknowledge.

Concern has been expressed in some quarters that in the face of the accumulation of data and other forms of information, people are now dealing with an 'info-glut', or data overload. In this age of opinion-expression and citizen journalism activities as part of Web 2.0 prosumption, a myriad of ways of representing events and constructing views of reality are available. Digital media users need to find some way of sifting through these opinions and representations and making sense of them. It is argued that there are simply too many forms of data to which individuals are now exposed, and it is difficult for people to assess which data are important, valuable and accurate and which are trivial or inaccurate. This is the case both for those entrepreneurial operators who seek commercial value from big data and for ordinary citizens. However, those who own the data stored in corporate archives have privileged access to these data and greater resources for making connections between them and interpreting their meaning (Andrejevic 2013).

A distinction between the 'big data rich' and the 'big data poor' was made by boyd and Crawford (2012) in pointing out the power relations inherent in differential access to digital data. Andrejevic (2013: 34–35) takes this further by predicting that what he describes as 'two different information cultures' will co-exist: one based on traditional information sources such as their own and others' experiences, news media and blogs, and the newer information culture offered by big data that relies upon computerised analytics for its comprehension. He contends that the new information culture has instituted new forms of social, economic and political disadvantage. Those with greater cultural and economic capital are able to make big data work in their favour, while others simply lack access to the benefits offered by big data. As this suggests, there remain limits to the contributions that people in general are able to make to the new digital knowledge economy, the authority they are able to develop and the benefits they are able to accrue. While the rhetoric suggests that platforms for prosumption serve to create 'new informational gatekeepers and data interpreters' (Ruppert and Savage 2011: 87) (that is, members of the digitally empowered public), the digitally engaged citizen as an ideal-type is configured through dominant and often continuing hierarchies of power and knowledge.

Some advocates of the open digital data movement are beginning to realise these issues and encourage people to develop a critical approach to the big data phenomenon itself: a 'critical citizen science' that goes beyond the notion of citizen scientists as sensor-based nodes in the Internet of Things (McQuillan 2013). As McQuillan (2012) puts it, critical citizen science involves people 'examining and questioning what represents their world inside the big data machine, and having the ability to intervene on their behalf of their preferred futures'. He asserts that once people start to engage with digital data, they will realise its 'obstinacy and material resistance' (McQuillan 2012). They will come to see the flaws and inaccuracies of digital data (the 'dirtiness' of the data), the assumptions and judgements that underpin them, the ways in which they are used for political purposes and that these forms of information and 'truths' are not as neutral and perfect as they are so often presented. They will be able to think about what kinds of data are most useful for their own purposes. McQuillan (2012) gives the example of the Counter Cartographies Collective, a group that attempts to 'queer' big digital data sets by using them for purposes unintended by the generators and archivers of the data.

THE NEGATIVE SIDE OF CITIZEN DIGITAL PUBLIC ENGAGEMENT

Encouraging citizens to participate in the creation of knowledge bears some significant risks and threats to other citizens' privacy and freedom. Practices of sousveillance and synoptic veillance are now integral elements of many users' interaction with digital technologies. Mobile and wearable computing devices enable users to constantly monitor and record both visual and audio data as they move around domestic and public spaces, as well as monitor geo-location details (Mann and Ferenbok 2013; Michael and Clarke 2013). Users of these technologies can watch each other constantly and record and then share their observations with many others using social media platforms (in some cases, thousands or even millions of others). People moving in public spaces become imbricated within the field of public vision, representing a new configuration of space, visuality and social or even criminal censure. The recordings that ensue become subject to moral interpretation as they are disseminated and tagged through digital media platforms (Biressi and Nunn 2003).

Beginning with the amateur video-filming of Rodney King being beaten by police officers in Los Angeles in 1992, the notion that citizen journalists and activists can take images and circulate them in the interests of public accountability has gathered momentum. The opportunity to act as a civil witness has increased exponentially in the age of ubiquitous and mobile computing. It is now extremely easy to take photographs or videos on one's device and very quickly upload them to social media sites for sharing and circulation (Byrne 2013; Kingsley 2008). The behaviour of figures of authority, such as police and security officers, may be placed under more public scrutiny by virtue of pervasive sousveillance on the part of private citizens, who can distribute the images or audio files they record on social media sites and gain wide exposure (Bossewitch and Sinnreich 2013).

The surveillance capacities offered by digital media can work to bolster social mores and identify wrongdoing, but can also be used for harassment, manipulation, stalking, voyeurism, mob activism and wrongful punishment or social exclusion. People engaging in these activities participate in acts of public shaming, in which individuals or groups deemed to have acted outside the boundaries of moral behaviour are held up for castigation and blame. This may quickly descend into vigilantism, sometimes in the absence of firm evidence that the individual who has been targeted has behaved criminally or otherwise reprehensibly (Byrne 2013; Kingsley 2008).

One such example occurred in the wake of the Boston marathon bombings in April 2013. Sunil Tripathi, a university student who had been reported missing for more than a month, was wrongly nominated as a suspect, much to his family's distress. One of the members of the social bookmarking site Reddit, who was working as part of a joint effort to comb through photographs to identify the bombers from blurry images from security cameras that were available online, decided that Tripathi resembled one of them. Very quickly, as this so-called identification was spread via other social media sites such as Twitter by journalists as well as other users, Tripathi became infamous. The Tripathi family's 'Help Us Find Sunil Tripathi' Facebook page was defaced by angry Reddit users and the family were forced to close it down. Tripathi's body was later found (he was presumed to have committed suicide in the days before the Boston bombings), and the real perpetrators of the bombing were identified.

The news media have traditionally exercised disciplinary power by 'naming and shaming' people who have come before the courts for criminal acts or otherwise gained public attention for wrongdoing. Now that many newspapers publish their news reports digitally, there is the potential for minor wrongdoings, offences and misdeeds to be reported online, circulated from the original source and remain in a digital format for perpetuity. Once an individual's name is linked many times on digital networks with criminal or antisocial behaviour, this association is impossible to eradicate. People's names, when entered into search engines, are immediately associated with the incident that garnered social media attention, even if it occurred years before or they were identified in error (Waller and Hess 2014).

Minor social *faux pas* have also been amplified by the circulation of shaming and acts of humiliation via social media (Kingsley 2008; Waller and Hess 2014). This has occurred frequently in relation to antisocial behaviours such as racist insults or urination in public spaces, for example, with the recording and digital sharing of such behaviours sometimes leading to police arrests. 'Twitter firestorms' are unleashed when individuals are identified in that social medium as behaving badly or criminally and then subjected to an intense degree of excoriation and attempts at shaming. I referred in Chapter 4 to Geoffrey Miller, the American academic who made an ill-judged offensive comment about fat students' supposed lack of self-control on Twitter. His remark was retweeted many times, often with negative appraisals of him appended, and he became known on the internet as 'the fat-shaming professor'. There are countless other examples, including the Destroy the Joint campaign against broadcaster Alan Jones that I described earlier in this chapter.

As the case of Sunil Tripathi demonstrated, sometimes social media sites not only spread erroneous 'news' but participate in making apparent 'breaking news'. The information disseminated on social media sites is taken very seriously by journalists working for major news organisations, who perpetuate the rumours in their own tweets and online 'breaking news' stories. The opportunities to create fraudulent content in the attempt to perpetuate a hoax or as part of propaganda efforts may hamper news gathering and humanitarian efforts. To use the example of the Boston Marathon bombings again, thousands of fake profiles were created on Twitter very soon after this event for the purpose of . malicious tweeting. The proportion of rumour dissemination and fake content among tweets was high. Fraudulent charity accounts were created and incorrect information was spread about the victims of the bomb blasts, including incorrect claims about children who allegedly had been killed and fake photos of them (Gupta *et al.* 2013).

This type of spreading of misinformation and rumour also occurred when Hurricane Sandy affected New York City in late 2012. Various fake images were created using digital image manipulation tools or taken from fictional materials such as films and art installations that were widely shared on Twitter and Facebook, as well as images of scenes that were represented as taken during the hurricane that were authentic but were actually of earlier events in New York City or other cities. These fake images included one of the Statue of Liberty surrounded by crashing waves that was from the 2004 film *The Day after Tomorrow*, another of threatening storm clouds over the city that predated the hurricane by a year and a digitally manipulated image falsely showing a shark swimming in flood waters in the city (Colbert 2012).

The reports of the deaths of various celebrities have also spread rapidly via Twitter, often forcing the celebrities themselves to make public protestations that news of their demise was premature. False Twitter accounts have been created and images and videos uploaded to social media sites in efforts to disseminate political propaganda or to slander political figures (Silverman 2012). Wikipedia entries are renowned for being manipulated by editors seeking to engage in pranks or to achieve political gain. April Fool's Day is a particularly popular date for Wikipedia hoaxes (see Wikipedia 2013). A common use of celebrity identity is evident in the phenomenon of celebrity fake porn, where people use Photoshop to digitally manipulate images of (mostly) female celebrities to represent them in fake pornographic poses and then post these images online.

Some writers, drawing on Castells's concept of network society, have used the term 'network(ed) journalism' to refer to the use by journalists of social and other digital media to create their news stories (Heinrich 2012). Journalists are increasingly using sources such as Twitter, YouTube, Flickr and Instagram to collect material on breaking news stories but are then confronted with the requirement to rapidly assess the validity and authenticity of the information uploaded on these sites. Citizen or crowd-sourced journalism and eyewitness accounts offer great possibilities for widening the scope of journalistic news–gathering, but they also offer significant pitfalls, such as those outlined above, as well as the sheer difficulty of dealing with the increased flows and speed of information emerging from sources such as social media and blogs (Heinrich 2012). Verification of social media sources and citizen journalism is now a significant part of journalistic work, and several major news organisations employ dedicated teams of journalists to do this. Journalists themselves can now be held to account by others, who can more easily expose any fabrications or inaccuracies in their reporting by presenting their own information and posting it online (Silverman 2012). In this context, the audiences for news reports are no longer positioned as the passive recipients of this news, but as active creators and sometimes news breakers who themselves are authoritative sources that require management by journalists seeking to compile a news report (Harrington and McNair 2012).

I have argued in this chapter that there are many complexities to digital veillance, digital activism, citizen digital public engagement and the rhetoric and strategies of openness. Digital activism and citizen participation in the construction of knowledge via digital media are able to achieve certain objectives but continue to take place in a context in which powerful commercial and state interests can delimit citizens' freedom of expression and action. The opportunity for citizens to use digital media to conduct their own strategies of veillance and create and circulate knowledge also may support the reproduction of false and misleading information, social shaming, vigilantism, social discrimination and hate speech. I have further contended that the project to achieve 'openness' of data is not as unproblematic as it may first appear. Here again, a critical and reflexive sociological approach is vital to investigate the manifold issues that lie beyond simple calls for increased citizen participation in the creation of digital knowledges and the protection of digital privacy.

CHAPTER 8

The digitised body/self

Various digital technologies have been developed to digitise the self or one's body. These include the sharing of photos on social media platforms, public profiles, blogs and comments written about themselves by social media users, and self-tracking devices that are used to monitor and measure aspects of everyday life and render these into data. These technologies facilitate the collection, sharing and dissemination of information and emotions that might in previous eras have been considered highly personal, including experiences of illness, surgery or the death of a loved one, information about one's moods or bodily functions, relationship break-ups, work difficulties and so on.

Digital sociologists and other digital media researchers have recognised the ways in which human embodiment and concepts of self-hood are represented and configured via digital technologies and digital social networks. It is not only the data or images produced via digital technologies that are important to research and theorise but also how the objects themselves – the devices, such as smartphones, tablet computers, gaming technologies and wearable devices – are used in practice. This chapter takes up theory and research from a diverse range of disciplines, including social computing, digital anthropology, media studies and cultural studies as well as sociology, to review the ways in which digital technologies are incorporated into everyday lives across a range of contexts.

INTIMATE COMPUTING

As I argued in Chapter 2, the concept of the cyborg, so popular in the early years of theorising computerised technologies, has lost much of its currency. Few of the new generation of scholars interested in digital media seem to refer to the established literature on the cyborg, perhaps because it seems no longer relevant. I would argue, however, that the very ubiquity and portability of new forms of digital technologies introduce potential ways of thinking about the digital device from the perspective of the cyborg body. By this, I do not mean the science-fiction version of the cyborg – that masculinised, aggressive sub-human exemplified by the figures of the Terminator or Robocop. Instead, I have developed the concept of the 'digital cyborg assemblage', which I see as a far more fluid and complex concept. The digital cyborg assemblage is the body that is enhanced, augmented or in other ways configured by its use of digital technologies that are worn, carried upon or inserted into the body, continually interacting with these technologies in dynamic ways. This concept draws upon Haraway's revision of her definition of the cyborg, in which she goes beyond the concept of the hybrid body to emphasise the need to highlight the ever-changing multiplicities of human embodiment and identities as they come into contact with nonhuman entities (Chapter 2).

We are more cyborgs than ever before, with our mobile and wearable technologies that many of us carry throughout our day, position close to our beds at night or even wear in bed, in the case of biometric self-tracking devices (see more on this below). We are both the literal and the metaphorical cyborgs outlined in Haraway's work. Indeed, our melding with our digital technologies, their incorporation into the envelopes of our bodies, has become so habituated that we no longer think of ourselves as cyborgs. Our bodies are literally constantly in physical contact with digital devices or rendered into digital formats via digital technologies. On the ontological level, our sense of self-hood and embodiment are implicated with digital technologies. We are entangled with the digital throughout our waking (and sometimes sleeping) hours. As digital devices become ever smaller and unobtrusive, their status as separate objects to our bodies/selves diminishes in importance. In the case of wearable computing, the devices are worn upon the body, as Google Glass, headbands, bracelets, clip-ons and jewellery. Some medical digital technologies are incorporated even more unobtrusively into the body, such as insulin pumps and ingestible tablets with microchips embedded into them that send out wireless signals from inside the body.

Such is the extent of our intimate relations with digital technologies that we often respond emotionally to the devices themselves and to the content contained within or created by these devices. The design of digital devices and software interfaces is highly important to users' responses to them. Devices such as iPhones are often described in highly affective and aestheticised terms: as 'beautiful' playthings, 'glossy and shiny' objects of desire, even as 'edible' or 'delicious'. Advertising for the iPhone and other Apple devices often focuses on inspiring child-like wonder at their beauty and magical capabilities (Cannon and Barker 2012). Affective responses to material objects are integral to their biographical meaning to their owners and their participation in intimate relationships. Writers on material culture and affect have noted the entangling of bodies/selves with physical objects and how artefacts act as extensions or prostheses of the body/self, becoming markers of personhood. Objects become invested with sentimental value by virtue of their association with specific people and places, and thus move from anonymous, mass-produced items to biographically inscribed artefacts that bear with them personal meanings. Over use and with time, such initially anonymised objects become personalised prosthetics of the self, their purely functional status and monetary value replaced by more personal and sentimental value (Miller 2008; Turkle 2007).

Two decades ago I and others were writing about the affective relationship that people had developed with their personal computers and their attempts to personalise and domesticate them. This scholarship identified the ways in which such objects are thought about, incorporated into selfhood and embodiment, their emotional meanings and resonances and their psychic investment in the self. My research in the 1990s demonstrated that personal computers were conceptualised as friends, work companions or even lovers, and were frequently given names or gender by their users. They were typically represented as anthropomorphic objects, as warm, soft and friendly, and, like humans, subject to birth and death, or to obesity or viral infection (Lupton 1995; Lupton and Noble 1997).

One decade ago, even before the advent of social media and the expansion in ubiquitous computing technologies, Bell (2004) was using the term 'intimate computing' to describe the ways in which digital technologies were acting as repositories of memories and intimate relationships and (via websites) means of communicating personal thoughts and beliefs to others online. She also commented on the use of devices as personal assistants or companions, helping users to manage and structure their everyday lives. Bell discussed the new closeness that users have with mobile devices and the emotional and personal resonances they have for many people. She commented further on the ways in which digital devices were becoming more 'knowing' about users and their lives as they collected intimate data about users and predicted tastes and preferences.

All of these dimensions have become intensified in the ensuing decade since Bell wrote that piece. The advent of devices which are easily portable, carried on or worn on the body suggests an even greater physical intimacy. Moreover, not only are such devices easily incorporated into bodily movement, they are connected to friendship and family networks via social media. Unlike the older unwieldy, desk-bound computers, people with mobile digital devices are able to be connected almost anywhere they travel, at any time of the day or night, and thus able to contact intimate others at any time or virtually anywhere. This ease of access and ability to track movement represent a pivotal change in the ways in which devices are incorporated into everyday life.

The boundaries between self and Other, human and machine, body and technology have become ever more blurred. Thus, in the latest advertising for the iPhone, the Apple website 'introduces' 'Siri', a feature embedded in the phone's technology that allows the user to 'converse' with the phone. Siri is described in the advertising as: 'The intelligent assistant that's there to help ... Siri understands what you say and knows what you mean'. The accompanying advertisement shows busy people engaging in various activities – jogging, driving, cooking – and talking to their phone, which replies to their queries with a personable and calm female voice. We are told to 'Talk to Siri as you would a person ... You're actually having a conversation with your iPhone'. These portrayals of the new iPhone's capabilities suggest a relationship with one's device that is not only embodied but affective, positioning the phone as the medium for a human-like personality who is able to respond to any request or demand while constantly remaining helpful and friendly.

Spike Jonze's film *Her* (2013) plays upon and extends this concept. The film combines science fiction with romantic comedy. In the film a lonely middle-aged man, Theodore Twombly, played by Joaquin Phoenix, develops a close relationship with the Siri-like female voice/personality emitting from his smartphone (played by Scarlett Johansson). Named Samantha, the voice of his computer operating system conveys intelligent insight and emotional warmth. Theodore develops a close relationship with Samantha to such an extent that he feels that he has fallen in love.

While we may not yet have reached this degree of intimacy with our devices or operating systems, there is no denying that those who use such technologies are increasingly coming to view them as extensions of their bodies. In Finland and Germany, mobile phones are referred to affectionately as 'little hands'; a telling linguistic choice that suggests their use as an additional part of the body (Paasonen 2009: 19). These devices touch our bodies and our bodies, in return, touch them, in many cases, for many hours a day. The devices rest upon our skin or we touch them ourselves, swiping, pressing and typing on keyboards as we interact with social media, make phone calls or write documents. The new iPhone 5s uses fingerprints instead of passwords, reacting directly to users' unique bodily configurations. As Balsamo (2012: 252) has remarked of her iPhone: 'Not merely an extension of my ear, as McLuhan would have argued, it is me. My body/myself – my iPhone/myself. I become the cyborg I always wanted to be'. Our bodies are shaped and moved in certain ways when we use digital devices: typing, swiping, holding, gazing. The design of the device constrains our physical actions, and our bodies, in turn, leave traces upon the device – sweat, body oils, food crumbs, signs of accidental damage when we drop or scratch the device.

BODIES/TECHNOLOGIES/SPACES

New ways of using and interacting with digital technologies have fundamentally changed the ways that we think about the 'space' of online interaction and experience. As a result, virtual reality is almost a nonsensical term in today's digitised world. The ubiquity and pervasive nature of computing, its entry into many spheres of everyday life and its portability have meant that nearly all 'reality' is now virtual, to the point that we no longer conceptualise it in these terms. Most digital technologies are continually connected to the internet, so we no longer go 'online' or 'offline'. Instead of 'entering cyberspace' from a specific location and using a formal means of connection to do so, we simply use our devices and check in on our emails and social media updates wherever we are located (Paasonen 2009).

New locative technologies mean that, far from entering cyberspace or virtual reality when we use digital devices, we are identified ever more obviously with the place and space we are physically inhabiting. Geo-locational software that locates the user and tailors the content to which the user has access (in some cases, blocking the user) has challenged the notion that cyberspace is non-geographical or placeless. It has become increasingly difficult for people to interact anonymously online and take on new identities. The internet now knows where you live. It also knows who you are, and many things about not only you but your friends and followers on your digital social networks (Rogers 2013).

Ubiquitous computing brings digital devices off the desktop and into public spaces that are already populated and inhabited with heterogeneous actors that may facilitate or detract from the connectivity of the device. This therefore raises the issues not only of the culturally inflected factors that influence digital infrastructures, but also of the spaces, both private and public, in which devices are used. Just as technologies are cultural configurations, so are spaces, and the interactions between the two are complex, unstable and dynamic (Dourish and Bell 2007). What Miller and Horst (2012: 25) describe as 'digital context' is also material: the places, spaces and people that are part of the environment in which digital technologies are used.

In addition to the participatory affordances of Web 2.0 technologies, the capabilities of 'smart' devices to be connected to the internet at any time and in almost any place and the presence of microchips in these devices that measure bodily movement and geo-location offer new ways to monitor and measure bodies and identify the spaces in and through which bodies travel. Kitchin and Dodge (2011) have formulated the concept of 'code/space', which represents the mutually constitutive nature of computer codes with spatiality. As they argue, in digital society spaces are increasingly designed and monitored with the use of computer software programs. Any space that is dependent on software to function as intended can be viewed as a code/space. They give the example of the contemporary supermarket, which is reliant upon the digital scanner and cash register for customers to purchase goods, and which produce data that then inform the supermarket what goods are popular and which require re-stocking. Through the use of customer loyalty cards operating through the digitised checkout system, the supermarket owners are able to monitor the purchasing habits of individuals. If this system crashes, the supermarket can no longer function as a supermarket. Human bodies (checkout operators, shelf stockers, supply truck drivers and customers) interact with the computerised programs to produce the coded assemblage (or alternatively the code/space) of the supermarket.

As a contemporary alternative to virtual reality the concept of 'augmented reality' has been proposed, in which it is acknowledged that everyday life is extended (augmented) by the use of technologies such as digital devices and software. There is no online or digital 'second self': the self configured through the digital is always already part of the self (Jurgenson 2012). Related to this term is that of 'augmented co-presence', which refers to the distributed nature of social relationships and physical locations on social media networks.

Using such features as geo-location details and images of the spaces in which they are located, social media users can establish a new sense of place that is a hybrid of physical and virtual co-presence (Hjorth and Pink 2014).

The use of digital devices also tends to blur spatial boundaries for their users. In combining a material object (the device such as the smartphone or tablet computer) with the information that flies between these objects and repositories such as digital archives and repositories, and also in connecting private spaces with public spaces (one may use the device at home but in doing so connect to others outside this domestic space), mobile media inhabit a liminal space (Beer 2012b; Schneider 2012). Smartphones such as the iPhone are supremely tactile and visual in their materiality, but also immaterial, thus blurring the boundaries as objects between the two. It is no longer possible to make definite distinctions between hardware and software. In such devices, touch, vision and immaterial objects of knowledge (digital data objects) are aligned (Schneider 2012). So too, the need to connect one's device to a broadband network when in public spaces and finding a strong enough signal bring together the visible with the invisible aspects of digital technologies, and avoiding encroaching on other users' wireless connections highlights 'the physicality of the virtual' (Dourish and Bell 2007: 424).

In engaging in locative media practices, users are able to inhabit one physical space while simultaneously engaging with others in other locations. They are establishing co-presences through practices that are social, mobile, locative and photographic all at the same time (Hjorth and Pink 2014). Using a mobile digital device, an individual may be located within a certain material space surrounded by other people ('present others'), but can 'exit' that space and relate to 'absent others' outside that space (Enriquez 2012: 60). A casual observation of the users of public transport demonstrates how digital devices are used in public spaces to enter private worlds. Enter any train or bus and many of one's fellow passengers can be seen using mobile digital devices to pass the time, often communicating with 'absent others' outside the physical space. Such use enables passengers to achieve private actions in public spaces and to evade interactions with the 'present others' sharing the material space (Enriquez 2012).

Recent research has focused on the new digital media technologies in investigating the embodied habitual practices of their use. For example, Pink and Leder Mackley (2013) used video ethnographies to explore the meaning of digital media as part of people's everyday sensory and affective embodied routines in their homes. They identified the ways in which these media contributed to concepts of the domestic setting 'feeling right' for the participants, or achieving the appropriate atmosphere and texture in their home surroundings. The researchers moved around participants' homes with their video cameras, recording the participants as they explained their domestic routines. They were particularly interested in the routines in which participants engaged in relation to energy use and conservation: practices such as switching off electronic technologies or plugging them in to recharge them each night, for example.

This research brings together three related analytical 'prisms' of behaviour in relation to digital media: environment/place, movement/practice and perception/sensory embodied experience. Based on their ethnographic research, Pink and Leder Mackley (2013) argue that people realise the extent to which their lives are saturated by digital and other media, but often this knowledge is embodied and affective rather than easily explained via the use of words (returning to the concept of the domestic space 'feeling right' at specific times of the day). By documenting with the use of ethnographic observation how people are engaging with media (so that the participants can demonstrate their practices rather than simply talk about them), such less obvious dimensions can be observed. People may 'feel right' if their radio alarm wakes them at the appropriate time each morning, if they watch television at the usual time and then switch it off before going to bed, if they check their emails and text messages on their smartphone last thing at night, and so on.

REPRESENTATIONS OF BODIES/SELVES ONLINE

People discuss and visually represent their (and others') bodies incessantly as part of using social media. The body is represented in ever finer detail on the types of digital networks and platforms that are now available for use. Social media sites such as YouTube, Tumblr, Pinterest, Instagram and Flickr focus on the uploading, curating and sharing of images, including many of bodies. Facebook and Twitter also provide opportunities for users to share images of bodies. Bodies receive much digital attention, particularly those of celebrities, but increasingly those of ordinary users. Female celebrities, in particular, are the subject of continual digital visualising by paparazzi and fans and constant commentary in social media and news sites on the appropriateness and attractiveness – or otherwise – of their bodies (Gorton and Garde-Hansen 2013).

Due to the plethora of online platforms and apps devoted to human anatomy, the internal organs and workings of the human body have moved from being exclusively the preserve of medical students and surgeons to being open to the gaze of all. Online technologies now allow anyone with access to a computer to view highly detailed visual images of the inside of the body. Although these images may have been produced for medical students and medical practitioners and other healthcare workers, they are readily available to the general public. Tapping in the search term 'human anatomy' will call up many apps on the Apple App Store and Google Play that provide such details. Many websites also provide graphic images of the human body. The Visual Human Project used computer technologies to represent in fine detail the anatomical structure of male and female cadavers. Each body was cross-sectioned transversely from head to toe and images of the sections of the bodies, using magnetic resonance imaging, computed tomography and anatomical images, were uploaded to a computer website and can also be viewed at the National Museum of Health and Medicine in Washington, DC.

All shapes and sizes of living human bodies are available for viewing online. Sites as diverse as those supporting people wishing to engage in self-starvation or purging (the so-called 'pro-ana' or 'thinspiration' sites), promoting cosmetic surgery, fat activists seeking to represent the fat body in positive ways that resist fat-shaming, those for people engaged in self-harming practices or body-building, for transgender people and tattoo or body-piercing devotees, not to mention the huge variety of sites devoted to pornography and sexual fetishes, all display images of a wide variety of body shapes and sizes and of bodies engaged in a multitude of practices that are both normative and go beyond the norm. In addition there are the sites that represent bodies undergoing various forms of medical procedures (there are many videos of surgery on YouTube), providing vivid images or descriptions of the ills and diseases from which bodies may suffer.

Social and other digital media have facilitated the sharing of images and descriptions of many varied forms of human life, from the very earliest stage of human development. A huge range of representations of embryos and foetuses, and indeed even the moment of fertilisation of a human ovum by a sperm cell, can be viewed on the internet. Such media as YouTube videos of conception and embryonic development and websites such as the Human Embryo Project featuring detailed images and descriptions of each stage of unborn development allow people to gaze upon and learn about the unborn human. Proud parents now routinely post obstetric ultrasound images of their unborn to social media sites to announce a pregnancy. Some parents who have experienced miscarriage, foetal loss or stillbirth use memorialisation websites or make videos to post on YouTube featuring ultrasound images, hand- or footprints of the dead unborn and even images of its dead body. As a result, via digital media the unborn human entity now receives a far greater degree of visibility than at any other time in the past (Lupton 2013a).

At the other end of the human lifespan, the dead are achieving a kind of online immortality. Just as with the online memorialisation of the dead unborn, a person's death can be announced and memorialised via a plethora of online media. A digital afterlife may be achieved using these technologies. For example, Facebook pages are now frequently used to memorialise people who have died. The dead person's own personal Facebook page may be used by others to communicate their feelings with each other about the person's death, or they may establish a dedicated Facebook Group to exchange thoughts and memories about that individual (Bollmer 2013; Brubaker *et al.* 2013).

Commercial websites have been established that provide 'afterlife online services', as one such website – the Digital Beyond – puts it, that help people 'plan for your digital death and afterlife or memorialize loved ones'. They encourage the bereaved to submit photos and stories about a dead person or provide an online site for people to store their own memorabilia about their lives or important documents in anticipation of their death, leave or send posthumous messages, plan their funerals and provide details of what should happen to their social media profiles after death. Such terms as 'digital estate' and 'digital assets' are used to denote important documents, images and other information that have been rendered into digital formats for storage and distribution following a person's death. Some services provide the facility for people to send email messages, images and audio or video recordings up to 60 years following their death. The LifeNaut platform allows people to create a 'mindfile': a personal archive of images, a timeline of their life, documents, places they have visited, and other information about themselves, as well as an avatar that will react and respond with their beliefs, attitudes and mannerisms. The company also provides a storage facility for preserving the individual's DNA material. All of these data are preserved for the benefit of future generations.

The increasingly digitised representation of people is highlighted in artist Adam Nash's collaborative art project Autoscopia. In this project the available online images for individuals are derived from web searches and configured into new, recombinant portraits of that individual (anyone can try it using their own name or any other person's name). These digitised portraits then enter into the internet via tweeted links, thus recursively feeding themselves back into the latest versions of the portraits. In this project, data-as-data (the digitised image data that are mined by the Autoscopia computer program from many parts of the internet) are remodulated for the purposes of the art project into a different type of image, one formed from many images.

This art project raises intriguing questions about the ways in which digital data forms can be configured and reconfigured (or in Nash's terms modulated and remodulated) that have implications more broadly for the power of digital data to configure embodiment. A digitised map, for example, demonstrating outbreaks of infectious diseases in certain geographical locations (as produced by the Health Map platform) is a modulation of various types of data that have been entered into the platform, whether from mining social media or by users themselves reporting their own illnesses. These visualisations are virtual body fragments, representing as they do various bodily sensations and signs reinterpreted as symptoms and mapped in geo-located form. Bodies themselves become represented as forms of disease in this mapping technology, their fleshly reality stripped down to their symptoms. Infectious diseases are also reinterpreted as digital objects via such technologies. They are constantly remodulated by new data inputs just as the digital portraits produced through the Autoscopia project continually reconstitute the 'reality' of an individual's visage.

Digital technology practices produce new and constantly changing forms of digitised cyborg assemblages. When engaging in digital technologies, bodies and selves become fragmented in certain ways as various types of data on our selves and our bodies are transmitted along specific pathways but then joined together in new formations (Enriquez 2012). Via these accumulations of data about individuals' bodies, the body is extended beyond the flesh into digital data archives. The data assemblages thus configured have separate, although intertwined, lives in relation to the fleshly bodies that they represent (Bollmer 2013).

The data assemblages that are configured from the diverse forms of data that are produced from our digital interactions are constantly shifting and changing as new data are added to them. Data doubles feed information back to the user in ways that are intended to encourage the user's body to act in certain ways. When individuals receive positive comments or likes from social media friends or followers on the images or information they post about their bodies, this may encourage them to continue in the enterprise of embodiment that they so publicised (whether this is a certain hairstyle, way of dress, use of cosmetics or fitness or weight-loss regime). If responses are negative or non-committal, users may represent their bodies or engage in different bodily practices in response. The flow of information, therefore, is not one-way or static: it is part of a continual loop of the production of bodily related data and response to these data. Digital data doubles support a reflexive, self-monitoring awareness of the body, bringing the body to the fore. They are part of the augmented reality of the digital cyborg assemblage.

SOCIAL MEDIA AND SELF-FORMATION

Previous chapters have identified the ways in which digitised watching takes place in ways that may be coercive, covert, discriminatory or exclusionary. When aspects of people's bodies and selves become increasingly subject to digitisation, the potential for ever more detailed veillance becomes evident. Indeed digitising the body/self may incorporate all of the forms of veillance outlined in Chapter 2. In the present discussion, however, I focus on voluntary watching practices as they are carried out in social media engagement and self-tracking strategies using digital devices. Many users of digital technologies voluntarily engage in practices of watching each other or monitoring themselves as part of social veillance and participatory veillance. There is always an implied audience for many forms of digital engagement, and most particularly the use of social media platforms. These practices of watching are often reciprocal: people expect others to observe and comment on their content and do the same for the people they follow or friend on social media networks (Marwick 2012).

I referred in Chapter 2 to the Foucauldian concept of the practices of the self, and noted that some digital media researchers have represented social media participation as new forms of such practices. Via social media, users engage in practices of ethical self-formation. Theresa Sauter (2013) locates the writing about the self that is part of Facebook status updates as the latest in a long history of such practices, from ancient Greek and Roman self-reflections to the Christian confessional writings, the autobiography of the Romantic era and the transgressive self-writing of the Enlightenment through to the modern tendency to interpret one's thoughts and experiences via psychoanalytic discourses and those emphasising the importance of openness and self-expression. The practices of self-formation that take place in social media sites are merely one way by which the modern individual engages in configuring selfhood. One feature of social media that differs from previous eras and technologies for self-writing and self-formation, however, is the potentially public nature of expressions of the self, the instantaneous responses from others that may eventuate and the permanent nature of any such content.

Some people view their content creation concerning their personal lives on sites such as Facebook as developing a 'personal brand'. This includes the images or descriptions about one's body that appear on such sites, and involves careful selection of these texts. Shaping one's persona can be a difficult enterprise in a context in which one's friends or followers may be from different areas of the user's life and may post content themselves that challenges the 'brand' the user wishes to present. Self-monitoring or self-censoring of the content one uploads is part of the presentation of the ideal body/self on social media. Users may have 'different online bodies' for different audiences or at different times of their lives, and juggling this can be a complex task, particularly when the Facebook Timeline feature preserves all their status updates in chronological order for any Facebook friend to review. This feature locks Facebook users into a particular narrative of their bodies that they may later regret or wish to change (Goodings and Tucker 2014). For some Facebook users, however, the Timeline feature provides a welcome record of their thoughts, appearance and interactions with others. As one Australian user commented: 'The visual diary aspect really appeals to me. The timeline aspect of Facebook is also very seductive. I used to keep a diary, but now I keep my diary in public and in a [computing] cloud' (quoted in Hjorth and Pink 2014: 49).

The shaping by the Facebook platform of the memories and past events recorded in individual users' profiles became particularly evident on the occasion of the platform's tenth anniversary in February 2014. Facebook members (at that point, more than a billion of them) were invited to access a personalised 'Look Back' compilation video, in which highlights of their most liked status updates and posted images since the time they first joined were selected and presented as a video set to music that members could share with their Facebook friends. The catch was that users had no control over what content was selected: it was all done for them by the Facebook algorithms, which chose 'personalised highlights' for each person who requested the video automatically.

The 'selfie' phenomenon (posting photographic self-portraits taken by oneself using a digital device) has become the archetypal representation of the body/self in online forums. The popularity of the selfie (at least among some social groups) demonstrates that some people enjoy the opportunity to shape their bodily image in online forums in ways that allow them full control of what the image looks like and where it will appear. It also represents the intensification of the digitisation of the bodies of 'ordinary' people in public forums. Many celebrities use the selfie as a self-promotional tool, as do world leaders and high-ranking politicians (for example, Barack Obama, the Clintons, David Cameron and Pope Francis), and people who take selfies are often accused of being narcissistic or vain. However, the selfie is also an everyday practice that often involves a mundane portrait taken to show others what that individual is doing at the time or to personalise a greeting or share an experience (Wortham 2013).

Taking and posting selfies is both an intensely personal practice as a means of representing the body/self on a popular social media image-sharing website and a communal practice that demonstrates cultural norms about who should engage in this practice and how they should present themselves. This is demonstrated by the Selfiecity website, developed as part of a research project led by Lev Manovich to investigate features of these self-portraits in different cultural and geographical locations. A random selection of thousands of selfies posted to Instagram from five cities in three continents – Bangkok, Berlin, Moscow, New York and São Paulo – is included in the project. The researchers used both data-mining and algorithmic software and human judgement (drawn from the Amazon Mechnical Turk labour force) to code elements of each image, such as age, gender, mood/emotional expression, eye, nose and mouth position and head tilting. Their findings reveal that more women than men in all cities take selfies, particularly in Moscow, more younger than older people post selfies to Instagram (median age 23 years) and that people smile in selfies more in Bangkok and São Paulo than in the other three cities.

While veillance technologies pre-existed the digital era, digitisation has resulted in new forms of participatory veillance. Social media sites afford users the opportunity to upload images such as selfies and textual information about themselves so that others can see and comment on these materials. The whole point of the types of self-reflection and self-formation that occur on these sites is to hold this content up to the scrutiny of others and to invite their responses. These devices and platforms cater to an increasing desire for scopophilia – the desire to be seen – in promoting sharing of information and observations about one's self (Lyon and Bauman 2013). Such activities and the resultant visibility to others can be enjoyed for the intimacy, playfulness and friendship they may create or support. When people want to share their data with others, others' watching becomes valued. These practices invite responses from other users (Bucher 2012; Marwick 2012). If other users like a Facebook status update or photo, favourite or retweet a tweet or read one's blog post, these are all measures of success as part of social media networks. Indeed lacking or losing visibility may be considered problematic for social media users, as this denotes lack of popularity, importance or interest in one's updates and other posts. In this context, 'visibility is a reward, not a punishment' (Bucher 2012: 1174).

As I observed earlier in this chapter, celebrities, including politicians and members of royalty, are subjected to intensive monitoring whenever they appear in public spaces (and sometimes in private domains), facilitated not only by the paparazzi profession but also by people wielding their mobile devices. Participatory, synoptic and sousveillance modes of watching operate here. Celebrities often voluntarily engage in social media as a means of promoting their 'brand', connecting with their fans, promoting a sense of intimacy and publicising news about their latest activities (Marwick and boyd 2011). Their number of Facebook friends or Twitter followers can be a marker of their global popularity (at the time of writing, Lady Gaga is competing with Justin Bieber for this measure of success and fame). Many politicians and world leaders have also employed social media sites as part of their attempts to bolster their support and disseminate news. Both President Obama and the Pope have Twitter accounts. (Obama's tweet announcing his re-election in 2012 is the second-most retweeted of all time.) Obama's success in his election and re-election campaigns has been attributed in no small measure to his campaign managers' judicious use of social media to garner electoral and financial support (Zavattaro 2010).

Famous people can exert a high degree of control over the content that they themselves generate and disseminate in social media. As objects of the gaze of others, however, they are also often under intense scrutiny as part of sousveillance and synoptic watching practices, and can attract high levels of criticism on social media forums (Marwick and boyd 2011). Mistakes or comments considered to be inappropriate that are made by well-known people on social media often 'go viral' and receive a heightened level of attention on social media sites which is then often picked up by news outlets and further disseminated as news. Visibility as a prized measure of popularity can often turn quickly into mass opprobrium and ridicule.

Users of social media sites may engage in practices of self-surveillance when deciding what content to post, so as to preserve or present a certain kind of desired selfhood and to preserve privacy (Goodings and Tucker 2014; Marwick 2012). Many users of social networking platforms are grappling with coming to terms with new ways of defining privacy in a context in which concepts of 'the public' and 'the private' are no longer confined to a spatial dimension. Notions of intimacy, solitude, the personal, the secret and the hidden are challenged by the confessional of social media sites such as Facebook and Twitter, in which participants' inner thoughts and private behaviours are often revealed to a large number of friends or followers, and frequently several times throughout the day. This phenomenon has been referred to as 'the privatization of the public and publicization of the private' (van Manen 2010: 1026).

Contemporary digital devices and software provide even greater capacity than ever to become part of people's personal biographies, given their ability to document and archive vast quantities of personal information about their users' lives. Taking selfies or photos of the places one is occupying can become a means of promoting sociability and bolstering relationships with others. This practice also bestows personal meaning upon places, adding social, emotional, psychological and aesthetic dimensions. New forms of intimacy are being created by the sharing of geo-location details and images (Hjorth and Pink 2014). Not only photos but personally written documents, social media status updates, favourite music, newspapers and books, lists of telephone numbers and email contacts and the like can all be stored on digital devices and their associated platforms.

I noted in Chapter 5 that such overtly anonymous features as search engine histories on one's digital device can be profoundly personal indicators of the searcher's habits, tastes, preferences, stage in the life cycle and social group membership (and indeed sexual proclivities if the user engages with online pornography or sexual chat sites). Balsamo (2012) similarly claims that in using her iPhone she leaves traces of herself; her self becomes an assemblage of her travels online. Her iPhone reflects herself back at herself in the data it provides on her tastes, opinions, social interactions, places she has visited (including material spaces as well as online sites), becoming 'my most intimate personal digital companion' (Balsamo 2012: 253).

Many of these personal details are now open to access by others on the internet. In the participatory and confessional culture of Web 2.0 prosumption, it has become common for people to talk about their lives in intimate detail, reveal aspects of their thoughts and behaviours that they might previously have kept to themselves, and to comment on others' revelations. The digital device may therefore be conceptualised as a 'gateway' or 'portal' into realms of personalised data and material, such as one's digital music collection or personal photographs (Beer 2008: 79). Beer (2012b: 366) further points out that, given the dual nature of mobile digital devices as both material objects and repositories of personal data, it can be difficult to distinguish which dimensions of the objects are creating an affective relationship. Is it the material object of the smartphone one holds in one's hand as one makes a call or sends a text to an intimate other, or the content of the call or text itself? In other words, do we love our phones as hardware or as portals to digital content or (more likely) some combination of both?

As an interview study of Australian young people who used digital technologies to collate their musical collection found, the 'immateriality' of digitised music files does not necessarily detract from the pleasure of maintaining such a collection or the role the collection plays in people's personal identities. Whether in traditional material form (such as a record, tape or CD) or purely digital, music collections can have strong affective and biographical meanings to their owners. Indeed the capacity for users to make personally curated playlists of their online collections to suit their mood or environment and to share their collections easily with others online, among the other affordances of digital music collection tools, may contribute considerably to the emotional, symbolic, social and personal meanings attributed to the music (Kibby 2009).

When platforms such as Facebook abruptly change their privacy settings or change the ways in which personal data are displayed or recorded, members may feel that their privacy has been violated, because information that previously was not emphasised may suddenly come to the fore (as happened in 2006 when Facebook introduced its 'News Feeds' feature). People who previously may have been comfortable with the ways in which their personal data were dealt with often respond to such changes by feeling confronted by new relationships between the public and the private (boyd 2008). The greater reliance one may have upon a particular technology, the more it is incorporated into everyday life, subjectivity and embodiment, the more one feels an emotional connection to it, the greater the potential for ambivalence (Lupton 1995). One study interviewing users of social media sites found that violations of privacy were common on such sites, particularly in relation to other users revealing personal details about the interviewee. The interviewees recounted such experiences as a boyfriend sharing detailed relationship information with a Facebook friend on their public wall, a confidante sharing sensitive financial information with a group of mutual friends and friends using an individual's Facebook page to gossip about her past experiences that she would rather have not made public. These breaches of privacy incited the emotions of distress, anger and shock from the individuals who had experienced them, particularly in response to friends or former partners betraying their trust (Houghton and Joinson 2010).

SELF-TRACKING AND QUANTIFYING THE SELF

Nowhere is the concept of self-imposed digital veillance more apparent than in the discourses and practices of self-tracking, life logging or quantifying the self. These concepts refer to the practice of gathering data about oneself on a regular basis and then recording and analysing the data to produce statistics and other data (such as images) relating to one's bodily functions and everyday habits. Some self-trackers collect data on only one or two dimensions of their lives, and only for a short time. Others may do so for hundreds of phenomena and for long periods. Such individuals often represent themselves as 'body hackers' or 'self-experimenters' who are using digital and other technologies to learn more about their bodies and their selves. People who engage in these practices often share the data they have collected about themselves on social media, but may also prefer to keep these data private or only share them with medical practitioners, care-givers or intimate others.

Like the practice of self-writing, the tracking and analysis of aspects of one's self and one's body are not new. People have been recording their habits and health-related metrics for centuries as part of attempts at self-reflection and self-improvement. What is indisputably new is the term 'the quantified self' and its associated movement, which includes a dedicated website with that title and regular meetings and conferences, as well as the novel ways of self-tracking using digital technologies that have developed in recent years. Several of the technologies of self-surveillance can be worn upon or carried upon the body. With their smartphones users can quickly and easily take a selfie or a photo of the food they are eating or the place they are visiting, or type in or dictate some comments on everyday experiences, and upload these to social media. Some life loggers wear tiny cameras that hang around their necks all day, automatically snapping hundreds of images. An array of 'smart objects' – for example, toothbrushes, ear buds, shoes, clothing, furniture and jewellery – are now becoming available for use that include sensors and microprocessors that can monitor and measure aspects of the self and the body.

The number and types of wearable digital devices are expanding quickly. In early 2014 it was estimated that there were 181 wearable devices currently on the market, divided into 43 for medical purposes, 86 for fitness, 13 for gaming, 10 for industrial purposes, 121 for life-style and 28 for entertainment (some devices falling into more than one category) (Vandrico Inc. 2014). Medical devices allow patients with chronic conditions to engage in self-monitoring at home, often sending data wirelessly to healthcare providers or care-givers. These and some fitness self-tracking devices also provide well people with the ability to monitor their own bodily functions such as physical activity, blood pressure, heart rate, body weight, blood glucose levels, brain activity and lung function. Some devices are able to pull together data from a number of sources. One of the latest is Sony's SmartBand SWR10, a digital life-logging wristband that is designed to be worn day and night. It connects to a smartphone wirelessly and also to Sony's Lifelog app, which enables the user to access other apps and platforms such as Facebook, and their phone to log such aspects as places visited, music listened to, people interacted with and games played as well as body biometrics such as sleep and exercise activities. It can notify the user of incoming phone calls and messages by vibrating, and connects to a camera so that users can log visual aspects of their day-to-day activities.

People engaged in various digital gaming and sporting activities can also use wearable devices to track their activities. Digital gaming technologies now frequently incorporate sensors that can monitor users' bodies. Digital headsets can be purchased for gaming purposes that detect electric signals in the wearer's brain. Nintendo's Wii gaming console involves a direct focus on engaging in fitness and sporting activities via the device. Wii Fit programs, which can detect and record body movements, allow for the recording, measuring and computing of physical activities and bodily features such as body weight, body mass index, body control, physical fitness indicators and balance. The latest versionof this game, Wii Fit Plus, allows for the development of customised exercise routines and for the intensity of the exercise and calories burned during exercise and one's 'Wii Fit Age' to be calculated. As such, this technology plays a dominant and overt role in configuring concepts of health, correct body weight and fitness levels, prescribing advice for improving and normalising these bodily dimensions (Miah and Rich 2008; Millington 2009).

While the terms 'the quantified self' and 'quantifying the self' first began as part of the official Quantified Self organisation and website, they have now spread more widely into popular culture to denote self-tracking practices more generally (Lupton 2013c). The concept of the practices of the self is again evident in the discourses on digital self-quantification or life logging. Generating detailed data about oneself using digital devices is represented as an undeniable good as part of the ethos of working upon the self. Part of engaging in data collection using self-tracking devices is the idea that the self-knowledge that will eventuate will allow users to exert greater control over their destinies. It is assumed that the data and the knowledge contained therein will help them achieve greater health, higher-quality sleep, greater control over mood swings, improved management of chronic conditions, less stress, increased work productivity, better relationships with others and so on (Lupton 2013c). The data that are collected from digital devices used for self-tracking are represented as offering certainty, while the body's perceptions were represented as untrustworthy, inexact, inaccurately mediated through human experience rather than being objective. In these representations, technology and the data it produces become portrayed as offering unique insights into the workings of the human body that individuals' unmediated haptic (physical) sensations cannot.

The valorising of data evident in discussions of the quantified self is itself part of the broader data–utopian discourse, particularly that discussing the benefits of big digital data. Unlike the apparently anonymous and mechanistically aggregated big digital data sets, the data produced by quantified selfers are frequently acknowledged to be human–made and customised, wrought from the personalised decisions and individual objectives of the people who gather the data. Quantified selfers work to produce their own data assemblages as an element of the project of selfhood. Part of what they seek to achieve is control over their data and the manner and extent to which they share their data with others, which the big data economy currently does not offer them.

These individuals have readily adopted the subject of the responsible, entrepreneurial citizen as it is privileged in neoliberal governmentality in seeking to take action to improve their lives and potential. Anthony Elliott (2013) argues that we are currently in an age of reinvention of the self and the body. The concept and practices of reinvention have become central to both private lives and organisations, and it is generally accepted that they are important endeavours. Reinvention is about transformation for the sake of personal growth, achievement, career success, health or wellbeing. Elliott (2013: 11) views the current focus on reinvention as part of a 'new individualism' that is particularly evident in developed countries. This new individualism involves concentrating on the self to the exclusion of social groups, organisations or communities. As part of the new individualism, self-reflection and critical self-examination are encouraged, viewed as ways of improving the self via therapeutic discourses and practices. Self-tracking practices are frequently represented as ways of achieving reinvention. They conform both to the notion of self-work and self-improvement that is part of the reinvention paradigm and to the new individualism in their focus on the self.

SEAMS IN THE CYBORG

Bell and Dourish (2011) refer to the mythologies and the mess of ubiquitous computing technologies. By myths they mean the cultural stories, values and meanings that are drawn upon to make sense of and represent these technologies. The types of myths surrounding new digital technologies tend to focus on their very novelty, their apparent divergence from what has come before them and their ability to provide solutions to problems. The mess of digital technologies inheres in the challenges to myths that suggest that they are infallible and offer an ideal solution to a problem: the 'practical reality' of their everyday use (Bell and Dourish 2011: 4). When digital technologies operate as we expect them to, they feel as if they are inextricably part of our bodies and selves. Inevitably, however, there are moments when we become aware of our dependence on technologies, or find them annoying or difficult to use, or lose interest in them. Technologies break down, fail to work as expected; infrastructure and government regulations may not support them adequately; users may become bored with using them or their bodies may rebel and develop overuse symptoms. There may be resistances, personal or organised, to their use, and contestations over their meanings and value (Lupton 1995; Miller and Horst 2012).

Freund (2004: 273) uses the term 'technological habitus' to describe the 'internalised control' and kinds of consciousness required of individuals to function in technological environments such as those currently offered in contemporary Western societies. The human/machine entity, he argues, is not seamless: rather there are disjunctions – or, as he puts it, 'seams in the cyborg' – where fleshly body and machine do not intermesh smoothly, and discomfort, stress or disempowerment may result. Sleep patterns, increasing work and commuting time and a decrease in leisure time, for example, can be disrupted by the use of technologies, causing illness, stress and fatigue. Our bodies may begin to alert us that these objects are material in the ways that they affect our embodiment: through eye-strain, hand, neck or back pain or headaches from using the devices too much (Lupton 1995).

People may feel overwhelmed by the sheer mass of data conveyed by their digital devices and the need to keep up with social network updates. Analyses of social media platforms such as Facebook are beginning to appear that suggest that users may simultaneously recognise their dependence upon social media to maintain their social network but may also resent this dependence and the time that is taken up in engaging with them, even fearing that they may be 'addicted' to their use (Davis 2012). Users may also feel 'invaded' by the sheer overload of data that may be generated by membership of social networking sites and the difficulty of switching off mobile devices and taking time out from using them (boyd 2008).

Technology developers are constantly working on ways to incorporate digital devices into embodiment and everyday life, to render them ever less obtrusive and ever more part of our bodies and selves. As the technical lead and manager of the Google Glass (a wearable device that is worn on the face like spectacles) project contends, 'bringing technology and computing *closer* to the body can actually improve communication and attention – allowing technology to get *further* out of the way' (Starner 2013; emphasis in the original). He asserts that by rendering these devices smaller and more easily worn on the body, they recede further into the background rather than dominating users' attention (as is so overtly the case with the current popular smartphone and tablet computers). Despite these efforts, Glass wearers have been subjected to constant attention from others that is often negative and based on the presumption that the device is too obvious, unstylish and unattractive, or that the people who wear them are wealthy computer nerds who do not respect the privacy of others. They have reported many incidences of angry responses from others when wearing Glass in public, even to the point of people ripping the device off their faces or asking them to leave a venue (Gross 2014). The design of digital devices, therefore, may incite emotional responses not only in the users themselves but also in onlookers.

Some people find wearable self-tracking devices not fashionable enough, or not waterproof enough, or too clunky or heavy, or not comfortable enough to wear, or find that they get destroyed in the washing machine when the user forgets to remove them from their clothing. One designer (Darmour 2013) has argued that if these technologies remain too obvious, 'bolting' these devices to our bodies will 'distract, disrupt, and ultimately disengage us from others, ultimately degrading our human experience'. She asserts that instead these objects need to be designed more carefully so that they may be integrated into the 'fabric of our lives'. Her suggested ways of doing this include making them look more beautiful, like jewellery (brooches, necklaces, bracelets, rings), incorporating them into fashionable garments, making them peripheral and making them meaningful: using colours or vibrations rather than numbers to display data readings from these devices.

Creative and physical labour is also an integral dimension of the materiality of human–technology enactments. I referred in Chapter 2 to the intellectual and creative labour involved in prosumption, and noted that this largely unpaid labour is provided as part of the ideals of the sharing subject and participatory democracy. While prosumers are not paid for this labour, the developers of the platforms to which they uploaded their content often profit handsomely from the data that are created. While prosumption is largely unpaid, paid workers who bid for freelance work on online platforms such as Amazon's Mechanical Turk and Freelancer.com are provided with very low recompense for their work, experience job insecurity and are granted none of the benefits offered by most other workplaces (Philip *et al.* 2012; Scholz 2013).

People also labour physically as part of the digital knowledge economy. There is a massive digital labour force involved in the physical production of digital devices: Apple alone employs half a million in their factories in two cities in China. These workers are paid, but not very well, and often work in conditions that are poor and exploitative. Many of the workers involved in the manufacture of digital technologies are physically affected by their manual labour. As discussed earlier, digital infrastructures such as servers, hard drives and data storage systems are material objects located in geographical spaces, and require continuing maintenance from human actors. For those who labour in mines to produce the minerals required and factories to make digital technologies, often in suboptimal conditions where they may be exposed to noxious chemicals, the materiality of the digital is omnipresent (Parikka 2013; Philip *et al.* 2012).

Various large, wealthy computer manufacturers have been accused of exploiting the workers in their Chinese factories. It has been claimed that these companies have suppressed or resisted attempts by workers to join trade unions, provide poor pay, force workers to labour for long hours and face continual economic insecurity and flout human rights. Workers are subjected to exhausting, repetitive work and exposure to chemicals, provided with cramped and crowded living conditions in the dormitories in which they are housed, and given inadequate safety protection. Some companies have been charged with using child labour in their factories. News reports of suicides by workers in some of these Chinese factories, including young workers producing Apple iPads, have drawn attention to the sub-standard conditions endured by these workers (Chamberlain 2011; Chen 2013).

As Parikka (2013) observes, for all the focus on the lightness and mobility of contemporary digital devices, their 'hardness', or the conditions in which many such devices are built, is obscured. He argues that there is a 'geopolitics of hardware', in which the working conditions of those who labour in mines and factories to make digital devices for people living in more advantaged regions are often removed from the sight of those who see only the gleaming, polished final products. Bodies produce these machines, and sometimes suffer for it; these bodies 'register the materiality of information technology production – and discarding – in lungs, brains, nervous systems, and more. They are indeed inscription systems for the "persistence of hardware"' (Parikka 2013). These observations demonstrate the dual meaning of hardware, both as tangible, touchable devices and as the products of hard labour on the part of those who make them.

I have argued in this chapter that digital devices and their associated software and platforms have become incorporated into the ontology and practices of embodiment and selfhood. There are four main dimensions to the ways in which human embodiment is enacted via the digital. First, human bodies are portrayed by digital media technologies using visual images and verbal descriptions: in medical surgeries, on websites, social media platforms, apps and news sites. Second, people touch and view digital devices and carry or wear them on their bodies. Third, the movements and activities of human bodies are monitored and tracked using digital devices that are able to upload data continuously to apps and platforms, including technologies that can locate bodies in space using global positioning systems, sense movements using embedded accelerometers and gyroscopes and collect detailed biometric data. And, fourth, human bodies manufacture digital devices and digital data through their intellectual and physical labour.

CHAPTER 9

Conclusion

I end with a brief summary of the main points of this book.

Why should sociologists be interested in theorising and researching digital technologies?

- Digital technologies are increasingly an integral part of everyday life for many people across the lifespan, whether or not they are aware of – or consent to – this.
- Social life is configured through and with digital technologies.
- Digital technologies are increasingly playing a major role in configuring concepts of selfhood, social relationships, embodiment, human–nonhuman relations and space and place.
- What counts as 'the social' is increasingly enacted via digital technologies.
- Digital technology use and practice are structured through social categories such as gender, social class, geographical location, education, race/ethnicity and age.
- Digital technologies are integral parts of contemporary social networks and social institutions such as the family, the workplace, the education system, the healthcare system, the mass media and the economy.
- Digital technologies offer alternative ways of practising sociology.
- Digital technologies are important both to 'public sociology' (engaging with people outside of academia) and 'private sociology' (personal identities and practices as sociologists).

Important insights that have been generated by sociologists of the digital include the following:

- Digital technologies and digital data objects are sociocultural artefacts.
- Digital technologies and digital data objects are shared accomplishments between human and nonhuman actors.
- Digital technologies have generated a new knowledge economy in which thought has become reified, public and commodified.
- Digital data objects have a social life of their own outside the archive, circulating in diverse forums and taking on new forms and value.
- Digital technologies have created new political relationships and power relations.
- Users of digital technologies are increasingly observers and documenters of their own lives, both consuming and creating digital data.
- People are constituted as dynamic digital data assemblages via their interactions with digital technologies.
- New forms of social research devices are generated by digital technologies.
- Digital technologies configure new forms of veillance.
- Digital media technologies can contribute to innovative ways of conducting sociology, generating a vision of a different kind of sociological sensibility.

I began this book with reference to contentions by some sociologists that big digital data sets and the increasingly distributed nature of social research among a diverse range of actors challenge sociologists' role as pre-eminent social researchers. I argue that rather than sociology being threatened by these changes, new opportunities have been generated to demonstrate that sociologists can offer valuable skills and insights and expand their authority in social research. Sociologists may not hold a monopoly over collecting and analysing data, but they are highly trained in maintaining a critical distance from simplistic assumptions about the benefits of digital technologies and the data they accumulate. Sociologists are able to stand back and take a provocative approach by identifying and asking difficult questions. In the face of those promoting ever-more detailed analysis of ever-greater data sets, a perspective that is able to both reflect on the social implications of big data and give meaning to these data is vital.

As the points above demonstrate, the new field of digital sociology goes well beyond an examination of the digital. It raises questions about what should be the focus and methods of contemporary sociological research and theorising. As such, sociologists writing about digital technologies are important contributors to debates about the future of sociology and how the discipline can remain vibrant, creative and responsive to new developments and social change.

DISCUSSION QUESTIONS

- What do big data offer society? What are the limitations and ethical considerations of big data? What are the implications for sociologists of the big data phenomenon?
- How would a Marxist/political economy perspective on prosumption compare with a Foucauldian perspective? What are the differences in the ways each theoretical position interprets prosumption? Are there any overlaps in these two perspectives' interpretations?
- List the manifold ways in which an individual might be tracked by digital veillance technologies in the course of an average day. What devices might this person use? What data might be collected about this person? How can this person know what data are being collected? To what extent can this person reject or resist these practices of dataveillance?
- Make a list of the positive and negative aspects of the various forms of digital veillance. What benefits can each provide to individuals or society? What are their potential limitations or harmful implications for individuals or specific social groups?
- How have concepts of privacy changed in response to digital technologies and dataveillance? What might the future of concepts of privacy look like? Do we need to rethink privacy in the digital age?
- In what ways might algorithms be said to possess power or authority? Give some examples of how this power/authority operates.
- In what ways might digital technologies and digital data objects be considered immaterial and in what ways are they material artefacts?
- Choose one digital media practice and discuss the ways in which it contributes to concepts of the self, the body or social group membership (e.g. 'selfies', self-tracking devices, blogging, tweeting, Facebook membership, online gaming, making videos for YouTube).
- What can digital sociology offer to the discipline of sociology? In what ways might it be unable to contribute to the discipline? What are its strengths and deficits?

APPENDIX: DETAILS OF THE 'ACADEMICS' USE OF SOCIAL MEDIA' SURVEY

I utilised the commonly used online survey tool SurveyMonkey to construct a brief questionnaire about academics' use of social media. The survey included both fixed-choice questions and open-ended questions that allowed respondents to write in their answers. The survey was opened on 1 January 2014 and closed after four weeks. I publicised it several times during this period, using a variety of social media, including Twitter, Facebook pages, LinkedIn and listservs of which I was a member. My tweets publicising the survey generated a high number of retweets, and although I cannot be sure how the respondents who completed the survey came across it, I would estimate that many did so via Twitter networks.

The survey was non-representative, relying on volunteers who heard about it through social media networks and then chose to complete it, rather than using probability sampling. Given this method of recruitment, there is a strong probability that the academics who responded were more likely to use social media for professional purposes than the general population of academics and were more favourably disposed towards such use than a randomly selected, representative sample. My findings, therefore, are not generalisable to the population of academics as a whole. They do, however, provide some interesting insights into what academics find useful, interesting, challenging or confronting about using social media in their work in higher education. This is especially true of the responses given to the open-ended questions.

A total of 711 academics completed the survey, two-thirds of whom were women. In terms of geographical region, the largest response was from the UK (37 per cent), followed by Australia/New Zealand (25 per cent), the US (20 per cent), continental Europe (10 per cent) and Canada (5 per cent). The remaining 3 per cent of respondents were from Ireland, the Caribbean and countries in Africa, Asia and South America. Most of the respondents were relatively junior in terms of their career stage: 33 per cent were early career academics and 27 per cent were postgraduate students. Mid-career academics comprised 24 per cent of the respondents, while only 15 per cent described themselves as senior academics and 1 per cent as retired or emeritus academics. Almost half of the respondents (47 per cent) were in the social sciences; 19 per cent were in medicine, public health or allied health areas; 16 per cent were in the humanities; and 12 per cent were in science, technology or engineering. The remaining 6 per cent were in education, commerce, the creative and performing arts, law, library science and archaeology, or described themselves as 'multidisciplinary'.

The full report can be found at www.canberra.edu.au/faculties/arts-design/attachments/pdf/n-and-mrc/feeling-better-connected-report-final.pdf.

BIBLIOGRAPHY

Ackerman, L. (2013) *Mobile Health and Fitness Applications and Information Privacy*. San Diego, CA: Privacy Rights Clearing House.

Ackland, R. (2013) *Web Social Science: Concepts, Data and Tools for Social Scientists in the Digital Age*. London: Sage.

Adams, S. (2011) Sourcing the crowd for health services improvement: the reflexive patient and 'share-your-experience' websites. *Social Science & Medicine*, 72 (7), 1069–1076.

Adema, J. (2013) Practise what you preach: engaging in humanities research through critical praxis. *International Journal of Cultural Studies*, 16 (5), 491–505.

Adkins, L. and Lury, C. (2011) Introduction: special measures. *The Sociological Review*, 59 (S2), 5–23.

Ahrens, J. (2013) Between 'me-time' and household duty: male and female home internet use. *Media International Australia*, 146, 60–68.

Aipperspach, R., Rattenbury, T., Woodruff, A., Anderson, K., Canny, J. and Aoki, P. (2006) Ethno-mining: integrating numbers and words from the ground up. Technical report, Department Electrical Engineering and Computer Sciences, University of California, Berkeley.

Ajana, B. (2013) *Governing through Biometrics: The Biopolitics of Identity*. Basingstoke: Palgrave Macmillan.

Allen, M. (2013) What was Web 2.0? Versions as the dominant mode of internet history. *New Media & Society*, 15 (2), 260–275.

American Association of University Professors (2013) *Academic Freedom and Electronic Communications Draft Report*. Accessed 30 May 2014. Available from http://www.aaup.org/report/academic-freedom-and-electronic-communications-2014

Anderson, K., Nafus, D., Rattenbury, T. and Aipperspach, R. (2009). Numbers have qualities too: experiences with ethno-mining. *Ethnographic Praxis in Industry Conference Proceedings*, 123–140.

Andrejevic, M. (2013) *Infoglut: How too Much Information is Changing the Way We Think and Know*. New York: Routledge.

Angwin, J. (2014) How I quit Google. *Time*. Accessed 27 February 2014. Available from http://ideas.time.com/2014/02/24/how-i-quit-google/?iid=ent-article-mostpop2

Angwin, J. and Valentino-Devries, J. (2012) New tracking frontier: your license plates. *Wall Street Journal*. Accessed 19 March 2014. Available from http://online. wsj.com/news/articles/SB10000872396390443995604578004723603576296

Anonymous (2013) Why marketers should care about the quantified self. *Ad Age*. Accessed 9 December 2013. Available from http://adage.com/article/glossary-data-defined/marketers-care-quantified/243840

Anonymous (2014) Power to the people (editorial). *Nature*, 261. Accessed 18 March 2014. Available from http://www.nature.com/news/power-to-the-people-1.14505?WT.ec_id–ATURE-20140116

Aslinger, B. and Huntemann, N. (2013) Digital media studies futures. *Media, Culture & Society*, 35 (1), 9–12.

Avaaz.org (2014) *2014 Vienna Declaration on Freedom of Information and Expression*. Accessed 5 April 2014. Available from https://secure.avaaz.org/en/petition/ The_2014_Vienna_Declaration_on_Freedom_of_Information_and_Expression_Petition/

Back, L. (2012) Live sociology: social research and its futures. *The Sociological Review*, 60 (S1), 18–39.

Back, L. and Puwar, N. (2012) A manifesto for live methods: provocations and capacities. *The Sociological Review*, 60 (S1), 6–17.

Bailey, J., Steeves, V., Burkell, J. and Regan, P. (2013) Negotiating with gender stereotypes on social networking sites: from 'bicycle face' to Facebook. *Journal of Communication Inquiry*, 37 (2), 91–112.

Ball, J. (2014) Angry Birds and 'leaky' phone apps targeted by NSA and GCHQ for user data. *Guardian*. Accessed 26 February 2014. Available from http://www. theguardian.com/world/2014/jan/27/nsa-gchq-smartphone-app-angry-birds-personal-data

Ball, K. and Murakami Wood, D. (2013) Political economies of surveillance. *Surveillance & Society*, 11 (1/2), 1–3.

Balsamo, A. (2012) I phone, I learn. In P. Snickars and P. Vonderau (eds) *Moving Data: The iPhone and the Future of Media*. New York: Columbia University Press, 251–264.

Barbour, K. and Marshall, D. (2012) The academic online: constructing persona through the World Wide Web. *First Monday*, 9. Accessed 27 September 2013. Available from http://firstmonday.org/ojs/index.php/fm/article/view/3969/3292

Barrett, M., Humblet, O., Hiatt, R. and Adler, N. (2013) Big data and disease prevention: from quantified self to quantified communities. *Big Data*, 1 (3), 168–175.

Bates, J. (2012) 'This is what modern deregulation looks like': co-option and contestation in the shaping of the UK's Open Government Data initiative. *Journal of Community Informatics*, 2. Accessed 16 November 2012. Available from http:// ci-journal.net/index.php/ciej/article/view/845/916

Baym, N. (2013) Data not seen: the uses and shortcomings of social media metrics. *First Monday*, 10. Accessed 8 October 2013. Available from http://firstmonday. org/ojs/index.php/fm/article/view/4873/3752

Beard, M. (2013) Internet fury: or having your online anatomy dissected online. *The Times Literary Supplement.* Accessed 3 August 2013. Available from http://times-online.typepad.com/dons_life/2013/01/internet-fury.html#more

Beer, D. (2008) The iconic interface and the veneer of simplicity: MP3 players and the reconfiguration of music collecting and reproduction practices in the digital age. *Information, Communication & Society*, 11 (1), 71–88.

Beer, D. (2009) Power through the algorithm? Participatory web cultures and the technological unconscious. *New Media & Society*, 11 (6), 985–1002.

Beer, D. (2012a) Open access and academic publishing: some lessons from music culture. *Political Geography*, 31 (8), 479–480.

Beer, D. (2012b) The comfort of mobile media: uncovering personal attachments with everyday devices. *Convergence*, 18 (4), 361–367.

Beer, D. (2012c) Using social media aggregators to do social research. *Sociological Research Online*, 3. Accessed 12 February 2013. Available from http://www.socresonline.org.uk/17/3/10.html

Beer, D. (2013a) *Popular Culture and New Media: The Politics of Circulation.* Houndmills: Palgrave Macmillan.

Beer, D. (2013b) Public geography and the politics of circulation. *Dialogues in Human Geography*, 3 (1), 92–95.

Beer, D. (2014) *Punk Sociology.* Houndmills: Palgrave Macmillan.

Beer, D. and Burrows, R. (2010) Consumption, prosumption and participatory web cultures: an introduction. *Journal of Consumer Culture*, 10 (1), 3–12.

Beer, D. and Burrows, R. (2013) Popular culture, digital archives and the new social life of data. *Theory, Culture & Society*, 30 (4), 47–71.

Beer, D. and Taylor, M. (2013) The hidden dimensions of the musical field and the potential of the new social data. *Sociological Research Online*, 2. Accessed 3 January 2014. Available from http://www.socresonline.org.uk/18/2/14.html

Bell, D. (2007) Cybercultures rewriter. In D. Bell and B. Kennedy (eds) *The Cybercultures Reader.* London: Routledge, 1–9.

Bell, D. and Kennedy, B. (eds) (2000) *The Cybercultures Reader.* London: Routledge.

Bell, G. (2004) Intimate computing? *IEEE Internet Computing*, 8 (6), 91–93.

Bell, G. (2006a) 'Satu keluarga, satu komputer' (one home, one computer): cultural accounts of ICTs in South and Southeast Asia. *Design Issues*, 22 (2), 35–55.

Bell, G. (2006b) The age of the thumb: a cultural reading of mobile technologies from Asia. *Philosophy & Technology*, 19 (2), 41.

Bell, G. (2011) Life, death, and the iPad: cultural symbols and Steve Jobs. *Communications of the ACM*, 54 (12), 24–25.

Bell, G. and Dourish, P. (2007) Yesterday's tomorrows: notes on ubiquitous computing's dominant vision. *Personal and Ubiquitous Computing*, 11 (2), 133–143.

Bell, G. and Dourish, P. (2011) *Divining a Digital Future: Mess and Mythology in Ubiquitous Computing.* Cambridge, MA: The MIT Press.

Best, K. (2010) Living in the control society: surveillance, users and digital screen technologies. *International Journal of Cultural Studies*, 13 (1), 5–24.

Bird, S.E. (2011) Are we all produsers now? *Cultural Studies*, 25 (4/5), 502–516.

Biressi, A. and Nunn, H. (2003) Video justice: crimes of violence in social/media space. *Space and Culture*, 6 (3), 276–291.

Boase, J. (2013) Implications of software-based mobile media for social research. *Mobile Media & Communication*, 1 (1), 57–62.

Bobkowski, P. and Smith, J. (2013) Social media divide: characteristics of emerging adults who do not use social network websites. *Media, Culture & Society*, 35 (6), 771–781.

Boehner, K., Gaver, W. and Boucher, A. (2012) Probes. In C. Lury and N. Wakeford (eds) *Inventive Methods: The Happening of the Social*. London: Routledge, 185–201.

Boellstorff, T. (2013) Making big data, in theory. *First Monday*, 10. Accessed 8 October 2013. Available from http://firstmonday.org/ojs/index.php/fm/article/view/4869/3750

Bollmer, G. (2013) Millions now living will never die: cultural anxieties about the afterlife of information. *The Information Society*, 29 (3), 142–151.

Bossewitch, J. and Sinnreich, A. (2013) The end of forgetting: strategic agency beyond the panopticon. *New Media & Society*, 15 (2), 224–242.

boyd, d. (2008) Facebook's privacy trainwreck: exposure, invasion, and social convergence. *Convergence*, 14 (1), 13–20.

boyd, d. (2012) Networked privacy. *Surveillance & Society*, 10 (3/4), 348–350.

boyd, d. and Crawford, K. (2012) Critical questions for big data: provocations for a cultural, technological, and scholarly phenomenon. *Information, Communication & Society*, 15 (5), 662–679.

Bracetti, A. (2012) The 10 most racist smartphone apps ever created. *Complex Tech*. Accessed 18 January 2012. Available from http://www.complex.com/tech/2012/01/the-10-most-racist-smartphone-apps-ever-created#1

Breslow, H. and Mousoutzanis, A. (2012) Introduction. In H. Breslow and A. Mousoutzanis (eds) *Cybercultures: Mediations of Community, Culture, Politics*. Amsterdam: Rodopi, vii–xx.

Breur, T. (2011) Data analysis across various media: data fusion, direct marketing, clickstream data and social media. *Journal of Direct, Data and Digital Marketing Practice*, 13 (2), 95.

Brignall, T. (2002) The new panopticon: the internet viewed as a structure of social control. *Theory and Science*, 1. Accessed 15 January 2014. Available from http://theoryandscience.icaap.org/content/vol003.001/brignall.html

Brophy, J. (2010) Developing a corporeal cyberfeminism: beyond cyberutopia. *New Media & Society*, 12 (6), 929–945.

Brubaker, J., Hayes, G. and Dourish, P. (2013) Beyond the grave: Facebook as a site for the expansion of death and mourning. *The Information Society*, 29 (3), 152–163.

Bruns, A. (2012) How long is a tweet? Mapping dynamic conversation networks on Twitter using Gawk and Gephi. *Information, Communication & Society*, 15 (9), 1323.

Bruns, A. (2013) Faster than the speed of print: reconciling 'big data' social media analysis and academic scholarship. *First Monday*, 10. Accessed 27 October 2013. Available from http://firstmonday.org/ojs/index.php/fm/article/view/4879/3756

Bruns, A., Highfield, T. and Burgess, J. (2013) The Arab Spring and social media audiences: English and Arabic Twitter users and their networks. *American Behavioral Scientist*, 57 (7), 871–898.

Bucher, T. (2012) Want to be on the top? Algorithmic power and the threat of invisibility on Facebook. *New Media & Society*, 14 (7), 1164–1180.

Bunge, J. (2014) Big data comes to the farm, sowing mistrust. *Wall Street Journal*. Accessed 17 March 2014. Available from http://online.wsj.com/news/articles/SB10001424052702304450904579369283869192124

Burawoy, M. (2005) For public sociology. *American Sociological Review*, 70 (1), 4–28.

Burgess, J. and Bruns, A. (2012) Twitter archives and the challenges of 'big social data' for media and communication research. *M/C Journal*, 5. Accessed 27 October 2013. Available from http://journal.media-culture.org.au/index.php/mcjournal/article/viewArticle/561

Burrows, R. (2012) Living with the h-index? Metric assemblages in the contemporary academy. *The Sociological Review*, 60 (2), 355–372.

Butler, P. (2012) How the Spartacus welfare cuts campaign went viral. *Guardian*. Accessed 18 January 2012. Available from http://www.theguardian.com/society/2012/jan/17/disability-spartacus-welfare-cuts-campaign-viral?guni=Article

Byrne, D. (2013) 419 digilantes and the frontier of radical justice online. *Radical History Review*, 2013 (117), 70–82.

Cammaerts, B. (2013) Networked resistance: the case of WikiLeaks. *Journal of Computer-Mediated Communication*, 18 (4), 420–436.

Cannon, K. and Barker, J. (2012) Hard candy. In P. Snickars and P. Vonderau (eds) *Moving Data: The iPhone and the Future of Medicine*. New York: Columbia University Press, 73–88.

Caplan, P. (2013) Software tunnels through the rags 'n refuse: object oriented software studes and platform politics. *Culture Machine*. Accessed 8 August 2013. Available from http://www.culturemachine.net/index.php/cm/issue/current

Carrigan, M. (2013) Continuous publishing and being an open-source academic. Digital Sociology. Accessed 22 December 2013. Available from http://digitalsociology.org.uk/?paged=2

Casilli, A. (2012) By leveraging social media for impact, academics can create broader support for our intellectual work and profession. LSE Impact of the Social Sciences. Accessed 25 January 2012. Available from http://blogs.lse.ac.uk/impactofsocialsciences/2012/01/25/leveraging-social-media-impact

Castells, M. (2000a) Materials for an exploratory theory of the network society. *British Journal of Sociology*, 51 (1), 5–24.

Castells, M. (2000b) *The Rise of the Network Society.* Vol. 1. Malden, MA: Blackwell.

Castells, M. (2012) *Networks of Outrage and Hope: Social Movements in the Internet Age.* New York: Wiley.

Center for Media Justice, ColorOfChange, Sum of Us (2013) *Consumers, Big Data, and Online Tracking in the Retail Industry: A Case Study of Walmart.* Accessed 18 May 2014. Available from http://centerformediajustice.org/wp-content/files/WALMART_PRIVACY_.pdf

Chamberlain, G. (2011) Apple factories accused of exploiting Chinese workers. *Guardian.* Accessed 27 March 2014. Available from http://www.theguardian.com/technology/2011/apr/30/apple-chinese-factory-workers-suicides-humiliation

Chapman, S. (2012) Hate mail and cyber trolls: the view from inside public health. *The Conversation.* Accessed 3 August 2013. Available from https://theconversation.com/hate-mail-and-cyber-trolls-the-view-from-inside-public-health-9329

Chen, M. (2013) Exploitation remains the name of the game at Dell's Chinese factories. *The World Post.* Accessed 27 March 2014. Available from http://www.huffingtonpost.com/michelle-chen/exploitation-remains_b_4243246.html

Cheney-Lippold, J. (2011) A new algorithmic identity: soft biopolitics and the modulation of control. *Theory, Culture & Society*, 28 (6), 164–181.

Christie, M. and Verran, H. (2013) Digital lives in postcolonial Aboriginal Australia. *Journal of Material Culture*, 18 (3), 299–317.

Citron, D.K. (2009) Law's expressive value in combating cyber gender harassment. *Michigan Law Review*, 108 (3), 373–415.

Citron, D.K. and Norton, H. (2011) Intermediaries and hate speech: fostering digital citizenship for our information age. *Boston University Law Review*, 91 (4), 1435–1484.

Colbert, A. (2012) 7 fake Hurricane Sandy photos you're sharing on social media. Mashable. Accessed 30 October 2012. Available from http://mashable.com/2012/10/29/fake-hurricane-sandy-photos

Copeland, P., Romano, R., Zhang, T., Hecht, G., Zigmond, D. and Stefansen, C. (2013) *Google Disease Trends: An Update.* Accessed 22 February 2014. Available from http://static.googleusercontent.com/external_content/untrusted_dlcp/research.google.com/en/us/pubs/archive/41763.pdf

Cottom McMillan, T. (2012) Risk and ethics in public scholarship. University of Venus. Accessed 4 August 2013. Available from http://www.insidehighered.com/blogs/university-venus/risk-and-ethics-public-scholarship

Cozza, M. (2011) Bridging gender gaps, networking in computer science. *Gender, Technology and Development*, 15 (2), 319–337.

Crawford, K. (2014) When big data marketing becomes stalking. *Scientific American.* Accessed 19 March 2014. Available from http://www.scientificamerican.com/article/when-big-data-marketing-becomes-stalking

Crawford, K. and Schultz, J. (2014) Big data and due process: toward a framework to redress predictive privacy harms. *Boston College Law Review*, 55 (1), 93–128.

Curran, G. and Gibson, M. (2013) WikiLeaks, anarchism and technologies of dissent. *Antipode*, 45 (2), 294–314.

Daniels, J. (2009a) Cloaked websites: propaganda, cyber-racism and epistemology in the digital era. *New Media & Society*, 11 (5), 659–683.

Daniels, J. (2009b) Rethinking cyberfeminism(s): race, gender, and embodiment. *Women's Studies Quarterly*, 37 (1/2), 101–124.

Daniels, J. (2013a) From tweet to blog post to peer-reviewed article: how to be a scholar now. LSE Impact of the Social Sciences. Accessed 11 December 2013. Available from http://blogs.lse.ac.uk/impactofsocialsciences/2013/09/25/how-to-be-a-scholar-daniels

Daniels, J. (2013b) Race and racism in Internet studies: a review and critique. *New Media & Society*, 15 (5), 695–719.

Daniels, J. and Feagin, J. (2011) The (coming) social media revolution in the academy. *Fast Capitalism*, 2. Accessed 12 March 2013. Available from http://www.uta.edu/huma/agger/fastcapitalism/8_2/Daniels8_2.html

Darmour, J. (2013) 3 ways to make wearable tech actually wearable. Co.Design. Accessed 15 March 2013. Available from http://www.fastcodesign.com/1672107/3-ways-to-make-wearable-tech-actually-wearable

Davenport, T. and Patil, D. (2013) Data scientist: the sexiest job of the 21st century. *Harvard Business Review Magazine*. Accessed 4 December 2013. Available from http://hbr.org/2012/10/data-scientist-the-sexiest-job-of-the-21st-century

Davies, T. and Bawa, Z.A. (2012) The promises and perils of open government data (OGD). *Journal of Community Informatics*, 8. Accessed 16 November 2012. Available from http://ci-journal.net/index.php/ciej/article/view/929/955

Davis, J. (2012) Social media and experiential ambivalence. *Future Internet*, 4 (4), 955–970.

de Almeida, A.N., Delicado, A., de Almeida Alves, N. and Carvalho, T. (2014) Internet, children and space: revisiting generational attributes and boundaries. *New Media & Society*. Accessed 30 May 2014. Available from http://nms.sagepub.com/content/early/2014/03/24/1461444814528293.abstract

DeLanda, M. (1991) *War in the Age of Intelligent Machines*. New York: Zone.

DiMaggio, P., Hargittai, E., Neuman, W.R. and Robinson, J. (2001) Social implications of the internet. *Annual Review of Sociology*, 27 (1), 307–336.

Dourish, P. and Bell, G. (2007) The infrastructure of experience and the experience of infrastructure: meaning and structure in everyday encounters with space. *Environment and Planning B: Planning & Design*, 34 (3), 414–430.

Doyle, A. (2011) Revisiting the synopticon: reconsidering Mathiesen's 'the viewer society' in the age of Web 2.0. *Theoretical Criminology*, 15 (3), 283–299.

Dredge, S. (2013) Yes, those free health apps are sharing your data with other companies. *Guardian*. Accessed 4 September 2013. Available from http://www.theguardian.com/technology/appsblog/2013/sep/03/fitness-health-apps-sharing-data-insurance

Drucker, J. (2014) Pixel dust: illusions of innovation in scholarly publishing. *Los*

Angeles Review of Books. Accessed 13 February 2014. Available from http://la reviewofbooks.org/essay/pixel-dust-illusions-innovation-scholarly-publishing/#.Ut2S9g7Doyk.email

Duggan, M. and Smith, A. (2013) Social media update 2013. Pew Research Center. Accessed 31 December 2013. Available from http://pewinternet.org/Reports/2013/Social-Media-Update/Main-Findings/Demographics-of-key-social-networking-platforms.aspx

Duhigg, C. (2012) How companies learn your secrets. *New York Times Magazine.* Accessed 16 February 2012. Available from http://www.nytimes.com/2012/02/19/magazine/shopping-habits.html?pagewanted=1&_r=2&hp

Dumbill, E. (2013) Making sense of big data. *Big Data*, 1 (1), 1–2.

Dunbar-Hester, C. (2010) Beyond 'Dudecore'? Challenging gendered and 'raced' technologies through media activism. *Journal of Broadcasting & Electronic Media*, 54 (1), 121–135.

Dunleavy, P. (2014) Why do academics choose useless titles for articles and chapters? Four steps to getting a better title. LSE Impact of the Social Sciences. Accessed 9 February 2014. Available from http://blogs.lse.ac.uk/impactofsocialsciences/2014/02/05/academics-choose-useless-titles

Dutton, W.H. and Blank, G. (2013) *Cultures of the Internet: The Internet in Britain.* Oxford: Oxford Internet Institute.

Dwoskin, E. (2014) Give me back my online privacy. *Wall Street Journal.* Accessed 25 March 2014. Available from http://online.wsj.com/news/articles/SB10001424052702304704504579432823496404570?mod=ITP_journalreport

Edwards, A., Housley, W., Williams, M., Sloan, L. and Williams, M. (2013) Digital social research, social media and the sociological imagination: surrogacy, augmentation and re-orientation. *International Journal of Social Research Methodology*, 16 (3), 245–260.

Elliott, A. (2013) *Reinvention.* London: Routledge.

Ellis, K. and Goggin, G. (2014) Disability and social media. In J. Hunsinger and T. Senft (eds) *The Social Media Handbook.* New York: Routledge, 126–143.

Elmer, G. (2003) A diagram of panoptic surveillance. *New Media & Society*, 5 (2), 231–247.

Enriquez, J.G. (2012) Bodily aware in cyber-research. In H. Breslow and A. Mousoutzanis (eds) *Cybercultures: Mediations of Community, Culture, Politics.* Amsterdam: Rodopi, 59–72.

Estes, H. (2012) Blogging and academic identity. *Literature Compass*, 9 (12), 974–982.

Eubanks, V. (2014) Want to predict the future of surveillance? Ask poor communities. *Prospect.* Accessed 26 February 2014. Available from http://prospect.org/article/want-predict-future-surveillance-ask-poor-communities

Eysenbach, G. (2011) Can tweets predict citations? Metrics of social impact based on Twitter and correlation with traditional metrics of scientific impact. *Journal of Medical Internet Research*, 4. Accessed 25 June 2013. Available from http://www.jmir.org/2011/4/e123

Farrell, D. and Petersen, J.C. (2010) The growth of internet research methods and the reluctant sociologist. *Sociological Inquiry*, 80 (1), 114–125.

Featherstone, M. (2009) Ubiquitous media: an introduction. *Theory, Culture & Society*, 26 (2/3), 1–22.

Fenwick, T. and Edwards, R. (2011) Considering materiality in educational policy: messy objects and multiple reals. *Educational Theory*, 61 (6), 709–726.

Firth, N. (2013) How open data empowers citizens of poorer nations. *New Scientist*, 2943. Accessed 16 November 2013. Available from http://www.newscientist.com/article/mg22029434.400-how-open-data-empowers-citizens-of-poorer-nations.html#.Uoa3cflmhca

Ford, S., Jenkins, H. and Green, J. (2013) *Spreadable Media: Creating Value and Meaning in a Networked Culture*. New York: New York University Press.

Foucault, M. (1979) *The History of Sexuality*. Vol. 1. London: Penguin.

Foucault, M. (1988) Technologies of the self. In L. Martin, H. Gutman and P. Hutton (eds) *Technologies of the Self: A Seminar with Michel Foucault*. London: Tavistock, 16–49.

Foucault, M. (1995) *Discipline and Punish: The Birth of the Prison*. Translated by A. Sheridan. 2nd edn. New York: Vintage Books.

Fox, S. and Boyles, J.L. (2012) *Disability in the Digital Age*. Washington, DC: Pew Research Center.

Fox, S. and Duggan, M. (2013) *The Diagnosis Difference*. Washington, DC: Pew Research Center.

Fraser, V. (2010) Queer closets and rainbow hyperlinks: the construction and constraint of queer subjectivities online. *Sexuality Research and Social Policy*, 7 (1), 30–36.

Freund, P. (2004) Civilised bodies redux: seams in the cyborg. *Social Theory & Health*, 2 (3), 273–289.

Friedman, E.J. (2007) Lesbians in (cyber)space: the politics of the internet in Latin American on- and off-line communities. *Media, Culture & Society*, 29 (5), 790–811.

Fuchs, C. (2011) Web 2.0, prosumption, and surveillance. *Surveillance & Society*, 8 (3), 288–309.

Fuchs, C. (2012) The political economy of privacy on Facebook. *Television & New Media*, 13 (2), 139–159.

Fuchs, C. (2014a) Book review: Manuel Castells, *Networks of Outrage and Hope: Social Movements in the Internet Age*. *Media, Culture & Society*, 36 (1), 122–124.

Fuchs, C. (2014b) *Social Media: A Critical Introduction*. London: Sage.

Fuchs, C. and Dyer-Witheford, N. (2013) Karl Marx @ Internet Studies. *New Media & Society*, 15 (5), 782–796.

Fuller, M. (2008) Introduction, the stuff of software. In M. Fuller (ed.) *Software Studies: A Lexicon*. Cambridge, MA: The MIT Press, 1–13.

Gabrys, J. (2011) *Digital Rubbish: A Natural History of Electronics*. Ann Arbor: University of Michigan Press.

Gajjala, R. (2003) South Asian digital diasporas and cyberfeminist webs: negotiating globalization, nation, gender and information technology design. *Contemporary South Asia*, 12 (1), 41–56.

Galligan, F. and Dyas-Correia, S. (2013) Altmetrics: rethinking the way we measure. *Serials Review*, 39 (1), 56–61.

Ganascia, J.-G. (2010) The generalized sousveillance society. *Social Science Information*, 49 (3), 489–507.

Gane, N. and Back, L. (2012) C. Wright Mills 50 years on: the promise and craft of sociology revisited. *Theory, Culture & Society*, 29 (7/8), 399–421.

Garrety, K., McLoughlin, I., Wilson, R., Zelle, G. and Martin, M. (2014) National electronic health records and the digital disruption of moral orders. *Social Science & Medicine*, 101, 70–77.

Gill, R. (2010) Breaking the silence: the hidden injuries of neoliberal academia. In R. Flood and R. Gill (eds) *Secrecy and Silence in the Research Process: Feminist Reflections*. London: Routledge, 228–244.

Ginsburg, F. (2012) Disability in the digital age. In H. Horst and D. Miller (eds) *Digital Anthropology*. London: Berg, 101–126.

Gitelman, L. (ed.) (2013) *'Raw Data' is an Oxymoron*. Cambridge, MA: The MIT Press.

Gitelman, L. and Jackson, V. (2013) Introduction. In L. Gitelman (ed.) *'Raw Data' is an Oxymoron*. Cambridge, MA: The MIT Press, 1–14.

Gleason, B. (2013) #Occupy Wall Street: exploring informal learning about a social movement on Twitter. *American Behavioral Scientist*, 57 (7), 966–982.

Goggin, G. and McLelland, M. (2009) Internationalizing internet studies: beyond anglophone paradigms. In G. Goggin and M. McLelland (eds) *Internationalizing Internet Studies: Beyond Anglophone Paradigms*. London: Routledge, 3–17.

Gooding, P. (2013) Mass digitization and the garbage dump: the conflicting needs of quantitative and qualitative methods. *Literary and Linguistic Computing*, 28 (3), 425–431.

Goodings, L. and Tucker, I. (2014) Social media and the co-production of bodies online: Bergson, Serres and Facebook's Timeline. *Media, Culture & Society*, 36 (1), 37–51.

Gorton, K. and Garde-Hansen, J. (2013) From old media whore to new media troll: the online negotiation of Madonna's ageing body. *Feminist Media Studies*, 13 (2), 288.

Graham, C., Laurier, E., O'Brien, V. and Rouncefield, M. (2011) New visual technologies: shifting boundaries, shared moments. *Visual Studies*, 26 (2), 87–91.

Grant, L. (2013) Understanding education through big data. DMLCentral. Accessed 25 October 2013. Available from http://dmlcentral.net/blog/lyndsay-grant/understanding-education-through-big-data

Greenwald, G. (2014) How covert agents infiltrate the internet to manipulate, deceive, and destroy reputations. *The Intercept*. Accessed 26 February 2014. Available from https://firstlook.org/theintercept/2014/02/24/jtrig-manipulation

Greenwald, G. and Gallagher, R. (2014) Snowden documents reveal covert surveillance and pressure tactics aimed at WikiLeaks and its supporters. *The Intercept*.

Accessed 18 February 2014. Available from https://firstlook.org/theintercept/article/2014/02/18/snowden-docs-reveal-covert-surveillance-and-pressure-tactics-aimed-at-wikileaks-and-its-supporters

Gregg, M. (2006) Feeling ordinary: blogging as conversational scholarship. *Continuum*, 20 (2), 147–160.

Gregg, M. (2009) Banal bohemia: blogging from the ivory tower hot-desk. *Convergence*, 15 (4), 470–483.

Gregg, M. (2011) *Work's Intimacy*. Cambridge: Polity.

Griffith, C., Heydon, G., Lamb, D., Lefort, L., Taylor, K. and Trotter, M. (2013) *Smart Farming: Leveraging the Impact of Broadband and the Digital Economy*. CSIRO and the University of New England. Accessed 22 March 2014.

Gross, A. (2014) What's the problem with Google Glass? *The New Yorker*. Accessed 28 March 2014. Available from http://www.newyorker.com/online/blogs/currency/2014/03/whats-the-problem-with-google-glass.html

Gupta, A., Lamba, H. and Kumaraguru, P. (2013) $1.00 per RT #BostonMarathon #PrayforBoston: analyzing fake content on Twitter. Paper delivered at the IEEE APWG eCrime Research Summit, San Francisco, 16–19 September.

Haggerty, K. and Ericson, R. (2000) The surveillant assemblage. *British Journal of Sociology*, 51 (4), 605–622.

Hakkarainen, P. (2012) 'No good for shovelling snow and carrying firewood': social representations of computers and the internet by elderly Finnish non-users. *New Media & Society*, 14 (7), 1198–1215.

Halavais, A. (2013) Home made big data? Challenges and opportunities for participatory social research. *First Monday*, 10. Accessed 8 October 2013. Available from http://firstmonday.org/ojs/index.php/fm/article/view/4876/3754

Halford, S. and Savage, M. (2010) Reconceptualizing digital social inequality. *Information, Communication & Society*, 13 (7), 937–955.

Halford, S., Pope, C. and Weal, M. (2013) Digital futures? Sociological challenges and opportunities in the emergent Semantic Web. *Sociology*, 47 (1), 173–189.

Hall, G. (2013a) *About Media Gifts*. Accessed 7 August 2013. Available from http://garyhall.squarespace.com/about

Hall, G. (2013b) *Media Gifts*. Accessed 7 August 2013. Available from http://www.garyhall.info/open-book

Hall, G. (2013c) The unbound book: academic publishing in the age of the infinite archive. *Journal of Visual Culture*, 12 (3), 490–507.

Hall, G. and Birchall, C. (2006) New cultural studies: adventures in theory (some comments, clarifications, explanations, observations, recommendations, remarks, statements and suggestions). In G. Hall and C. Birchall (eds) *New Cultural Studies: Adventures in Theory*. Edinburgh: Edinburgh University Press, 1–28.

Hands, J. (2013) Introduction: politics, power and 'platformativity'. *Culture Machine*. Accessed 5 February 2014. Available from http://www.culturemachine.net/index.php/cm/issue/current

Haraway, D. (1985) Manifesto for cyborgs: science, technology, and socialist feminism in the 1980s. *Socialist Review*, 80, 65–108.

Haraway, D. (2012) Awash in urine: DES and Premarin® in multispecies response-ability. *WSQ: Women's Studies Quarterly*, 40 (1), 301–316.

Hargittai, E. and Hinnant, A. (2008) Digital inequality: differences in young adults' use of the internet. *Communication Research*, 35 (5), 602–621.

Harrington, S. and McNair, B. (2012) The 'new' news. *Media International Australia*, 144, 49–51.

Hartmann, M. (2013) From domestication to mediated mobilism. *Mobile Media & Communication*, 1 (1), 42–49.

Hay, S., George, D., Moyes, C. and Brownstein, J. (2013) Big data opportunities for global infectious disease surveillance. *PLoS Medicine*, 4. Accessed 3 December 2013. Available from http://www.plosmedicine.org/article/info

Heinrich, A. (2012) What is 'network journalism'? *Media International Australia*, 144, 60–67.

Helmond, A. (2013) The algorithmization of the hyperlink. *Computational Culture*, 3. Accessed 12 November 2013. Available from http://computationalculture.net/article/the-algorithmization-of-the-hyperlink

Hill, K. (2012) 'Google Now's' terrifying, spine-tingling, bone-chilling insights into its users. *Forbes*. Accessed 26 August 2013. Available from http://www.forbes.com/sites/kashmirhill/2012/07/03/google-nows-terrifying-spine-tingling-bone-chilling-insights-into-its-users

Hintjens, H. (2013) Screening in or out? Selective non-surveillance of unwanted humanity in EU cities. *Surveillance & Society*, 11 (1/2), 87–105.

Hjorth, L. and Pink, S. (2014) New visualities and the digital wayfarer: reconceptualizing camera phone photography and locative media. *Mobile Media & Communication*, 2 (1), 40–57.

Hochman, N. and Manovich, L. (2013) Zooming into an Instagram city: reading the local through social media. *First Monday*, 7. Accessed 10 March 2014. Available from http://firstmonday.org/ojs/index.php/fm/article/view/4711/3698

Holmwood, J. (2007) Sociology as public discourse and professional practice: a critique of Michael Burawoy. *Sociological Theory*, 25 (1), 46–66.

Holmwood, J. (2010) Sociology's misfortune: disciplines, interdisciplinarity and the impact of audit culture. *British Journal of Sociology*, 61 (4), 639–658.

Holmwood, J. (2011) Sociology after Fordism: prospects and problems. *European Journal of Social Theory*, 14 (4), 537–556.

Horning, R. (2013) Safe in our archives. The New Inquiry. Accessed 24 May 2013. Available from http://thenewinquiry.com/blogs/marginal-utility/safe-in-our-archives

Horst, H., Hjorth, L. and Tacchi, J. (2012) Rethinking ethnography: an introduction. *Media International Australia, Incorporating Culture & Policy*, 145, 86–93.

Houghton, D. and Joinson, A. (2010) Privacy, social network sites, and social relations. *Journal of Technology in Human Services*, 28 (1/2), 74–94.

Howard, P. and Hussain, M. (2011) The upheavals in Egypt and Tunisia: the role of digital media. *Journal of Democracy*, 22 (3), 35–48.

Hughey, M. and Daniels, J. (2013) Racist comments at online news sites: a methodological dilemma for discourse analysis. *Media, Culture & Society*, 35 (3), 332–347.

Humphreys, S. and Vered, K.O. (2014) Reflecting on gender and digital networked media. *Television & New Media*, 15 (1), 3–13.

Humphry, J. (2011) Making an impact: cultural studies, media and contemporary work. *M/C Journal*, 6. Accessed 10 March 2014. Available from http://www.journal.media-culture.org.au/index.php/mcjournal/article/viewArticle/440

Hurwitz, J., Nugent, A., Halper, F. and Kaufman, M. (2013) *Big Data for Dummies*. Hoboken, NJ: John Wiley & Sons.

Ingeno, L. (2013) That wasn't research. *Inside Higher Ed*. Accessed 3 July 2013. Available from http://www.insidehighered.com/news/2013/07/03/review-board-finds-professors-tweet-was-not-research

IntelPR (2013) Future of technology may be determined by millennial malaise, female fans and affluent data altruists. *Intel Newsroom*. Accessed 18 October 2013. Available from http://newsroom.intel.com/community/intel_newsroom/blog/2013/10/17/future-of-technology-may-be-determined-by-millennial-malaise-female-fans-and-affluent-data-altruists

International Telecommunication Union (2013) *Measuring the Information Society*. Accessed 15 January 2014. Available from http://www.itu.int/en/ITU-D/Statistics/Documents/publications/mis2013/MIS2013_without_Annex_4.pdf

Jagoda, P. (2013) Gamification and other forms of play. *Boundary 2*, 40 (2), 113.

Jarrett, K. (2014) The relevance of 'women's work': social reproduction and immaterial labor in digital media. *Television & New Media*, 15 (1), 14–29.

Jenkins, H. (2014) Rethinking 'rethinking convergence/culture'. *Cultural Studies*, 28 (2), 267–297.

John, N. (2013) Sharing and Web 2.0: the emergence of a keyword. *New Media & Society*, 15 (2), 167–182.

Joiner, R., Gavin, J., Brosnan, M., Cromby, J., Gregory, H., Guiller, J., Maras, P. and Moon, A. (2012) Gender, internet experience, internet identification, and internet anxiety: a ten-year followup. *Cyberpsychology, Behavior and Social Networking*, 15 (7), 370–372.

Jurgenson, N. (2012) When atoms meet bits: social media, the mobile web and augmented revolution. *Future Internet*, 4 (1), 83–91.

Kamel Boulos, M., Resch, B., Crowley, D., Breslin, J., Sohn, G., Burtner, R., Pike, W., Jezierski, E. and Chuang, K.-Y.S. (2011) Crowdsourcing, citizen sensing and sensor web technologies for public and environmental health surveillance and crisis management: trends, OGC standards and application examples. *International Journal of Health Geographics*, 1. Accessed 30 May 2013. Available from http://www.ij-healthgeographics.com/content/10/1/67

Kavada, A. (2014) Introduction. *Media, Culture & Society*, 36 (1), 87–88.

Kelly, A. and Burrows, R. (2011) Measuring the value of sociology? Some notes on performative metricization in the contemporary academy. *The Sociological Review*, 59 (S2), 130–150.

Kendall, L. (2011) 'White and nerdy': computers, race, and the nerd stereotype. *Journal of Popular Culture*, 44 (3), 505–524.

Kibby, M. (2009) Collect yourself: negotiating personal music archives. *Information, Communication & Society*, 12 (3), 428–443.

Kingsley, D. (2008) Keeping a close watch – the rise of self-surveillance and the threat of digital exposure. *The Sociological Review*, 56 (3), 347.

Kinman, G. and Wray, S. (2013) *Higher Stress: A Survey of Stress and Well-being among Staff in Higher Education*. University and College Union. Accessed 22 November 2013. Available from http://www.ucu.org.uk/media/pdf/4/5/HE_stress_report_July_2013.pdf

Kirkpatrick, R. (2011) Data philanthropy: public and private sector data sharing for global resilience. Global Pulse. Accessed 28 May 2013. Available from http://www.unglobalpulse.org/blog/data-philanthropy-public-private-sector-data-sharing-global-resilience

Kirkup, G. (2010) Academic blogging: academic practice and academic identity. *London Review of Education*, 8 (1), 75–84.

Kitchin, R. (2014) Engaging publics: writing as praxis. *Cultural Geographies*, 21 (1), 153–157.

Kitchin, R. and Dodge, M. (2011) *Code/Space: Software and Everyday Life*. Cambridge, MA: The MIT Press.

Kitchin, R., Linehan, D., O'Callaghan, C. and Lawton, P. (2013) Public geographies through social media. *Dialogues in Human Geography*, 3 (1), 56–72.

Lambert, A. (2013) *Intimacy and Friendship on Facebook*. Houndmills: Palgrave Macmillan.

Langois, G. and Elmer, G. (2013) The research politics of social media platforms. *Culture Machine*. Accessed 8 August 2013. Available from http://www.culturemachine.net/index.php/cm/issue/current

Lapenta, F. (2011) Locative media and the digital visualisation of space, place and information. *Visual Studies*, 26 (1), 1–3.

Laplante, P. (2013) Who's afraid of big data? *IT Professional*, 15 (5), 6–7.

Lash, S. (2005) Lebenssoziologie: Georg Simmel in the information age. *Theory, Culture & Society*, 22 (3), 1–23.

Lash, S. (2006) Life (Vitalism). *Theory, Culture & Society*, 23 (2/3), 323–329.

Lash, S. (2007) Power after hegemony: cultural studies in mutation? *Theory, Culture & Society*, 24 (3), 55–78.

Latour, B. (1987) *Science in Action*. Cambridge, MA: Harvard University Press.

Latour, B. (2005) *Reassembling the Social: An Introduction to Actor-Network-Theory*. Oxford: Clarendon.

Latour, B., Jensen, P., Venturini, T., Grauwin, S. and Boullier, D. (2012) 'The whole is always smaller than its parts' – a digital test of Gabriel Tarde's monads. *British Journal of Sociology*, 63 (4), 590–615.

Law, J. and Ruppert, E. (2013) The social life of methods: devices. *Journal of Cultural Economy*, 6 (3), 229–240.

Lazer, D., Kennedy, R., King, G. and Vespignani, A. (2014) The parable of Google Flu: traps in big data analysis. *Science*, 343 (6176), 1203–1205.

Leetaru, K. (2011) Culturomics 2.0: forecasting large-scale human behavior using global news media tone in time and space. *First Monday*, 9. Accessed 10 September 2013. Available from http://firstmonday.org/ojs/index.php/fm/article/view/3663/3040

Lesk, M. (2013) Big data, Big Brother, big money. *IEEE Security & Privacy*, 11 (4), 85–89.

Letouze, E. (2012) *Big Data for Development: Challenges and Opportunities*. New York: UN Global Pulse.

Liu, J. and Adie, E. (2013) New perspectives on article-level metrics: developing ways to assess research uptake and impact online. *Insights*, 26 (2), 153–158.

Löfgren, O. (2014) Routinising research: academic skills in analogue and digital worlds. *International Journal of Social Research Methodology*, 17 (1), 73–86.

LSE Public Policy Group (2013) *Open Access Perspectives in the Humanities and Social Sciences*. Accessed 27 December 2013. Available at http://blogs.lse.ac.uk/impactofsocialsciences/files/2013/10/Open-Access-HSS-eCollection.pdf

Luckman, S. (1999) (En)gendering the digital body: feminism and the internet. *Hecate*, 25 (2), 36–47.

Lupton, D. (1994) Panic computing: the viral metaphor and computer technology. *Cultural Studies*, 8 (3), 556–568.

Lupton, D. (1995) The embodied computer/user. *Body & Society*, 1 (3/4), 97–112.

Lupton, D. (2012) M-health and health promotion: the digital cyborg and surveillance society. *Social Theory & Health*, 10 (3), 229–244.

Lupton, D. (2013a) *The Social Worlds of the Unborn*. Houndmills: Palgrave Macmillan.

Lupton, D. (ed.) (2013b) *The Unborn Human*. Open Humanities Press. Available from http://www.livingbooksaboutlife.org/books/The_Unborn_Human

Lupton, D. (2013c) Understanding the human machine. *IEEE Technology & Society Magazine*, 32 (4), 25–30.

Lupton, D. (2014a) The commodification of patient opinion: the digital patient experience economy in the age of big data. *Sociology of Health & Illness*. Available from http://onlinelibrary.wiley.com/doi/10.1111/1467-9566.12109/full.

Lupton, D. (2014b) Quantified sex: self-tracking sexual and reproductive embodiment via digital technologies. *Culture, Health & Sexuality*. Available from www.tandfonline.com/doi/abs/10.1080/13691058.

Lupton, D. and Noble, G. (1997) Just a machine? Dehumanizing strategies in personal computer use. *Body & Society*, 3 (2), 83–101.

Lupton, D. and Noble, G. (2002) Mine/not mine: appropriating personal computers in the academic workplace. *Journal of Sociology*, 38 (1), 5–23.

Lupton, D. and Seymour, W. (2000) Technology, selfhood and physical disability. *Social Science & Medicine*, 50 (12), 1851–1862.

Lupton, D. and Seymour, W. (2003) 'I am normal on the net': disability, computerised communication technologies and the embodied self. In J. Coupland and R. Gwyn (eds) *Discourse, the Body, and Identity*. Houndmills: Palgrave Macmillan, 246–265.

Lury, C. and Wakeford, N. (2012a) Introduction: a perpetual inventory. In C. Lury and N. Wakeford (eds) *Inventive Methods: The Happening of the Social*. London: Routledge, 1–24.

Lury, C. and Wakeford, N. (eds) (2012b) *Inventive Methods: The Happening of the Social*. London: Routledge.

Lyon, D. and Bauman, Z. (2013) *Liquid Surveillance: A Conversation*. Oxford: Wiley.

Mackenzie, A. (2005) The performativity of code: software and cultures of circulation. *Theory, Culture & Society*, 22 (1), 71–92.

Mackenzie, A. and McNally, R. (2013) Living multiples: how large-scale scientific data-mining pursues identity and differences. *Theory, Culture & Society*, 30 (4), 72–91.

Mackenzie, A. and Vurdubakis, T. (2011) Codes and codings in crisis: signification, performativity and excess. *Theory, Culture & Society*, 28 (6), 3–23.

MacKenzie, D. (2013) Social media helps aid efforts after Typhoon Haiyan. *New Scientist*. Accessed 12 November 2013. Available from http://www.newscientist. com/article/dn24565-social-media-helps-aid-efforts-after-typhoon-haiyan. html?cmpid=RSS NSNS 2012-GLOBAL online-news#.UoKUCflmhcZ

Madden, S. (2012) From databases to big data. *IEEE Internet Computing*, 16 (3), 4–6.

Madianou, M. and Miller, D. (2012) *Migration and New Media: Transnational Families and Polymedia*. London: Routledge.

Mager, A. (2009) Mediated health: sociotechnical practices of providing and using online health information. *New Media & Society*, 11 (7), 1123–1142.

Mahrt, M. and Scharkow, M. (2013) The value of big data in digital media research. *Journal of Broadcasting & Electronic Media*, 57 (1), 20–33.

Maitzen, R. (2012) Scholarship 2.0: blogging and/as academic practice. *Journal of Victorian Culture*, 17 (3), 348–354.

Mann, S. and Ferenbok, J. (2013) New media and the power politics of sousveillance in a surveillance-dominated world. *Surveillance & Society*, 11 (1/2), 18–34.

Manovich, L. (2012) Trending: the promises and challenges of big social data. In M. Gold (ed.) *Debates in the Digital Humanities*. Minneapolis: University of Minnesota Press, 460–475.

Manovich, L. (2013a) *Software Takes Command*. London: Bloomsbury.

Manovich, L. (2013b) The algorithms of our lives. *The Chronicle of Higher Education*.

Accessed 17 December 2013. Available from http://chronicle.com/article/ The-Algorithms-of-Our-Lives-/143557

Manyika, J., Chui, M., Brown, B., Bughin, J., Dobbs, R., Roxburgh, C. and Byers, A.H. (2011) *Big Data: The Next Frontier for Innovation, Competition, and Productivity*. McKinsey Global Institute. Accessed 15 January 2014. http://www. mckinsey.com/insights/business_technology/big_data_the_next_frontier_for_ innovation

Marcus, G. (2006) Assemblage. *Theory, Culture & Society*, 23 (2/3), 101–106.

Markham, A. (2013) Undermining 'data': a critical examination of a core term in scientific inquiry. *First Monday*, 10. Accessed 8 October 2013. Available from http://firstmonday.org/ojs/index.php/fm/article/view/4868/3749

Markham, T. (2014) Social media, protest cultures and political subjectivities of the Arab Spring. *Media, Culture & Society*, 36 (1), 89–104.

Marres, N. (2012) The redistribution of methods: on intervention in digital social research, broadly conceived. *The Sociological Review*, 60 (S1), 139–165.

Marres, N. and Weltevrede, E. (2013) Scraping the social? Issues in live social research. *Journal of Cultural Economy*, 6 (3), 313–335.

Martin, H. (2011) Digital gender divide or technologically empowered women in developing countries? A typical case of lies, damned lies, and statistics. *Women's Studies International Forum*, 34 (6), 479–489.

Marwick, A. (2012) The public domain: social surveillance in everyday life. *Surveillance & Society*, 9 (4), 378–393.

Marwick, A. (2014) How your data are being deeply mined. *New York Review of Books*. Accessed 9 January 2014. Available from http://www.nybooks.com/ articles/archives/2014/jan/09/how-your-data-are-being-deeply-mined

Marwick, A. and boyd, d. (2011) To see and be seen: celebrity practice on Twitter. *Convergence*, 17 (2), 139–158.

Mayer-Schonberger, V. and Cukier, K. (2013) *Big Data: A Revolution That Will Transform How We Live, Work, and Think*. New York: Houghton Mifflin Harcourt.

McCarthy, M. (2013) Experts warn on data security in health and fitness apps. *British Medical Journal*, f5600. Accessed 27 February 2014. Available from http://www. bmj.com/content/347/bmj.f5600

McCormick, T. (2013) Gamification: anthropology of an idea. *Foreign Policy*, 201, 26–27.

McCowen, D. 2013. Concerns over Big Brother insurance. *Sydney Morning Herald*, 21 September, 11.

McFedries, P. (2013) Tracking the quantified self. *IEEE Spectrum*, 50 (8), 24.

McQuillan, D. (2012) Big data capabilities and citizen glitching. *Internet.artizans*. Accessed 15 November 2012. Available from http://www.internetartizans.co. uk/bigdatacapability

McQuillan, D. (2013) Open sensor networks and critical citizen science. *Storify*. Accessed 29 November 2013. Available from http://storify.com/danmcquillan/ opentech-2013-sensor-networks-and-citizen-science

Meleo-Erwin, Z.C. (2011) 'A beautiful show of strength': weight loss and the fat activist self. *Health*, 15 (2), 188–205.

Merithew, C. (2004) Women of the (cyber) world: the case of Mexican feminist NGOs. *Journal of Interdisciplinary Gender Studies*, 8 (1/2), 87–102.

Mewburn, I. and Thomson, P. (2013) Why do academics blog? An analysis of audiences, purposes and challenges. *Studies in Higher Education*, 38 (8), 1105–1119.

Miah, A. and Rich, E. (2008) *The Medicalization of Cyberspace*. London: Routledge.

Michael, K. and Clarke, R. (2013) Location and tracking of mobile devices: uberveillance stalks the streets. *Computer Law & Security Report*, 29 (3), 216–228.

Michael, K. and Michael, M.G. (2013) The future prospects of embedded microchips in humans as unique identifiers: the risks versus the rewards. *Media, Culture & Society*, 35 (1), 78–86.

Michael, M. (2012) De-signing the object of sociology: toward an 'idiotic' methodology. *The Sociological Review*, 60 (S1), 166–183.

Michael, M. and Gaver, W. (2009) Home beyond home: dwelling with threshold devices. *Space and Culture*, 12 (3), 359–370.

Michel, J.-B., Shen, Y.K., Aiden, A.P., Veres, A., Gray, M., Pickett, J., Hoiberg, D., Clancy, D., Norvig, P., Orwant, J., Pinker, S., Nowak, M. and Aiden, E.L. (2011) Quantitative analysis of culture using millions of digitized books. *Science*, 331 (6014), 176–182.

Miller, D. (2008) *The Comfort of Things*. Cambridge: Polity Press.

Miller, D. (2011) *Tales from Facebook*. Malden, MA: Polity Press.

Miller, D. and Horst, H. (2012) The digital and the human: a prospectus for digital anthropology. In H. Horst and D. Miller (eds) *Digital Anthropology*. London: Berg, 3–35.

Millington, B. (2009) Wii has never been modern: 'active' video games and the 'conduct of conduct'. *New Media & Society*, 11 (4), 621–640.

Mitchell, A. (2013) Take back the net: institutions must develop collective strategies to tackle online abuse aimed at female academics. LSE Impact of the Social Sciences. Accessed 8 August 2013. Available from http://blogs.lse.ac.uk/impactofsocialsciences/2013/07/24/take-back-the-net-female-academics-online-abuse

Mitchell, P. (2000) Internet addiction: genuine diagnosis or not? *Lancet*, 355 (9204), 632.

Moreno, M., Goniu, N., Moreno, P.S. and Diekema, D. (2013) Ethics of social media research: common concerns and practical considerations. *Cyberpsychology, Behavior and Social Networking*, 16 (9), 708–713.

Muller, B. (2008) Securing the political imagination: popular culture, the security dispositif and the biometric state. *Security Dialogue*, 39 (2/3), 199–220.

Murdoch, T.B. and Detsky, A.S. (2013) The inevitable application of big data to health care. *Journal of the American Medical Association*, 309 (13), 1351.

Murthy, D. (2013) *Twitter: Social Communication in the Twitter Age*. Oxford: Wiley.

Natale, S. and Ballatore, A. (2014) The web will kill them all: new media, digital utopia, and political struggle in the Italian 5-Star Movement. *Media, Culture & Society*, 36 (1), 105–121.

Neal, D. (ed.) (2012) *Social Media for Academics: A Practical Guide*. Oxford: Chandos.

Newell, C. and Goggin, G. (2003) *Digital Disability: The Social Construction of Disability in New Media*. Lanham, MD: Rowman & Littlefield.

Newsom, V. and Lengel, L. (2012) Arab women, social media, and the Arab Spring: applying the framework of digital reflexivity to analyze gender and online activism. *Journal of International Women's Studies*, 13 (5), 31–45.

Nichols, L. (2009) Toward a renewed sociology of mass media and popular culture. *American Sociologist*, 40, 147–148.

Nippert-Eng, C. (1996) *Home and Work: Negotiating Boundaries through Everyday Life*. Chicago, IL: University of Chicago Press.

Noble, G. and Lupton, D. (1998) Consuming work: computers, subjectivity and appropriation in the university workplace. *The Sociological Review*, 46 (4), 803–827.

Olphert, W. and Damodaran, L. (2013) Older people and digital disengagement: a fourth digital divide? *Gerontology*, 59 (6), 564–570.

Olson, P. (2013). Teenagers say goodbye to Facebook and hello to messenger apps. *Guardian*. Accessed 10 November 2013. Available from http://www.theguardian.com/technology/2013/nov/10/teenagers-messenger-apps-facebook-exodus

Orton-Johnson, K. and Prior, N. (eds) (2013) *Digital Sociology: Critical Perspectives*. Houndmills: Palgrave Macmillan.

Oxford Internet Institute (2013) *Age of Internet Empires*. Accessed 7 October 2013. Available from http://geography.oii.ox.ac.uk

Paasonen, S. (2009) What cyberspace? Traveling concepts in internet research. In G. Goggin and M. McLelland (eds) *Internationalizing Internet Studies: Beyond Anglophone Paradigms*. New York: Routledge, 18–31.

Paasonen, S. (2011) Revisiting cyberfeminism. *Communications*, 36 (3), 335–352.

Palmås, K. (2011) Predicting what you'll do tomorrow: panspectric surveillance and the contemporary corporation. *Surveillance & Society*, 8 (3), 338.

Parikka, J. (2013) Dust and exhaustion: the labor of media materialism. *CTheory*. Accessed 2 November 2013. Available from http://www.ctheory.net/articles.aspx?id=726

Pavone, V. and Esposti, S.D. (2012) Public assessment of new surveillance-oriented security technologies: beyond the trade-off between privacy and security. *Public Understanding of Science*, 21 (5), 556–572.

Payne, R. (2012) Virality 2.0: networked promiscuity and the sharing subject. *Cultural Studies*, 27 (4), 540–560.

Penley, C., Ross, A. and Haraway, D. (1991) Cyborgs at large: interview with Donna Haraway. In C. Penley and A. Ross (eds) *Technoculture*. Minneapolis: University of Minnesota Press, 1–26.

Pew Research Center (2014) *The Web at 25 in the US*. Washington, DC: Pew Research Center.

Philip, K., Irani, L. and Dourish, P. (2012) Postcolonial computing: a tactical survey. *Science, Technology, & Human Values*, 37 (1), 3–29.

Pinder, D. (2013) Dis-locative arts: mobile media and the politics of global positioning. *Continuum*, 27 (4), 523–541.

Pink, S. (2009) *Doing Sensory Ethnography*. London: Sage.

Pink, S. and Leder Mackley, K. (2013) Saturated and situated: expanding the meaning of media in the routines of everyday life. *Media, Culture & Society*, 35 (6), 677–691.

Polonetsky, J. and Tene, O. (2013) Privacy and big data: making ends meet. *Stanford Law Review*. Accessed 4 September 2013. Available from http://www.stanford-lawreview.org/online/privacy-and-big-data/privacy-and-big-data

Pooley, J. and Katz, E. (2008) Further notes on why American sociology abandoned mass communication research. *Journal of Communication*, 58 (4), 767–786.

Postill, J. (2008) Localizing the internet beyond communities and networks. *New Media & Society*, 10 (3), 413–431.

Postill, J. (2013) The uneven convergence of digital freedom activism and popular protest. Unpublished paper.

Postill, J. and Pink, S. (2012) Social media ethnography: the digital researcher in a messy web. *Media International Australia*, 145, 123–134.

Procter, R., Vis, F. and Voss, A. (2013) Reading the riots on Twitter: methodological innovation for the analysis of big data. *International Journal of Social Research Methodology*, 16 (3), 197–214.

Public Administration Select Committee (2014) *Statistics and Open Data: Harvesting Unused Knowledge, Empowering Citizens and Improving Public Services*. London: House of Commons.

Rainie, L. and Madden, M. (2013) 5 findings about privacy. Pew Research Center. Accessed 24 December 2013. Available from http://networked.pewinternet.org/2013/12/23/5-findings-about-privacy

Rapp, L., Button, D., Fleury-Steiner, B. and Fleury-Steiner, R. (2010) The internet as a tool for black feminist activism: lessons from an online antirape protest. *Feminist Criminology*, 5 (3), 244–262.

Räsänen, M. and Nyce, J.M. (2013) The raw is cooked: data in intelligence practice. *Science, Technology & Human Values*, 38 (5), 655–677.

Richards, N. and King, J. (2013) Three paradoxes of big data. *Stanford Law Review*, 66 (41), 41–46.

Richardson, H.J. (2009) A 'smart house' is not a home: the domestication of ICTs. *Information Systems Frontiers*, 11 (5), 599–608.

Ritzer, G. (2014) Prosumption: evolution, revolution, or eternal return of the same? *Journal of Consumer Culture*, 14 (1), 3–24.

Ritzer, G., Dean, P. and Jurgenson, N. (2012) The coming of age of the prosumer. *American Behavioral Scientist*, 56 (4), 379–398.

Robinson, L. (2009) A taste for the necessary: a Bourdieuian approach to digital inequality. *Information, Communication & Society*, 12 (4), 488–507.

Rogers, R. (2013) *Digital Methods*. Cambridge, MA: The MIT Press.

Rose, J., Mackey-Kallis, S., Shyles, L., Barry, K., Biagini, D., Hart, C. and Jack, L. (2012) Face it: the impact of gender on social media images. *Communication Quarterly*, 60 (5), 588–607.

Rosen, J. (2012) The right to be forgotten. *Stanford Law Review*. Accessed 21 November 2013. Available from http://www.stanfordlawreview.org/online/privacy-paradox/right-to-be-forgotten

Rosenzweig, P. (2012) Whither privacy? *Surveillance & Society*, 10 (3/4), 344–347.

Ruppert, E. (2011) Population objects: interpassive subjects. *Sociology*, 45 (2), 218–233.

Ruppert, E. (2012) The governmental topologies of database devices. *Theory, Culture & Society*, 29 (4/5), 116–136.

Ruppert, E. (2013) Rethinking empirical social sciences. *Dialogues in Human Geography*, 3 (3), 268–273.

Ruppert, E. and Savage, M. (2011) Transactional politics. *The Sociological Review*, 59 (S2), 73–92.

Ruppert, E., Law, J. and Savage, M. (2013) Reassembling social science methods: the challenge of digital devices. *Theory, Culture & Society*, 30 (4), 22–46.

Salovaara, A., Helfenstein, S. and Oulasvirta, A. (2011) Everyday appropriations of information technology: a study of creative uses of digital cameras. *Journal of the American Society for Information Science and Technology*, 62 (12), 2347–2363.

Sauter, M. (2013) 'LOIC will tear us apart': the impact of tool design and media portrayals in the success of activist DDOS attacks. *American Behavioral Scientist*, 57 (7), 983–1007.

Sauter, T. (2013) 'What's on your mind?' Writing on Facebook as a tool for self-formation. *New Media & Society*. Accessed 30 May 2014. Available from http://nms.sagepub.com/content/early/2013/07/05/1461444813495160.abstract

Savage, M. (2010) Unpicking sociology's misfortunes. *British Journal of Sociology*, 61 (4), 659–665.

Savage, M. (2013) The 'social life of methods': a critical introduction. *Theory, Culture & Society*, 30 (4), 3–21.

Savage, M. and Burrows, R. (2007) The coming crisis of empirical sociology. *Sociology*, 41 (5), 885–899.

Savage, M. and Burrows, R. (2009) Some further reflections on the coming crisis of empirical sociology. *Sociology*, 43 (4), 762–772.

Savage, M., Devine, F., Cunningham, N., Taylor, M., Li, Y., Hjellbrekke, J., Le Roux, B., Friedman, S. and Miles, A. (2013) A new model of social class? Findings from the BBC's Great British Class Survey experiment. *Sociology*, 47 (2), 219–250.

Schneider, A. (2012) The iPhone as an object of knowledge. In P. Snickars and P. Vonderau (eds) *Moving Data: The iPhone and the Future of Media*. New York: Columbia University Press, 49–60.

Scholz, T. (2013) Introduction: why does digital labor matter now? In T. Scholz (ed.) *Digital Labor: The Internet as Playground and Factory*. New York: Routledge, 1–9.

Seymour, W. and Lupton, D. (2004) Holding the line online: exploring wired relationships for people with disabilities. *Disability & Society*, 19 (4), 291–305.

Shahani, A. (2012) Who could be watching you watching your figure? Your boss. All Tech Considered. Accessed 29 January 2013. Available from http://www.npr.org/blogs/alltechconsidered/2012/12/26/167970303/who-could-be-watching-you-watching-your-figure-your-boss?

Shepard, M. (2013) Minor urbanism: everyday entanglements of technology and urban life. *Continuum*, 27 (4), 483.

Silverman, C. (2012) A new age for truth. *Nieman Reports*, Summer. Accessed 13 November 2011. Available from http://www.nieman.harvard.edu/reports/article/102762/A-New-Age-for-Truth.aspx

Singer, N. (2013) On campus, a faculty uprising over personal data. *New York Times*. Accessed 14 September 2013. Available from http://www.nytimes.com/2013/09/15/business/on-campus-a-faculty-uprising-over-personal-data.html?smid=tw-nytimeshealth&seid=auto&_r=0

Smith, K. and Jeffery, D. (2013) Critical pedagogies in the neoliberal university: what happens when they go digital? *Canadian Geographer*, 57 (3), 372–380.

Smith, M. (2013) Theses on the philosophy of history: the work of research in the age of digital searchability and distributability. *Journal of Visual Culture*, 12 (3), 375–403.

Soriano, C.R.R. (2014) Constructing collectivity in diversity: online political mobilization of a national LGBT political party. *Media, Culture & Society*, 36 (1), 20–36.

Starner, T. (2013) Google Glass lead: how wearing tech on our bodies actually helps it get *out* of our way. *Wired*. Accessed 23 December 2013. Available from http://www.wired.com/opinion/2013/12/the-paradox-of-wearables-close-to-your-body-but-keeping-tech-far-away

Sutherland, T. (2013) Liquid networks and the metaphysics of flux: ontologies of flow in an age of speed and mobility. *Theory, Culture & Society*, 30 (5), 3–23.

Sutrop, M. and Laas-Mikko, K. (2012) From identity verification to behavior prediction: ethical implications of second generation biometrics. *Review of Policy Research*, 29 (1), 21–36.

Swan, M. (2013) The quantified self: fundamental disruption in big data science and biological discovery. *Big Data*, 2. Accessed 2 March 2014. Available from http://online.liebertpub.com/doi/abs/10.1089/big.2012.0002

Tang, L. and Sampson, H. (2012) The interaction between mass media and the internet in non-democratic states: the case of China. *Media, Culture & Society*, 34 (4), 457–471.

Terras, M. (2012) The verdict: is blogging or tweeting about research papers worth it? LSE Impact of the Social Sciences. Accessed 3 May 2013. Available from http://blogs.lse.ac.uk/impactofsocialsciences/2012/04/19/blog-tweeting-papers-worth-it

Thomas, S. (2013) *Technobiophilia: Nature and Cyberspace*. London: Bloomsbury.

Thomson, P. (2014) Coles reveals sharing of customers' data. *Sun-Herald*. Accessed 9 March 2014. Available from http://www.smh.com.au/national/coles-shares-personal-flybuys-and-online-data-20140308-34efw.html

Thrift, N. (2005) *Knowing Capitalism*. London: Sage.

Thrift, N. (2006) Re-inventing invention: new tendencies in capitalist commodification. *Economy and Society*, 35 (2), 279–306.

Tufekci, Z. and Freelon, D. (2013) Introduction to the special issue on new media and social unrest. *American Behavioral Scientist*, 57 (7), 843–847.

Turkle, S. (2007) *Evocative Objects: Things We Think with*. Cambridge, MA: The MIT Press.

UN Women (2013) UN Women ad series reveals widespread sexism. Accessed 21 October 2013. Available from http://www.unwomen.org/en/news/stories/2013/10/women-should-ads

Ungerleider, N. (2013). Colleges are using big data to predict which students will do well – before they accept them. *Fast Company*. Accessed 21 October 2013. Available from http://www.fastcoexist.com/3019859/futurist-forum/colleges-are-using-big-data-to-predict-which-students-will-do-well-before-the

Uprichard, E. (2012) Being stuck in (live) time: the sticky sociological imagination. *The Sociological Review*, 60 (S1), 124–138.

Uprichard, E. (2013) Big data, little questions? *Discover Society*, 1. Accessed 28 October 2013. Available from http://www.discoversociety.org/focus-big-data-little-questions

Urban, J., Hoofnagle, C. and Li, S. (2012) Mobile phones and privacy. Unpublished paper. Berkeley Centre for Law and Technology Research Paper Series.

Vaidhyanathan, S. (2011) *The Googilization of Everything (and Why We Should Worry)*. Berkeley: University of California Press.

van Deursen, A. and van Dijk, J. (2014) The digital divide shifts to differences in usage. *New Media & Society*, 16 (3), 507–526.

van Dijk, J. (2010) Book review: Castells, M., *Communication Power*. *Communications*, 35 (4), 485–489.

van Dijk, J. and Hacker, K. (2003) The digital divide as a complex and dynamic phenomenon. *The Information Society*, 19 (4), 315–326.

van Manen, M. (2010) The pedagogy of Momus technologies: Facebook, privacy and online intimacy. *Qualitative Health Research*, 20 (8), 1023–1032.

Vandrico Inc. (2014) Wearable tech market insights. Accessed 27 March 2014. Available from http://vandrico.com/database

Vaughn, J. (2013) As big data use explodes, Verizon strategist explores the 'data self'. *TechTarget*. Accessed 8 August 2013. Available from http://searchdatamanagement.techtarget.com/feature/As-big-data-use-explodes-Verizon-strategist-explores-the-data-self

Ventura, P. (2012) *Neoliberal Culture: Living with American Neoliberalism*. Farnham: Ashgate.

Verran, H. (2012) Number. In C. Lury and N. Wakeford (eds) *Inventive Methods: The Happening of the Social*. London: Routledge, 110–124.

Vis, F. (2013) A critical reflection on big data: considering APIs, researchers and tools as data makers. *First Monday*, 10. Accessed 27 October 2013. Available from http://firstmonday.org/ojs/index.php/fm/article/view/4878/3755

Wade, L. and Sharp, G. (2013) Sociological images: blogging as public sociology. *Social Science Computer Review*, 31 (2), 221–228.

Wajcman, J. (2004) *TechnoFeminism*. New York: Wiley.

Wallace, N. and Whyte, S. (2013) Supermarket spies. *The Sun-Herald*, 15 September, 3.

Waller, L. and Hess, K. (2014) The digital pillory: the shaming of 'ordinary' people for minor crimes. *Continuum*, 28 (1), 101–111.

Waterman, K. and Hendler, J. (2013) Getting the dirt on big data. *Big Data*, 1 (3), 137–140.

Watson, S. (2013) You are your data and you should demand the right to use it. *Slate*. Accessed 13 December 2013. Available from http://www.slate.com/articles/technology/future_tense/2013/11/quantified_self_self_tracking_data_we_need_a_right_to_use_it.html

Weaver, S. (2011) Jokes, rhetoric and embodied racism: a rhetorical discourse analysis of the logics of racist jokes on the internet. *Ethnicities*, 11 (4), 413–435.

Webster, F. (2005) Making sense of the information age. *Information, Communication & Society*, 8 (4), 439–458.

Wellcome Trust (2013) *Summary Report of Qualitative Research into Public Attitudes to Personal Data and Linking Personal Data*. Accessed 3 March 2014. http://www.wellcome.ac.uk/stellent/groups/corporatesite/@msh_grants/documents/web_document/wtp053205.pdf

Weller, M. (2011) *The Digital Scholar: How Technology is Transforming Scholarly Practice*. London: Bloomsbury Academic.

Weller, M. (2013) The battle for open: a perspective. *Journal of Interactive Media in Education*. Accessed 23 December 2013. Available from http://jime.open.ac.uk/jime/article/view/2013-15

Werbin, K. (2011) Spookipedia: intelligence, social media and biopolitics. *Media, Culture & Society*, 33 (8), 1254–1265.

West, E. (2014) Consumer subjectivity and US health care reform. *Health Communication*, 29 (3), 299–308.

Wikipedia (2013) List of hoaxes on Wikipedia. Accessed 13 November 2013. Available from http://en.wikipedia.org/wiki/Wikipedia

Williams, L. (2013) Academic blogging: a risk worth taking? *Guardian*. Accessed 13 December 2013. Available from http://www.theguardian.com/higher-education-network/blog/2013/dec/04/academic-blogging-newspaper-research-plagiarism

Williamson, B. (2013a) Programming power? Does learning to code empower kids?

DMLCentral. Accessed 14 November 2013. Available from http://dmlcentral. net/blog/ben-williamson/programming-power-does-learning-code-empower-kids

Williamson, B. (2013b) *The Future of the Curriculum: School Knowledge in the Digital Age.* The John D. and Catherine T. MacArthur Foundation Reports on Digital Media and Learning. Cambridge, MA: MacArthur Foundation.

World Economic Forum (2011) *Personal Data: The Emergence of a New Asset Class.* Accessed 2 July 2013. Available from http://www3.weforum.org/docs/WEF_ITTC_PersonalDataNewAsset_Report_2011.pdf

Wortham, J. (2013) My selfie, myself. *New York Times.* Accessed 27 March 2014. Available from http://www.nytimes.com/2013/10/20/sunday-review/my-selfie-myself.html?pagewanted=1&_r=0&smid=pl-share

Wynn, J. (2009) Digital sociology: emergent technologies in the field and the classroom. *Sociological Forum,* 24 (2), 448–456.

Zavattaro, S. (2010) Brand Obama: the implications of a branded president. *Administrative Theory & Praxis,* 32 (1), 123–128.

Zickuhr, K. (2013) *Who's Not Online and Why.* Washington, DC: Pew Research Center.

WEB RESOURCES

Autoscopia: http://www.autoscopia.net/about.html

BSA Digital Sociology: http://digitalsociology.org.uk

Computational Culture (online open-access journal): http://computationalculture.net

Culture Digitally blog: http://culturedigitally.org

Cyborgology blog: http://thesocietypages.org/cyborgology

Data.gov: http://www.data.gov

Digital Methods Initiative (online course and media analysis tools compendium): https://www.digitalmethods.net/Digitalmethods/WebHome

Digitize Me, Visualize Me, Search Me (open-access online book edited by Gary Hall): http://www.livingbooksaboutlife.org/books/Digitize_Me,_Visualize_Me,_Search_Me#World_of_Data

DMLCentral (Digital Media and Learning): http://dmlcentral.net/about

Every Minute of Every Day: http://everyminuteofeveryday.org.uk

FibreCulture Journal (online open-access journal): http://fibreculturejournal.org

First Monday (online open-access journal): http://firstmonday.org/ojs/index.php/fm/index

Global Pulse: http://www.unglobalpulse.org/about-new

Hybrid Pedagogy: A Digital Journal of Learning, Teaching, and Technology: http://www.hybridpedagogy.com/

Internet.artizans: http://www.internetartizans.co.uk

ISTC Social (Intel's Science and Technology Center for Social Computing): http://socialcomputing.uci.edu

LSE Impact of the Social Sciences blog: http://blogs.lse.ac.uk/impactofsocialsciences

Media Gifts: http://www.garyhall.info/journal

Our Mobile Planet: http://www.thinkwithgoogle.com/mobileplanet/en

Oxford Internet Institute: http://www.oii.ox.ac.uk

Pew Research Center: http://www.pewinternet.org

Phototrails: http://phototrails.net

Quantified Self: http://quantifiedself.com

Scrutiny blog (Tarleton Gillespie): http://tarletongillespie.org/scrutiny

Selfiecity: http://selfiecity.net/#

Social Media Collective Research blog: http://socialmediacollective.org

Software Studies Initiative: http://lab.softwarestudies.com

Surveillance Studies network (including the online open-access journal *Surveillance Studies*): http://www.surveillance-studies.net

The Digital Beyond: http://www.thedigitalbeyond.com/online-services-list

The Digital Self (the author's Scoop.it collection): http://www.scoop.it/t/the-digital-self

The Digitised Academic (the author's Bundlr collection): http://bundlr.com/b/the-digitised-academic

The Social Life of Big Data and Algorithms (the author's Bundlr collection): http://bundlr.com/b/the-social-life-of-algorithms

The Sociology of the Digital (the author's Bundlr collection): http://bundlr.com/b/the-sociology-of-the-digital

The Sociology of the Quantified Self (the author's Scoop.it collection): http://www.scoop.it/t/the-sociology-of-the-quantified-self

Thinking Culture blog (David Beer): http://thinkingculture.wordpress.com

This Sociological Life (the author's blog): http://simplysociology.wordpress.com

Triple C (online open-access journal): http://www.triple-c.at/index.php/tripleC/index

Visible Human project: http://www.nlm.nih.gov/research/visible/visible_human.html

We the Data: http://wethedata.org/#home

INDEX

419eater.com 138
2014 Vienna Declaration on Freedom of Information and Expression 152

Academia.edu 70, 80
academic blogging 70, 71–2, 76, 77, 89–90
academic journals 80, 89
academics 15, 16, 18–19, 66–92; digital public sociology 66–72; gift economy 77–9; metric assemblages and audit culture 79–83; new forms of publishing 68, 77–9, 90–2; openness and circulation of knowledges 83–92; research on the digitised academic 72–7; survey on use of social media 73–5, 77, 192–3
access to digital technologies 118, 123–4, 134–5, 155
activism, digital 19, 148–50; critical perspectives 154–9; use of social media 133, 134
actor network theory 23, 46
ad-blocking tools 152
adigitals 122
Adkins, L. 106
affective labour 131–2
affective relationship 166–7
afterlife online services 173
age 120, 125–6
agriculture 98
Ahrens, J. 131
Aipperspach, R. 52–3

algorithmic authority 49–50, 100–5, 112
algorithmic identities 103–5
algorithmic veillance 36
algorithms 11, 26, 88–9, 100–5
altmetrics 80
Amazon 11
American Sociological Association 14
Amsterdam Real-Time project 52
Anderson, K. 52
Andrejevic, M. 158–9
Angwin, J. 116
anonymity 144–5
Anonymous 148, 156
Apple 166, 186; iPhone 166, 167, 168, 179
application program interfaces (APIs) 60–1
appropriation 38–9
apps 109, 113, 114; racist 138–9; sales of information from 97–8; young people and use of 126
Arab Spring 133, 156, 157
archetypes 129–30
archives 31–3
Asian countries 135–6
assemblages 23–4, 25, 26; and algorithmic authority 100–5; digital cyborg 165, 174–5; metric 26, 79–83; in research 48–9; surveillant 26, 34, 35
attacks, verbal 85–6, 137–40
audit culture 79–83

Learning
to Labor in
New Times

The *Critical Social Thought* Series
edited by Michael W. Apple, University of Wisconsin—Madison

Learning to Labor in New Times

Edited by

Nadine Dolby and Greg Dimitriadis
with Paul Willis

RoutledgeFalmer
NEW YORK AND LONDON

Published in 2004 by
RoutledgeFalmer
29 West 35th Street
New York, NY 10001
www.routledge-ny.com

Published in Great Britain by
RoutledgeFalmer
11 New Fetter Lane
London EC4P 4EE
www.routledgefalmer.com

10 9 8 7 6 5 4 3 2 1

Library of Congress Cataloging-in-Publication Data

Learning to labor in new times / edited by Nadine Dolby and Greg Dimitriadis.
       p.   cm. — (Critical social thought)
    Includes index.
    ISBN 0-415-94854-1 (alk. paper) — ISBN 0-415-94855-X (pbk. : alk. paper)
    1. Willis, Paul E. Learning to labour. 2. Youth—Employment. 3. Working class—
Education. I. Dolby, Nadine, 1964– II. Dimitriadis, Greg, 1969– III. Willis, Paul E.
Learning to labour. IV. Series.
    HD276.G7W5435 2004
    306.3'6'0835—dc22
                                                            2004041867

Contents

Acknowledgments

This book began as two panels at the 2002 meeting of the American Educational Research Association. We would like to thank Barry Fraser, then chair of the International Relations Committee, for his enthusiastic support. The panel participants—and the audiences—generated an enormous amount of energy and excitement about the work, and were the inspiration for developing a more sustained examination of the impact of Paul Willis's research and scholarly work on educational research over the last quarter century. We thank everyone who participated and the authors whose essays appear in this collection.

We thank the Office of the Vice-President for Research at Northern Illinois University for publication assistance. Joe Miranda and Catherine Bernard at RoutledgeFalmer were dedicated and wholly supportive—we are grateful for their commitment to this project. Samar Haddad provided outstanding support in the production process. Nadine would like to thank Stephen for his understanding during a hectic period of our lives, and for supporting her and this work. Greg would like to thank all his colleagues and students in the Graduate School of Education and the Department of Educational Leadership and Policy at the University at Buffalo.

Foreword

STANLEY ARONOWITZ

When I first read Paul Willis's *Learning to Labor* my first response was: Finally, someone has addressed schooling outcomes for working-class kids not as an instance of failure or victimhood. Instead Willis shows that working-class kids more or less consciously reject the cultural and political implications of buying into the curriculum and accepting school authority. In standard sociological terms, far from being labeled as "losers," the lads are exercising "agency" by choosing to "fail." I wrote the preface to the American edition of the book in these terms. My preface was, to say the least, incomplete. As several articles in this collection demonstrate *Learning to Labor* is suggestive in several additional dimensions. Because industrial labor has traditionally been associated with "manly" endeavor and intellectual labor has a distinctly feminine connotation, the "lads'" rebellion against school authority, in the first place against the classroom teacher, is an assertion of masculinity. As Willis himself points out, this gendered gesture mediates the lads' rebellion because it helps reproduce male superiority within gender relations as well as reproducing class relations.

Subsequently others, including myself, have situated Willis's superb ethnography in its historicity. Their entrance into the factory to which the lads gleefully escape after leaving school reproduces the class structure, but also reproduces the oppositional working-class culture inherited from their families, neighborhoods, and peers. Although in a wider context forms of working-class association are considered "sub" cultures, this does not

ix

proceed from a presupposition of inferiority to the dominant middle-class aspirations of social climbing and consumerism. In fact, the bonds of (male) class solidarity are forged on the shop floor as well as at the sites of working-class public spheres: the pub, the union hall, and noninstitutional sites such as the street corner. But the factory jobs that were still available in the early 1970s, when Willis engaged the lads, are now gone not only from the Midlands and from Hammertown—the city that is the sight of his study—but from many major industrial cities in Britain, continental Western Europe, and the United States. As subsequent studies of working-class life in cities demonstrate (notably Jay McLeod's *Aint No Makin' It* and William Julius Wilson's *When Work Disappears*, both about Chicago, among many others including my own analysis, with William DiFazio, *The Jobless Future*), those who leave school without acquiring a credential are almost invariably consigned to low-paying service jobs or long-term, sometimes permanent unemployment. And in many cities of the United States where the working class is composed mainly of Blacks, Latinos, and Asians, despite shrinking job opportunities, the patterns Willis discerns generally hold. Contrary to some observers like Moynihan and Glazer, Wilson, and anthropologists such as Oscar Lewis, it is not the "culture of poverty" that leads to and derives from the formation of an "underclass" of permanently unemployed people; casual and contingent work is the product of a new labor-market regime of Global Capitalism.

The historicity of Willis's great ethnography consists in its location in time and space. Since the late 1970s the political economy of global capitalism has radically altered conditions of life. The decentralization of production to all corners of the planet's geography has led to the disappearance of good jobs in the metropoles of the United States and other industrially developed societies, not only in low- and intermediate-technology industries, but also in high-tech sectors. The tale of the losses in textiles, garments, steel, and other major production industries is by now a commonplace. But in the last few years the easy assumption that services on the one hand and computers on the other would do more than take up the slack has suffered crushing repudiation. In 2003 no significant economic sector has elided massive reorganizations and steep job losses, but high-tech is no exception. After an explosion of hard- and software computer and computer-mediated manufacturing from the 1960s to the 1990s and the concomitant dot.com, boom both of which created employment for low-, moderate-, and fairly high-paid work, the turn of the 21st century has witnessed a pronounced bust. Chip makers have laid off low-paid Latino women in Silicon Valley just as software firms have shed computer programmers and engineers in the Microsoft Seattle empire and Silicon Alley in Manhattan. Recession tells only part of the story. Some of the best jobs have migrated to India and China, where, owing to good technical and scientific universities, engineers and computer scientists and technicians have proven able to design world-class equipment and software and earn a tenth of the salaries of their United States counterparts.

But overriding these considerations, the new regimes of computer-mediated industrial and service production—and the inability of labor unions to protect wages and benefits—have accelerated productivity, which far exceeds the economic growth rate, revealing the purpose of technological change: to reduce labor costs. Even without recession and job migration over time, cybernetic technologies reduce factory and service jobs absolutely and reduce them relative to the expansion of the labor force, even in growth periods. In the years between 2000 and 2003, even as the labor force grew by 3 percent the United States lost almost 3 million jobs, mostly in manufacturing, but increasingly in the services, including retail and wholesale trades and especially in financial services.

Having said this, working-class kids still drop out of school at alarming rates, while many others grimly hang in because they are well aware that there is no alternative to obtaining a credential of some sort, even if the credential carries no specific occupational qualifications. On the other hand, American colleges, technical institutes, and universities have, perhaps unwittingly, contributed to depressed salaries for credentialed computer workers by overproducing them in relation to the sagging job market. The hype of the 1990s—that computers would lead to almost infinite job and income opportunities—brought hundreds of thousands of students into a field that produced tens of thousands of good jobs. Armed with their associate and bachelor's degrees, many qualified computer technicians and programmers were delivered to a job market that offered only a small number of real jobs, but much part-time, contingent, and temporary work that usually carried no health benefits. For young people the first years of the new century have been disasterous. Many ended up waiting tables, working as construction laborers at nonunion sites, vainly trying sales, or entering rapidly declining financial services sector as licensed brokers, but with few clients. And others simply withdrew from the labor force and took work in the underground or informal economy.

The new working-class jobs—coded as forms of "professional" labor—bring with them neither good wages and benefits, nor do they reproduce working-class culture. As the first generation to have earned a postsecondary credential, many working-class kids have been inducted into the value systems and expectations of the salaried middle class, but without acquiring the accoutrements. Class identities have become ambiguous. Even as they seek professional and technical jobs, many retain their ties with the neighborhood and with their families because they have learned that the academic promises for social mobility have proven to be ephemeral. Yet, with some exceptions, neither the family nor the neighborhood provides a secure anchor missing in their work situations. Economic dislocation has pulled many families apart as siblings, frustrated with the dearth of jobs in their hometowns, move away in search of a better future, leaving parents and grandparents behind. And in the major cities of New York, Boston, Chicago, Los Angeles, and San Francisco, gentrification has driven millions from their once scorned ghetto and slum communities that nevertheless provided a sense of place for the Black and Latino working poor and the unemployed. What from outside appeared as ravaged neighborhoods were—and remain for many of their inhabitants—a haven in the heartless world, impoverished conditions notwithstanding.

Contemporary youth are frequently caught between still potent, although disintegrating, social networks of their childhood and youth and the stark reality that there are no good working-class jobs. Even as the struggle over loyalties never abates while they remain skeptical about the chances for good jobs, let alone genuine social mobility, school is perceived by a significant fraction of them as a necessary option. Needless to say, many working-class kids, Black, Latino, and white drop out of college because elementary and high schools have not prepared them, in either literacy or numeracy terms, for technical and scientific occupations much less the liberal arts.

Students who drop out of high school and community and senior colleges do not disappear from the face of the earth. Some, especially women, find full-time subprofessional or administrative jobs in government or in the health and education sectors. They work in so-called "caring" occupations such as nonprofessional nursing, dietary departments of schools and hospitals, and in commercial and residential building maintenance. These are now the "good" working-class jobs because they are usually unionized, provide health benefits, and are relatively protected from layoffs.

But most of them constitute the working poor. Contrary to ordinary belief, most work full-time for wages that are below the bogus official poverty line. They are the customers of the thousands of food pantries and kitchens because their meager take-home pay needs to be reserved for rent, which has skyrocketed almost everywhere in the Northeast and on the West Coast as well as in some cities of the heartland. Typically they live at home with their parent(s), relatives, and siblings. If they are fortunate to live in public housing, living conditions, although crowded, are somewhat better than in the tenements that, as everyone knows, were built to be slums. Or four or five take an apartment in order to pay the rent. And of course a certain number of dropouts enter the informal economy. They work off the books for subminimum wages or engage in illegal trade, mostly of drugs, and a few do become petty thieves.

In every state the period of deindustrialization corresponds to the burgeoning prison systems, which today house more than 2 million residents, the highest number and percentage of the population of any industrial country. Most are incarcerated for victimless crimes such as drug use and drug dealing and, in many states, are obliged to serve prolonged mandatory sentences. Prison culture may be brutal but it is the culture of the oppressed. For young Black and Latino men, often the consequence of their antiauthoritarian revolt is to find themselves, sooner or later, in the so-called criminal "justice" system, either as inmates, parolees, or probationers. According to some students of the process, a third of all Black men between 16 and 25 years old can expect to be within the purview of the criminal justice system sometime in their adolescent or adult lives.

Prisons are awful places, but, like families, neighborhoods, and peer groups, they are, perhaps, more important educational sites than the schools. For what Paul Willis has taught us—and this may be the most important contribution of *Learning to Labor*—is that schools are in constant competition for the hearts and minds of youth with powerful, oppositional cultural sites that regard schooling from an adversarial perspective. That in the context of urbanism the current form of these cultures is often coded in racial rather than class terms does not erase the fact that for the overwhelming majority of Blacks, Latinos, and Asians, segregation and economic deprivation are both class and race issues. More to the point, the constellation of circumstances—jobs or the lack thereof, segregated neighborhoods, common cohabitation in prisons, social relationships that form communities of class/race solidarity—reproduces an oppositional, if not an explicitly working-class culture, the representations of which in the media, rap music, and other popular forms are as ubiquitous as they are misapprehended by the dominant social formations.

CHAPTER 1

Learning to Labor in New Times
An Introduction

NADINE DOLBY AND GREG DIMITRIADIS

This book grew out of two panels at the 2002 annual meeting of the American Educational Research Association that honored the 25th anniversary of the U.S. publication of *Learning to Labor*, and the indispensable contribution of Paul Willis to educational research worldwide. Willis's many contributions during his (still flourishing) career speak to the importance of everyday worlds and lives, and to his commitment to ensuring that youth's realities—of school, of work, of home, of community, and of media culture—are consistently at the forefront of our agendas for research, and for political change. From the seminal *Learning to Labor*, to his more recent work on a major policy document, *The Youth Review*, Willis repeatedly insists that what youth *do* is important: they function as political actors, and they are not simply dupes of a wholly reproductive class system.

Several words continually reappear in the copious amounts of literature devoted to the study and critique of Willis's work over the past quarter century: *class, education,* and *ethnography.* An exploration of these three connected aspects of his writing and research structures this volume's engagement with his work. Such an emphasis is particularly appropriate at this moment, as all three terms are undergoing profound, substantive changes that reconfigure the way that educational researchers will approach their work in this century. First, as we discuss throughout this introduction and the book, "class"—as an explanatory category and

1

a site of identification—is reemerging as a key locus of academic inquiry.[1] Second, "education" as a public good is under threat globally, as corporate practices and privatization are increasingly accepted as the norm (Apple, 2001; Klein, 2000; Stromquist, 2003). Finally, "ethnography," as a practice is reshaping itself in light of decades of harsh critique, so that it can continue to be a significant force in academic practices that help us to understand, and transform, social and cultural worlds. In this introduction, we map theses three trajectories in Willis's work, and then introduce the essays in this volume. As is evident throughout this volume, Paul Willis's remarkable contributions to the rich literature on class, education, and ethnography are formative sparks that will undoubtedly mold how educational researchers make sense of, and attempt to influence, this new terrain.

Learning to Labor: Twenty-Five Years Later

Learning to Labor: How Working Class Kids Get Working Class Jobs is arguably one of the most significant educational research studies of the 20th century. The book was originally published in Britain in 1977 by Gower Press. Since that time, it has been reprinted nine times in Britain, published in a separate U.S. edition in 1981, and published in German, Swedish, Finnish, Japanese, Spanish, Portuguese, and Korean. Based on an ethnographic study of a group of working-class boys in a secondary school in an industrial area of England in the 1970s, Willis's analysis of the lads' role in the production and reproduction of their position in the working class stands as major contribution to multiple fields, including education, anthropology, sociology, cultural studies, and political science. Within education, Willis's work precipitated a major shift in the way that researchers have come to understand the school as a site of political, social, and cultural struggle, and the way that youth's identities are constituted within schools, ground largely in their own particular autonomy.

Through the 1970s, the dominant approach to class analysis in education had been structural (see Morrow & Torres, 1995). Bowles and Gintis's influential *Schooling in Capitalist America* (1976) was perhaps the most important text in this regard. For Bowles and Gintis, schools had a key functional role in the reproduction of capitalism, preparing young people to take their places in a differentiated class hierarchy. Schools operated on what they called a "correspondence principle," and were anything but a meritocracy. One's class position was determined by family income rather than one's achievement in school. Schools helped, more often than not, to create and justify the *illusion* of meritocracy, but not its reality. For Bowles and Gintis, the pedagogical experience was about learning to take one's place in the capitalist system.

Ultimately, or "in the final instance," capitalism was reproduced. There was little room for transformative action, for an understanding of human agency, or for the rearticulation of ones circumstances.

Willis's *Learning to Labor* came out of a very different kind of history and academic tradition. Although Bowles and Gintis were both economists, trained in statistical methods, Willis situated himself within the more interpretive, humanistic, and ethnographic tradition of the Birmingham School for Cultural Studies. Here, there was an effort to understand the cultural dimensions of everyday life, how people lived through the structural conditions they found themselves in. There was, of course, a stress on agency and creativity in this regard, and an effort to understand social structures from the ground up.

Learning to Labor is an ethnography of working-class youth in an industrial town Willis calls Hammertown, conducted between 1972 and 1975. Hammertown is, for Willis, an "archetypal industrial town." It had first been industrialized over 200 years before Willis began his work (p. 6). As Willis explains, the total labor force in this town was about 36,000, with an extremely high percentage—79%—involved in manufacturing. Half of these jobs were in metal and metal goods, wherease the other half included the production of bricks, pottery and glass, and food, beverages, and tobacco.

For this study, Willis followed a small group—about 12—of working-class youth throughout their school day. He attended classes and leisure activities and at points accompanied them onto the shop floor. He interviewed individual youth, recorded group discussions, and interviewed parents, senior masters at the school, the youth's teachers, and career officers. As the study was multisited, Willis also interviewed and spent time with a smaller cohort of other youth.

Willis's findings are, by now, well known. These working-class boys create a culture of resistance and opposition to authority. As Willis writes, "The opposition is expressed mainly as style. It is lived out in countless small ways which are special to the school institution, instantly recognized by the teachers, and an almost ritualistic part of the daily fabric of life for the kids" (p. 12). These boys spend their days "dosing, blagging, and wagging." Above all else, "having a laff" is key. "Opposition to the school is principally manifested in the struggle to win symbolic and physical space from the institution and its rules and to defeat its main perceived purpose: to make you 'work'" (p. 26). These boys enact everyday resistances to all symbols of school authority—teachers as well as conformist youth.

Willis powerfully documents the emergence of an aggressive, White working-class masculinity. The youth in his study violently mark out the boundaries of their lives: They are aggressively territorial about their neighborhood and are quick to fight. The lads are also sexist and racist. Young women must be sexually attractive, but "giving in" to sex devalues them immeasurably. Courtship is complicated business. "The referent is the home—dependability and domesticity—the opposite of the sexy bird on the scene. If the initial attraction is based on sex, the final settlement is based on a strange denial of sex" (p. 44). A kind of "domestic code" rules the day (Weis, 1990). In racial terms, the boys define themselves against Asians and West Indians, seeing both as "foreign," "smelly," and "dirty" yet still differentiated (and threatening) in sometimes divergent ways.

Willis displays the counters of an emergent White working-class masculinity. He focused on these young men's resistance to school authority and the way they were able to subvert dominant culture on a local level through devaluing school life. Crucially, it also means that they are invested in masculine kinds of labor activities, the kinds of work associated with manual labor and heavy industry. Perhaps Willis's most important insight is that these young men are complicit in their own class reproduction. The kinds of dispositions they generate in school prepare them for life on the shop floor. In addition to the immediate financial rewards, they are more likely to "have a laff" on the shop floor. The culture of resistance generated in school is entirely continuous with work culture. It is a cruel irony. In one of the book's more trenchant moments, Willis asserts:

> For no matter what the larger pattern of working class culture and cycle of its continuous regeneration, no matter what the severity of disillusionment amongst "the lads" as they get older, their passage is to all intents and purposes irreversible. When the cultural apprenticeship of the shopfloor is fully worked out, and its main real activity of arduous production for others in unpleasant surroundings is seen more clearly, there is a double kind of entrapment in what might be seen, as the school was seen before, as the prison of the workshop. Ironically, as the shopfloor becomes a prison, education is seen retrospectively, and hopelessly, as the only escape. (p. 107)

This is only one of the study's most enduring findings. Along with this class reproduction, however, is the notion that there are cracks in this edifice. Reproduction is never total. In what Willis refers to as moments of "partial penetration," the lads understand that they are positioned as abstract labor. These are key insights: insights about the nature of the lads' labor and their control over it. However, as noted, these penetrations are largely subverted by their own resistant practices.

Youth, Common Culture, and The Ethnographic Imagination

One of the most sustained legacies of *Learning to Labor* is its focus on youth's agency. Though the lads' resistance and "victory" was pyrrhic, Willis drew attention to the importance of scrutinizing youth's everyday lives and practices through ethnography. In Willis's later work (*Profane Culture* [1978], *Common Culture* [1990], and *The Ethnographic Imagination* [2001]) he specifically extends and examines the substantive and methodological implications of what he terms youth's everyday cultural lives. The "ethnographic imagination perspective" that Willis develops is one that acknowledges the "art" of everyday life, that understands people make sense out of their lives in creative ways and that there are moments of penetrating insight worth exploring and documenting (Willis, 2001, p. xx). Youth are a critical focus for understanding contemporary societal dynamics, for, as Willis notes, youth are at the forefront of confronting and negotiating the new modes of technological and human transformation at the core of modernization. He writes,

> Young people respond in disorganized and chaotic ways, but to the best of their abilities and with relevance to the actual possibilities of their lives as they see, live, and embody them. These responses are actually embedded in the flows of cultural modernization, but to adult eyes they may seem to be mysterious, troubling, and even shocking and anti-social. (Willis, 2003, p. 391)

Yet, as Willis reflects, it is not enough to simply document or record the minutiae of youth's everyday lives, as if it existed in some pretheoretical world. Instead, researchers must creatively bring this experiential material into "some relation to theory," thereby "maximizing the illumination both of wider change and of the ethnographic data" (2001, p. 114). Indeed, Willis implores us to avoid the twin dangers in contemporary social scientific work—the danger of presenting empirical material divorced from theoretical reflection, as well as the danger of theoretical reflection divorced from an engagement with the empirical.

For Willis, there is something irreducible about the human experience. Reflecting on *Learning to Labor*, he noted that he had "a 'common sense' view which knew that your identity was always *more* than class, gender, or ethnicity, involving a whole set of points about the way you lived, how you fitted in, who you knew, what the myriad of your personal and domestic relations were: these things were separate from the theories that I picked up specifying obvious binary divisions" (Mills & Gibb, Appendix, this volume). Ethnography is a way at getting at some of this cultural complexity, a way to reflect on experience in ways that go beyond easy categories and distinctions.

Ultimately, this kind of work points us to a broader project that looks to understand the ways people creatively deal with their realities, which is one of the enduring lessons of *Learning to Labor*. Willis's politics center on capturing this spark "of creativity or aspiration"—which is at the core of the lads paradoxical "moment of partial penetration"—and using it to propel us into the terrain of new possibilities. Here we find Willis's hope, as he reflects that this spark is "routinely lost, distorted or alienated or turned into reified forms" though "never quite lost" (Mills & Gibb, Appendix, this volume).

Willis has spent much of the past few years extending these concerns, studying young people's cultural lives. In particular, his influential *Common Culture* documented the multiple uses to which a group of young people put popular culture, or, as he writes, the "common culture" that young people create and sustain. Willis, for example, celebrates the ways that young people subvert dominant music and fashion industries by taping music from the radio for free and buying secondhand clothes and using them in exciting and interesting ways. He also documents the ways in which an all-pervasive media culture has come to wholly saturate the rituals of everyday life,

> The omnipresent cultural media of the electronic age provide a wide range of symbolic resources for, and are a powerful stimulant of, the symbolic work and creativity of young people. . . . The media enter into virtually all of their very creative activities. But whilst the media invite certain interpretations, young people have not only learnt the codes, but have learnt to play with interpreting the codes, to reshape forms, to interrelate the media through their own grounded aesthetics. They add to and develop new meanings from given ones. (Willis, 1990, p. 30)

Willis does much to highlight the work that young people invest in popular culture and the ways in which popular culture is occluding contemporary school culture for many. If *Learning to Labor* focused largely on school life, *Common Culture* was a more fully contextualized look at young people's creative lives as they traverse a wider range of spaces. Indeed, one of the major implications of *Common Culture* was its impulse to decenter "school" as the most relevant node in young people's lives and open up a much wider range of texts and sites for study.

Willis's expansive engagement with the lives of young people, it's critical to note, is imperative to developing policy from below. Just as Willis challenges the official role that schools play in young people's lives, he also opens up a space for us to ask what kind of policies make sense from "the ground up." This was also a vital part of *The Youth Review* compendium he helped to put together. The study, undertaken in Wolverhampton and sponsored by the Labour party, was an effort to understand the effects of unemployment on local youth, asking one of the most persistent new questions about work and class: What happens to the working-class when work disappears? As Willis reflects, this study indexed the "new social condition" of youth, and, consistent with his commitments to youth's realities and agency, asserted that "policies could be derived from the actual existing condition of the youth, rather than from the view of the powerful as to how they should change or be formed" (Mills & Gibb, Appendix, this volume).

Willis in New Times

At the time of publication, and shortly thereafter, *Learning to Labor* was critiqued for privileging class analysis over the persistent dynamics of gender and race. Most notably, Angela McRobbie charged that Willis overlooked the lives of young girls, reinforcing the lads' own sexist stereotypes. She wrote:

> Questions around sexism and working-class youth and around sexual violence make it possible to see how class and patriarchal relations work together, sometimes with an astonishing brutality and at other times in the 'teeth gritting harmony' of romance, love and marriage. One of Willis's "lads" says of his girlfriend, "She loves doing fucking housework. Trousers I brought up yesterday, I took 'em up last night her turned 'em up for me. She's as good as gold and I wanna get married as soon as I can."
> Until we come to grips with such expressions as they appear across the subcultural field, our portrayal of girls' culture will remain one-sided and youth culture will continue to "mean" in uncritically masculine terms. Questions about girls, sexual relations and femininity in youth will continue to be defused or marginalized in the ghetto of women's studies. (McRobbie, 1991, p. 18)

McRobbie's critique was incisive, and one that resonated with then-growing interest in questions of "identity" and "recognition" in the academy. In the United States in particular, although the mantra of race, class, and gender was often evoked, it was questions of race and gender that moved to the center of academic analysis. Although there are varying perspectives on why class analysis slipped off of the agenda of the left in the 1980s and 1990s (see Peter McLaren & Valerie Scatamburlo-D'Annibale, chap. 3, this volume), one of the most certain realities is that the "working class" was harder to find and locate as a political movement and social force. Politically, the

Thatcher and Reagan "revolutions" of the late 1970s and 1980s largely articulated working-class concerns to a rightist agenda that appealed to White, nativist sentiments, at the same time that the clout of labor declined, and the structural conditions of the economy changed. The new social movements of the 1960s and 1970s sutured identities around gender, race, sexual orientation, and disability, displacing any sense of collective identities that were specifically linked to class location—despite the fact that movements based on social identities were often fractured and ultimately rendered powerless by latent class splits.

The late 1990s and the turn of the 21st century have bred a new set of realities, and a new set of contexts vis-à-vis class and capitalism and their relationship to schooling. Willis brilliantly documented a particular moment in the historical narrative of capitalism—a moment that has now evaporated, to be replaced with a story that is more complex and, in many respects, more troubling. First, it is clear that the structural conditions of capital have shifted dramatically since Willis's study of a small industrial town. Corporations in "First World" nations such as the United States, the United Kingdom, and Australia have largely closed domestic operations and industrial production, moving operations to free trade zones and "Third World" countries where they exploit a largely destitute, Black, nonunionized workforce that is desperate to simply stay alive. This literal relocation has been devastating to the economic health of the White working class, who may now look back on the lads' situation with nostalgic longing, for at least the lads had a job awaiting them. Today's working class in the industrialized world is largely employed in low-wage jobs with no possibility of advancement, overwhelmingly, Black, often immigrant, and largely female. Second, such changes also reflect the material changes in the constitution of capitalism, as "productive labor" fades as the real basis of the economic structure, to be replaced with an age where the economy is largely driven by the circulation of capital through the fluctuations of markets. As Benjamin Lee and Edward LiPuma (2002) argued, the shifts in the way that capital is imagined has material consequences for its function, changes that have rapidly accelerated in the 30 years since the Bretton Woods agreement, which created enormous transformations in international financial markets. Such changes have also had implications for the cultural imaginings of modernity (Appadurai, 1996), the relationship between culture and capital (Jameson & Miyoshi, 1998; Lowe & Loyd, 1997), and the constitution of human and economic communities (Castells, 2000; Ong, 1999; Sassen, 2001, 2002).

Of course, these global repositionings also have implications for the ways that scholars theorize about the relationship between school, work, class, and capital, and how we make sense of youth's school and work identities. For example, Lois Weis's (1990) study of a White working-class high school in a deindustrializing area of the United States examines what happens to working class identities when there is no work, a theme that is also probed in several of Stanley Aronowitz's latest books (Aronowitz, 2001; Aronowitz & Cutler, 1998). Although Willis's study assumed a close relationship between the state, the economy, and the schools, such linkages are no longer as strong, as economies and educational systems are increasingly positioned within global, not national, contexts (Apple, 2003; Burbules & Torres, 2000; Stromquist & Monkman, 2000). Despite these powerful and often over-whelming forces, Willis's work reminds us that sparks proliferate, and that we must continually look to youth and their creativity to understand the potentials that exist at any specific moment. For example, as Naomi Klein (2000) demonstrated, there is a growing anticorporate sentiment among young people today. Within the context of schooling, Willis (2003) recently argued that educational researchers must focus attention on what he terms the "third wave" of cultural modernization, in which commodities are central to creative processes of identity, and to the revamped terrain of social and political relations and power.

Willis's work matters because it taps into questions that are at the core of any contemporary research or practice that is concerned with (re)building what Michael Apple termed "thick democracy" in a historical era when citizenship has become conflated with consumption (2003, p. 12; Dolby, 2003). For example, how do we define and think about the working-class in the context of changed state power, new global formations, and empire; how do youth still "learn to labor" under these conditions; and how can schools, as sites of power and struggle, change these realities? As Paul Willis demonstrates through his work over the last 25 years, the everyday lives of ordinary people—the literal and metaphorical "streets" of the world—are at the center of the answers (Willis, 1990).

The Essays

The essays in this volume are divided into three sections. In the first section, Madeleine Arnot, Peter McLaren and Valerie Scatamburlo-D'Annibale, Michael Apple, and Fazal Rizvi engage with the complexities of *Learning to Labor*, taking up both its limitations and possibilities within its own histor-ical moment, and as we reflect on it from the vantage point of 2004. In the second section, Jane Kenway and Anna Kraack, Lois Weis, Kathleen Nolan and Jean Anyon, and Cameron McCarthy probe *Learning to Labor*, and Willis's other works, for their relevance for "new times," how we might retain and reinvigorate Willis's insights about class into the remarkably different economic, cultural, political, and cultural landscape that we face, and the ways that Willis's work can motivate and inspire a new generation of educational scholars. The volume concludes with reflections from Paul Willis, and David Mills and Robert Gibb's 2001 interview with Paul Willis, "'Centre' and Periphery.'"

Section I: Reflecting on *Learning to Labor*

In Section I, authors focus their reflections and analysis on Willis's work. Although *Learning to Labor* provides the anchor for this section, other texts are also discussed, within a broad framework of assessing the impact of *Learning to Labor* for educational theory, analysis, and policy.

Madeleine Arnot's chapter, "Male Working-Class Identities and Social Justice: A Reconsideration of Paul Willis's *Learning to Labor* in Light of Contemporary Research," opens the volume with a discerning analysis of *Learning to Labor*, examining three different readings of the book, and then placing *Learning to Labor* within the context of contemporary research on male working class identities. Arnot's thorough essay carefully interrogates many of the historical and contemporary critiques of the book, specifically in regard to the intersection of gender and class in Willis's work.

Although Arnot's work explores the intersection of gender and class, the second chapter of the volume returns us to the "abiding centrality of class." In "Paul Willis, Class Consciousness, and Critical Pedagogy: Toward a Socialist Future," Peter McLaren and Valerie Scatamburlo-D'Annibale explore the political trajectories and possibilities that emanate from several of Willis's works, including *Learning to Labor*, *Common Culture*, and *The Ethnographic Imagination*. McLaren and Scatamburlo-D'Annibale argue for a politics that moves beyond the defetishizing of cultural practices into the development of the working-class consciousness that is evident in Willis's analysis. Drawing on Willis, McLaren and Scatamburlo-D'Annibale aim to resituate class as both a lived culture and an objective existence, and to use this positioning to move towards a socialist future.

The concluding two essays of this section analyze Willis's work for what can be understood about yet another intersection: this time, between class and race. In his contribution to this volume, "Between Good Sense and Bad Sense: Race, Class, and Learning from *Learning to Labor*," Michael Apple begins by tracing the influence of Paul Willis's work on his own intellectual development, noting that Willis's theoretical insights have helped to shape Apple's notions of "good" and "bad" sense, and the contradictions inherent in various positionalities, such as race and class. In the essay, Apple develops this analysis through an extended critique of BAEO, the Black Alliance for Educational Options, an alliance of African American parents and teachers who are supporters of the neo-liberal policy of school vouchers. Apple concludes by observing that Willis's work provides a critical touchstone for educational research in the future, as scholars strive to critically engage the understandings provided by the last two decades of "post" analysis without sliding back into a reductive class analysis.

In the final chapter in this section, "The 'Lads' and the Cultural Topography of Race," Fazal Rizvi complicates *Learning to Labor* through questioning the relationship between the "lads" and the racial "others" who populated their lives. Reflecting on his own experience in England as a "racial other" at the time, Rizvi interrogates Britain's colonial history and postcolonial present, and uses Stuart Hall's idea of "new ethnicities" to theorize the impact of new, hybrid cultural forms on the subjectivities of Willis's lads—past, present, and future. Rizvi concludes by arguing that racial relations, in Britain and elsewhere, must be understood within a global framework, one that recognizes both the entrenched racial antagonisms of the present, and the spaces of hybrid, dynamic identities that simultaneously flourish.

As a group, these essays reflect on the multiple contributions of Paul Willis's work to educational research over the past 25 years, and the continued relevance of his analysis for understanding the dynamic and intricate intersections between class, education, and the economy.

Section II: Learning to Labor in New Times

In Section II, "Learning to Labor in New Times," authors collectively interrogate how global economic shifts—including the massive shift away from industrial economies toward service-based ones—have registered attendant cultural, gender, and racial dynamics on the quotidian lives of 21st century citizens. Indeed, one of Willis's central insights was to show how "the lads' " gendered and racialized identities were imbricated in their ideas about labor itself. The four chapters in this section ask what happens when the reality of work itself changes, what "identity work" happens and why.

Jane Kenway and Anna Kraack's chapter, "Reordering Work and Destabilizing Masculinity," looks at how young men have responded to the shift to deindustrialized economies in two Australian locales. According to Kenway and Kraack, generations of men have "earn[ed] respect and reputation by performing a job well and diligently and by working hard to earn a decent wage." The move to a service economy is often seen as a move to "feminized" labor, potentially destabilizing these notions of male selfhood. Kenway and Kraack interrogate the dynamics at two different sites in Australia, comparing and contrasting responses. In the first example, Putland, men largely hold onto their ever-antiquated ideas about the labor market, internalizing many of their failures. In the second example,

Paradise, younger generations of men look to a growing tourist industry, potentially redefining their notions of labor and gender.

In the following chapter, "Revisiting a 'Moment of Critique': Class, Gender, and the New Economy," Lois Weis revisits the participants in her earlier study, *Working-class Without Work*. In this earlier study, Weis famously discussed a "moment of critique" in her teen working-class female participants—the burgeoning idea that they could not rely on men to take care of them, that they needed to achieve their own education and career. In this follow-up study, Weis reinterviewed these (now) young adults to see how this critique played out in their lives. She highlights the experiences of two young women, Judy and Suzanne. Although distinct in many ways, each young woman, in fact, actualized many of her earlier dreams and aspirations for an education and career. However, neither was able to fully disentangle themselves from the patriarchal gender relations they grew up with. In particular, neither was able to fully escape the brutality of male abuse, whether from husband or partner.

Both Kenway and Kraack and Weis show how changing economic contexts have reworked traditional notions of gender. In the next chapter, "Learning to Do Time: Willis's Model of Cultural Reproduction in an Era of Postindustrialism, Globalization, and Mass Incarceration," Kathleen Nolan and Jean Anyon move the discussion more explicitly to the terrain of race. Here, Nolan and Anyon extend Willis's discussion of school, work, and social reproduction for working-class White youth, to the terrain of contemporary Black youth. For these youth, incarceration is an increasingly prevalent reality, largely supplanting the role and importance of school. The authors situate the rise of incarceration with multiple and varied pressures of globalization, including the rise of the prison industry, as well as the growth of a "surplus" population of underskilled youth. Drawing on compelling ethnographic data, they argue that young people are more and more embodying dispositions—echoes of Willis's lads' "having a laff"—that will prepare them for a lifetime of intermittent incarceration. They end, however, on a hopeful note, noting that the cultural manifestations of urban youth are being articulated to larger political movements.

Finally, Cameron McCarthy's chapter, "Thinking About the Cultural Studies of Education in a Time of Recession: *Learning to Labor* and the Work of Aesthetics in Modern Life," brings this section to a close. Here, McCarthy argues for the role and importance of aesthetics in everyday life. The kind of material reproduction that Willis assumed in his work has been supplanted for many marginalized youth. More and more, the imagination is a material fact, as is the complex self-fashioning that is linked to global popular culture. According to McCarthy, Willis's "nationally and geographically inscribed lads" are largely being replaced by a more complex set of identifications and affiliations—"the new representational technologies are the centers of public instruction providing the forum for the work of the imagination of the great masses of the people to order their pasts and present and plot their futures."

Taken together, these chapters extend the implications of Willis's work to more context-specific treatments of social and cultural reproduction. These articles all affirm the importance of material realities while looking beyond them, to the variability of life for contemporary global subjects.

Section III: Critical Ethnography, Culture, and Schooling: Paul Willis Reflects on *Learning to Labor*

The book concludes, in Section III, with Paul Willis's reflections, "Twenty-Five Years On: Old Books, New Times." In his reflection, Willis calls for a new commitment to ethnographic research that ranges across a wide swath of cultural sites, restoring the primacy of the everyday in critical analysis of new times.

Notes

1. Note, for example, the significant interest in Michael Hardt and Antonio Negri's *Empire* (2000).

References

Appadurai, A. (1996). *Modernity at large: Cultural dimensions of globalization.* Chicago: University of Chicago Press.

Apple, M. (2001). *Educating the "right" way: Markets, standards, god, and inequality.* New York: RoutledgeFalmer.

Apple, M. (2003). *The state and the politics of knowledge.* New York: RoutledgeFalmer.

Aronowitz, S. (2001). *The last good job in America: Work and education in the new global techno-culture.* Lanham, MD: Rowman & Littlefield.

Aronowitz, S., & Cutler, J. (1998). *Post-work: The wages of cybernation.* New York: Routledge.

Bowles, S., & Gintis, H. (1976). *Schooling in capitalist America: Educational reform and the contradictions of economic life.* New York: Basic Books.

Burbules, N. & Torres, C. (2001). *Globalization and education: Critical perspectives.* New York: Routledge.

Castells, M. (2000). *The rise of the network society* (2nd ed.). Oxford, UK: Blackwell.

Dolby, N. (2003). Popular culture and democratic practice. *Harvard Educational Review 73*(3), 258–284.

Hardt, M., & Negri, A. (2000). *Empire.* Cambridge, MA: Harvard University Press.

Jameson, F., & Miyoshi, M. (Eds.). (1998). *The cultures of globalization.* Durham, NC: Duke University Press.

Klein, N. (2000). *No logo.* New York: Picador.

Lee, B., & LiPuma, E. (2002). Cultures of circulation: The imaginations of modernity. *Public Culture, 14*(1), 191–213.

Lowe, L., & Lloyd, D. (Eds.). (1997). *The politics of culture in the shadow of capital.* Durham, NC: Duke University Press.

McRobbie, A. (1991). *Feminism and youth culture: From Jackie to just seventeen.* Boston: Unwin Hyman.

Morrow, R., & Torres, C. (1995). *Social theory and education: A critique of theories of social and cultural reproduction.* Albany: State University of New York Press.

Ong, A. (1999). *Flexible citizenship: The cultural logics of transnationality.* Durham, NC: Duke University Press.

Sassen, S. (2001). *The global city: New York, London, Tokyo* (2nd ed.). Princeton, NJ: Princeton University Press.

Sassen, S. (Ed.). (2002). *Global networks, linked cities.* New York: Routledge.

Stromquist, N. (2003). *Education in a globalized world: The connectivity of economic power, technology, and knowledge.* Lanham, MD: Rowman and Littlefield.

Stromquist, N., & Monkman, K. (Eds.). (2000). *Globalization and education: Integration and contestation across cultures.* Lanham, MD: Rowman and Littlefield.

Weis, L. (1990). *Working class without work: High school students in a de-industrializing economy.* New York: Routledge.

Willis, P. (1981). *Learning to labor: How working class kids get working class jobs.* New York: Columbia University Press. (Original work published 1977)

Willis, P. (1978). *Profane culture.* London: Routledge & Kegan Paul.

Willis, P. (1990). *Common culture.* Milton Keynes, UK: Open University Press.

Willis, P. (2001). *The ethnographic imagination.* Cambridge, UK: Polity Press.

Willis, P. (2003). Foot soldiers of modernity. *Harvard Educational Review, 73*(3), 390–415.

Reflecting on *Learning to Labor*

CHAPTER 2

Male Working-Class Identities and Social Justice

A Reconsideration of Paul Willis's Learning to Labor *in Light of Contemporary Research*

MADELEINE ARNOT

The publication of Paul Willis's *Learning to Labor* in 1977 represented a landmark in the study of social identities and social justice in education. When first published, Willis's seminal thesis about why working-class boys get working-class jobs was described on its back cover as "an uncompromising book which is certain to provoke considerable controversy." Twenty-five years later, the book is still one of the most cited sociology texts in the study of education. The fact that this text has been read and reread in the very different decades of the 1970s, 1980s, and 1990s and now in the new century is indicative of the power of its analysis. In an extraordinary way, Willis's text links the "problem" of working-class education, which has framed social democratic policy discourses since 1944, with contemporary concerns about identities, culture, and social change. Rereading Willis at this critical stage in the field of sociology, I want to argue, has significance beyond the immediate concerns of the book. The various rereadings of the book, only some of which I refer to in this chapter, exemplify some of the complex theoretical and methodological shifts in critical educational theory. I argue that, despite the numerous rigorous criticisms of Willis's theory of working-class culture and the social-cultural reproduction of working-class inequalities, the themes of his study still represent an important symbolic marker in the study of gender and social class identities and in the development of critical research methodologies associated with transformative politics. Arguably, the book also represents a more grounded and situated analysis of identity than is currently on offer. Rereading the text therefore proffers the chance to reflect critically on the current theoretical project on social identities, social justice, and schooling.

I begin that discussion by illustrating three rather different readings of the book, before exploring how male class identities are now being researched and related to issues of social justice.

Connecting Identity, Agency, and Structure

Willis's research was conducted with a group of 12 working-class boys attending Hammertown school in the huge industrial conurbation in the Midlands. At the time, the town was working class with only 8% classified as professional middle class. The population was around 60,000 with one of the highest activity rates in the country. Women were especially active in this town, and most members of the labor force (some 79%) were involved in manufacturing in metal and metal goods; the rest worked in food, drinks, and tobacco industries, mechanical engineering, vehicles, bricks, pottery and glass, and distribution. Unemployment in the early 1970s in this area was only 1% under the national average. As Willis noted, Hammertown was "something of an archetypal industrial town. It has all the classic industrial hallmarks as well as those of modern monopoly capitalism in conjunction with a proletariat which is just about the oldest in the world" (p. 6).

The Hammertown "lads" studied by Willis had developed their own strong "antischool" culture—a culture that they had developed creatively out of the materials, resources, and insights available to them. Their praxis—the creative development, transformation, and reproduction of aspects of the larger culture—paradoxically and critically led them to certain kinds of work. The effect was "the manual giving of their labor power" to the structures of Western capitalism. This giving, "a compact with the future" as Willis described it, took working-class destiny and reformed it into new purposes. Part of that process involved what he called the "partial penetration" of the "really determining conditions of existence of the working class" (p. 3), which belied official versions given to them by the school and society.

> The tragedy and the contradiction is that these forms of "penetration" are limited, distorted and turned back on themselves, often

unintentionally, by complex processes ranging from both general ideological processes and those within the school and guidance agencies to the widespread influence of a form of patriarchal male domination and sexism within working class culture itself. (Willis, 1977, p. 3)

Using his data, Willis offered an explanation about the failure of the educational system to improve the chances of these lads. Central to his analysis was the role of labor power, and in Part 2 of the book, Willis explored the relationship of patriarchy (and to a lesser extent racialism) to capitalism. The meaning of laboring and labor power to these "young non–academic and disaffected males" was understood in the context of the logic of these other social divisions. Thus Willis demonstrated empirically how the working class cultural pattern of the educational failure of manual working-class children was different from other middle-class and working-class patterns found in schools—it had its own logic, experiences, relationships, choices, and decisions. In this analysis, the extraordinary conjunction of structural and subjective possibilities were brought together in the description of the experiences and identifications of one particular group of youth.

Learning to Labor therefore spoke to the concerns of social justice, which, at the time, were focused on male working class educational experiences and offered an analysis of class identities that resonated with the sociological discourses then current. Willis himself described how the book "hit a certain time in academic history, a certain time in Marxism, in cultural studies, educational sociology, a certain time in educational politics around an emerging disillusionment and disenchantment with the promises of comprehensive schooling" (Willis, quoted in Mills & Gibb, Appendix, this volume). The analysis went to the heart of the liberal democratic merito-cratic ideals of schooling which in the post war settlement offered schools a contradictory dual repertoire (CCCS, 1981)—the pursuit of economic growth coupled with the desire to encourage greater social equality and cohesion. This dual repertoire at the center of Labour's reform efforts brought together vocational and liberal discourses within the school. Economic rationalism was coupled the promotion of the individual skills and competencies with the tapping of working-class pools of talent and the promotion of a more educated society. In contrast, Willis's research exposed the injustice and forms of "institutional repression" (Willis, 2000, p. 38) associated with such a repertoire for manual working-class boys. Creden-tialism, the boys understood, could no more lead to the "dismantling of the whole class society" (p. 38) than it could improve the chances of the manual working class. According to Willis,

> Prevented from pursuing alternative flowerings of their capacities or subversive courses of growth, credentialism enslaves their ["the lads"] powers and seeks to trap them in the foothills of human development. . . . From the collective point of view, lived out in the culture of "the lads," the proliferation of qualifications is simply a worthless inflation of the currency of credentialism, and advance through it, a fraudulent offer to the majority of what can really mean something only to the few (pp. 38–39)

However, the consequences of revealing such "institutional repression" underlying the functioning of meritocracy through certification were not necessarily negative. Curiously, Willis's account of the transitions of the young working-class male into manual labor confirmed to teachers that not only could they not be held directly responsible for working-class failure but also that by hearing the collective voices of "the lads," teachers could begin to address the realities of the boys' lives and intervene on their behalf in transformative ways. Distancing himself from the more deterministic func-tionalism of social/cultural reproduction theory, Willis positioned himself within what he saw as the radical educational practice that was being nurtured by the Centre for Contemporary Cultural Studies at Birmingham University at that time. Reflecting on his work, he wrote:

> If we have nothing to say about what to do on Monday morning everything is yielded to a purist structuralist immobilising reduc-tionist tautology: nothing can be done until the basic structures of society are changed but the structures prevent us making any changes. . . . To contract out of the messy business of day to day problems is to deny the active, contested nature of social and culture reproduction: to condemn real people to the status of passive zombies, and actually cancel the future by default. To refuse the challenge of the day to day . . . is to deny the continuance of life and society themselves. It is a theoretical as well as a political failure. (Willis, 1977, p. 186, quoted in Skeggs, 1992, p. 182)

Willis firmly believed that, by using ethnographic methods to explore in depth the forms of human creativity or "art" and their social consequences, the possibility existed of radicalizing teachers' practice and addressing the injustices associated with capitalism as a economic and social form. In his more recent book *The Ethnographic Imagination* (Willis, 2000) he described how the study of social "penetrations," such as those of the "lads," is a means of widening and deepening the "always contingent and reflexive body of knowledge about humankind" about "how humans use resources for meaning-making in context." "Cultural practices of meaning-making are intrinsically self-motivated as aspects of identity making and self-construction: in making our cultural worlds we make ourselves" (Willis, 2000, p. xiv). In *Learning to Labor*,

> the ethnographic study of culture therefore had a general role to play in pointing to injustice and in contributing to, maintaining and extending norms of social justice and human decency. There are specifically internal connections here for a perspective attuned to the lived penetrations of social agents, i.e. understanding what *in situ* practices themselves 'say' about social justice. (Willis, 2000, p. 120)

Collecting of voices of those who might otherwise be silent must be done, according to Willis, in the spirit of "respecting, recording, illuminating and learning from forms of sensuous subordinate meaning making and self-making, even as they may be distorted and constrained by their unpropitious conditions" (p. 120). The ethnographer, in Willis's eyes, may give those studied potential power through the politics of "naming," and might "open up the invisibility of symbolic work, and thereby offer opportunities for the redirection or limitation of the reproductive consequences of lived penetrations"[1] (p. 121). Other namings could thus be put into circulation in official discourses, thus "interrupting or denying the smooth functioning of expert government regulation and the legitimisation of inequality" (p. 121). Referring to contemporary worlds, such ethnographic studies can develop greater theoretical understandings of the impact of the structures, social relationships, and "behind back" social change that generate new kinds of desires and new kinds of survival and thus new kinds of identity expressed in new kinds of collectivity and new kinds of politics (p. 121).

Such ideals, however, were never likely to be achieved easily nor in a linear fashion. Indeed, through describing in such vivid detail the ways in working-class "lads" worked on and with material circumstances and their "objective possibilities," *Learning to Labor* suggested that the egalitarian efforts of school could be diverted and even negated by the self-reproduction of working class subordination. The pleasure with which the "lads" took in having "the laff," fun and the pisstake (Willis, 2000, p. 38), their "tumble out of (rather than transition from) school" (p. 41) their random selection of jobs and their "resistant dignity" (p. 39) were shown to prepare them for the logic of labor under capitalism—"an intended and conservative reproduction" of the social structure. Critical modernist and later postmodernist educators in the United Kingdom and abroad not surprisingly received the book with a certain amount of ambivalence.

Nevertheless, the power of Willis's text lay in the richness of his account of the survival of the "lads" and in the potency of his analysis of social inequality. Its sociological legacy in the fields of education and youth cultural studies can be found in the continuing focus on the extraordinary creativity of various groups of youth in responding to their positionality. Indeed, the analysis of creativity in identity construction, identifications, and alliances arguably has now become the major focus of sociological studies. At the same time, the relevance of *Learning to Labor* has been greatly affected by poststructuralist readings of such a "modernist" and politically committed agenda (Skeggs, 1992).

Methodological Agendas for Social Justice

In retrospect, it is easy to see why *Learning to Labor* was seen as methodological and theoretical turning point, paving the way not just for critical ethnographies but also later for poststructuralist readings of identity and identity work. It was described as a key marker in the development of social scientific epistemology integrating an analysis of structure and agency that was unprecedented. The critical ethnographic methods employed by Willis were interpreted, initially, as a significant epistemological break with the structures of positivism and rational theory (although arguably these had already been challenged by Hargreaves [1967] and by Lacey's [1970] studies of school life). As Wexler (2000) recently commented, Willis's analysis of the reproduction of inequality moved away from more "neutral, atheoretical" studies of boys, "adding empirical quality to a more general theoretical introduction of critical theory to education" (p. 98). This critical methodology could be taught to new generations of social researchers interested in the experiences and identities of young people, particularly during the transition between school and work.

Willis's political agenda, however, was later challenged by a number of methodological and political critiques. Beverley Skeggs's (1992) review of *Learning to Labor* commented on the extent to which Willis's political project had committed the reader to a highly romanticized celebratory view of the working-class "lads." She pointed to the "seductive" nature of the text—noticing its use of rhetorical devices such as the use of "we," its encouragement to evolve a personal response to the subjects before discussing the sociological theory about their situation (the division between the first and second parts of the book), the use of dramatic incidents that would "do a soap opera proud," the vicarious access to an unfamiliar world, the appeal of Willis's political commitment with its celebration of agency over structure and domination, his optimism and the sympathy he generates for "the lads" and their "having a laff." However, the consequences led to "a reconfirmation" for middle-class socialists "of the revolutionary potential of the working-class—if only they weren't so sexist and racist" (1992, p. 188).

Poststructuralist and postmodernist rereadings of the study went further and questioned the extent to which the book was a methodological turning point. Poststructuralist and postmodern feminists, in particular, pointed to the various ways in which Willis's project had left unresolved central questions about, for example, the role of theory, especially in relation to central questions about agency, identity, and praxis. From this approach, Willis was read as trapped within the narratives of critical theory in the mid 1970s. Using a postmodern yardstick, Patti Lather (1991), for example, criticized Willis for his a priori use of neo-Marxist theory. She argued that there was no sense of the ways in which Willis's perspective as researcher might have been altered by the data. The role of theory was therefore presented as "non-dialectical, unidirectional, an imposition that disallows counter patterns and alternative explanations" (p. 67). The methodological stance of such critical Marxist theory was that it essentially privileged externality, created a unitary analysis of "the lads," and left the researcher paradoxically in a politically neutral position, distanced from his subject.

Ironically, Willis was taken to task for his failure to develop any further dialogue or praxis with the boys in his study. Gore argued that, although Willis pointed to "the productive aspects of power," he had concluded with "elucidation of the oppressive structures which kept the lads in their class position" (Gore, 1993, p. 96). She argued that concept of "partial penetration"—the ability of people to pierce through cultural contradictions in incomplete ways that did not lead to ideology critique—was itself incomplete because it did not offer insights into the possibilities for intervention. Thus, although the "language of possibility" had its beginnings in such a text, the move from an awareness of structural constraints to transformative work had not been made. Strong tensions still existed between the "'discursive foci on critique and possibility'" (Gore, 1993, p. 96).

Thus, although Willis had identified the area of resistance to authority as an important corrective to the overly deterministic correspondence, he was seen as maintaining a quasi-positivist or scientific realist approach to research. Without problematizing the research process itself, the dangers of objectification, and the distanced relationship between subject and object (Lather, 1991), Willis had apparently reproduced "covert forms of positivism" or a "scientific realist approach to research" that had led in the final instance to the sustaining of an "essential male gaze of social subordination and domination as knowledge practice" (Wexler, 2000, p. 98).

The consequences of such readings of Learning to Labor were substantial. On the one hand, Willis's theory of class resistance through youth cultural forms took hold of the sociological and political imagination (Brown, 1988)—its emphasis on identity construction became the dominant sociological research paradigm. On the other hand, as a result of such criticisms, Willis's book was understood to represent a modernist text *par excellence* by a new generation of social scientists trained in post-Enlightenment thinking. The consequence arguably, as Beverley Skeggs noted, was that the political and theoretical integrity of Willis's analysis "has been lost in much of the game playing of postmodern discourse" (1992, p. 193).

Masculinity as Class Opposition

A different, more positive reading of *Learning to Labor* has been proffered by those concerned with the processes of gender identity formation. In the context particularly of the development of a sociology of masculinity, Willis's book represents a major break with past theories of gender socialization. Willis had, in effect, shown how identity construction—the production and construction of gender identities—could be researched. Since the publication of *Learning to Labor*, as Connell (1995) argued, few have doubted that the social construction of masculinities is a systematic socially negotiated process. Nor have they been able to avoid the complex interface between the social structure and culture. Paradoxically, in this context, *Learning to Labor* did not pave the way just for critical ethnographies but also for poststructural readings of gender identity and gender identity work.

As Connell (1995) noted, Willis's contribution was to place the study of gender well within the analysis of working-class cultures in education, at the interface between schooling and the economy and shop floor culture and within the study of antischool cultures. Significantly, the book focused not just on class specificity but also on "a study of masculinity in practice." For Connell, Willis's study and Andrew Tolson's (1977) seminal text *The Limits of Masculinity* were the first of their kind. Both suggested that school was the site in which multiple masculinities were generated, often in opposition to school authority relations, curriculum structures, and forms of discipline. Since then, many studies have explored the range of subject positions inhabited by boys inside and outside schools (e.g., Brown, 1988; Mac an Ghaill, 1994; Sewell, 1997, 1998). Thus, even though the formal dichotomy of "lads" and ear'oles was soon challenged by Brown's (1987) ethnography of "ordinary" working-class boys—those who wanted to "get on" and "get out" of their destinies—his study and the many others that followed focus on the *relational* world of boys. Boys were shown to be actively shaping gender relations as much as social class relations and to be constructing their masculinity within the fluid relations of gender, ethnicity, class, age, and sexuality. Rather uniquely, as early as the 1970s, Willis had brought together the study of class, gender and race relations, in a complex and sophisticated way. It is not without cause that almost every study of masculinity at some point uses Willis's research as a reference point.

Willis had also shown the ways in which different masculinities and indeed particular forms of (heterosexual/White) hegemonic masculinity were created, regulated and reproduced within the same school. According to Connell, Willis had effectively demonstrated

> the *relations* between the different kinds of masculinity: relations of alliance, dominance and subordination. These relationships are constructed through practices that exclude and include, that intimidate, exploit and so on. There is a gender politics within masculinity. (Connell, 1995, p. 37)

After Willis, school studies focused on patterns of hegemonic masculinities rather than socialization. Cultural differentiations rather than just economic differentiation, as Connell noted, became central to the study of working-class identity formation.

Ahead of its time, *Learning to Labor* explored the contradictory and negative consequences of gender and, to a lesser extent, race on White working-class boys' identities. Willis offered pivotal insights into how masculinity/sexuality could become the key to social class resistance to unjust systems. Willis described his work as "creative explorations and rearticulation of received dominant social codes and reproduction: working-class/middle-class, Black/White, male/female. Binaries can be played off against each other and miscegenated or ironically positioned to reveal third terms" (Willis, 2000, p. 37). The dualism of masculine and feminine, which contemporary poststructuralist writers such as Bronwyn Davies (1989) saw as central to the discursive framing of identities in modern society, was explored through Willis's analysis. In *Learning to Labor*, he considered how such dualisms work for working-class lads who are trapped within the objective structures of capitalism. His analysis of the "lads'" culture demonstrated that forms of social class (antischool) resistance that are based on the celebration of traditional sexual identities ultimately confirm the cycle of social class reproduction (MacDonald, 1981/2002, p. 153). It is this insight that arguably still has not been challenged. His research showed that boys were adopting, adapting, reworking, and fashioning gender dualism rather than being socialized into one or other category. The lads' "identity work" involved them critically in the inversion of the mental/manual divide associated with capitalist economies, and the matching of hard physical labor with what we would now call the "narrative superiority of masculinity."

The way in which such dualism worked in the school setting was configured by the realities of schooling for working-class male youth. Willis saw that "the lads" understood what was the price of conformism to the state educational agenda for the manual working classes. Conformism would entail collusion by the working classes in their own educational suppression. As Willis argued, the working-class "lad" "must overcome his inbuilt disadvantage of possessing the wrong class culture and the wrong educational decoders to start with" (Willis, 1977, p. 128). To conform, however, would have meant the emasculation of the working-class youth. These English "lads" celebrated their masculinity against school norms of docile, conforming and diligent pupils. By labeling such pupils as effeminate and "cissies"—the ear'oles—"the lads" affirm their pugnacious and physical masculinity in an antischool culture. They thus confirm their respect for their masculine identity, derived from their families and peer group, and see its fulfillment in hard, physically demanding manual jobs. A critical aspect of *Learning to Labor* therefore is the discussion of what Willis called the "*cross-valorization* of manual labor with the social superiority of masculinity" (p. 148). In an account that has many resonances with contemporary poststructuralist discussions of identifications, disidentifications, and subject positionings (e.g., Skeggs, 1997), Willis describes the identity work of "the lads." He commented that not all divisions should be viewed as oppressive:

> For "the lads," a division in which they take themselves to be favoured (the sexual) overlies, becomes part of, and finally, partially changes the valency of a division in which they are disadvantaged (mental/manual power). (Willis, 1977, p. 148)

According to Willis, "the lads" invert the mental–manual hierarchy and transpose it onto the gender dualism and male–female hierarchy. In effect, the mode of production and class oppression are reproduced in part through the equivalence established between the mental/manual division of labor and between masculinity and femininity. This also paves the way for the reproduction of male manual labor power on the factory floor:

> The important inversion however is not achieved within the proper logic of capitalist production. Nor is it produced in the concrete articulation of the site of social classes of two structures which in capitalism can only be separated in abstraction and whose forms have now become part of it. These are patriarchy and the distinction between mental and manual labour. *The form of the articulation is of the cross-valorisation and association of the two key*

terms in the two sets of structures. The polarisation of the two structures become crossed. Manual labour is associated with the social superiority of masculinity and mental labour with the social inferiority of femininity. In particular manual labour is imbued with a masculine tone and nature which rends it positively expressive of more than its intrinsic focus in work. (p. 148)

Willis's analysis of the struggle of the working class male in the context of a dominant class culture resonated well with that of Bourdieu (1977), who argued at that time that working-class men have much to lose through educational success in such a culture.[2] Protecting themselves from social mobility and indeed from emasculation, working-class men find ways of expressing their sexuality. Bourdieu argued that biological (male/female) and gender (masculine/feminine) determinations "exert their influence on linguistic (or sexual) practices and imagery through the structure of homologous oppositions which organise the images of the sexes and classes" (Bourdieu, 1977, p. 51, quoted in MacDonald, 1981/2002; Arnot, 2002). What is at stake in acquiring dominant linguistic and cultural forms is not just the accusation of class disloyalty, but also the negation or repudiation of masculine sexuality defined in terms of virility, pugnacity, and self-assertion. Taking on bourgeois culture (a way of speaking, self-presentation through gesture, dress, and so forth) also implies a particular relation to one's body—hence, the different names for part of the body (the femininity and daintiness of *la bouche* against the roughness and violence of *la gueule)* in bourgeois and working-class speech. By inverting the classification between class cultures, Bourdieu argued, working-class men celebrate their masculine sexuality and their physical (manual) culture by punctuating their language with "coarse" and "crude" words and "broad and spicy stories"—a theme that also emerges strongly in *Learning to Labor* and, interestingly, in contemporary poststructuralist research on boys' laddish behavior in schools.

In ways that resonate well with contemporary concerns about localized social identities, Willis argues that the interconnections he uncovered between gender and class were specific to particular positionings of youth. In an interview, he demonstrated his awareness of the formation of multiple identities and multiple articulations of these binary categorizations. He commented thus:

I wasn't arguing that a certain working class male masculinity was forever linking manualism and masculinity, but that these were different binary systems with their own histories, and that in other situations, you might have different articulations of gender, patriarchal and capitalist categories. There is a real instability in the way that gender systems and capital systems or capital relations are articulated with each other. (Willis, quoted in Mills & Gibb, in this volume)

Gender Relations, Identities, and Family Life

Although Willis's classic had exposed the "brutality of capitalist productive relations" (McRobbie, 1980, p. 41), its social justice agenda arguably had failed to address the extent of male power over women and White oppression of Black groups within the working-class. Thus although setting a new agenda around concepts of masculinity, Willis had neglected to explore more fully those empirical data that demonstrated precisely the complex interaction between masculinity and femininity and its harsh consequences for working-class women. Angela McRobbie, for example, paid homage to the extraordinary creativity of Willis's study of male adolescents. At the same time she also saw that, through the language of adolescent male sexuality embedded in these texts, Willis had illustrated (but had not sufficiently analyzed) the ways in which class and patriarchal relations work together, "sometimes with an astonishing brutality and at other times in the teeth-gritting harmony of romance, love and marriage" (p. 38). McRobbie argued, like other cultural theorists of the time, that Willis failed to come to grips with working-class male cultures. She commented that

> "the lads" may get by with—and get off on—each other alone on the streets but they did not eat, sleep or make love there. Their peer group consciousness and pleasure frequently seem to hinge on a collective disregard for women and the sexual exploitation of girls. (McRobbie, 1980, p. 40)

What McRobbie found striking was how "unambiguously degrading to women is the language of aggressive masculinity through which "the lads" kick against the oppressive structures they inhabit" (p. 38). Willis was taken to task for his failure to comment critically on, for example, the way a female teacher's authority was undermined by being labeled a "cunt," the way "the lads" mime masturbating of a giant penis for amusement, their litany of sexual obscenities, and the way they publicly expressed their disgust for menstruation (jam rags) at every opportunity. The violence of the imagery, the cruelty of the lads' sexual double standard, the images of sexual power and domination become the lads' last defensive resort. By dignifying these racist, sexist, and homophobic "lads" in their degradation, McRobbie and later Skeggs (1992) argued that Willis's project failed to understand the articulation of male power and domination.

Feminist critics also pointed to the impression gained in *Learning to Labor* that male manual work depended solely on the cultural reproduction of machismo from father to son,[3] the male pride in physical labor and contempt for pen pushing. Willis had thus failed to integrate these aspects of working-class culture into a full account of the working-class family. Like most cultural theorists of the time, the family was outside the sphere of analysis. It was represented in some ways as a "softer sphere in which fathers, sons and boyfriends expect to be, and are, emotionally serviced" (McRobbie, 1980, p. 41). The private experiences (relations with parents, siblings, and girlfriends) behind "the lads'" hard outer image, and their immersion in working-class culture outside the public sphere, were largely ignored. As McRobbie noted, working-class culture "happens as much around the breakfast table and in the bedroom as in the school and in the workplace" (p. 44).

This debate still resonates with current writing on masculinity. Recently, Willis (quoted in Mills & Gibb, Appendix, this volume) recognized the strength of this feminist critique about the reduction of patriarchal relations to class, the underestimating of the importance of the home and domestic relations, and the uncritical reproduction or celebration of "sexist conventions, forms and prejudices." Yet, 25 years after this analysis of *Learning to Labor*, the internal dynamics of family life still tend not to be seen by social and cultural theorists as significant as economic factors in framing youth identities. The more the family takes center stage, the more likely it is that gender identities are located not just within the division of labor, but also within two other axes of gender power identified by Connell (1987)—that of *power relations* and what he called *cathexis* (emotional/sexual selves and attachments). These latter two axes are beginning to emerge in accounts of gender identities (in particular studies of masculinity), although unfortunately the connection to social justice is often not made explicit.

A more fully *sexed* notion of working-class culture that Angela McRobbie so powerfully called for is only now the subject of most contemporary social justice research on identities and education. Christine Heward (1996), for example, challenged contemporary scholarly work on masculinity which still tends to relate masculinity, to particular "normative understandings of family relations." These normative models tend to take up the theme of father–son relations as critical to the development of male gender identity and mother–daughter relations as critical to female gender identity. Freudian psychoanalysis and Parsonian sex-role theory, she argued, have legitimated this view of the sexual division of labor in the family. As a result, there is still little analysis of how masculinities are negotiated, experienced, and worked on in relation to more holistic notions of the psychosocial gendered power dynamics of family life.

As Heward pointed out, a boy's identification with his father (even if the father was absent most of the time) was seen as central to the construction of masculinity, which was understood in the context of "the world of work and power." Willis, like Tolson (1977), had built his theory of the "lads" using the father's position in the labor market and class culture as "an important differentiator in the construction of masculinities" (Heward, 1996, p. 36). Using seven male biographies, Heward demonstrated how "the ambivalence and alienation which characterise father–son relations" are in fact rooted in the "vast range of complexities of power, emotion and sexuality nexus *within* families." Each biographical example illustrates how the dynamics between mothers and fathers and the son's negotiations of those dynamics are problematic, contested, and unpredictable. Thus young men's experiences of family life are deeply shaped by both parents. Heward argued:

> The importance of mothers in the process of identity formation should be acknowledged rather than dismissed as anti-models who have performed their initial nurturing function. (Heward, 1996, p. 48)

The relations of self to structure in this analysis become far more complex than just the gender and generational transmission of working-class work cultures. Gender regimes and power relations, particularly in the family and workplaces, are being transformed for example by women "turning away from exploitative male heterosexuals." Intimate relations have been transformed, child-care regimes have changed, and female and male patterns of employment and work cultures have shifted. As Heward argued, "women and relations between men and women are a potent source of change in intimate relations" (p. 48)—thus, it would seem essential today that in order to understand today's "lads" we must look to the third of Connell's elements— that of emotional life and to explore "intra and inter family gender relations within structural contexts." "This would permit a wide variety of outcomes to be envisaged and make mothers integral rather than peripheral to the process of constructing masculinities" (Heward, 1996, p. 48).

Other recent research of working-class boys in English secondary schools has highlighted the centering of mothers in boys' lives. For example, in their analysis of the contemporary practice of masculinity in schools, Nayak and Kehily (2001) highlighted the contradictory role of mothers in working-class boys' humor. Like Willis's findings, "having a laff" for these boys represents one of the means by which different positions of domination and subordination among boys are established and regulated, allowing some boys to exert power over others. Humor is used as an "unofficial resource" in the culture of manhood. In Willis's analysis such humor had significance as preparation for the styles and rituals of male shop floor culture, or a form of class cultural resistance. However, today such humor has become the means by which White working-class heterosexuality is affirmed. "Wind ups, joke telling, funny stories, spontaneous gags, mimicry," Nayak and Kehily found, become the "unseen forms of communication, validating or rejecting male forms of behaviour" (p. 111). Young men are "hardly learning to labor." Having a laugh today is "every bit as dedicated to counter culture of humour as 'lads' in Willis's study, but it is less about gaining power and more about feeling entitled to it."

> We contend that heavy industrial humour may become a means of recuperating masculinity in a post industrial economy. The values embedded in schoolboy pranks, jokes and funny stories then act as symbolic codes which young men may learnt to 'be masculine' *in the absence of secure manual work*. [my emphasis added] (Nayak & Kehily, 2001, p. 112)

Where Willis observed the *class significance* of such humor, Nayak & Kehily saw cussing, blowing matches, ritualized insults, and funny/spicy stories as the undercurrents at work behind English *heterosexual masculinity*. Significantly such behavior reinforces hypermasculine egos by exploring the deepest sexual taboos about sons' relationship with their mothers. The ritualized insults play with the idea of their mothers as slags, sluts, and whores. These highly personal comments are a source of great distress for some boys, some of whom are reduced to tears in public. However, by mobilizing sexist discourses of power such as mother cussing, boys achieve superior positions in the group. They could even collude with male teachers' jokes about their mothers being "slags."

Arguably, contemporary sociological research has taken Willis's acknowledgement of working-class family culture further and has queried the powerful association between fathers and son as the only influence on the construction of working class male identity. Clearly, fathers play a major role in representations of working class masculinity, but the construction of male heterosexuality is also played out within the emotional relationships of parents and other family members. Recent poststructuralist research on masculinity has therefore developed even further the insights Willis introduced into the study of gender identities, although not necessarily within the same discourse of social justice.

Contemporary "Lads" in a Performance Discourse

Willis's ethnographic study of the response of working class youth to their schooling and their social and economic positioning exposed the social contradictions of postwar illusions of meritocracy. From a policy perspective, *Learning to Labor* offers a unique platform from which to consider the nature and extent of contemporary sociocultural and economic inequalities. Following Willis, we can now ask: Does the school with all its performance and standardizing cultures now include rather than exclude such working-class youth? Has the individualizing of educational achievement led to the transformation of such young men who had previously prepared themselves, in resistance, for their destinies as unskilled manual labor?

The book, it seems, has greater, not less, relevance in the current school climate in the United Kingdom when the processes of social exclusion have become even more acute than in the more lenient times of full employment and social democratic philosophies. Today, young men in the manual working-classes (those who are variously called "status zero" or the "under-wolves," Wilkinson & Mulgan, 1995) have even less investment in the economic future, even less prospect of making the transition into continuous work of the sort described by Willis in the late 1970s. Paradoxically, with the heightened pressure on young people today through competitive, tightly regulated, and divisive performance driven school systems, research in the United Kingdom suggests that today's "lads" appear to be pushed to even more extreme alternative cultures, and there appears to be a spread of a laddish behavior (although not working-class culture) among other groups of boys.

Willis's theory of class reproduction was challenged, as he himself recognized (Willis, 1979; Willis, Bekenn, Ellis, & Whitt; 1988),[4] by the loss of male labor in manufacturing industry in the United Kingdom. By 1989, the three great industrial sectors made up only 25% of jobs in the country, whereas the service sector accounted for 15 million jobs—almost 70% of employment. Such economic restructuring and the contraction of manufacturing industry in the United Kingdom had the greatest impact on those boys whose fathers worked in factory or other industrial jobs. The loss of their fathers' jobs was to reduce young men's expectations of finding "real work" (Haywood & Mac an Ghaill, 2001; Mac an Ghaill, 2001). The collapse of the youth labor market, the replacement of factory work with new technologies, and the expansion of the service industries all fundamentally affected the opportunities for these young men's employment after school. Willis's lads could no longer expect the conventional transitions from school to work through traditional apprenticeships and familial contacts.

Evidence from more recent studies of working-class masculinities (Mac an Ghaill, 1994; Sewell, 1997, 1998) suggests that the reforms of schooling from the late 1980s to the mid 1990s exacerbated rather than reduced school resistance. By increasing emphasis on performance and on competition within and between schools, and by raising the stakes in terms of compliance to a school culture that was class oriented, schools were more rather than less likely to be viewed as hostile institutions, especially because the sorting and selecting functions of schools were made more visible. The new school ethos bore little relationship to the realities of economic dysfunction and community breakdown. As Haywood and Mac an Ghaill (1996, 2001) argued, in areas in which working-class youth are already marginalized, surveilled, and excluded from the productive life of the society, the reconstruction of schooling according to market principles was most likely to force confrontations between young Black and White working-class boys and their teachers. It was these confrontations that created and sustained counterhegemonic masculinities among such youth that were both antiacademic and antischool.

Mac an Ghaill's (1994) ethnographic research in Parnell Comprehensive School in a predominantly working-class inner-city industrial area also in the Midlands confirmed the presence of a group of what he called "Macho Lads" who celebrate a powerful version of heterosexual machismo not dissimilar to that of "the lads" in Willis's study. As Haywood and Mac an Ghaill argued, deindustrialization creates "a crisis in White working-class forms of masculinity." The responses of the macho lads to the new ethos of schooling involves celebrating alternative sources of gender power. Gender power based on what Mac an Ghaill called *hyper-masculinity* is not so much the mechanism through which they could celebrate manual labor, but appeared to be the main source of their identity (Mac an Ghaill, 1994, p. 71). Still inverting the values of the school system, still retaining highly traditional gender values, today's "lads" now choose to celebrate the three Fs—*fighting, football, and fucking* (see also Connell's [1989] account of unemployed White working class men in Australia and Canaan's [1996] study of predominantly White working-class youth in the Midlands). In short, these "lads" cope with the multiple uncertainties of their position by promoting an exaggerated concept of heterosexual masculinity. By "behaving badly," they regain control of their lives.

Contemporary White and Black "lads" thus appear to find ways of celebrating manhood without relying on a work identity. The generational connections between hard male physical labor and working-class masculinity described by Willis are not always possible, although as Mac an Ghaill argued, White working-class lads in Parnell School still held onto outdated modes of masculinity that centered around traditional manual waged labor. In contrast, the Afro-Caribbean and Asian Macho Lads in Parnell School appeared to have less commitment to work in the locality and were more used to unemployment and economic insecurity. In Mac an Ghaill's analysis the major difference between "the lads" of the 1970s and "the lads" of the 1990s appeared to be in terms of the purposes/significance of their counterschool culture.

Male heterosexuality was found to have played a major role in shaping the responses of a group of African Caribbean boys to school (Sewell, 1997, 1998). In order to succeed, aspiring Black youth had to assume a form of "racelessness" and lose their community and ethnic identity to avoid the wrath of their teachers. The reaction to this racelessness was the counter-promotion of a new Black identity, which took the form of what bell hooks (1993) called "phallocentric masculinity" among those who found comfort from exclusion in hedonism and an antischool Black machismo. Yet these African Caribbean "lads" who were in "retreatism or rebellion" were not necessarily less positive about learning than girls. However, teachers in this case study had not only gendered these boys, but were obsessed with the dangers of Black male sexuality.

What has therefore become a major issue in current research on social justice issues is *the norm of male heterosexuality*. Today, a much preferred theoretical position for most masculinity researchers is that of poststructuralism, which offers insights into "a certain game of truth" (Martino, 1999, p. 240). From such a Foucauldian perspective, researchers can think about the various ways boys are inserted into the "game of truth" in which they learn about what it is to be "man" (p. 240). In this context, masculinity becomes a range of practices, a form of performativity that can shift in different locales, occasions, moments, and sites. There is no a priori theory of the subject. Instead, the focus is in how boys constitute themselves as male subjects. The emphasis is on the cultural techniques of boys, the "polymorphous techniques of power" (Foucault, 1978, quoted in Martino, 1999, p. 240), which they experience and sometimes own. From a Foucauldian perspective, the analysis has shifted away from the class significances of working-class masculinity to the various statuses given to masculinity in a particular school culture, an analysis of how the desires of adolescent boys are channeled and relayed, and how the hierarchy of valorized and subordinated masculinities come into being (Martino, 1999, p. 242).

Increasing interest in this aspect of male power has led to a multitude of projects on white and Black male heterosexuality among working-class youth in school (see Frosh, Phoenix, & Pattman, 2002; O'Donnell & Sharpe, 2000; Arnot, et al., 1999). The argument now put forward is that this dominant hegemonic form of masculinity has been encouraged by schools, promoted extensively by the media (*Men Behaving Badly, Loaded*) and taken up now by a variety of different boys. Displaying styles of behavior and modes of identification that ape "the lads'" culture of the 1970s, all sorts of other schoolboys have been found to exploit similar aggressive forms of heterosexual and racist masculinity as that found among Willis's manual working-class "lads." Politicians since the 1990s have publicly declared *laddism* to be the cause of male working-class educational failure and the reason for all boys' alleged underachievement (Francis, 1999; Raphael Reed, 1999). What was understood in Willis's analysis to be a class cultural response to the conditions of material existence of the working classes and of the nature of schooling within capitalism is now being represented as a characteristic of masculinity itself, irrespective of social class.

For some, the explanation for this extension of laddishness from the working classes to other social groups including even middle-class children is found (paradoxically) in the *remasculinization* of schooling, with its new cultures of competition, standards, performance, and exclusions (Mac an Ghaill, 1999). Jackson (2002), for example, argued the adoption of laddish behavior is much stronger because of the changes in the educational system, which are generating increased insecurity and pressure. Although boys appear to be using sexist and heterosexist discourses to frame their masculinity vis-à-vis femininity, she argued that from a social-psychological perspective, laddishness is also about coping with the fear of academic failure in a dominant culture of performavitity. Middle-class boys might appropriate the culture of Willis's "lads" because of the advantages of adopting the styles of disengagement and indifference of White working-class boys in such a heightened competitive environment. Some of the strategies that Becky Francis (1999) found boys now associate with "laddish-ness" involve procrastination, intentional withdrawal of effort and rejection of academic work, the appearance of effortless achievement, and disruptive behavior. The presence of a competitive performance-oriented culture generates anxiety especially among boys whose gender identity needs to be based on achieving power, status and superiority.

Heywood and Mac an Ghaill (2001) argued that the shift from "soft welfare" to harder market economies has lead to the restructuring of teaching, which, in turn, has emphasized hierarchies of domination and subordination. They suggested that the restructured authority system, intensified surveillance, disciplinary codes, curriculum and testing, stratifi-cation technologies, and the allocation and knowledge selection processes have resulted in a range of new, hierarchically ordered masculinities. New discourses of entrepreneurialism and new masculine authoritarianism are being replaced by modern forms of "technical bureaucratic knowledge." In this context, there is less socialiability between teacher and taught, and chil-dren "are now conceptualised as value added knowledge containers." The play of masculinities in school in this contemporary context therefore repre-sents a complex dynamic that appears to have less oppositional and thus has less transformative political potential. However, as Reay (2002) recently argued, there is little evidence to suggest that traditional working-class masculinities and such performance cultures in schools can in the end be reconciled politically. One cannot easily transform the other. For that to happen, those promoting working-class male educational success would need to address the centrality of masculinity as an identity forged out of deep traditional patterns of socialization.

Conclusions

The debate about family life, cathexis, and also "Laddishness" in schools, to some extent, has shifted away from Willis's account of working-class boys preparing to go into working-class jobs in their locality. The concept of "the lads" has been extended in the media, in politics, and even in boys' popular worlds to represent "all boys." As a result it is difficult to retrieve the touchstone of critical engagement signified by the class cultural studies of the 1970s. The transformative project developed in the critique of social democracy is not clearly reflected within the critical analyses of the globalized economy and performance-based choice cultures of schooling in the current decade. The relationship of young people's meaning making and official discourses of education, between critique and possibility, is not as clearly expressed; it is often implicit.

Paradoxically, although Willis's seminal text became a symbolic marker of modernist methodologies and narratives, at the same time arguably it anticipated, through the wealth of its description and theoretical insight, the development of poststructuralist tradition of studies of masculinities. As I have shown, many of the themes of contemporary poststructuralist work on masculinities were originally represented in *Learning to Labor*—most notably the working through of social classifications and dualisms, the nature of meaning making and identity construction, the situated relational worlds of identity formation, and the complex cross-articulations of class, race, sexuality and gender. The epistemological break therefore was not necessarily as strong as it has been represented. At the same time, I want to argue that some of the strengths of Willis's analysis are precisely the weaknesses of contemporary accounts of gender.

Contemporary research on masculinities might suggest that Willis's analysis is less relevant in today's more fluid society. The argument would be that monocausal analysis of power such as the social reproduction model with its concerns about rational subjects and predictable power relations and the "romance" of working-class male creativity in the face of degradation could not adequately cope with the complexity of experience among contemporary boys. Can such a theory really account for the responses of boys to the restructured globalizing economy? Poststructural research on school based masculinities, on public discourses around masculinity, and on male narratives and biographies suggests that we need more a more dense, complex, and social psychological analysis of power plays in schools, families, and communities. As we have seen, since the publication of *Learning to Labor*, there has been what has been called a "biographical turn" (Coffey, 2001) among those interested in social identities. There is now a greater interest in how an individual's "self-identity is constructed and negotiated through complex social processes" (p. 53). More attention is being paid to the creation of "choice" biographies, away from normative biographies.

This new phase, which Stanley and Morgan (1993) call the "biographising of social structure and the structuralising of biography," can, however, also lead to romanticizing the individual, the personal, and their stories. Although schools are now seen as key sites for the "active construction, production and reproduction of biographies and identities," only some studies are good at ensuring that "personal narratives, individual lives and experiences are located within the situated, political and local contexts of education and schools" (p. 57). Indeed, as leading masculinity scholars such as Mac an Ghaill (1999) admit, the poststructuralist approach, although immensely valuable, cannot easily read the significance of the collective forms that masculinity take within new economies.

Willis's insights should be at the center of our thinking about a society in which qualifications matter even more than before and the social exclusion of the manual working classes is even harsher. Willis's critical ethnography was never just an ethnography, nor just an example of social-cultural reproduction theory. His work causes us to reflect on how far society has changed since the 1970s, how much we, as social scientists, have developed our analysis of the meaning of education for different groups of youth, how much we have gained and lost methodologically. But *Learning to Labor* also asks us to consider how we too might develop what Bernstein (1996) called "a generative theory" about the relationship between schooling and the economy—research questions that can be, as we have seen addressed and readdressed time and again. I would like to conclude by quoting from *Learning to Labor*. In today's context, the following observations about the relationship between identities and the social justice "impulse" are especially meaningful.

> Masculinity must not . . . be too simply posed. It has many dimensions and edges. In one way it is a half-blind, regressive machismo which brings self-destructive violence, aggression and division to relationships within the working class. In another way imparting something of what lies behind it, masculinity expresses impulses which can be progressive.
>
> Behind the expression of masculinity lies an affirmation of manual labour power and behind that (though mediated and distorted) a sense of the uniqueness of the commodity of labor

power and of the way in which the general abstract labour unites and connects all kinds of concrete labour.

The masculine disdain for qualification, for all its prejudice, carries still a kind of "insight" into the divisive nature of certification, and into the way in which mental work and technicism are mobilised ideologically primarily to maintain class relations rather than to select the most efficient or to increase productive efficiency. (Willis, 1977, p. 152)

Acknowledgments

The first draft of this chapter was presented at the American Educational Research Association, New Orleans, April 1–6, 2002, at the session celebrating 25 years since the publication of *Learning to Labor*. I would like to thank Nadine Dolby and Greg Dimitriadis for their invitation to participate in this symposium. I am also very grateful to Paul Willis for his comments on the first draft and for sending me the interview with Mills and Gibb and *The Ethnographic Imagination*. My thanks to Carol Vincent for giving permission to reprint large sections of this article, which was first published in her edited collection *Identities & Social Justice* (London: RoutledgeFalmer, 2003).

Notes

1. More than consciousness raising which Willis considered to be potentially vacuous.
2. Willis argued in an interview with Mills and Gibb (Appendix, this volume) that he was much influenced by Bourdieu, although interestingly he was not familiar with this particular article by Bourdieu, which coincidentally explored the same ground (personal communication).
3. It is relevant to note that Willis's childhood was shaped by the father–son relationship. He was brought up by his father alone after his mother's death when he was 9. Willis described his father as having played a vital role in transforming a working-class culture into a process of social and intellectual growth (Willis, quoted in interview with Mills and Gibb, in this volume).
4. See Willis's own studies of male unemployment (Willis et al., 1988).

References

Arnot, M. (2002). *Reproducing gender? Essays on educational theory and feminist politics.* London: RoutledgeFalmer Press.

Arnot, M., David, M. & Weiner, G. (1999). *Closing the gender gap: Postwar education and social change.* Cambridge: Polity Press.

Bernstein, B. (1996). *Pedagogy, symbolic control and identity: Theory, research, critique.* London: Taylor & Francis.

Bourdieu, P. (1977). The economics of linguistic exchange. *Social Science Information,* 16(6), 661.

Brown, P. (1987). *Schooling ordinary kids: inequality, unemployment and the new vocationalism.* London: Tavistock.

Brown, P. (1988). Education and the working class: A cause for concern. In H. Lauder & P. Brown (Eds.), *Education in search of a future* (pp. 1–19). Barcombe, Lewes: The Falmer Press.

Canaan, J. E. (1996). "One thing leads to another": Drinking, fighting and working-class masculinities. In M. Mac an Ghaill (Ed.), *Understanding masculinities* (pp. 114–125). Buckingham: Open University Press.

Centre for Contemporary Cultural Studies. (1981). *Unpopular education: Schooling for social democracy in England since 1944.* London: Hutchinson.

Coffey, A. (2001). *Education and social change.* Buckingham: Open University Press.

Connell, R. W. (1987). *Gender and power.* Cambridge: Polity Press.

Connell, R. W. (1989). Cool guys, swots and wimps: The interplay of masculinity and education. *Oxford Review of Education*, 15(3), 291–303.

Connell, R. W. (1995). *Masculinities.* Cambridge: Polity.

Davies, B. (1989). The discursive production of male/female dualism. *Oxford Review of Education*, 15(3), 229–241.

Foucault, E. (1978). *The history of sexuality, Vol. 1* (R. Hurley, Trans.). New York: Vintage.

Francis, B. (1999). Lads, lasses and (new) Labour: 14–16-Year-old students' responses to the "laddish behaviour and boys" underachievement debate. *British Journal of Sociology of Education*, 20(3), 355–371.

Frosh, S., Pheonix, A., & Pattman, R. (2002). *Young masculinities.* London: Palgrave.

Gore, J. (1993). *The struggle for pedagogies.* New York: Routledge.

Hargreaves, D. (1967). *Social relations in a secondary school.* London: Routledge and Kegan Paul.

Haywood, C. & Mac an Ghaill, M. (1996). What about the boys? Regendered local labour markets and the recomposition of working class masculinities. *British Journal of Education and Work*, 9(1), 19–30.

Haywood, C., & Mac an Ghaill, M. (2001). The significance of teaching English boys: Exploring social change, modern schooling and the making of masculinities. In W. Martino & B. Meyenn (Eds.), *What about the boys* (pp. 234–237). Buckingham: Open University Press.

Heward, C. (1996). Masculinities and families. In M. Mac an Ghaill (Ed.), *Understanding masculinities* (pp. 35–49). Buckingham: Open University Press.

Hooks, B. (1993, August 15). Hard Core rap lyrics stir backlash. *New York Times.*

Jackson, C. (2002). "Laddishness" as a self-worth protection strategy. *Gender and Education*, 14(1), 37–51.

Lacey, C. (1970). *Hightown grammar: The school as a social system.* Manchester: Manchester University Press.

Lather, P. (1991). *Getting smart: Feminist psychology and pedagogy in the postmodern.* London: Routledge.

Mac an Ghaill, M. (1994). *The making of men: Masculinities, sexualities and schooling.* Buckingham: Open University Press.

Mac an Ghaill, M. (1999). New cultures of training: Emerging male (hetero) sexual identities. *British Education Research Journal*, 25(4), 427–443.

MacDonald, M. (2002). *Schooling and the reproduction of class and gender relations.* Reprinted in M. Arnot. Reproducing gender? Essays on educational theory and feminist politics. London: RoutledgeFalmer. (Original work published 1981.)

Martino, W. (1999). "Cool boys," "party animals," "squids" and "poofters": Interrogating the dynamics and politics of adolescent masculinities in school. *British Journal of Sociology of Education*, 20(2), 239–263.

McRobbie, A. (1980). Settling accounts with sub–culture. *Screen Education*, 34, 37–50.

Nayak, A. & Kehily, M. J. (2001). "Learning to laugh": A study of schoolboy humour in the English secondary school. In W. Martino and B. Meyenn (Eds.) *What about the boys? Issues in masculinity in schools* (pp. 110–123). Buckingham: Open University Press.

O'Donnell, M., & Sharpe, S. (2000). *Uncertain Masculinities.* London: Routledge.

Raphael Red, L. (1999). Troubling boys and disturbing discourses on masculinity and schooling: A feminist exploration of current debates and interventions concerning boys in school. *Gender and Education*, 11(1), 93–110.

Reay, D. (2002). Shaun's story: Troubling discourses of white working class masculinities. *Gender and Education*, 14(3), 221–234.

Sewell, T. (1997). *Black masculinities and schooling: How Black boys survive modern schooling.* London: Trentham Books, (pp. 111–127).

Sewell, T. (1998). Loose canons: Exploding the myth of the "Black macho" lad. In D. Epstein, J. Elwood, V. Hey, & J. Maw (Eds.), *Failing boys: Issues in gender and achievement.* Buckingham: Open University Press.

Skeggs, B. (1992). Paul Willis, *Learning to Labour*. In M. Barker & A. Beezer (Eds.), *Reading into cultural studies* (pp. 181–196). London: Routledge.

Skeggs, B. (1997). *Formations of class and gender*. London: Sage.

Stanley, L. & Morgan, D. (1993). Editorial. *Sociology*, 27(1), 1–4.

Tolson, A. (1977). *The limits of masculinity*. London: Tavistock.

Wexler, P. (2000). *Mystical society: An emerging social vision*. Boulder, CO: Westview Press.

Wilkinson, H., & Mulgan, G. (1995). *Freedom's children: Work, relationships and politics for 18–34 year olds in Britain Today*. London: Demos.

Willis, P. (1977). *Learning to labour: How working-class kids get working-class jobs*. Farnborough, Hants: Saxon House, Teakfield.

Willis, P. (1979). Shop floor culture, masculinity and the wage form. In J. Clarke, C. Critcher, & R. Johnson (Eds.), *Working class culture* (pp. 185–198). London: Hutchinson.

Willis, P., Bekenn, A., Ellis, T., & Whitt, D. (1988). *The youth review: Social conditions of young people in Wolverhampton*. Aldershot: Avebury.

Willis, P. (2000). *The ethnographic imagination*. Cambridge: Polity Press.

CHAPTER 3

Paul Willis, Class Consciousness, and Critical Pedagogy
Toward a Socialist Future

PETER McLAREN AND VALERIE SCATAMBURLO-D'ANNIBALE

Paul Willis's *Learning To Labor*, published in 1977, marked a pivotal moment in the history of educational criticism.[1] As Stanley Aronowitz acknowledged in his introduction to the book, Willis's work represented a significant contribution to radical and Marxian-inspired analyses of the function of schools while nonetheless challenging some of their basic presuppositions. In what was to be acknowledged as one of the most significant ethnographies of working-class youth culture, a pathfinding work that connected a humanistic study of everyday life with a sophisticated macropolitical analysis of the workings of ideology and social power, Willis sought to understand how ordinary, everyday mainstream cultures were produced and to explore the expressions of resistance that were aimed at dominant social forms. *Learning to Labor* uncoils in compelling detail the ideological tensions between an oppressed group (working-class "lads") and the status quo (middle-class, white-collar "ear'oles") in order to demonstrate the dynamic processes involved in the production, reproduction, and transformation of cultural meanings that constitute class-based ideology. Scuppering much of the ethnographic conventions of the time, Willis's ethnographic study, both in theory and method, demonstrated how lived culture and the rituals of everyday school life among primarily nonelite

groups contributed to the shaping of capitalist structures and social relations of power and privilege. One of the most noteworthy aspects of Willis's
work was its implacable openness to "experience" as well as its attempt to
explore a theoretical basis for activist struggle (see Willis, 1978).

Willis argued that the lads' culture drew on the broader working-class
and factory cultures and social heritage to which these young men had been
introduced and exposed in their homes, neighborhoods, and communities.
Their resistance to, and contempt for, the "official" knowledges presented to
them in school were derived from and influenced by the features of
Hammertown's broader working-class tradition. Contrary to the many
myths ensconced in the rhetoric of "meritocracy," the lads were consciously
but uncritically aware that their own cultural and economic location in the
larger social totality was the best guide to their futures—they realized, in
short, that they would probably not get "good" jobs. The lads' culture, therefore, led them to "reject, ignore, invert, make fun of, or transform most of
what they [were] given in careers lessons" (Willis, 1977, p. 92). Rather than
treating the lads as passive subjects deprived of agency, Willis contended that
the lads were not simply channeled into jobs but rather were actively (if not
defiantly) embracing their future in the realm of "unskilled" labor. Paradoxically, their resistance to the conformity encouraged within the educational
setting also functioned to reproduce them as laborers in the workforce—in
other words, the cultural practices that were interpreted as expressions of
resistance in school situations were concomitantly serving as forms of
accommodation to working-class futures. The pioneering aspect of Willis's
work, however, was that he insisted that the processes by which working-
class youths ended up with working-class jobs were far more complex than
previous theorists had suggested. But more than this, Willis argued that the
ability and eagerness of the lads to resist demonstrated at least a partial (if
not sufficient) recognition of their social locatedness and the way in which
they were economically situated as members of an oppressed class. This, of
course, created at least the possibility of attaining the kind of class
consciousness that would refuse to capitulate to at least the most orthodox
features of capitalism's requirements.

Willis's *Learning to Labor* was, of course, one of several projects
conducted under the auspices of the Birmingham Centre for Contemporary
Cultural Studies during the 1970s. At the time, the work of the center as a
whole was undoubtedly influenced by various strands of Marxism. In virtually all of its work, class was a central concept that was considered and
analyzed not only in terms of its cultural aspects (i.e., people's beliefs, values,
practices) but also *in relation to economic realities*. The earliest manifestations of cultural studies were, therefore, shaped substantially by social class
and its attendant issues/concerns. Since then, as contemporary cultural
studies have assumed an increasingly postmodern coloration, class (along

with Marxism) has been generally consigned to the "discard tray labeled 'modernity'" (Milner, 1999, p. 114). Although the conflation of Marxism with modernity is, in and of itself, problematic enough given that Marx was one of the sharpest critics of liberal modernity (cf. Wallerstein, 1995), the dismissal of class as a so-called "modernist" category is even more disturbing because class as a category was never really dissolved in the bubbling vat of postmodern theory, despite claims to the contrary. Nonetheless, the category of class has been marginalized not only within the prevailing precincts of cultural studies but also in what routinely passes for "radical" social theory. Talking about class is "unpopular" and presumably not "sexy enough for the intelligentsia," whose members seem more enthralled by the "intellectual eroticism" of studying difference (Munt, 2000, pp. 3, 7). As Collini (1994, p. 3) aptly noted, in the "frequently incanted quartet of race, class, gender and sexual orientation, there is no doubt that class has been the least fashionable ... despite the fact that all the evidence suggests that class remains the single most powerful determinant of life-chances."

Discussions of the working class, so central to Willis and other founding figures of cultural studies, now tend to "stick in the throat like a large chunk of stale Hovis" (Anthony, cited in Munt, 2000, p. 3), and academics seem particularly squeamish when the subject is raised. To speak of the working class and/or working class culture at a time when the topic of social class has been deemed defunct by the sentinels of intellectual fashion is often viewed as somewhat naive, nostalgic, even perverse. Issues of class and explorations of class consciousness belong, or so we have been told, to an earlier era; notions of class are no longer "central to the current fashion in cultural studies" (Lave, Duguid, & Fernandez, 1992, p. 258). In a presumably "post"-everything society, the "problem" of class has been supplanted by "new" concerns with identity and difference—categories that are considered more appropriate to the "postmodern" condition. Today, a rather uncritical and ahistorical postmodern "pluralism" reigns supreme.

As a partial result of the conceptual shift within social theory, and cultural studies in particular, it is not surprising that Willis's study subsequently became a target of criticism. *Learning to Labor* was critiqued for its class reductionism and its almost exclusive focus on working-class males, their experiences and their forms of resistance. It has also been the object of unsupple accusations by positivists for not constituting an adequate sample for making generalizations across wider communities and groups, and feminists have charged that the study ignored cultural forms of patriarchy. Additionally, Willis's classic study has been plagued by charges of romanticizing working-class culture. The alleged structural functionalism (or functional structuralism, take your pick) of his theorizing has been traced to an epistemic essentialism and dualism. His sweeping dialectic of freedom/determination has been chastised for its presumed ahistoricism and utopianism. Yet despite these criticisms—and possibly, in part, because of them—*Learning to Labor* continues to be his most influential text—one that (a) represented a landmark in the annals of critical educational discourse; (b) created a seismic shift in the tectonic plates of educational ethnography; and (c) foregrounded the centrality of class issues/relations in the analysis of school cultures, pedagogical practices, and material conditions. We are not, however, interested in rehashing the critiques of Willis's work with the intent of defending it or contributing to the governing themes of his critics. Rather, we are concerned with identifying some political trajectories that emanate from Willis's work, for he has provided some interesting fodder for radical educationalists committed to engaging (rather than cavalierly dismissing) the legacy of Marxism at a time in U.S. history when Marxism has all but disappeared as a legitimate problematic out of which analysis and social action can proceed.

The Abiding Centrality of Class

Despite the lack of attention accorded to the category of class in contemporary scholarly narratives, everyday life is saturated with class relations. Class never went "away," and its marginalization in the academy and in realm of educational and cultural studies "merely alludes to the success of entrenched beliefs in liberal pluralism" (Munt, 2000, p. 10). This marginalization is, of course, a symptom of the larger tendency—namely, the suppression of Marxism—by erstwhile "post" and "ex" Marxists. Indeed, for years, Marxism has been maligned by the prevailing centers of intellectual power, which tend to reject it in what San Juan (2003) calls "reflex epithets" as "totalizing," "reductionist," and even "repressive." Today, the critique of Marxism by cultural studies has "become a series of unthinking reflexes and slogans that are mobilized to dismiss historical materialist critique as quickly as possible" (Katz, 2000, p. 51). In many respects, class has actually been hidden from analytic and political view by the "postmodern" turn in cultural studies. Although we would not dispute that cultural studies has made great inroads in addressing the previous dearth of cultural investigation into gender, sexuality, "race," and ethnicity, it has come at a considerable cost and has led to an evacuation of the key concern that gave birth to cultural studies in the first place—namely, a profound commitment to overcoming capitalist exploitation. Recently, Andrew Milner (1999, pp. 10–13) addressed the abandonment of class in academic and political discourses, despite the array of empirical data that provides ample evidence of the continued existence of class and people's identification with it (in both a positive and negative sense), where the daily realities of inequality in society speak not only to deep structural divides but also to economic and cultural exploitation and oppression. Milner (1999) in fact argued that the more class has become theoretically abstract and/or dealt with in a metatheoretical sense, the more it has been marginalized and, in some instances, completely obliterated from the theoretical and political canvas. The vogue is toward textual readings of class at the expense of grounded, ethnographic investigations.

We view this as a disturbing theoretical and political development, for it seems to domesticate the radicalism that informed the earliest manifestations of the cultural studies project. Rather than posing a challenge to dominant ideological formations and indeed to capitalism, post-Marxist, postmodern cultural studies (at least in the American academy) have become "an Establishment organon" (San Juan, 2002, p. 222) and have evolved into an apologetic narrative that reinscribes the banality of liberal pluralism. Our own work in recent years has attempted to redress this tendency (McLaren, 1998, 2000; McLaren & Farahmandpur, 1999, 2000; Scatamburlo-D'Annibale & McLaren, 2003). Our approach has not been one of defeatism nor triumphalism but one of emphasizing the strategic centrality of class in theorizing the "social." We argue that given the entrenchment of neo-liberal globalization practices and the global dominance of U.S. military and economic power, class is as important a category and explanatory instrument as it ever was, perhaps even more so. We believe that the ongoing significance of Willis's work can point us in the direction of a more sustained emphasis on class consciousness and class struggle within educational research. In this context, Palmer's comments could not be more apposite:

> Class, as both a category of potential and becoming and an agency of activism has thus reasserted its fundamental importance. More and more of humanity now faces the ravages of capitalism's highly totalizing, essentializing, and homogenizing impulses. . . . There are no answers separate from those of class struggle, however much this metanarrative of materially structured resistance intersects with special oppressions. Class has not so much fallen as it has returned. It had never, of course, gone anywhere. *Identified* as simply one of many plural subjectivities, class has actually been obscured from analytic and political view by poststructuralism's analytic edifice, erected at just the moment that the left is in dire need of the clarity and direction that class, as a category and an agency, a structure and a politics, can provide. The legacy of Marxism in general, and of historical materialism in particular, is to challenge and oppose this obfuscation, providing an alternative to such material misreadings, building an oppositional worldview that can play some role in reversing the class struggle defeats. (Palmer, 1997, p. 72)

We reject the notion put forward by postmodernists and poststructuralists that class is simply about habits and behavior, cultural status, or social prestige, or that is primarily a language sign whose meaning is overpopulated with referents and therefore "undecidable." Class is both a lived culture and an objective entity. It has an objective existence as an empirical category and a subjective existence in terms of the way in which it is lived.[2] The progenitors of cultural studies well understood this, even though they tended to emphasize (and in some cases, overemphasize) the subjective dimensions of class in response to the perceived economism of certain versions of Marxist theory. Yet in their rush to avoid the "capital" sin of "economism," many contemporary cultural and educational theorists have fallen prey to an uncritical and ahistorical "culturalism" that has severed the links between culture and class in a profoundly problematic manner. Unlike earlier theorizations that bridged a cultural approach and the Marxist concept of class struggle, the very notion of class struggle and the very idea that Marxism still has something to teach us is considered passé. In the contemporary post-Marxist climate, those who dare speak of class tend to be Weberians who "ignore discussions of capital and labour"; as such, there has been a "tendency to depoliticize class analysis so that it naturalizes social divisions" and replaces the "engine of protest" with a "resigned, imperceptible social organism" (Munt, 2000, p. 3). Because there is no evidence that class has withered away in either the United States or Britain, there is no convincing argument that class analysis can be consigned to the proverbial dustbin of history. On the contrary, at a time when we are in the midst of returning to the "most fundamental form of class struggle" (Jameson, 1998, p. 136) in light of global conditions, class analysis must be foregrounded. This can and must be done at different levels. On the one hand, there is a need to return to concrete sites of class experience and to theorize out of them, for they represent forms of situated knowledges that may provoke the forms of class consciousness necessary in the struggle against capitalist exploitation. On the other hand, we cannot discard the notion of class as an objective phenomenon. Dominant postmodernist formulations tend to view class as one among a diversity of semiotically constructed identities and just another form of "difference." In other instances, class is associated with the process of consuming commodities as a "lifestyle event" or focuses on their circulation. Against such puerile conceptualizations, we believe it is imperative to acknowledge that class is directly connected to where a person is located within the capitalist division of labor and that it is labor that is the source of value (Allman, McLaren, and Rikowski, 2003). Capitalism is a system based on the imposition of "universal commodification, including, centrally, the buying and selling of human life-time" (Dyer-Witheford, 1999, p. 9). Furthermore, class is not simply another ideology that serves to legitimate oppression. Rather, class denotes "exploitative relations between people mediated by their relations to the means of production" (Gimenez, 2001, p. 24). Although all categories are social, "class is the quintessence of the social"; unlike other categories, class cannot be determined "except by the position of the individual in society, and cannot be reproduced except through participation in the functioning of the economic system.... Class ... was created by capitalism and is reproduced together with it, and for this reason poses a real danger to it" (Kagarlitsky, 2000, p. 95).

Such an understanding of class has largely been marginalized in excessively "culturalist" narratives that confuse class (which has an objective status) with class consciousness, which is undoubtedly shaped and conditioned by social and cultural factors. Acknowledging this dimension of class does not undermine the subjective aspects of class as lived culture and lived experience, but it does point out that classes do not simply come into being by subjective fiat. Furthermore, the "objectivity of capitalist exploitation" cannot be relativized by "treating it as a mere reflex of hermeneutic self-understanding" (Harvey, 1998, p. 9) or as a mere discursively articulated subject position.[3] Unfortunately, educational discourse on the "left" has been awash in "postmodern" platitudes that sublimate class and valorize uncritical and fetishized notions of "difference" while marginalizing socialist alternatives to the social universe of capital. In an effort to counteract what we perceive to be politically domesticating and depotentiating tendencies in North American educational criticism, we argue elsewhere (Scatamburlo-D'Annibale & McLaren, 2003; McLaren & Farahmandpur, 2001) for the increasing relevance of Marxist analysis by locating the struggle for educational reform within current struggles against the globalization of capitalism and the conditions that produce the material armature of the imperial state. In doing so, we foreground the importance of working toward the socialization of productive property. Despite post-Marxist claims to the contrary, Marxist theory still has a key role to play in generating ideas that challenge intellectual orthodoxies and rationalizations for educational inequalities.

Expressive Practices and a Grounded Marxist Aesthetics

Throughout Paul Willis's innovative and expansive *oeuvre*, not only has he demonstrated an abiding interest in class consciousness and its potential role as a weapon against capital, but he has also revealed an unyielding conviction that Marxist criticism can bring about a world less populated by economic exploitation and social injustice. These features of Willis's work operate dialectically within his overall project as a Marxist scholar: Working-class consciousness can be "educated" by Marxist theory, while Marxist theory can, at the same time, be both bodied forth and conceptually deepened by those emboldened in their daily praxis by working-class consciousness. For Willis, understanding human action stipulates grasping its dialectical relation to social and symbolic structures. He has been especially attentive to how systems of intelligibility are produced within cultural formations and how ideological hegemony is maintained internally to specific group cultures within identifiable historical moments, such as the present era of disaggregated and fragmented identities. Of course, he is most concerned with ways of challenging existing ideologies, hegemonic relations, and institutional orthodoxies through the creative operations of nondominant cultural formations.

To engage in a systematic and detailed examination of the production and reproduction of conflictual and contradictory cultural formations exercised by various social classes at specific historical moments, and to preoccupy oneself with how these formations contribute to the reproduction of and resistance to existing capitalist social relations, is a lifelong research endeavor, and it is no surprise that Willis often takes pains to clarify and revise his work when the occasion demands. Few theorists comprehend as well as Willis what is at stake politically when, at the metropolitan heart of the capitalist empire, the commodity reigns supreme. Willis understands only too well that commodities are always produced in excess of human need, and this poses a specific problem for the reproduction of cultural life and for the reproduction of capitalist social relations in particular. Specifically, Willis is interested in the dynamism constitutive of cultural production resulting in what he calls "sensuous meaningfulness" or "the bodily oil of lived presence" (Willis, 2000, p. 31). He is concerned most of all with what he terms "expressive practices" linked to "living cultures." Although these cannot be apodictically linked to the immanent and historically produced situations and logics of economic production, it is, nevertheless, highly likely that such practices are connected to these logics. His work has led him to formulate moments of resistance as forms of "embedded logics in rebellious impulses or social counter-forces" (1990, p. x). It is within these impulses and forces that capitalism as a living dynamic, rife with contradictions, can best be understood.

Willis comprehends the contradictions of capitalism as both sites for cultural struggles as well as other types of nondiscursive struggles, and also as "sources for change and expansion" (1990, p. x). Here Willis sees the prickly processes of cultural reproduction tied up in the development and maintenance of "the 'teeth-gritting' harmony of capitalist formations" while at the same time, paradoxically, operating as "critical resistant or rebellious forces" (1990, p. xi). Willis reveals how working-class students produce living critiques of their identity formation within capitalist culture and in doing so explains how their "penetrations" cannot always be understood as a form of critical reflexivity. In fact, they most often take expressive forms communicated in and through their bodies. As Willis argued:

> I would never argue that the lads' culture in *Learning to Labor* is socialist though I would argue that it contains materials that must be dealt with in any socialist reconstruction. The point of my ethnography was precisely to show the profane complexity of cultural experience, only a small part of which—partially, selectively, differently at different moments of the argument—is explicable in our theoretical forays. For me culture is a very commodious and profane conceptual bag. It is much, much broader than ideology. I would never equate the two. My notions of cultural practices and cultural production ... produce *living* critiques and penetrations of dominant ideology only as a small (though critical) part of their total effective presence. They often do so in eccentric, collectively unspoken rather than individually verbal ways, and almost as the byproduct of the application of sensuous human capacities to immediate ends. I hesitate to use the word "cognition" at all to describe such processes. Furthermore, the in-built limiting structures here embedded as they are in sensuous, concrete forms are not in any conceivable sense a question of "false consciousness." It is not a mistaken or false perception, for instance, to experience class exploitation as concretely mediated and mitigated (for white men) and changed through gender and race power. These things are "real," too. (1990, p. x)

Central to cultural reproduction of the social relations of capitalist societies is the process of cultural production, a process that undergoes various stages of transformation. Cultural formations and expressive modalities are the shape-shifters of the postindustrial era, although not in a metaphysical sense; rather, they are continually transforming themselves into something else, only to return again, like the proverbial rag-and-bone shop of the repressed, in an expanded and enlarged aspect of their original state, refleshed, resignified, recathected, often with a vengeance. Willis is keenly interested in the internal relations of expressive practices—enacted while on the dole, in dance clubs, in the mall, in the classroom, or in the local pub—focusing on their critical content, their cultural production, and how cultural production is implicated in the larger process social reproduction. His center of inquiry can be said to revolve around the following axis: How do cultural commodities relate to the creative capacities and practices of the individuals who create them, and to the process of commodification in general?

In *Common Culture*, Willis discusses "symbolic work" (work that rests on the development of expressive labor power) to draw attention to the active and productive nature of cultural consumption, the "making whole" through binding fragments together, thereby defetishizing (remaking) commodities. We engage in symbolic work through our cultural practices of purchasing commodities. Our identification with the object appears to be the product of the commodity-in-itself that is purchased, but in reality it is the social effects of the purchase that we mistake for the magical attributes of the commodity. In other words, we often confuse the effects of the purchase of a commodity for the identity that we believe the commodity bestows upon us. We mistake our self-identity achieved through our purchase of the commodity for the effects of our expressive labor power. What people often confuse with the act of purchasing is, in reality, a purchasing effect, which is not a quality of their own symbolic labor. Symbolic work, as theorized by Willis, involves the transformation of commodities through the process of productive consumption; this involves the expenditure of expressive human labor to produce expanded value. In this process, alienated and fetishized meanings are converted into new contextual meanings and embodied satisfactions that were not previously available to the consumer. This process functions to expand the use value of the commodity over its exchange value through a form of defetishization. When we are faced with the production of expanded expressive labor power through the productive consumption of cultural commodities that is at odds with the repressive disciplines of the labor process, we have, according to Willis, participated in an act of resistance.

Willis has always been interested in communicative action, in the culturalization of the body, but it is in his later works, *Common Culture* (1990), and *The Ethnographic Imagination* (2000), that these interests are most fully explored. Willis begins with the assumption that no commodity is ever completely fetishized. If this were the case, communication would be impossible. He ends with the conviction that communication is only truly possible when fetishization breaks down. In other words, a given commodity must be defetishized in order to offer communicative and cultural use values. Cultural commodities, observes Willis, possess an in-built stability; there is a "double naturing" or self-repairing quality about them; they are continually extinguished and renewed, never escaping the process of fetishization, but never being reduced to that process, either. Cultural commodities are for use, not for ownership. They seduce, they offer the promise of community but never deliver on that promise. As consumers, we become addicted to the failure of the commodity, by its fraudulent claims, by its enticing promises. You can't get commodities to sign a contract, but you still take them up on their offer. What makes them creative is that they remain unfettered by historical norms of consumption and they are preloaded with expressivity. Words are never eaten the same way, and they taste differently depending on the combinations that are put in the mouth; but the best part is that they can be spit out and stripped of their dominating power before they arrive at their final destination in the stomach. Commodities are linked to the logic of capitalist production in terms of their availability within contexts of prior communicative meaning and symbolic appropriation—that is, in relation to their specific human role within communicative and cultural meaning systems which are inherently social.

Willis achieves a theoretical dynamism in *The Ethnographic Imagination* that surpasses much of his previous work. His writing appears less turgid and is crafted in a more self-consciously poetical style. On the one hand, his writing still betrays a textual heavy-handedness and arcane theorizing and trumpery that has become the signature of many postmodern writers, with ideas and concepts laboriously troweled onto the surface of his text until it appears to collapse under the weight of its own ideas; on the other hand, there are moments when his own expressive style is refreshingly probing, resembling the wordplay of a loutish Leavisite hanging out with fellow wordsmiths in the local pub, playing the theoretical dozens with the street-wise deftness of a homeboy from South Central LA. *The Ethnographic Imagination* is a work that stalks the meaning of cultural objects and artifacts from the dark alleys of cultural criticism, cautiously approaching its subject matter from various theoretical angles and trajectories, yet never veering from the central question: How does human "praxis" rearrange the "objective possibilities" of a cultural object or material form? Carefully fashioning a transgressive aesthetic sensibility, Willis traverses the lost territory between particular signifiers and emotional expressivity with the hard-scrabble earnestness of a shop steward. This is especially evident, for instance, in his discussion of working-class speech codes as a process of making words into fists, a process that is populated by a politics of subversion and freighted with creative alternatives to official representations and naturalized ideological accounts.

In *The Ethnographic Imagination* Willis nominates resistance as a "grounded aesthetics." Grounded aesthetics is simply a modality of living through a creative defetishization of cultural commodities, and the relocation of their social meaning. Grounded aesthetics highlights how "vertical" structures within capitalism that employ abstract reason and mentalized communication and that treat human beings as objects to control can be detached for "lateral" use and circulation for expressive resistance. Willis is able to boast an optimism of the will precisely because he is absolutely sold on the fecundating power of human creativity and on ethnography as a means of understanding how such creativity works in commercialized human culture. Willis sees ideological and institutional processes as producing the alienated individual of postmodern culture from above but symbolic work as producing the subject from below. He also sees the expanding and creative nature of expressive labor power as a basis for critiquing instrumental labor power, thereby challenging the capitalist labor processes and forming a basis for collective organization and a struggle on behalf of common interests. This can only occur when symbolic work is made less invisible. Because cultural production is not self-conscious enough of its own constitutive processes, informal meaning-making can help strengthen mental/manual divisions characteristic of capitalist societies.

A Critical Pedagogy of Class Consciousness

Willis undoubtedly ranks among the most prominent Marxist cultural theorists, especially in terms of the relevance of his work for education. Nonetheless, we would be remiss if we did not share some reservations we have concerning the overall trajectory of his work. In attempting to examine social life from the inside out, Willis is, at times, overly preoccupied with the expressive nature of meaning-making, particularly within the semiautonomous spaces of mediated cultural formations, or structures of mediation. There often tends to be an undialectical overemphasis on abstract labor and the production of fetishized social relations (both mediated aspects of communicative activity and resistance to reified or alienated aspects of the same activity). These fetishized social relations are tied up with the alienation produced between the worker and the commodity he or she produces but also, as Marx pointed out in his labor theory of value, with those that enable individuals to misperceive everyday social intercourse as a relation between things. This, in our view, provokes Willis at times to elevate cultural formations responsible for "alienation effects" over and above material relations of production. Although Willis is clearly aware that such cultural formations are "structured" by capitalism as a specific system of social/production relations, these relations appear much less central to his work. We don't believe that capital can be defeated through fighting within and against its mediated forms. Resistance requires more than the defetishization of commodities. It requires the very overturning of the generalization of commodity production itself and the dereification of capital and the nation state; that is, it requires overturning the historical and material conditions that shape bourgeois ideology and our imprisonment within it (see Allman, McLaren, Cole & Rikowski, 2003). It requires creating the social and material conditions that can help to shape and educate class consciousness in the pursuit of socialist futures. Especially at a time of deepening social and economic crisis, punctuated by imperialist wars of aggression and conquest, resistance requires a democratic and centralized class struggle in order to transform state power and abolish the very value form of labor that not only gives class society its ballast, anchoring it in the process of commodification, but also its conditions of possibility.

We believe that Willis's grounded aesthetics needs to be complimented by a larger strategy for socialist transformation, one that proceeds from an assessment of the objective factors and capabilities latent in the current conditions of class struggle (see McLaren 2003). The worldwide social movement against anti–corporate globalization and the anti-imperialist/antiwar movements preceding and following the U.S. invasion of Iraq, have provided new contexts (mostly through left-wing independent publications and resources on the internet) for enabling various publics (and nonpublics beyond the institutions that serve majority groups) to become more critically literate about the relationship between current world events and global capitalism (see Pozo, 2003 and Moraes, 2003). Following an engagement in these new opportunities for analysis, it is possible to forge a vision of possible futures for humanity and the development of an understanding of what, exactly, stands between us and the realization of that vision. It is likely that the changes that we seek will not be possible without a massive social revolution consolidated around the wider struggle against imperialism, in support of human rights, and a search for a socialist alternative to capital. This will require a socialist "education" of working-class consciousness. And this, in turn, means challenging the mediated social forms in which we live and learn to labor.

One way of scrutinizing the production of everyday meanings so that they are less likely to provide ballast to capitalist social relations is to study working-class consciousness. It is here that Willis's work can be especially productive. Bertell Ollman (1993) noted that more systematic and effectively theorized studies of working-class consciousness remains to be done, given that most current studies of working-class consciousness have been derived from non-Marxist approaches. A key point to remember, according to Ollman, is that class consciousness is much more than individual consciousness writ large. The subject of class consciousness is, after all, class. Viewing class consciousness from the perspective of the labor theory of value and the materialist conception of history, as in Ollman's account, stipulates that we view class in the context of the overall integrated functions of capital and wage labor. And although people can certainly be seen from the functionalist perspective as embodiments of social-economic functions, we need to expand this view and understand the subjective dimensions of class and class consciousness. Ollman follows Marx's advice in recommending that in defining "class" or any other important notions, we begin from the whole and proceed to the part (see also the writings of Ilyenkov, 1977, 1982a, 1982b).

Class must be conceived as a complex social relation in the context of Marx's dialectical approach to social life. It is important in this regard to see class as a function (from the perspective of the place of a function within the system), as a group (qualities that are attributed to people such as race and gender), and as a complex relation (i.e., as the abstracted common element in the social relationship of alienated individuals). A class involves, therefore, the alienated quality of the social life of individuals who function in a certain way within the system. The salient features of class—alienated social relation, place/function, and group—are all mutually dependent.

Class as function relates to the objective interests of workers; class as group relates to their subjective interests. Subjective interests refer to what workers actually believe to be in their own best interests. Those practices that serve the workers in their function as wage laborers refer to their objective interests. Ollman summarized class consciousness as "one's identity and interests (subjective and objective) as members of a class, something of the dynamics of capitalism uncovered by Marx (at least enough to grasp objective interests), the broad outlines of the class struggle and where one fits into it, feelings of solidarity toward one's own class and of rational hostility toward opposition classes (in contrast to the feelings of mutual indifference and inner-class competition that accompany alienation), and the vision of a more democratic and egalitarian society that is not only possible but that one can help bring about" (Ollman, 1993, p. 155). Ollman underscored (correctly in our view) the notion that explaining class consciousness stipulates seeking what is not present in the thinking of workers and what is present. It is an understanding that is "appropriate to the objective character of a class and its objective interests" (1993, p. 155). But in addition to the objective aspect of class consciousness we must include the subjective aspect of class consciousness, which Ollman described as "the consciousness of the group of people in a class in so far as their understanding of who they are and what must be done develops from its economistic beginnings toward the consciousness that is appropriate to their class situation" (1993, p. 155). But what is different between this subjective consciousness and the actual consciousness of each individual in the group? Ollman wrote that subjective consciousness is different from the actual consciousness of the individual in the group in the following three ways:

> (1) It is a group consciousness, a way of thinking and a thought content, that develops through the individuals in the group interacting with each other and with opposing groups in situations that are peculiar to the class; (2) it is a consciousness that has its main point of reference in the situation and objective interests of a class, viewed functionally, and not in the declared subjective interests of

class members (the imputed class consciousness referred to above has been given a role here in the thinking of real people); and (3) it is in its essence a process, a movement from wherever a group begins in its consciousness of itself to the consciousness appropriate to its situation. In other words, the process of becoming class conscious is not external to what it is but rather at the center of what it is all about. (Ollman, 1993, p. 155)

Class conscious is therefore something that Ollman described as "a kind of 'group think,' a collective, interactive approach to recognizing, labeling, coming to understand, and acting on the particular world class members have in common" (1993, p. 156). Class consciousness is different from individual consciousness in the sense of "having its main point of reference in the situation of the class and not in the already recognized interests of individuals" (1993, p. 157). Class consciousness is something that exists "in potential" in the sense that it represents "the appropriate consciousness of people in that position, the consciousness that maximizes their chances of realizing class interests, including structural change where such change is required to secure other interests" (1993, p. 157). Ollman stresses that class consciousness "exists in potential," that is, "class consciousness is a consciousness waiting to happen" (1993, p. 187). It is important here not to mistake class consciousness as some kind of "abstract potential" because, in contrast, it is "rooted in a situation unfolding before our very eyes, long before understanding of real people catches up with it" (1993, p. 157). Class consciousness, then, is not something that is fixed or permanent but is always in motion. The very situatedness of the class establishes its goal—it is always in the process of becoming itself, if we understand the notion of process dialectically. Consequently, we need to examine class from the perspective of Marx's philosophy of internal relations, as that "which treats the relations in which anything stands as essential parts of what it is, so that a significant change in any of these relations registers as a qualitative change in the system of which it is a part" (Ollman, 2003, p. 85).

Willis captures this dynamics of class when he writes:

Non-class categories may tell you more empirically about a person, but they do not "move" or develop by themselves. To understand principles of change or how those categories combine or develop over time, to make sense of the picture, to historicize it we need the dynamism of economic relations. To be crude, class explains more about them than they can explain about it. Socially received and atavistic, often still unnamed or analyzed, categories provide the sea, class the currents. Class and productive relations and commodity production provide nodal points of influence, confluence, and change that allow us to organize and see the empirical "wholes" in more ordered and interlinking ways. (2000, p. 112)

It is precisely in mapping out and explaining these "nodal points" that Willis's work can offer us a deeper understanding of the formation and education of class consciousness. Although the former nodal points Willis describes as "manual wage labor and masculinity, spatial concentration, white-collar/blue-collar, work/leisure, collectivity" have not deserted Willis's work, the new nodal points that interest him include the conditions of cultural practices such as their "different relations to language and to embedded forms of sensuous meaning; different access to and different types of relationships, with resources available for symbolic work and for the development of the expressive self" (2000, p. 112). But again, too often Willis's focus on how capital is "lived" in the sensuous domain of the fetishized cultural object and its dialectical relation to individual and group identity and fails to account sufficiently for the role of production in generating the value form in which labor is produced. It is here that Willis's work could benefit from a more dialectical approach like the one pioneered by Ollman. Willis's work as it stands could be more effectively deployed as a strategic weapon in the struggle against capital if it assumed a more world-historical, international, multicultural, and anti-imperialist perspective. Such a perspective would still be grounded in the social dimension of meaning-making but within the context of a wider counteroffensive against economic and environmental degradation brought about by globalized capitalism's imperial blitzkrieg. The glimmerings of what a postcapitalist socialist society might look like are as yet unbirthed in Willis's overall political project.

Having said this, we agree that where Willis's work can provide an especially significant contribution to the existing work on class consciousness resides in the challenge of according "sufficient weight to the social relations in which people produce and reproduce the means of material life without reducing everything to these" (McNally, 2001, p. 113). Here Willis's empirical and theoretical work can help to establish what David McNally called "the dialectical determination among the internally related elements that constitute a social whole" (2001, p. 113). Willis's contributions to our understanding of commodity fetishism can be especially fruitful in helping us fathom the dialectical relationship that obtains between ideological class divisions and the forces of production and between the inner laws of capital and cultural and subjective processes. In the broadest sense, it can enable us to situate with more analytic precision the struggle over the meaning and the inner dialectical quality of the commodity within wider social, cultural, and historical processes and formations (keeping in mind that there are aspects of Willis's work that could themselves be improved with a more directed focus on the totality of capitalist social relations). In this regard, Willis emphasizes the importance of linguistic translation in helping to undress the hidden processes of symbolic work both as a means to resist the deleterious aspects of ideological fetishism and as a way of creating new inroads to political self-fashioning. Here we recognize in Willis's work a suggestive strategy for taking received meanings from bourgeois commodity culture and, as Volosinov (1986) would put it, contesting their "tenure." In this context, Willis's work provides a crucial avenue for exploring the formation and functioning of the conflicting ensembles of social and cultural relations, moral assumptions and obligations, and forms of social activity and discourse that make up the contemporary "moral economy" among working-class groups (see Thompson, 1963, 1991). We suggest that much of the contemporary work on commodity culture and class consciousness could be deepened if undertaken with an eye to exploring the connections between Willis's work and those of the Bakhtin School of the 1920s that includes V. N. Volosinov (1986), M. M. Bakhtin (1981, 1984), and P. N. Medvedev (Medvedev & Bakhtin, 1985). We also discern a fruitful complementarity between Willis's use of aesthetics as a form of resistance and the work of Walter Benjamin (1968, 1999), especially in light of Benjamin's materialist theory of language and his understanding of how, in the words of McNally (2001, p. 224), "bourgeois society tries to efface the human body, beginning with the fetishism of the commodity." Like Benjamin, Willis believes that degraded bodies in our society can trouble significantly the formation of capitalist commodification and become sites for resistance and revolt. McNally noted appositely, after Benjamin, that "a precondition of emancipation is that repressed desires must enter into the language of everyday life and that the latter must recover the language of the body and of things" (2001, p. 225). If it is true that the pathways to liberation must make their way through the language of the body, then surely these bodies, and the way they are enfleshed with the capacity to recall memories long repressed and dreams long forgotten, constitute the most important resource in forming the larger collective body of class-conscious workers necessary for class struggle to achieve its goal.

Because Marx lays bare "relations among what is, what could be, what shouldn't be, and what can be done about it" (Ollman, 2003, p. 82), Ollman argued that Marxism constitutes "science, critique, vision and recipe for revolution" simultaneously "with each of these qualities contributing to and feeding off the others" (2003, p. 82). It is by approaching Marxism with this description in mind that one can best assist educators in exploring the causeways of revolutionary consciousness and praxis (Allman, McLaren, & Rikowski, 2003). It is precisely by utilizing Marx in this fashion that Willis's work can be strategically employed by radical educators bent on developing cultural strategies within forms of lived culture that can move defetishization into new creative contexts for sundry ad hoc struggles alongside, within, and against commodity culture (see Ollman, 1971). The key objective for critical educators is not only to become involved in making the process of cultural commodification less invisible to those whose subjectivities are formed within it, but to become involved in creating the kinds of social, political, and educational conditions that not only can assist in the defetishization of cultural practices but can shape the development of working-class consciousness (McLaren, 2000).

So much that we have learned about the ethnographic imagination from Willis's work can be brought to bear in new and productive ways on the study of class consciousness and its transformation into new forms of socialist resistance. Such an engagement can afford educators new ways of broadening the struggle for new resources of meaning-making and self-making, extending the norms for social transformation, and advancing the struggle for a socialist future.

Notes

1. Many of us have viewed ourselves as fellow-travelers of Willis, on the bumpy and uncharted road to liberation—what Raymond Williams called *The Long Revolution*—which can most effectively be brought about by socialist renewal. Willis had been riding the rails of socialist research for years while many of us were still cutting our graduate school teeth on his *Profane Culture*, delighting ourselves in his theoretical renditions of the Teddy Boys, Mods, and Rastas, and debating the strengths and weaknesses of indexical, homological, and integral levels of cultural relations among motor bike boy culture (not to mention integral circuiting). During the British invasion of graduate schools of education in the 1980s, commandeered by the Birmingham School of Contemporary Cultural Studies, any radical doctoral student worth her (or his) salt who was not familiar with the works of Paul Willis, Phil Corrigan or his brother, Paul, Stuart Hall, Richard Johnson, Angela McRobbie, or Dick Hebdige was unable to participate with any credibility in the weekly brown-bag seminars or lunchtime conversations in the graduate student lounge. Those of us who were lucky enough to have our doctoral work read and encouraged by Willis, or other visitors from the United Kingdom to the radical campuses of the day, felt more than lucky: We were blessed.

2. In *The 18th Brumaire of Louis Bonaparte*, Marx proposed a clear distinction between the objective fact of class position and the subjective fact of class consciousness. In this discussion of the French peasantry, Marx (1984, p. 124) argued that:

    In so far as millions of families live under economic conditions of existence that separate their mode of life, their interests and their culture from those of the other classes, and put them in hostile opposition to the latter, they form a class. In so far as there is merely a local interconnection among these small-holding peasants, and the identity of their interests begets no community, no national bond and no political organization among them, they do not form a class.

3. For a lengthier exposition of our approach, see Scatamburlo-D'Annibale and McLaren (2003).

References

Allman, P., McLaren, P., & Rikowski, G. (2003). After the box people: The labour–capital relation as class constitution and its consequences of Marxist educational theory and human resistance." In J., Freeman-Moir and A. Scott (Eds.), *Yesterday's dreams: International and critical perspectives on education and social class* (pp. 149–179). Christchurch, New Zealand: Canterbury University Press.

Bakhtin, M. M. (1981). *The dialogic imagination: Four essays* (M. Holquist, Ed.; C. Emerson & M. Holquist, Trans.). Austin: University of Texas Press.

Bakhtin, M. (1984). *Problems of Dostoevky's poetics* (C. Emerson, Ed. & Trans.). Minneapolis: University of Minnesota Press.

Benjamin, W. (1968). *Illuminations* (H. Arendt, Ed.). New York: Schocken Books.

Benjamin, W. (1999). *Selected writings, Volume 2: 1927–1935* (M. Jennings, H. Eiland, & G. Smith, Eds.). Cambridge, MA: Belknap Press of Harvard University Press.

Collini, S. (1994). Escape from DWEMsville. *Times Literary Supplement*, 4756 (May 27), 3–4.

Dyer-Witheford, N. (1999). *Cyber-Marx: Cycles and circuits of struggle in high-technology capitalism.* Urbana and Chicago: University of Illinois Press.

Gimenez, M. (2001). Marxism, and class, gender and race: Rethinking the trilogy. *Race, Gender & Class*, 8(2), 23–33.

Harvey, D. (1998). The practical contradictions of Marxism. *Critical Sociology*, 24(1, 2), 1–36.

Hill, D., McLaren, P., Cole, M. & Rikowski, G. (2002). *Marxism Against Postmodernism in Educational Theory.* Landham, MD: Lexington Books.

Ilyenkov, E. V. (1977). *Dialectical logic: Essays on its history and theory.* Moscow: Progress.

Ilyenkov, E. V. (1982a). *Leninist dialectics and the metaphysics of positivism.* London: New Park.

Ilyenkov, E. V. (1982b). *The dialectics of the abstract and the concrete in Marx's Capital.* Moscow: Progress.

Jameson, F. (1998). *The cultural turn.* London: Verso.

Kagarlitsky, B. (2000) *The return of radicalism.* London: Pluto Press.

Katz, A. (2000). *Postmodernism and the politics of "culture."* Boulder, CO: Westview Press.

Lave, J., Duguid, P., Fernandez, N. & Axel, E. (1992). Coming of age in Birmingham: Cultural studies and conceptions of subjectivity. *Annual Review of Anthropology*, 21, 231–249.

Marx, K. (1984). *The 18th Brumaire of Louis Bonaparte.* New York: International. (Original work published 1869.)

McLaren, P. (1998). Revolutionary pedagogy in post-revolutionary times: Rethinking the political economy of critical education. *Educational Theory*, 48(4), 431–462.

McLaren, P. (2000). *Che Guevara, Paulo Freire, and the pedagogy of revolution.* Boulder, CO: Rowman & Littlefield.

McLaren, P., & Farahmandpur, R. (1999). Critical pedagogy, postmodernism, and the retreat from class: Towards a contraband pedagogy. *Theoria*, 93, 83–115.

McLaren, P. & Farahmandpur, R. (2000). Reconsidering Marx in post-Marxist times: A requiem for postmodernism? *Educational Researcher*, 29(3), 25–33.

McLaren, P., & Farahmandpur, R. (2001). The globalization of capitalism and the new imperialism: Notes towards a revolutionary critical pedagogy. *The Review of Education, Pedagogy & Cultural Studies*, 23(3), 271–315.

McLaren, P. (2003). Critical pedagogy in the age of neoliberal globalization: Notes from history's underside. *Democracy and Nature*, 9(1), 65–90.

McNally, D. (2001). *Bodies of meaning: Studies on language, labor, and liberation.* Albany: State University of New York Press.

Medvedev, P. N., & Bakhtin, M. (1985). *The Formal method in literary scholarship: A critical introduction to sociological poetics* (A. J. Wherle, Trans.). Cambridge, MA: Harvard University Press. (Original work published 1928.)

Milner, A. (1999). *Class: Core conceptual concepts.* London: Sage.

Moraes, M. (2003). The path of dissent: An interview with Peter McLaren. *Journal of Transformative Education*, 1(2), 117–134.

Munt, S. (Ed.). (2000). *Cultural studies and the working class.* New York: Cassell.

Ollman, B. (1971). *Alienation: Marx's conception of man in capitalist society.* New York: Cambridge University Press.

Ollman, B. (1993). *Dialectical investigations.* New York: Routledge.

Ollman, B. (2003). Marxism, this tale of two cities. *Science & Society*, 67(1), 80–86.

Palmer, B. (1997). Old positions/new necessities: History, class, and Marxist metanarrative. In E. M. Wood & J. B. Poster (Eds.), *In defense of history: Marxism and the postmodern agenda* (pp. 65–73). New York: Monthly Review Press.

Pozo, M. (2003). Toward a critical revolutionary pedagogy: An interview with Peter McLaren. *St. John's University Humanities Review,* 58–77.

San Juan, E., Jr. (2002). *Racism and cultural studies: Critiques of multiculturalist ideology and the politics of difference.* Durham, NC: Duke University Press.

San Juan, E. (2003). Marxism and the race/class problematic: A re-articulation. *Cultural Logic.* http://eserver.org/clogic/2003/sanjuan.html.

Scatamburlo-D'Annibale, V., & McLaren, P. (2003). The strategic centrality of class in the politics of "race" and "difference." *Cultural Studies/Critical Methodologies, 3*(2), 148–175.

Thompson, E. P. (1963). *The making of the English working class.* London: Gollancz.

Thompson, E. P. (1991). *Customs in common.* London: Merlin.

Volosinov, V. N. (1986). *Marxism and the philosophy of language* (L. Matejka & I. R. Titunik, Trans.). Cambridge, MA: Harvard University Press.

Wallerstein, I. (1995). *After liberalism.* New York: New Press.

Willis, P. (1977). *Learning to labor.* New York: Columbia University Press.

Willis, P. (1978). *Profane culture.* London: Routledge and Kegan Paul.

Willis, P. (1990). Foreword. In D. E. Foley (Ed.), *Learning capitalist culture: Deep in the heart of Tejas* (pp. vii–xii). Philadelphia: University of Pennsylvania Press.

Willis, P. et. al. (1990). *Common culture.* Milton Keynes: Open University Press.

Willis, P. (2000). *The ethnographic imagination.* Cambridge: Polity.

CHAPTER 4

Between Good Sense and Bad Sense
Race, Class, and Learning from Learning to Labor

MICHAEL W. APPLE

In *Models and Mystery* (Ramsey, 1964), Ian Ramsey made a distinction between two kinds of models. The first, "pictorial models," seek to show the world "as it really is." Such models, although useful, are usually relatively undynamic and risk becoming reified representations of reified people and processes. The second, "disclosure models," enable us to see the people and processes in wholly new and considerably more dynamic ways. In the (often overused) Kuhnian sense of the word, they provide for and signify paradigm shifts (Kuhn, 1970). Only a very few works in the fields of sociology, cultural studies, and education can be said to have provided powerful disclosure models. But if I were asked to nominate truly lasting contributions, ones that continue to deserve to be read today, within that select few would be *Learning to Labor* (Willis, 1977, published in the United Kingdom as *Learning to Labour*). Indeed, along with, say, the scholarship of Bourdieu and Bernstein, Paul Willis's work stands as an achievement that has not only stood the test of time but remains among the most compelling analyses of how class can be understood. Indeed, I would want to claim that its basic approach provides some of the essential building blocks for a critical analysis of many of the dynamics of differential power and experience with which all of us are concerned.

Paul Willis has been a friend and colleague for over 20 years. Because of this, some of what I say must be partly autobiographical, not because my

61

perspectives should be privileged above others', but because like many others in the field my own work was changed in fundamental ways by *Learning to Labor*.

I need to return us to the intellectual/political world within critical educational studies of the mid-1970s in order to restore our sense of Paul Willis's unique contribution. In the United States, as in many other nations, critical sociological work on schooling was dominated either by the reductive and economistic readings of the relationship between schools and society of Bowles and Gintis (1976) or by the somewhat more critical culturalist readings of people such as myself and Jean Anyon (Anyon, 1979; Apple, 1979). With varying degrees of complexity, the emphasis was on the schools' role in economic and cultural reproduction and on the debates over base and superstructure and structure and agency (Apple, 1982a, 1982b). As the tradition grew in sophistication, such reproduction was seen as contested and not always successful (Apple, 1982b; Apple & Weis, 1983), and more attention began to be paid not only to content but to the form and organization of knowledge, pedagogy, and evaluation and the principles that underpinned them, and to the ways all of this was actually experienced by students and teachers (Apple, 1982b). *Learning to Labor* became crucial in this project. Even when it was not overtly cited (which by and large it almost always was), it provided the conceptual door for others to go through. Certainly this was true in my case.

The first edition of my book *Ideology and Curriculum* was published in 1979, although the manuscript had been completed in 1977. In the final chapter, after the entire book was spent on analyzing the structures of cultural domination in the curriculum and in schooling in general, I argued—correctly, but in a conceptually and politically underdeveloped and somewhat naive manner when I look back on it now—that "ideological reproduction" was not all that was going on. Students and teachers were not puppets. Culture was neither epiphenomenal, nor unimportant; it counted in crucial ways and provided significant resources in hegemonic and counterhegemonic struggles.

During the period of time in which I was completing the final draft of the manuscript, I was lecturing in England. Colleagues there spoke to me about *Learning to Labor*. I bought it and read it immediately. Over the following months, it became increasingly clear to me that each time I wanted to more fully understand the relationship between culture and economy in education, to more fully grasp the materiality of cultural form and content and the political dynamics in which it played such a constitutive part, I was using a set of lenses that in large part were influenced by my reading and rereading of Paul's work. I sensed that, at the time, his analyses had a relatively underdeveloped theory of the role of the state in structuring the very arena in which the schools and their definitions of "official knowledge" and "legiti-mate" social and pedagogic relations played a large part (see, e.g., Apple, 2000; Apple et al., 2003) and that it romanticized the possibility of using the lived culture of youth in developing a political response to oppressive reali-ties, in "disarticulating" them from one set of positions and "rearticulating" them to a more progressive set of positions and collective actions. But these issues seemed minor compared both to the things that his work disclosed and to the doors that it opened to the entire realm of cultural studies inside and outside of education, such as the influential tradition of critical cultural analysis that came out of the Centre for Contemporary Cultural Studies at Birmingham. Anyone looking at the books of mine that immediately followed (Apple, 1982b, 1986)—with their focus on lived culture, on the contradictory meanings and results of resistance, on the realities of cultural production that, while influenced by political economy, could not be reduced to it, on the ways in which gender, race, and class were linked in fully contradictory ways—couldn't fail to see the influences on me that were embodied in both Willis and the CCCS.

Yet, thinking back on Paul's work and its influences on me then has also made me recognize the continuity of such influence. It is not simply "in the past." His analyses provided me with the epistemological and conceptual tools that formed the basis of a considerable portion of the work I do *now*. I can trace the development of a number of my own projects to the rather Gramscian understanding of the contradictory formations involved in "common sense" that has played such an important role in Willis's own work over the years. Whether one calls them "penetrations" (a concept that proved to be troublesome because of its masculinist tendencies) and "limi-tations" as Paul did, or elements of "good" and "bad" sense in tension as I have done, our modes of being in and understanding the world are seen as contradictory. Habitus and body hexis are constitutively contradictory, filled with elements of real understandings that both help and hurt at one and the same time. Thus, concepts that have such a long history in, say, Marxist (and other) perspectives, such as "false consciousness," are to be rejected both as simplistic and as ungrounded in lived and embodied culture of identifiable people and movements as they go about their daily lives.[1]

Let me say more about this. For example, it would not be possible to understand my work over the entire past decade—in, for example, *Cultural Politics and Education* (1996), *Official Knowledge* (2000), and *Educating the "Right" Way* (2001)—without understanding its historic genesis in parts of *Learning to Labor* and *Common Culture*. My agenda has been to demon-strate how the formation of hegemonic (and later counterhegemonic) alliances has been accomplished, how people can be "hailed" or pulled under the leadership of a new hegemonic bloc, what I have called "conservative modernization" (Apple, 2001; see also Dale, 1989/1990). This creative process of disarticulation and rearticulation can *only* be accomplished if dominant groups work off of and on the elements of real understanding of social and educational problems that are already there within social groups and movements. The formation of ideological umbrellas cannot be done without this process. And a critical understanding of the creative work that neo-liberals and neo-conservatives have been engaged in so successfully in education, in the economy, in the political sphere, and elsewhere can best be gotten at by analyzing the ways in which there have been discursive connections made with the elements of good sense that people have.

In reflecting on this, I recognize then that in many ways, at the very core of the critical research I have done both on rightist social movements and on how to interrupt them is the perspective I first encountered in *Learning to Labor*. Perhaps the best way of documenting how these influences continue to have an impact on my work and that of my students is to give a elaborated example. The example has to do with the current move to the right in education and so much else in our societies. It concerns the intersection of race and class and the politics of educational policy and how identities can be constructed and reconstructed so that they are connected to social movements that wish to transform society.

Mapping Conservative Modernization

This is both a good and bad time in the world of educational policy. On the one hand, there have been very few periods when education has taken such a central place in public debates about our present and future. On the other hand, an increasingly limited range of ideological and discursive resources dominates the conceptual and political forms in which this debate is carried out. These debates are occurring on an uneven playing field, one on which what were formerly seen as rightist policies have now become "common sense" (Apple, 2000, 2001). Yet such conservative policies have a different kind of cachet today. There is a sense that these are not only things that will protect a romantic past; these policies are now often seen as "radical" but necessary solutions to an educational system that is out of control and is no longer responsive to the needs of "the people."

Thus, a new kind of conservatism has evolved and has taken center stage in many nations. "Conservative modernization" is decidedly not simply a mirror of previous rightist movements. Although parts of these positions may have originated within the New Right, they are now not limited to what has traditionally been called the Right. They have been taken up by a much larger segment of government and policymakers and, as shown in this section of this chapter, have even been appropriated by groups one would least expect to do so, such as African American activists. How are we to understand this? In answering this question, although my focus here is largely on the United States, the tendencies I describe have implications well beyond one nation.

The concepts we use to try to understand and act on the world in which we live do not by themselves determine the answers we may find. Answers are not determined by words, but by the power relations that impose their interpretations of these concepts. Yet there are key words that continually surface in the debates over education. These key words have complicated histories, histories that are connected to the social movements out of which they arose and in which they are struggled over today. These words have their own histories, but they are increasingly interrelated. The concepts are simple to list: markets, standards, accountability, tradition, God, and a number of others. Behind each of these topics is an assemblage of other words that have an emotional valence and that provide the support for the ways in which differential power works in our daily lives. These concepts include democracy, freedom, choice, morality, family, culture, and a number of other key concepts. And each of these in turn is intertextual. Each and every one of these is connected to an entire set of assumptions about "appropriate" institutions, values, social relationships, and policies.

Think of this situation as something of a road map. Using one key word—markets—sends you onto a highway that is going in one direction and that has exits in some places but not others. If you are on a highway labeled *market,* your general direction is toward a section of the country named *the economy.* You take the exit named *individualism* that goes by way of another road called *consumer choice.* Exits with words such as *unions, collective freedom, the common good, politics,* and similar destinations are to be avoided if they are on the map at all. The first road is a simple route with one goal—deciding where one wants to go without a lot of time-wasting discussion and getting there by the fastest and cheapest method possible. There is a second route, however, and this one involves a good deal of collective deliberation about where we might want to go. It assumes that there may be some continuing deliberation about not only the goal, but also even the route itself. Its exits are the ones that were avoided on the first route.

There are powerful interests that have made the road map and the roads. Some want only the road labeled *market,* because this supposedly leads to individual choice. Others will go down that road, but only if the exits are those that have a long history of "real culture" and "real knowledge." Still others will take the market road because for them God has said that this is "his" road. And finally, another group will sign on to this tour because they have skills in mapmaking and in determining how far we are from our goal. There's some discussion and some compromise—and perhaps even some

lingering tension—among these various groups about which exits will ultimately be stopped at, but by and large they all head off in that direction.

This exercise in storytelling maps onto reality in important ways. The
first group is what is appropriately called *neo-liberals*. They are deeply
committed to markets and to freedom as "individual choice." The second
group, *neo-conservatives*, has a vision of an Edenic past and wants a return
to discipline and traditional knowledge. The third, one that is increasingly
powerful in the United States and elsewhere, is what I call *authoritarian
populists*—religious fundamentalists and conservative evangelicals who
want a return to (their) God in all of our institutions.[2] And finally, the
mapmakers and experts on whether we got there are members of a particular fraction of the managerial and professional *new middle class*.

In analyzing this complex configuration of interests around conservative
modernization, we need to act on what Eric Hobsbawm described as the
historian's and social critic's duty. For Hobsbawm, the task is to be the
"professional remembrancers of what [our] fellow citizens wish to forget"
(Hobsbawm, 1994, p. 3). That is, it requires us to detail the absent presences,
the there that is not there, in most rightist policies in education. How does
their language work to highlight certain things as "real" problems, while
marginalizing others? What are the effects of the policies that they have
promoted? How do the seemingly contradictory policies that have emerged
from the various fractions of the Right, aspects of which have now taken on
a life of their own at times—such as the marketization of education through
voucher plans, the pressure to "return" to the Western tradition and to a
supposedly common culture, the commitment to get God back into the
schools and classrooms of America, and the growth of national and state
curriculum and reductive national and state (and often "high stakes")
testing—actually get put together in creative ways to push many of the
aspects of these rightist agendas forward?

In a number of recent books, I have critically analyzed why and how this
has occurred. Along with others (see, e.g., Whitty, Power, & Halpin, 1998;
Gillborn & Youdell, 2000), I have examined a range of proposals for educational "reform" such as marketization, standards, national/statewide
curricula, and national/statewide testing. This critical examination has
demonstrated that, even with the often good intentions of the proponents of
many of these kinds of proposals, in the long run they may actually exacerbate inequalities, especially around class and race. Furthermore, they may
paradoxically cause us both to misrecognize what actually causes difficult
social and educational problems and to miss some important democratic
alternatives that may offer more hope in the long run (see, e.g., Apple, 2000,
2001; Apple & Beane, 1999; Apple et al., 2003).

It is helpful to think of this as having been accomplished through the use of a vast socio/pedagogic project, a project that has actively—and in large part successfully—sought to transform our very ideas about democracy. Democracy is no longer a political concept; rather, it is wholly an economic concept in which unattached individuals—supposedly making "rational" choices on an unfettered market—will ultimately lead to a better society. As Foner (1998) reminded us, it has taken decades of creative ideological work to change our commonsense ideas about democracy. Not only does this change fly in the face of a very long tradition of collective understandings of democracy in the United States, but it has also led to the destruction of many communities, jobs, health care, and so many other institutions not only in the United States but also throughout the world (Greider, 1997; Katz, 2001). Hidden assumptions about class and a goodly portion of the politics of whiteness may make it hard for us to face this honestly (see Fine, Weis, Powell, & Wong, 1997).

But let me stop myself here. I should have put two words in the last sentences of the preceding paragraph—*us* and *we*—in quotation marks. Who is the "we"? Does it include all those who have been hurt by that combination of neo-liberal and neo-conservative polices that now play such an important role in our discourse in education? If these policies have a disproportionate and negative effect on, say, the working class and on people of color—as they seem to do—should we assume that, for example, all persons of color will recognize this and will reject both the policies and their underlying ideologies? That this is not the case is the subject of the rest of this chapter as I employ models strongly influenced by Willis's approach to understand how and why this may not be the case.

Strange Allies

Given the history of their struggles both for redistribution and recognition, it would be very difficult to integrate historically disenfranchised social groups, especially people of color, under the umbrella of conservative modernization (Apple, 2000; Fraser, 1997). However, this does not make it impossible. As I noted in the introduction to this chapter, one of the ways in which hegemonic alliances are built is through a process in which dominant groups creatively use the elements of "good sense" (what Willis had called "penetrations") that disenfranchised groups possess and then attach their neo-liberal and neo-conservative agendas to these elements (Apple, 2001). Unfortunately, the partial success of such a strategy among those groups who are often counted as "despised others" (Fraser, 1997) in our societies is a subject that many progressives would like to forget. Yet there is increasing evidence that there are growing numbers of members of "minority" groups, conservative women, and gays and lesbians who are activists in neo-liberal and neo-conservative movements, and to a lesser extent in authoritarian populist religious movements. (Of course, given the crucial role that Black churches have played in the historical struggles for justice [West, 1982], it would be surprising if there were not elements of such sentiments within African American communities.)

There have been exceptions to this relative neglect. In a recent book, Dillard (2001), for example, critically examined a number of the key actors within conservative circles who themselves are members of historically oppressed groups, but who—for a variety of personal and political reasons—give vocal support to neo-liberal and neo-conservative causes. Aggressively "free" market policies, a rejection of affirmative action and the use of race and/or gender as a category in public decisions, mobilizing for public funding for religiously based schooling, welfare "reform," and a host of similar issues provide the centers of gravity for these individuals. Many of the figures on which she focuses will be familiar to those on the United States side of the Atlantic: Dinesh D'Sousa, Thomas Sowell, Clarence Thomas, Linda Chavez, Glenn Loury, Richard Rodriguez, and similar national spokespersons of conservative causes. Each of these figures is a person of color. Among them are well-known academics, journalists, government officials, and a justice of the Supreme Court. Other figures may be familiar only to those readers who have closely followed the cultural and political debates on the Right in the United States over such things as educational policy, sexuality, affirmative action, and welfare reform: Star Parker, George Schuyler, Andrew Sullivan, Elizabeth Wright, Bruce Bawer, and Susan Au Allen, among others.[3]

There is of course a history of dominant groups using—or at least giving visibility to—"minority" voices to "say the unsayable" in the United States and elsewhere (Lewis, 1993, 2000). Thus, for example, Ward Connerly, a prominent conservative African American businessman and a vocal member of the Board of Regents of the University of California, has taken a very visible stand against affirmative action. For him, government involvement is actually harmful to Black Americans. "While others are assimilating, Blacks are getting further and further away from one nation indivisible" (quoted in Dillard, 2001, p. 50). His insistence on "individual merit" and his rejection of state intervention for the cause of equality has clearly been employed by the larger, and mostly White, conservative movement to legitimate its own policies. As a prominent conservative spokeswoman put it, "You can't have white guys saying you don't need affirmative action" (Dillard, 2001, p. 15). Powerful neo-liberal and neo-conservative movements both inside and outside government circles, hence, can steadily expand the realm of what is in fact sayable by prefacing what would otherwise be seen as consistently racist positions with a quote from a well-known

Black spokesperson. One of the most articulate critics of such moves states that this enables dominant economic, cultural, and racial groups "to cannibalize the moral authority of minority voices by skirting responsibility" (Dillard, 2001, p. 20).

Because of this very history of dominant groups employing the selective voice of the "other" to legitimize its actions, there has been a concomitant history of regarding those members of minority communities who openly affiliate with conservative movements as "pariahs." They have been dismissed as either "traitors" or "sell-outs," and even seen as "self-loathing reactionaries who are little more than dupes of powerful white ... conservatives" (Dillard, 2001, p. 4). Although these labels are powerful indeed, many conservative persons of color see themselves very differently. In their self-perception, they are "crusading rebels" against a state and a liberal elite within the ranks of their own communities whose own self-understanding as "helping the people" actually mystifies policies that work to destroy the very moral and social foundations of their communities. Here they can also turn to a rich history of nationalist, self-help, and conservative moral principles within these communities as a source of "authenticity" and legitimacy (Dillard, 2001, p. 13).

Of course, there *are* internally developed conservative traditions within, say, communities of color, many of which have made lasting contributions to the very existence and continuity of the cultures within these communities (see, e.g., Lewis, 1993, 2000). However, given the fact that so much of the conservative tradition in the United States was explicitly shaped by racist and racializing discourses and practices,[4] and by a strongly anti-immigrant heritage as well, and given the fact that much of the current neo-liberal and neo-conservative attacks on the public sphere have had disproportionate effects on the gains of poor communities and on communities of color, the current existence and growth of such movements among dispossessed groups is more than a little striking. This makes their current iterations all the more interesting.[5] As I show later, neo-liberal and neo-conservative economic, political, and cultural movements *and* some of the African American groups that have been connected to them are both seeking to redefine the relations of power in particular social fields, with education being a prime site where these relations of power are being worked through (Bourdieu, 1984). A complex process of discursive and positional disarticulation and rearticulation is going here, as dominant groups attempt to pull dispossessed collectivities under their own leadership and dispossessed groups themselves attempt to employ the social, economic, and cultural capital usually possessed by dominant groups to gain collective power for themselves. As will be evident, the label "conservative" cannot be employed easily in understanding the actions of all of the dispossessed groups who do ally themselves with conservative causes without at the same time reducing the complexity of the particular social fields of power on which they operate.

Perhaps the most interesting example of the processes of discursive and social disarticulation and rearticulation that one could find today involves the growing African American support for neo-liberal policies such as voucher plans (see, e.g., Moe, 2001). A key instance is the Black Alliance for Educational Options (BAEO), a group of African American parents and activists that is chaired by Howard Fuller, the former superintendent of Milwaukee public schools, one of the most racially segregated school systems in the United States. BAEO provides vocal support for voucher plans, "choice" (a sliding signifier whose meaning has increasingly become fixed around issues of vouchers in the United States when it is used in political discourse), and similar conservative proposals. It has generated considerable support within Black communities throughout the nation, particularly within poor inner-city areas, and has an identifiable presence in 27 cities within the United States.[6] The fact that the Supreme Court of Wisconsin has ruled that the Milwaukee voucher plan is constitutional and the U.S. Supreme Court recently ruled that the Cleveland voucher plan is also constitutional gives more legal and political legitimacy to BAEO's efforts, since both plans were officially aimed at providing the "right to exit" for inner-city and largely "minority" residents.

A sense of the language that underpins BAEO's commitment can be seen in the following quote:

> Our children are our most precious resource. It is our responsibility to love them, nurture them and protect them. It is also our responsibility to ensure that they are properly educated. Without a good education, they will [not] have a real chance to engage in the practice of freedom: the process of engaging in the fight to transform their world. (BAEO web site)

BAEO's mission is clear. "The Black Alliance for Educational Options is a national, nonpartisan member organization whose mission is to actively support parental choice to empower families and increase educational options for Black children" (BAEO web site). Its position is even clearer in its manifesto:

BAEO Manifesto
Current systems of K–12 education work well for many of America's children. But, for far too many children, the current systems do not work well at all. A high percentage of these children are poor children of color living in urban areas. For these children, the old

educational strategies and institutional arrangements are not preparing them to be productive and socially responsible citizens. This requires that we dramatically change our teaching and learning strategies and create new governance and financial structures.

BAEO believes we must develop new systems of learning opportunities to complement and expand existing systems. We need systems that truly empower parents, that allow dollars to follow students, that hold adults as well as students accountable for academic achievement, and that alter the power arrangements that are the foundation for existing systems.

BAEO understands that there are no "silver bullets" or "magic wands" which will instantly make things better for our children. BAEO is also not anti-public school. However, we do believe that parent choice must be the centerpiece of strategies and tactics aimed at improving education for our children. We must empower parents, particularly low-income parents, to make the best choices for their children's education.

Consider the potential impact of this power in the hands of families who previously have had little or no control over the flow and distribution of the money that drives the policies and procedures of the educational systems of this country. Consider how the absence of this power means that their children will remain trapped in schools that more affluent parents, some of whom oppose parental choice, would never tolerate for their own children. Consider how this power shift may change the shape of the future for their children.

BAEO will bring together the ideas, aspirations, energies, and experiences of all generations in this struggle. (BAEO web site)

The use of language here is striking. The language of neo-liberalism (choice, parental empowerment, accountability, individual freedom) is reappropriated and sutured together with ideas of collective Black freedom and a deep concern for the community's children. This creates something of a "hybrid" discourse that blends together meanings from multiple political sources and agendas. In some ways, this is similar to the long history of critical cultural analyses that demonstrate that people form bricolages in their daily lives and can employ language and commodities in ways undreamed of by the original producers of the language and products (see, e.g., Willis, 1990, 2000).

Although this process of rearticulation and use is important to note, it is equally essential to recognize something that makes the creative bricolage in which BAEO is engaged somewhat more problematic. A very large portion of the group's funding comes directly from conservative sources such as the Bradley Foundation. The Bradley Foundation, a well-known sponsor of conservative causes, has not only been in the forefront of providing support for vouchers and privatization initiatives, but also is one of the groups that provided significant support for Herrnstein and Murray's book *The Bell Curve* (1994), a volume that argued that African Americans were on average less intelligent than Whites and that this was genetic in nature. Thus, it would be important to ask about the nature and effects of the connections being made between rightist ideological and financial sources and BAEO itself. It is not inconsequential that neo-liberal and neo-conservative foundations provide not only funding but media visibility for "minority" groups who support—even critically—their agendas.

The genesis of such funding is not inconsequential. Many of the strongest proponents of vouchers and similar plans may claim that their positions are based on a belief in the efficiency of markets, on the fear of a secularization of the sacred, or on the dangers of losing the values and beliefs that give meaning to their lives. However, historically, neither the economic nor the moral elements of this critique can be totally set apart from their partial genesis in the struggles over racial segregation, over busing to achieve integration, and in the loss of a federal tax exemption by conservative—and usually White only—religious academies. In short, the fear of the "racial other" has played a significant role in this discursive construction of the "problem of the public school" (Apple, 2001). Does this mean that groups such as BAEO are simply being manipulated by neo-liberal and neo-conservative foundations and movements? An answer to this question is not easy, but even with my cautions just stated it is certainly not a simple "yes."

Strategic Compromises?

It is important not to engage in reductive analyses here, ones for example that assume that simply because a group's funding comes from a specific source, therefore all of its own agendas will be fundamentally determined by where it gets its money. This is certainly not always the case. Indeed, in public forums and in discussions that my colleague Tom Pedroni and I have had with some of leaders of BAEO, these leaders have argued that they will use any funding sources available so that they can follow their own specific program of action. They would accept money from more liberal sources, but Bradley and other conservative foundations have come forward much more readily.[7] In the minds of the leaders of BAEO, the African American activists are in control, not the conservative foundations. Thus, for BAEO, they see themselves as strategically positioning themselves in order to get funding from conservative sources. What they do with this funding, such as their strong (and well advertised in the media) support for voucher plans (although this support too is contingent and sometimes depends on local power relations), is wholly their decision. For them, the space provided by educational markets can be reoccupied for Black cultural and/or nationalist politics and can be employed to stop what seems to them (more than a little accurately in my opinion) to be the strikingly ineffective, and even damaging, education of Black children.[8]

However, although I have a good deal of respect for a number of the leaders of BAEO, it is important to remember that they are not the only ones strategically organizing on this social field of power. Like BAEO, groups affiliated with, say, the Bradley Foundation also know exactly what they are doing and know very well how to employ the agendas of BAEO for their own purposes, purposes that in the long term often may run directly counter to the interests of the majority of those with less power at both the national and regional levels. Is it really in the long-term interests of people of color to be affiliated with the same groups who provided funding and support for books such as Herrnstein and Murray's (1994) *The Bell Curve*? I think not, although once again we need to recognize the complexities involved here.

I am certain that this kind of question is constantly raised about the conservative stances taken by the people of color who have made alliances with, say, neo-liberals and neo-conservatives—and by the activists within BAEO itself. When members of groups who are consistently "othered" in this society strategically take on identities that support dominant groups, such questioning is natural and I believe essential. However, it is also crucial to remember that members of historically oppressed and marginalized groups have *always* had to act on a terrain that is not of their choosing, have always had to act strategically and creatively to gain some measure of support from dominant groups to advance their causes (Lewis, 1993, 2000; Omi & Winant, 1994). It is also the case that more recently national and local leaders of the Democratic Party in the United States have too often assumed that Black support is simply *there*, that it doesn't need to be worked for. Because of this, we may see the further development of "unusual alliances" over specific issues such as educational policies. When this is coupled with some of the tacit and/or overt support within some communities of color not only for voucher plans but for antigay, antiabortion, pro-school-prayer, and similar initiatives, the suturing together of some Black groups with larger conservative movements on particular issues is not totally surprising (see Dillard, 2001).

The existence and growing power of committed movements such as BAEO, though, do point out that we need to be careful about stereotyping groups who may publicly support neo-liberal and neo-conservative policies.

Their perspectives need to be examined carefully and taken seriously, not simply dismissed as totally misguided, as people who have been duped into unthinking acceptance of a harmful set of ideologies. There are complicated strategic moves being made on an equally complex social field of power. I may—and do—strongly disagree with a number of the positions that groups such as BAEO take. However, to assume that they are simply puppets of conservative forces is not only to be too dismissive of their own attempts at social maneuvering, but I also believe that it may be tacitly racist as well.

Saying this doesn't mean that we need to weaken our arguments against marketization and privatization of schooling. Voucher and tax credit plans (the later ultimately may actually be more dangerous) will still have some extremely problematic effects in the long term. One of the most important effects could be a *demobilization* of social movements within communities of color. Schools have played central roles in the creation of movements for justice. In essence, rather than being peripheral reflections of larger battles and dynamics, struggles over schooling—over what should be taught, over the relationship between schools and local communities, over the very ends and means of the institution itself—have provided a crucible for the *formation* of larger social movements toward equality (Apple et al., 2003; Hogan, 1983). These collective movements have transformed our definitions of rights, of who should have them, and of the role of the government in guaranteeing these rights. Absent organized, community-wide mobilizations, these transformations would not have occurred.

This is under threat currently. Definitions of democracy based on possessive individualism, on the citizen as only a "consumer," are inherently grounded in a process of deracing, declassing, and degendering (Ball, 1994). These are the very groups who have employed struggles over educational access and outcomes to form themselves as self-conscious actors. If it is the case, as I strongly believe it is, that it is the organized efforts of social movements that ultimately have led to the transformation of our educational system in more democratic directions (Apple, 2000), the long-term effects of neo-liberal definitions of democracy may be truly tragic for communities of color, not "only" in increasing inequalities in schools (see, e.g., Apple, 2001; Gillborn & Youdell, 2000; McNeil 2000), but in leading to a very real loss of the impetus for *collective* solutions to pressing social problems. If all problems are simply "solved" by individual choices on a market, then collective mobilizations tend to wither and perhaps even disappear. If history is any guide here, the results will not be pleasant. Thus, although short term support for neo-liberal and neo-conservative policies may seem strategically wise to some members of less powerful groups, and may in fact generate short-term mobilizations, I remain deeply worried about what will happen over time.[9] It is the long-term implications of individuating processes and ideologies, and their effects on the necessity of larger and constantly growing social mobilizations that aim toward substantive transformations within the public sphere, that need to be of concern as well. For we need to remember that—although in *Learning to Labor* Paul Willis focuses on the possibility of working on "penetrations," on the elements of "good sense" that people have, to form progressive movements—given the unequal balance of forces and the conservative discourses that now circulate so widely in society, progressives may *not* be the movements that will be the most successful in the process of disarticulation and rearticulation.

A concern over the effects of individuation that such "choice" programs may ultimately bring is unfortunately actually mirrored in the (already limited) literature on Black support for neo-liberal and neo-conservative policies. All too much of the critical literature on such "strategic alliances," even such work as Dillard's compelling book (2001), tends to focus on individuals, rather than on larger social movements. As I noted earlier, it is social movements that historically have had the power to transform social and educational policy and practice. An emphasis on individuals does humanize the issues that are in contention and it does allow us to see the people behind the Rightist presence within marginalized communities. However, this very focus causes us to miss the dynamics that have led to the growth of groups such as BAEO and to the strategic moves that are being self-consciously made on the unequal social fields of power in which educational policy operates. This doesn't vitiate the strength of what such analyses of the growing conservative tendencies among some "othered" communities have given us. However, the question is not whether it is possible to build a Rightist-led coalition that will include elements of "multiculturalism." Indeed, as I have shown in this part of the chapter, such a process is in part already being successfully attempted. Instead, the questions we must constantly ask are the following: At what cost? At whose expense? We do know, for example, that the integration of some elements of communities that have historically been seen as "the other" has occurred, that certain elements have been brought under the umbrella of conservative modernization. For instance, some Latino/as, Asian Americans, gays and lesbians, and others have given their support to what are surprisingly conservative causes. Although perhaps overstating her arguments for political reasons, Dillard, for example, is at her most perceptive when she sees that the roots of the support of conservative positions among some members of oppressed groups may often be based in not wanting to "be Black." It is worth quoting her at length here.

> [One] point on which Latino, Asian-American, women, and homo-
> sexual conservatives seem to agree is the desire, to restate the matter

> bluntly, not to be like blacks—members of a group that persists in pressing for collective redress from the government rather than pursuing the path of individualism, upward mobility, and assimilation. That some Latino and Asian-American conservatives have engaged in this narrative is troubling. If Toni Morrison is even partially correct in asserting that previous waves of immigrants have embraced (white, middle-class) American identity "on the back of blacks," then there is reason to fear that new immigrants will seek to replicate this pattern. In the process, the already tense relationships among African-Americans, Latinos, and Asian-Americans could degenerate. That some African-American conservatives, a contingent that remains predominantly middle and upper-middle-class, appear content to follow suit—to assimilate on the backs of the black poor—is doubly disturbing (Dillard, 2001, p. 182).

Although I do not think that her arguments are as applicable to groups such as BAEO, for many other persons and organizations with which she does deal Dillard's points need to be taken very seriously. For the implication of such arguments is that the major losers in the shifting discursive terrain surrounding race and identity may very well prove once again to be poor Blacks. Once more, they will be pathologized. Their voices will be silenced. And they will continue to be "everybody's convenient and favorite scapegoat" (p. 182). Given the central place that race has played in the development of the neo-conservative movement of "return" and the neo-liberal movement of "choice" (Apple, 2001), we should not be surprised if rightist multiculturalism promises more of the same, but covered in a new and seemingly more diverse discourse.

"Not wanting to be Black" does not explain the support of vouchers by groups such as BAEO, however. Instead, it is the very fact of *being Black*, of recognizing and fighting against their social and cultural positioning as the ultimate "other," that has caused them to seek out strategic—some might say heretical—alliances with some of the main tendencies that, paradoxically, have been in the forefront historically in supporting such positioning. In *Educating the "Right" Way* (Apple, 2001), I called for thinking heretically about possible alliances that might subvert parts of the agendas involved in conservative modernization. Whether BAEO's "heretical actions" actually do subvert such agendas and the racial stratification of schools remains to be seen. I fear that they may not. But one must also ask what choices they in fact do have, given the structures of inequality that currently exist. Not recognizing the strong elements of good sense in their persistent struggles to understand and act on a world organized around a politics of racialization is simply inadequate.

Conclusion

In this chapter, I have documented the ways in which Paul Willis's work has had a continuing influence on my own, especially his recognition of the crucial importance of the contradictory tensions between "good" and "bad" sense in people's common sense and his recognition of the problem of employing the elements of good sense of oppressed people to disarticulate them from previous alliances and rearticulate them to new collective movements. I gladly recognize this publicly, in his role both as a friend and as someone who has helped to teach me a way of understanding the world and the politics of lived culture that, once one understands the world this way, one cannot easily return to previous models. For me and for many others, this kind of "disclosure model" is lasting.

At the same time, I have instantiated this understanding in a concrete example. I have examined a growing phenomenon—the growth of seemingly conservative sentiments among "despised others." At the core of my analysis is not only an interest, shared with Willis, in seeing the rich complexity of the politics of lived action, however. My arguments also center on a deep concern about what is at stake for all of us if rightist multiculturalism succeeds in redefining what and whose knowledge is of most worth and what our social and educational policies are meant to do. No matter what one's position is on the wisdom of BAEO's strategic actions, the entire case provides a crucial example of the politics of disarticulation and rearticulation, on the ways in which social movements and alliances are formed and re-formed out of the material and ideological conditions of daily life, and of the politics of discursive reappropriation (Apple, 2001; Hall, 1996).[10] Thus, an analysis of such movements is important both in terms of the balance of forces and power involved in specific educational reforms, but also in terms of more general issues concerning the processes of social transformation and agency. A critical but sympathetic understanding of groups such as BAEO may enable us to avoid the essentialism and reductionism that enters into critical sociological work on the role of struggles over the state and over the connections between culture and power (Apple et al., 2003). It can provide a more nuanced sense of social actors and the possibilities and limits of strategic alliances in a time of conservative modernization (see Apple and Pedroni, in press).

Although I support the struggles of groups such as BAEO and have a good deal of sympathy with their critique of the current functioning of public (state supported) schools, I have very real worries about whether they can control the uses to which their support of neo-liberal policies will be put. Yet, having said this, there may be some salutary effects of their efforts to mobilize around vouchers.

If the common school loses its legitimacy among significant numbers of people within communities of color—and there is some evidence that this may be happening within some communities (Moe, 2001)—this may force a reexamination of the unequal ways schools are currently financed in the United States, where a school's funding is dependent on the local tax base and its very real inequalities. It also may create the conditions in which teachers and their unions may have to work much more closely with local communities than is the case now simply in order for teachers to maintain their legitimacy in the eyes of people of color. I say this knowing that, oddly enough, this might provide evidence for parts of the neo-liberal case about school markets. Fear of competition among teachers and other educators then may have hidden effects that may, finally, lead to even more support among them for needed changes in schools.

Having said this, however, I predict the opposite. Although these changes may occur, it is unfortunately just as likely that the effects will be ones less positive in their long-term consequences. Less funding will be given to public (state supported) schools. A politics of blame will evolve in which parents who have no choice but to keep their children in underfunded and highly policed inner-city schools will be seen as the source of the problem of the common school. Much depends on the balance of forces at the time. Given what I and others have shown about the often-negative results of the combination of neo-conservative and neo-liberal reforms in schools, I am not sanguine about what will happen. At the very least, though, we need to be aware that the complicated politics and strategic maneuverings that are occurring on the terrain of educational policy will have complicated, contradictory, and unforeseen results. The example of BAEO signifies the beginning, not the end, of this story.

Although I have focused on the growth of strategic alliances between "despised others" and conservative forces in the United States, I predict that such alliances may not be limited to this one nation.[11] This may be disturbing to many progressively inclined educators, and this leads to my final point. Any groups that disagree with BAEO about the wisdom of supporting vouchers and of making tactical alliances with the Right have a task that goes well beyond simply criticizing their position or their strategy. Critics of their positions and strategies must have a detailed and in depth understanding both of what generates their anger at public (state supported) schools and at the lack of responsiveness that all too many school systems have shown to communities of color and the poor and working class for decades. The conditions to which groups like BAEO are responding are *real* and immensely destructive on real children in real communities (see, e.g., Kozol, 1991). Thus, those who worry about BAEO must ask what they themselves are for. They need to redouble their own efforts to end the racial contract that underpins "our" economic and political institutions (Mills, 1997), to work even harder to provide the economic and cultural conditions that would make African American parents have faith in their schools, and to challenge the ways in which a politics of "whiteness" underpins so much of the daily life of this society. Simply saying no to BAEO, then, is not enough. Indeed, I would claim that it is a racializing act itself unless it is accompanied by powerful antiracist actions.

A Final Word on Paul Willis

In recognizing my (and our) debt to Paul Willis, I have focused my attention on the ways in which race and class intersect in complex ways here, with the primary attention being given to race. Yet I cannot end this chapter without noting that there are other equally crucial reasons for us to continue to return to *Learning to Labor*. This has to do with the turn to the "post" in much of the current critical scholarship in education today. As I have argued at much greater length elsewhere, such a turn has proven to be immensely productive (see, e.g., Apple, 1996, 1999). Indeed, the reader will undoubtedly have noticed my own debt to selective parts of post positions in this chapter—a focus on identity, on discourse, on an anti-essentializing problematic, for example. However, the often unreflective turn to the post also has had some unfortunate effects. Today, for instance, when there often is either an evacuation of class in all too much critical educational and cultural research or a return to the reductive and economistic readings of class so reminiscent of Bowles and Gintis, critical work could be revitalized by returning—critically—to *Learning to Labor*. Class, not only as a set of structural positions and locations, but profoundly as a vital and lived *project*, can return in its most sophisticated forms. Granted we will need to recognize that "it" is filled with contradictions and intersected by a multitude of dynamics surrounding gender, sexuality, "race," "ability," age, region, religion, and colonial and postcolonial relations and histories—but class analysis needs to be returned. Some of us may like to think of class as a "text," as a discursive construct that is by its very nature reductive and essentializing, and that it simply speaks to one more instance of a power/knowledge nexus. I believe that this is itself a dangerously essentializing position to take. It may be a bit reductive for me to say that class can only be considered this way by those who do not recognize the materialities of their own class positions, who have the luxury of not having to deal with the "worlds of pain" involved in being excluded from the supposed benefits of "our" postmodern universe of hybridity and "choice." But it would be salutary to consider what it means—analytically and personably/politically—to take such a position on class.

In the meantime, returning to *Learning to Labor*, with its silences acknowledged, would be a fine first step in how one creatively understands the ways in which elements of good and bad sense operate in people's daily lives. The act of going back to Paul Willis's work would also enable us to recapture our sense of what class means and how it works—and of how it is connected to other constitutive dynamics over and through which we struggle to create an education that is worthy of its name. That too would be one way of demonstrating our continuing respect for what Paul Willis accomplished.

Acknowledgments

I thank David Gillborn, Steven Selden, and in particular Tom Pedroni for their perceptive comments on the issues raised in this essay. Tom Pedroni has offered important conceptual, historical, and empirical suggestions and criticisms. A number of my arguments are indebted to his own ongoing investigation of BAEO and the complexities of African American educational politics (see Pedroni, 2003). Sections of this chapter have appeared in the *London Review of Education*.

Notes

1. See Willis's reflections on these issues in Willis (2000).
2. The term "authoritarian populism" originally comes from the compelling work of Stuart Hall. Unlike Hall, however, I would prefer to limit its use to a particular group of people who make up the "religious right." For more on this, see Hall (1980) and Apple (2001).
3. Although her analysis could be more detailed and subtle in certain places, Dillard (2001) does a good job of detailing the "structures of feeling" of conservative affiliations among a number of people who usually are not expected to take such position. She deals with a wide range of different forms of conservative leanings: from the economy, the legitimacy of activist government, the politics of the body, and the role of religion in public affairs on the one hand, to questions dealing with what knowledge should and should not be taught as "legitimate" and, say, the place of race in university admissions on the other.
4. "Progressive" traditions in the United States were not free of such racializing and racist logics. See, for example, Selden (1999).
5. That, say, a number of African American groups, ones that are making alliances with distinctly conservative movements, exist and are growing says something very important about the fascination with identity politics among many progressive scholars and activists in education and elsewhere. Too often writing on identity (wrongly) assumes that identity politics is a "good thing," that people inexorably move in progressive directions as they pursue what Nancy Fraser would call a politics of recognition (Fraser, 1997). Yet any serious study of rightist movements demonstrates that identity politics is just as apt to take, say, angry and retrogressive forms—antigay, racist nativism, antiwomen, etc. For many such people, "we" are the new oppressed, with that "we" not including most people of color, feminists, "sexual deviants," immigrants, and so on (see, e.g., Kintz, 1997, and Blee, 2002). Yet, as I noted earlier, even people within these "despised" groups themselves may take on such retrogressive identities.
6. BAEO is a heterogeneous organization. Much, though not all, of BAEO's leadership is from the middle class, but it does have a good deal of grass-roots support. Where it specifically meets and intersects with Rightist organizations, those who interact with such organizations tend not to be among the poor and working class. However, a class analysis is not sufficient

here. Racial solidarity may come first; race fundamentally mediates class relations. Thus, the issue of the class position of BAEO's leadership needs to be thought about in complex and subtle ways. I thank Tom Pedroni for this point.

7. In this regard, Tom Pedroni's ongoing research on BAEO is of considerable importance (see Pedroni, 2003).

8. In this regard, the political issue they are facing is in some ways similar to the debates over "market socialism." Can economic and political forms developed under the auspices of less progressive tendencies and power relations be employed to further goals that are organized around a very different set of ideological sentiments? See, for example, Bardhan and Roemer (1993) and Ollman (1998).

9. Dillard (2001) herself is very fair in her assessment of what the implications of such support may be. She nicely shows the contradictions of the arguments and logic of the people she focuses on. In doing so, she draws on some of the more cogent analyses of the relationship between democracy and the maintenance of the public sphere on the one hand and an expansive and rich understanding of what it means to be a citizen on the other. Readers of her discussion would also be well served to connect her arguments to the historical struggles over the very meanings of our concepts of democracy, freedom, and citizenship such as that found in Eric Foner's illuminating book, *The Story of American Freedom* (1998), but Dillard's discussion is substantive and useful. It also serves as a reminder of the continuing importance of a number of democratic and critical writers such as Hannah Arendt (1973, 1990), whose work, although not perfect by any means, unfortunately is no longer read as often as it should be.

10. An analysis of groups such as BAEO could enable us to extend the range of Basil Bernstein's work on *recontextualization* as well (see Bernstein, 1990).

11. Heidi Safia Mirza's ongoing work on the role of schooling in communities of color in England is very interesting in this regard.

References

Anyon, J. (1979). Ideology and U.S. history textbooks. *Harvard Educational Review, 49*, 361–386.

Apple, M. W. (1979). *Ideology and curriculum.* Boston: Routledge and Kegan Paul.

Apple, M. W. (Ed.). (1982a). *Cultural and economic reproduction in education.* Boston: Routledge and Kegan Paul.

Apple, M. W. (1982b). *Education and power.* Boston: Routledge and Kegan Paul.

Apple, M. W. (1986). *Teachers and texts.* New York: Routledge.

Apple, M. W. (1996). *Cultural politics and education.* New York: Teachers College Press.

Apple, M. W. (1999). *Power, meaning, and identity.* New York: Peter Lang.

Apple, M. W. (2000). *Official knowledge* (2nd ed.). New York: Routledge.

Apple, M. W. (2001). *Educating the "right" way: Markets, standards, God, and inequality.* New York: Routledge.

Apple, M. W., & Beane, J. A. (1999). *Democratic schools: Lessons from the chalk face.* Buckingham: Open University Press.

Apple, M. W., et al. (2003). *The state and the politics of knowledge.* New York: Routledge.

Apple, M. W., & Weis, L. (Eds.). (1983). *Ideology and practice in schooling.* Philadelphia: Temple University Press.

Apple, M. W., & Pedroni, T. (in press). Do vouchers make strange bedfellows? Conservative alliance building among the dispossessed. *Teacher College Record.*

Arendt, H. (1973). *The human condition.* Chicago: University of Chicago Press.

Arendt, H. (1990). *On revolution.* New York: Penguin Books.

Ball, S. (1994). *Education reform.* Buckingham: Open University Press.

Bardhan, P., & Roemer, J. (Eds.). (1993). *Market socialism: The current debate.* New York: Oxford University Press.

Bernstein, B. (1990). *The structuring of pedagogic discourse.* New York: Routledge.

Blee, K. (2002). *Inside organized racism: Women in the hate movement.* Berkeley: University of California Press.

Bourdieu, P. (1984). *Distinction.* Cambridge: Harvard University Press.

Bowles, S., & Gintis, H. (1976). *Schooling in capitalist America.* New York: Basic Books.

Dale, R. (1989/1990). The Thatcherite project in education. *Critical Social Policy, 9*(1), 4–19.

Dillard, A. D. (2001). *Guess who's coming to dinner now: Multicultural conservatism in America.* New York: New York University Press.

Fine, M., Weis, L., Powell, L., & Wong, L. M. (Eds.). (1997). *Off White.* New York: Routledge.

Foner, E. (1998). *The story of American freedom.* New York: Norton.

Fraser, N. (1997). *Justice interruptus.* New York: Routledge.

Gillborn, D., & Youdell, D. (2000). *Rationing education.* Philadelphia: Open University Press.

Greider, W. (1997). *One world, ready or not.* New York: Simon and Schuster.

Hall, S. (1980). Popular democratic vs. authoritarian populism. In A. Hunt (Ed.), *Marxism and democracy* (pp. 150–170). London: Lawrence and Wishart.

Hall, S. (1996). On postmodernism and articulation. In D. Morley & K-H Chen (Eds.), *Stuart Hall: Critical dialogues in cultural studies* (pp. 131–150). New York: Routledge.

Herrnstein, R., & Murray, C. (1994). *The bell curve.* New York: Free Press.

Hobsbawm, E. (1994). *The age of extremes.* New York: Pantheon.

Hogan, D. (1982). Education and class formation. In M. W. Apple (Ed.), *Cultural and economic reproduction in education* (pp. 32–78). Boston: Routledge and Kegan Paul.

Katz, M. B. (2001). *The price of citizenship.* New York: Metropolitan Books.

Kintz, L. (1997). *Between Jesus and the market.* Durham, NC: Duke University Press.

Kozol, J. (1991). *Savage inequalities.* New York: Crown.

Kuhn, T. (1970). *The structure of scientific revolutions.* Chicago: University of Chicago Press.

Lewis, D. L. (1993). *W. E. B. DuBois: Biography of a race, 1868–1919.* New York: Henry Holt.

Lewis, D. L. (2000). *W. E. B. DuBois: The fight for equality and the American century. 1919–1963.* New York: Henry Holt.

McNeil, L. (2000). *Contradictions of school reform.* New York: Routledge.

Mills, C. (1997). *The racial contract.* Ithaca, NY: Cornell University Press.

Moe, T. (2001). *Schools, vouchers, and the American public.* Washington, DC: Brookings Institution.

Ollman, B. (Ed.). (1998). *Market socialism: The debate among socialists.* New York: Routledge.

Omi, M., & Winant, H. (1994). *Racial formation in the United States* (2nd ed.). New York: Routledge.

Pedroni, T. (2003). *Strange bedfellows: African American participation in the Milwaukee school choice coalition.* Unpublished PhD dissertation, University of Wisconsin, Madison.

Ramsey, I. (1964). *Models and mystery.* London: Oxford University Press.

Selden, S. (1999). *Inheriting shame.* New York: Teachers College Press.

West, C. (1982). *Prophesy deliverance!* Philadelphia: Westminster Press.

Whitty, G., Power, S., & Halpin, D. (1998). *Devolution and choice in education.* Buckingham: Open University Press.

Willis, P. (1977). *Learning to labour.* Westmead: Saxon House.

Willis, P. (1990). *Common culture,* Boulder, Westview.

Willis, P. (2000). *The ethnographic imagination.* Cambridge: Polity Press.

CHAPTER 5

The "Lads" and the Cultural Topography of Race

FAZAL RIZVI

Twenty-five years after its publication I can still recall my first encounter with Paul Willis's landmark book, *Learning to Labor* (first published as *Learning to Labour,* 1977). It made a huge impression on me: Not only did it challenge some of my deeply held neo-Marxist assumptions about social reproduction and education, it also helped me to think through some of the experiences I had teaching mathematics in the mid 1970s, in a high school at the northern outskirts of Manchester, England—in a town not unlike Hammertown, depicted so powerfully by Willis from the perspective of the "lads." Willis provided a powerful ethnographic account of the lads as they sought to make sense of their experiences at school, located within a community in England's declining industrial heartland, and their futures in and out of employment.

The school in Manchester where I taught was also located in an urban community, which was characterized by declining employment opportunities for the White working-class youth, on the one hand, and increasing levels of postcolonial immigration, leading to a great deal of racial unrest, on the other. I found myself within this complex "cultural topography of race," to use a term used by Willis to describe the social dynamics of race relations at Hammertown. However, the problem in my case was that the "the lads" at my school found it difficult to place me within their preexisting cultural topography of race—mostly because I was the only non-White teacher at the school. They had been told that I had come to their school from Australia but that I was born in India. Yet as far as they were concerned, I looked like a South Asian and therefore the racist term "Paki" clearly applied to me. Somewhat problematically, however, I did not readily fit the stereotypes the lads had of "the Pakis." There was something different about me—to begin with, I was their teacher. Within a few weeks of my being at that school the lads found a way out of their dilemma. Because I was no ordinary "Paki," I acquired a nickname: "Super Paki." As a young teacher who had only recently arrived in England, I found this name both personally disturbing and deeply contradictory. On the one hand, I viewed it as overtly racist and offensive. Yet, on the other hand, I could not but be flattered by the affection the term was meant to express toward me. I was also somewhat amused by the lads' sense of humor.

It was within the context of this experience that I first read *Learning to Labor*. Willis's rich analysis provided me with some of the resources I needed to theorize about the nickname I had been given, along with a number of other racist encounters I had at the school. It helped me to understand that, as a teacher, I embodied the school's authority, which although it was recognized by the lads was simultaneously resisted and opposed, although not in any direct fashion, but always through "having a laff," "taking the piss," and "dossing." This opposition, as Willis (1977, p. 12) put it, was "expressed mainly as a style." Just as the lads were creative in the ways in which they differentiated themselves from the norms of the school, they also sought to define me as different from the other "Pakis," who were subjected to more ridicule than I. I was admired for not being like the other "Pakis" but was also disliked for the way I had embodied the received English cultural norms that were expressed through my authority at the school.

The lads' relationship to me was characterized by a deep ambivalence that expressed a degree of respect but also involved a substantial measure of cultural disdain, especially when I asserted my authority and insisted that lads perform the learning tasks to which they were mostly hostile. On these occasions, they did not hesitate to apply the stereotypes to me. As Willis (1977, p. 152) suggested, these stereotypes involved a "clear demarcation between groups and a derogatory view of other racial types." These stereotypes were "simply assumed [by the lads] as the basis of this or other action: it is a daily form of knowledge in use." This knowledge discursively cast people within a cultural topography of race that defined everyone as either "us" or "them," with relatively clear sets of social characteristics, expectations, and entitlements applying differentially to each group.

This topography applied as much to the labor market as it did to interracial relations within the school. Thus, the lads understood the labor market to be fundamentally divided along class, gender, and race lines. As Willis (1977, p. 152) argued, racial division provided the lads with "an ideological object for feelings about the degeneracy of others and superiority of the self." The West Indian males were entitled to jobs that were dirty, messy, and unsocial, requiring masculine assertiveness, whereas Asians were placed at the opposite end of the cultural scale, in jobs that required them to be "cissy," passive, and lack aggression. This racist differentiation clearly served to divide the working class both materially and ideologically. This constituted one of the ways in which the lads were complicit in reproducing the logic of "the complex social definition of labor power under capitalism," despite their oppositional culture and "partial penetration" (Willis, 1977, p. 126).

Perhaps the most important of Willis's many insights in *Learning to Labor* is his theorization of this complicity. The lads understood perfectly how their oppositional practices at school condemned them to poorly paid jobs and perhaps even to unemployment; they nonetheless rejected the middle-class values and the academic practices of school as irrelevant to their lives. The complicity did not arise out of a false consciousness, involving a simple reproduction of their class position within the grand narrative of capitalism. The lads were not dupes, lacking any agency: quite the contrary. In their everyday lives they had a reasonably good understanding of the prevailing structures of power, and a working knowledge of how to live with it, even if this helped produce unfavorable social outcomes for them. The lads examined and solved everyday problems with deftness and dexterity, often with a great deal of creative imagination.

In *Learning to Labor*, Willis used the term *penetration* to account for the ways in which counterschool culture saw through the meritocracy and individualism of schooling, allowing and helping the lads to develop realistic assessments of the pessimistic futures they confronted in manual labor. They lived with this realization with a great deal of reflexivity about the structural forces that affected their lives. These forces were seen not only as determinants but also "as sources of what is to be known and discovered in the possibilities of experience" (Willis, 2000, p. 35). In his recent book *The Ethnographic Imagination*, Willis argued that fun and pleasure, "the laff," are powerful creative resources for, and mechanisms of, penetration, through which the lads confronted "the power of institutional command, drawing out, developing and reproducing powers and abilities and a cultural world of reference not defined by institutional roles." Thus, the cultural topography of race included having fun at the expense of those who were considered racially different. Both collectively and individually, the lads extended a great deal of creative effort to making sense of the consequences for them of patterns of immigration that changed their social milieu and life chances. However, they did this thinking within the cultural topography of race the defined the racial order in Britain at that time, but not unreflexively.

And so it was with my nickname. The term "Super Paki" enabled them to attach a new social identifier to me without disturbing their existing cultural topography of race. In a sense, it demonstrated their narratives of race to be reasonably flexible, even if it remained trapped within the dominant stereotypes. It showed their interpretive frameworks to be dynamic, capable of modification and change in the face of new social conditions, personal interactions, and political circumstances. In *The Ethnographic Imagination* (2000), Willis reflected further on this interpretative process in an effort to elucidate his larger notion of cultural production by focusing on the active and productive nature of cultural practices that are seldom passive but are located within the flows of the broader cultural topography and are intended to make situated personal and collective meanings.

In this way, Willis avoids the dangers of essentialism in the earlier reproduction theories of education and culture (Bowles & Gintis, 1975, for example), by viewing the cultural topography of race as continually changing, being challenged, interrupted, and reconstructed, involving, often in ways that are contradictory, complex structural processes on the one hand and the processes of imagination and creativity on the other.

The cultural topography of race is thus historically specific. The discourses and cultural practices inherited from the past and the broader culture are reconstituted and rearticulated in processes through which people struggle to make sense of their everyday lives, both seriously and cynically—in the case of the lads, with a great deal of joviality and fun. The racial categories that people use are thus not homogeneous and static but are given concrete form by the specific social relations and the historical context in which they are embedded. They are continuously changing, often through processes of resistance and contestation as people attempt to understand their social circumstances differently. On occasions, they construct new patterns of social relations, whereas in other circumstances particular practices persist, often through the use of new code words and new ideological forms that obscure old discriminatory behavior.

If cultural topographies of race represent distinctive spatio-temporal modalities of racial discourse and practices, with their own history and structures of meaning, then Willis's ethnography in *Leaning to Labor* is a historically specific one, located within a particular social and economic context, involving a range of key assumptions about the production of meaning, identity and social outcomes. Indeed, Willis (2000, p. 86) himself acknowledged that he "caught 'the lads' in *Learning to Labor* at the end of what was perhaps the last golden period of working-class cultural coherence and power in a fully employed Britain." Implicit in Willis's analysis in *Learning to Labor* is the view that this cultural coherence and power was racially organized, and was much threatened by large-scale immigration during the 1970s. The "lads" expressed this anxiety through various overt and covert practices of racism.

The cultural topography of race Willis described in *Learning to Labor* is thus specific to Britain's colonial history, postcolonial immigration, and the strength of its working-class traditions. In the last 25 years Britain has become transformed into another kind of society. It has experienced massive losses of manual industrial work available to the working classes. Over 4 million manufacturing jobs have been lost. The new jobs that have emerged for the working classes are largely lower paid service jobs—casual, part-time, low-paid, and insecure, especially for young people, older workers and ethnic minorities. This structural feature of society has had major implications for the cultural topography not only of class but also of gender and race. Fundamental economic and social changes since the mid 1970s, Willis (2000, p. 85) argued "have certainly made the reproductive balances of British society more jagged, cynical and unstable." They have had important implications for gender forms, identities, and relations. For the working class, masculinity has become disconnected from particular forms of labor.

Similarly, the racial signifiers that were once assumed by the lads have become destabilized and highly contradictory. The "lads" had assumed that it was "natural" that people belonged to supposedly different "races," which constituted distinct and separate communities. For them, the boundaries of inclusion and exclusion were based on the imagined community of Britain as a nation. But this interpretive framework for the signification of race is no longer as clear-cut, changed perhaps irredeemably not only by economic and social changes but also by highly localized antiracist activism in Britain, on the one hand, and the contemporary processes of globalization, on the other.

In what follows, I examine some of these changes in order to determine the ways in which the transformed cultural topographies of race now require new ethnographic practices, which do not describe a particular locality within its own terms, but also investigate its relationship to the broader global processes, as has been argued by a range of recent authors, including Doreen Massey (1994), Michael Burawoy et al. (1999), and Michael Smith (2001).

As a geographer, Massey attempted to show how concepts of space and place are relevant to any ethnographic examination of social relations and cultural practices. She argued that changes in the world economy can be characterized in a number of ways, from modernism to postmodernism, from industrial to postindustrial manufacturing to services, and from Fordist to post-Fordist. However, each of these characterizations indicate the "prevailing uncertainly about the shape of the new"—the uneven extension of the boundaries of economic relations in both intensity and scope (Massey, 1994, pp. 157–158)—which is one of the key processes at the heart of globalization of capital. This has resulted in "the stretching out of different kinds of social relationships over space," creating new relations of power: relations imbued with meaning and symbolism. These new global relations of power, argued Massey, have implications for the ethnographic study of localities, which can no longer avoid taking into account global processes.

As sociologists, Burawoy and his colleagues (1999) similarly argued for the need to understand identities and relations in global terms. Making a distinction between "global imperialism" and "global postmodern," Burawoy suggested that under the former, class, gender, race, and nation constituted "relatively stable and enduring subjects," possessing "a certain insularity and essentialist character" (p. 346). Under global postmodernism, on the other hand, boundaries have broken down and identities proliferated. Gender and class relations are no longer "given" but have to be negotiated. The experiences of migration and the rebellion of the second- and third-generation ethnic experiences challenge and break through conventional boundaries. Buroway et al. (1999, p. 347) added that "these experiences become more common as migration cuts national identity adrift from states, building new diasporas within fluid boundaries." The children, born and raised in Britain, of immigrant parents and grandparents have a radically different kind of relationship to their local communities, and to the global diasporic networks that play an increasingly significant role in their lives. Globalization has not only transformed the nature of work and labor markets but has also created new conditions for intergroup relations and for thinking about social identities (Castells, 1997). In such a context, ethnographic practice requires globalization to be grounded in specific locations, and localities need to be globally articulated.

In *Learning to Labor*, the lads viewed "Jamaicans" and "Pakis" as relatively homogeneous groups, culturally apart from themselves. There was little evidence of social mixing, except in ways that were antagonistic. Assumed was a context of immigrants as newly arrived without a significant voice of their own. Interethnic friendships were almost nonexistent. The nature of interethnic relations in Britain has now changed markedly. Ethnic groups are no longer see themselves or are mostly treated as racially homogeneous, as was the case in Hammertown. Close friendships across cultures now exist widely, as does a substantial degree of alignment between White and immigrant oppositional youth cultures. It is therefore impossible now to understand the cultural orientation of the White working class without also theorizing its complex relationship with changing dynamics of race relations in Britain. I agree with Angela McRobbie (1996), who argued that we cannot fully understand contemporary youth cultures without looking critically at the issue of how these cultures are constituted *relationally*. To do this, we cannot simply focus on the White working-class youth without also determining how other cultural groups relate to them—how subjectivities with different cultural histories intersect with each other to produce new subjectivities, more so now than ever before, in contexts created by global flows of ideas and people and a postcolonial cultural politics that rejects the idea of an authentic racial subject.

Stuart Hall used the notion of "new ethnicities" to capture the cultural transformations now taking place in Britain wrought by migration. Hall (1996, p. 441) considered the ways in which immigrant communities have represented themselves in response to their "common experience of racism and marginalization in Britain." Especially through arts and writing, they have contested the stereotypical and derogatory representations of Black people at large with positive images of the Black community. They have resisted unifying modes of representation by highlighting the "extraordinary diversity of subjective positions, social experiences and cultural identities." Cultural identities are presented as multiple and mobile, with their own inner tensions. This has inevitably entailed "a weakening or fading of the notion that 'race' or some composite notion of race around the term Black will either guarantee the effectivity of any cultural practice or determine in any final sense it aesthetic value" (Hall, 1996, p. 443). Hall suggested that this creates a challenge for the Black communities, of how to construct a radical politics that works with and through difference, which is able to build those forms of solidarity and identification that makes common struggle possible but which does not presuppose any homogeneity of identities. Black communities have had to think about the dynamic nature of their identity under the new conditions of fluidity, hybridity, and mobility.

However, these conditions pose a challenge, equally, to the White working-class youth—of how to engage politically with the increasingly confident ethnic communities who reject totalizing systems of representation but nonetheless work collectively to contest racial inequalities. As John McLeod (2000, p. 225) pointed out, the emergence of "new ethnicities" in Britain has "altered the ways *all* people in one location, not just those constructed as 'diasporic communities'" have to consider questions of difference. Indeed, all oppositional divides between "native inhabitants" and "diasporic peoples," "majority" and "minority" are threatened with dissolution. This does not suggest the demise of traditional social categories, but rather the need to reconsider how the processes of racialization now occur and how racialization of particular groups of people is converted into the discursive and institutional practices of racism.

The communities that the lads had once assumed as their own, in which immigrants were uniformly regarded as outsiders, now have to be renegotiated and rearticulated. As Massey (1994) noted, communities acquire their particularity not from some long-internalized history or culturally embedded character, but from the specific interactions and articulations of contemporary social relations, social processes, and understandings. Place making is shaped by conflict, difference, and social negotiation among differently situated and at times antagonistically related social actors, some of whose networks are locally bound whereas others transcend national boundaries. Unlike the immigrants of an earlier generation, diasporic people now increasingly work both within their geographically specific locality, but also through networks that are not necessarily anchored in Britain but may have a transnational reach. Their sense of their locality is tied to the crisscrossing of transnational circuits of communication, and to the crosscutting of local and translocal social practices. Arjun Appadurai (1996) used the term *ethnoscape* to describe the landscape of mobile persons who now constitute the shifting world that characterizes communities like Hammertown. The cultural topography of such towns is reconstituted by tourists, immigrants, exiles, refugees and other moving groups, affecting the politics of identity, place and difference.

The community that the "lads" once inhabited was assumed to be characterized by continuity and stability. Theirs was a cohesive community in which immigrants were considered intruders and were regarded as inferior. This mode of cultural representation was based on a particular politics of difference, informed by the assumptions of power asymmetries that had emerged out of a history of colonialism. Akhil Gupta and James Ferguson (1997) identified three dimensions of contemporary cultural production that have complicated this always-idealized communitarian narrative. First, the growing economic, sociocultural, and informational interdependence across linked spaces is undermining the notions of discrete, autonomous self-contained local cultures. Second, the ubiquitous discourses and practices of postcolonialism are producing a variety of new hybrid practices that problematize the very notion of "authentic cultural traditions." And third, the boundary-penetrating processes of globalization are facilitating the social construction of "communities in the making," as imagined spaces, often occupying the same geographical locale.

These trends necessarily entail new processes of inclusion and exclusion, that is, processes that create "Otherness." In constructing the Other, a group recognizes itself through its selective memory of a common past, involving continual attempts to imagine, assert, and redefine its boundaries, in ways both routine and creative. Identity formation is characterized by its two constitutive dimensions of self-identification and affirmation of difference. Of course, under the social conditions of capitalism, this politics of difference is often an antagonistic one. With increasing mobility of people across national boundaries, the Other is both strange and increasingly in our midst. Julia Kristeva (1991, p. 20) called this "the hidden face of our identity." She has suggested that the stranger, the foreigner, is not only among us, but also *inside us.* This is an enormously significant insight. It suggests that as a result of regular cultural contact, be it physical or virtual, we acquire some of the characteristics of the Other, which has the consequence of at once creating a sense of existential unease and foreboding. In fearful anticipations, said Kristeva (1991, p. 13), the stranger looms as a powerful persecutor against whom "we" solidify to take revenge . . . must we not stick together, remain among ourselves, expel the intruder, or at least keep him in "his" place.

A number of recent theorists have discussed this politics of racial antagonism and resentment, under the global conditions of mobility. In this context, more creative discourses and practices of racism emerge, which cannot be "read off" with any predetermined logic of racial differentiation. Rather racism is best viewed as a dynamic ideological form that is continuously changing, being challenged, interrupted, and reconstructed, and that often appears in contradictory forms. Its cultural production can be expected to be complex, multifaceted, and historically specific. We need to avoid any assumption of simple historical duplication because ideologies are never only received but also constructed and reconstructed by people responding to their material and cultural circumstances in order to both understand and represent them and act in relation to them. As such, the politics of racial antagonism, like other forms of cultural politics, are created by people to find their way out of the dilemmas of everyday life they confront, produced by the conditions of rapid and continuous change.

There is nothing historically necessary about this politics. The emerging postcolonial confidence of subjugated groups need not necessarily produce resentment. Indeed, the new cultural topography of race is producing a space, at an intersection of borders, where as Avtar Brah (1996, p. 209) pointed out, "all subjectivities become juxtaposed, contested, proclaimed, or disavowed; where the permitted and the prohibited perpetually interrogate, and where the accepted and the transgressive imperceptibly mingle even while these syncretic forms may be disclaimed in the name of purity and tradition." This suggests that the outcomes of cultural intermingling are entirely contingent. Indeed, as Angela McRobbie (1996, p. 43) observed, the cultural forms produced by the new Black ethnicities in Britain have often "reached out and touched" many often socially subordinate, White young people, both male and female.

Willis provided ample evidence of the vital creativity in the production of cultural practices, but also pointed out that this creativity is ideologically laden and deeply affected by the prevailing social conditions of existence. In an era of globalization, these conditions point both to the deepening of racial antagonism, embodied in the new discourses of conservative restoration, but also to the real possibilities of antiracism, involving creative cultural practices of critical reflexivity and action.

References

Appudarai, A. (1996). *Modernity at large: Cultural dimensions of globalization.* Minneapolis: University of Minnesota.

Bowles, S., & Gintis, H. (1975). *Schooling in capitalist America.* London: Routledge.

Brah, A. (1996). *Cartographies of diaspora: Contesting identities.* London: Routledge.

Burowoy, M. et al. (1999). *Global ethnography.* Berkeley: University of California Press.

Castells, M. (1997). *The power of identity.* Oxford: Blackwell.

Gupta, A., & Ferguson, J. (1997). *Culture, power and place: Explorations in critical anthropology.* Durham, NC: Duke University Press.

Hall, S. (1996). New ethnicities. In D. Morley & K.-H. Chen (Eds.), *Stuart Hall: Critical dialogues in cultural studies* (pp. 441–449). London: Routledge.

Kristeva, J. (1991). *Strangers to ourselves.* New York: Harvester Wheatsheaf.

Massey, D. (1994). *Space, place and gender.* Minneapolis: University of Minnesota Press.

McLeod, J. (2001). *Beginning postcolonialism.* Manchester: Manchester University Press.

McRobbie A. (1996). Different youthful subjectivities. In I. Chambers & L. Curti (Eds.), *The postcolonial question* (pp. 30–46). London: Routledge.

Smith, M. P. (2001). *Transnational urbanism: Locating globalization.* Oxford: Blackwell.

Willis, P. (1977). *Learning to labour: How working class kids get working class jobs.* Aldershot, Hampshire, UK: Gower.

Willis, P. (2000). *The ethnographic imagination.* Cambridge, UK: Polity Press.

Learning to Labor in New Times

CHAPTER **6**

Reordering Work and Destabilizing Masculinity

JANE KENWAY AND ANNA KRAACK

Learning to Labor (Willis, 1977, first published as *Learning to Labour*) tells of a time when there were steady jobs available even for nonacademic, low-achieving, school-disaffected, White working-class boys and when there was an identifiable British working class to be reproduced through schooling and work. It tells of work in "Hammertown" in the British Midlands in the early 1970s in conditions close to full employment. The Willis study seeks to explain the reproduction of the male working class and the role of "the lads" and their education therein. Willis explains how cultural and institutional forms contribute to social reproduction. He illustrates how, in their manner of resisting school, the lads readied themselves for factory work and excluded themselves from opportunities for social mobility through education. Economic circumstances have changed dramatically since *Learning to Labor*, and this leads to somewhat different questions. What are contemporary economic conditions and what happens to working-class masculinity under such conditions? Such questions have prompted a number of studies in Britain designed, in effect, to empirically and theoretically update the issues addressed in *Learning to Labor* and indeed to address some of its absences. These studies include Mac an Ghaill, (1994), Arizpe and Arnot, (1997), O'Donnell and Sharpe (2000), and McDowell (2000, 2002).

This chapter complements such work, foregrounding "the prism of space" (Urry, 1994, p. 14). It focuses on two localities and on the reordering of work

95

and the destabilizing of local working class masculine identities and rela-tionships. It asks, how do nonacademic, school-disaffected, White working-class boys respond to such detraditionalization and with what effects? It draws from a wider study (Kenway & Kraack, in progress) that considers youthful masculinities and gender relations in marginalized, stig-matized, but also sometimes romanticized and exoticized places outside of Australia's capital cities.[1] This broader study points to the intersections between the changing social and cultural base of place, and identities, rela-tionships, and inequalities as they are increasingly caught up in, and also attempt to stand apart from, globalizing flows. With its focus on the "global-izing local," this research links ideas associated with critical (Willis, 2000) and global (Burawoy et al., 2000) ethnography, and we call our approach critical local/global ethnography.[2] This chapter arises from 3 months of fieldwork in two localities. In-depth semistructured interviews were carried out with 36 young people; weekly, for 6 weeks, the 24 males were each interviewed, and the 12 females were interviewed fortnightly. Loosely structured focus and affinity group discussions were held with mothers, fathers, community members, teachers, youth workers, and welfare service providers. Informal conversations were held with a wide range of local people. The researcher also spent time at a variety of community and youth-specific locales (e.g. the school, beach, and main street) and events (e.g., sporting matches, discos, local carnivals). We use pseudonyms for all localities and participants.

The Contemporary Economic Order

The working world of Willis's lads is set against a backdrop of economic security and predictability in England. From World War II through to the late 1960s the global economy prospered and Britain's industrialized economy thrived with it (Currie, 1983). Yet in the late 1960s/early 1970s, underlying structural, industrial and economic weaknesses became evident in the global economy (Hall, 1983) and the British economy was rendered unstable. Indeed, since the days of "the lads," economies in various parts of the world have altered in remarkable ways. We begin with an overview of contemporary economic conditions.

Structural shifts in the economy in "First World" countries have involved a move away from primary and secondary to tertiary industries, particularly to the service sector. This has been variously described as a shift from Fordist to post- or neo-Fordist, or from industrial to post- or deindustrial produc-tion (Bauman, 2000; Harvey, 2000). These shifts have often included the closure, restructuring and downsizing, and indeed "off-shoring" of "heavy" manufacturing industries. Further, the center of economic gravity has altered and has become more global and less national and local. Survival needs and the drive for competitiveness have led small businesses to either close or to join bigger ones and bigger businesses to become international or global. Many public enterprises have become private and have then followed this pattern (Beresford, 2000). Local business sensibilities have been replaced either by national or by nonterritorial sensibilities. Global corporations have an increasing presence everywhere. Workplace restructuring has usually included the reduction of the workforce, intensification (longer working hours, increased productivity, and less pay), casualization, and technological enhancement. New approaches to management include an increased sensitivity to risk. Despite the neo-liberal rhetoric about leaving economic growth to market forces and despite various practices of deregulation, governments have acted as mediators among global, regional, national, and local economic trends. They have sought to sustain national and state economies by steering them in particular directions away from certain industries and business practices and toward others. This takes the form of policy advice, various deregulating and regulating practices, sundry incentives and disincentives, and strong intervention in the ideological climate.

As Massey (1995, p. 189) explained, there exists a "geography of production" and this involves a "spatial divisions of labour." Different patterns of economic activity in different locations and uneven economic growth and decline mean that the broad patterns associated with economic globalization as described earlier and the associated changes in the world of work are manifest somewhat differently in different places. Deindustrialization is not evenly spread, and there is an increasing tendency to relocate production from "First World" to "Third World" countries or to distribute it across multiple sites (Harvey, 2000). Further, as economic production in "First World" countries is increasingly dematerialized and veers toward the production of services and symbolic goods as described by Lash & Urry (1994), those places involved in primary and secondary material production are economically undermined. They are particularly subject to the flight of capital, and the associated downsizing or closure of local private and then public industries and services. The economic base of place is also altered by ecological globalization. In the interests of environmental sustainability, governments now undertake risk management in local economies. Together these factors have disrupted local economies and led local entrepreneurs to develop new industries in an attempt at local economic recovery.

Contemporary Workers

In these circumstances workers' conditions have been reconfigured and their identities challenged. The "First World" global work order consists of a small labor elite (the highly skilled, highly privileged professions) and an increasing number of people in casual, poorly paid and insecure work (May, 2002). The key features of desirable workers for the contemporary "First World" work order include mobility (they must not be rooted in place), flexibility (they must be prepared to work in any mode, at any time, for any pay), increased expertise (they must have more technical rather than manual knowledge and skill), and increased cultural (style) and social (networks) capital. Loyalty to tradition, location, and social class are understood by "industry" as impediments to growth. Indeed, as Bauman pointed out, "technological progress is measured by the replacement and elimination of labour" (Bauman, 1998b, p. 65).

The literature on the implications of deindustrialization for subgroups of working class school boys shows how these groups reinscribe themselves around academic achievement, high- and low-status vocational courses, and indeed around "new work areas such as business, design, media, and information technology" (O'Donnell & Sharpe, 2000, p. 134). This literature points to the ways that some young working class males are inventing themselves as "new workers" and to the fact that some others, particularly those who subscribe to working-class "macho masculinities," are not. However, such research offers little sense of the gendered ways in which pertinent young males get around the identity problems that arise in the so-called feminized work and labor markets. The casual work now available to them is not only insecure and poorly paid and difficult to class, but often invokes the "feminine" other to the working-class masculine described by Willis in his discussion of "labour power and patriarchy" (1977, p. 149). The term *feminization of work* commonly refers to the trend for an increasing number of workplaces to emulate the work and working conditions that have historically pertained to the "female" retail and service sectors. This involves the gendered convergence of labor market and work experiences and is part of what Bakker (1996, p. 7) called the "gender paradox of restructuring," involving the "contradictory effects of the dual process of gender erosion and intensification." We next show how working class masculinity is imbricated within this dynamic.

Detraditionalizing Masculinity in the "Globalizing Local"

For many years the main economic base of the two Australian localities discussed here has been power generation in the country city of Putland and fishing and timber in the coastal town of Paradise. The history of work in each location is closely tied up with what is conventionally thought of as men's work and with particular manifestations of masculinity. Males earn respect and reputation by performing a job well and diligently and by working hard to earn a decent wage—by, as Willis put it, "Doing a hard job well and being known for it" (1977, p. 52). Logging, fishing and industrial work all require "heroic" (Willis, 1977, p. 150), hard, sometimes grueling physical labor and involve various kinds and degrees of manual skill and physical toughness. In addition, logging and fishing occur out in the elements and involve battling with nature and extracting its bounty. They entail physical danger and call into play the camaraderie that arises from shared risk. In contrast, the industrial work associated with the power industry in Putland involves the mastery of machinery, and males develop close affinities on the shop floor. The masculinities invoked here equate with what Vashti Kenway (2001, pp. 7–8), drawing on Connell (1995), called "hegemonic industrial working class masculinity." As she points out, this includes "a 'hard bodies,' 'hard emotions' response to the world. [And] a mode of embodiment that signifies strength, mobility, autonomy, solidarity and a capacity to dominate space." Putland and Paradise have historically developed their self-concept around a particular place-based version of "hegemonic industrial working-class masculinity," which is central to the manner in which identities, work, and all relationships are valued. Others' work plays no part in the identities of each place and is either ignored or belittled for its softness and lack of physicality. The broad economic changes just outlined have, however, challenged each locality's character and the identities and relationships of local people, who have, in the words of Bauman (1998a, p. 18) "watched helplessly, the sole locality they inhabit moving away from under their feet." As we will now explain, the various reactions of White working class males are similar to those discussed in O'Donnell and Sharpe, (2000, p. 127); generally they are defensive, reactionary, progressive, uncertain, and confused. Yet there are also different patterns of effects in both places.

"Men Were Put on the Scrap Heap"

Located near rich deposits of brown coal that are excavated for the production of electricity, Putland was once a thriving "power town," providing over 85% of the State of Victoria's electricity (Local Government Board, 1994). But the neo-liberal privatization and deregulation reform policies pursued by successive Victorian state governments since the late 1980s have undermined Putland's economic base. The privatization and restructuring of the State Electricity Commission have involved major job losses (Kazakevitch, Foster, & Stone, 1997). This has had a significant social and psychological impact on the locale.

Before this restructuring, male jobs were plentiful, secure, and well paid, and there was intergenerational employment for males. Sally, a youth service worker, explained, "You could always get work at the SEC. It was slow, easy and comfortable. You didn't need an education, you started at the bottom and just worked your way up." Boys whose fathers worked at a power station were almost guaranteed an apprenticeship. Our conversations with local people are suffused by a melancholy discourse of loss and defeat, and this flows into pessimistic views about the present and future of Putland. Sometimes this discourse is also taken up by the young, who portray Putland as a "ghost town," a "lonely city."

"The mark of the socially excluded in an era of time/ space compression is immobility," argued Bauman (1998a, p. 113). According to Bauman, the excluded are those who have been "left behind," constrained by space, and also those who have no choice but to move. Putland is caught up in the class and gender politics of such mobility and immobility. With the downsizing of the power industry came worker redundancy and the search for new employment. The local working class has been disrupted and the industrial foundations of workers' identities have been lost. Some men have used their redundancy payouts to start small local businesses. Some survived; many failed. Others have searched for work locally, but, unable to find it, have reluctantly "gone on the dole." Others feel they have no tolerable choice but to leave their families and to join the many "mobile" and "flexible" new workers displaced and on the move due to economic globalization. Some have found work elsewhere and fled with their families. Other families have stayed behind "because the kids are settled here and they have a house here," Sally made clear. "This is having a big impact on families," Georgina (a service worker) explained. Fathers are away for various stretches of time. Moreover, as some of the boys and girls told us, even those fathers who are still working in Putland are not necessarily a strong presence at home. Those with small businesses work very long hours and are commonly, as Ted (age 14), noted, "too busy to be worried about us kids."

The families who have stayed in Putland are the "locally bound"—left behind as capital and influence have flown. They have to do what Bauman (1998a, p. 8) called the "wound licking, damage repair and waste disposal." The gendered dynamic to being "locally bound" in Putland is a clear example of "gender intensification" (Bakker, 1996) for females. The absence of fathers means that more family work falls on mothers, whether they are in paid employment or not. This work includes dealing with the psychological fallout of neo-liberal economic globalization, the emotional upheaval that often accompanies the forced loss of men's jobs, status, and identity, and the subsequent stresses of change. Predictably, though, despite the implications for women, children, and families and indeed for the town itself, this changing economic context is largely framed as a "crisis" for men and boys by many of local adults. Elizabeth, a long-time local, observed, "Men were put on the scrap heap. There was a feeling that they were useless."

There is a general view that when fathers lose their jobs and cannot get work, this impacts particularly on sons. The fact that significant numbers of hard-working, able-bodied men were not wanted by their employer and even by many subsequent potential employers cast serious doubt on their worth and on their particular ways of being male. Both were socially surplus and disposable. However, such deeply entrenched ways of being male are not so easily disposed of by the males themselves, and notions of worthwhile work and the admirable worker remain from the past and indeed across the generations. Local ideologies of masculinity have not been weakened even though there is no economic base to support them. This is evident in the hopes of quite a sizable proportion of young adolescent males and in their views of education (see Kenway & Kraack, in progress, chap. 5, for other standpoints).

Local middle-class entrepreneurs consider education an important part of an economic renewal strategy for Putland. There are moves afoot to establish an Education Precinct on the regional campus of Monash University. This proposal builds on ideas about the vocationalization and technologization of the secondary school, which, incidentally, also set the scene for Mac an Ghaill's 1994 study of "macho lads" and "academic achievers" in England. The Precinct is also based on the notion of borderless and "lifelong education," a notion informing the Australian government's attempts to build a globally competitive "knowledge economy." The idea is that upper secondary schooling, vocational education and training, and university courses are provided on one campus, thus allowing students to move relatively easily across the three types of provision. Such options for educational mobility were not available to the lads and their peers in *Learning to Labor*. But had they been, the lads probably would have scorned them. Certainly, similar boys in Putland don't accept such ideas. They expect to leave school as soon as possible and to get an apprenticeship. "Having a trade is like having a job for life," said Ted (age, 14), who doesn't care what sort of work he gets after he leaves school as long as it is a trade. For these boys, school is either a place where they wait, impatiently and often disruptively in a manner similar to Willis's lads, until they can legally leave and take up an apprenticeship. Or it is where they get the "hands-on" or practical knowledge necessary to prepare them for an apprenticeship. Such boys love the "tech shed" at school, but not what is described as paper-work—"too much" writing or "too much" theory. Terry, age 15, is typical.

> I am not really interested in any of the stuff like being a lawyer or accountant ... I want something that is hands on. I hate sitting there and doing nothing.... If there is paperwork and stuff involved I will do it, but I would rather be out in the machine shop doing something than inside the shop writing on paper.... It just seems more challenging to be out in the workshop.

As Collinson and Hearn (1997) observed, from the point of view of male manual workers, paperwork is not real work, and indeed, although Terry did not say so, it is also seen as effeminate. Further, like the working-class males in Willis's study, for these boys "practice is more important than theory" (Willis, 1977, p. 56).

There is a popular view among boys like Terry (and their parents) that doing "hands-on" at school and then going into a trade are what ordinary boys do—especially boys who are "good with their hands but not their heads." Yet, as teachers and youth workers tell us, many contractors cannot afford to take on apprentices and the restructuring of the power industry has dramatically reduced the apprenticeships offered in the district. Further, those few that are available locally through the Commonwealth Government's New/Modern Apprenticeship Scheme are highly competitive and this involves "lots of aptitude, medical and psyche tests." "Nonacademic" students compete against the high academic achievers and usually miss out. Missing can cause family conflict, especially between fathers and sons. Some fathers cannot admit that a trade is no longer "a job for life," even though this notion has been so patently undermined by the Putland experience. The continuities between school, work, and home experienced by the lads in *Learning to Labor* do not exist for such boys in Putland either socially or culturally. Although men's work has been detraditionalized in Putland and the material base for it has all but vanished, the values associated with traditional hegemonic working-class masculinity have proved very difficult to dislodge. Indeed, they provide intergenerational camaraderie between fathers and sons. But the boys who subscribe to such values are undergoing what Mac an Ghaill (1994) called a crisis of "working class masculinity" and what O'Donnell and Sharpe (2000, p. 134) more accurately described as "a crisis of macho working-class masculinity."

Despite the restructuring of Putland's economy and the changed nature of local employment, many fathers cannot *unlearn* the attitudes associated with regular skilled manual employment and local hegemonic working-class masculinity. Indeed, they have become melancholic figures living in the past and sidelined in the present.[3] Having a job is tightly connected to self-respect, while lacking one is shameful and attracts disdain. Many fathers and sons hold these views. Take the case of Brett (age 13), whose father works at Power Bricks, where the number of workers has dropped dramatically over recent years. Unlike many of his friends' fathers, Brett's has not been made redundant. He describes those who lost their jobs as "slack," "lazy," and "soft." His father's continued employment affirms his view that his father is superior. He boasts that his dad can "work rings around the other guys." He works hard and doesn't "bludge" off the social welfare system.

In Putland, earning an income and financially supporting the family are masculine imperatives. Unemployment is associated with laziness, weakness, and passivity—in fact, with a lack of masculinity. This view of masculinity is a key element in local social constructions of the unemployed and of the associated politics of resentment directed at those who have been 'left behind' in place, but out of work and who suffer "enforced immobility" (Bauman, 1998a, p. 121). Indeed, as we have shown elsewhere (Kenway & Kraack, 2003) the economic and existential uncertainties associated with economic globalization have contributed to deep divisions among those on the lower rungs of the global economy in Putland and elsewhere. The sense of working-class collectivity, solidarity, and its predictable reproduction across generations so evident in *Learning to Labor* is now seldom evident in Putland. Meanwhile, the boys who constitute this fraction of Putland's working class face the prospect of either joining the "bludgers" they despise, of undertaking a form of education and work that they also despise, or of joining the growing ranks of those who have little choice but to move.

"What Future Is There for Boys with Aprons?"

The story of globalization in Paradise has some things in common with the Putland story but also involves some significant differences associated with what Beck (1992) called "risk society" and Giddens (1994, p. 20) called "high consequence risk." The key themes in Paradise are associated with the government's regulation and "risk management" of the timber and fishing industries in the interest of environmental conservation. Although "the state" has deliberately loosened its grip in Victorian Putland, it has tightened its grip over Paradise in New South Wales (NSW) (Bochner & Parkes, 1998). In addition, the flight of global capital has meant the closure of the Heinz cannery processing plant. Overall, there have been significant job losses (Eden Business Challenge, 2000).

Paradise has suffered social dislocation similar to Putland. Again, a town has been severely shaken; there is talk of a town dying. A middle-aged male timber worker puts it bluntly: "Paradise is a working man's town but it has no jobs." A study of the social impact of the changes to the Paradise timber industry identified higher levels of stress and insomnia, increased use of prescription drugs, feelings of powerlessness, heightened fear of family breakup and of not being able to meet financial commitments, and higher levels of physical and verbal violence (Bochner & Parkes, 1998, pp. 18–20). Again, the despondency is not restricted to adults. Many young people feel that they have no future due to the lack of jobs, and their subsequent feelings of worthlessness are exacerbated by the strong local work ethic. Prior to the closure of the cannery there was a sense of hope and, indeed, quite strong resistance to the globalizing forces associated with environmental regulation. This was evident in a truck blockade of parliament house in Canberra in the early 1990s and in similar protests in Sydney against the NSW government. The government and "the greenies," "ignorant" city dwellers, "outsiders with no understanding of local issues," were seen as the root of the problem.

The town is now split. According to Grant (age 15), "The loggers don't like the greenies, the fishos don't like anyone, the greenies don't like the fishos or the loggers." And then there are the "druggos," the "alternative life-stylers," and the "hippies," all of whom want to "close down the chip mill" and "get rid of jobs," many boys tell us. Generally, environmental regulation and the Save the Forest Campaign conducted by environmental activists were seen as an attack on the values associated with local lifestyle and on the timber cutters themselves. As Bochner and Parkes (1998) showed, the timber workers felt confused about their negative public image and suffered an overall loss of self-dignity that left them feeling resentful of outside interference. This spilled over into serious conflict with environmental activists, and many stories were shared with us about the provocative behavior of greenies and equally the hostile and sometimes violent behavior of those who opposed them.

There are several implications of this economic and social upheaval for intergenerational relations among males. The first has strong parallels with Putland. Before the restructuring of the timber and fishing industries, boys found it easy to follow their fathers into work. However, now there are not even enough jobs for the current work force. Even so, some fathers have difficulty understanding why their sons are finding it so hard to get a job, when they just "walked" into their jobs once they were working age. There is a form of denial here, and this is manifest in the quite commonly held view that "If you're prepared to put in the hard yards [the hard work], you'll always get a job." Thus, some fathers are inclined to blame young men for their lack of work.

To achieve respect in Paradise, young men must gain employment. Those without work are often constructed as "just plain lazy" and are an embarrassment and annoyance to their fathers. Witness this father's comments about his son: "I get out of bed about seven or eight a.m., but he doesn't get out of bed until ten a.m., and he will just sit around the house all day in his boxers and watch TV." He proudly described the change in attitude of his older son once he got a job:

> My eldest bloke, when he was going to work with forestry, he was up at half past six, and that was unheard of. He just used to get up himself, yeah. That really surprised me. Used to be a fight every morning to get him out of bed. (Fathers' focus group)

The context of globalized restructuring of traditional industries and rising unemployment is unaccounted for in such fathers' constructions of young males.

However, whatever their opinion of greenies and governments, some fathers are heeding their lessons about the future.

> I come from a long line of timber cutters. I followed my father into the industry. But I am not going to let my sons follow me. . . . It's just not acceptable these days—because of the greenies and because it is a dying industry. (Fathers' focus group)

Environmentalism is also putting some young men off these primary industries. James, age 16, typifies this view.

> The chip mill, all the major industries like the fishing, . . . they can't go on forever the way they are doing it, . . . and that is why I don't want to be a fisherman. The industries are going to be gone eventually, and the same with logging. . . . So it is just a waste of time getting a job in logging.

Clearly, the young males of Paradise are negotiating some powerful and conflicting local, state, and global forces associated with the world of work. To be valued as males in the local culture, they are expected to have work, but there is not enough work for all of them, and the available local work is insecure casual work either in the traditional local industries or in the fledgling tourist industry. Further, they have grown up in an atmosphere hostile to outsiders and the outside world and this implicitly discourages them from migrating elsewhere for work. Yet to stay locally is to be subject to a depressed economy and culture. If they seek to reinvent themselves in tune with the tourist industry, this is seen to subscribe to "ritzy" values that are alien to this "working man's town" and worse still to the feminine values associated with women's work. Boys who do so put others' perceptions of their masculinity at risk. Note the remarks of a long-time male resident (aged 65):

> This town is made up of the Ockers, you know like the timber industry, the bush fellas and the fishermen. They are hard working types. . . . They work with their hands and they can't be turned into office boys. They'd be out of place if this became a big tourist industry. There is an outdoor working culture. Their jobs have diminished. There are tourism jobs for girls, but that doesn't help a hard working person.

So what do boys do when they leave school? They do what they can and they do things to affirm themselves. Some, but not many, leave town for further study or work, some get casual work when it is available, some go on the dole, and some get into trouble. And, of course, those who stay in town but remain outside the full-time workforce have time on their hands and many go surfing. Despite all its masculine virtues, fathers do not regard surfing as a valuable way for their under- or unemployed sons to spend their abundant time. Furthermore, some senior teachers associate surfing with what they scornfully call "beach culture," which is seen to distract local boys from the serious work of schooling.

Ironically, beach culture, differently defined of course, is the basis for the multipurpose wharf that local entrepreneurs hope will soon be built and rescue the Paradise economy. Certain local residents also see tourism as the answer to their town's plight, although others vigorously oppose it unless it is the sort of tourism that involves "those who'd want to come here and get their hands dirty" (elderly local male). Further, some local educational entrepreneurs have developed a marine studies program at the high school. This program includes units of study such as diving, safe boating, and Coxin's certificates, and provides students with a qualification to undertake work in any marine area, from deck handing on a fishing boat to running tourist charter boats. This is stroke of brilliance. It builds young males into the expanding tourist industry in ways that draw on the masculinities most valued in Paradise. But masculine values are also being detraditionalized.

Many young people, like James mentioned earlier, see the old industries as dying and obsolete and are turning to the hospitality industries. Garth (age 14) exemplifies this trend:

> These days you have to get into hospitality, the retail trade. . . . I know one [friend] who wants to drive boats up in the islands. . . . He said his brother drives boats for some fishermen, and it is a charter type thing. . . . Another friend wouldn't mind being a chef.

Garth is also adjusting his views of the gendered division of labor and is redefining as masculine, work that has traditionally been defined as feminine. Adkins (1997) called this process *retraditionalization*. Garth thinks that retail work is for women but that "In the hospitality trade, its better to be a man, like in the kitchen or something like that." Despite their fathers' views about the threats to their masculine identity, some Paradise schoolboys have embraced tourism and are taking up courses and work experience that will lead them to a career in hospitality. "The two most popular choices at school are now marine studies and hospitality courses," a teacher reports. But, again, this is not how the fathers necessarily see it. Fathers who have invested in the forms of masculinity associated with hard physical outdoor labor find it difficult to respect sons who undertake such "feminized" work:

> They are pointing kids to hospitality and stuff like that at the high school. I guess that's directly related to losing the industries we're losing and trying to put something else in there. But they're getting boys in there when they should be trying to learn how to do something with their hands. What future is there for boys with aprons? (Fathers' focus group)

Conclusion

Learning to Labor is a book of its time and place. We have written of more recent times and other places that nonetheless carry strong traces of the working-class masculinity discussed by Willis. Indeed, we have shown how each locality's traditional culture and identity has arisen from men's classed work and how the masculinity associated with such work still holds sway, particularly in Putland. However, contemporary economic trends have clearly destabilized local working-class work and demoralized local working-class men. As a consequence, the reproduction of working-class masculinity has been ruptured. By and large, working-class boys no longer get working-class jobs and cannot reproduce their fathers' class cultures. However, despite this, some try to do so and others try to make them. Memory and custom have collided with the present, and such collisions are personally and poignantly manifest in tense intergenerational relationships between some fathers and sons and also in the intensification of women's emotional labor.

Young males are caught on the cusp of the old and the new and react differently to the competing imperatives involved. Even though they cannot walk into work as did Willis's lads, nonacademic, White working-class boys in Putland still subscribe to traditional views about masculinity and work and refuse to reinvent themselves for the new educational and economic order. These boys neither seek nor find viable alternative versions of manhood. Indeed, in monocultural Putland there are few alternatives, and anyway to subscribe to alternative masculinities would be to psychologically wound their already wounded fathers and to go against local common sense about meaningful work. Even the prospect of joining the working-class-without-work, be they locally bound or mobile, does not encourage these boys to develop alternative forms of expertise or to be flexible about their gender identities in ways that might equip them for alternative labor markets. However, there is also evidence of an emerging detraditionalized masculinity in the more diverse and dynamic culture of Paradise. This involves some young males turning to the tourism and hospitality industries and ideologically leaving behind notions of the working class. Yet, even in relation to such nontraditional work these young men sometimes retraditionalize it in gender terms. They do this by either picking up more "masculine" aspects of such work or by reinscribing the traditionally feminine work they do as masculine. Overall, across both locations, we see that hegemonic working-class masculinity and its cross-generational reproduction have been profoundly destabilized, and the traditional gender order of each place is both eroded and, paradoxically, intensified.

Acknowledgment

We thank Vashti Kenway for her contributions to this chapter.

Notes

1. This 3-year study was funded for 1999–2001 by the Australian Research Council's Large Grant scheme and was called *Country Boys in Uncertain Times and Places*.
2. For an extended discussion of this approach to ethnography and the debates within which it is immersed see Kenway and Kraack (in progress).
3. We acknowledge here Vashti Kenway's (2001) work on masculinity and melancholia in "Brit Grit" films.

References

Adkins, L. (1997, July). *Community and economy: The retraditionalisation of gender*. Paper presented at "Transformations: Thinking through feminism," Institute for Women's Studies, University of Lancaster.

Arizpe, E., & Arnot, M. (1997, April). *The new boys of the 1990s: A study of the reconstruction of masculinity in relation to economic restructuring*. Paper presented at the American Education Research Association Conference, Chicago.

Bakker, I. (Ed.). (1996). *Rethinking restructuring: Gender & change in Canada*. Toronto: University of Toronto Press Inc.

Bauman, Z. (1998a). *Globalisation: The human consequences*. Cambridge, UK: Polity Press.

Bauman, Z. (1998b). *Work, consumerism and the new poor*. Buckingham: Open University Press.

Bauman, Z. (2000). *Liquid modernity*. Cambridge, UK: Polity Press.

Beck, U. (1992). *Risk society—Towards a new modernity*. London: Sage.

Beresford, Q. (2000). *Governments, markets and globalisation: Australian public policy in context*. St. Leonards: Allen and Unwin.

Burawoy, M., Blum, J. A., Sheba, G., Gille, Z., Gowan, T., Haney, L., Klawiter, M., Lopez, S. H., Riain, S., & Thayer, M. (2000). *Global ethnography: Forces, connections, and imaginations in a postmodern world*. Berkeley: University of California Press.

Bochner, S., & Parkes, L. (1998). *The psychological effects of the timber industry in the Eden region of New South Wales: A critical review of social impact studies conducted between 1991–1995*. Report prepared for the NSW Forest Products Association, Sydney, NSW.

Collinson, D., & Hearn, J. (1997). "Men" at "work": Multiple masculinities/multiple workplaces. In M. Mac an Ghaill (Ed.), *Understanding masculinities* (pp. 61–77). Buckingham: Open University Press.

Connell, R. W. (1995). *Masculinities*. St Leonards: Allen and Unwin.

Currie, D. (1983). World capitalism in recession. In S. Hall & J. Martin (Eds.), *The politics of Thatcherism* (pp. 79–105). London: Lawrence and Wishart.

Eden Business Challenge. (2000). *Business plan—February 2000.* Eden, NSW: Barclay & Donaldson Services.

Giddens, A. (1994). *Beyond left and right: The future of radical politics.* Stanford, CA: Stanford University Press.

Hall, S. (1983). The great moving right show. In S. Hall & J. Martin (Eds.), *The politics of Thatcherism* (pp. 19–39). London: Lawrence and Wishart.

Harvey, D. (2000). *Spaces of hope.* Edinborough: Edinborough University Press.

Kazakevitch, G., Foster, B., & Stone, S. (1997). *The effects of economic restructuring on population movements in the Latrobe Valley.* Canberra: Department of Immigration and Multicultural Affairs.

Kenway, J., & Kraack, A. (2003, March). *The politics of resentment and mobility: Local/global power geometries.* Keynote address given at the Gender and Education conference, Sheffield, UK.

Kenway, J., & Kraack, A. (in progress). *Masculinity beyond the metropolis.* Hampshire and New York: Palgrave.

Kenway, V. (2001). *Dodos, dinosaurs and men: Representations of melancholy masculinities in* Brassed Off, Billy Elliot *and* The Full Monty. Honors Dissertation, Melbourne University, Melbourne, Australia, 2001.

Lash, S., & Urry, J. (1994). *Economies of signs and space.* London: Sage.

Local Government Board. (1994). *A vision for Gippsland: Gippsland area review, Interim Report.* Victoria: Local Government Board.

Mac an Ghaill, M. (1996). "What about the boys?": Schooling, class and crisis masculinity. *Sociological Review, 44*(3), 381–397.

Massey, D. (1995). *Spatial divisions of labour: Social structures and the geography of production.* London: Macmillan.

May, C. (2002). *The information society: A skeptical view.* Cambridge: Polity.

McDowell, L. (2000). Learning to serve? Employment aspirations and attitudes of young working class men in an era of labour market restructuring. *Gender, Place and Culture, 7*(7), 389–416.

McDowell, L. (2002). Masculine discourses and dissonances: Strutting "lads," protest masculinity, and domestic respectability. *Environment and Planning: Society and Space, 20,* 97–119.

O'Donnell, M., & Sharpe, S. (2000). *Uncertain masculinities: Youth, ethnicity and class in contemporary Britain.* London & New York: Routlegde.

Urry, J. (1995). *Consuming Places.* London: Routledge.

Willis, P. (1977). *Learning to labour: How working class kids get working class jobs.* Hampshire: Gower.

Willis, P. (2000). *The ethnographic imagination.* Cambridge: Polity Press.

CHAPTER 7

Revisiting a 1980s "Moment of Critique"
Class, Gender, and the New Economy

LOIS WEIS

December 1985

I want to go to college for four years, get my job, work for a few years, and then get married. I like supporting myself. I don't want my husband supporting me. I like to be independent. (Judy Rankin, Class of 1987 Homecoming Queen)

January 2001

My mom hit a point where she came to me and said, "Please Judy, I don't know what to do to stop it, but I just don't wanna be seeing you in your grave." (Judy Rankin Smithers, Class of 1987 Homecoming Queen)

Beginning with my ethnographic investigation of Freeway High (*Working Class Without Work*, Routledge, 1990), and culminating with intensive follow-up interviews with these same students in 2000–2001, I track a group of the sons and daughters of the workers of "Freeway Steel" and similar such industries over a 15-year time period. Exploring identity formation among American White working-class male and female students in relation to the school, economy, and family of origin, *Working Class Without Work* captures

111

the complex relations among secondary schooling, human agency, and the formation of collective consciousness within a radically changing economic and social context (Bluestone & Harrison, 1982). Most widely known, I suggest in the volume that young women exhibit what I call a "glimmer of critique" regarding traditional gender roles in the White working-class family and that young men are ripe for New Right consciousness given their strident racism and male dominant stance in an economy that, like that immortalized in the justly celebrated *The Full Monty* and the BBC serial *The Missing Postman* (Walkerdine, Lucey, & Melody, 2001), offers them little.

Now, 15 years later I return to these same students (35 of the original 51 were reinterviewed in 2000–2001), as they (and we) meet in *Class Reunion* (Weis, 2004), a study firmly embedded in what Michelle Fine and I call "compositional studies" (Weis & Fine, 2004)—a broadly based theory of method in which analyses of public and private institutions, groups, and lives are lodged in relation to key economic and social structures. Through a careful look at the high school (ages 14–18) and young adult years (ages 18–31) of the sons and daughters of the industrial proletariat in the northeast "rust belt" of the United States, I track the remaking of this class fraction through careful and explicit attention to issues that swirl around Whiteness, masculinity, femininity, representations, and the new economy. Reflective of the triplet of theoretical and analytic moves that Michelle and I put forward as signature of our work (Weis & Fine, 2004)—deep work within one group (over a 15-year time period in this case), serious relational analyses between and among relevant bordering groups, and broad structural connections to social, economic and political arrangements—I argue in the broader study that the remaking of the American White working class can only be understood in relation to gendered constructions within itself, the construction of relevant "others" as uncovered ethnographically—in this case African Americans and Yemenites ("Arabians")—as well as deep shifts in large social formations, most particularly the global economy.

Here I focus on a slice of the larger study, interrogating data collected at two points in time in light of Paul Willis's contributions regarding what he called "penetrations." "Penetrations," which Willis coined in *Learning to Labour* (1977) and later affirmed in *The Ethnographic Imagination* (2000), refer to "impulses within a cultural form towards the penetration of the conditions of existence of its members and their position within the social whole but in a way which is not centrist, essentialist or individualist" (1977, p. 119). Willis moved beyond "penetrations" to what he called "limitations": those "blocks, diversions and ideological effects which confuse and impede the full development and expression of these impulses" (p. 119). "The rather clumsy but strictly accurate term 'partial penetration,'" continued Willis, "is meant to designate the interaction of these two terms in a concrete culture.

Ethnography describes the field of play in which the impulses and limitations combine but cannot isolate them theoretically or show them separately" (p. 119).

In this chapter I turn my attention to the possibilities opened up by one such cultural "penetration" over time, using, by way of example, the young Freeway women's "glimmer of critique" that I flagged in the mid 1980s. To be clear, by critique I mean narrative data that represent a critical awareness or knowledge of class structures, racism, sexism and/or the globalizing economic in interpersonal and/or structural relations. This, I would argue, parallels Willis's concept of "penetration," thereby enabling me to probe carefully, using data collected at two points in time from the same individuals, where such cultural "penetrations" sit as the young women move toward adulthood in a radically changing economic and social context.

Here I move through working-class White women's lives not on a wholly theoretical level but on a more practical lived level, as they have families and assume positions as wage laborers. Given their "moment of critique" during adolescence, the question is, what elements of critique, or "penetration" in Willis's parlance, were young White working-class women able to live out and sustain as they plunge toward adulthood?

Freeway, 1985 and Beyond

> Best are the freedom dreams. Steering wheels so real in the hand, the spring of the accelerator, gas tanks marked FULL. . . . We take the freeways, using the fast lanes, watch for signs saying San Francisco, New Orleans. We pass trucks on great interstates, truck drivers blowing their airhorns. We drink sodas at gas stations, listen to country music stations, we pick up Tijuana, Chicago, Atlanta, GA, and sleep in motels where the clerk never even looks up, just takes the money. (Fitch, 1999, *White Oleander*, p. 348)

Young women, unlike their male counterparts in working class Freeway, take a stab at reworking gender while still in high school (Weis, 1990). Unwilling to accept the lives of their mothers and grandmothers as their own, Freeway High White girls strut forward, exhibiting an inchoate sense of "girl power" while attempting to remake the class/gender intersection more to their liking, engaging, it can be argued, in a process of the "re-making of girls and women as the neoliberal subject: a subject of self-invention and transformation who is capable of surviving within the new social, economic and political system" (Walkerdine et al., 2001, p. 3). For the Freeway youth, this means a female based income, one earned in the public wage labor sector; a perhaps ill-defined sense of independence ("the freedom dream"); and a life that can conceivably move forward comfortably even if they experience the divorce now so commonplace in their community—a phenomenon that virtually every young woman comments on in the 1980s.

Energized by the possibility of a life markedly different from that of their mothers, young women generate a female version of life in a working-class community under the new economy. Given kaleidoscopic changes in the global economy (Reich, 1991, 2002) and the virtual excisement of the former industrial proletariat, their men would no longer be able to "support" the family through earning the working-class family wage packet, at one and the same time as corporate America seeks female labor in a wide variety of service positions. These young women are, in addition, desirous of continuing their schooling, not ensnared by its hegemonic working-class masculine coding as negative (Arnot, chap. 2, this volume; Arnot, 2002; Connell, 1995; Reay, 2002; Weis, 2004; Willis, 1977), and look forward, for the most part, to some form of postsecondary education in spite of the fact that they, like the young men, bounce through the contradictory code of respect in relation to school knowledge and culture (Sennett & Cobb, 1972) while in high school (Weis, 1990, 2004). Finding it psychologically easier than their men to land on the substance side of this class-embedded contradiction with respect to schooling, young Freeway women exploit a myriad of educational opportunities. As the men in their lives experience increased unemployment and what they see as underemployment—the economic sector with which they are historically linked being virtually excised—White working-class women are reveling in the moment of possibility in economic and cultural terms (that "freedom dream") that they desire.

Data suggest that 1985 young White Freeway women envision their lives very differently from girls in previous studies and very differently than investigators such as Lillian Breslow Rubin (1976) and Glen Elder (1974) suggested that their mothers and grandmothers do. Articulating a challenge to the Domestic Code, they suggest strongly that the domestic is not primary; wage labor is. If patriarchy rests on a fundamental distinction between men's and women's labor and the domination of women in both the home/family sphere and the workplace, these girls exhibit the glimmerings of a critique of that. They understand to the point of being able to articulate that too many negative consequences result if one depends on men to the exclusion of depending on oneself, and this suggests the necessity of engaging in long-term wage labor. Significantly, they do not offer the part-time wage labor solution (Valli, 1986) and/or flights into fantasy future (McRobbie, 1978) so characteristic of girls in previous studies. In this sense, then, their emerging collective identity embodies a critical moment of critique of an underlying premise of patriarchy, that being that women's primary place is in the home/family sphere and that men will, in turn, take care of them. In so doing, they question the basis of the "family wage," which the young men in 1985 Freeway voraciously affirm (Weis, 1990). Indeed, as numerous investigators point out, the "family wage" ideology lies at the very heart of industrially based White working-class male identity (Arnot, chap 2., this volume; Connell, 1995; Nayak, 2001; Reay, 2002; Walkerdine et al., 2001; Willis, 1977, 2000).

As men struggle to cope with the changes that confront them, clinging, through high school, to a fantasy future linked to the patriarchal family/work site of past years (Weis, 1990), women, in contrast, "positively face the prospect of self transformation" (Walkerdine, et al., 2001, p. 20). Like the postman's wife in the BBC serial who "comes to life after her husband's disappearance" (after being laid off, her husband traverses the country delivering "one last letter"; she, on the other hand, becomes an interior decorator of some note), the young Freeway women face the prospect of transforming themselves with gusto, moving quickly to remake themselves in the face of educational and workforce opportunities.

By way of example, of those interviewed in 1985, 48% of the women completed their BA as of 2001, as compared with 29% of the men. Every single woman interviewed in 1985 and reinterviewed in 2001 pursued some form of higher education, whether 4-year university, comprehensive college, community college, or nursing school. Men, on the other hand, have a far less noteworthy record in the education arena, with 50% attending some form of postsecondary education and less than half completing their intended program. Both the men and women are from similar family circumstances: 79% of men come from families that owned their own homes in Freeway while they were growing up (the great symbol of working class stability), whereas a comparable 76% of the women come from such homes. All the women but one currently work in the wage labor sector, with jobs like respiratory therapist, teacher, registered nurse, licensed practical nurse, chemical engineer, catering manager, paralegal, vascular technician, waitress (simultaneously a full-time student in a teacher education program), social worker, and health plan representative. Compared with the Freeway men whom I interviewed (Weis, 2004), the women have moved into postsecondary education and accompanying skilled positions with some dexterity. The question must be asked, though, to what extent does this represent a lived-out challenge to the gender regime deeply embedded in the White working-class community? What is challenged by this "moment of critique"/cultural penetration, and what remains the same?

Here I offer brief portraits of two young women in 1985, all grown up by 2000. Judy, who we met in the chapter header, a former homecoming queen whose working-class life seemed so perfect when I met her in 1985, reveals how the brutality of her patriarchally bound existence as a teenager rendered her life pure hell. All smiles, kindness, and exuberant beauty, a fine student in the context of Freeway High, which prepared students only minimally for college entrance, Judy lets us in on her secret—only too happy to do so in order to help the next generation of young women, her niece included, who she fears is entrapped in the same vicious dynamic as she was.

Suzanne, still angry at her drunken father who off-loaded his pain on a human triangle encircling herself, her mother, and all Black Americans, lived, as it turns out, in a home totally out of control in the 1980s. Suzanne had few friends and a sarcastic mouth, set in sharp contrast to Judy's, yet Suzanne also had her secrets. She had a boyfriend who was 13 years older than she was and a father who flew into drunken rages at all hours of the day and night. Both from working-class families filled with sharp secrets, Judy and Suzanne, as emblematic of White working-class Freeway women, lived "worlds of pain" (Rubin, 1976), although Judy projected a "good girl" image whereas Suzanne exuded venomous "bad girl" anger. Both, however, wanted out of life as they knew it. Striving for a job, space, and time, neither saw the ostensibly soft hand of male support as desired, or as a solution to their problems. What I did not know when they were teenagers (although I knew them fairly well) was the deeply rooted male brutality—both physical and emotional—that laced their existence. In retrospect for each, it is the pain linked to physical and emotional violence that they desperately wished to escape: An envisioned job, a metaphoric ride on the "freedom train," was seen as a way out.

The stories that follow illustrate the pain and brutality that fester barely beneath the surface of this class fraction, spearheading, at least in part, a critical moment of critique regarding gender roles and relations among White working-class women in the mid 1980s. To be sure, the opening up of the economy to women and the larger middle-class and virtually unacknowledged (by this group) women's movement offer important contexts for the young White working-class women's expressed desires and subsequent actions. But, as I argue here, it is the seen and felt brutality that in large part triggers the critique; the changing context enables the critique to land, rather than being wholly stalled, or turned inward on self.

Although they were teenagers in the mid 1980s, and unable to articulate the linkages, it is clear from an adult perspective, mine as well as theirs, that the brutality underlying patriarchal domesticity in White working-class communities is much of what these women wish to escape. As such, their stories must be read as emblematic of what such a moment of critique can become—what a movement of women at the end of the century, whether understood this way or not, is able to build toward as the American White working class remakes itself against the kaleidoscopic backdrop of changes in the U.S./world economy.

Judy

JUDY: We had a lot of ups and downs—the steel plant was closing. A lot of ups and downs, just with the steel plant and my Dad being out of work and that type of thing. And my mom went to work when I was eight, just for that reason. And she felt guilty about it forever, and still probably does. But otherwise I think we were pretty normal. I mean, my mom tried her best to do everything she could for us. Took us on trips and did that type of thing. We lived in a very small apartment though.

LOIS: So this must be like a palace to you [her current house which is not in Freeway but sits on a large plot of land in a fairly rural area].

JUDY: This is my dream home [laughs] . . . yeah, this is truly, yes, this is. Actually my husband grew up in a nicer house than I did [in a first-ring suburb], but we grew up in a little apartment that was three bedrooms and one bathroom and it was very small [for five of them].

LOIS: When you were in high school you did talk to me about your dad being laid off. Do you reflect back on that at all?

JUDY: At times, yeah. Especially now with having kids [one 3-year-old and one 2-months old]. I think back . . . like I said, I remember the first time my mom really talked about going back to work and how guilty she felt leaving me when I was eight. And like now . . . when I think back about how my Grandmother used to come, or my Grandfather would come down [they lived upstairs] if I was sick because my Mom had to go to work, and take care of me, and my Mom wouldn't have done it if my Dad wasn't laid off at the time. Because actually it was more when I was in junior high school when a lot of it was going on.

LOIS: What did your mom do when she went to work?

JUDY: She's actually still doing it. She works . . . it's almost like an accountant, but she doesn't have an accounting degree. And it's called Jacobbi's now. It used to be called Augustine Electric. So she worked there. Still does. Now I'm happy for her 'cause she does it. It's definitely her pride and joy. She does very well at it and she loves it. Loves the freedom of money finally. . . .

When my dad was laid off, and then go back, and he would get unemployment, I think it bothered him a lot. But my dad's not the type that would go out and get another job. Not that he *couldn't* do it. I don't know. He just, he didn't. Because there was like, the steel plant was all he did and all he knew. And that's, I mean, I can never see him even like going to Home Depot to work because I don't think he has enough self-confidence. I don't know if that's what it is, but even now, with being retired. The steel plant opened back up but under a different name for a little while. And they called him, and he went back for a few months and then stopped. He was getting paid garbage money and he was standing in oil and it just wasn't his thing. He didn't go back after that. So, but he was in his late fifties when the steel plant closed finally [completely], and he retired. He was, pretty much collected unemployment, and I mean, I think he just had hoped that it would always be there and it would be fine. . . . My dad used to do like little projects around the house . . . the house we lived in was four apartments. It was actually my dad's dad's house. And when he passed away, my dad and his brother got the house, so they split it . . . and my dad would do little things around the house. Type of fixer up things. Not decorative or major projects, but just putter around. As far as like laundry, cooking . . . [laughs] . . . he didn't do any of that, really. Yeah, he was just home a lot. That was it. I mean, there was definitely some tough problems there. I mean with my dad and my mom. And so for a while it was very rough. And I think it all stems back from that. Plus my dad was injured in the steel plant. He had his fingers cut off. So that had a big psychological effect on my father. I mean, I didn't like to go back to think about when I was growing up and like, now, like I said, I've been thinking about it. And I think that [his injury] played a big part of it, and he probably should have done something to even get out of there [the steel plant], but he didn't. It's just, like I said, that's all he knew. And if it was up to him I think he'd still live there [in Freeway—in the same house]. . . . Yeah, he just wanted to stay in his little world.

LOIS: Can you describe for me where you live now?

JUDY: Oh, it's tremendously different [laughs]. This is like my own little piece of heaven here, actually. I just wanted property, 'cause, well, in Freeway the house next to us, you could stick your arm out the window and it was right there. You heard everything. Everybody heard everything. And I just wanted space. So now we own thirteen acres . . . and the house is, to me, it was huge compared to where I grew up.

Almost from rags to riches would be the way in which Judy describes her life—a life that began in a run-down section of Freeway and meandered to a beautiful home on Salk Island. She, a 2-year college graduate and radiologic technician in a local hospital, and her husband, a construction worker, have pieced together a materially comfortable life 20 miles from Freeway, one that rests largely for him, and partially for her, on the skills and contacts embedded within the White working-class community. Her husband's job as a construction worker represents the culmination of a set of skills obtained as a youth, and he now works for a family friend. Judy works at General Hospital, a job known to her courtesy of her sister-in-law who also works there. It is these skills and contacts that not only helped Judy and Ron obtain jobs, but also enabled them to build their home (the contractor, for example, is a family friend and her husband and his friends did much of the work themselves), a scenario duplicated by many of the "settled livers" interviewed in 2000[1] (Weis, 2004).

Judy and Ron's present "settled" lifestyle is as dependent on Judy's job as her husband's, for it is the two-income family and the collective production of domesticity that enables the necessary cobbling together of resources, both human and material. The young Freeway women's teenage desire to "be independent," "get a job," "not live off a man," and "live my own life" has encouraged these women to seek postsecondary education with a vengeance (Fine & Weis, 1998), as well as work in a wage labor capacity. Ironically, of course, it is the very desire to escape brutality and dependence on a male breadwinner that has enabled/encouraged familial dependence on the two-income family. Thus, young women's push for "independence" *has* served to alter gender relations in the family, at least to some extent. In this sense, then, these women have lived out the "moment of critique" around patriarchy and wage labor articulated in high school. They are not wholly economically dependent on a man. Rather, men and women are now economically dependent on one another if a comfortable family lifestyle is to be attained.

On another level, however, the youthful moment of critique has not necessarily interrupted male brutality in women's lives, even though, as I suggested earlier, it is the brutality that in large part catapulted this set of changes to begin with—a brutality that sweeps through the White working class with a vengeance (Fine & Weis, 1998). Although the new economic and social context enabled White working-class women to at least imagine exiting lives laced with home-based violence, Judy, like many others, harbored a dark secret, one that she took great pains to conceal.

Judy: My [other] brother is an electrical engineer. He actually did go away to school, just for a couple of years. Ended up coming back and finished up at State College. And he got a job and was doing really well, and my sister, the same thing. *And I wanted that.* And then I think going around to . . . like in our senior year when you had the chances to see colleges, or like college representatives would come, and sometimes these girls would come in and they're all dressed up and I'm like, "That's what I want. I wanna be like that. I wanna have a career and be independent and just be like that." *Do* something instead of being a stay-at-home mom. Or . . . I'm not saying there's anything wrong with that either [being a stay-at-home mom], but I just wanted, I wanted that . . . I guess, the self-esteem and self-confidence in myself. I didn't wanna depend on anybody. And the not depending on anybody thing I think comes from [everything] with my dad and how my mom and dad were, and I just didn't wanna be like that. I didn't wanna live a life like that.

Lois: How were they? You've talked about that twice now. . . .

Judy: They had their rough times. My dad at times was abusive to my mom. More physically than mentally. Mentally he was fine. I think it was . . . now thinking back on it . . . I think it was just problems he had from the steel plant and all that. But . . . sorry [she is crying]. Yeah, and it was bad [crying] . . . that's why I said, I just wanted bigger and better. My family and my kids . . . and I have a wonderful husband.

Lois: You're so lucky.

Judy: I am. He's wonderful. He knows all about it, so . . . I wouldn't even think that [the abuse] would ever even happen here. I know it wouldn't, and I love that comfort, knowing that it wouldn't.

Lois: Do you think that's one of the reasons why you wanted to get out of there?

Judy: Yeah, I think like . . . get me outta here [Freeway] and I'll forget all about those horrible times. That's how my mom deals with it, because when we talk or, my dad was getting a little funny actually a month ago. That's why this is . . . [laughs] . . . a little upsetting. It was getting a little on edge again, and I was, I was getting nervous again about it, and I brought it up to my Mom. And she'll almost act like it didn't happen. Or she'll say like, "It wasn't that bad." And then like I have these vivid memories and I'm like, "What do you mean it wasn't that bad? How can you say it wasn't that bad when we spent nights locked in the bathroom 'cause it was the only door in the house that locked" type of thing, you know? And I was more like, "Oh, how could this be happening."

Lois: Was he drinking?

Judy: No. You almost wish it did [explain it] 'cause you had a reason, you know? Or it's easier to get help that way. His was definitely . . . I mean, I don't know if he ever had a nervous breakdown. Now I think that's probably what happened at some point in time. And I think he probably needed help but never did anything about it. And my mom hid it from everybody. I don't think anybody knew. I mean, she would just call in sick to work . . . she had black eyes. I remember her laying on the couch with the black eyes and stuff, and she would just call in sick to work, and nobody would know. . . .

That was like a big part of my childhood, 'cause I remember it always being there. I don't remember a point when it wasn't. Yeah . . . I wanted out of there [Freeway] for that reason, I'm sure.

Lois: Did anybody try to tell him to get help?

Judy: He's not open to that . . . I mean . . . and it happened when we were older. I called the cops twice. And there was a whole embarrassing thing, 'cause of course, the front pages of the local newspaper, and they would put the Sheriff's Reports in there. And it said, "Domestic, 25 Seneca" in there. And I remember somebody came in school the next day and said, "What happened at your house?" And I made up this whole story about these people living upstairs had this fight. And I was like, "This is terrible." I was embarrassed. I acted like it didn't happen. Maybe it was in my thinking [that] I didn't *want* it to happen. And now when I think, thinking about it, me and my sister and brother have turned out pretty good [laughs], considering how bad it was. . . .

So, I'm sure that was why I wanted out of Freeway. 'Cause going through there, I mean there are memories that come back, you know. I mean, yes, I have great memories through high school and stuff, and that's what you focused on. And I guess that's part of why you try to stay positive and try to view things positively because you wanted to leave all that behind and make a better life for yourself.

Judy and her family fell victim to the abusive elements festering within White working-class male culture. Although she sees her current marriage as more than she could ever have hoped for, her escape from Freeway, and simultaneously Carl, her low-key Freeway high school boyfriend, led her down a treacherous path, one laced with abuse. Meeting Mike in college, she envisioned him as a way of "getting out of the Carl situation" and moving along the road to new experiences, although her first step in this direction was to hook up with another man from Freeway, who, as it turns out, was exceedingly brutal. Having met at a local softball game, she and Mike dated for 3 years, she still smarting from the pain.

JUDY: I guess when it first started happening, yeah, it's just like that little push, little shove, and I didn't . . . I guess I just didn't think of it, and I didn't think that it was gonna go anywhere. And then as it got worse I think I was more like, "I can't believe this is happening." You know, it's not real, or it's gonna stop. And I was ignoring it, probably how my mom just like ignored things [the abuse] and didn't do anything. I just let it go. And I could say that I was in love with him. Definitely. I mean, if he wasn't like that, we'd probably still be together. . . .

He was unbelievably jealous. Unbelievably. I mean I couldn't even look at somebody the wrong way sometimes and he would start. He was just very obsessive type of thing. And then I got to the point where people started finding out. My mother started questioning and, you know, I'd have bruises. He did stuff in front of all my friends. We went to Chowder Point and it was really bad there. And that actually distanced most of my friends because most of them were just like, "Judy, you need to get out of it," and "Judy, why are you still going out with him? If you go out with him, we're not gonna bother with you guys anymore 'cause we don't wanna deal with it." And that's kinda what happened. And I did. I stayed with him and there was definitely a few years there that I was not as close with everybody because of it. . . .

My parents were upset . . . my brother saw something . . . when he [Mike] hit me . . . and he [brother] got really upset and called Mike's parents. And I knew it was, it was just out of control. He [Mike] was out of control. But at one point he was going for counseling. I actually had him talked into that, and he was doing it, so I'm thinking to myself . . . I can do this, I can change him, it'll get better. And I think that was stemming from my father, thinking, you know, "I can help this, I know. It can get better." And I wound up getting to the point where I had to get restraining orders and stuff. Actually I had to get two restraining orders. Yeah, I got one and then, of course, I wound up going back to him. But then, when I started going to County Community College we separated for like nine months. I ran into him at a bar and he's like, "Judy, I wanna talk to you." We started talking. He seemed genuine and sincere and then we started dating. But something wasn't right there, and then he started again. And then he actually attacked me . . . right in front of all these people, and scratched my car and all this stuff. And that was when I was like, "I've had it." I already had enough self-confidence and I think my self-esteem was back so that I was like, "No, I don't need this. I'm not gonna put up with this." And I got another restraining order at that point and that was when we severed our ties. And I did, I mean, he lived four houses away from me growing up, and then I wound up moving to that apartment [her parents' apartment in Freeway], and I was in college and I ran into him a few times there. . . . I mean we talked a couple of times and then a couple of times in the middle of the night he'd come to my apartment. And then I just wanted nothing to do with him. And I was happy to say that at that point, because at one point I would have probably have done anything for him.

LOIS: And if you had a niece who was in this situation, what would you tell her to do?

JUDY: I have two. We're approaching this point. I guess [I'd tell them] always be self-confident. To really look for help and hopefully they'd have a friend or someone that they could talk to that would always be there and stand by them. And not leave them to be . . . like [thinking] this is all you have, you know? To let them know that there is more out there. To be so much more self-confident themselves that they don't need that; they don't need anybody. Honestly, I would love to talk to girls in these situations because I've been there, and I know how hard it is, and I know how hard it is to get out. *And just do it!* I mean, it was really bad there for a while. My mom hit a point where she came to me and said, "Please Judy, I don't know what to do to stop it, but I just don't wanna be seeing you in your grave."

Two restraining orders later (one was useful; the other was not), Judy exited this situation. Terrified to go to a battered women's shelter because her one phone call to Safe Haven led to a connection with someone she knew on the other end of the line, Judy took years to extricate herself from abusive relationships. Spending her entire childhood hiding the abuse in her family, and later as a young adult fleeing those who might know her and label the abuse for what it was, this mid 1980s homecoming queen harbored her secrets well. Crying as she took the blood-red roses at her high school prom, Judy, a young woman determined to "support herself" and "be on her own," like virtually all of the young women I interviewed in 1985, lurched from the violence of her home to violence embedded within young love. Now a radiologic technician whose income enabled the construction of her dream house, Judy walked a path strewn with sharp rocks. Part of a collective expression of "a moment of critique" among White female working-class youth in the mid 1980s, she continued forward toward her dream, but she, like most of the working-class White women I worked with when they were teenagers, was unable to escape fully the physical brutality associated with men in her life. Looking around her kitchen filled with wonderfully happy cut-and-paste glittery pumpkins produced by her family, she reflects on her struggles and triumph.

Suzanne

Suzanne, in contrast to Judy, has no children and is not married. Informing me in 1985 that "Marriage was invented by somebody who was lucky if they lived to be twenty without being bit by a dinosaur," she retains her feisty sarcasm 15 years later. But Suzanne also has a story to tell. Currently a seventh-grade math teacher in a city middle school, she, like Judy, lived her dream of "not being trapped." As she said in high school, "Back when they [parents] were kids, like . . . girls grew up, got married, worked for a couple of years after graduation, had two or three kids, had a white picket fence, two cars. Things are different now. . . . You've got to do it [make a good life] for yourself. I don't want to be Mrs. John Smith. I want to be able to do something." Besides, she tells me in 1985, "You can't rely on them [men]—it's like, I know a lot of older guys, they drink all the time."

SUZANNE: Dad spent most of my growing up years either at work—he's a city firefighter and also worked at Macey Boiler Works—or at a bar for seventy to eighty percent of my growing up time. Mom went back to work when I was about eleven or twelve years old. When she went back to work it was very part-time [she is a waitress]. There's a lot of family conflict because of dad being so unavailable. Mom found comfort elsewhere. I ended up getting involved with somebody much older than me in high school ... I met Joe [long pause] probably eighth grade summer, going into freshman year. I met him when I was thirteen. We became involved, sexually involved, at sixteen, but he was much older than I was. He was about seven years older than I was at the time. He was 21 when we met. We ended up being together pretty much on, most of the time, for about eight years. Yeah, it was very long-term. Did not end well. It was very ugly. . . .

As I look back on it, quite honestly, parts of the relationship were extremely destructive. Parts of it were very instructive in that I learned a lot, especially sex. He was the first one that I was ever with. He was very active, and had no problems teaching me everything he knew, for better or worse. And, of course, you know, of course you're learning something and you take a certain pride in learning how to do something well. And I look back, though, it was destructive, in that in a way he developed into a father figure for me. I would look to him for guidance when I really should have had a father to look to for guidance. We would get into extremely heated arguments. I mean, oh! It was a very passionate relationship on all levels, not sexually passionate ... if we fought, we fought all out! I mean, we threw everything that we could at each other. He was good at throwing things back at me, and I was never as good at throwing things back at him as he was to me. He would remember something I had done six months, a year, two years earlier, and throw it back in my face. . . . You know, now I have the wisdom of knowing better and I can say that it [the entire relationship] was blamed on my father and his drinking because I couldn't run to him [for support]. First of all, I didn't have a male adult in my life to learn how adult men treated adult women. My father's the kind that would come home and yell and scream. You know, he's gonna "sell the house, kill the dog" ... you know ... usually it was only after he had been drinking. Mom has typical dependencies for spouses of alcohol abusers. You know, the whole co-addictions. She's addicted to nerve pills to retain her sanity. And, of course, if he took something out on her, she would take it out on me. If he took something out on me, I took it out on her. If they took something out on me, I took it out on Joe. So there was the whole interaction of things going on. And the further away from high school that Joe and I got, the more brutal our arguments about things would become. It eventually got to the point where he would scream at me, "You have nothing to say! Don't even say anything; you have nothing to say about this!" And eventually it became true. I had nothing to say.

Like Judy, Suzanne centers on her father as the source of current and past problems, a centering that rests squarely on abuse associated, in Suzanne's case, with alcohol. Her relationship with her father, or more accurately the lack thereof, colors her relationship with all men, and she attributes her destructive involvement with Joe to this source.

It is certainly true that individuals from a variety of social classes, both men and women, abuse alcohol. It is also true that such abuse saturates a family, causing untold damage to all family members—partners as well as children. What is striking about the Freeway data in this regard, however, is its very *layered typicality*; whether with respect to physical violence or obvious alcoholism, a very high proportion of the White women I knew in 1985 narrate, as adults, a set of family encounters with alcohol and/or domestic violence that spans generations. This mirrors what Demi Kurz (1995) uncovered as well as what Michelle Fine and I discussed in *The Unknown City* (1998), where an overwhelming majority (92%) of the White working-class women we interviewed across two cities reported childhood abuse (physical or sexual) and/or adult domestic abuse (aimed at themselves or a sister) at the hands of a father, a mother's boyfriend, or the woman's husband or her boyfriend. Contrary to the Norman Rockwell images of a family sitting down to eat dinner, these women's lives drown in various forms of abuse, leaving them too emotionally bereft, in many instances, to deal with the festering anger among the men who continue to surround them.

For Suzanne, the "not talking" with her father, for example, continues well into her adult years:

SUZANNE: Dad and I are better off not talking about anything controversial whatsoever. Dad's not capable of having an intelligent conversation; he just doesn't have the resources.

LOIS: You told me that when you were in high school. Has anything changed?

SUZANNE: No, nothing! It's funny that I was that articulate in high school! Yeah, he's just not capable of having an intelligent conversation with someone.

LOIS: Did anyone ever try to get him into a program? Or rehab?

SUZANNE: Oh, God, no! You're just asking for trouble. I can remember having an argument with my father, this was the first time I ever moved out of this house. It was in the springtime of '94, because it was right around

Valentine's Day and it had gotten to the point . . . I had gone into a rather severe depression that semester [in college]. This was after the first time I dropped out of college. Because this was '94, just before I graduated . . . the second time I went back. And in the spring of '94 around Valentine's Day, things in this house were horrendous. I was not functioning at all. And I had to function somewhat because I just had to get out of the house. This is not a house that you can just stop functioning in, because as soon as you stop functioning, it gets very ugly. I moved out of this house. I moved in with a girlfriend out in Centreville, and I'm pounding out of my room with my things and screaming at my father . . . because my father was home, drunk as usual, Mom was at work, and I looked at him and I said, "What do you care about? All you do is sit on a barstool and watch the world go by. You don't care what happens in here!" And he turned to me and looked at me and he said, "I've earned my right to drink." I thought, you know, fine. You've earned your right to drink. You've earned the right to not have a family, because you don't have one. And, you know, from that day on, I realized there's no point in ever trying to get him to stop. I don't want him to stop. I wish to God he'd drink himself into his grave, quite frankly. Or at least move away from here and not come back, because he's more damaging than he is anything else. I can't say that I wish him dead. My mother can. I can't. . . .

Lois: Your mom ever say anything to you about not getting married because of her own situation?

Suzanne: Never. Well, she didn't have to say, "Don't marry a man that drinks." No, she would prefer that I was married, because she is under the impression that I cannot take care of myself, you know, with the debt that I have and the disasters that seem to happen [she is a teacher but has lost two jobs], she just doesn't think I can take care of myself. And she thinks I need someone to do that for me, which I don't agree with.

Whether Suzanne "needs someone to take care of her" or not is not at issue here. What is important is that Suzanne has lived out her teenage dream—she is "independent," earns her own money, is not married, and has no children. In her 1985 words, she is not "Mrs. John Smith" crawling behind a "white picket fence." For Suzanne and the other 1985 Freeway girls, "Best are the freedom dreams," and Suzanne has lived this "freedom."

On the down side, Suzanne was in a highly abusive relationship with a man 7 years her senior from the time she was 16: a relationship that began, although nonsexually, when she was 13. She hates her father, who continues to drink, verbally abusing her, her mother, and all Black Americans when drunk. She attributes her own destructive relationship with Joe to the fact that she has no father. Within the last 2 years Suzanne has suffered two nervous breakdowns, having lost one teaching job and enduring seemingly endless bad encounters with men. At one point last summer, she could not get up from the couch for a full week—she just lay there, crying.

Suzanne did not emerge unscathed from the "freedom" train—she and a high proportion of the young Freeway women continue to suffer under the men of their class, as it is the men of their class whom they meet and interact with. I asked her at one point where she meets men. She responded that she goes to bars. "Which bars?" I said. "Oh, you know," she responded, "the ones that people like me go to—the guys are rough, not very educated, and like to have fun. I don't go to bars that educated guys go to." "Why?" I asked. "I don't feel comfortable there," she responded. "I need to be with people who are from places like Freeway." Suzanne is a seventh grade math teacher in a city school. Her social class of origin—her class-embedded *habitus* (Bourdieu, 1993) and accompanying assertions of physical male dominance—travels with her.

The hand of the male is not soft for Judy, Suzanne, or the majority of the Freeway girls, now women. The bruises, Black eyes, thrown plates of spaghetti, angry phone calls at three o'clock in the morning—all encircle life with men they have come into contact with over the years, beginning, in many instances, with their fathers. In the case of Carla, a third woman in the cohort sample, her mother "just knew"—there was something mean about Tom (Carla's former boyfriend who beat her mercilessly). She was right. One drunken night he called her up after slamming her daughter's head against the wall, threatening, "You better say goodbye to your daughter because this is the last time you're ever gonna hear from her."

Concludsion

Juxtaposing the deeply etched youthful desire for "independence" against the women's now held full-time and relatively stable positions in the labor force, the question arises, what came of, and was able to come of, the moment of critique packed within modal working-class female culture as it emerged during the high school years? In other words, where can such a "cultural penetration" deposit, and why?

Significantly, all live to an appreciable extent their fantasy of not being wholly dependent on a man, yet a very high proportion of the women, like Suzanne and Judy, experience horrific episodes of abuse at the hands of men. Certainly not all of the Freeway women have experienced such violence either during their youth or since high school, but most have, to the point where those who have not lived through violent episodes are the exception rather than the rule, signifying the very *layered typicality* of the experience. Although Freeway men may live distanced from their expressed high school desire to set up patriarchal families in which they labor outside the home/family sphere and women reside within it and tend to it (Weis, 1990), the physical brutality that is all too common speaks to an underlying male desire to control and dominate their women.

For women, then, the lived-out "moment of critique" has not wholly been able to challenge all that goes on in the private sphere, although this certainly was their teenage desire. The new collective unit (the family of varying forms; Weis, 2004) on which working-class men and women are now totally dependent if a "stable" life is to be accomplished is punctuated by raw physical male power, much as the working- class collective of old was punctuated by raw bursts of violent capitalist power, as supported by the state. Both the fundamental site of collectivity *and* essential punctuating moves of physical power, as a disruption to this site, have altered under the new economy.

In 1985 the Freeway girls offered the glimmerings of critique of women's place in both the home/family sphere and that of wage labor, challenging the notion that their primary role is to take care of their husbands' children in return for which their husbands' family wages will support them, thus challenging the secret guarantee of the family wage: sacrifice, reward, dignity (Willis, 2000). Additionally, they pierced the notion that they must account to men—that they must listen as men tell them what to do, where to go, when to have children, and what to buy, thus chipping away at the ideology of thoroughly separate spheres for women and men and the accompanying notion that they must occupy a subordinate role.

It is arguably the case, then, that the Freeway girls' identity must be understood in terms of a radically changed economy as well as in relation to altered understandings of women as a sexual class in general, even though the resurgence of the women's movement has been spearheaded and certainly colonized by the middle class. Some of the middle-class struggles have clearly filtered down to these girls, and their beginning critique of women's place must be seen as linked to these broader struggles in key ways. The language of "independence," for example, is tied discursively to a middle-class women's movement and picked up by working-class girls, whether they consciously identify with this movement or not.

What working-class Freeway women have not been able to do, however, is escape the violence associated with the ways in which patriarchy plays out historically and continues to play out in this particular class fraction. It is this element of class association and embeddedness, this *habitus* if you will (Bourdieu, 1993), that the daughters of the industrial proletariat have not, as a collective, been able to escape. Indeed, it is arguably the case that such abuse is on the rise as working-class men move away from older patriarchal notions in some part of their lives yet retain violent elements meted out in the domestic realm. Given that longitudinal physical abuse data are difficult to read because any rise in such abuse may signal greater frequency of abuse or simply more extensive reporting of such abuse, it is difficult to establish with any certainty whether or not abuse in working-class communities is on the upswing as a result of changes in the economy and family structure. In a frightening turn of events, though, it is conceivable that the physical cruelty of White working-class men (whether more extensive than in the past or not) becomes their last defensive resort—their last solidly and visible patri-archal stand in a world that has stripped them of alternative forms of power. Under this scenario, the power left to them, as a group, is their physicality, and they employ it, whether consciously or not, to stake out a form of continued dominance vis-à-vis women and children in the home.

This underscores points made by Angela McRobbie (1980) and more recently Madeline Arnot (chap. 2, this volume). As Arnot notes, what McRobbie found most striking was how "unambiguously degrading to women is the language of aggressive masculinity through which (Willis's) lads kick against the oppressive structures they inhabit" (p. 38, as cited in Arnot). *Learning to Labor*, which can be read as a classic piece on White working-class masculinity (Arnot, chap 2., this volume), is peppered with references of utmost brutality against women, suggesting that "the violence of the imagery, the cruelty of the lads' sexual double standard, the images of sexual power and domination become the lads' last defensive resort" (Arnot, chap 2., this volume). Given changes in the world economy that render substantial *economically* based male power in the White working class less and less likely, it is arguably the case that raw physical power becomes the last line of defense, building on already existing sensibilities regarding women in this class fraction (Nayak, 2001; Reay, 2002). Certainly, many White working-class husbands and fathers (some of whom are currently married to the Freeway women) do not fall victim to this brute physicality as an expression of desired and yet stripped down dominance and superiority. Yet data suggest that enough of these women have experienced such raw physical abuse so as to render violence against women typical.[2]

Critique, then, such as that expressed by the young Freeway women, although not necessarily "fizzing out" as some of our earlier short-term studies suggested (Weis & Fine, 1996), takes different shape and form by gender, and, I am quite certain, moves forward in the real world in markedly different ways. Paul Willis's extraordinarily insightful set of understandings around the theoretical constructions associated with penetration, partial penetration, and limitation, useful as they are, *play over time*. What I am suggesting here is, not only do they play differently over time for men and women, but that a "moment of critique" such as I stumbled on in the mid 1980s is multifaceted, with long-term follow-up studies allowing us to unravel the "sticking power" of varying elements of such critique in concrete political, economic, cultural and discursive settings.

The Freeway girls "all grown up" in 2000–2001 reveal that although their mid 1980s moment of critique enables some semblance of control over work and family life, it does not enable them to escape the male-based physical abuse of this class. Ironically, although it is the skills and contacts embedded within White working-class *habitus* that enable the "accomplishment" of "settled" life within this specific class fraction under the new economy, a topic that I take up at much greater length elsewhere (Weis, 2004), it is, at one and the same time, the physical domination as embedded within this same *habitus* that "causes" the violence noted here. Thus, both "good" and "bad" elements of White working-class *habitus* are carried on the backs of women (and men, of course) as they move into the 21st century, carving, with men, a new class fraction under the restructured economy.

Notwithstanding occupational segregation and the continued "double burden" (wage labor/family) of women across social class context, the White working class has moved into the 21st century with women figuratively working side by side men in both the home/family sphere and the public sphere so as to bring in income and raise the next generation. Just below the surface of this newly minted collective, however, rests the potential physical dominance of the White working-class man, a dominance intensified perhaps by a deep and targeted sense among White working-class men that their masculinities are under siege in the new global economy. The apparent seamlessness with which this new White working class fraction is accomplished, then, is, on closer scrutiny, perhaps being shredded from the inside.

Notes

1. Here I am employing an updated version of the "hard" versus "settled" living binary embedded within the literature on the white working class (Howell, 1973). I explore this at length in *Class Reunion* (Weis, 2004).

2. I want to make it clear here that White working-class identity as expressed within my original ethnography addresses what can be seen as *modal* cultural forms. Diane Reay (2002) recently took me to task for my apparent "homogenization" of White working-class male forms, suggesting that such homogenized accounts of White working-class masculinities not only ignore difference within masculinities but leave this class to "bear the weight of White racism and male sexism" (Reay, 2002, p. 222). I agree with her latter point wholeheartedly. When we point fingers at this group and locate racism and sexism within it, we ignore the differently coded but nonetheless real racism and sexism within the middle and upper middle classes, for example, as well as racism and sexism embedded within economic and state policies, which are most definitely not crafted by the White working class (but may, nonetheless, benefit them as "Whites"). This is obviously not my intent, but I recognize that

a focus on one group inadvertently tends to "black out" the ways in which these same characteristics may be embedded within another group or broad-based policies. Michelle Fine and I have taken up this point elsewhere (Fine & Weis, 1998), arguing strongly that White working-class men and women, and particularly men, often bear the brunt of broad class-based racism and sexism simply because they speak out whereas others offer more coded versions of similar sentiments.

With respect to Reay's point about homogenization, I do not mean to imply that all men and women from the White working class live out the stories presented in any of my writing or *necessarily* exhibit the range of characteristics embedded within the stories. However, I do suggest that these are *modal* stories—that a *significant* proportion of the specified group could tell a similar story, as evidenced by Reay's own admission that "my own childhood and adolescent experience of white working class masculinities was one scarred by violence, both physical and verbal abuse plus the more symbolic but equally damaging violence of deeply entrenched sexism and racism within the male dominated coal mining community I used to be part of" (p. 222). Again, then, I do not mean to imply that there are not varying masculinities or femininities within this class cultural group. Obviously there are. What I do suggest though, in line with a range of scholars such as R. W. Connell (1995), Kenway and Fitzclarence (1997), and others, is that particular masculinist constructions are highly valued—or hegemonic—thereby providing the center with which and against which all other competing masculinities (or femininities) must emerge. My point in this chapter, then, is not that every White working-class woman has the experience outlined here, but rather that my data suggest its very typicality, a typicality that should not be ignored as we focus on the adult "living out" of culturally rooted "penetrations" observed during teenage years (metaphorically ours and actually theirs).

References

Arnot, M. (2002). *Reproducing gender: Essays on educational theory and feminist politics.* New York: Routledge Falmer.

Bluestone, B., & Harrison, B. (1982). *The de-industrialization of America.* New York: Basic Books.

Bourdieu, P. (1993). *Sociology in question.* London: Sage.

Connell, R. W. (1995). *Masculinities.* Cambridge, UK: Polity Press.

Elder, G. (1974). *Children of the Great Depression.* Chicago: University of Chicago Press.

Fine, M., & Weis, L. (1998). *The unknown city: The lives of poor and working class young adults.* Boston: Beacon Press.

Fitch, J. (1999). *White oleander.* London: Virago Press.

Howell, J. (1973). *Hard living on Clay Street.* Garden City, NY: Anchor Press.

Kenway, J., & Fitzclarence, L. (1997). Masculinity, violence and schooling—Challenging poisonous pedagogies. *Gender and Education, 9,* 117–33.

Kurz, D. (1995) *For richer, for poorer: Mothers confront divorce.* New York: Routledge.

McRobbie, A. (1978). Working class girls and the culture of femininity. In Women's Studies Group (Ed.), *Women take issue* (pp. 96–108). London: Hutchinson.

McRobbie, A. (1980). Settling accounts with sub-culture. *Screen Education, 34,* 37–50.

Nayak, A. (2001, May). *Ivory lives, race, ethnicity and the practice of Whiteness in a northeast youth community.* Paper presented at the Economic and Social Research Seminar Series: "Interdisciplinary Youth Research: New Approaches," Birmingham University, U.K.

Reay, D. (2002). Shaun's story: Troubling discourses of white working-class masculinities. *Gender and Education. 14*(3), 221–234.

Reich, R. (1991). Why the rich are getting richer and the poor poorer. In *The work of nations* (pp. 208–224). London: Simon and Schuster.

Reich, R. (2001). *The future of success.* New York: Alfred Knopf.

Rubin, L. (1976). *Worlds of pain.* New York: Basic Books.

Sennett, R., and Cobb, J. (1972). *The hidden injuries of class.* New York: Vintage.

Valli, L. (1986). *Becoming clerical workers.* Boston: Routledge and Kegan Paul.

Walkerdine, V., Lucey, H., & Melody, J. (2001). *Growing up girl: Psychological explorations of gender and class.* New York: New York University Press.

Weis, L. (1990). *Working class without work: High school students in a de-industrializing economy.* New York: Routledge.

Weis, L. (2004). *Class reunion: The new working class.* New York: Routledge.

Weis, L., & Fine, M. (1996). Narrating the 1980s and 1990s: Voices of poor and working class White and African American men. *Anthropology and Education Quarterly, 27*(4), 1–24.

Weis, L., & Fine, M. (2004). *Working method.* New York: Routledge.

Willis, P. (1977). *Learning to labour: How working class kids get working class jobs.* Westmead, England: Saxon House Press.

Willis, P. (2000). *The ethnographic imagination.* Cambridge, UK: Polity Press.

CHAPTER 8

Learning to Do Time
*Willis's Model of Cultural Reproduction in an Era of
Postindustrialism, Globalization, and Mass Incarceration*

KATHLEEN NOLAN AND JEAN ANYON

This chapter examines Paul Willis's cultural reproduction model, explicated in *Learning to Labor* (first published as *Learning to Labour*, 1977), and offers an analysis of the importance it holds as a critique of urban public schools in the current context of postindustrialism, globalization, and the mass incarceration of people of color—particularly Black men—in the United States. Willis's contention that working-class youth, by opposing the dominant school culture, act as agents not only in the reproduction of working-class culture, but in the reproduction of their own class position, is as relevant today as it was over 25 years ago. However, oppositional behavior in school—when enacted by Black urban youth in poverty neighborhoods in the United States—does not lead to the shop floor. Rather, in this postindustrial era of mass incarceration, oppositional behavior by working-class youth of color in educational institutions often leads them directly into the criminal justice system.

The chapter first describes how the phenomenon of mass incarceration in the United States was created. Although it is difficult to identify the myriad causes of mass incarceration, we hold that there is a relationship between such trends as deindustrialization and globalization, and the need for the management and control of a population that has become economically superfluous—particularly in urban, deindustrialized zones. In our analysis, race and class are central. The chapter next explores the changing role of urban public schools in the new social and economic circumstances. Urban public schools, we argue, have become increasingly connected to the criminal justice system and to the production of mass incarceration of youth of color therein. This "school/prison continuum" has developed through the use of academic policies such as high-stakes testing, disciplinary policies such as "zero tolerance," the use of high-tech security apparatus and police officers in schools, and the establishment of a multitude of intermediary institutions that house youth as they move between educational and custodial facilities. A most important step in this "prison track" is that truancy and the kind of oppositional behavior displayed by Willis's lads, when committed by U.S. youth of color in schools, is criminalized.

However, it is not only oppositional youth who get criminalized. Dominant media representations that depict urban youth of color as dangerous criminals and the source of urban chaos and the media's sensationalist coverage of school violence serve to demonize inner-city youth of color as a group. These media representations generate fear of young Black men and other youth of color and support school discipline policies, such as zero tolerance, that place even youth of color who accommodate to school protocols in jeopardy of being constructed as troublemakers—or worse, criminals.

We posit finally that Willis's model of cultural reproduction, as a dialectic between opposition and reproduction, offers today a much needed sense of possibility for political action. Although laden with contradictions, the cultural productions of youth of color, at times, can lead to youths' reclaiming their individual and collective identities, social critique, and the possibility of organized resistance.

The Social Context

In 2000, the prison population of the United States exceeded 2 million for the first time. Currently, about 6.6 million Americans are incarcerated, on probation, or parole—an increase of 258% since 1980. The ratio of incarcerated people is now 702 per 100,000 people (in contrast to 97 per 100,000 in 1972), the highest reported rate of incarceration in the world. The explosion in the number of people involved in the criminal justice system has had its most dramatic effects on communities of color, especially African American men. In fact, about two-thirds of the people in prison are racial and ethnic minorities, and about half of the prison population is African American, although they represent only about 13% of the total population (Mauer, 1999). Among African American men, the most adversely affected population is men between the ages of 16 and 25. An astounding one out of every three young Black men are either incarcerated or otherwise involved in the criminal justice system, and for the first time in decades, there are more Black men headed to prison than to college (Justice Policy Institute, 2000).

The number of children (those under the age of 16) involved in the juvenile justice system has also increased (Zimring, 2001). Moreover, national statistics reveal alarming patterns of bias against African American and Latino youth. They are overrepresented in the juvenile and criminal justice system, and are subject to harsher treatment than whites. For example, African American youth are more likely than Whites to be "waived" into adult court. They are more likely to be detained, and six times more likely to be incarcerated than White youth for the same offense (Jones & Yamagata, 2000).

The rise in the prison population began in the 1960s, but the dramatic shift in adult incarceration occurred over a decade later, in the early 1980s. This increase marked a new era in the American criminal justice system. An increase in the juvenile population involved in the criminal justice system followed a decade later and continued throughout the 1990s (Zimring, 2001). Although there is some debate about the causes of this phenomenon, we argue that it is the result of complex interactions of economic, political, historical, and discursive forces.

Loic Wacquant (2002) posited that since the inception of the United States, there have been four racialized economic institutions: slavery, Jim Crow, the ghetto, and—beginning in the late 1960s—what he calls the hyper-ghetto/prison. Within this framework, Wacquant offers an historical analysis of the capitalist classes' interest and investment in institutions created for the management of forced and low-wage labor and racial containment (see also Wacquant, 2001).

As early as the 1920s, African Americans living in the South were drawn to Northern industrial cities seeking employment and escaping the Jim Crow South. By the 1950s, Southern Blacks were migrating to Northern industrial cities at unprecedented rates. Although employers actually encouraged migration and sought to hire Black workers at times, such as during World War I when there was a dearth of European immigrant labor, Black workers were more often excluded from skilled jobs by employers and trade unions (Anyon, 1997). Nevertheless, for the most part, the 1940s and 1950s marked a period of economic expansion, and African Americans in urban neighborhoods enjoyed more employment opportunity and autonomy than they had as Southern sharecroppers.

The decades after World War II were also characterized by housing discrimination, the construction of new highways that tore through working-class urban neighborhoods, and federally subsidized White suburbanization. These trends contributed to the economic and social isolation of people of color in American "ghettos" (Anyon, 1997).

Economic shifts that occurred in the in the postwar years destabilized urban neighborhoods and—in conjunction with the economic crisis and emergence of a service economy in the 1970s—were root causes of the soon-to-emerge phenomenon of mass incarceration. These changes translated into the loss of millions of jobs. From 1967 to 1987, Philadelphia lost 64% of its manufacturing jobs and Chicago lost 60%. New York lost 58% of its manufacturing jobs, or 520,000 in absolute numbers (Wilson, 1996). Although jobs in service industries increased, their wages were considerably lower than manufacturing jobs. Unemployment rose and real wages have decreased—disproportionately effecting African Americans and Latinos (Wilson, 1996). In 1999, almost a *third* (29.5%) of Black men, almost *half* (40.7%) of Black women, almost *half* of Hispanic men (40.3%), and *more than half* of Hispanic women (51.8%) earned poverty wages working full-time, year-round (Anyon, forthcoming). If one calculates the individuals, rather than families, who made less than 200% of the poverty level in 2001 ($17.40/hour or $36,192/year), the results are as follows: 84.3% of Hispanic workers, 80% of Black workers, and 64.3% of White workers made wages at or under 200% of the official poverty line (Anyon, forthcoming).

Moreover, a smaller percentage of African American men are working now than in recent decades. Only 52% of young (aged 16 to 24), noninstitutionalized, out-of-school Black males with high school degrees or less were employed in 2002, compared to 62% 20 years ago (Anyon, forthcoming). In contrast, the labor-force activity of comparable White and Hispanic males has been steady over the last two decades, and employment among young Black women has increased significantly (Anyon, forthcoming).

The employment rate of young, less educated Black males is much lower in cities than in suburbs, and the gap widened over the last decade. The employment rate for young, less educated Black men living in central cities (46.99%) is now 16 percentage points lower than that for their suburban counterparts (63.09%) (Anyon, forthcoming, p. 4). The employment rate for young Black male high school graduates dropped by over four times as much in cities (9 percentage points) as in suburbs (2 percentage points) over the course of the 1990s (Anyon, forthcoming).

These economic shifts, coupled with dramatic cuts in social services in the 1980s and 1990s, led to dire material conditions and the social isolation of working-class African Americans and other people of color in inner-city areas (Wilson, 1996).

Other scholars complicate the notion of social isolation by expounding on the new economic and spatial arrangements found in urban areas as a result of globalization. They emphasize the interconnectedness between increased concentrations of poverty, immigration, processes of uneven development, gentrification, and the simultaneous creation of "hyper-anaesthetized bourgeois play zones" (Parenti, 2000), or "glamour zones" (Sassen, 1998)—such as SoHo in New York City. All of these, it is argued, are elements of the "global city" (Sassen, 2001).

Globalization is characterized by the worldwide primacy of financial and speculative capital, the creation and integration of flexible systems of production of goods and services, increased international mobility of workers, and the bifurcation of national economies into rich and poor (Sassen, 1998; see also Lipman, 2001).

Although many characteristics of globalization occur on the global scale, others are local—and it is the racial, class, and spatial arrangements that appear in urban neighborhoods and cities that are most important to this analysis. First, there has been a hardening of economic stratification due to changes in the labor market. Many cities have seen an increase in both high paying professional, managerial, and technical jobs on the one hand, and low-wage, informal, transient, and part-time employment in the service sector, on the other hand. This has created a polarization of class divisions along racial, ethnic, and gender lines (Sassen, 2001).

Second, globalization has changed urban geography through an intensi-fied process of uneven local development. There have been both an increase in concentrated poverty and great increases in wealth in global cities like New York and Chicago, and in what Sassen calls "second tier" cities as well, creating high-income areas that abut very poor neighborhoods. Thus, everyday interactions between rich and poor may be increased. Low-income workers—who in most cities are people of color—traverse upscale commer-cial and entertainment zones as service workers or as consumers. And gentrification, the process by which the depreciation of property value in depressed urban areas makes investment profitable, coupled with the desire of some high-income professionals to live near financial centers, has created a situation where high-income workers increasingly move into poverty areas. This not only causes the displacement of low-income families, but heightens calls for increased surveillance and heavy policing of those who remain.

Parenti (2000) pointed to a major contradiction within the American economic system: "Capitalism always creates, needs, surplus populations [to keep wages down], yet faces the threat of political, aesthetic, or cultural disruption from those populations" (p. 239). The threat residing in an unruly reserve pool of labor is great, given the bifurcation of wages and the polarization of classes and races, uneven local development, and massive unemployment and underemployment in central cities across the country. Recent dramatic increases in the prison and criminal justice populations are attempts to manage this contradiction.

The sharp increases in poverty in American cities in the 1980s (Jargowsky, 1998) and cuts in social services were accompanied by a dramatic increase in the sale of drugs on inner-city streets in the form of crack cocaine. The "drug problem" gave politicians and pundits a way to respond to economic and social problems that were plaguing the city: Declare a "war on drugs." This is the most immediate cause of the explosion in the number of people incarcerated in the United States.

Some specific policy changes that accompanied the "war on crime" were the introduction of mandatory sentencing and three-strikes policies, and more stringent parole regulations. New York State's Rockefeller Drug Laws, passed in 1973, were considered among the toughest in the country (Mauer, 1999). Throughout the 1980s, many other states subsequently passed similar laws. These laws mandated mandatory prison terms and limits to plea bargaining. Federal legislation, such as the 1984 Sentencing Reform Act and the Anti-Drug Abuse Acts of 1986 and 1988, greatly expanded the use of mandatory minimum sentencing (Mauer, 1999; Zimring, 2001). Finally, the first three-strikes laws appeared in 1993 and the federal truth-in-sentencing law came in 1994.

These laws deeply weaken the social fabric of urban communities as hundreds of thousands of people of color enter the criminal justice system. A number of White rural communities, on the other hand, received somewhat of an economic stimulus, in the form of new prisons (Gilmore, 1998; Parenti, 2000).

Concomitant with changes in the political economy, by the 1970s the field of criminal justice had changed as well. The efficacy of the rehabilitation model dominant during the 1960s was questioned. In addition, many criminologists who were concerned about equity in sentencing contended that individualized treatment led to bias in sentencing, and therefore uniform sentencing procedures should be adopted (Garland, 2001). Soon the discourse of rehabilitation and the liberal emphasis on the individual treatment of the "disadvantaged" offender were replaced by discourses of retribution, punishment, and social pathology.

The current "tough on crime" rhetoric and focus on retribution can be seen as an extension of political maneuvers dating back to the 1960s—beginning perhaps with Richard Nixon's "law and order" discourse of 1968—which spoke to people's fears of growing racial tensions and social protest; this discourse was also aimed at feminists who were demanding safety on the streets (Mauer, 1999). By the 1970s, politicians had identified crime as an important political issue. Crime control became a "wedge issue," along with welfare, affirmative action, and immigration, used by conservative politicians to capture the vote of working-class Whites (Tonry, 1999).

Likewise, high taxes, inflation, and declining economic performance caused anxiety among the new middle classes, which triggered the major political realignment and shifts in public opinion around the issue of crime control just described (Garland, 2001).

The media have supported this new discourse through a dramatic increase in coverage of urban crime and the proliferation of representations of Black and Latino urban men as a "new class of superpredators." Although crime dropped by 20% from 1990 to 1998, crime news on network television increased 83%. Moreover, television networks overrepresent people of color as perpetrators and Whites as victims, and Black suspects are less likely than White suspects to be identified by name, consequently creating an image of the Black criminal as indistinct from other Black people (Dorfman & Shiraldi, 2001). Black youth, in particular, are perhaps constructed as the most dangerous element of the urban "underclass," as "young Black male" has become synonymous with crime in the media (Dorfman & Shiraldi, 2001).

Thus, the rationale provided by authorities and the media for mass incarceration does not implicate poverty or unemployment; it has become, instead, a "value rationale"—one that is expressive and moralistic (Garland, 2001). Young men of color (and teen-aged mothers on welfare) have come to represent the moral crisis in America, and young people of color in urban areas are blamed for the social and economic problems of our time. Increased levels of repression are justified on moral grounds, and control becomes a prevailing cultural theme (Garland, 2001).

The Urban School

In the 1970s, reproduction theorists who shaped radical educational theory demonstrated how schools, as predominantly ideological institutions, served to reproduce social class stratification (Althusser, 1971; Bourdieu & Passeron, 1977; Bowles & Gintis, 1976). Although these models were helpful in understanding the school's role in maintaining the class structure, they did not take into account human agency and the possibility of resistance (but see Anyon, 1980).

Willis's model of cultural reproduction offered a more dialectical notion of reproduction, in which students are not passive receptacles of the dominant ideology but play an active role in reproduction as they engage in shaping their own cultural responses to their conditions. Willis's working-class lads reject school culture because they see through the myth of meritocracy. They know that, as members of the working class, there is little chance that they will enter the middle class. Willis refers to these insights as "penetrations," or "impulses within a cultural form towards the penetration of the conditions of existence of its members and their class position within the social whole" (Willis, 1977, p. 119).

These penetrations, however, are only partial; they do not represent a critical working class consciousness. Here Willis uses the notion of limitations. That is, cultural penetrations are "repressed and prevented from going further (and in fact often paradoxically link the lads more fully to an unequal economy) by the contradictions built into [the lads'] actions" (Apple, 1995, p. 91). For example, the lads' celebration of manual labor and rejection of mental labor ultimately exclude them from middle-class jobs.

We argue that Willis's model is still relevant today. Nevertheless, within the context of globalization, urban impoverishment, and demographic polarization, the functions of schooling for working-class students of color have shifted. Thus, we ask: What is the function of schooling for Black students and other students of color in the current context of postindustrial impoverishment? And what is the relevance of Willis's model of cultural reproduction for these youth in the current context?

To answer the first question, we consider discursive shifts and policy changes that have occurred in the field of education in the past few decades. The changes in educational discourse have reflected discursive changes in the larger society and in fields "contiguous" to education, such as the criminal justice system. Liberal educational practices of the 1960s that acknowledged social inequalities and the need for civil rights had, by the 1980s, given way to discipline-oriented policies in the field of education that pathologized whole groups of people, as in criminal justice.

The 1980s saw a renewed emphasis on the Western canon and basic skills training, and fierce attacks on multicultural and bilingual education. Conservatives such as Charles Murray (1984) overtly advocated coercive policies—claiming that students, particularly working-class Blacks and other minorities, needed to be disciplined. Thinking behind these trends involved the stereotype that working-class people of color were culturally deprived.

In the 1990s, neo-liberal educational policies meshed with economic privatization and marketization tendencies, with similar and supporting results. In the new framework, the public must be convinced not only that the unregulated marketplace is the truest expression of individual freedom, but that the marketplace must be expanded into every sphere of life—including education—freeing it from the inefficient and dysfunctional public domain (Apple, 2001). The implementation of choice plans—vouchers, magnet schools, and privately owned charter schools—then becomes the commonsense approach to education reform.

However, privatization schemes ultimately have led to the intensification of social divisions along racial, ethnic, and class lines, and increased polarization of and in neighborhoods (Apple, 2001; Lipman, 2001, 2002). This happens as middle and upper-middle-class (typically White) parents—and some from the working class—that is, those with the social and cultural capital required to negotiate systems of choice—ensure that their children benefit from the new schools while leaving the most economically and socially disenfranchised students to languish in the poorest schools.

Moreover, the corporate logic embedded in privatizing enterprises has shifted the focus away from liberal education reform policies, such as decreasing class size and creating more culturally relevant curriculum, to a focus on increasing productivity while minimizing spending (House, 1998). Funding for enrichment programs has been cut while new systems of accountability, that is, the implementation of labor discipline practices, have moved the full burden for educational success onto students, teachers, and low-level administrators.

Today, one of the most significant policy initiatives is high-stakes standardized testing: standardized exams that students must pass in order to be promoted or graduate. High-stakes testing holds appeal for both conservatives and neo-liberals because on the one hand they help to carry out the conservative agenda by maintaining tight control over what constitutes "official knowledge," while on the other hand these exams fit nicely into the new corporate logic as they help to shift blame for school failure onto students, foster competition, and create new markets within the burgeoning testing industry.

Moreover, high-stakes testing has worked to maintain racial and economic inequality in America's cities by fostering highly regimented and superficial rote learning in schools serving students who have historically underachieved on standardized tests, that is, African Americans and other students of color (Apple, 2001; McNeil, 2000; Lipman, 2001). The requirement that poorly prepared students in urban schools pass these tests in order to graduate has been linked with increasing dropout rates. In some urban high schools, the dropout rate is as high as 70%, and those who drop out have increased chances of future incarceration (Coalition for Juvenile Justice, 2001).

Current education policy, then, aligned with the needs of the market, has reinforced and strengthened the school's role in the reproduction of social stratification, along class and racial lines, that was illustrated to us decades ago (Anyon, 1980). The heightened social stratification that results from current education policy does not establish a direct link between schools and the criminal justice system, but it certainly does create at least two distinct groups of students—those prepared for high-paying professional jobs, and those who must vie for the low-wage service jobs or enter the illegal economy. Not surprisingly, our prisons are full of young people who belong to the latter group—many of whom read well below grade level, do not have high school diplomas, have been placed on the lowest academic tracks, and have spent years in underfunded, underachieving schools (Coalition for Juvenile Justice, 2001).

The more direct link between schools in low-income urban neighborhoods and the criminal justice system is created by current "zero-tolerance" policies and practices. The term *zero tolerance*, which entered the public discourse in the early 1980s in relation to the new drug laws, found its way into educational policy rhetoric partly in response to a few highly publicized school shootings that occurred in middle-class White suburbs. In the mid 1990s, the federal government responded to public concern over what the media labeled "the national crisis of school violence" by implementing strict security guidelines for public schools. Zero-tolerance policies have since led to dramatic increases in exclusionary practices—suspensions and expulsions (Skiba, Michael, & Nardo, 2000). Moreover, zero-tolerance policies have increased the flow of some students into the juvenile or criminal justice system through the establishment of a close working relationship between school personnel and the police and the installation of high-tech security apparatus.

Other practices within school walls have led to the flow of students into the criminal justice system. Some studies identify the subjective views of White teachers and the cumulative effects of discriminatory, disciplinary action as major factors in the overrepresentation of students of color in school discipline cases (Ferguson, 2001; Skiba et al., 2000). Moreover, as in the criminal justice system itself, Black and Latino students are more likely to be punished than their White counterparts for the same offenses (McCarthy & Hoge, 1987; Skiba et al., 2000). Thus, Black and Latino students are more likely to enter the criminal justice system, as it has become increasingly common for disciplinary problems to be referred to the police.

Urban high schools, however, have not all witnessed the same levels of increased repression. For the most part, only large urban public high schools in poor areas have been prisonized through the use of security apparatus and police surveillance. Students in these schools, regardless of whether they have ever committed a crime, are at times subject to bodily searches, metal detectors, and referral to the police for small, nonviolent school infractions that were once handled internally. Thus, whole school populations are criminalized.

The school/prison continuum, however, does not rest solely on individual teachers' racist assumptions and new school discipline codes. The continuum is also supported by new intermediary institutions that manage the stages between school and prison. The establishment of alternative educational sites for students charged with certain disciplinary offenses in New York, and probationary schools for youth barred from regular high schools on release from incarceration in Philadelphia, are two such examples. Some of these intermediary institutions are private ventures, thus carrying out dual functions—educational exclusion and capitalist expansion. Intermediary institutions serve to solidify the connection between schools and prisons, creating a more totalizing system of control.

We are arguing, then, that although urban public schools have long been used, at least in part, to control the "dangerous classes," this historically repressive element of schools—that serves to physically contain and direct students' bodies—has now been for all intents and purposes "merged" with the criminal justice system.

Here, we have been most concerned with the atmosphere within those schools that have become prisonized—many of which were the large comprehensive high schools of a few decades ago from which each year cadres of workers would flow.

Willis's Model of Cultural Reproduction

One of Willis's most significant contributions to radical educational theory, his attention to the cultural level, is essential to an analysis of schooling today. Willis does not explicitly address the repressive elements of schooling; instead, his framework is consistent with the notion that schools are ideological institutions that serve to justify their own existence through a discourse of social mobility. However, his focus on the everyday lives and the cultural practices of youth can help to illuminate the repressive function of schooling we have been describing. Although schools today still maintain ideological functions, the everyday interactions between school officials and working-class students of color belong in the repressive realm. Bringing in security guards to handle disruptive behavior, walking through metal detectors, and police escorts of truant students to the principal's office are interactions that, in part, define many urban public schools today, and these daily events express the repressive nature of schools, not their ideological role.

Indeed, a new school culture has emerges in urban schools with a police presence, high-tech security apparatus, and zero-tolerance policies. Students become used to procedures like hallway sweeps, book-bag and locker searches, "pat down" and frisks, that treat them like criminals (McCormick, 2000). Prison metaphors used by teachers, administrators, and even students characterize a significant portion of the dialogue: "Students are on 'lockdown'" and "That one [referring to a third grade student] has a cell at Rikers with his name on it" (Nolan, unpublished research in progress).

Moreover, ongoing research by Kathleen Nolan indicates that some students, particularly the most marginalized ones who may already have experience in the criminal justice system, typically see little difference between prison and school. They describe both places as hostile environments where students gain nothing and teachers most often misunderstand them. The significant difference between school and prison for these youths are that they are able to leave the school building at 3:00 p.m., whereas in prison it is "24/7." In these ways, in this educational context, urban students are "learning to do time."

Willis's model of cultural reproduction—as it moves the theoretical lens onto the everyday cultural practices of youth—also offers a framework for understanding young people's own role in reproduction of their class positions. Like Willis's lads, many working class students of color, as we have mentioned, understand schools as out of touch with their lived experiences and irrelevant to their future lives. Nolan (ongoing research) has found, particularly as high-stakes tests such as the New York State Regents exams drive curriculum, that many working class students are dreadfully bored. Often at the mere mention of the exams, students' heads drop to their desks as they grumble their objections.

Sometimes, the students with the strongest critiques choose to dropout (Fine, 1991). At other times, students remain in school and find ways to cope. Like Willis's lads, many of our students attempt to win space from school and its rules by "having a laff." "Having a laff" can take on particular importance for today's students who find school not only irrelevant but hostile and prisonlike. So students find creative ways to interrupt the humdrum of exam preparation by telling jokes, cutting or walking out of class to roam the hallways, or passing around notes or magazines whose content is far more interesting to students than the drone of their teachers. Willis posits that the purpose of having a laff is to beat boredom and fear and overcome hardships, and we would argue that many of today's working-class youth of color, in the context of high-stakes testing, dismal employment prospects, and street violence, experience levels of boredom, fear, and hardship that far surpass the levels experienced by the lads.

Unfortunately, "having a laff" in an urban fortress such as a large comprehensive urban high school can get students labeled as troublemakers and send them down a slippery slope. This occurs when students engage in destructive pranks such as throwing other students' belongings out the window, as well as when students do something as minor as disrupt the teacher with an inappropriate comment. It is the school's overreaction to these minor offenses—often calling in the police—that has served to criminalize whole school populations. Thus it is that low-income students of color who engage in oppositional behavior—no matter how insignificant—

participate in the reproduction of themselves not as workers but as a probable criminalized class, subject to the possibility of incarceration and the exclusion from civilian jobs.

Willis notes that "having a laff" is not always an effective method of conquering boredom; violence, on the other hand, is the "ultimate way of breaking a flow of meanings" (p. 34). He posits that violence regulates a kind of honor among working-class youth, and is "the fullest if unspecified commitment to a blind or distorted form of revolt" (p. 34). Although violence has taken on quantitatively and qualitatively new forms in many urban American schools, the notion of violence as a means of claiming honor and a form of resistance is still prevalent in the more critical literature on school violence today (Dance, 2002; Giroux, 1983).

Indeed, in recent years, a growing number of ethnographies have been motivated by Willis's work, providing new analyses of students' oppositional behavior, school violence, and discipline in current U.S. circumstances. One such ethnography is *Tough Fronts* by Janelle Dance (2002). According to Dance, young African American boys and other youth of color who are not involved in illegal behavior often assume "tough fronts" anyway, as a temporary strategy for surviving the streets.

Postures of toughness assumed in the streets are then brought into schools—both for protection against peers and as a form of resistance to schooling. School officials and law enforcement agents may misinterpret tough fronts and engage youth as if they were troublemakers or criminals, excluding them from opportunities to enhance their academic performance (Dance) and often setting them on a track toward the criminal justice system.

In Dance's analysis, the image of the low-income urban Black male as tough "emanates from both mainstream society and the streets" (p. 5). Put another way, she argued that as low-income Black youth are bombarded with oppressive stereotypes of themselves as gangsters, some youth come to perceive themselves as tough, or in need of becoming tough, and assume gangsterlike postures—ultimately participating in their own alienation from the dominant school culture. Like Willis's work, then, Dance's ethnographic research illustrates the interplay between social structural forces and students' agency.

Dance's analysis, however, also reminds us that despite the significance of students' role in social reproduction, disruptive behavior and criminal activity are not necessary ingredients in the exclusion of working-class youth of color from educational opportunity and jobs. As Dance pointed out, the vast majority of working-class students of color are not violent. And students who do not appear tough—those with more academic demeanors—can be criminalized by school personnel. Just as Willis's lads demonstrated group solidarity through clothing choices, language use, and other cultural expressions, working-class youth of color today have also formed a collective identity, and, like oppositional behavior and "tough fronts," the cultural expressions of working-class youth of color, no matter how innocuous, have been associated with criminal behavior by people who are part of the dominant culture. A young Black man—even a studious one—who chooses to wear baggy jeans and a do-rag is often immediately perceived by teachers, prospective employers, or a police officer as a gang member or a drug dealer, thus—by his own manner of dress—participating in his exclusion from educational and employment opportunities.

There are also significant differences worth noting between Willis's and Dance's work. First, unlike Willis's lads, the working-class Black youths in Dance's study do have mainstream American dreams and aspirations, and she argues that counterschool cultural exploits are not linked to pride in working-class heritage as much as they are to the desire to maintain peer respect.

Second, although Dance emphasized structural forces and students' agency in her analysis, her major policy recommendation is a call for "down" teachers, that is, teachers who understand or are willing to learn about the pressures of street culture and do not devalue "the cultural assets necessary for surviving urban streets" (p. 145). Willis, on the other hand, is concerned with economic structures, students' agency and their own role in reproduction, and the possibility agency implies for resistance. Thus, his analysis does not lead to specific school-based policy recommendations, but instead suggests the importance of the political organization of the working class.

Another recent ethnography that examines the culture of working-class youth of color, as well as school violence and discipline, is John Devine's *Maximum Security* (1996). Although Dance focused on the fact that the majority of students who choose to assume gangsterlike postures are not criminals, John Devine, in his ethnography, emphasized the very real violence and criminal behavior that spills into schools from the streets. In fact, Devine critiqued Willis for framing violence as a form of resistance that can be characterized as "boisterous merry-making" during which no one actually gets hurt and no blood is ever shed (p. 139). He went on to argue that Willis fails to appreciate that street culture in school "possesses its own (de)formative power that is capable of transforming the student into an instrument of violence" (pp. 139–140).

Although Devine demonstrates great insight into the level to which street violence has escalated in some schools and the school's role in exacerbating violence, he neglects to acknowledge that Willis's study was conducted in a very different social and economic context. Perhaps Willis simply did not find the same level and forms of violence that Devine and his research assistants documented in an urban public high school in the United States in the early 1990s. Moreover, the acts of violence Willis describes did not typically lead a young person into incarceration as they so often do today.

Nevertheless, Devine's analysis is not completely inconsistent with Willis's, and in fact, he owes much to Willis's framework. That is, although Devine does not view violence as a form of resistance in the same way Willis does, his analysis remains on the cultural level and points to the students' role in social reproduction.

Thus, we argue that Devine's and Dance's books, along with other such books, owe a great deal to Willis's work, yet within the new economic, social, and cultural context, these books offer their own updated, or at least somewhat revised, analyses of oppositional behavior, violence, and resistance.

Up to this point, we have emphasized structural determinants and the interplay between institutional practices and students' own behavior in the production of a criminalized class. However, we would be remiss not to refer to the possibilities that Willis's model of cultural reproduction offers us. In an era marked by the unmitigated use of physical control, staggeringly high unemployment rates, deteriorated material conditions for people of color, and media representation of youth of color as criminals, rap and Hip Hop music, which more than anything else have helped to shape the new Black youth culture (Kitwana, 2002), offer a context within which creative identities and social critique can develop. For example, we see young people using Hip Hop texts and rap music "to construct locally validated selves and senses of community" (Dimitriadis, 2001, p. 5). In other words, young people are using rap in creative ways, to define themselves and make meaning of their worlds. This helps them cope with their difficult material conditions and provides a forum for the development of social critique. For example, although not without serious contradictions, rap music is replete with social commentaries on the irrelevance of schools and police brutality. This focus on the cultural productions of youth and their creative uses challenges nihilistic and fatalistic depictions of working-class Black youth and, as Willis suggests, points to the possibility of resistance.

Bakari Kitwana moves beyond an analysis of the cultural productions of Black youth and other youth of color to examine the activism of what he calls the "Hip Hop generation." He argues that there are some significant differences between the activism of the civil rights generation and the activism of today's youth, which finds its form within the postindustrial context we have described. That is, youth in general and Black working-class youth specifically lack the mass political movement that characterized their parents' activism. Instead, they tend to organize themselves on smaller scales around single issues that are indicative of today's political and economic reality—police brutality, the death penalty, college tuition hikes, and mandatory minimum sentencing, to name a few.

Although these single-issue movements are not often rooted in a broader radical agenda, they certainly cannot be overlooked for their radicalizing potential. Although the insights of today's working-class youth of color, like Willis's lads, are often partial and do not constitute a collective working-class consciousness leading to (radical) political action, some working-class youth of color today, particularly ones with experience in the criminal justice system, may be closer than ever to the articulation of a radical social critique and political action. Young people in organizations such as Youth Force or the Prison Moratorium Project often appear to understand the connections between the increased investment in prisons, defunded urban schools, and staggeringly high unemployment rates in communities of color. And as working-class youth of color continue to experience both the exclusion from economic and educational opportunities and the heavy weight of the repressive hand of the state, there is perhaps an even greater chance that the cultural penetrations of youth will lead to a critical class (and race) consciousness and political action than Willis had ever imagined for his lads.

References

Althusser, L. (1971). *Lenin and philosophy.* New York: Monthly Press Review.

Anyon, J. (1997). *Ghetto schooling: A political economy of urban educational reform.* New York: Teachers College Press.

Anyon, J. (1980). Social class and the hidden curriculum of work. *Journal of Education, 162,* 67–92.

Anyon, J. (forthcoming). *Social policy, urban education, and a new civil rights movement.* New York: Teachers College Press.

Apple, M. (1995). *Education and power.* New York: Routledge.

Apple, M. (2001). *Educating the "right way": Markets, standards, god, and inequality.* New York: Routledge Falmer.

Bourdieu, P., & Passeron, J. C. (1977). *Reproduction in education, society and culture.* Beverly Hills, CA: Sage.

Bowles, S., & Gintis, H. (1976). *Schooling in capitalist America: Educational reform and the contradictions of economic life.* New York: Basic Books.

Coalition for Juvenile Justice. (2001). *Abandoned in the back row: New lessons in education and delinquency prevention.* CJJ 2001 Annual Report. Washington DC.

Dance, L. J. (2002). *Tough fronts: The impact of street culture on schooling.* New York: Routledge Falmer.

Devine, J. (1996). *Maximum security: The culture of violence in inner-city schools.* Chicago: University of Chicago Press.

Dimitriadis, G. (2001). *Performing identity/ performing culture: Hip hop as text, pedagogy, and lived practice.* New York: Peter Lang.

Dorfman, L., & Shiraldi, V. (2001, April). Off balance: Youth, race, and crime in the news. *Building Blocks for Youth.* Washington, DC: Justice Policy Institute.

Ferguson, A. A. (2001). *Bad boys: Public schools in the making of Black masculinity.* Ann Arbor: University of Michigan Press.

Fine, M. (1991). *Framing dropouts: Notes on the politics of an urban public high school.* Albany: State University of New York Press.

Garland, D. (2001). *The culture of control: Crime and social order in contemporary society.* Chicago: University of Chicago Press.

Gilmore, R. W. (1998). Globalisation and U.S. prison growth: from military Keynesianism to post-Keynesian militarism. *Race and Class, 40,* 2–3.

Giroux, H. (1983). *Theory and resistance in education: A pedagogy for the opposition.* South Hadley, MA: Bergin and Garvey.

House, E. R. (1998). *Schools for sale: Why free market policies won't improve America's schools and what will.* New York: Teachers College Press.

Jargowsky, P. A. (1998). *Poverty and place: Ghettos, barrios, and the American city.* New York: Russell Sage Foundation.

Justice Policy Institute. (2000, August). *Cellblocks or classrooms? The funding of higher education and corrections and its impact on African American men.* Washington, DC: Author.

Kitwana, B. (2002). *The Hip Hop generation: Young Blacks and the crisis in African-American culture.* New York: BasicCivitas Books.

Lipman, P. (2001). Bush's education plan, globalization, and the politics of race. *Cultural Logic: An Electronic Journal of Marxist Theory and Practice, 4*(1). Available online at http://eserver.org/clogic/4–1/lipman.html.

Lipman, P. (2002). Making the global city, making inequality: The political economy and cultural politics of Chicago School Policy. *American Educational Research Journal, 39*(2).

Mauer, M. (1999). *Race to incarcerate: The sentencing project.* New York: New Press.

McCarthy, J. D., & Hoge, D. R. (1987). The social construction of school punishment: Racial disadvantage out of the universalistic process. *Social Forces, 65,* 1101–1120.

McCormick, J. (2000). Aesthetic safety zones: Surveillance and sanctuary in poetry by young women. In L. Weis & M. Fine (Eds.), *Construction sites: Excavating race, class, and gender among urban youth* (pp. 180–195). New York: Teachers College Press.

McNeil, L. (2000). *Contradictions of school reform: Educational costs of standardized testing.* New York: Routledge.

Murray, C. (1984). *Losing ground: American social policy, 1950–1980.* New York: Basic Books.

Parenti, C. (2000). *Lockdown America: Police and prisons in the age of crisis.* New York: Verso.

Poe-Yamagata, E., & Jones, M. (2000, October). *And justice for some.* Building Blocks for Youth Initiative. Washington, DC: Justice Policy Institute.

Sassen, S. (1998). *Globalization and its discontents.* New York: New Press.

Sassen, S. (2001). *The global city: New York, London, Tokyo* (2nd Ed.). Princeton, NJ: Princeton University Press.

Skiba, R., Michael, R., & Nardo, A. C. (2000, June). *The color of discipline: Sources of racial and gender disproportionality in school punishment* (Report No. SR1). Research Policy Report.

Tonry, M. (1999, October). Why are U.S. Incarceration rates so high? *Crime and Delinquency, 45*(4).

Wacquant, L. (2001). Deadly symbiosis: When ghetto and prison meet and mesh. *Punishment and Society, 3*(1), 95–134.

Wacquant, L. (2002, January/February). From slavery to mass incarceration: Rethinking the "race question" in the United States. *The New Left Review, 13,* 41–60.

Willis, P. (1977). *Learning to labour: How working class kids get working class jobs.* New York: Columbia University Press.

Wilson, W. J. (1996). *When work disappears: The world of the new urban poor.* New York: Knopf Books.

Zimring, F. (2001, March). The new politics of criminal justice: Of "three strikes," truth in sentencing, and Megan's Laws. *Perspectives on Crime and Justice: 1999–2000 Lecture Series.* NCJ 184245. Washington, DC: National Institute of Justice.

CHAPTER 9

Thinking About the Cultural Studies of Education in a Time of Recession
Learning to Labor *and the Work of Aesthetics in Modern Life*

CAMERON McCARTHY

> What strikes me is the fact that in our society, art has become
> something which is related only to objects and not to individuals
> or to life. . . . But couldn't everyone's life become a work of art?
> (Michel Foucault, quoted in Sarup, 1996, p. 87)

In this essay I call attention to a specific thematic dimension of the concep-
tualization of work and reproduction in modern life raised (but also
repressed) in Paul Willis's germinal ethnography *Learning to Labor,* (first
published as *Learning to Labour,* 1977) and in the cultural studies of education research literature that Willis's now legendary volume precipitated.
This aspect of work and reproduction concerns the role of the imagination
and aesthetics in critical cultural and economic processes central to modern
existence: that is, the mobilization and organization of capitalism and its
late-20th century and new millennial global transformations, as well as the
historically variable counterhegemonic response of the working-class poor
of both the metropole and the periphery to these developments. This essay
engages Willis's *Learning to Labor* as a critical point of departure for
thinking about the work of aesthetics in the fates and fortunes of the
marginalized proletariat in the peripheries of the First and the Third

151

Worlds.

Indeed, nowadays, when I think of *Learning to Labor*, I cannot help thinking of the rising tide of denunciations of cultural studies both from the Left and the Right, particularly Judith Williamson's extraordinarily blunt rejection of "Left-wing academics picking out strands of subversion in every piece of pop culture from Street Style to Soap Opera" (Williamson, 1986, pp. 14–15). Of course, the radical academic world is saturated with bad-faith punditry, soothsaying, and the empiricist declarations of Cassandras. As, perhaps, a compensatory reflex, we are genre prone. No sooner is a new theoretical line of inquiry announced than a whole new congregation gathers, a field of affiliation is declared, even as its enemies, theorists on the other side, gather, lying in wait in the shadows. Well, the end is always near, at the closest "post." Reading/writing/researching radicals live precarious lives, and so forth. But there is something nagging in Williamson's statement; it concerns the attack on texts and textualism, the opposition of that fatal couplet "text" versus "experience," and the attendant cynicism about the politics of everyday life and popular investments in taste and style. These are all issues that are raised directly or obliquely in Willis's work, particularly his recent *The Ethnographic Imagination* (2000).

It is therefore not my purpose to defend cultural studies on these grounds here. I do, however, want to take up the matter of aesthetics, not simply in terms of the narrow scenario of what its conceptual status or place might be vis-à-vis the economic and so forth. Neither, certainly, am I speaking of aesthetics as elite or maverick practices of creativity, refinement, or taste. What I wish to discuss is something else altogether. I want to talk about a central energy in modern life associated with the production, reception, and circulation of representations and images and the diffusion of knowledge and information. I want to talk about the rising importance of the materiality of immateriality. I want to speak about the centrality rather than marginality of the diffusion of practices of self–fashioning in life sustaining processes and objectives. I am speaking about the work of the imagination in ordinary life. Here imaginary practices are understood as social practices of meaning production in the context of modern life, defined as it is by time–space compression, disembeddedness, disjunctures, and radical flows consequent upon the intensification of globalization and the separation of culture from place (Giddens, 1990). The idea here is to link the aesthetics of existence to economy and power—to think of these dynamics, in the context of globalization, as coarticulated. I want to maintain that the worlds of the metonymic Pakis, Jamaicans, and the Lads—the working-class youth protagonists of *Learning to Labor*—are deeply related, integrated into the processes of globalization in which the work of the imagination plays a pivotal role, co-coordinating the fragments of the materials of everyday life, even in their industrial strength. I want to extend the discussion of aesthetics to speak of an anthropology of politics, pulling the whole ascetic firmament of Marxist politics down to the everyday.

Customarily, cultural studies and neo-Marxist scholars of education writing on urban life have tended to place aesthetics on the boundaries of critical practices, treating aesthetics as a surplus set of practices that could only be made fully relevant when added on to a more concentrated attention to economy and politics. I argue here against this tradition. Instead, I maintain that aesthetic practices now underwrite the fiber of everyday modern life. As Arjun Appadurai (1996) usefully pointed out in *Modernity at Large*, aesthetic practices are no longer to be simply understood as the practices exclusive to the artist, a maverick citizen creating images about the past, present, and the future of human existence. Rather, aesthetic practices are linked to the work of the imagination of ordinary people and connected even more earnestly to the work of capitalism and its organization and reorganization on a global scale. Contrary to the neo-Marxist thinking, aesthetic practices are at the epicenter of lived experience and commodified and institutional processes of modern societies. These practices of performing and shaping self and community are now broadly diffused throughout society. These practices provide the language of cultural translation and revivification of identities. And they cultivate, provoke, and register the turbulent rearticulation of difference and multiplicity in our age. Our lives are now (self-)governed in concert with massive processes of textual production and simulation associated with media and educational systems and other institutional apparatuses of the state and global capital. Theses processes work in tandem to produce technologies of truth and identification that serve to transform concrete individuals into cultural citizens whose lines of loyalty and affiliation now exceed the territory and social geography of the nation-state (Miller, 1998).

As C. L. R. James (1993) alerted us in *American Civilization*, popular aesthetic practices constitute a great window on contemporary life, revealing central societal contradictions, tensions, and discontinuities between the individual and community:

> To put it more harshly still, it is in the serious study of, above all, Charles Chaplin, Dick Tracy, Gasoline Alley, James Cagney, Edward G. Robinson, Rita Hayworth, Humphrey Bogart, genuinely popular novels like those of Frank Yerby (*Foxes of Harrow, The Golden Hawk, The Vixen, Pride's Castle*), men like David Selsnick, Cecil deMille, and Henry Luce, that you find the clearest ideological

expression of the sentiments and deepest feelings of the American people and a great window into the future of the modern world. This insight is *not* to be found in the works of T. S. Eliot, of Hemingway, of Joyce, of famous directors like John Ford or Rene Clair. (James, 1993, p. 119)

In the 20th century, modern aesthetic practices received their full amplification in popular forms of life—particularly in the emergence of television, film, radio, newspaper, and new genres of music like jazz—and not so much in the classical or establishment cultures that are now valorized in the selective tradition that informs the organization of aesthetic knowledge in schooling. Of course, postcolonial intellectuals have been making this argument for sometime. This, after all, was the burden of the Latin American and Caribbean writers' forum of Intellectual and Cultural Workers (George Lamming, Gabriel Garcia Marquez, and others) who had very publicly opposed the Reagan government invasion of Grenada in 1983. They insisted, as did Arnaldo Roche-Rabell of Puerto Rico, that aesthetics were imbricated in economy and politics and that artistic militancy is critical to production of democracy (Roche-Rabell, 1996). This, too, is the critique of Reinaldo Arenas of the excesses of communist government in Cuba in the film *Before the Night Falls* (2000). The work of aesthetics is crucial to any formula for democratic transformation, as Derek Walcott maintains in "What the Twilight Says" (1970).

I want to speak on these matters, not from the heroic status and point of view of the Lads, but from the perspective of the, perhaps, antiheroic, postcolonial subjects—the West Indians and Asians, the metonymic "Pakis" and "Jamaicans," the petrified Third World spectators of metropolitan subcultural lore—witnesses to the birthing of the White working class into the modern industrial society as bricoleurs, flaneurs, and the like.

First, I want to discuss the entanglement of aesthetic discourses in the diffusion of modernization and developmentalism to the Third World. Second, I want to point as well to the deepening role of aesthetics in the organization of capitalism in the new millennium in which we live. Third, I discuss briefly the crisis of language that the aestheticization of everyday life has precipitated in neo-Marxist efforts to grasp the central dynamics of contemporary societies. The latter development has led to a depreciation of the value and insightfulness of neo-Marxist analysis in our time. We live in an era in which old metaphors associated with Marxism—concepts such as "class," "economy," "state," "production," "reproduction," "resistance," "the labor/capital contradiction," "reality" and "fiction," "ideology" versus "truth," "materiality" and "immateriality"—are being worn down by the transformations of the past decades in which the saturation of economic and political practices in aesthetic mediations has proceeded full pace (Klein, 2000). Let me now turn to a discussion of the historical context of the integration of aesthetics into commerce.

The Marriage of Aesthetics and Economy

The long shadow of the integration of aesthetics and economics in the elaboration of the capitalist order can be tracked back to before the turn of the 20th century in the production of new markets for the ever-expanding range of capitalist goods and services and the generation of consumer durables. These "luxuries" of personal style were in their everyday utility, if not necessity, expanding middle-class consumption patterns to the working class. A growing market in cheap *luxury* items allowed others (the lower and working classes) to purchase the symbolic accoutrements of status (Ewen, 1988, p. 59). Within this set of developments, deepening patterns of aestheticization of advertising, the imbuement of commercial products with sensuality, flair, and feeling, and so forth generated a leveling effect in the processes of class representation and helped to transform agrarian and immigrant actors into the new acquisitive urban subjects. The working class could try on the uniforms of the upper classes, explore their ways of life through the illumination of bric-a-brac, and, through consumer credit and loans, acquire the imitation furniture, jewelry, and items of leisure that mirrored aristocratic existence. Aesthetic practices integrated into economic form were now performing the pedagogy of molding the new subjectivities of the modern age—less in collision with capital in the classical 19th-century sense identified by Friedrich Engels in *The Condition of the Working Class in England* (1845/1987) but more in the besotted communion with the spectacular array of consumer products capitalism had strewn in their wake. "Progress," the narrative of one's life trajectories and imagined futures of linear accumulation, would now be marked by the range and capacity of one's consumption. To be a true citizen in the modern society was to be a dedicated consumer.

This model of progress, proletarianized and internationalized by the middle of the 20th century, would be taken full scale to underdeveloped countries around the globe, embodied in Coke and Pepsi ads, the family-size Coca Cola drink, the cultural translation performed by the films, musicals, popular songs, and so on that entered the Third World through cinema houses, and especially radio and newspaper, cartoons, and the lure of the new sleek-looking surfaces of the consumer durables and household appliances. Here, retail and hire purchase practices of the lower orders summarized the needs of the masses for something more than material want. These practices of borrowing today and paying tomorrow underlined a fueled working-class interest in comparative affluence, taste, and leisure— a desire to expand and materialize freedom by codifying taste and style and by integrating the aesthetic and erotic, leisure and pleasure practices into their rigorously subordinated lives defined by industrial parks and in agrarian obligation.

Musicals such as *The King and I* (1956) and *The Sound of Music* (1965) and soap operas such as *Portia Faces Life* (a radio soap opera that was started in 1940s and later taken up for television broadcasting by CBS in the 1950s) offered aesthetic solutions to the problems of necessity and want in the Third World. These popular cultural productions propagated ideas such as the inviolability of contract and the value equivalence involved in the process of exchange of labor power for wages. They extended a shimmering imaginary plane of existence linking the metropolis to the periphery latent with needs and saturated with unfulfilled desires. These aesthetic works suggested that Third World life, linked to tradition and agrarian organization and imagination, was flawed, oppressive, backward (a neo-Marxist claim as well!). This type of enlightenment narrative was propagated, for example, in highly popularized musicals such as the *The King and I*. Circulated through radio and television, *The King and I* made popular the modernization dilemma of the old traditions of Siam (what is now Thailand) versus the suppressed wish fulfillment of Siam's people, particularly their capacity for individual action and choice. *The King and I* ultimately set the capriciousness of the absolutist state against the visions of constitutional democratic nation-state. The way out of cultural miasma and backwardness to enlightenment was provided in the person of an English schoolteacher, Anna, who would carry out the work of cultural incorporation and translation. The cultural and philosophical forms of modernization—the right to private property, the capacity of the workers to sell their labor power, and the deification of Western democratic traditions—are all underscored in this musical in which a half-naked king, with Anna's help, must reconstitute his relations to his subjects and retool himself as a comprador agent of capitalism's expansion in southeast Asia.

The aestheticization of the economic—capitalism with a human face— sold the Third World on the modernization theories of Western policy intellectuals such as Daniel Lerner, Harold Lasswell, and William W. Rustow. The "passing of traditional society," as Lerner (1958) called it, involved that fearful asymmetry of contractual agreement to exploitation and excavation of the resources of the native and her land, along with state-enforced guarantee of the privileged status of the right to private property that multinationals and mercantile local elites so intensely craved. The development gap between the Third World and the First could be jumped by the expansion of the consumerist culture of possessive individualism and the infrastructure of industrialized production to "overseas" territories. Just as new streets were being paved for industrialization by invitation in Puerto Rico and Barbados, the sweet middle-class life of the "Brady Bunch" and later the "Partridge Family" presented itself through television as the embodiment of the one and only true heaven, as the buoyant end game in the struggle for happiness (Lasch, 1991). Why couldn't a woman be more like a man (*My Fair Lady*, 1964)? Why couldn't we Third World Siams be more like the enlightened West?

It was, in part, this logic of modernization, the embeddedness of the developmentalist project, the dream of plenitude and progress, the work of the imagination of ordinary Third World people that delivered the Pakis and the Jamaicans to the land of the Lads in pursuit of the Holy Grail of the better life and the material rewards of capitalism. What we confront in the ocular opposition of the immigrant other to the Lads in *Learning to Labor* is this abridgement of a continuous line or movement of disembeddedness, displacement, and transformation in an imaginative and spatial geography that extends the aspirations of the Jamaicans, the West Indians, the Pakis, the Indians and Bangladeshis from the periphery to beachheads in Brixton and Manchester, and elsewhere in England. The full significance of what this movement would mean in the changing terms of globalization was indeed far more fully recognized in the popular films *The Full Monty* (1997) and *Billy Eliot* (2000). To understand these dynamics more clearly, we must now turn to a consideration of the role of aesthetics in everyday life.

Aesthetics and Everyday Life

The role of aesthetics in everyday life has deepened in the last few decades with the rising importance of computerization and media-driven technologies. The work of aesthetics is not simply now embodied in the selling of messages and images but in the very construction of products and constituencies of affiliation in the new millennium. It is that whole area of stylization of the self, self-regulation, surveillance, and the self-management of everyday life, that Foucault discusses in his *History of Sexuality* volumes. But the processes of aestheticization also reach deeper into the marketing and circulation of goods and services, the proliferation of labels and the redirection of difference and diversity towards the new vending machines of choice. As the author of *No Logo* (2000) Naomi Klein insisted, it is the aesthetics of entrepreneurial identities and labels, logos and brands, that has displaced the manufacture of products as the heart and soul of what makes post-Fordist capitalism tick:

> The astronomical growth in the wealth and cultural influence of
> multinational corporations over the last fifteen years can arguably
> be traced back to a single, seemingly innocuous idea developed by
> management theorists in the mid-1980s: that successful corpora-
> tions must primarily produce brands, not products. (Klein, 2000,
> p. 3)

Everywhere, smart capital is running away from the materialization of
dense product inventories, costly overheads, and static models of factory
organization, and opting instead for the cultivation of new bonds of
consumer affiliation and labeling, relying on the faithful consumer to spawn
markets by parading the labels of branded distinction in their natural habi-
tats. The consumer's body has become the canvas of commodity fetishism.
And it is in this framework of cultural oversupply that the modern
consumer tries on new identities and directs and redirects practices of self-
correction and self-modulation. Transnational corporations such as
Starbucks, Borders, and Nike now brand new ecumenical communities with
their labels, like so many tattoos on the social/global body. And so, ethnic,
class, and gendered communities are now coalescing around practices of
consumption and patterns of taste rather than around production relations
or ancestry, or geography, or biology (Bourdieu, 1984; Dolby, 2001). The
language of the new aesthetically branded world now registers the new
ecumenical orders of feeling and the organization of affect and taste. As
Manuel Castells tells us in *The Rise of the Network Society* (2000), these
ecumenical orders overlap with the traditional collectivities of class or race
or gender, but in the most frenetic and unpredictable of ways. This new
aestheticism has generated a new cannibalism as the modern actor seeks
refuge in ever more savage intensities and hybridities. Attachments to
subject positions are now more precariously saturated. The old authentici-
ties of class and race rooted in place, ancestry, economy, and so forth have
been swept away by the new developments associated with electronic mediation, mass migration, and the rapid movement of economic and cultural
capital across borders.

This has meant, for example, the end of the auratic status of race. That is
to say, for instance, that the notion of race as residing in origins or in
"biological" or "cultural" unity has been broken, overwhelmed by the
immense processes of hybridity unleashed in contemporary life. These
processes of migration, electronic mediation, and globalization have had the
effect of separating culture from place. Difference has therefore become an
abstract value that can be dirempted from specific ("authentic") groups and

settings in ways that combine and recombine, narrate and renarrate cultural forms and passionate attachments. For example, clothing designer magnates like Tommy Hilfiger, drawing on the critical disciplinary expertise in demography, ethnography, semiotics, social psychology, art, and design, now appropriate elements of, say, inner-city Hip Hop culture and style, reordering and infusing these styles into a broad-banded appeal to a new ecumenical community of hip youth from a wide array of class and ethnic backgrounds. In the process, Hilfiger shamelessly sells a version of the inner city back to the inner city itself. Aestheticization breaks down the symbolic realms of insulation separating Black youth from White ones and so forth, cracking the codes of youth desires and elaborating a new community of Pepsi drinkers, Gap hipsters, and Nike shoe devotees among a wide array of ethnic cross-dressers. These new ecumenical communities are themselves dynamic and unstable, constantly changing as new aesthetic resources, systems of ready-made representation, and over-the-counter personas can now be used to generate very new and different genres and lines of affiliation. We are living in a new context in which aestheticization as a strategy of existence has spread throughout the body politic. One in which the oblique powers of capital and the state work toward the reordering of identities, uprooting stabilities associated with the labor process as well as private and public spaces beyond the shop floor. Capitalists, and some right-wing strategists, may now understand these logics of multiplicity better than the Left, deploying multiculturalism and integrating difference into the division of labor and the labor process at warped speed and appropriating new sources of value from the Lads and their adversaries in new asymmetries and alliances of production and consumption. W. E. B. Dubois's psychological wage is now spread around the world, indexing ever new avenues of difference and intraclass subordination in the stratification of taste and culture among the lowest of the low. All of this has placed a special interpretive strain and test of relevance on the analytical powers of neo-Marxist scholarship in education.

Neo-Marxist Scholarship and the Shifting Terrain

This shifting terrain of identity and affiliation has overtaken neo-Marxist scholarship in education. Categories and metaphors that had been relied on in the past to unscramble social relations and dynamics now seem challenged by the new circumstances of contemporary education, work, and leisure. The formation of interests, distinctions, needs, and desires seems now to be so susceptible to an endless array of permutations. The framework of analysis that linked education to capitalist employers, to factories, to the nation-state, and so forth is no longer serviceable, as the coordination of economic and symbolic production is now rearticulated along multiple sites in a global process of marketing, branding, and outsourcing of goods and services. Much of the limitation of contemporary neo-Marxist discourses in addressing the dynamic movement of cultural and economic capital today has to do with a tendency toward a residual structuralist realism that both reifies and privileges notions of an authentic working class, a territorially bounded nation-state and an economy understood in terms of the language of commodity production and accumulation. What these theorists need to recognize, as Naomi Klein (2000) suggested, are the new trends that point to a deepening reorganization of capital. Within these developments, symbolic mobilization is now an ascendant practice. Capitalist industries are divesting in inventories of commodities and investing in cultivating label affiliation, brand loyalty, and esprit de corps among the consuming population. Style and taste are now driving the economic as ecumenical communities are fabricated in the uniforms of Nike or Gap or Hilfiger. It is the royal consumer whose newly dressed body serves as a mobile billboard for the corporate enterprise of Nike, Starbucks, Borders, Adidas, and others. The new consumer is the new citizen, whose aesthetics of existence are now ever more deeply imbricated in a universalization of the entrepreneurial spirit and the propagation of the redemptive neoliberal value of choice. Nowhere do we see this cultural morphing of capital and the citizen more than in schooling. Students now approach their school and university curricula as the savvy consumer shopping for courses. And courses are weighted by educational administrations on the basis of their "drawing power"—the numbers of enrollees per class (Miyoshi, 1998).

We have reached a stage in this new millennium where the old "conflict" versus "consensus" metaphors do not seem to apply. Instead of models based on conflict and resistance, social groups are being increasingly defined by overwhelming patterns of transnational hybridities, new forms of association and affiliation that seem to flash on the surface of life rather than to plunge deeper down into some neo-Marxist substructure. Paul Willis's nationally and geographically inscribed Lads are now being replaced by Jenny Kelly's Afro-Canadian youth, who are patching together their identities from the surfeit of signs and symbols crossing the border in the electronic relays of U.S. television, popular music and cyber culture (Kelly, 2003). Postapartheid South African youth now assign more value to markers of taste—Levi and Gap jeans, Nikes or Adidas, rap or rave—than ancestry and place in their elaboration of the new criteria of ethnic affiliation (Dolby, 2001). All these developments are turning the old materialism versus idealism debate on its head. It is the frenetic application of forms of existence, forms of life, the dynamic circulation of and strategic deployment of style, the application of social aesthetics that now governs political rationalities and corporate mobilization in our times. The new representational technologies are the centers of public instruction providing the forum for the work of the imagination of the great masses of the people to order their pasts and present and plot their futures. The massive work of textual production is a socially extended project producing the cultural citizen in the new international division of labor.

Conclusion

Ultimately, then, the issues I am exploring here go beyond a consideration of *Learning to Labor*, they reach out into a new field of questions. How should we understand the dynamics affecting the separation of culture from place in modern life? How do we understand the heightened and intensifying role of aesthetics practices in the everyday lives and fortunes of people? How can we intervene in the ever-changing present? Some of the answers to these questions lie at the frontera of a negotiation of neo-Gramscian and Foucauldian perspectives on the work of culture in modern life and the expanding networks of knowledge and power that circulate in the new information technologies and their central involvement in popular identity formation, agency, and transgression. Here, too, the narrow nationalistic project that has defined cultural studies to this date needs a retooling in postcolonialism and transnationalism to remind us that the everyday lives and fortunes of people in the metropolitan center are now fully articulated to the peripheries of the modern world—Kingston to Brixton, Lahore to Oldham, Kabul to New York. I am framing my responses this way because I think we are confronting the way in which neo-Marxist, even cultural Marxist, scholarship has looked at questions of culture and power: that is, within the fatal couplets of base/superstructure or production/consumption. Within the latter frame of reference, aesthetics of everyday life always seem to be linked to "consumption" understood as a crass, unthinking activity. And consumption seems always to be doing the work of dissipating the agency and emancipatory promise of the oppressed. Even when neo-Marxists theorized consumption through notions of lived and commodified culture emphasizing "resistance," that resistance always seemed marginal or a poor substitute or proxy for production-driven politics. This is in part why the perpetrators of 9/11 surprised both the Left and the Right, organizing beneath our noses and rearticulating the tools, symbols, and technologies of the everyday with devastating effect: Box cutters, fax machines, crop dusters, tap water, commercial flights, a pair of fundamentalist shoes, matches, all now harbor new terrors and uncertainties, as Greg Dimitriadis and I have argued elsewhere (Dimitriadis & McCarthy, 2002). It reminds me of having conducted a war of maneuver with the Barbados health care system regarding my father's health care by phone, e-mail, and letters. Here, deploying the politics of diplomacy within my large family in getting decent care for 86-year-old Dad enlarged both my sense of family and my opposition to the Barbados bureaucracy.

Marxists have always advanced notions of resistance to power, notions of transformation, that involve a bulldozing masculinist logic that targets the state, the shop floor, and the commanding heights of capital as the indisputable markers of radical action. This is a model of change that projects onto the working class a status of folk other, the noble savage of rebellious middle-class fantasies of capturing power as an object of repression and seizure. This formula of change read from the economy onto culture and subculture ignores the enormous transitional costs that will be borne by the working class within this transformative regime. This model of politics and change speaks the language of vanguardism and edicts, assigning to the subaltern a very limited degree of reflexivity and creativity. I am arguing instead for the vital need to anthropologize Marxist politics as C. L. R. James suggested in his book *American Civilization* (1993).

Thinking about power in these terms involves thinking about change within the terms of modulation, rearticulating and redirecting the terms of the center–periphery thesis that dominates neo-Marxist optics on social formation toward envisioning the materialization of new communities and investment in the work of the imagination, working with and against constraint, in the struggle for happiness. Ultimately, then, the pursuit of aesthetics of everyday life calls our attention to latent possibilities in modern social spaces and points to the negotiation of constraint in modern life. It calls attention to the enormous pedagogical role that can and must be undertaken in the domain of the popular arts and textual production and within the field of the active imagination of the broad masses of the people across the divide of center and periphery.

References

Appadurai, A. (1996). *Modernity at large: The cultural dimensions of globalization*. Minneapolis: University of Minnesota Press.

Bourdieu, P. (1984). *Distinction*. Cambridge, MA: Harvard University Press.

Castells, M. (2000). *The rise of the network society* (2nd ed.). Oxford: Blackwell.

Dimitriadis, G., & McCarthy, C. (2002). Urban renewal: Gordon Bennett's *Notes to Basquiat* (9/11). In G. Bennett (Ed.), *Notes to Basquiat* (pp. 1–4). Adelaide, Australia: Greenaway Art Gallery.

Dolby, N. (2001).*Constructing race: Youth, identity, and popular culture in South Africa*. Albany, NY: SUNY Press.

Engels, F. (1987). *The condition of the working class in England*. London: Penguin. (Original work published 1845).

Ewen, S. (1988). *All consuming images*. New York: Basic Books.

Giddens, A. (1990). *The consequences of modernity*. Cambridge, UK: Polity Press.

James, C. L. R. (1993). *American civilization*. London: Blackwell.

Kelly, J. (2003). *Borrowed identities*. New York: Peter Lang.

Klein, N. (2000). *No logo*. London: Flamingo.

Lasch, C. (1991). *The true and only heaven: Progress and its critics*. New York: W. W. Norton.

Lerner, D. (1958). *The passing of traditional society: Modernizing the Middle East*. New York: Free Press.

Miller, T. (1998). *Technologies of truth*. Minneapolis: University of Minnesota Press.

Miyoshi, M. (1998). "Globalization," culture and the university. In F. Jameson & M. Miyoshi (Eds.), *The cultures of globalization* (pp. 247–272). Durham, NC: Duke University.

Roche-Rabell, A. (1996). Under a total eclipse of the sun. In R. Hobbs (Ed.), *Arnaldo Roche-Rabell—The uncommonwealth* (p. 44). Seattle: University of Washington Press.

Sarup, M. (1996). *Identity, culture and the postmodern world*. Athens: University of Georgia Press.

Walcott, D. (1970). What the twilight says. In D. Walcott (Ed.), *Dream on Monkey Mountain and other plays* (pp. 3–40). New York: Farrar, Straus and Giroux.

Williamson, J. (1986, September). The problems of being popular. *New Socialist*, pp. 14–15.

Willis, P. (1977). *Learning to labour*. Westmead: Saxon House.

Willis, P. (2000). *The ethnographic imagination*. Cambridge, UK: Polity Press.

Critical Ethnography, Culture, and Schooling:
Paul Willis reflects on *Learning to Labor*

CHAPTER 10

Twenty-Five Years On
Old Books, New Times

PAUL WILLIS

I owe many thanks to Nadine Dolby and Greg Dimitriadis, who spotted a couple of years ago the looming 25th anniversary of the publication of *Learning to Labor* and have put so much work, effort, and good will into organizing, editing, compiling, and publishing this excellent volume. Thank you! I cannot say that I had noticed the approach of this milestone[1] until Nadine sent me an email suggesting the possibility of the AERA panels. My immediate thought was, "Christ, we are ageing at the same pace, 25 years . . . what kind of an old codger does that make me?" But the idea was excellent. The panels gave me much food for thought, and I am delighted that this book sees the light of day with its many wonderful contributions from people whose work I have long admired or am happy to learn from now.

It has been something of a salutary experience, though, as well as a privilege, to focus on writing a response to the chapters of this volume and to try to survey 25 years of my own chaotic life as somehow "intellectual development." In a way, the book has led its own strange and often schizophrenic public life variously separate from my own private wanderings, which have included a long period away from academe in practical policy engagements (see Appendix). How could I make sense of the dizzying range of responses to the book over the last 25 years and relayed here now? What, anyway, was the purpose of such an exercise? In the event, rather than try to respond to individual positions or chapters, or to attempt thorough academic surveys (painstakingly accomplished any way in many of the chapters), or to attempt an implausible "developmental" periodization of my own life and times, I have plumbed for a very personal route of trying to reclaim, develop, and apply some of the themes and emphases of *Learning to Labor* that, at the risk of idiosyncracy and self-referentiality, seem to me as of most use for understanding the current conjuncture. In doing this I do not write within any one discipline—education, sociology, cultural studies, anthropology—but in a spirit of multi- or postdisciplinarity. This is essential, in my view, to the future of ethnography and its continued vigour. The journal, *Ethnography*,[2] that I jointly founded and jointly edit is also devoted to breaking down and transcending barriers between the disciplines, especially sociology and anthropology. It is focused on connecting and encouraging the work of ethnographers worldwide, no matter what their disciplinary homes.

Although I do not refer to them in detail, I have the chapters published here very much in my thoughts as I write, and have learned from them as well as finding constructive disagreements. Often, actually especially in disagreement, they have reminded me of what it is that I really want to communicate to a new generation of scholars. Nor do I pass up the opportunity of replying to critics more generally, not as a settling of accounts, names, chapters, verses, but in the spirit of more fully developing positions, which are of use, I hope, to future ethnographers. I have divided my comments into two basic sections; the first pursues a theoretical clarification of perspectives essential to the ethnographic enterprise, and the second is devoted to grappling with the complexities of the new situation, in many ways so profoundly changed since "back in the day" when I did the research for *Learning to Labor*.

I have not devoted a specific section to a discussion of the family of methods that constitute the practice of ethnography, but, in different ways, the whole piece is aimed at showing the irreplaceable importance of ethnography to understanding various dimensions of the new situation of crisis and epochal change effecting not only schooling but societies quite generally. Very much in mind I have the hope of encouraging researchers, Ph.D. students in particular from across the disciplines, to attempt the unnerving task of the ethnographic evocation of the experiences and cultures of others, so carrying on and enhancing a very important tradition. My comments are meant to give them heart and focus.

The Ethnographic Theoretical Sensibility

Cultures and Class: A Three-Stage Model

First of all, prefacing the complexity of the theoretical model I outline next, what I take from all of the chapters and very much roll forward from

Learning to Labor, what I ask all ethnographers to take renewed heart in, is the importance of the embattled term and concept of "culture." The more it is criticized, the more we need it. Why do we need this portmanteau term? Because it designates materially symbolic patterns and associated practices of human meaning making in context, which cannot be reduced to a reflex of something else—individual psychology, "discourses," or the economy. It is its own thing. In one way I am a simple empiricist: Write down what happens, take notes about what people do and say, how they use objects, artifacts, and symbolic forms in situ. Do not worry too much about the endless debates concerning ethnographic authority and the slippages of discursive meaning understood from an abstract post structuralism. Tell me something—I know all the method problems—tell me, tell your readers, something about the world. We launched the journal *Ethnography* in part addressed to an old-fashioned notion of ethnography and ethnographic articles having some empirical data in them, rather than endless method-ological discussions where we learn everything about the sacred bourgeois formation of the writer and nothing about the profane formation of the subject. I seem to hear subjects screaming silently from the margins of the page, "but what the hell about us?"

Since I wrote *Learning to Labor*, the importance of culture, understood as just outlined, has become even more important. No sociological, anthro-pological, educational, or cultural studies research project, no policy initiative can make sense without asking in some form or another: "What is the culture of the people with whom we are dealing?" "How do they make sense?" "How does the world look to them?" "What do they make of us looking at them?" So, culture is worth recording in its own right but, *pace* my apparent empiricism, enjoys a further purchase because it also is a theoret-ical site. If your problem is understanding the relation of structure and agency; if your problem is understanding new formations of the social order; if you are looking at the new social functions of schooling; if you are looking at reproduction, how classes get replaced over time; if you are looking at the formation of labor power, how the subjective capacities of individuals are formed up and applied to productive processes: All these things require a cultural moment and analysis. An ethnographic sensibility implies a theoretical sensitivity to the importance of culture and human experience in human affairs.

At the heart of the concerns of *Learning to Labor* and coming rapidly up the agenda again and what I would like to focus on specifically here is the complex theoretical relations of culture(s) to social class (see Nadine Dolby & Greg Dimitriadis's Introduction, the chapter by Michael Apple, and Peter McLaren & Valerie Scatamburlo-D'Annibale's chapter). All the preceding questions conceal associated questions of class: How are those without power taken up into positions where power is exercised over them? How do social agents "see" and embody the structured world of power, both resisting and reproducing it in complex ways. For me, these things are achieved in and through the radical unprefigurability of culture, which, because things are not fixed, also gives an option for politics and hopes for making a difference, for making it different next time. So for me, questions of culture and class and politics are inextricably interwoven.

That is saying a lot. Let us pause a little, take a good breath, and step back to unravel this complexity somewhat.

What do I mean more precisely by class and how it relates to culture? The issues are complex and it is necessary to play a little game, a three-stage construction in our thought processes. This is not to attempt to paint a picture of the world more accurately, explaining its workings better than others. It is to try to provide a glimpse of the kind of underscaffolding that might make for the possibility of better three-dimensional picture painting. Patience is required; the early stages of the construction are meant to be tools for thinking, not mighty foundations for a better model. The whole construction only has a hope of being put to work usefully when all stages are finally put together in their unified, interconnected, and therefore continuously interdependent and self-modifying operations.

Stage 1. For analytic purchase, the first theoretical construction, it is important to be able to locate certain "basic" class elements as being, so to speak, "precultural"—again, it must be stressed, not as putative reflections of the way "things really are" but as a provisional analytic device in thought. How can we think of a "precultural" world? For a moment let us exercise our imaginations, hit an imaginary button to freeze the world so that its complex and dialectical relations of parts, normally in ceaseless and relativised motion, are stopped in our thoughts. Let us begin to unpack the complexity by blowing up the frozen elements in a splay diagram. What are the elements in our blown up diagram that relate to class? We are ignoring, for a moment, all the "color de rose" of the individual participants: the colors, smells, and passions of their everyday practices and cultures. In the gray and economistic world that remains, *class* for me designates the *positions* of agents in groups and their *relationships* to each other in systematic groups. What separates the groups is the possession of power and/or capital. Working class subjects are in subordinate *positions*: They have no power and capital. Their *relationships* with those who do have power are ones of domination through the exercise of this power: crudely, being told what to do—most notably and importantly in production (the subsumption of labor power in capitalist labor processes overseen by owners or managers) but also across a wide swathe of institutions, educational ones not least, where some form of "necessity" (direction) reigns. This "economistic" or "precultural" level of analysis is necessary, although actually quite limited in its own terms (most of the "moving" picture of human affairs has been frozen), in order to guard against *everything* being elided into the notion of culture and its horizontal differences. For "culture" to be effective as a notion, to give it some "go" and to show the *social* work that it accomplishes, there must be some things that are "not culture"; this is actually to show precisely the *autonomy* of culture, that is, *the manner of its autonomy with respect to something else.* Of course I know that "in reality" culture not only conditions economic relations but actually dynamically and transformingly embody them to bring about a fully human living system—what happens when we finally hit the button to start everything moving again. But unless there is a moment in our analysis that separates larger forces and relations we are in danger of presenting a depthless view of the world, which is not saved by a radical patina added to cultural descriptions rhetorically invoking emancipation and liberation.

Stage 2. Still the economistic level of analysis *is* only of limited value. So let us hit our imaginary button again, the second stage, to set the working class agents in motion, holding the rest of the picture still frozen. Let us restore the color and irreducible humanness to subordinated and dominated groups and focus on what is specific about the *cultural* elements of our splay diagram. What I want to focus on here is the specificity of culture as the active process of "meaning-making" of social agents, their "making sense." But of what? Of many things possibly, but I would argue in particular of their economic *positions* and *relationships*.[3] At least in part, cultural practices are about forging viable identities and strategies for human dignity, development, and becoming in relationship to and through their conditions of existence, in so doing at their own level making sense of economistic *positions* and *relations*[4] (so renewing them, changed, in their always already-ness). But these practices do not operate in the abstract or conjure up meanings from thin air. They need symbolic materials; the processes and activities do not proceed only as electric currents within individual brains. There is a production process at the cultural level, a *cultural production*,[5] that you could say is similar to material production in the labor process whereby humans engage in sensuous practices working on raw materials to produce new or refashioned things fit for useful human purpose. In this case the "products" are meanings and expressions useful in themselves but also, in one way or another, useful for making sense of economistic *positions* and *relations*, those things first isolated in our splay diagram.

In trying to really focus on this *cultural production* of our second stage, comprehend the way in which it relates to the still frozen elements of structure, I find it useful to deploy, again, the notion of *penetration*. The cultural practices of *cultural production*, I argue, function to "penetrate" or "see into" their conditions of existence (*positions* and *relations*) as part of the cultural calibration of how identities and actions can be best developed in their light, the constraints and enablements they supply. I take forward from *Learning to Labor*, therefore, the notion of "penetration," after all these years still troublesome for its masculinist associations but, for lack of alternative, used again here and in my recent *The Ethnographic Imagination*. Especially in relation to the difficulties of setting aside its sexist connotations, I am grateful for Madeleine Arnot's clear exposition and treatment of the term in her chapter. The term tries to capture, at one moment of analysis, the impetus to reveal the structural elements on which cultures depend, their conditions of existence. These are the "insights" of embedded folk knowledges, of common sense, of what I have sometimes referred to as "grounded aesthetics." Lois Weis refers to it in her chapter as "critical moments of critique," Michael Apple as "good sense." The results of the *work* of cultural production can never be prefigured in advance.

Here is the radical source of the creativity and unprefigurability of cultural practices and forms. It is agents, not academics, who make the *penetrations*. So academics can never come up with fully adequate "outside" explanations. It is not possible in advance and from "objectivist" outside surveys of, or armchair theories about, the "determination" of structural forces or cultural systems to deduce the forms of these *penetrations*, either of what or how (both very possibly pointing toward "undiscovered" aspects of structure) they focus on or the lived forms of their embodiments and practices. Here is indicated, again, of course, the supreme importance of "being there," of ethnographic witness and an associated theoretical sensibility. Cultural forms are of intense interest for the postdisciplinary ethnographer not because they preserve a set of quaint customs and hypostasised self-maintaining values to be recorded for ethological and historical record but because they contain a certain cruciality in context, embedded and lived insights with respect to their own conditions of existence. To be interested in an ethnographic account of subculture, for instance, is to make some kind of an epistemological break. If you believed some kinds of Marxism or post-structuralism, you would not bother going to the field. If you believed institutional, ideological accounts of what kids do, you would not bother going to the field. If you were interested in "discourses" and their internal instabilities, you would not go to the field. The whole point of doing so is to try to understand how particular subjects are making sense of themselves and their situations in ways that cannot be prefigured and that might "surprise" you.[6] And that making sense must be of something, not of the moon, not of the stars, but of their daily life and the conditions of existence of their daily life, of their own situation and its possibilities. This is the very business of ethnography for me. What sense is this culture making of its situation? What sense are you making of that sense making, recognizing that there is a possibility of a break, a difference, a form of local knowledge, created by actors upon conditions of course but, nevertheless, never reducible to what is supplied from outside, ideologically. Through the mediations of the counterschool culture, "the lads" of *Learning to Labor*, for instance, *penetrate* the individualism and meritocracy of the school with a group logic that shows that certification and testing will never lift the whole working class, only inflate the currency of qualifications and legitimize middle-class privilege. They frame the giving of their labor power in wearing circumstances without "career" illusions, judging the minimum that is necessary, so avoiding the double indignity of living their practical subordination twice, once really and again in ideology. Cultural and psychic capacities so released are made available for other uses: fun, diversion, "having a laff."

The "raw materials" for processes of *cultural production* and their attendant *penetrations* come in a wide variety of forms, plastic, oral, textual, musical, and from a wide variety of sources, historical and contemporary, local and mediated, commoditized and non-commoditized. The textual "treasure troves" of history should not be underestimated, nor the funds of oral history and advice passed on from elders. Ideological accounts and texts also play a variable part. Many of the symbolic resources used in cultural production have not been named yet by social science classification but are the interstitial stuff of ethnographic accounts of real lives in progress. But the particular traditions and continuities provided by social inheritances in the well-trodden classifications of sex, gender, race, ethnicity, and age are of the most particular importance. They both organize other kinds of symbolic material and supply their own symbolic meanings.[7] Because they are subject to the work of *cultural production*, all of these resources can be made into new shapes and put into new articulations producing new hybrid forms. Again it is a supremely ethnographic question to ask how resources are combined, through what practices, for what purposes.

Stage 3. Let us come to the third and final stage of our mental constructions, hitting the button again to put structure and culture in dynamic and connected motion again. A further crucial point about the cultural level for me is that processes of "making sense" of structural location not only "reveal" aspects of them but also act to reproduce them in supplying the living, moving, embodied forms through which they (*positions* and *relations* structured according to power) are maintained and reproduced. In the case of "the lads," for instance, the forms in which their very penetrations were made also prepared them, ironically, for insertion into the lower orders of the economic structure. Although highly relevant in opposing and penetrating the demands of the school, the antimental animus of the counterschool culture also becomes a kind of second nature for "the lads" that continues to orient bodily style, attitudes, and values during the transition from school to work and long after. This pattern impels them toward a certain kind of culturally mediated and experiential form of meaning making throughout their lives. The danger is that this antimental attitude leads to the whole world being divided into two—the mental and the manual. It makes all jobs involving mental work, now and for the future, seem to be simply boring paperwork—"Who wants to spend their day pushing paper around?" This makes hope for a "second-chance" return to higher education much more difficult and unlikely. The lads' antimentalism reconciles them and those like them to manual work and often to job hopping between dead-end jobs—now interspersed with long spells of unemployment, or even permanent unemployment—for the rest of their lives.

Although the "precultural" relations of power may be profoundly modified by their cultural embodiment, they continue in some form within basic limits set by the necessary maintenance of basic *positions* and *relations*. They live again to structure the next round of human "meaning-making" which in turn helps to reproduce structural relations and positions, and so on and so on.[8] It is in this continuous dialectic of renewal and the reformation of the old (tout ça change, tout c'est la même chose) that social structures should be understood from an ethnographic point of view, leaving far behind the static "economistic" stage with which we started.[9] Key ethnographic questions, therefore, concern not only how far cultural practices "make sense" of structural location but also how far these same practices ironically contribute toward the maintenance through time of those very power relations and interests. These questions also raise in their train political questions of the broadest hue: In future circles of these mutual relations, how might the balance be switched more to the advantage of the dominated, and under what conditions might the *penetrations* of cultural production be turned into outright political opposition and radical interruption of the reproduction of inherited structural relations?

Theoretical Integrity in a Postdisciplinary World

Above all other methodologies, ethnography invites in a postdisciplinary perspective. Ethnographic data needs a dialectical relation to theory, broadly considered, in order to bring out its sinews in relation to urgent issues and nitty-gritty questions. We should be eclectic in considering the possible relevance of all theories. But even in a postdisciplinary world not *all* theories are equal with respect to the tasks and dilemmas of ethnography. Beware of ethnographers who never met a theory they did not like! What I want to say about *penetrations* and culture is not ecumenical, not infinitely plastic. There are positions, in my view, that are not compatible with an ethnographic view of culture as meaning making from below. I often feel that *Learning to Labor* and my work generally are pushed around rather too much, considered without respect to its context and ends, unfairly critiqued for not doing, and sometimes strangely praised for doing, what it cannot do and does not attempt.

This not the same thing as asking for disciplinary consistency. Often the same issues and difficulties are approached in similar or usefully complementary ways from quite different disciplines; often within the same discipline can be deeply contradictory perspectives. Perhaps ethnographic practice will lead the way to new formations of intellectual practice focused on coherency of approach, explanation, and object, rather than academic schools.

My position is that, in general, ethnography needs *generative* not outside explanatory theory (see Michael Apple's chapter). The tiresome debates between the "culturalists" and the "structuralists," between so-called populists and political economists, pivot not on whether the former are without theory but on the differences in type between their theories, implicit or explicit. Although I see it as important to include structural factors, along the lines just outlined, there is nevertheless a line of radical indeterminacy necessary to ethnographic perspectives. In ever-decreasing circles, structural and structuralist theoretical social scientists of one kind or another run themselves ragged trying to track down cascading chains of determination to explain the relations of all levels, often bracketing out all possibility of creativity at the "lowest" levels of their models. In so doing they produce, knowingly or not, "objectivist" and "outside" accounts, because any recognition by them of an indeterminate subjective element allowing elements of agentive choice, except as an illusion to be "explained," would defeat the purpose of prediction and explanation. Ethnography and qualitative work then become simply a hunt for exemplifications of what it has already been decided should be there, no "surprises." In my view, some theoretical appreciation of a few simple and open-ended *generative* mechanisms (creativity, penetration, reproduction) implanted, not in the analyst's head but in the "real" world, repeating over and over for different groups with different although not unpatterned outcomes, is enough to encompass myriads of observable results that madden the objectivists to further theoretical involutions but that lead the ethnographer out to the field to be "surprised."

What I am arguing is a severe qualification on some Marxist notions of ideology, which see meaning as coming from outside to "interpellate" their subjectivity. My position almost inverts aspects of such Marxism. If you like, ideology can also flow in the other direction, with subjugated subjects and positions of subjugation enjoying epistemological resources, through their cultural forms, to seek contradictions in ideology or to retell its stories in somewhat different ways from a subordinate interest and point of view.

What I am arguing is also not compatible with many versions of post-structuralism. As Madeleine Arnot's chapter points out so deftly and as I have learned from her, it is interesting to note that in some ways *Learning to Labor* shares with poststructuralism, almost precursively, some interests in the workings and reworkings of symbolic articulations (see next section also). But for me they are produced in living and active ways rather than internally and textually. Ethnography is about observing the use of objects and artifacts and the conjunctions of discourses and being "surprised" about their new articulations, not in textual forms but as they are worked on, used, shaken and stirred for purpose in living ways through practices on the profane grounds of history. Intersections, reversals, unexpected combinations, repositioning within unlikely context, inappropriate exaggerations in inappropriate contexts, reversals in polarity, monitoring others for affects of enacting particular discourses and their recombinations and reordering in that light—all these practice-based workings of discourses are the stuff of ethnography and can yield contents, meanings, ideas of difference just hanging in the air that exploit the always slipping, never properly to be known relations between signifier and signified. Meanings so produced are not assimilable back to relations of dominance or the contents and "subject positions" of any one discourse "structured in dominance." Here is perhaps an unlikely field of cooperation between "humanist" ethnographic practices and "antihumanist" poststructuralisms. But the ethnography must keep paramount the practices of *cultural production* in concrete situated context. Practice bends all kinds of symbolic resources, recalcitrant as they may be and following whatever internal "grammars," to perform not their own internal scripts but some kind of referentiality in context as use for social purpose. Isolated discourses considered in the abstract, even if they are considered in hybrid relations, always have a dominant reference, implicit collusions with the mental/manual divide rendering as mental constructions and representations what are crucial conjunctions where it is practice that makes the difference for subordinated groups. In the end, ethnography is concerned with acting subjects and their "surprises"; otherwise, everything could be read out from discursive forms. Without an ethnographic anchor, poststructuralism can advocate a diversity and a creativity altogether without a subject. I am absolutely for showing the complexity and variability of the subject with respect to the forming up of symbolic systems, but, nevertheless, I still posit some kind of social subject formed enough to act and to have a hand in shaping their own culture.

Of course, the trump card of poststructuralism is its critique of essentialism. Humanist positions and perhaps especially ethnographic writings are seen as assuming, in one way or another, that meanings and senses of the self, self-identities, arise "expressively" and automatically from centered human beings. Although accepting the strictures against essentialism, I do not accept that ethnographic approaches must automatically fall prey to them. Indeed, against the poststructuralists, it could be argued that they can fall prey, in their turn, to a discursive essentialism where meaning is reduced to the internal operations and slippages of symbolic systems, at best mutely "performed," rather than arising from their articulations with context and practice, often utterly changing the import of their internal codes. Discursive approaches attempt to locate "genes" of information in symbolic forms, but they are as far off as genetic biology is from producing or comprehending the flows of human life and living human beings as they commit the flat packs of genetic information to the sensuous concourses and confluences of material life, profane, lived, real.

My position is simply that we do not need to go to the internal relations of the arbitrary signifiers of discourse to confound a presocial scientific essentialism. The argument about the *penetrations* of cultural forms is not that they come from fully formed preexisting unified subjects, making individual cognitions directly intended to reveal their conditions of existence. *Penetrations* come about almost randomly in the profane, corporeal, and un-prefigurable operations of cultural forms as they reconnoiter the land in a de facto kind of way, scraping it in the pursuit of their own fullest development in their own terms and for their own potentials and objectives. "Identities" do not predate this but are formed and re-formed in practice. The ways in which structural positionality is *penetrated*, explored, exposed, by "the lads" in *Learning to Labor* do not constitute the direct purpose or function of the counterculture, nor are they the referents of the discourses through which it works. Very often, working-class cultural forms expose aspects of social structure "unconsciously." Because of the subordinated historic positions and relations that working-class agents occupy, they cannot call forth their own necessary and self-determined "pure," "class-expressive" culture. They work on and through a variety of discourses and "found" symbolic resources, exposing in them *through practice* surprising potentials, previously unimagined "double edges," meanings never meant to be there and certainly not marked through like writing in seaside candy rock "working-class culture" (see endnote 5). In surviving and working through, making the best of, imposed conditions, living cultures expose aspects of social structure basically eccentrically and indirectly, almost accidentally. The immediate objectives of "the lads," for instance, is not to further the class struggle but to pursue fun, diversion, "the laff," and "having a go" at disliked figures or restrictive aspects of the specific and concrete regime of the school as it faces them. They are not trying to be good class warriors; they are trying to be good "lads." In pursuit of that some sort of "lived penetrations" of individualism and meritocracy and the nature of labor, power and laboring under capitalism are accomplished, but these are still only *cultural* revelations. They are not verbally articulated and have to be analyzed almost as the hidden premises on which cultures depend, unconscious assumptions that their members make about how the world works as far as they are concerned. *Penetrations* need a whole other stage of decreasing likely political and intellectual work and the mediations and preconditionality of a working class political party in order to become *political* entities (a gap in the otherwise excellent commentary in the chapter by Peter McLaren & Valerie Scatamburlo-D'Annibale).

All that said, it is absolutely part of my argument that relevant and socially generative *penetration*s, once formed by whatever hidden process of logic, help to determine the vivacity and longevity of cultures and are extended, continuously "reselected" if you like, in their operations for reasons quite different from the randomness of their causation. They socially "mark" a culture as producing a social as well as a cultural effectivity, helping them thereby to make better "sense"—in the way of the viability of identities and practices, freeing up psychic and real space—than other available cultural or official options. This "marking" also makes them more likely to be pitched into social antagonisms and is also fuel for negative stereotyping and social prejudice against them. Again, though, it is important to emphasize that this is a social "marking," not a Marxist or pure class marking, not a branding (as some have taken me as saying) as "working-class hero culture." A working-class hero may well be something to be, but it is an essentialist construction of discourse not one of ethnographic presentation and analysis. If *penetrations* were indeed straight and true then we would not be condemned to the parochial analysis of ironic reproductions. We could proceed straight to emancipation.

There is a further antiecumene point with respect to poststructuralist and postmodernist positions on methodology and "reflexivity." The formulations and prescriptions I am giving now require some responsibility to be taken on by the analyst, a responsibility to undertake an interpretative stage for which all parties to the fieldwork relationship are not equally prepared. Against fully reflexive positions I argue that fieldwork relationships are necessarily asymmetric and that the responsible ethical and intellectual recognition and response to this should be not a faux equalitarianism but a responsible working through of the advantages, training, and wider perspectives that the analyst brings. For me, this responsibility entails some degree of the provisional adoption of an epistemological realism in portraying how cultures are materially placed (stage one of my construction). What are the conditions of existence on which cultures depend and that they are attempting to *penetrate*? What external ideologies are being *penetrated*? If you go wholly down the self-reflexive road, if you go down a complete dialogical relativism in methodology—everybody's account is equal—you cannot generate such contextual accounts of culture. Every form would be equal, every text equal. You would not be able to indicate which are *penetrations*, which are *reproductions*, and you would not be able to identify which of the governing conditions of existence in a particular area are important for those *penetrations* and *reproductions*.

This is not to argue against reflexivity as a theoretical and political self-consciousness. We must always engage "points of view" on our own "points of view," be aware that collected data and associated theoretical advances are specific outcomes of our research questions and starting out theoretical orientations. Different research questions and different theoretical orientations would produce different analyses and findings. This is reflexivity not as a personal confession but as the awareness of the productivity of our research questions and theoretical resources. It is a quality of "rich" ethnographic texts, though, that they offer and contain capaciousness, reflecting the indeterminacy of their cultural subject matter. They present forms of life, "unnecessary" detail and contexts beyond what is relevant to any particular theory about them, so allowing other or even contradictory theories to utilize their data. This is a further reminder that we are not observing the world directly but in a particular universe of concern. The researcher is situated in context just as surely as are the agents they researchers observe.

Gender

Gender relations and associated symbolic meanings and practices are crucial to the full understanding of any cultural form. In terms of the articulation of symbolic systems, the shared concerns of ethnographic and poststructuralist perspectives, perhaps the two most important systems, with race/ethnicity a close third, to be explored for the specific manner of their interrelations are those of gender and class. The ways in which gender relations, the male/female division, map on to other kinds of divisions are at the heart of *Learning to Labor*. I did think, 25 years ago, that this was perhaps one of the main "scientific" findings of the book, that gender categories overlaid and changed the meaning of capitalist categories, particularly the mental/manual divide, and that the latter, in turn, conditioned the meanings of gender forms. This was, if you like, again, a very early poststructuralism in precisely arguing, against subsequent major misunderstandings of the book, that this form of working class culture was not inevitable and arising in some essential way from the "nature" or genetic culture of those working-class lads, but that it was precisely a construct, a particular form of masculinity in relation to a particular division of labor and in relation to a particular mental/manual division and in relation to a particular state formation at a particular time. Of course, where I part company from post-structuralism, these articulations did not take place in the abstract or from an internal discursive causation or motor. Masculinity was mobilized in a class context because of the work it could accomplish for "the lads" in relation to the urgent issues facing them as they saw them. Symbolic structures of masculinity help to embody and give an extra force to their school resistance. Masculinity gives them an axis of power over women, but it also gives them a realistic basis for feeling at least some ambiguous superiority over other less successful males, such as teachers and "ear'oles" (conformists). This response has a definite logic and is effective against the attempted domination of the school, and it gives alternative nonmental grounds for valuing the self and a whole solid, sometimes formidable, presence to resist belittling. But just as practice in context precedes the articulations of gender and class, so real social effects follow in train. As I argue in *Learning to Labor*, once formed, "hard" or "tough" masculine identities and the patterning of social relations that follow prove highly inflexible, intractable, and durable (see Lois Weis's chapter). Masculinity and its reflexes henceforth help to organize the same repertoire of defensive/offensive responses no matter what the situation. Furthermore, the antimentalism generated in the school and the masculinity of the lads become intertwined with their sense of themselves and their own vital powers. For "the lads," a manual way of acting in the world is a manly way, whereas a mental way is effeminate. These gendered associations reinforce and lock each other, producing a disposition and sensibility that may, quite literally, last a lifetime. In a final sealing of their subordinate fate, mental work becomes not only pointless "paper pushing" but also "sissy" work for "the lads." Even higher paid mental work is considered "sissy" from "the lads'" point of view. Exhausting, exploited, and increasingly low paid, manual work can somehow be seen in a masculine register, which prevents its true brutality from showing through.

It is still the case that students are forced into the unnatural atmospherics of the school, which pressure cooks together different social and symbolic relations regardless of how individuals are supposed to survive psychically, although through their very suffering gathering symbolic resources around them in order to build some kind of viable cultural identity, not least in gender terms and as bulletproof as possible—storing up particular trouble for working-class males mismatched for available jobs (see the chapter by Jane Kenway & Anna Kraack). But none of this is ordered in the genes or in the lap of the historical or economic gods. In different circumstances, all of these articulations could be ordered differently. That opens up a contingent cultural politics.

So, it was and still is a bit surprising and disappointing to be attacked so comprehensively by some feminists (for details, see Nadine Dolby & Greg Dimitriadis's Introduction and Madeleine Arnot's chapter). Of course, they have attacked what they see as uncritical reproduction of the insulting terms and behavior of "the lads" as well as or as part of an attack on my supposed essentialism. I accept that I could have shown more reflexivity in how sexist behaviors were presented in the book, but my point here is that the analysis was, overall, deeply gendered, especially for a class-based treatment of social relations. I am not trying to award myself full retrospective feminist credentials. I reproduced sexist terms too unconsciously and I think it is probably right that I "discovered" (was "surprised" by) a sexed class on the ethnographic way to trying to understand more fully, more humanistically, the brutality of capitalist relations. My object was to try to understand how capitalism works at a human level, how male labor power was inserted into factory production in concrete detail under the economic conditions and social relations prevailing then. But along the way, responding to the data and in order to get a more robust analysis, I took up seriously the whole question of the symbolic articulations of gender relations. In this the book foresaw and perhaps in a small way helped to inititiate the academic field of masculinity studies. I welcome that with one important caveat. The whole point of my analysis in *Learning to Labor* was to highlight the articulation of gender forms to other forms, not least to class, the mental/manual divide, and the institution of the school. It seems to me that it might become a blind alley to look at masculinity only for its own sake. Although floated off into a separate academic realm, masculinities cannot be seen as making themselves in a vacuum. They form always in some institutional, class, and power context and in relation to other discourses and symbolic resources. So, if you like, the gender dimension needs to come on home, back to structured contexts and its articulations with other kinds of symbolic relations in order to really make progress. Not least, as we see a resurgence of interest in class analysis it is vital for a full ethnographic understanding and presentation to see class categories as always inseparably intertwined with and conditioned by gender and that gender, in turn, is profoundly shaped by class.

Culture and Schooling in the 21st Century: New Times

As all the chapters of this volume evidence, things have certainly changed in the United Kingdom, the United States, and worldwide since *Learning to Labor* was published. The papers in this volume demonstrate a whole host of changes very clearly. Perhaps the most dramatic change has been in the material conditions of the working class (see particularly the chapters by Jane Kenway & Anna Kraack, and Kathleen Nolan & Jean Anyon). Within the so-called "core" countries there has been a deep and profound worsening of their economic position. It is perfectly possible that I caught "the lads" at the last gasp of a certain kind of real, if always subordinated, working-class power and celebration in England; almost from the moment the book was published, the conditions got worse. In the late 1970s and early 1980s the United Kingdom became the first industrialized country to experience massive losses of the manual industrial work that had previously been available to the working classes. This trend is now firmly established across the old industrialized world. In the United Kingdom over half of the manufacturing jobs that existed in the 1970s have been destroyed, with a slightly larger reduction in related trade union membership. At the same time, there has been a virtually epochal restructuring of the kind of work available. Taken together, the new customer service call centers and the hotel and catering industries now employ more than double the number of workers as the old "smokestack" industries—cars, ship building, steel, engineering, coal mining.

The whole working class has been badly affected by the diminution in both the quality and quantity of jobs available, especially young people, older workers, and ethnic minorities. Perhaps especially in the United States, where the minorities now make the majority of the working class in some major cities, race stereotyping and prejudice increase the likelihood of economic exclusion for Black and Latino groups as well as adding extra barbs of stigma to the condition of unemployment. From the point of view of the working class and from all its age and ethnic constituencies, work opportunities have shifted away from relatively abundant, well to reasonably paid skilled or semiskilled industrial work, to much lower paid service and out-of-reach white-collar work. For reasons of culture and disposition only too well analyzed in *Learning to Labor*, the new high-tech jobs and the higher level training and educational programs designed to fill them are irrelevant to most of the displaced and to be displaced manual industrial workers. A new and developing feature is that the state has also intervened much more massively in the operations of the labor market and a reregulation of collapsing traditional transitions from school to work. For many working-class youth, the choice is now workfare, being forced into low-wage labor, or street survival with jail as the likely terminus. This is a state-mandated attempt to regulate and reform the labor power of the working class wholesale, attempting to make "idleness" impossible just as work disappears.

The objective probabilities of a reliable and decent wage through manual work have been radically decreased, then, for substantial parts of the working class, and the threat of its removal has become a permanent condition for all workers. I would argue that the old expectations often continue in some form but have been thrown into permanent crisis. There are still plenty of male working-class kids, like "the lads," who are perhaps more willing than ever to take on exploited manual work in traditional masculine and antimentalist ways (see the chapter by Jane Kenway & Anna Kraack), but there is not enough work to go around, and many are left in suspended animation on varieties of state schemes and dead end training programs. Many simply disappear from the radar screens. These dramatic changes have destroyed or substantially weakened working-class paths from school to work and have shaken the material foundations of traditional working-class cultural forms.

In many ways we are now entering an epochal and possibly catastrophic social void.[10] We are seeing in the current "postindustrial revolution" a shake out of especially male industrial labor on a scale similar to that of the shake out of agricultural labor in the first industrial revolution. In England, the first country to experience the industrial revolution, this shake out was accompanied by mass internal migration from the country to the city. Although lived through suffering, massive dislocation, and countless personal tragedies, this constituted, ultimately, a way out of the "void" as it faced displaced peoples then. Displaced "landless laborers" moved to the new cities, forming there new urban relations and cultures, through struggle and possibility finding and making new psychic, cultural, institutional, and material homes. But when you are displaced from the city, where do you go? What cities are the new mostly male "workless workers" bound for? If you have just arrived with diasporic bags unpacked, where do you go? Cities of the sky? Derelict cities of dead and alienated souls hovering over the decaying city centers where once they were welcome? Falling into its cracks and crannies, making new cities of the sidewalk? Cities of vastly expanded penal institutions? Signed "Training Centers," cities of state warehouses for the unemployed? Schooling as we know it was developed for the expanding Victorian cities of the first industrial revolution; what of schooling now for the new ghostly cities of the postindustrial revolution?

Apace with these profound material changes effecting the world of work has been a profound social recomposition of working class communities and of "labor supply" for the vastly different (or disappearing) kinds of jobs available. In some ways inversely reflecting the decline in demand for male manual labor power, women across all classes are achieving higher education levels and rates of labor force participation. Continued waves of migration, now politically driven as well as economically, flow into the metropolitan centers, cumulatively changing and forever their race/ethnic compositions and expanding labor supply even as the "proper jobs" dry up. Britain also now has a very substantial third generation of predominantly Asian British and African Caribbean British youth who, even though now facing actually a tougher labor market unless very well qualified, do not willingly accept the conditions their grandparents suffered in silence, and who contest every day ignorant presuppositions and insulting stereotypes about their "outsideness" and supposedly homogeneous racial identities (see Fazal Rizvi's chapter in particular). With newfound ethnic confidence and in new ways they exploit electronically freed-up resources of global diasporic networks and often commodity-borne postcolonial hybrid and syncretic forms to adapt to and explore their current conditions, not least original and creative ways of occupying and surviving the new cities of the mind and institution.

In some ways the scale and direct effects of the mass movement of people across the globe are often exaggerated. Over 97% of people live and work in countries where they were born.[11] But for the majorities, even if they are still, symbolic borders pass them. Not least this redraws the cultural map for the White working class, for those such as "the lads" of *Learning to Labor*. They are having to recognize themselves, often unwillingly or with resentments, as a newly "marked" ethnic group as they lose or can no longer automatically take for granted the advantages conferred by colonialism and participation in the durable formations of the first industrial revolution and its (White) proletarian inheritances of a decent industrial wage. Economic leveling, especially in the light of renewed ethnic confidence among non-Whites, brings a whole set of visible comparative and relational issues: cultural questions of otherness and difference, similarity and solidarity, for identities no longer resting on what they took unconsciously to be categorical, historical and economic advantages. Now they are revealed to be similarly subject to the much larger relations of subordination that always trapped those on whom they so recently looked down. Here lie potentials for new forms of White antiracism, for racial solidarity, for racial cultural borrowing in diverse forms of White ethnicity, as well as for possible pits of resentment to fuel more conscious and virulent forms of racism replacing the old unconscious and taken-for-granted forms of superiority.

Alongside these material and social changes, further complicating their own internal dynamics, has been an accelerating epochal change at the specifically cultural level whereby symbolic resources, from whereever derived, have been commoditized and their communicative and useful potentials subject to fetishisation. Of course, commercialized cultural forms were of great interest to the lads of *Learning to Labor*, so this is not a new development. But the sheer weight of commercial provision, the massive increase in broadcast TV channels, the faltering of public service, or at least of its ethic, accumulate to render quantitative into qualitative change. Commoditization of objects, artifacts, and cultural services has become the norm. New global electronic forms of communication are sidelining old sensuous communities—face-to-face interactions with known others— with now literally hundreds of TV channels available through digitalization. This is furthered by the huge growth of commercial leisure forms. The post-modern cultural epoch is characterized by this qualitative expansion of commodity relations from the meeting of physical needs—food, warmth, and shelter—to the meeting and inflaming of mental, emotional, expressive, and spiritual needs and aspirations. You could say that the predatory productive forces of capitalism are now unleashed globally not only on nature but also on human nature.

At the level of culture, young people are becoming less defined by neigh-borhood and class and more defined by these new relations of commodity and electronic culture. Even as their economic conditions of existence falter, most young working-class people in the United Kingdom would not thank you now for describing them as working class. They find more passion and acceptable self-identity through music on MTV, wearing baseball caps, branded sneakers and designer shirts, and socializing in fast-food joints than they do through traditional class-based cultural forms.

You could say that the commodization and electrification of culture has produced a double articulated crisis of "the void": Not only are the mate-rial conditions of the working class profoundly changed, but the cultural resources and forms through which that crisis may have been understood and responded to have been eroded and devalued. Fetishism has removed the "ghostly cities" further into the spectral. Although exaggerated and sometimes mythologized now, too easily forgiven for their racism and sexism, the traditional forms of British working class culture, for instance, did at least give a corporeal and embedded sense of the self in relation to a larger group and a logic for understanding the relations of that larger group to other groups, not least dominating ones. Just as this domination deepens dramatically and material conditions change profoundly for the worse, the means for placing the self and understanding are plunged into crisis as well. It is certainly conceivable that if the old cultural forms, and their institutional extensions and expressions, had held there would have been much stiffer resistance to, or much better collective settlements made within, the multiple crises now engulfing the working class. As it is, market-led processes of individuation have helped to render structural change and deepened subjugation apparently into matters merely of personal misfortune.

Understanding New Times

So we are faced with a bewildering new world of contradictory influences, a profound crisis of the old and faltering births of the new. The collapse of industrial employment in the core countries continues apace with the postmodern separation of time, place, and culture. The commodified aestheticization of everyday existence and materials accompanies the mass movement of peoples across the globe. New postcolonial diasporic social relations and the development of "new ethnicities" in the "core" economies accompany gravely worsened economic conditions for all those, Black or White, with only their manual labor power to sell. I recognize all of these trends, but if it is immodest, forgive me, I still see ethnographic practices with *Learning to Labor* as a model and *The Ethnographic Imagination* as some sort of guide as providing highly relevant ways of proceeding.

Unsurprisingly given the diversity and complexity, the different facets of the new situation are considered in fragmented ways with different disciplines highlighting different fragments. Cultural studies has developed to highlight the creativities of consumption and the new possibilities for postcolonial identities. "Boring" sociology focuses on broken transitions and the destroyed inheritances of the working class and working-class culture. What is needed is a bringing together again of sociology and cultural studies, anthropology too, although in some ways the latter has always fared better from an interdisciplinary point of view. Although cultural studies has celebrated freedoms in the realm of choice and identified fluidities and possibilities in the making of new ethnic identities, these identities and formations, for the most part (although see the chapters by Kathleen Nolan & Jean Anyon and Jane Kenway & Anna Kraack), have not been grounded with respect to their articulations and productiveness within realms that are still determined by necessity, especially, for instance, school, work, and/or state schemes. The question for me is: How does the necessary connect with the voluntary under new conditions?

Ethnography shows the grounds on which this consolidation might take place. At a minimum, and as a precondition, it stresses agency and insists always on a role for subordinated groups producing their own cultures and understandings. Crudely, ethnographers always ask, what is the meaning-making from below? Too often, profound changes are seen as passive processes, described in gerund terms from above—nobody, no acting subjects are really responsible. Globalization, who does it, who suffers, who cares, it's *globalization*, stupid. Downsizing—nobody is doing the sacking, it's just a process—nobody knows where it comes from. Restructuration? "Oh yeah, it's a modern condition of the world." As Tony Blair is fond of saying on hearing of the latest factory closure, "It's sad but that's the nature of the modern world we live in, isn't it?" There is no agency there, it is just happening. In my hometown of Wolverhampton, "relicization" is the most recent word I have heard used to describe what is happening to our industrial inheritance—whole sectors of the city have become industrial relics, empty wastelands apparently only because another dratted "-ization" has been on the loose. These are all top-down views. Desperately, urgently, we need the view from underneath. What does it feel like for the working class to be "relicized"? What are the subjective understandings on the shop floor for those who teeter on the edge of "relicization," who remain for the moment in the old but now sped up, globalized, and Japanized factories?

Ethnography further reminds us that real social agents live simultaneously, and in the same life space, the dislocations of "the void" together with the recompositions of the social together with the commoditization of communicative social relations. Ethnographic work must encompass the interpenetrations of these too often separated worlds as they constitute the practical field on which agents live and act. How is "relicization" understood through and in relation to new social representations and identities, through a world of commodity communication whose materials are out of reach for the new workless, barely in reach for the new armies of the working poor keeping their heads just above water in seas of symbolic plenty?

Against the gloom, cultural theorists, my part, too, are right to emphasize that in the train of the new commodity relations and their erosion of traditional cultural forms have come new possibilities, emergent forms that although so far promising much less for institutional development than the old forms of solidarity must be scrutinized for their social possibilities, clues to social becoming. Among these is the emergence of an, albeit damagingly individualized, "expressive subject" (see the chapter by Peter McLaren and Valerie Scatamburlo-D'Annibale for an excellent exegisis as well as critique!). This concerns individuals taking for themselves—on the alien and profane grounds of the commodity—something that only the elite has enjoyed as part of their sacred privilege. This privilege entails the formation of sensibilities to mark oneself culturally as a certain kind of person—rather than simply an unconscious carrier of traditional markers of class, race, and gender—or to "choose" to belong to these categories in transformative, distinctive, mannered, celebratory, or self-conscious ways. This is to take part in self-formation on relatively autonomous expressive grounds, rather than to be formed from outside on automatically ascribed grounds. The connection of the "given self" to *variable* external symbolic forms reflects the desire not just to take up social or material space in a way governed by others, but also to *matter* culturally. Of course, these *cultural productions* are subject to future rounds of commoditization as market researchers scour the streets for the next inner-city fashion to sell to the inner city. But there is an inescapable moment of meaning-making from below here that, through the very promiscuity of the restless commodity, also aids processes of change, hybridity, and syncretism. The changes of race and gender composition and especially the new assertiveness and confidence of previously "invisible" or "representationally fixed" groups produce complex changes for all representations of social difference, multiple opportunities for ethnic, gender, and class "cross-dressing" (see Cameron McCarthy's chapter) as ordinary possibilities for social agents to intervene in the symbolic orders of their own social universes.

But for me the urgency remains. How are the new orders of symbolic experience related to structural features of contemporary experience, to the *positions* and *relations* of a deepening oppression that seem oddly to be have been made invisible by the new surface diversity of social and cultural forms? I propose that an indispensable tool here is class analysis as explored in the first part of this chapter.

The issue is not one of the "objective" disappearance of class, but one of the disappearance of the once relatively clear lines of connection, shown in *Learning to Labor*, for instance, between class positions, class cultures, and class identities. There are no longer, if there ever were, totalizing systems of representation (see Fazal Rizvi's chapter). And there are simply more groups, so to speak, within the working class, and, mostly depending on luck (but also perceptions about them in the labor market), very divergent economic prospects for them. Within the different groups are very many more discursive, symbolic, and socially symbolic resources feeding into their *cultural productions*. But an important feature of the latter continues to be the effectiveness with which they explore and exploit their conditions of existence. What is needed, what was unified in *Learning to Labor*, is the bringing together of class perspectives with the focus on culture, albeit now less centered and more diverse.

Diversities and creativities are celebrated too often for themselves and for their apparently free-floating ontologies. They are connected up only horizontally and in the abstract through loose associations of similarities in form and potential. My argument is that within the different forms we need to ask: What are their *penetrations* and *reproductions*? What *positions* and *relations* lie beneath the diverse surface forms that might share convergent *penetrations* about them? How do they all converge in a social reproduction of polarizing structures that depress the prospects for all subordinated groups? What are the hopeful mismatches and ragged edges between *penetrations* and *reproductions* in situated context?

In the first section of this chapter I argued that the old working-class cultural forms were nothing like as solid, homogeneous, purposive, or class-expressive as they are now held to be, portrayed in mythic, if surpassed, form, with *Learning to Labor* sometimes held up (thereby suppressing its current theoretical and political messages) as a nostalgic and sentimental icon. Against that, I say, again, that the *penetrations* of "the lads" were not essentialist or directly "class-expressive." They worked indirectly and eccentrically with respect to the direct purposes and phenomenal flows of their culture. So it should be no surprise now that current forms do not declare themselves on their foreheads to be "working-class culture" but are nevertheless speaking to and revealing of class-related contexts of subordination. It is therefore no big step to analyze them in the same way as I analyzed the counterschool culture of "the lads."

Of course, class processes, impulses and responses may be clothed and coded in other ways. Not least in the U.S. context, for instance, racism adds weight and form to structural oppression, but race and ethnic belongings and traditions also supply the phenomenal forms and symbolic resources for survival and expressions, including resistant ones, for Black and Latino groups. These as well as other oppositional themes are commodified and through the mediations of popular culture (see endnote 5) put into capitalist circuits both of accumulation *and* of the spread of ideas and symbols, many subversive, thus supplying materials for the *cultural production* of much wider groups. So, there is certainly much more grist to the mill of the *cultural production* of young people and all social agents, but the questions remain the same: What is articulated and *penetrated* and *reproduced* with respect to their structural *positions* and *relations*; are the cultures under question *socially marked* in any way, and if so, what is the social work they accomplish?

Here is a broad agenda for ethnographic cultural research and one in which we should have real confidence in the likely productivity of our findings. How are *positions* and *relations* lived and understood? How are the requirements of economic and state systems met? What kinds of labor power or withdrawal of labor power are required? What are the new relations of exploitation and how are they actually embodied in living, breathing, and cultured, clothed bodies? What happens *culturally* in the welfare offices? What happens *culturally* in work placement and training schemes? What happens *culturally* in McDonalds? What happens culturally in the still existing but sped up Fordist factories?

Schools

From a general point of view of understanding social change through to the pedagogic interest, schools are important sites for ethnographic investigation. Along with work and state-mandated sites of labor market regulation, they constitute a very important and continuing realm of necessity where diverse cultural forms and a whole range of identities are brought together by force to face inescapable and urgent questions structured in one concrete site. Schooling continues to supply its own set of forces and contradictions that school-based cultures must survive and work through, thus further profoundly effecting identities within them. Students are thrust into a realm of necessity with little or no control over the terms of their presence or participation, but with greater "choices" than ever over how they register and understand the possibilities and confinements of school. The contradictions of individualism and meritocracy carry over, actually in much deeper ways, from the days of *Learning to Labor*. The "new" floating resources of the imaginary world of commodity culture, changing gender relations and identities, diasporic cultural networks, postcolonial cultural topographies, syncretic and hybrid combinations of all these, are here located in very anchored "old" situations. Added now to the complexity of school is an extra layer of difficulties and contradictions to be made sense of, those produced by the disappearance of manual industrial work. Are schools training for work, for the dole, or for endless state schemes to follow, and what sense do any of them make from which student points of view? The impulses of cultural response, old and new—conformism through instrumentality through disassociation, through resistance— are likely to show some continuity with previous cultural forms, but are also likely to be clothed and articulated in some new ways with attendant and specific forms of *penetration* and *reproduction* (see the chapter by Kathleen Nolan & Jean Anyon).

The ethnographic impulse forces you to be broad empirically if not entirely ecumenical theoretically. In the pursuit of the ethnographic presentation and understanding of school-based cultures, I would certainly add many more symbolic resources to the mix, discourses new and old, symbolic relations ushered in by the mass movement of peoples, and the increased range of possible articulations between class forms, gender, and ethnicity, not least those brokered through the now dominant relations of the commodity. But the project for understanding the complexities is kind of similar: to repeat, what are the *cultural productions* within the specific site, what the *penetrations,* what the *reproductions,* what the ragged edges?

In the new context, it is more difficult than ever to outline positive programs for schooling and pedagogic strategies for the betterment of subordinate groups. Compared with the old Victorian schools with one roof over one purpose, the roofing of schooling now covers a multitude of different trajectories, arrivals, departures. Schools are continuously buffeted by changes, internal and external to their operations, continuously cutting their sails to differently blowing storms. They are having to become more "marketized," focusing on high-status testing preparing labor power for jobs in the new "weightless economy" (see Michael Apple's chapter), but, in working-class and inner-city neighbourhoods they are also having to grapple with a variety of cultural responses from those who are excluded or exclude themselves from these opportunities, as well as attempting to deal, although ever more unsuited to welfare roles, with pathological manifestations of the profound dislocations of community, poverty, and suffering associated with unemployment. Caught between these objectives, it is harder than ever to see schooling, in an earlier modernist liberal way, as a unified force for the emancipation of the whole working class. Are schools to train working-class students to compete with each other ever more vociferously for the ever diminishing supply of "proper jobs?" Are they to prepare them, or some of them (which ones?) for coping with a hostile state in a life without work? Are they to prepare them for contractual submission to an ever-extending succession of training schemes? Prepare the rest for jail?

There are many interesting guides in this volume to the new functions and formations of schooling, bleak additions to the traditional functions of preparation of industrial labor power where schools also provide fodder for jails (see the chapter by Kathleen Nolan & Jean Anyon) and permanent unemployment (see the chapter by Jane Kenway & Anna Kraack). We need more studies showing the cultural complexities of schooling, particularly of the new roles of cultural consumption in school.[12]

What of pedagogy? What is to be done now on Monday mornings? Often I am seen as too pessimistic and concentrating on resistant or, in one way or another, deviant pupils. Of course my belief is that we should not underestimate the continuing importance and potentials of school for all students and that we should continue to protect its freedoms and necessities as a site at least partly removed from the deeper necessities, exploitations, and exclusions of the world of work and now unemployment. Although we must never underestimate the complexity of how schools function differentially and for whom and to what purpose, it is still the case that schools are the major source of skills necessary in the labor market and the main avenue for student chances of a "proper job." Through all the contradictions and counter forces, schools must continue to offer all working-class students the best possible individual opportunities and highest expectations for educational advance, ignoring all provocations and rejections. Maximum possible resources—the more difficult the school, the higher the budget—should be mobilized to support teachers in their heavy tasks, giving them maximum time out of class and in sociologically informed and literate support groups to maintain a social as well as a pedagogic professionalism that refuels their ability to see behind the insults often thrown at them.

In any particular student there is likely to be a conflict between horizontal cultural influence and individualized aspiration. Bracketing out the ambiguities of seminar debate, in the classroom teachers must seek to supply safety, inducements, and appropriate contexts to encourage the students to take and keep to the individualistic routes and what they offer, not only for upward mobility, but increasingly, through evidence of conformist attitudes, for the very possibility of a decent permanent job. Actually, many students from working-class backgrounds still lean instinctively toward the school, especially in their early years, and pursue its individualistic promises even at the cost of some local cultural embarrassment, rejection, lack of belonging, or complex "double-agent" dealing. There have to be safeguards, protections, and supports for those who take this sometimes rocky road. For the resistant or disaffected, traditional and experimental attempts to explore and lay bare (in sympathetic, not damning frustrated, prediction) likely future reproductions may reconnect some students to an individualistic path. Within the fluidity and dynamic tensions of the new articulations of race and gender, fractures in the formations of subordinate culture (e.g., White lads ethnically disaffected, perhaps, from the resistant White culture) may throw up groups for whom there is real subjective point in and objective possibilities for meritocratic advance, less solidaristic cultural roadblocks in the way. They should be identified and supported, for schooling may be their only hope.

To be clear, my position has never been against schooling, against learning, or against personal intellectual development. It should never be forgotten that the problem with knowledge and mental activity in schools is not that there is something "wrong" with knowledge and mental activity or that students from subordinated backgrounds are not interested in them— in their own ways and through their own practices they clearly are. "Dumbness" is celebrated nowhere. The problem is that the current social and institutional contexts and arrangements for the transmission of knowledge and mental skills produce fields of social opposition against them. The "ideal" productions of "educated selves" are targets rather than models for subjectivities produced through general experiences of surviving everyday subordination. Although often given its instrumental dues, mental work is hobbled for many because it is articulated so closely with indiviualism and meritocracy within the compulsory school, complicit with hierarchized labor markets and oppressive capitalist labor processes. But once students find a bridge across institutional and cultural hazards, they can find a world of knowledge, mental development, and expression that can be appropriated and appreciated in autonomous ways. It is these destinations that always have to be borne in mind, all bridges kept open, built anew and multiplied. They are not only crossings to disclose, they also install whole new landscapes.

I know that I will be in trouble here with some readers and even with some coauthors. So far my discussion of pedagogy deals only with individualistic forms of knowledge and does not meet, in like terms, those culturally articulated forms that proceed with a social or collective knowledge and guide many students. This continuing mismatch is indeed an ironic condition for guaranteeing the renewal of nonconformist cultures. But our societies, certainly in Britain and America, are further off than ever from operating public and economic policies that protect collective interests and guarantee safety, security, and development for all. Educational institutions are absolutely not wired into such collective horizons. They are thoroughly and for the moment inextricably mired in the capitalist relations of the market economy and capitalist labor market. Falling off the meritocratic academic ladder now is to risk falling a very long way indeed, possibly into the spectral cracks of the miserable cities of the postindustrial revolution. Neither I nor you, the likely professional readers of this book, would contemplate that possibility as an alternative in our own lives, nor for the futures of our own children. Do we owe anything less to the children of others? It is not the role of teachers to stand by while students culturally grease up the bottom rungs of the only ladders that might save them. We must put our weight and feet on that bottom rung to help them up and stabilize it for them.

At the same time, for all the difficulties and respecting student abilities to handle contradiction, just as we do, and recognizing that the school is not just a pedagogic instrument but a field of *cultural production*, I argue strongly that along with the maximum attempts to keep students on individualized tracks should run curricular and extracurricular provision for exploring collective logics, programs that deal with social justice, not least exposing schooling's role in the reproduction of deepening class divisions in capitalist societies. This may open fields of mental life that can be developed for themselves, ironically also for individualistic advance. But their purpose is to explore the however distant prospects of social advance towards emancipation and a world free from the unequal *positions* and *relations* which restrict the free expressive and cultural development of all. For all the reasons discussed throughout this chapter, this may seem utopian given all the forces buffeting the school. Even where allowed, the formal and systematic teaching of systematic critical perspectives may fare no better among those who really need it than does the mainstream curriculum. I am absolutely for demands for radical streams within the main curriculum but would also ask for, possibly in relation to and as feeders for them, some lifelines into informal cultures. What are the ways of finding a way through here, not by building bridges over the cultural "blocks" but by going through them, utilizing them, the mental life of their *penetrations?* An important feature of the class analysis I proposed in the first half of this chapter is that *penetrations* are never fully assimilated back into social reproduction. There is what I have called throughout a "ragged edge," precisely a mental contents to be experimentally mined and recovered and then connected to systematic critical thought. The working-class distrust of meritocracy and un-illusioned appropriation of what it is to give manual labor power continues. New formations of ethnicity are, in part, adapted to the conditions and possibilities of their new locations, what do their cultural and identity politics say about the ideological architecture and *positions* and *relations* of modern capitalism. What is the nature of their social "marking"? Can it be so hard to break open the "secrets" of cultural reproduction when reproduction in general now proceeds in so many brutal, coercive, and open ways compared to the days of *Learning to Labor?* Can it be so difficult to make connections?

I do not have any magic "social pedagogy" bullets to offer. I will close, though, with two modest suggestions. What is usually referred to as the field of "popular culture" offers many possibilities. For all their individualizing and fetishizing tendencies, commodity communication and expressive forms reflect crucial features of the cultural universes of the young including oppositional themes, if sometimes liminal. They also bring new hybrid and ethnic resources to the lived and creative rearticulations of received social representations, not least in sites such as the school. A recent special issue of the *Harvard Educational Review* (see endnote 12) is devoted to exploring the pedagogic potentials of popular culture and contains many useful ideas and possible lines of approach. Cultural commodity forms and their uses in context are sites of intense interest for most young people and offer, both the texts and their appropriation, fields for imaginative pedagogic practices to connect up their relevance with lived *penetrations* and with wider critical perspectives and analyses. Further, informal education sites can offer access to cultural commodities on terms controllable by young people, maintaining a critical difference from private sites of consumption in their recognition of informal *cultural production* and in their attempts to connect it with more formal expression: speaking, writing, singing, recording, and filming.

Second, I would recommend new or further use of critical ethnographic texts, or fragments of texts, or performances related to texts, in school settings. Exposing similar, although not copresent, cultural forms to them can pique even resistant student interest and show the commonality of separated cultures, drawing together a cultural membership in to an awareness of a wider social membership indicating interests in common. Reading or hearing cultural texts in more formalized contexts can produce an othering and distance that dignifies and releases popular cultural practices from invisibility in the everyday, (see endnote 5) so aiding the prospects of a more systematic analysis of *cultural production,* exposing their critical impulses for connection up to wider critical perspectives.

Here is where I end as I began, beating the drum for ethnography. Knowing that the tasks I set myself are difficult and incomplete, I pass the baton to others, stressing again as I did at the beginning of the chapter the broad impact and importance of ethnography. This is what I hope to be the legacy of *Learning to Labor*, that critical ethnography should play an expanded part in registering and analyzing the profound changes we are living through and provide useful tools for social and cultural understanding and emancipation in these "new times" so distant from when the book was published.

Notes

1. Mention should also be made of a parallel though slightly later and unconnected approach by Wiel Veuglers of the Dutch organization SISWO that also resulted in an excellent day conference, *Learning to Labour: Twenty-Five Year Anniversary Symposium*, in Holland in October 2002, the proceeds of which have not been published but that have also informed my reflections here.
2. For a full description of the mission of the journal, see P. Willis and M. Trondman (2000). Manifesto for ethnography. *Ethnography* 1(1), (5–16).
3. I do not discount aspects of the directly constraining and determining power of structural forces not only over *positions* and *relations*, but also how they are understood. My essential point here is that I do not see the relationship of structure to culture as only one of *direct determination*, structures are also things to be explained and discovered, so to speak, in the reverse direction. There is a convoluted, inconclusive, and extensive debate on whether *positions* or *relations* should predominate in class analysis; how to define and measure them in relation to production (Marxist perspectives) or to wider market, social and status considerations (Weberian approaches); and on how far economic class entities determine or correlate with cultural, voting, and attitudinal "outcomes." My position is that many of the difficulties and dead ends of this debate can be seen to arise in trying to scientifically locate as real entities what are for me only notional "precultural" elements. I would argue that the unpredictable ways and measures in which cultural relations and cultural productions take up, embody, change, and reproduce which (never actually existing) "precultural" forms are themselves determining factors and not simply dependent variables or "outcomes" so imparting a "spirit" to the machine, which will always confound "machine mathematics." For a comprehensive review of the class analysis debate, see Mike Savage, *Class Analysis and Social Transformation* (Buckingham: Open University Press, 2000).
4. For clarity of exposition I am focusing here on the cultural practices of subordinated and dominated groups (for short, working-class culture[s]). But of course the middle class or powerful groups "move" within their own cultural production and with the power to legitimize their own positions, relations, and cultures through institutional power. So we have to bear in mind that subordinate groups "make sense" not only of economic positions and relationships but also of a variety of cultural and ideological ways in which these and the cultures of others are fleshed, justified, and represented, if you like also making sense of ideological relations.
5. See *The Ethnographic Imagination* (Polity, 2000) for a fuller exploration.
6. For a discussion of "surprise," see P. Willis, "Notes on Method" in S. Hall, D. Hobson, A. Lowed & P. Willis (eds.), *Culture, Media, Language* (London: Hutchinson, 1980), pp. 88–95.
7. I know that these categories constitute not only repertoires of possible symbolic meaning but also sources of *position* and *relation* with respect to their own symbolic stakes and often material interest. The valiancy of these symbolic resources and how their availability over time has been continuously reproduced come from active contestation of meanings and identity within their own terms and boundaries. As I explore in the section on gender, the "full picture" needs to show a complex dynamic of the interrelationship of different kinds of relationships. It would also be perfectly reasonable to posit a feminist version, for instance, of structural *positions* and *relationships* where class traditions could be seen as supplying

symbolic raw materials for "making sense" of gender. Why do I prioritize class? The basic social classifications of gender, and race as well, do in some sense have more importance than class categories, say more empirically about a person. But for me they are more "inert" than categories of class; the latter change them more than they change it. The organizing drive of the capitalist world system comes from an imperative of class organization at bottom derived from economic motives and organization. In the end, in order to better understand the formations of race and gender (locating what may well be most of human experience), or more precisely to comprehend their direction of change and source of internal tension, we need to locate them with respect to *more dynamic* class relations that work through them.

8. Although it is only tangentially the focus of this volume, frequent criticisms of *Common Culture* (P. Willis et al., Open University, 1990) accuse it of "cultural populism": a celebration of the creativities of common culture unrestricted by a consideration of structural forces and constraints. Indeed, that book does more or less restrict itself to a consideration of informal cultures in "sites of choice" rather than "sites of necessity," and this does dispose analysis toward a horizontal plane, limiting its ability to show the cycles presented here. This was in large measure determined by its (policy addressed) funding from the Gulbenkian Foundation, heterogeneous range of fieldwork, and aim to intervene in policy debates (much clearer in its sister volume, *Moving Culture*, P. Willis, Gulbenkian Foundation, London, 1990) concerning youth's creativity in order to widen arts funding opportunities for youth groups beyond their traditional focus on the received and legitimate arts. The book gives an over-reading to the autonomies of culture, but, against the critics, I would argue that it in no way contradicts the possibility of the analysis of the cultural exploration of social and economic conditions of existence and their ironic reproduction. It certainly shows the diversity, complexity, and nonreducibility of the cultural forms through which this has to be understood.

9. This is why those criticisms of *Learning to Labor* that complain about my use of "off-the-shelf" Marxism are wide of the mark. Of course there have to be provisional starting points where views are "borrowed" (no analysis springs fully formed either from the analyst's head or from the empirical world), but these are then modified or refined and put in better working order through the practice of fieldwork, its "surprises," and successive rounds of dialectical and mutual influence between theory and evidence. (see "Manifesto for Ethnography" for a fuller account of this process).

10. I thank Mats Trondman for introducing this term to me in our long discussions about the current crisis.

11. See: Humanity on the move: The myths and realities of international migration." *Financial Times*, July 7, 2003, p. 9.

12. See the Special Issue, "Popular culture and education," *Harvard Educational Review, 73*(3), Fall 2003.

"Centre" and Periphery—
An Interview with Paul Willis*

DAVID MILLS AND ROBERT GIBB

Paul Willis was a student and research fellow at the Centre for Contemporary Cultural Studies in Birmingham from 1969 to 1981, publishing his doctoral research on Hippy and Biker subcultures as *Profane Culture* (1978). He is best known for his book *Learning to Labour* (1977), a ground-breaking ethnographic study of the shaping of working-class masculinities within a British classroom. He has also worked and published extensively in the field of youth policy (1986, 1988, 1990a, 1990b). His most recent work is *The Ethnographic Imagination* (2000), and he is also senior founding editor of the new journal *Ethnography*.

As students of anthropology, our motivation for the interview was primarily undisciplined curiosity. What had given rise to the studied ignorance displayed by British anthropology towards the politicised deployment of "its" methodologies within cognate disciplines? And why, everywhere else, had a set of debates that began within a small prefab hut outside the Arts building at the University of Birmingham remained so mythologised? The interview helped us answer both these questions. More importantly, it provides a historicised sense of the everyday administrative and intellectual

---

*Centre and Periphery—An Interview with Paul Willis, by David Mills and Robert Gibb, was originally published in *Cultural Anthropology*, 16(3), 2001. Reprinted with permission of the American Anthropological Association.

routines that lay behind the Centre's published work. The pedagogic practices developed within the Centre—such as a postgraduate-led, collaborative working environment—are rarely acknowledged as the precursor to the subsequent theoretical innovations. For as long as classroom power relations and the politics of learning remain an under–examined aspect of academic life this situation is likely to remain—some labours are less easily learnt.

We met with Paul Willis in his hometown of Wolverhampton in the so-called "Black Country" (named from the sooty legacy of its role as a cradle of the industrial revolution) over a day in May 2000, and this co–written transcript is taken from our wide-ranging conversations. These ranged from personal reflections on his own life-narrative, through an optimistic discussion of the possibilities of shaping local government policy, to some trenchant comments on contemporary trends within anthropology and academia. We have edited and arranged it under three broad headings— "Childhood and Education," "Teaching and Research" and "Ethnography and Theory." Paul recently described himself as an "intellectual vandal," and his own iconoclasm looms large in this dialogue. This is a highly consistent iconoclasm nonetheless. His unwavering insistence on a model of humanistic creativity, regardless of the vagaries of intellectual fashion, together with his commitment to linking theory to policy and practice, mark out a courageous model for an engaged academic career.

Part 1: Childhood and Education

School Days

Following the example of Learning to Labour, *can we start with your childhood and school experiences? How formative were these for your subsequent career and intellectual projects?*

I was born in 1945 in Wolverhampton where I still live, an industrial town not far from Birmingham in the English Midlands. I guess my cultural background was working-class, perhaps *petit bourgeois*. My father was a carpenter who became a "general foreman" and went on to work for the local authority as a building inspector. He then developed his own small property business.

My mother died when I was very young, nine. My father was an incredible engine of competence, production and responsibility: a single parent looking after two kids, myself and my brother who was four years older than me, and going flat out to make an economic success of his life. We were a very close if depleted nuclear family unit, very masculine ambience and bonding. He, my father, was both very ambitious for his family, "I'm doing what's good for the Willis's," and very optimistic in a classically "modernist from below" kind of way, viewing life through a rational lens of everything-was-getting-better-through-the-powers-of-science-and-labour. Academically ambitious for his kids, that didn't stop him forcing us out to work with him onto building-sites from very shortly after my mother died. "Forced," that's the wrong word, it was simply expected. In the family was a sense—typical of that period—of rising expectations, a gathering sense of control over nature, of the world, of your future—perhaps in our case a very masculine and vigorous sense of these things. In school too, a rational and practical application was all. . . . In different ways all of our activity was practical and scientific and in everything we were encouraged to work hard, not least at school.

I went to a co–ed "grammar school." These were the days of the "11+ exam," a selective exam taken by all at age 11 where 15 percent or so were selected to go on to elite grammar schools. My father backed up my grammar school selection and relatively elite education. He felt it was all part of the plan [laughs], things working out perfectly. So what's my background? A very particular version of upward aspiration: a classic Hoggartian "scholarship boy" story of being selected through a grammar school system to go into a good, privileged education. I was in fact the only boy ever from my grammar school then to go on to Cambridge.

Did that make you, in the language you describe as employed by "the lads" in Learning to Labour, *an "ear-'ole"?*

Looking back on it, it was clear that I had to make the best of a contradictory situation. There was a very high emphasis on achievement and doing well, and at the same time this school was overwhelmingly working-class. There were tough cultures, and clear divisions between those who were exceptionally hard-working and those who were rather less so. I was often frightened in school. I was so embarrassed when the French teacher picked on me and forced me to try to say things in French which I simply thought I couldn't, to derision from the teacher and other pupils. It put me off languages *for life*. I used to be quaking behind the desk—would I be picked on next?

Later on I enjoyed school, or at least found it more manageable, partly because of sport, particularly Rugby Union Football. The school had switched from soccer to rugby in an attempt to improve its image, look posh like a Public School (the British title for privately-funded schools), to get fixtures with them, hoping something would rub off on us. I was big and athletic, well strong anyway, and was selected for the first team when I was only fifteen. This was unusual, playing with eighteen year olds, a big difference at that age. It felt like a massive breakthrough, especially when the extremely strict and frightening and over-bearing gym teacher, Mr Jones, suddenly started calling me by my nick-name, which was "Will." Of course for the teachers you were just "Willis." Suddenly, evidently because of the surprise promotion to the first team, there I was being called in front of mates, in front of girls, women, "*Will*, I'll see you on Saturday then!" I was a man amongst the other boys of my age. I think sport and especially physical-contact sports were and still are a very big area where you can have subcultural kudos *and* academic kudos. Teachers could play on that. Deviance was contained, even given an acceptable masculine register that made conformism, or over-conformism, seem effeminate. Throughout my early career Rugby was an important vehicle for the expression of a certain kind of independence, muscularity, for not being an ear-'ole, but in a way which didn't jeopardise my academic standing.

You decided to specialise in the sciences at A-level?

I was good at the sciences throughout my school career, and got the school prize for physics after "O"-level (oddly enough, choosing *The Rubaiyat* by Omar Khayyam as my prize). I guess in some way the scientists were also the rugby-players, and the Arts were for the girls. And it was *definitely* sissy to be interested in poetry and drama. I remember, quite by chance, an old auntie died and I had a book of Byron's poetry, an antique Victorian bound issue, bequeathed, or at least passed on to me. Dad brought it home one night, this was when I was sixteen or so, and I started reading it at bedtime. I remember being thoroughly moved by Romantic poetry. I had a major crisis half-way through the lower-sixth, whilst I was doing Physics, Maths and Chemistry. I was *quite* a good physicist and I think it's still in me a bit; there are certain kinds of theorising I like if they are elegant and successful and cut through stuff. But I just wasn't *that* interested. Meanwhile I was really moved by the Romantic poetry which seemed to speak to *me* in my adolescent uncertainties as well as in my struggles over identity: was I a big masculine, rugby-playing scientist or a budding entrepreneur still forced out at weekends to work on the building sites with my father … ?

Or a poet?

Well, yes, I was trying to write poetry. I have to give my father credit: once I explained my dilemma to him, he was open and he didn't force me. He found it odd and he didn't know what was going to become of me, and the school didn't like it much. Anyway, after consultations all around and something of a family crisis, I switched to the arts: literature, history, geography. It was a wafer-thin decision, I could easily have thought "I'm being silly" and stuck with the Physics and the Chemistry. And you know, it would have been a different life-course to say the very least. But it suddenly seemed to suit me and within eighteen months I'd got an "A" in English and within twenty months I was sitting in Cambridge studying literature.

Cambridge

It was my father's fault! After the "A"-level results he said: "You know you've got these "A"s, so why aren't you going to Oxford or Cambridge?" But our school had no tradition of Oxbridge entry which is still a highly specialist route, so during the summer of 1963 I wrote around to all the Oxford and Cambridge colleges—including the women's colleges because I didn't know which were which—asking if there was a chance of sneaking in at the last minute? Both St. Peter's of Oxford and Peterhouse of Cambridge offered me places within the space of four or five weeks. I chose Peterhouse.

Was Cambridge a shock?

Yeah, I guess so. It had all been rather sudden but my actual experience of Cambridge on an intellectual level was *extremely* and almost immediately disappointing. I very quickly realised that I just didn't know what was happening. I didn't understand the lectures, the famous Oxbridge tutorial system just didn't work for me. I quickly formed the impression that the tutors thought I was a Black Country, working-class "oik" who had wandered into the place by some terrible mistake, perhaps from a training programme for the unemployed up the road or something. Within weeks there was a comment in the Junior Common Room (JCR) suggestions book from an old Oxbridge, public-school twit saying that the "JCR had noticeably deteriorated this term with the arrival of people who seem unable to speak the King's English." And I was quite sure that it was for me. Still, I don't know quite how I managed to wind up in Peterhouse, which continues to be a bastion of old right-wing Tories and Whig historians. Why on earth? I don't know. I've never asked, I never questioned. I *was* an ingénu, an innocent wandering into an old, privileged bastion both in the social life of the college and, oddly, in the subject, which, within a term of going, had lost me. . . .

Because of its scholasticism?

Yes, though at the time I experienced it simply as my inadequacy. I just felt inadequate. After feeling that I'd almost magically found the centre of things, me at the centre, I was out on the edge again. The small group seminars and close reading sessions were both a revelation and source of total depression. We'd get an unseen piece of poetry or literature and you'd have to comment on it and try to place it. The historical knowledge, in depth, of literature and verbal confidence and polish which the public school kids had was simply frightening. The truth is I just knew about Shakespeare and the Romantic Poets. I couldn't have even sat down and given you a period, a periodicity, a schema of the different stages, genres and types of English. I was just completely out of my depth and worse, frightened to open my mouth. And I couldn't see rhyme or reason in how the lecture system worked. I just couldn't link up the lectures with the weekly essays I was supposed to be writing and with the close reading sessions. Again, this is reading *back in* a social scientific category: I now see all of those difficulties as related to my relative lack of cultural capital. I must have been a bright working-class kid to have got there, and aspiring to something or other, but basically got flattened by English. Having had a sense of myself as rather literate and rather intelligent, I began to think I was a bit of an idiot basically.

I got a third in my first year, which was embarrassing given that I was supposed to be grooming myself for a glittering career. I didn't want to go back after the summer vacation. I was far happier in my home town where my friends were. However, I stuck with literature, partly thinking it was a question of work to try to develop the knowledges others had. Slowly I got better, finally ending up with a 2:2. Trying to jump through their hoops but not knowing quite what the hoops were.

As it was, rugby saved me again socially. I got into the College team as "pack leader," even had a trial for the University, scoring a try which was reported in the local press of my home town and proudly reported at the Speech Day of my old school. I still preferred coming home to Wolverhampton. I missed the bustle, the double decker buses, the lack of pretension, I missed the disco, I missed a wide range of friends as well as my girlfriend, Val, who subsequently became my first wife.

Did your friends change their attitude towards you after Cambridge?

I don't think so, because my immediate friends were also scholarship kids off to University too. My immediate group was classic working-class, grammar-school selected, upwardly-aspirant, many of whom I still know and see. At the same time, of course, part of the advantage of the town and one of the reasons why I've stopped here is that I knew and know a whole variety of other groups: neighbourhood-based, through my father, school friends who didn't spiral up, etc. Within those groups I think I was seen as changing, even now people say to me that my accent has changed, become posh even though I still speak with an evident Midlands lilt. I never attempted to change my accent, but nor was I politically above it, it was just something that happened.

Birmingham

How did you come across the Centre for Contemporary Cultural Studies at Birmingham? What made you want to go to do post–graduate work?

Having decided I wasn't a particularly academic person, I had in mind my father's trajectory—going from working-class to small businessman—so I applied to Manchester Business School and got in there with a bursary.

Along with accountancy, operational research, business planning I also studied industrial sociology and industrial social-psychology. I remember being impressed with Tom Lupton and a psychologist there. Suddenly I was bright and clever and top of the class again which was wonderful.

I began to think that I'd found a métier in social science. I was offered a grant to continue to do a Ph.D. in Manchester. But because my Wolverhampton girl-friend of the time was finishing college in London, I applied to the London School of Economics and from there came a bursary for an M.Sc in Industrial Relations. I'd become a bit of a hippy, shoulder length hair, interested in things, "the revolution in the air," interested in social science but seeing it as basically manipulative, telling the bosses how to kick the asses of the workers but in more sophisticated and clever ways. I became interested in "culture" in a general kind of way, not least because of the ferment around me, and wondered if I could re-tune my re-awakened academic abilities to my *real* interests. I don't quite know how I found out about Birmingham, and the newly launched Centre for Contemporary Cultural Studies (CCCS) which was looking at contemporary culture. Even then it had a *very* trendy image, well for me anyway. Probably through the staff at LSE, or maybe the lecturers at Manchester.

So you were one of the first students when you started?

Yes, maybe the third or fourth year of students, a very early crop, a fledgling class. I had no chance of a grant. But I went down, was interviewed and accepted by Stuart Hall as a self-financing part-time student. I wanted to do serious work on cultural change, cultural development, cultural resistances to old forms of working. Though I had enjoyed my return to Wolverhampton, I also saw in the Centre a way of getting out of my previous class, cultural restrictions and experiences in Wolverhampton, or of finding a new relation to them. Within any biography there's the terrific role of sheer accident, what you hear about and when. Happenstance explains a lot. Negative "avoidance factors" also play a role. I just didn't want a "proper job."

I was also *very* attracted by Stuart and by Stuart's emphasis on multidisciplinarity. "I'm not interested whether you're a sociologist or an English person or whatever, Paul. What I *am* interested in is that you want to look at youth culture and music and at how young people live now." And that seemed like a liberation compared with the very restrictive experiences I'd had at a number of institutions as well as Cambridge.

What was the working culture like, amongst the students and the staff at the Centre? Were your peers more important than your supervisors?

I was actually Richard Hoggart's student for the first year, 1968–9. Then he went off to UNESCO. He was very busy, and we had our first supervision over lunch. I remember him saying, in the lunch queue I think: "Paul, it's very important to immerse yourself in the destructive element, and don't rush into anything too quickly. Unless you feel very confused you can't then put together a new thing. So I'm not going to ask you exactly what you're going to do or what your theory is." That was good. Keats called it "negative capability," being able to live with uncertainty but still have a sense of direction. I think it's such an important thing, you know, in a good research project, a tolerance for chaos whilst willing coherence, living on that edge. If you know exactly what you want or what you're going to prove, then you go to the field for a few exemplifications and you write what you always knew. But if you are willing to get disoriented and confused, which can feel, well, disorienting and confusing, it's not necessarily a bad thing, out of it can come real gems. Of course, if you carry on just being confused [laughs] it's a bad thing, but at a certain stage and grappling with a new topic it's vital. So that was an early impression for a then 23 year old: "Immerse yourself in the destructive element, Paul, don't formulate. . . ."

Did you have to justify your approach or topic or style of work?

No, not at the beginning. No, I just did it. A very important reason for that was of course that I was paying for myself, I was part-time, forking out hard earned cash, after tax, to pay the fees. So coming from what seemed like a very elongated, privileged existence at Cambridge, Manchester and London with good grants, by the time I got to the Centre I was teaching in four different places to support my studies. You could easily pick up part-time teaching in those days: "Communications" at Aston University; "English for Business" at Birmingham College of Commerce; and "English as a Second Language" at Handsworth Tech, and Wolverhampton Poly teaching "General studies." And I was selling ice-cream from an ice-cream van during Easter and summer vac's, weekends. I was really working very hard, not at all a full-time student floating around the Centre. I was unusual at the Centre, for I was a local boy. I used to drive over from Wolverhampton (14 miles away)—and didn't feel particularly elite or special in terms of my conditions of life and types of daily social contacts. By my second year at the Centre I was married with a newborn baby, with all the pressures that brings. I didn't feel like an elite person. I hadn't done well at Cambridge and I'd been a bit of a vagrant, carpet bagging full-time student afterwards. I had to be *very* effectively organised to get around all my different teaching, and *very* practically organised to be in the field. I wasn't in the Centre anything like 100% of the time. I was there when I wanted to be, to benefit directly from especially Stuart Hall, or when I had to be, for the so-called Theory Seminar for instance.

Part 2: Teaching and Research

1968 and the CCCS

Did you get involved in the student uprising at Birmingham?

I wasn't directly involved with the eruptions at LSE during 1967–68. I left LSE in the Summer of 1968. The big Birmingham sit-in was Autumn '68 which I *was* involved in. I had a feeling, a bit like the original feeling for Keats and Byron, but social now, that there was something in the air, something happening in everyday culture and social relations. Things would never be the same again. I joined in the occupation of the Great Hall of the University, sat in on planning meetings, relished the atmosphere. Centre students, were leading lights of the sit-in. Especially Jack Hayward, and Larry Grossberg, both American students at the Centre for a year. Larry, I remember, pony tail right down his denimed back, opinionated, was a *major* instigator. My recollections of the actual events are dim. I was rushing around teaching everywhere to earn a living, selling ice-cream, getting back to Wolverhampton, so I was a part-time student revolutionary, popping in and out to do my teaching and to keep my own private life together. Stuart, most *definitely* in a contradictory position as a full-time employee of the University, was a major figure in the sit-in, a memorable and major speaker in front of huge masses of students and exciting rallies. The Centre and that group of students who had just arrived were very involved. Courses were cancelled, the entire proceedings of the Centre were suspended, all time and energy was given over to arguments over strategy and political discussions of what the demands were or should be or could be. A very exciting period. Richard telling me to be confused and now the world was really turned upside down. Embarrassingly I think for Richard Hoggart, always down to earth and courteous, his baby, the Centre, had become the think-tank for the student revolution.

How much lasting change was there within universities? From the institution's viewpoint, didn't it all blow over, to a certain extent?

Well, I don't know, I forget some of the specific demands now. But there was certainly student representation, student councils were instituted and there was *far* more student in-put into curriculum development, although how long-lasting that was is debatable. In terms of the Centre, "blow over," *absolutely not!* We were the permanent revolutionary council of the sit-in extended indefinitely—in our minds at least. Stuart was very brave, as well as conditioned in a certain degree of paranoia, in coping over a very long period with the feeling that he was camping out in an enemy institution. But from that moment, especially after Richard left, the Centre was very clearly a pioneer in a different kind of pedagogical relation. *I* was perfectly clear that Stuart felt that he was protecting us from the institution and that the Centre was some kind of experiment—although we all thought it was an experiment that would expand and take over the world. Somehow I was simultaneously centre and periphery. Against what I said just about feeling "normal," non-privileged, you could say that along with other students I also shared some sense of the importance of being at the centre of things. A failed "scholarship boy," I was now recruited to the revolution, being groomed for something or other returned now in radical guise. Whereas before I thought I'd be joining the establishment, then this happened, and through accidents of history, personal inertias against other kinds of future as much as anything else, I moved into a radicalised position. I felt that I was really part of some important movement in those years and Stuart was *the* charismatic leader, taking great risks with his own career trying to put into practice within our tiny, micro-institution many of the feelings and principles of the student movement, *especially* the notion of being open in terms of disciplinary areas and being led by student interests, connected *outwards*.

To what extent did Stuart Hall define the focus of the Centre?

In a remote control kind of way perhaps, also, of course controlling and maintaining the general parameters and political ambience. Not substantively. Collectively we really did control most of the administrative processes, certainly the areas of work, reading and research. There was no question but that it was a collectively-controlled process. We certainly felt that. Though looking back on it, we probably did exactly what Stuart wanted a lot of the time. This arrangement was a secret from the university: if the administration knew, there would be dire consequences, such as being closed down, especially after Richard Hoggart had gone. That first year was a very strange inter-regnum. After the sit-in and after '68, Richard went. I have no evidence but I wonder whether Richard went *because* of the sit-in. He could see he'd got this nest of radicals, the nest that he's never known what to do with since. In one way he must have been pleased, for his entrepreneurial actions in setting up the Centre led to the formation of cultural studies—and *The Uses of Literacy* was and is a very important book in that. But I think he must have felt cause for alarm when it ran in to a kind of continuation of New Left battles in different form.

After Richard, Stuart took on a new kind of institutional role; rather than just the archival, professorial relations that Richard was used to, he was attempting to foment academic revolution from below. Business meetings were every Monday, where Stuart would open the books and say what was happening, what the University was on about to him. All the crucial issues and processes of admissions were collectivised. Admission criteria were discussed as rationally as possible, political, subject area, academic. Groups of students interviewed candidates. Curriculum-wise students chose areas, topics and texts collectively, though with advice from Stuart. I remember him advising caution about getting seriously into Marxism because it was not something you could easily get out of again or readily adapt to an eclectic frame. I also remember him saying, many times, that quality was essential, depth of understanding and rigour of argument were to be the weapons of persuasion, not political assertion.

Has the subsequent fetishisation of that period surprised you? The way in which it's been mythologised?

I don't know. The real lessons may have been entirely forgotten. I think it still carries lessons around pedagogy, and around how we might organise intellectual work, lessons from a long-lasting academic experiment in genuinely collective work. Oddly there is most to learn from what were experienced as the failures within a stuttering but still continued experiment.

What was the "Theory Seminar"?

Our early attempts to define "culture," to find relevant disciplines and methods and approaches developed into what we called the Theory Seminar, where we went through intellectual traditions in a reasonably systematic way. After the impetus of the student sit-in, we tried to carry some of the principles of collective work into this Theory Seminar. I don't remember exactly, but I think we started off with literary theory, structuralism, then sociology, I remember Berger and Luckmann, moving eventually into an engagement with Marxism. But it hit the buffers and basically failed. The attempt to really work through a coherent position on what culture was and what a method was, and adapting them to a radical programme, just proved impossible. People couldn't agree, and there wasn't a coherent heart to it all. Compromising, we moved from what we called a "tight collective" to a "loose collective." We split into working-groups, we called them Work Groups. So those who were interested in literature and the Humanities went into the Literature Group; heavy-weight theorists went into the Ideology Group; later feminism, "race" groups and so on. We just couldn't all agree.

Were these political differences, or theoretical differences?

The principal problem, as I recall, was that we couldn't agree on a central theoretical core, but as you can well imagine, theoretical differences were associated with political differences, which were associated with different political positions, in some cases sectarian positions. At times things were quite tense, or I experienced them so. These devolved work groups met often without a member of staff for a whole year and were, of course, self-directed. But something very important remained from the "tight collective." You had to report back at what we termed the Centre Presentations, every summer, on what the hell you'd been up to. The place still had that sense of, you know, this ambition, some sense of a major project. Only now it was really focussed and productive. You would be *judged* at the Centre Presentations, so you pulled your finger out, stopped up all night preparing and writing. People used to get absolutely *terrified* about making their presentation, both to show that they'd been up to something—which of course they had been—and perhaps more importantly to in some way justify it as part of the project, to justify it with respect to other positions. And, looking back, it is simply extraordinary how many of those presentations from working-groups, which might have been working with only a few students, subsequently became books or issues of *Working Papers in Cultural Studies.* So I think we stumbled upon a fantastically productive way of working. Some framework of overall direction and commitment, substantial autonomy; collective pooling of ideas and critique, and terror motivating individuals to work to a deadline. Odd combinations of centre and periphery again. A stable instability of collectivism and rampant individualism.

Learning to Labour

How was your own work, both with the hippies and the "lads," received in the working groups of the Centre?

I felt throughout that my fieldwork was seen as unscientific, humanistic and rather subjective. The major area where I felt a palpable, sometimes personal, sense of critique was in a Marxist attack on agency and subjectivity, almost an orthodoxy on the inadequacy of humanistic positions. I felt that I had to justify myself, take the issues seriously. In another place, you would have been allowed to continue in the humanist track of your own concerns. At the Centre there was, through the continuing plenary sessions in every summer term, a sense of trying to bring things back together in some co-ordinated and central, critical, cultural studies approach. But still I felt sectored off.

None-the-less in terms of my development it was very important that I was in a Centre which had some central collective purpose together with a space for autonomous work. Although there wasn't really a strong ethnographic tradition at the Centre, that particular mix of autonomy and purpose was what kept me at my last. The Centre presentations posed question after question for me, trenchant questions which I couldn't ignore. I was at the periphery taking the centre very seriously.

Did you carry on defending your own project as these critiques developed? Did you feel you had to keep defending your way of "squaring the circle"?

Well, I was accused of working with a banal or un-theorised sense of subjectivity and agency, and that I was kind of assuming an answer without stating the main puzzle. By assuming a sense of subjectivity and creativity I was short-circuiting, deliberately ignoring or simply altogether overlooking the Althusserian position on interpellation. I was working from the assumption that "the lads" were creative, rather than trying to explain the conundrum that they felt so against all the contrary evidence. I felt that hanging on to that creativity was the main concern, and I still think it is, although the terms of the argument have undoubtedly changed. I don't know whether I defended my position so much as stuck with it *sotto voce*. I do remember Stuart, in response to a Work Group presentation I was involved in, saying "What Paul calls creativity I call survival."

There is a very strong continuity throughout your work in your ideas around creativity.

I suppose that's my story. I had an initial interest in individual artistic activity, feeling that was at the centre of things, but drew a blank in the boring, aesthete, refined textual version of that. It continued as an impetus to find the same thing in ordinary life: some form of holding the centre and the periphery again perhaps. And there is a longer-term politics to seeing some spark of creativity or aspiration or aesthetic motivation within absolutely, everyday, common experience. Rather than it being a contin-uous, visible, presence, this is routinely lost, distorted or alienated or turned into reified forms, folding back in oddly repressive ways according to circumstance in different sites, institutions and situations. Never quite lost though, always recoverable, that's the point. I think in every intellectual work, one tries to preserve the core, an impetus, a subconscious stream of the will to know or to state or to argue for.

The lesson of the Centre was that the humanistic assertion of human creativity had to live in those same four walls of the Centre with *very* tough Marxist notions around reproduction and class continuities. And then *certainly* there was the feminist critique of me at the Centre. How I'd ignored patriarchal divisions, reduced them to class ones. And especially some sense of my under-estimating the importance of the home: as the factory was the site of capital conflicts, that the home too might be the site of gender conflicts, that my own methods were mostly related to work and schools and didn't take enough account of domestic relations. There was a move in one of the feminist Centre Presentations to critique, even outlaw, naturalistic ethnography like *Learning to Labour* because it was seen as uncritically reproducing rather than condemning and deconstructing sexist conventions, forms and prejudices.

Actually, in *Learning to Labour* I did think I was working in a way that took account of patriarchal categories and feminist critiques. This was another pressure I felt I was working against, not by refusal, but by creative internal extension, invention and appropriation. I still feel that some of what I'd been trying to argue hasn't been taken seriously by feminists, which was an attempt to see how gender divisions overlapped onto especially manual-mental divisions within capitalism. I wasn't arguing that a certain working-class male masculinity was forever linking manualism and masculinity, but that these were different binary systems with their own histories, and that in other situations you might have different articulations of gender, patriarchal and capitalist categories. There is a real instability in the way that gender systems and capital systems or capital relations are articulated with each other.

Right now there is a terrific disruption in the apprenticeship model, reshaping modes of social reproduction formed over a very long period of industrialisation. And we are seeing a crisis or reformulation of how important binary systems of thought relating to gender and relating to class and relating to location are recombining. I would very much argue that some of that ethnographic, theoretical Marxism continues to be relevant, not in an all-time depiction of a certain working-class masculinity, but precisely in freeing up the terms of the analysis, so that different articulations and combinations are possible. So that there might be a gentler, working-class masculinity, or there might be a masculinity which is freed from proletarianism. And to my mind, I had taken the feminist point about systems of patriarchy. Whether I've taken it properly methodologically back into the home or quite what a method is for the home I don't know.

It must have been quite hard for you—you had to be brave to defend your position again and again?

Yeah, though you shouldn't get too heroic a notion of how I defended myself. Throughout the period I lived in Wolverhampton and drove over to Birmingham: in the early part of the period I was working in four institutions and selling ice cream; in the second part where I was a Research Fellow working on *Learning to Labour* I was out doing fieldwork, or I was in Wolverhampton having a *very* normal life. And all of those were supports for an alternative subjectivity, one which I didn't have to sustain or fight for in the Centre. There was always a centre of gravity or base or some lead in my bottom which was related to other identities. And you *could* argue that this maintained a certain humanism as well as a certain interest in field practice. I wasn't an active, discursively and intellectually fully-armed, fully-referenced, fully kitted-out, Centre warrior fighting in each of those Marxist, feminist and anti–racist revolutions. I understood the implications for subjectivity of the arguments around interpellation, around gender, around "race." I could see all that, but I *also* had, and it's embarrassing to say it, a "common sense" view which knew that your identity was always *more* than class, gender or ethnicity, involving a whole set of points about the way you lived, how you fitted in, who you knew, what the myriad of your personal and domestic relations were: these things were separate from the theories that I picked up specifying obvious binary divisions. If you're in the field and trying to understand the way a pub works or a factory works, then there's a million other things going on around humour, around language, around personality types, around taking-the-piss—and where you're just not clever enough to have worked out all the binaries, all the binaries producing other terms or still other binaries. A good fieldworker *knows* something's important without being able to say: "This is an example of class. This is an example of gender. This is an example of "race."

How do you feel about Learning to Labour's subsequent reception?

Learning to Labour is, in many ways, an odd book. I didn't think it would travel very far, I thought it was "only" a monograph which I was very relieved to get published. I got a poor deal out of the publishers, but it was very surprising how quickly it succeeded and sold a lot of copies. It was a bit of an accident, perhaps, that it hit a certain time in academic history, a certain time in Marxism, in cultural studies, educational sociology, a certain time in educational politics around an emerging disillusionment and disenchant- ment with the promises of comprehensive schooling. It's gone to several editions now and numerous translations. It is selling more than ever, certainly in Japan, Germany, the U.S. of course. I was recently in Korea, where there was a briskly selling pirate edition. I saw the book as an ethnog- raphy of creativity and social consequence in unexpected place. It continues to hit a variety of debates, issues and interests, travelling out of Cultural Studies altogether. Perhaps its natural home has become anthropology which is both odd and gratifying.

Amongst anthropologists, do you think Learning to Labour was more influen- tial in America, because of its broader and more inclusive anthropological tradition, in comparison to Britain?

I don't know. I can't speak authoritatively about anthropology. Certainly in the U.S. the book registered early on in anthropology. I had several take- ups and invites from U.S. anthropology departments, and that was not the case until recently in British anthropology. In the British case now this may be a partly paranoid, partly justified reaction to the advance of cultural studies. Maybe they've opened their doors to me to protect themselves from other sources. Perhaps my work is discussed as a reverse Trojan horse within cultural studies, to indicate that the best part of the enemy has been doing exactly the same anyway!

Policy, Politics and the University

Can you tell us about how you got involved in working for Wolverhampton council, and how The Youth Review *(1986) came about?*

During the Thatcher cuts and contractions of the early 1980s I lost my research fellowship at the CCCS and was unemployed for about a year. I was involved with the local Labour party here in Wolverhampton and they asked me to do a review of youth unemployment. Their idea was to try to formu-late and implement effective policies for the enormous crisis engulfing the town, we were falling into the yawning gap of mass unemployment—this town has lost half of its manufacturing jobs since 1979. Thatcher's strategy was to use monetarism, the high pound and international capital to outflank and discipline workers and trade-unions. The closure of British Steel and other plants hit this town very hard. There was a particular concern about youth unemployment. I used that opening to try to do a thorough account of the local impact of unemployment in a whole variety of ways, with a sample survey and ethnographic studies of social groups of young men, young women, African–Caribbeans and Asians. I had three research assis-tants paid for by the council: the research grew and grew. I also did a review of all the main local agency departments, ten I think, in relation to what I called the "new social condition" of youth. I believe that this was the first comprehensive review of the local impact of post–industrial mass unem-ployment in developed context.

Rather than start with the usual internal departmental reviews, we were trying to show the crisis from the point of view of youth and *then* move on to how the local authority departments might adapt to the new situation and the new needs of youth. Don't forget that the Black Country was the Silicon valley of the Industrial revolution. You could say that in 1979 and the early 1980s it saw the beginning of the post–industrial revolution, that vacuum still waiting to be filled. Other places saw the new industrial revolu-tions. This is a crisis that we are *absolutely* still working through. A region and a population that over 200 hundred years had adapted to the rhythms and exploitations and disciplines and powers of the industrial wage, suddenly lost its centre. Relatively settled patterns of social and cultural reproduction were thrown into crisis. It was almost as if Mrs. Thatcher wanted to push areas like this quite literally over the brink.

What was your experience of engaging with policy-makers? Did you try and define an agenda, or argue that policy-work should make a space for what you call "sensuous creativity"?

I can't say that I talked about "sensuous creativity" but that was the resource from which I was working and hoped to liberate. Politics is to some extent a dirty business. From the point of view of getting change at the local level and perhaps feeding something through to the national level, I felt it was important to have a big slab of evidence to give to local politicians. The *Youth Review* was a very chunky document, containing hard and soft data. I stressed the importance of taking the perspective of young people against departmental and professional perspectives and inertias, and for building in systematic forms of youth representation. In terms of making changes happen it was important to work politically, seek alliances, open up new channels of political influence. I helped form a youth council. Involved in distributing funds for cultural activities, it also supplied representatives of a new political committee called the Youth Affairs Committee. This political committee wasn't just interested in what's normally at the *bottom* of usually the education committee's agenda, ie. youth clubs and youth leisure and sporting activities, but it also took reports on housing, policing, social services, education and so on. The Youth Affairs Committee and the youth council still exist. The fundamental spirit of *The Youth Review* was to re-orient the local state to the needs and problems of youth, rather than what has predominated since, which is to use the state to reform youth as more useable and low priced labour power for internationalised capitalist labour markets.

I tried to suggest to the voluntary sector as well as to the state that poli-cies could be derived from the actual existing condition of the youth, rather than from the view of the powerful as to how they should change or be formed. It is wrong to think that there is a right royal road that connects through from ethnography to policy. I think it can play an important role, but the question of politics, in so far as you are involved in politics when you are doing fieldwork, is a very broad front indeed. We used all kinds of methods. One of them was certainly to do sample surveys, so you could show in big numbers what was happening. This was combined with quali-tative work, so you could begin to try and develop an agenda that was made by the needs of young people. You can't simply stick a microphone in a seminar and ask them what they want; by the fact of their structural situa-tion they are confused and disoriented when it comes to formulating public positions. Nevertheless you can use an ethnographic technique to look at the forms of their lives and to an extent speak on their behalf. There continue to be whole sets of issues around training and education, cultural provision, housing, for many working-class youth on very low wages. For example, whether they have low-paid jobs or no jobs they find it impossible to get into an increasingly privatised flat market. Why the hell isn't the state dealing with that issue?

How did you feel about using ethnography in this new setting?

I'm not claiming wonderful successes, but I am claiming some direct communication of real needs and that the youth affairs perspective has, for example, registered housing needs as central to the youth condition and has met at least some housing needs of young people in special singles developments.

To try to focus a bit, in my view the work for *The Youth Review* was almost the opposite of the colonial encounter which spawned anthropological ethnography. Now don't forget my accidental drop into anthropological methods relieved me, as I see it, almost entirely of colonial bad faith and guilt. On the other hand it has saddled me with a humanist urge, perhaps a white working-class or petit bourgeois take on whatever human creativity is supposed to be. Far from being associated with colonial agency, trying nostalgically to preserve, in a dis-connected backwards-looking and elite kind of way, a threatened or perhaps imagined past, I thought I was helping the "people" in their current struggles to formulate their position in order to make demands on the local state in an emergent set of social relations. I was *within* the circuit of as a contending force rather than trailing its dominant elements.

I don't know though, it's complicated. You could say that I was concerned with a disappearing way of life and I was paid for by the colonial adminis-tration—though is the Labour party really a similar organisation? It is also true that there was a situation of fear after the 1981 riots and there was a worry all over the country about youth rebellion. As with the colonial paymaster, there was an issue of intelligence for social control.

But there was a very genuine feeling in the Labour Party that we were spending a lot of money on local services, youth provision and education and that it could be made more relevant to "*our* kids." There was a sense of the whole region being set against wider powers. If you genuinely take in feeling from below, even with a reformist programme, there are definitely changes that are worth making to make structures, provisions and services more in line with real and emergent conditions as experienced and lived.

If you look back now, what difference do you think you've made? This is a ques-tion partly about your vision, your ways of seeing. In your new book, you describe yourself at one point as an "intellectual vandal." At another, you say that there are no large projects any more, only cultural gardening jobs. Looking back on your different projects, would you want to say that one has had more impact than another? Has Learning to Labour *been more influential than* The Youth Review?

It is very difficult for me to bill myself as having been effective in any particular way. Think back to some of the idealistic self-promotions of ourselves at the Centre—that we were organic intellectuals about to change the world! In fact we moved within a short tight circuit of influencing each other and ultimately perhaps some other intellectuals, but not really the real world. I would be embarrassed about claiming identifiable effects on anything other than what I've done in immediate contexts and circumstances. You can certainly bear in mind possible longer range effects and argue for certain versions of them, but it's by no means obvious how things will work out. There are the struggles within intellectual practice which are well worth having, and then there are the consequences of how we see the world within our own practices.

My work has been about trying to grasp in an ethnographic way what it means to live and act out structurally given conditions of existence and changed structural positions. A lot of kids won't be in permanent work now. They'll be in a mosaic of study-schemes and very low-paid part-time work, sometimes scrounging off parents then back into another state scheme. That's a whole new role, or much extended regular role, for the state. The state sector is going to become a whole terrain of experience, not as a part of a transition, as an early part, but as a continuing condition of experience. Blair has also talking about 50% of 18 year-olds going on into Higher Education. There is developing a whole new type of student body. Surprisingly, perhaps, because in this country now students have to pay their own way and their own fees, there continues to be a strong demand for sociology, media studies and cultural studies as well as or instead of vocational studies, training for IT etc. It's hard to see the meal tickets at the end of social studies, but there is still this clear demand. Socially relevant ethnography, my own work included, can offer very useful curricular and project materials for these new spaces, allowing students to recognise, dignify and analyse their own private experiences and cultural practices—often a motive, sometimes mis-recognised, for an interest in social studies. Ethnography can help in developing a certain kind of self-reflexivity, not so much in being aware of oneself, as being aware of the conditions of possibility of the self, the self as an historical as well as existential construct. I have a history of letters from workers and others who had read *Learning to Labour* in various contexts, who had already encountered it in classes, or by accident, one in a prison library, and who have re-understood their own experiences of ten years and more before, and become more mentally and socially attuned. There is a diffuseness about intellectual work which we simply shouldn't underestimate: texts do take on their own lives. There is a special poignancy in ethnography, about reported experience which can make itself live again, or re-ignite in different ways, elements within the experiences of the reader, in the experience of reading. This is a way of digging out the relations between selves and their mediated conditions of existence; of contemplating the possible meanings of living *changed* conditions of existence. It's a way of identifying what may be controllable as well as identifying the continuing power of cultural anachronisms even when we don't know what the "synchronisms" might be.

Do you think this sort of work is still possible in Blairite, sound-bite, focus-group Britain?

The general policy framework, structurally, has been moving against the left, and against a kind of radical policies that try and understand issues systematically from below. The Labour party, which was a major hope for connecting through to influences or interests from below, has become detached from the working class. In many ways it is continuing a kind of Thatcherite project, connecting with the masses through advertising techniques. But Blairism, focus group-ism and political marketing doesn't exhaust the political or policy field. In all kinds of ways the state is and will be involved with managing the population, and there are huge issues for everyone, not least state agents of one kind or another, about how this is done—intellectually, culturally, personally politically. What is the state's role to be in managing explosive new developments in: new technologies; exploding communications; floods of cheap or without cost information; nano-technologies and new manufacturing; exponential rises in computer power and artificial intelligence; micro-biological control of genetic make-up. What is to be the shape of the *inevitable* state involvement in the interactions of these things with commercial interests and the commodisation of all kinds of human provision? Even more important still, what will be the state's involvement in managing the social relations of the emergent trends of this brave new world, especially in managing those left out, economically and culturally, but who could still ruin the party for the rest? There *could* be liberating dimensions of a new governance in so far as *practical* aspects of feelings from below are registered and become part of the operation of power, and can mine, twist and develop from there. Whereas under New Labour, it's hard to see how we're not just a branch of multi-national capital with the state trying, without fully knowing what it's doing, to train workers to attract international capital. But there are many dimensions. Don't forget that state sectors are still hugely important—45 pence in every pound spent in this country is spent by the state, mostly locally or through the local state. Questions of politics and governance at a local level—of how the population is enrolled under these conditions—are very important topics indeed, especially with the increased importance of culture and subjective experience. There is a feeling that you have to take into account peoples' views. Even if you do manipulate them in the end, you can't do it in old top-down ways, especially in face to face service and institutional locations. There are new discourses around, of human rights, which are in part an articulation of the way people really have changed. People aren't prepared to be ascribed identities, I'm a worker, she's a whatever. Everyone, in a very incoherent way, is struggling for their own piece of action. How are these cultural trends and the technical/economic trends to collide? Economic disenfranchisement is juxtaposed with strange cultural enfranchisements. That is where critical ethnography can be very important, to get more thought-out, integrated policy options, especially in local government; options which both attend to the cultural impetus and keep the redistributive questions alive.

You talked of the implications of 50% of 18-year-olds being in higher education, and of people staying in state-sector provision throughout their lives. What are your feelings about the potentials and risks of these changes for the future of the university?

A lot of the educational/training discourses in the U.K. about attracting inward investment to Britain are very instrumentalist. Improving our "human capital," "competitive advantage" etc., etc. The global situation has changed the parameters within which the game is played out: within the official discourses there is a never-ending game enforced of apparently increasing the value of labour power to multi-national capital. Meanwhile in local areas, the situations of people going into HE (higher education) are far more diverse. It still amazes me that working class middle-aged women will sign up to do sociology and cultural studies, with very few apparent employment prospects, rather than IT or personnel management, the skills from which they might expect to have 20 years reasonable income and material security. They are doing it for personal development, doing it to make sense of their previous personal and cultural history, and doing it, to use my old humanistic terms, in search of some sort of creativity in their own lives and possible futures in ways which aren't entirely linked to labour market outcomes. I think this whole area can be a huge opportunity for sociological studies, cultural studies and anthropology, using critical ethnography as a live action research project to understand what the new transitions/destinations/mosaics and possibilities are within the logic of cultural practice and experience, so that involvement in higher education is intrinsically interesting and enjoyable, and relates to forms of consciousness raising and development which needn't be vacuous or rely on the worn-out old cliches of "race, class and gender." If cultural studies had developed in a different way, through the early fermenting period had fashioned a cultural studies ethnography, rather than splintering into several idealist camps, cultural studies might really have become *the* form of adult education.

Anyway, the current situation. Education is enmeshed in an unequal struggle between contending views of labour power, you might call them instrumental vs. expressive, with the former calling all the shots. Peoples' experiences and motivations, especially on a local level, might however relate more readily to an expressive labour power, and if you were clever enough you might be able to combine them all up, because developed expressive labour power may be a very valuable resource for many employers.

How to play the future? I don't know. Defend institutional positions, defend subject positions, try to argue that expressive labour power is an economic resource, all of those are possibilities. The sector will undoubtedly further fragment between the "elite" and the "new" universities, and "e-unis" will rise. We are going to head more towards an American situation. But my own view on local universities is that they should be real universities, and that they shouldn't be glorified further education colleges, intellectually franchised only to teach other peoples' research. Part of that local relevance must be in, by any standards, high quality work, where policy and ethnographic interests can come in and combine.

Part 3: Ethnography and Theory

"Being There": Tape-Recorders and Ethnographic "Data"

I caught I think the first technological wave of ethnographic work. I was very short of time (this is 1968, with everything else that was happening in my life), and I was desperate to get out into the world to see what was happening. It was the classic, first-time, cold contact ethnographic encounter. There was a famous pub right in the centre of the hippy scene in Birmingham and I asked the bartender who were the big hippies, the people who were on the hippie scene. And he told me, he introduced me to some of them, saying I was doing a project for a Ph.D. on music and hippy culture, and needed more information. I hadn't done any methods courses, I didn't see myself as an anthropologist, I knew I just had to have data. So I said do you mind if I record the discussions? They didn't have portable tape-recorders and cassettes at this period at all, or not that I knew about anyway. The Centre had just spent a small fortune on a massive, top quality reel to reel tape-recorder which was like a suitcase, and I carried this huge suitcase around the hippy pads, stuck it on the table, unpacking great spools of tape. Talk about unobtrusive methods! I saw it at the time as "For god's sake get something, get some data!" I'd got so little time, I wanted to have a form of working where I could get data and use it, do it quickly.

Did you not feel you could just take notes? Did you feel you had to have some tapes?

Yes. To have data for some confidence that I'd got something, the feeling of being in the field and filling up with data as efficiently as possible. A store of data, a bit like a store of money, against the rainy theoretical day. You could figure out how to use it later, though you didn't know how to use it then, in the future you would have a store of data. Making hay when you could. I was taking notes as well, and making notes, especially early stabs at theoretical explanation. Though I also remember having piles of notes from the field, the hippies, and looking through and thinking "God, I haven't got enough! What am I going to say about this?" Haven't you had that feeling in the field? It arose from a real insecurity that I didn't have enough, the importance of getting a store of data that you could go through later was simply crucial to me. I think it would be a very interesting line to figure out when tapes came in, and whether they change field practice, or make people lazy? I think I'm partly responsible for cultural studies' over-reliance on verbal responses, and on a cultural studies notion of a very quick, dirty raid which is discursively based. First of all you turn to the tape-recorder, and you've got a project if you've got an hour's conversation. Then if you are just going to use a few words anyway, why not just remember a few things that somebody said to you in the pub [laughs]. So you could imagine it as the beginning of the corrosion of serious fieldwork.

But at the same time, I think it's a very good example of how technology can be fantastically useful. We are very poor now at exploiting modern technology: visuals, moving images and video you know. Sometimes the fly-on-the-wall documentaries, docu-soaps and much of popular culture is about using visual means to represent everyday experience, whereas with the professionals, if you're not using your pen and your notebook, you're still not a real anthropologist.

But the problem there is that the tape-recording becomes ethnography per se. That somehow a tape stands for fieldwork.

Yeah, I think that is a negative thing, duplicating the limits of the docu-soaps in a way. Though you can also fall down by mistaking the notebook for the field, or its meanings. The antidote to all of this is the flexible and open use of theory. Of all of the questions about how theory relates to ethnography, I think the crucial point of ethnography is its flexibility; that you can, almost unconsciously, test theories and hypotheses as you go through in the field. But it's also the case that some form of that takes place afterwards in your own data analysis, so that listening to your tape and seeing what main categories develop out of your tapes, how they relate to your existing thinking, is a way of getting onto something, getting traction.

It's nice when you're able to go back to the field to refine this, but even within the data there is a similar dialectic going on, where even if you can't go back to the field, you nevertheless go back to other bits of data, or you look through fieldnotes with a new sensitivity to issues that you didn't have at the time you wrote the data. Data should never be a congealed block simply waiting to be turned over to readers like toppling a concrete slab their way.

This is another route back to the importance of an open notion of what's relevant in the field and an open theoretical notion so that you record things that seem to you to be interesting and important, even if at that point you can't say why. It may well be that at a later stage in/of the data processing and analysis, you do know why you had a hunch that this was important, but you didn't have a proper theoretical reason for why it was important at the time.

On Multi-Sited Ethnography

Part of the reason your ethnography was taken up within anthropology was the perception within the discipline that we hadn't looked at class. This links to the question of doing what has come to be talked about as "multi-sited ethnography," of how you do ethnographic work of larger systems, of capitalism or globalisation, which seems to be even more pressing now than it was then.

I worry a little bit about multi-sited ethnography, and some American forms of anthropology. Through the new journal, *Ethnography*, I am learning about contemporary trends in the discipline. Many anthropologists are responding to the post–modern turn by adopting a version of contemporary history. You get a bit of political economy as an overall view of the country, you get a bit of institutional history, and then you get a snap of someone sitting on a verandah with somebody from a development agency. This is a kind of super-sophisticated journalism. The specific anthropological eye becomes the over-viewing eye of contemporary history. I see why this happens and it has a role. But I just don't want to lose the focus on situated human creativity, on "chunky" ethnography. With a lot of modern anthropology you don't quite know why you've been told stuff. It's interesting, it's a good story, but so what? What's the question or puzzle that the writer is wrestling with, and *from what vantage point*? What's specific about the mode of enquiry? The worry about the local-ness and the worry about narration, how the data is communicated, should not lead us to desert chunky, close, fine-grained, finely detailed, sensuous ethnography and head off towards an attempt to contain all levels of determination within a single descriptive frame.

There are other routes to understanding how the locality relates to the global, other routes of narration. There may be short circuits between global capitalist domination and some of the internal intricacies of experience. It is very important to record concentrated detail about subjectivity, about experiential intimacies, whatever the difficulties of representation and natu-ralness. Amongst other things this is in order to have a chance to be able to link them in theoretically reflexive ways, in compelling and nuanced ways, in ways that produce an "Ah-ha" effect, to a dimensionality and depth in how structural determination, change and continuity are understood and presented. The ways we live now are formed *both* through structuring forces and the increasing power and apparent viability of internal experiences and very local practices. There seems to me to be a danger in multi-sited ethnog-raphy and overview ethnography where external determination, influence and life-force, that which drives the whole thing forwards, is presumed as some kind of reservoir of global water. Waterfalls cascade down through a number of levels, starting off as global history, and you give that as a section, and then it flows into a national arena, then it dribbles down into politics and institutions. A bit more water dribbles down onto the town and the local economy, and a bit more dribbles down onto trade unions and a bit more water dribbles down onto specific sites and *finally* you get to creative groups and individuals and you've got no water. Certainly no counter-flows. One way of dealing with the problems is to try and understand the short circuits, to try and understand, for instance, commodity fetishism in the commoditised materials and communications which surround us and what it means for subjectivity. That stretches both to the global and to the highly particular. This would be, for me, a structural "force" that can be named at the subjective level, and analysed interactively there, rather than traced through millions of mediations. It is very odd that whilst everything is provided, nothing made locally, we've never held intimacy as more impor-tant. Yet you won't get to that intimacy by starting with global capitalism and then to national capitalism then Blairite politics etc.

Just as there is a kind of reductive and flattening "do-it-all" political economy, there is also a flattening "discursive-ism" still prevalent. If you focus just on narratives and discourses, then you understand consciousness and subjectivity on a very artificial and self-justifying rationalising level, insulating yourself from the possibility of recording and understanding sensuous activities and processes as containing depth and dynamism as well as subtlety and ambiguity. People are moved by passions that they can't explain. They are involved with musics, technologies, situations, things, that help them to hold and develop an expressive sense of themselves, sensu-ously, which might often be in tension with their discursive "positions."

Rather than a flow of structural determinations, economic and symbolic, trickling down, there is something around culture and consciousness and subjectivity at a particular stage of history struggling in its own creative ways to make sense of the mediations around intensely private and intimate experience. Even in the Third World which is going through a rapidly

concertina-ing period of not only industrialisation but also the industrialisation of consciousness, the mediating levels may be as much determined
by subjective changes as by larger structural changes. Of course I believe in
and support "global ethnography." How else did it start? We can't now leave
"globalisation" to capitalists and abstract theorists. But we need to try to
define what *we* mean.

If the result of the critique of empiricism is to lessen the focus on
concrete local experience and its own ways of dealing with world changes,
then we've lost. We must really maintain a dialectical open-ness to the mid-
range institutions being as influenced by culture and subjective change as by
macro-change. Not least they have to adapt to try to control and contain
pressures, restraints and resistances "from below." The journalists and historians and economists can do an equally good job of painting the overall
picture, but the particular anthropological or ethnographic contribution
should be to continue to focus on experience. Of course multi-sited studies
and methodologies are important to a larger understanding, but they
shouldn't be of multiple depth-less differences abstractly draped on a
second-hand political economy clotheshorse. They should show how the
same or similar tendencies are played out dialectically *in experience* and *local
practices* in different ways according to power, location and interest.

Theory, Ethnography, and Ethics

Who would you say has most influenced your theoretical position?

So far as I've got a coherent theoretical position it has developed from my
own interests, empirical interests, political interests and from protecting my
humanism from, or justifying it with respect to, other theoretical positions.
My recent book, *The Ethnographic Imagination* (2000), is in some ways my
first attempt to systematise and theorise a position. *Profane Culture* grew out
of the struggles to understand the biker culture within a humanist early
cultural studies paradigm. The *Ethnographic Imagination* grows out of
struggles to try to understand ethnographic specificity in relation to the the
take-over of cultural studies and much of social science by linguistic paradigms and post–structuralism (which is a simplification but there's truth in
it), re-thinking my naive practices in *Profane Culture*, for instance, in the
light of subsequent debates. Staking out the possibility of fieldwork on
sensuousness from my point of view.

For graduate students and people at the beginning of their career,
"Theory" constitutes a major dilemma, you know: "Am I a Marxist?" "Am I
a Bourdieuan now or a symbolic interactionist?" "An ethnomethodologist?"
"A semiologist?" I have difficulties with all those categories. My own view is
that ethnographers should have a healthy independence. I'm not against any
of the theories actually. I've learned a great deal from all of the theoretical
revolutions of the Centre, and I learn a great deal from the incredible range

of Bourdieu's work now. But if I *hadn't* got my own groundings in a humanistic creativity and some, however limited, examples of my own field experiences to draw upon to, it would be very difficult not to get sucked into theory. Funnily enough I think Bourdieu would say something rather similar about his early Algerian fieldwork. The problem is if you're, for example, just a Bourdieu disciple before the fact of fieldwork, it's even *harder* to do creative fieldwork; you would be using a Bourdieuan system and looking for exemplifications and illustrations. Back to the importance of Hoggart's "immersion in the destructive element" again.

So, I am against joining a school. Grad students tend to feel that they need to belong to a school, it's very difficult not to get sucked in, to find a patron, theoretically and sometimes concretely. It's slightly dangerous in my view. The commitment of the ethnographer should in some way be to his/her topic and set of small "p" politics and priorities. Being principledly eclectic, rather than putting all their eggs into one basket. Theorists cluster, they are often saying rather similar things. Bewitched by their own importance, perfecting their own "unique selling propositions" they are just very, very clever at generating further relevant categories, salami slicing against the opposition. This can get in the way of sensuousness. You end up more bothered about figuring out what a theorist means rather than figuring out what culture means. You should only use theory if it creates illumination, casts light on things, help you to present a phenomenon more fully *in itself.* Too many ethnographies are shackled rather than liberated by theoretical obeisance. If there aren't illuminating categories around, don't shy away from developing or adapting your own categories in relationship to the world, which is *undoubtedly* developing ahead of us and developing forms, binaries, sensuousness, emergences, cultural forms which *aren't* going to fit easily into prior categories. The over-reification of theories and theorists is a big problem.

How do you get your own Ph.D. students to engage with theory without being overwhelmed by it?

By asking why they are interested in the topic and then reminding them of Hoggart's advice to me. By saying that I want, for all of the naturalistic dangers, to have some account of the topic that interests them. By encouraging wide readings and trying outs. This is where the intellectual vandal comes in. Try on lots of different theorists in however a primitive form and don't genuflect to Bourdieu or Marx or Althusser or Bhabha or Spivak, you know. Don't be a pedant! To try to get the essence of what they're saying in practical and useable form and throw the concept at what interests *you,* and see if sticks. If it is illuminating and interesting, fine, then remodel the concept, be a bit less of a vandal. If it doesn't fit, try throwing something else.

Has it been lonely doing the sort of intellectual work you've done? Has it been hard for you to stick to your guns, stick to your eclecticism?

Good question. If you asked me if I was an intellectual, I'd say no. I'd say I'm a person who lives in Wolverhampton and who does intellectual *work* some of the time. The work is not at the centre. I earn some of my money in the academy. I have some sense of a centre of existence or identity—not that I know what it is, I certainly wouldn't want to glorify it—that's *not* defined by the academy. If I were a person more defined by the academy it might be not just lonely but impossible to plough my furrow. But it's another kind of loneliness, oddly bringing its own kinds of solidarity, which insulates me from academic paranoi, from taking its endless debates too seriously. I don't know, aren't all ethnographers to an extent facing a problem? Being worldly and not worldly. Convinced of the necessity of fieldwork; inescapably doubting the human integrity of the human contracts it entails. Whether or not they join a theoretical school, they know this *dreadful* contradiction of the exploitative relations within the ethnographic encounter. You're a voyeur, you're trying to look around corners. You're also to an extent ventriloquizing the people you're talking with to make your account. You're undertaking an unequal exchange which is capitalistic in its own way, because it *appears* to be an equal exchange, but in fact it's *very* unequal. You take from trust-like and reciprocal relations something which is then one sidedly and academically "marketised" as public, exchangeable: ripped out of local use value for a particular kind of exchange value. You take it off and cash it in in the academy, such as *Learning of Labour* becoming a book that sells 100,000 after twenty years. I have all of these guilts. I'm driven still, though more in theory than practice at this point, to concrete interactions because that is the only way of trying to understand creativity, sensuousness, specificity, even though the very action undermines that with its second order motives.

These multiples of the normal social atmospheric pressure, uniquely felt by the fieldworker, sometimes make me think of our method as a kind of symbolic tank or submarine. Field roles are a bit like tanks or submarines, splendidly useful vehicles for getting to strange or dangerous places. You'll never know, till you try, how quickly a vehicle can become a death trap. You *are* the research instrument. That's the point. But also, by that, you are making of yourself an enclosure that can be crushed.

You don't often don't mention this other side, the ethical impossibility of ethnography. Isn't that the other angle of the ethnographic imagination, its impossibility ... ?

Maybe that's the debt that the imagination tries to pay off. What I'm saying specifically here, though, is that I've felt solidarity with ethnographers no matter what their leanings because I think we *are* in some kind of secret club, whose rites of passage and membership fees consist of handling unexpressed guilt. Perhaps it's mephistophelean. The higher the fees, the higher the achievement. I can feel the electricity, the tension when it's present, but invisible in a text; part of a fatefulness in how experience is described; experience *really* registering as *implicated* witness; part of the undischargeable debt which turns into a kind of politics agonisingly without closure.

I don't care whether they're called anthropologists, Marxists, ethnomethodologists or linguists. I do feel an *immediate* sympathy and solidarity with anybody who has attempted to the very odd thing of joining in a social situation for reasons which are entirely unique to our little club, and which may well be suspicious to social agents: our peripheral membership of a social group as the *centre* of something else. Though it never ceases to amaze me how open and honest people are when *you* know that *you* are trying to peer round corners. You are not trying to do dirty deals in a conscious capitalistic way as in exploiting surplus-value, but you've got these driven feelings, as I said before, not least, to "get some data." If I've got an academic home, it is with people who know that moral dilemma. You could almost say that theoretical schools are very unimportant compared with that. Also, yeah, I resent some of the pure theorists. I want to *force* them to go out and face those moral dilemmas. Get them by the scruff of the neck, "this is what you're talking about." Not that academic thing of, you know: "Show me some empirical data." Rather: "Have you *really* been in a situation where you're trying to generate data, relevant to the theory you're talking about, from the people you're talking about?" Especially doing that with people who aren't like you, safely encamped in seminar groupings, or about whom you want to say something critical or difficult for them to hear. On the one hand, can we possibly do social science *without* talking to and granting equal *interactive* humanity to the people we're talking about? On the other hand, *how* can we do that without, at some level, exploiting them? You know, under existing social relations, honesty forces us to be dishonest. That leads to a discussion of the commitments and pay-offs and politics of why we put ourselves in moral jeopardy to start with. There is a compromised but unmistakeably unique energy behind this framing and justifying that which seperates us from "the suits" of the social sciences. And it is this shared knowledge of the energies of moral jeopardy which is my solidarity within this strange group.

Acknowledgments

We would both like to thank Paul Willis for his support of this project. David Mills would also like to acknowledge the financial support of the Leverhulme Trust and the British Academy.

References

Hoggart, R. (1957). *The uses of literacy.* London: Chatto and Windus.

Willis, P. (1977). *Learning to labour: Why working class kids get working class jobs.* Farnborough: Saxon House.

Willis, P. (1978). *Profane culture.* London: Routledge and Kegan Paul.

Willis, P. (1986). *Youth and community education. The future role and organisation of local government*; Education Working Paper 2.4. Institute of Local Government Studies, Univeristy of Birmingham, Birmingham, UK.

Willis, P. (with S. Jones, J. Canaan, & G. Hurd). (1990a). *Common culture.* Buckingham: Oxford University Press.

Willis, P. (1990b). *Moving culture: An enquiry into the cultural activities of young people.* London: Calouste Gulbenkian Foundation.

Willis, P. (2000). *The ethnographic imagination.* Oxford: Polity Press

Willis, P., Bekenn, A., Ellis, T., & Whitt, D. (1988). *The youth review: Social conditions of young people in Wolverhampton.* Aldershot: Avebury.

Willis, P. (2001). Tekin' the piss. In D. Holland & J. Lave (Eds.), *History in person.* Santa Fe, NM: SAR.

Notes on Contributors

Jean Anyon teaches social and educational policy in the Doctoral Program in Urban Education at the Graduate Center of the City University of New York. Her last book, *Ghetto Schooling: A Political Economy of Urban Educational Reform*, was positively reviewed in the *New York Times* and in over 20 other publications, and is widely used and cited. She has written many scholarly pieces on the confluence of social class, race, and education. Several of her articles are classics, and have been reprinted in over 40 edited collections. Her forthcoming book is entitled *And We Are Not Yet Saved: Social Policy, Urban Education, and a New Civil Rights Movement*.

Michael W. Apple is John Bascom Professor of Curriculum and Instruction and Educational Policy Studies at the University of Wisconsin–Madison. Among his recent books are *Educating the "Right" Way: Markets, Standards, God, and Inequality* and *The State and the Politics of Knowledge*.

Madeleine Arnot is Reader in Sociology of Education and Fellow of Jesus College at the University of Cambridge. She has published extensively on the gender, race and class relations in education and has been actively involved in promoting equality policies and citizenship education. Her recent books include *Closing the Gender Gap* (with G. Weiner and M. David, Polity Press, 1999); *Challenging Democracy: International Perspectives on Gender, Education and Citizenship* (edited with J. Dillabough, Falmer, 2000), and *Reproducing Gender? Essays on Educational Theory and Feminist Politics* (RoutledgeFalmer, 2002).

Stanley Aronowitz is Distinguished Professor of Sociology and Urban Education at the Graduate Center, City University of New York. His latest books are *How Class Works* (Yale, 2003) and, with Heather Gautney, *Implicating Empire* (Basic, 2002).

Greg Dimitriadis is Assistant Professor in the Department of Educational Leadership and Policy at the University at Buffalo, SUNY. Dimitriadis is the author of *Performing Identity/Performing Culture: Hip Hop as Text, Pedagogy, and Lived Practice* (Peter Lang) and *Friendship, Cliques, and Gangs: Young Black Men Coming of Age in Urban America* (Teachers College Press). He is first coauthor, with Cameron McCarthy, of *Reading and Teaching the Postcolonial: From Baldwin to Basquiat and Beyond* (Teachers College Press). He is first coeditor, with Dennis Carlson, of *Promises to Keep: Cultural Studies, Democratic Education, and Public Life* (RoutledgeFalmer).

Nadine Dolby is Assistant Professor of Comparative/International Education and Foundations of Education at Northern Illinois University. She is author of *Constructing Race: Youth, Identity and Popular Culture in South Africa* (State University of New York Press), and has published in numerous educational journals, including *Harvard Educational Review, Teachers College Record, Educational Researcher*, and the *British Journal of Sociology of Education.* She is the recipient of a "Rising Scholar" award from the Kellogg Forum on Higher Education for the Public Good.

Robert Gibb received his PhD from the University of Edinburgh in 2001. He has carried out research on antiracist associations in France, with a focus on the relationship between antiracism, republicanism, and party politics. He was the Leach/Royal Anthropological Fellow at the University of Edinburgh in 2001–2002 and is currently working on a research project funded by the British Academy entitled *"Spontaneity" and "Organisation": Anti-Racist Mobilisation in France During and After the 2002 Presidential Elections.* He has published in the *Journal des anthropologues,* the *International Journal of Francophone Studies*, and *Migrations-Société,* and has a book *The Politics of Anti-Racism in Contemporary France* forthcoming with the publisher Berg.

Jane Kenway is Professor of Education at Monash University in Melbourne, Australia. Her most recent book is: Kenway, J. & Bullen, E. (2001). *Consuming Children: Entertainment, Advertising and Education* (Open

University Press). Her forthcoming books with Peter Lang include *Globalizing Public Education: Policies, Pedagogies and Politics* (with Michael Apple and Michael Singh, editors) and *New Generations: Arts, Humanities and the Knowledge Economy* (with Elizabeth Bullen and Simon Robb). She is currently completing *Masculinity beyond the Metropolis* with Anna Kraack.

Anna Kraack is currently studying law at the University of Otago in New Zealand. Prior to this she studied rural sociology and worked for 3 years at the University of South Australia as Research Fellow on the Australian Research Council project *Country Boys in Uncertain Times and Places*.

Peter McLaren is a Professor in the Division of Urban Schooling, Graduate School of Education and Information Studies, University of California, Los Angeles. His most recent books include *Che Guevara, Paulo Freire, and the Pedagogy of Revolution* and (with Dave Hill, Mike Cole, and Glenn Rikowksi), *Marxism Against Postmodernism in Educational Theory*. His forthcoming book, *Red Seminars: Pedagogies for Unlearning Capitalist Culture*, will be published in 2004.

Cameron McCarthy teaches mass communications theory and cultural studies at the Institute of Communications Research at the University of Illinois at Urbana.

David Mills is Anthropology Coordinator at the Centre for Learning and Teaching Sociology, Anthropology and Politics at the University of Birmingham. He no longer works in the Department of Cultural Studies and Sociology after the university pressured all of its existing staff into taking compulsory redundancy in June 2002. As well as completing a political history of social anthropology, he is currently carrying out research into disciplinary knowledge practices in contemporary UK higher education.

Kathleen Nolan is a Student in the PhD Program in Urban Education at the City University of New York Graduate Center. She is a recipient of the Spencer Social Justice and Social Development Fellowship. Her research interests include the political economy of incarceration and the relationship between urban public school policy and the criminal justice system. Kathleen taught ESL (English as a Second Language) and English at South Bronx High School for 4 years. Currently, she teaches at the City College of New York in the Bilingual Education program and mentors teachers in the area of reading and writing in a second language. Her chapter "The Power of Language: A Critique of the Assumptions and Pedagogical Implications of

Howard Gardner's Concept of Linguistic Intelligence" will be published in *Multiple Intelligences Reconsidered* (editor Joe L. Kincheloe, forthcoming).

Fazal Rizvi is Professor of Educational Policy Studies at the University of Illinois at Urbana-Champaign. Before coming to America he held a number of academic and administrative positions in Australia. He has written on issues of globalization and educational policy, democratic reforms in education, and the politics of race and multiculturalism. He is currently researching student mobility across national boundaries and the internationalization of higher education.

Valerie Scatamburlo-D'Annibale, an award-winning author and educator, is an Assistant Professor and Chair of the Graduate Program in Communication and Social Justice at the University of Windsor. Her first book, *Soldiers of Misfortune: The New Right's Culture War and the Politics of Political Correctness*, received the American Educational Studies Association's 2000 Critics Choice Award. She has also published in a wide variety of journals and edited collections in the areas of social theory and critical pedagogy.

Lois Weis is the Author or Coauthor of numerous books and articles pertaining to social class, race, gender, and schooling in the United States. Her most recent books include *Silenced Voices and Extraordinary Conversations: Re-Imagining Schools* (Teachers College Press, 2003, with Michelle Fine); *The Unknown City: The Lives of Poor and Working Class Young Adults* (Beacon Press, 1998, with Michelle Fine); *Speed Bumps: A Student Friendly Guide to Qualitative Research* (Teachers College Press, 2000, with Michelle Fine); and *Beyond Black and White: New Faces and Voices in U.S. Schools* (State University of New York Press, 1997, with Maxine Seller). She sits on numerous editorial boards and is the editor of the Power, Social Identity and Education book series with SUNY Press.

Trained in literary criticism at Cambridge, **Paul Willis** received his PhD in 1972 from the Centre for Contemporary Cultural Studies at Birmingham University, where he remained as Senior Research Fellow until 1980. During the 1980s he served as youth policy adviser to Wolverhampton Borough Council in the English Midlands. There he produced *The Youth Review* (published by the Council and Ashgate [1988]), which formed the basis for youth policy in that city and for the formation of the democratically elected Youth Council, both still functioning. During the 1990s Paul served first as Head of the Division of Media, Communications and Cultural Studies and then as a member of the Professoriate at the University of Wolverhampton.

Currently he is Professor of Social and Cultural Ethnography at Keele University. He has held a variety of consulting posts, including membership in the Youth Policy Working Group of the Labour Party (1989–1990); at the English Arts Council (1992–1993); and at the Tate Gallery of the North (1995–1996). In 2000, he cofounded the Sage journal, *Ethnography*. Paul Willis's work has focused on the mainly but not exclusively ethnographic study of lived cultural forms in a wide variety of contexts, from highly structured to weakly structured ones, examining how practices of "informal cultural production" help to produce and construct cultural worlds "from below." Currently he is working on conceptual and methodological ways of connecting or reconnecting a concern with identity/culture to economic structure, with particular reference to "shop floor culture." Books: *Profane Culture, Learning to Labour, The Youth Review, Common Culture, The Ethnographic Imagination.*

Index